W9-CCW-444

CLASSICS IN PSYCHOLOGY

CLASSICS IN PSYCHOLOGY

A NOTE ABOUT THE AUTHOR

GUY M. WHIPPLE was born in Danvers, Massachusetts, in 1876, scion of five generations of farmers. He received his Ph. D. from Cornell in 1900 and taught successively at Cornell, Missouri, Illinois, Carnegie Institute of Technology, and Michigan. His principal interests were in educational, developmental and learning psychology, but he also published works in several other areas. In his later years he turned increasingly toward editorial work, founding the *Journal of Educational Psychology,* editing the National Society for the Study of Education *Yearbooks,* and working full-time for D. C. Heath, Publishers. His *Manual* went through three editions and was for many years the standard reference on procedures in mental testing. Whipple also published seven other books in educational psychology before his death in 1941.

MANUAL OF
MENTAL AND PHYSICAL TESTS

BY

GUY MONTROSE WHIPPLE, PH.D.

Parts I and II

94688

ARNO PRESS
A New York Times Company
New York ★ 1973

Reprint Edition 1973 by Arno Press Inc.

Reprinted from copies in
The University of Illinois Library

Classics in Psychology
ISBN for complete set: 0-405-05130-1
See last pages of this volume for titles.

Manufactured in the United States of America

———————◆———————

Library of Congress Cataloging in Publication Data

Whipple, Guy Montrose, 1876-1941.
   Manual of mental and physical tests.

   (Classics in psychology)
   Reprint of the 2d ed., published in 2 v.,
1914-15, by Warwick & York, Baltimore.
   1. Psychology, Physiological. 2. Mental
tests. I. Title. II. Series. DNLM: LB1121
W573m 1914F]
LB1121.W5 1973   370.15   73-2997
ISBN 0-405-05169-7

MANUAL OF MENTAL AND PHYSICAL TESTS

Part I: Simpler Processes

[SECOND REVISED AND ENLARGED EDITION]

MANUAL OF
MENTAL AND PHYSICAL
TESTS

Part I: Simpler Processes

A BOOK OF DIRECTIONS
COMPILED WITH SPECIAL REFERENCE TO THE EXPERIMENTAL STUDY
OF SCHOOL CHILDREN IN THE LABORATORY
OR CLASSROOM

BY

GUY MONTROSE WHIPPLE, PH.D.

ASSISTANT PROFESSOR OF EDUCATIONAL PSYCHOLOGY
CORNELL UNIVERSITY
AUTHOR OF "A GUIDE TO HIGH SCHOOL OBSERVATION," "QUESTIONS IN
GENERAL AND EDUCATIONAL PSYCHOLOGY"
"QUESTIONS IN SCHOOL HYGIENE"

BALTIMORE, U. S. A.
WARWICK & YORK, Inc.
1914

PREFACE TO THE SECOND EDITION.

One need not be a close observer to perceive how markedly the interest in mental tests has developed during the past few years. Not very long ago attention to tests was largely restricted to a few laboratory psychologists; now tests have become objects of attention for many workers whose primary interest is in education, social service, medicine, industrial management and many other fields in which applied psychology promises valuable returns. It is a source of gratification to me that this book has been a positive factor in furthering this development of mental tests, and that it has found sufficient favor, both with academic investigators and teachers and with those engaged in the immediately practical task of mental examination, to exhaust the first edition in an unexpectedly short time.

Opportunity has been taken of this necessity for a new edition to make extensive revision and alterations in the text. The attempt has been made to eliminate a number of confusing typographical errors; a new and better system of abbreviations for titles of periodicals has been introduced; the directions for conducting the tests have been modified where ambiguity was felt; numerous tables and graphs have been added; the section upon the treatment of measures has been expanded; and several new tests have been inserted. These changes have so increased the material as to make it desirable to divide it into two parts, the first dealing with simpler, the second with more complex processes. The numbering of the original tests has, however, been retained for various reasons.

It would have been quite difficult for me to have undertaken to improve the text had I not received valuable assistance from many of my colleagues and co-workers. In especial I wish to record my indebtedness to Dr. Otto Bobertag, of the *Institut für angewandte Psychologie,* Professor C. Spearman, of London, Professor S. P. Hayes of Mount Holyoke College, and Mr. D. K. Fraser, of Cornell University.

G. M. W.

Ithaca, N. Y.,
    February, 1914.

PREFACE TO THE FIRST EDITION.

Hitherto the literature of mental and physical tests has been scattered in numerous journals; the results obtained by different investigators have too often not been compared; indeed, in many cases where the methods have been divergent, comparison has been impossible. In consequence, there have been no recognized standards of procedure and none of performance. Nevertheless, I believe that the time has now come for the taking of an account of stock, and for the systematization of the available materials. This conviction, which is the outgrowth of my own interest in the experimental study of mental capacities, an interest that has been with me during the past ten years, has been confirmed by many suggestions from colleagues and friends, who have pointed out that a manual of directions for mental tests would meet a real need, and might further the cause of investigation. More particularly, at the instigation of Mr. C. H. Stoelting, of Chicago, who has undertaken to supply the apparatus and materials prescribed in this volume, I began, in March, 1906, to prepare a small handbook of mental tests. The impossibility of adequate treatment of the subject in small compass has, however, necessitated the expansion of that early undertaking into the present work.

In the introductory sections of this volume, I have sought to show the general purposes of mental tests, to lay down rules for their conduct, and to explain the methods of treating data. In this connection I discuss the calculation of measures of general tendency, measures of variability, indexes of correlation, and other statistical constants.

In the body of the volume, I have brought together, for specific treatment, some fifty of the most promising tests. In every case, my plan has been to sketch the development of the test, to prescribe a standard form of apparatus and method of procedure, to explain the treatment of the data secured, and to set forth the results and conclusions thus far obtained.

The tests that I have selected may not prove, ultimately, to be those of most value, but they are, I think, numerous enough, and varied enough in type, to furnish a working basis for investigations for some time to come.

In the choice of materials and methods, I have sought to follow a middle course; on the one hand to avoid the use of costly instruments of precision and of the elaborate methodology of the psychological laboratory, and on the other hand, to avoid the inexactness of make-shift apparatus and the unreliability of casual, unsystematic observation. My idea has been to supplement the exposition of the standard apparatus and method of procedure by suggestions for variations of apparatus or of method, so that each test will be carefully standardized, yet will retain a sufficient degree of flexibility.

Doubtless, to some readers, the instructions for the conduct of the tests will seem unnecessarily lengthy and detailed; but experience has convinced me that faulty results are to be traced, in quite the majority of instances, to the neglect of some seemingly trivial detail in the arrangement of the experimental conditions; so that instructions can scarcely be made too explicit in a manual of directions in which standardization is the object.

In explaining the treatment of data, my aim has been to make clear the arithmetic of the various formulas, without insisting, in every case, upon acquaintance with the mathematical reasoning upon which the formula is based.

And when I speak of "the results and conclusions thus far obtained," I speak with the intent to make clear what, I am sure, is made evident more than once in the text, that this book presents, not a closed chapter in the experimental investigation of mental activity, but a program of work to be done.

My acknowledgments for aid should be numerous and ungrudging. These have been made in part in the text, but in many instances, material assistance has, perforce, gone without explicit acknowledgment. I wish, however, to make clear my indebtedness to C. H. Stoelting Co., for the loan of numerous cuts, to Dr. Guy L. Noyes, of the University of Missouri, for assistance in the tests of vision, to Dr. H. H. Goddard, of Vineland, N. J., for the adaptation of the Binet-Simon tests to American conditions, to my colleague, Professor I. M. Bentley, as well as to my wife and to my mother, for the reading of proof, and to my colleagues, Professors Charles DeGarmo and E. B. Titchener, for almost daily advice and encouragement.

The inscription of the book to Professor Titchener is in token of my special debt to him as a teacher and as an expositor of the scientific method of attack in the solution of the problems of mental life.

GUY MONTROSE WHIPPLE.

Cornell University,
    June, 1910.

TABLE OF CONTENTS

CHAPTER VII. TESTS OF ATTENTION AND PERCEPTION

INDEX OF FIGURES

INDEX OF TABLES

INTRODUCTORY

CHAPTER I

The Nature and Purpose of Mental Tests[1]

When we speak of a mental test we have in mind the experimental determination for a given individual of some phase of his mental capacity, the scientific measurement of some one of his mental traits.

The mental test in some respects resembles, in some respects differs from the typical research-experiment of the psychological laboratory. Like this latter, the test is superior to the casual observation of everyday life because it is purposeful and methodical: it thus possesses all the merits common to experimental investigation at large, viz: the control of conditions (including the elimination of disturbing, and the systematic isolation of contributory factors), the possibility of repetition, and the possibility of subjecting the obtained results to quantitative treatment.

The primary difference between the research-experiment and the test-experiment is really one of aim. The test has a diagnostic, rather than a theoretical aim: its purpose is not to discover new facts, principles or laws for the science of psychology —though such a result may indirectly be attained—but to analyze, measure and rank the status or the efficiency of traits and capacities in the individual under examination. Again, unlike the typical research-experiment, the mental test ordinarily places little or no emphasis upon introspective observation by the subject, in part because of its relatively short duration, in part because it is frequently applied to inexperienced

---

[1]The tests with which this volume is concerned are mainly mental tests. Since, however, the intimacy of the relation between mind and body makes it well-nigh imperative to study their interrelations, attention has been paid to the more important anthropometric measurements and to those tests of physical capacity that have most frequently been used in the search for correlations of psychical and physical ability.

subjects who are incapable of aught but the most elementary introspection, but more especially just because it is concerned less with the qualitative examination or structural analysis of mental processes than with the quantitative determination of mental efficiency; because, in other words, it studies mental performance rather than mental content.

There is, however, danger of laying too much stress upon this distinction between quantitative and qualitative examination. Those, like Myers and Andrews, who see in mental tests nothing but statistics of performance, and who contend that in the absence of introspection it is impossible to get any information upon mental content, have failed entirely to appreciate how significant for qualitative exploration are tests when handled by a competent investigator who puts less emphasis upon mere accumulation of figures than upon the patient search for qualitative aspects of mental life implicit in the outcome of his investigations. To disregard these possibilities of the test-experiment is not only a loss, but also a positive source of danger to the progress of science, for it tends to suggest, if not to encourage the superficial execution of the tests themselves, especially on the part of untrained laymen—witness the present tendency to hand over to classroom teachers or psychologically untrained medical inspectors the diagnosis of the mental status of school children by the Binet-Simon tests.

The purposes for which mental tests have been developed are, of course, varied, but, roughly speaking, we may distinguish a theoretical interest on the part of laboratory psychologists, and a practical interest on the part of those who are concerned with mind at work in everyday life.

Historically, it appears that most of the tests now in use have originated in the psychological laboratory, either in the natural course of the development of experimental psychology as a system, e. g., the usual tests of sensory discrimination, or as a consequence of special attempts to study mental capacity, particularly the interrelations of various mental capacities and of mental with physical capacities. It is, we think, not too much to hope that in time the application of mental tests will bear rich fruit in this field. We may hope that the skillful study of mental functions by the test-method may supply us with a satisfactory account of the nature and interrelations of mental functions, just as the typical introspective experiment has been able to furnish an account of the structural make-up of mind. If we could, to take an instance, obtain an exact science of mental functions so that we could know the unit-characters of mind as the biologist knows, or expects to know, the unit-characters of plants and animals, the study of mental inheritance would be carried appreciably forward.

Outside the laboratory an active and very natural interest in mental tests has been exhibited by those who are busy with practical problems to the solution of which the scientific study of mind may be expected to contribute. It is, naturally, the educator to whom the development of a significant and reliable system of mental tests would most appeal, since he is concerned with the development of just those capacities of mind that these tests propose to measure.

It was a practical educational problem, for instance, that motivated the work of Binet and Simon, whose system of serial graded tests is just now to the forefront of popular interest. Of late, too, hopeful beginnings have been made in the application of mental tests to vocational guidance, whether in the selection of people for positions or the selection of positions for people. But the magnitude and complexity of these tasks, particularly of the second, is far greater than commonly supposed.

And this leads us to point out that there has been, unfortunately it seems to us, a disposition in some quarters to speak as if a science of mental tests were already achieved; as if, for instance, a child's native ability could now be measured as easily as his height, or as if his suggestibility or his capacity for concentration of attention could be determined as readily as his skull circumference or his breathing capacity. To make such assertions is surely misleading, for, as the study of the tests herein embodied will show, there is, at the present time, scarcely a single mental test that can be applied unequivocally as a psychical measuring-rod. The fact is we have not agreed upon methods of procedure; we too often do not know what we are measuring; and we too seldom realize the astounding complexity, variety and delicacy of form of our psychical nature.

Paradoxical as it may seem, these are the reasons, we believe, that render the elaboration of a scientific system of mental tests a possibility, for, if the all-too-evident lack of agreement in the results of the investigations already made is not attributable to faulty or divergent methods, or to clumsiness and ignorance—if, in other words, the discrepancies are inherent and ultimate—then we never can have a science of mental tests.

What we need is not new tests, though they are welcome enough, but an exhaustive investigation of a selected group of tests that have already been described or proposed. In particular, we need more than anything else, at least from the point of view of application, the establishment of norms of performance for these tests—norms that are based upon investigations in which standard and prescribed methods of procedure have been followed in a rigid and undeviating manner. We need, for every mental test that has proved its worth, data from a sufficiently large number of individuals of all stages and types of mental development to supply a standard table of distribution by percentile grades like the tables already available for some of the commoner anthropometric measurements.

This book is an attempt to assist in the realization of this need. It presents a program of work, rather than a final system of results.

REFERENCES.[2]

(1) B. R. Andrews, Auditory tests. *AmJPs*, 15:14-56.

(2) L. P. Ayres, Psychological tests in vocational guidance. *JEdPs*, 4:1913, 232-7. (Also published separately, Russell Sage Foundation, New York City.)

(3) H. Münsterberg, Psychology and industrial efficiency. Cambridge, 1913.

(4) C. S. Myers, The pitfalls of 'mental tests.' *BrMedJ*, Jan. 29, 1911. (Also published separately. Pp. 8.)

(5) W. Stern, Die differentielle Psychologie in ihren methodischen Grundlagen. Leipzig, 1911. Especially Ch. 6.

(6) W. Stern, Die psychologischen Methoden der Intelligenzprüfung und deren Anwendung an Schulkindern. Leipzig, 1912. (Eng. trans. to appear in *EdPsMon*, Baltimore.)

(7) F. L. Wells, The principle of mental tests. *Sci*, 38:1913, 221-224.

[2]Consult the *List of Abbreviations* for the exact titles of the periodicals cited in these and subsequent references.

CHAPTER II

General Rules for the Conduct of Tests

The following general rules may be laid down at the outset:

(1) The essential and fundamental principle underlying the conduct of scientific tests is the *standardization of conditions*. This does not mean that expensive apparatus or instruments of precision are always necessary, but simply that the conditions under which a test is given to one person or to one group of persons must be identically followed in giving the same test to another person or group. We cannot always make the conditions ideal, but we can at least try to keep them constant. *If the conditions are varied, they must be varied intentionally and for a definite purpose.*

(2) *No detail in the 'setting' of a test is too trivial to be neglected.* This is, of course, merely a restatement of the previous principle in another form. It is noteworthy that the lack of accordance between the results obtained by different investigators in the use of what is ostensibly the same test almost invariably turns out to be due to seemingly trivial variations in the method of administering the test.

In particular, attention may be called here to such matters as the time of day at which the experiment is made, the nature of the instructions that precede the test, the emotional attitude of the participants toward the investigation, their ability exactly to comprehend what is wanted of them (of which more hereafter) and their willingness to do their best throughout the test. It is well to write out the preliminary instructions and to memorize them, after first making a trial in order to see if they are perfectly intelligible. Thus, for instance, to say to one class of school children: "Cross out all the *e*'s on this paper while I take your time with a watch," and to another class: "Cross out all the *e*'s on this paper as fast as you can" may mean the same thing to the experimenter, but it will not bring the same results from the classes under investigation, because in the second case the idea of fast work has been more strongly emphasized.

A special difficulty that arises here may be too readily overlooked by the untrained examiner. The subject of a test is thrown by the examiner's instructions into what may be termed a 'set' or an 'attunement' for the work before him. Now, even if each subject be given precisely the same verbal directions, it is entirely possible that these directions may be interpreted differently by different subjects. Moreover, this attunement is quite as likely to be affected by the 'atmosphere' of the experiment, the general setting in which the work is carried on, as by the verbal instructions themselves. With children this difficulty may be quite serious. Anyone who has watched a succession of children enter the laboratory for mental testing must have been struck by these differences of attitude: one child is excessively timid, another is excited, a third is apathetic, a fourth is full of curiosity, and a fifth is strongly imbued with a competitive spirit. The skilled experimenter is on the watch for these signs and adapts his manner and his instructions in the effort so to compensate the tendencies that underlie them as to produce, so far as may be possible, the same final attunement.

The principle of rigid adherence to predetermined instructions has yet another exception. It may be quite worth while to vary instructions, like any other phase of the conditions of the test, provided the variation be done intelligently, for a purpose, by a trained experimenter. It is, indeed, precisely by this shifting of conditions that the first-class investigator can transcend the bare gathering of quantitative statistics and gain an insight into the qualitative aspects of mental life. Many boastfully 'exact' investigations would have more psychology in them had their authors known how to vary conditions and then, of course, to watch the results for concomitant variations in them. In short, then, the novice in mental testing neither realizes how disturbing slight changes in the experimental conditions can be, nor, on the other hand, how much of psychological interest can be discovered by intentional variation of the conditions.

(3) The examiner, *E,* should be on the look-out for external signs of the way in which the subject, *S,* responds to the test,

i. e., for indications of readiness, of quick comprehension, of a competitive spirit, or of *ennui*, fatigue, distraction, shift of attention, trickiness or deceit. The record-blanks should have a space for the recording of remarks of this nature. When tests are conducted individually, it is surprising how much can be gleaned in regard to S's mental traits by these indirect hints. In particular, whenever the object of the test is to examine the correlation of some physical or mental trait with S's general intelligence, it is largely upon this sort of observational record that E must depend for his estimate of this general intelligence, even though the test be supplemented by school marks, the estimates of teachers, and similar devices.

(4) No test should be undertaken by E until he is perfectly familiar with its nature, its purpose and its administration. Especially if it involves the use of apparatus, he should familiarize himself with the manipulations until they become automatic.

(5) No test should be undertaken until S is perfectly clear as to what is required of him. Since most mental tests are of an unfamiliar character, something beside explicit instructions, however clearly put, is needed to enable the average S to undertake the test under proper conditions. Ordinarily, a brief period (say 1 to 5 minutes) of *fore-exercise* is needed to remove timidity, excitement or misunderstanding. If this preliminary exercise is properly arranged (especially by being based upon material not used in the test proper, and by being of the same length and character for all S's), it does not introduce a serious practise error, while it does decidedly facilitate the test. In some cases, however, as, for instance, when the facility of adaptation to the test-conditions is itself an object of investigation, the fore-exercise should be omitted.

(6) Most mental tests may be administered either to individuals or to groups. Both methods have advantages and disadvantages. The *group method* has, of course, the particular merit of economy of time; a class of 50 or 100 children may take a test in less than a fiftieth or a hundreth of the time

needed to administer the same test individually. Again, in certain comparative studies, e. g., of the effects of a week's vacation upon the mental efficiency of school children, it becomes imperative that all S's.should take the tests at the same time.

But, on the whole, and especially when careful analytic work is contemplated, the group method, save for the preliminary trial of a method, is out of place. There are almost sure to be some S's in every group that, for one reason or another, fail to follow instructions or to execute the test to the best of their ability. The individual method allows E to detect these cases, and in general, by the exercise of personal supervision, to gain, as has been noted above, valuable information concerning S's attitude toward the test. Moreover, with the group method E must be content with bare quantitative performance: he has no opportunity for the skillful adaptation and variation of the attunement that we have mentioned; he can only surmise what has lain in S's mind between instruction and performance, between stimulus and response, nor can he tell what effect the compulsion to work with other S's may have had upon any given S. The objection that individual work takes too much time is, as one psychologist has put it, as laughable as would be the defence of a chemist that he had distilled several different fluids in the same flask without washing it—"to save time."

(7) One phase of the group vs. individual procedure demands special attention, viz: the problem of time-control. In many, if not in most tests, efficiency is measured, at least in part, by the rate at which the assigned work is performed. Now, in theory, rate or speed might be measured either by the amount of work performed within a given time or by the time taken to perform a given amount of work, in other words, by a *time-limit method* or by a *work-limit method*. In practise, however, we often find it difficult to arrange the material of a test in such a way as to make the task of equal objective difficulty at every portion of the test, and, even when this is possible, subjective variations may appear because of the fact that

different S's accomplish different amounts of work.[1] There is no doubt, therefore, that the work-limit method is to be preferred to the time-limit method: it is better, in other words, that every S should be asked to perform the same work and to measure his efficiency in terms of elapsed time than to require every S to work for the same time and to measure his efficiency in 'ground covered.' But the time-limit method is compulsory in all tests of this order undertaken by groups, so that this constitutes yet another serious objection to the group-method.[2]

(8) This leads naturally to a consideration of other difficulties that arise in scoring individual performance. Special difficulties are considered later in the discussion of the tests in which they appear, while the methods of handling measurements in general are treated in the following chapter. Attention is called here, however, to a fundamental problem, viz: *the relation of quantity of work to quality of work.* These two factors appear in nearly every test of mental efficiency, and the question arises: shall efficiency be measured in terms of quality, excellence, delicacy or accuracy of work, or shall it be measured in terms of quantity, rate, or speed of work? To this question no general answer can be given. Roughly speaking, quantity and quality of work probably tend, at least for a given S, to be inversely related. Whenever this relation can be demonstrated, it is theoretically, and often, indeed, actually possible to convert the two measures into a single index of 'net efficiency'— an index that is much desired for the study of general com-

---

[1]To take a concrete case, suppose E tries to conduct the "opposites" test upon a group of S's by the time-limit method. He must stop the work of all S's at the same moment. Suppose Subject A has written 10 and Subject B 20 opposites. Does it follow that B is twice as efficient as A? It certainly does not if, say, the 9th and the 10th terms on the list are more difficult than the rest, even if they are more difficult only to B. Again, it is more than twice as hard to name 120 as to name 60 words at random in three minutes. Failure to perceive this simple fallacy of counting as statistically equal, different portions or sections of an extended task is all too evident in the work of many investigators.

[2]Since the above was written the author has been able to use the work-limit method successfully with groups of reliable S's by the aid of a newly devised time-clock.

parative relations. In other instances it has been proposed[1] so to adjust the conditions of the test as to throw the emphasis so strongly upon quantity or upon quality of performance that the unemphasized factor may be neglected. In yet other instances, it seems necessary to keep both an index of quantity and an index of quality, and to make reference to both in subsequent comparative study.

(9) *Whether speed is a legitimate index of mental efficiency in general,* even when measured by the method of work-limits with individual S's may perhaps be questioned. It is true that in many instances it seems most obvious, and is extremely tempting to compare the work of different S's in terms of speed. But, in the author's opinion, we have been led astray by this temptation. Certainly, if we seek to evaluate the complex 'higher' mental functions, speed is not the primary index of efficiency, as is borne out by the evidence that speed and intelligence are not very highly correlated. Even with simpler tests, the quality of the work may be lost sight of, if rate of work is the only criterion of excellence: some S's become feverishly and nervously excited and get the idea that the faster they work, the better; others are naturally critical and hesitate to proceed until they feel sure of themselves; others are habitually leisurely in their mental activities and will not 'speed up' unnecessarily. Again, the time recorded for performing a given task is often quite equivocal, because it includes a number of irrelevant factors whose quantum is unknown, particularly motor activities of various kinds. As a general rule, it may be said that *time measurements become more significant and reliable in proportion as the task becomes more mechanical and less intellectual.*

(10) As already intimated, the use of group-tests nearly always implies the use of *written responses.* When speed of performance is then used as a measure of efficiency, a perfectly obvious and often very serious source of error is introduced, for it is next to impossible, particularly with children, to measure or even to estimate the fraction of the total time that has been

---

[1]For an illustration of both of these methods for obtaining a single index, see the Cancellation Test.

expended upon the writing: the process of writing 'telescopes' to an unknown extent into the other activities set in play by the test. And, moreover, even when speed is not regarded as significant, most S's will make a shorter and a different response to a test when they write than when they report orally.

For these reasons *mental tests should, so far as possible, be adapted for oral, instead of for written responses,* particularly if efficiency is to be measured in terms of speed. If written work be unavoidable, it should be reduced to the very minimum of simplicity.

(11) In the past not enough attention has been paid to the *desirability of repeating tests.* It is true that any repetition introduces the factor of practise and that this factor may exert a varying and undetermined influence. On the other hand, it is equally true that the outcome of a single application of a test may be very misleading: it may be affected by S's special attunement, by his mood, by some chance accident of expression or by mere whim. Indeed, it has been recently argued by one writer that the low degree of correlation between various mental traits found by many workers in correlational psychology is directly due to their failure to repeat the tests until the initial irregularities have disappeared. And it would follow, in his opinion, that, while simple preliminary tests might serve very well for detecting extreme departures from the mode, "in the determination of individual differences within the large middle range of the curve of distribution * * * we shall find it necessary to determine the individual's 'limit of practise' in the various tests before we shall secure diagnostic results which will be verified by the individual's subsequent achievement in daily life."[1] Again, now that interest is directed so much toward the question of 'types,' it seems particularly necessary to caution against the fallacy of taking the

---

[1]H. L. Hollingworth, Correlation of abilities as affected by practice. *JEdPs*, 4:1913, 405-414. The reader will find a divergent conclusion expressed by C. Burt (Experimental tests of general intelligence, *BrJPs*, 3:1909, 94-177, especially 168-9), who declares "the correlation is highest on the first occasion, that is to say, when the task is newest"—referring to the correlation between experimental tests and general intelligence.

result of a single test as a positive indication that S falls into this or that type—because, of course, belonging to a type really implies the possession of a persistent tendency.[1]

(12) When it is desired to determine for a given S his efficiency in a given mental direction, *e. g.,* in memorizing, discriminating, observing, reasoning, synthetizing, inventing, and like functions, it must be borne in mind that, at least when the function is of a 'higher' and more complex order, *more than one test must be used.* The results of correlation psychology are proof that a series of tests that seem, all of them, to test the same mental function actually need not exhibit a high index of correlation. Nor can we regard any mental function as so clean cut, distinct and open to isolation that any single mental test can fully and finally map its form and dimensions. As Ebbinghaus has remarked: "There are no paragraphs in mind," and if there were, we might add, we could not record them by any single observation. *A fortiori,* to try to concoct a single and final test of such a comprehensive capacity as "general intelligence" becomes doubly absurd. Our general rule would be, then: use as many tests as possible and combine their data (quantitatively, if that prove feasible) to obtain a resultant value. Naturally, the tests must be selected with great care.

(13) In the application of any test, it is usual first to secure certain *preliminary data* concerning S's personal history. Thus, in the experimental study of school children, E will find it advisable to record (*a*) name of the pupil in full, (*b*) sex, (*c*) date of birth, (*d*) name of school, (*e*) grade, (*f*) date, (*g*) hour. Other items, less uniformly recorded, but often of interest, are the following: (*h*) general health, (*i*) color of eyes and hair, (*j*) right or left-handedness, (*k*) name of teacher, (*l*) names and address of parents, (*m*) nationality of parents, (*n*) date of birth of parents, (*o*) occupation of parents, (*p*)

[1] An excellent illustration of the need of caution here is afforded by the work of Binet when he was studying the mental constitution of his daughter, Armande (*L'étude expérimentale de l'intelligence*). It will be recalled that Armande, on being asked why she now responded in a vein quite at variance with her previous replies, said: "I don't like to put things that way now; it would seem silly." That Binet, who was eager to establish the hypothesis of 'types,' had the courage to chronicle this incident, is one more testimony to the integrity of his scientific conscience.

number of children in family and their sex, (*q*) number of pupil in children of his family, (*r*) medical history of the pupil and his family, (*s*) obvious developmental defects or physical peculiarities, (*t*) details of personal habits, such as sleeping, eating, drinking, smoking, exercise, work, etc., (*u*) conduct in school, (*v*) proficiency in school work. For clinical work there will be added, of course, other anamnesic data appropriate to the case in hand.[1]

In *recording age* it is best to note the exact date of *S*'s birth. Unfortunately, direct comparison of the results of different investigators has at times been rendered difficult on account of disparity in the method of recording age. Thus, in arranging statistical tables, a boy 9 years and 7 months old would by some be classed in the group of 9-year-olds, by others in the group of 10-year-olds, as being nearer 10 than 9. A third method, which has the advantage of being clear to the reader and not confusing to *E*, is to put all *S*'s at or past a given birthday into a single group, the age of which is specified as that birthday, plus a half-year, *e. g.*, all *S*'s between their 9th and 10th birthday comprise the 9.5-year-old group, since their average age tends, of course, to approximate 9.5 years.

---

[1]For an excellent syllabus illustrating the data usually recorded for clinical examination of children, consult E. B. Huey, Backward and feeble-minded children. *EdPsMon*, Baltimore, 1912, ch. vi.

CHAPTER III

THE TREATMENT OF MEASURES

The immediate results of the application of mental and physical tests are very apt to be obscure or unintelligible until they have been ordered and systematized by proper statistical treatment. It is the purpose of the present chapter to explain the most common methods by which this systematization is accomplished.[1]

A. MEASURES OF GENERAL TENDENCY

In many cases it is unnecessary, if not impossible, to keep in view the individual measurements of an extended series. We naturally seek to condense these values into a single representative value. Any single measure that affords us such a summary of a series of measurements may be termed a 'representative measure' or a 'measure of general tendency.' There are three such measures in common use—the average or mean, the median, and the mode.

1. The Mean

(a) The *ordinary arithmetical mean* (M), more often termed the *average* in psychological measurements, is computed by dividing the sum of the several measurements or magnitudes (m) by their number (n).

Hence:
$$M = \frac{\Sigma\, m}{n}. \tag{1}$$

---

[1] The reader will find more extended discussions of measurement methods in the following: Brown, Yule, Galton, Thorndike, Titchener, Sanford, Wissler, Spearman, C. B. Davenport, E. Davenport, Merriman and Elderton (see the end of this chapter for exact references). Technical papers upon correlation formulas by Pearson, Yule and others will be found in various numbers of *Biometrika*, the *Proc. of the Royal Soc.* of London, and in the *Phil. Transactions* of the same body.

The mean is the most familiar measure of general tendency, and it is the most precise, because it is affected by all measurements in proportion to their size. It has, however, some disadvantages: its computation requires more labor than that of the median or the mode, and, as will be shown later, it may fail after all to afford a truly representative value. Examples of arithmetical means are scarcely needed, but may be found in Tables 1 and 2, and elsewhere.[1]

(b) In dealing with a large number of measures a short cut may be furnished by a special application of what is known as the *weighted arithmetical mean*. Its use may be made evident by the following hypothetical case. Suppose it were desired to ascertain the average height of 1000 12-year-old boys. By the ordinary method we should be obliged to record each measure exactly (say, within 1 mm.) and to add the entire 1000 measurements. To utilize the weighted arithmetical mean, we divide the range of height into a limited number of groups of, let us say, 2 cm., and record simply the number of cases that fall into each group, *i. e.*, the frequency of each group. Thus in Table 3, there are in the 6th group 58 measurements lying between the limits 135 and 137 cm. The weighted mean can now be found very simply by multiplying the value or magnitude representing each group by the corresponding frequency (1×126; 5×128, etc.) and dividing the sum of the products by the sum of the frequencies (1000).

The formula for the weighted arithmetical mean is therefore:

$$M = \frac{\Sigma (m \cdot f)}{\Sigma f},$$

or:

$$M = \frac{\Sigma (m \cdot f)}{n}. \tag{2}$$

---

[1]The computation of M may be greatly lessened by assuming a convenient approximate value, and correcting subsequently to the true value. For illustrations, see Davenport (6, p. 429), Thorndike (32, ch. iv) or Yule (38, ch. vii).

TABLE 1

Strength of Grip, in Hectograms, 50 boys. (*Whipple*)

ORDER	RIGHT HAND				LEFT HAND				RANK COMPARISONS			
	NO.	STAND-ING	d	d²	NO.	STAND-ING	d	d²	G	D	D²	xy
1	30	158	−125	15625	30	138	−135	18225	—	0	0	16875
2	17	175	−108	11664	17	163	−110	12100	—	0	0	11880
3	52	193	− 90	8100	1	175	− 98	9604	—	6	36	7470
4	39	197	− 86	7396	48	180	− 93	8649	—	2	4	7568
5	10	197	− 86	7396	7	180	− 93	8649	—	9	81	5246
6	43	200	− 83	6889	39	185	− 88	7744	—	2	4	6889
7	1	205	− 78	6084	16	190	− 83	6889	4	4	16	7644
8	40	206	− 77	5929	43	190	− 83	6889	—	4	16	5236
9	3	208	− 75	5625	52	190	− 83	6889	—	1	1	5550
10	7	210	− 73	5329	3	199	− 74	5476	5	5	25	6789
11	6	210	− 73	5329	6	200	− 73	5329	—	0	0	5329
12	48	220	− 63	3969	40	205	− 68	4624	8	8	64	5859
13	42	225	− 58	3364	15	210	− 63	3969	—	6	36	2204
14	2	225	− 58	3364	10	212	− 61	3721	—	2	4	2842
15	19	225	− 58	3364	19	215	− 58	3364	—	0	0	3364
16	37	226	− 57	3249	2	224	− 49	2401	—	10	100	741
17	15	235	− 48	2304	50	235	− 38	1444	4	4	16	3024
18	8	244	− 39	1521	8	235	− 38	1444	—	0	0	1482
19	14	244	− 39	1521	42	235	− 38	1444	—	6	36	507
20	51	245	− 38	1444	23	242	− 31	961	—	1	1	1192
21	50	248	− 35	1225	51	244	− 29	841	4	4	16	1330
22	41	262	− 21	441	45	245	− 28	784	—	2	4	273
23	25	262	− 21	441	9	253	− 20	400	—	14	196	− 735
24	23	267	− 16	256	41	260	− 13	169	4	4	16	496
25	12	269	− 14	196	14	260	− 13	169	—	5	25	− 98
26	44	270	− 13	169	37	260	− 13	169	—	1	1	78
27	29	273	− 10	100	44	267	− 6	36	—	2	4	− 20
28	9	280	− 3	9	34	270	− 3	9	5	5	25	60
29	45	290	+ 7	49	29	275	+ 2	4	7	7	49	− 196
30	36	294	11	121	12	280	7	49	—	10	100	594
31	11	296	13	169	32	282	9	81	—	3	9	312
32	28	301	18	324	20	290	17	289	—	4	16	576
33	32	310	27	729	13	290	17	289	2	2	4	243
34	31	313	30	900	11	297	24	576	—	1	1	810
35	20	315	32	1024	31	300	27	729	3	3	9	544
36	34	320	37	1369	28	305	32	1024	8	8	64	− 111
37	24	323	40	1600	25	308	35	1225	—	4	16	2520
38	16	325	42	1764	26	315	42	1764	31	31	961	−3486
39	35	330	47	2209	38	325	52	2704	—	3	9	3854
40	13	346	63	3969	36	327	54	2916	7	7	49	1071

It is clear that this weighted mean approaches the ordinary mean in accuracy in proportion as the number of classificatory groups is increased.

TABLE 1 (Continued)

ORDER	RIGHT HAND				LEFT HAND				RANK COMPARISONS			
	NO.	STAND-ING	d	d^2	NO.	STAND-ING	d	d^2	G	D	D^2	xy
41	38	348	65	4225	24	336	63	3969	2	2	4	3380
42	46	350	67	4489	35	355	82	6724	—	3	9	7035
43	33	353	70	4900	49	362	89	7921	—	1	1	7140
44	26	375	92	8464	33	375	102	10404	6	6	36	3864
45	21	375	92	8464	46	378	105	11025	—	2	4	12236
46	18	403	120	14400	18	400	127	16129	—	0	0	15240
47	27	430	147	21609	21	406	133	17689	—	2	4	26019
48	49	440	157	24649	5	443	170	28900	5	5	25	13973
49	5	440	157	24649	27	450	177	31329	1	1	1	26690
50	22	508	225	50625	22	490	217	47089	—	0	0	48825
Sums		14164	3104	293004		13651	3165	315221	106		2098	280118
Aver.		283	62.1	5860.1		273	63.3	6304.4				

TABLE 2

Values Derived from the Data of Table 1

MEASURE	FORMULA	VALUE	
		Right Hand	Left Hand
Mean	1	283.0	273.0
Median	3	269.5	260.0
A. D.	4	62.1	63.3
S. D.	5	76.6	79.4
S. D.	6	77.3	80.2
S. D.	7	77.8	79.3
P. E.	10	51.7	53.6
P. E.	11	52.1	54.2
P. E.	12	50.7	52.0
P. E.	13	52.5	53.5
C.	16	0.27	0.29

TABLE 3

Distribution of the Heights of 12-Year-Old Boys (Hypothetical)

Centimeters	126	128	130	132	134	136	138	140	142	144	146	148	150	152	154	156	158	160
Deviation	-16	-14	-12	-10	-8	-6	-4	-2	0	2	4	6	8	10	12	14	16	18
Frequency	1	5	14	24	39	58	96	120	150	142	123	88	63	36	23	12	5	1

Weighted mean = 142.9   Median = 142.9   Mode = 142.

2. *The Median*

The *median* or *central value* is, literally, the middlemost of
a group of measurements arranged singly in ascending or
descending order, or the measure above and below which lie an
equal number of individual measurements. It is expressed,
therefore, by the formula:

$$\text{median} = \text{the } \frac{n + 1}{2} \text{ measurement.} \qquad (3)$$

In practise the median may or may not coincide with some
actual measurement; more often than not it is an interpolated
value. To compute its value we must first arrange the measures serially (if any magnitude is repeated two or more times,
the number of such repetitions must, of course, be indicated).
To find the middlemost measure when interpolation is needed,
we may proceed by a simple method which may be illustrated
by reference to Table 3. Here, since there are 1000 measurements, we seek the value of the 500.5th masurement. The first
8 groups (126 to 140 cm.) represent 357 measurements. The
value desired, the 500.5th measurement, therefore lies in the
9th group of 150 cases and is the theoretical value between the
143d and the 144th measurement in this group. We have, therefore, to take $\frac{143.5}{150}$ of the range of magnitude covered by the 9th
group (2 cm.), and add this to the lower limiting value of the
group, 141 cm. (because the value 142 comprises measures
ranging from 141 up to 143 cm.), so that we obtain for the
median the value, 141 + 1.9 = 142.9.

The great merit of the median is the ease with which it can

be determined: in short series it is not even necessary to arrange the measures serially, as one-half of the measurements may be checked off by inspection. Its primary disadvantage is that it gives little weight to extreme deviations and may fail entirely to represent the type, yet, in many psychological observations, it is precisely these extreme deviations which are most suspicious, so that this tendency of the median to lessen the significance of extreme measures may prove a positive advantage.

In general, the longer the series or the more symmetrical the distribution of its values, the more nearly does the median approximate the mean.

3. The Mode

If a number of measurements are distributed in ascending or descending order, a *mode* is a measure that appears more frequently than do measures just above or below it in the series. There may be several modes in a distribution, though usually there is but one, and we may then define the mode as the commonest single value, or the commonest condition.

Many statistical arrays find a better representative value in the mode than in the average. Thus, when we speak of the "average American citizen," we really have in mind the typical citizen, the one most frequently met with. To borrow an illustration from Rietz (6, p. 684): "If a community has 10 millionaires, but all the other citizens are in poverty, an arithmetical average might give the impression that the people of the community are in good financial condition, while really the 'average citizen' is in poverty." The primary use of the mode is, therefore, *to characterize a type*.

Strictly speaking, we may have an empirical mode, as indicated in a given array, and a theoretical mode, which would be the most frequent condition in a theoretical distribution. The latter is difficult to compute and not often employed. If an array is very irregular, there is, in strictness, no mode or type at all, or at least the indicated mode has little significance.

In Table 3, it is clear that the mode is 142 cm., because this measure appears 150 times, and no other measure is so frequent.

B.   MEASURES OF VARIABILITY

It is a common fallacy to rest content with the statement of the general tendency of measurements. Even in supposedly accurate and scientific determinations, we may find the quantitative expression limited to averages, c. g., "the mean temperature for September," "the average weight of 12-year-old boys," etc. But it is evident that the average gives no indication of the distribution of the individual measures from which it is obtained, no indication of the extent to which these measures vary or deviate from the average, no information as to how homogeneous is the material that the average represents. The September temperature may have been seasonable and equable or there may have been some days of frost and some days of sweltering heat. Again, if five individuals weigh 80, 65, 60, 40, and 55 kg., respectively, and five others 62, 59, 60, 61, and 58 kg., respectively, then the mean weight of either group is 60 kg., but one group is distributed very closely around the mean, whereas the other group exhibits such marked deviations from it that M (or any other general tendency measure) has little or no significance as a representative value.

From this it follows that we need not only measures of general tendency, but also measures of the variability or tendency to deviation of measurements, and that these latter are of well-nigh equal importance.

There are three common measures of variability[1]—the average deviation, the standard deviation, and the probable error.[2]

---

[1] Besides these measures, range of variability is sometimes indicated roughly by stating the maximal and minimal measurements, in conjunction with M. This gives us, at least, information as to the extremes of deviation.

[2] It is well to avoid confusion here at the outset. The average deviation (A. D.), as used by the statisticians, is identical with the mean variation (m. v.) of experimental psychology. The standard deviation (σ) is called the average error by Sanford, the mean error by Merriman, and the error of mean square by others.

1. The Average Deviation (Mean Variation)

The average deviation, *A.D.*, of a series of measurements, m, is the arithmetical mean of their separate deviations, d, from their mean, M (or some other measure of central tendency), taken without regard to sign.

Hence:

$$A.D. \text{ or } m.v. = \frac{|M - m_1| + |M - m_2| + \ldots |M - m_n|}{n},$$

or:

$$A.D. = \frac{d_1 + d_2 + \ldots d_n}{n},$$

or:

$$A.D. = \frac{\Sigma d}{n}. \tag{4}$$

Reference to Table 1 will render this process clear: there the average right-hand grip is 283; the weakest boy has a grip of 158, hence he deviates 125 units from the average; the strongest has a grip of 508, hence he deviates 225 units from the average. The first 28 boys rank below average, and their deviations, for a reason that will be clear later, are considered in the table as minus deviations. So far as the *A.D.* is concerned, however, all the deviations are added without regard to sign and their sum, 3104, is divided by the number of cases, 50, yielding a mean variation of 62.1 hectograms. If the median were selected as the representative value, the variability would, of course, be computed similarly with a new series of d's.

If the individual deviations are not to be made use of subsequently, as in correlation work, a very neat short-cut to the computation of the *A.D.* may be made in the following manner.[1]

---

[1] See Dunlap (7) for further suggestions concerning the use of the adding machine in this method.

Let $M = $ the mean,
    $N = $ the total number of measures,
    $N_{-M} = $ the number of measures less than the mean,
    $N_{+M} = $ the number of measures greater than the mean,
    $\Sigma_{-M} = $ the sum of the measures less than the mean,
    $\Sigma_{+M} = $ the sum of the measures greater than the mean.
Then $A.D.$ may be found by either of the formulas

$$A.D. = (\Sigma_{+M} - M \cdot N_{+M}) \div .5N, \qquad (4a)$$
$$A.D. = (M \cdot N_{-M} - \Sigma_{-M}) \div .5N. \qquad (4b)$$

Thus, for the right-hand grip, Table 1, Formula 4a becomes $A.D. = (7785 \text{-} 283 \cdot 22) \div 25 = 62.3$.

2. *The Standard Deviation (Error of Mean Square)*

This measure of variability is preferred by many experimenters and is practically the only one employed by statisticians, as it is thought to be more accurate than the average deviation, but it is much more laborious to compute. It is the square root of the average of the squares of the individual deviations.

$$S.D., \text{ or } \sigma = \sqrt{\frac{d^2_1 + d^2_2 + d^2_3 + \dots d^2_n}{n}},$$

or:

$$\sigma = \sqrt{\frac{\Sigma (d^2)}{n}}. \qquad (5)$$

If n is small, the formula is often modified by writing $n-1$ in place of n:[1]
Hence:

$$\sigma = \sqrt{\frac{\Sigma (d^2)}{n-1}}. \qquad (6)$$

The application of Formula 5 is illustrated in Table 1, 5th and 9th columns, where the squares of the individual deviations are shown in detail. The sum of these squares for the right-

---

[1] For the reasons for this substitution, consult Merriman (p. 71). It is evident that the effect of the substitution becomes progressively less as n increases: as will be seen in Table 2, the difference between Formula 5 and Formula 6 is practically negligible when $n = 50$.

hand grip is 293,004. This is divided by 50, giving 5860.1, the square root of which is 76.6, the σ desired.

The *S. D.* of a given series is somewhat larger than its *A. D.* Theoretically, and practically if the distribution be 'normal' (in the sense to be explained) and the observations sufficiently numerous, the relation is constant at

$$\sigma = 1.2533 \ A. \ D. \tag{7}$$

Conversely,

$$A. \ D. = 0.7979 \ \sigma. \tag{8}$$

As shown in Table 2, the *S. D.* computed by Formula 7 is closely similar to that computed by Formula 6.

3. The Probable Error

The probable error, *P. E.*, of a single measure is an amount of deviation both above and below *M* (or median or mode) that will include one-half of the individual measures; that is, it is a value such that the number of deviations that exceed it (in either direction from *M*) is the same as the number of deviations that fall short of it.[1]

The *P. E.* is approximately two-thirds the *S. D.*, or more exactly:

$$P. \ E. = 0.6745 \ \sigma \tag{9}$$

By reference to Formula 5 this becomes:

$$P. \ E. = 0.6745 \ \sqrt{\frac{\Sigma \ (d^2)}{n}}, \tag{10}$$

---

[1]The term 'probable error' is often a source of confusion to those unfamiliar with its use in mathematics. For a descriptive term, we might call it the 'median deviation,' since it is that deviation that is found midway from the representative value in either direction. The magnitude in question is not, of course, the *most* probable error, neither is it, in a certain sense, a 'mistake.' It is rather a 'probable sampling error:' we are unable to measure every possible instance of the thing we are studying, but must content ourselves with a restricted number of samples, usually so taken as to be 'random samples.' The *P. E.* serves to indicate the reliability of these random samples, the degree to which they probably depart from the true universal values. That the *P. E.* implies a symmetrical distribution of the samples is indicated in its definition and will be made clearer in a subsequent section.

or, for a small number of cases (Formula 6) :

$$P.E. = 0.6745 \sqrt{\frac{\Sigma (d^2)}{n-1}}. \tag{11}$$

In practise we may find the $P.E.$ approximately, if the dis- tribution be assumed to be normal (see under D, below), by counting off one-fourth of the cases from either end of a series of measurements, and halving the difference between the two values thus found.

$$P.E. = \frac{m_{\frac{3}{4}n} - m_{\frac{1}{4}n}}{2}. \tag{12}$$

Thus in Table 1, these limits lie at the 12th and a half and the 37th and a half measurements, and have, for the right-hand grip the values 222.5 and 324, respectively; hence, $P.E. = 324 - 222.5 \div 2 = 50.7$—a value that is approximately the same as the values of $P.E.$ computed by Formulas 10, 11, and 13 (Table 2). By Formula 11, $P.E. = 0.6745 \times 77.3 = 52.1$. Cor- responding values are given in Table 2 for the left-hand grip as distributed in Table 1. Still other values might be computed on the basis of the median instead of the mean.

By combination of Formulas 7, 8, and 9, we may obtain for a normal distribution :

$$P.E. = 0.8453 \, A.D. \tag{13}$$
$$S.D. = 1.4825 \, P.E. \tag{14}$$
$$A.D. = 1.1843 \, P.E. \tag{15}$$

The first of these is illustrated in Table 2.

4. The Coefficient of Variability

If it is desired to compare the variability of one series of measurements with that of another, it will be found that, as a rule, their respective measures of variability cannot be com- pared directly, because they are based upon different units or at least upon different measures of general tendency, but the relations of the two measures of variability to their respective measures of general tendency can be directly compared. In other words, we can compute two coefficients of variability (C) by dividing in each series a measure of variability by a representative measure, *i. e.,* either *S. D., A. D.,* or *P. E.,* may be divided by either mean, median, or mode. Unless otherwise specified, it may be assumed that *S. D.* is divided by *M.* Hence:

$$C = \frac{\sigma}{M} \tag{16}$$

Thus, in Table 1, for strength of right hand, $C = 77.3 \div 283 = .27$ and for strength of left hand, $C = 80.2 \div 273 = .29$, hence the latter series is slightly more variable.

5. *Variability of Measures of General Tendency*

The measures of variability just discussed serve to inform us of the variability of the distribution of the individual measurements around the mean, mode or median. But since our opportunities for securing data are limited, it follows that even averages may fail to be absolutely exact measures of the general tendency of the trait under measurement. To revert to the hypothetical data of Table 3, we were there able to obtain an *M*, 142.9 cm., of the height of 12-year-old boys: it must be evident that if we could have measured a million boys we should feel surer that the *M* then obtained was the true one, or that if we had measured only ten boys of that age we should not have felt at all sure that the average thus obtained was truly representative of the height of 12-year-old boys. We need, therefore, a measure of the reliability of *M*, so that we may have some idea as to how far the actually obtained *M* is likely to differ from the ideal or true *M*, or, reversely, how many measurements we need to secure an *M* that will have any desired or assigned degree of reliability.

To illustrate, suppose we did measure 1,000,000 boys in 1000 groups of 1000 measurements each; if we then averaged each group we should obtain 1000 *M*'s, each representing the central tendency of a group chosen by random sampling: we should then expect these 1000 M's to be closely similar, but not identical, and we could distribute them like a series of individual measures and determine the variability of this distribution. In practise, the variability of M is found by a formula that takes into consideration the variability of the distribution which M represents and the number of cases on which it is based.

Any formula for the variability of a distribution can be converted into a formula for the variability of the mean of the distribution by dividing the formula in question by the square root of the number of measurements. Thus, if Formula 4 be expressed as $A. D._{dis.}$ and the average deviation of the mean by $A. D._M$, we obtain

$$A. D._M = \frac{A. D._{dis.}}{\sqrt{n}}. \tag{17}$$

Similarly, Formulas 5 or 6 yield

$$\sigma_M = \frac{\sigma_{dis.}}{\sqrt{n}}. \tag{18}$$

More frequently used, however, is

$$P. E._M = \frac{0.6745\,\sigma}{\sqrt{n}}. \tag{19}$$

6. Variability of Differences between Means

One of the commonest problems in the application of tests is the determination of a difference between the averages of two sets of data. Thus, the average capacity of boys might be compared with the average capacity of girls in a given test. The circumstance that the one average is higher than the other does not of necessity indicate a true difference: it is imperative first to determine the degree of reliability that attaches to the difference. The neglect of this obvious check is one of the most conspicuous faults in many published results. Yet the computation is perfectly simple: the variability of a difference between two means is the square root of the sum of the squares of the variabilities of these means. Any one of the measures of variability may be employed.

Let D be the difference between two means, M_1 and M_2: let n_1 be the number of cases in the first, n_2 in the second series of measurements and the remaining values be similarly designated by the subscripts 1 and 2.

By reference to Formula 17 we obtain

$$A.D._D = \sqrt{\left(\frac{A.D._{dis.1}}{\sqrt{n_1}}\right)^2 + \left(\frac{A.D._{dis.2}}{\sqrt{n_2}}\right)^2} \text{ or } \sqrt{\frac{A.D._1^2}{n_1} + \frac{A.D._2^2}{n_2}}$$ (20)

From Formula 18, similarly,

$$\sigma_D = \sqrt{\frac{\sigma_1^2}{n_1} + \frac{\sigma_2^2}{n_2}},$$ (21)

and from Formula 19

$$P.E._D = \sqrt{\frac{P.E._1^2}{n_1} + \frac{P.E._2^2}{n_2}}$$ (22)

In case, however, the difference in question is a difference between the averages of two series of measurements that might stand in correlation (whether positive or negative, complete or incomplete), Formula 22 should be replaced by the following formula, in which r is the coefficient of correlation (explained later on) between the two series:

$$P.E._D = 0.6745\sqrt{\frac{\sigma_1^2 + \sigma_2^2 - 2r\sigma_1\sigma_2}{n}}.$$ (22a)

In illustration[1] we apply this formula to the data of Table 1 in order to see whether the difference between right-hand and left-hand grip is a chance or a significant difference. Substituting for r its value 0.92 (as computed below) and for σ_1 and σ_2 the values found by Formula 6 (Table 2), we obtain P. E. = 3.0, or not quite one-third the magnitude of the difference, 10, which thus gains a satisfactory degree of reliability.

---

[1]For a more detailed but simple example of the application of this formula, consult W. H. Winch, Inductive versus deductive methods of teaching. *EdPsMon*, No. 11, Baltimore, 1913 (statistical note, pp. 7-10).

7. *Other Measures of Variability*

As in the case of the measures of general tendency and of differences in general tendency, so with the measures of variability, they likewise diverge from the true values because we are forced to limit ourselves to restricted or random samples of the facts we are recording. The degree of this divergence, *i. e.*, the reliability of measures of variability may be discovered, approximately at least, by dividing any one of these measures by $\sqrt{2n}$. To take a single case:

$$\sigma_{var.} = \frac{\sigma_{dis.}}{\sqrt{2n}} \tag{23}$$

C. THE GRAPHIC REPRESENTATION OF MEASUREMENTS

A series of measurements, as we have seen, can be expressed adequately by a single representative value only when that value is accompanied by some measure of variability. Even these two values may fail to express the series completely, since they are, after all, only symbols for the convenient summarizing of general tendency and variability, whereas a complete numerical expression of a series of measures would imply the tabulation of all the data of the series. Such a tabulation is for the most part impracticable, or at least of little significance, because of the difficulty of grasping the nature of the series by the inspection of a mass of figures.

The use of the graphic method, however, supplies a most serviceable and effective means of showing at a glance all of the important features in the distribution of a series of measurements and likewise of relations between series of measurements.

1. *The Plotting of Frequencies: Graphs of Distribution*

The most usual form of graph for illustrating the distribution of a series of measurements is constructed as follows:

Draw two lines, *OY* and *OX* (Fig. 1) in the form of coördinate axes, *i. e.*, with *OY* perpendicular to *OX*. Upon the horizontal, or x-axis, lay off convenient intervals corresponding to the units of measurement of the series to be plotted; upon the vertical, or y-axis, lay off intervals corresponding to the frequencies of the series.

The choice of the scale units is largely arbitrary. The intervals of the two axes need not be the same, nor need different graphs, save for purposes of direct comparison, be plotted to the same scale. In general, a scale should be selected that will bring the surface easily into view as a whole and that will render conspicuous the features that are under consideration. Thus, if one is studying rate of increase or decrease, a scale should be selected that affords a fairly steep curve in order to emphasize its rise and fall. 'Squared' or cross-section paper (usually laid off by mm. on sheets 15x20 cm.) may be purchased for curve-plotting, and will be found invaluable for this work.

In illustration, the numerical table of frequencies above (Table 3) is turned into a surface of frequency upon the axes just mentioned (Fig. 1). We mark off on the x-axis, it will be seen, 18 equal intervals corresponding to the range of dimensions, 126, 128, ... 160 cm. Upon the y-axis we mark off equidistant intervals for the range of frequencies from 1 to 150. We next locate the series of 18 points. The first point lies vertically above the 126-cm. mark at a distance equal to 1 of the vertical units; the second lies vertically above the 128-cm. mark at a distance equal to 5 vertical units, etc. By joining the 18 points thus located, the resulting line evidently gives in a single visual impression the distribution that was expressed numerically in Table 3. Any point in this line is fixed by stating its abscissa or distance from the y-axis, and its ordinate, or distance from the x-axis.[1]

Now, it would have been equally feasible to have considered the values in Table 3 in terms of their deviation from the mean, median or mode, and with little or no change in the curve. Take, for simplicity, the mode, 142 cm., as the representative value. Erect an ordinate of the value of 150 at a point **M** on the x-axis (Fig. 1); intervals to the right of this ordinate may now represent positive deviations ($+2, +4 + 6$, etc.) while those to the

---

[1]The 'curve' is sometimes so drawn as to form the tops of a series of columns erected at the intervals on the base-line, instead of by joining the single points as here described. See, for example, Fig. 2.

left represent negative deviations (— 2, — 4, — 6, etc.), as indicated in Table 3.   It thus becomes possible to represent negative values graphically.

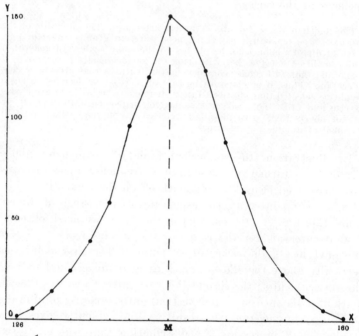

FIG. 1.   GRAPHIC REPRESENTATION OF THE DISTRIBUTION OF TABLE 3.

2. *The 'Smoothing' of Distributions*

Ordinary measurements are subject to numerous disturbing factors; our units of measurement are often coarse; our opportunities for securing data are always restricted; variable factors of one sort or another obtrude themselves—and these disturbances produce irregularities in the resultant data.   The obtained distribution, in other words, does not coincide with the true distribution, *i. e.,* with the distribution that would theoretically appear under ideal conditions.   Thus, in Table 3, chance may have led to the measurement among the 1,000 cases studied, of more boys of a certain height, say 144 cm., than we should ordinarily have encountered in measuring 1,000 pupils

taken at random. Or, to take an instance of a striking artificial distortion, in the census returns, people who are 39 or 41
years of age show a tendency to report their age as 40, so that
the age of 40 has an unnaturally large frequency.

Minor deviations from the theoretically expected distribution may be counteracted if we are constructing a frequency
graph by 'smoothing' the curve, i. e., by drawing the connecting
line in the form of a true curve rather than a broken straight
line: such a curve will pass in the neighborhood of the several
points which have been located by the numerical data, but will
not necessarily pass exactly through these points.[1] The result
is a graph that shows how the data would presumably have been
distributed if the factors which produced the distortions and
irregularities were eliminated.

TABLE 4

The Numerical Smoothing of the Distribution of Table 3

Centimeters	126	128	130	132	134	136	138	140	142	144	146	148	150	152	154	156	158	160
Original	1	5	14	24	39	58	96	120	150	142	123	88	63	36	23	12	5	1
Smoothed	2	6	14	26	40	64	91	122	137	138	108	91	62	41	24	13	6	2

In tabular work these deviations may be counteracted by a
simple arithmetical process. Replace each frequency except the
two extreme ones by the mean (to the nearest integer) of the
given frequency and the one just below it and the one just
above it; replace the two extreme frequencies by the mean (to
the nearest integer) of the given frequency taken two times
and the adjacent frequency taken once. If necessary, a second
smoothing may be made of the values obtained by the first
smoothing.

The values of Table 3 do not exhibit marked irregularities, as
is evident from their graphic distribution in Fig. 1: the process
of smoothing may, however, be illustrated by the treatment in
Table 4.

---

[1] For graphic work the curve may most readily be drawn with the aid
of the celluloid 'curves' or the flexible splines sold for this purpose by
dealers in drafting instruments.

D. NORMAL AND OTHER TYPES OF DISTRIBUTION: THE PROBABILITY SURFACE AND ITS APPLICATIONS[1]

1. The Normal Frequency Surface

Assume that errors of observation have been eliminated and that a large number of measurements of some psychological trait or capacity have been secured: experience has shown, and theoretical considerations likewise indicate, that as a rule these measurements will distribute themselves in the form of a symmetrical bell-shaped curve—variously known as the probability curve, the curve of error, Gauss' curve, or the normal frequency surface—the salient characteristics of which are a maximal frequency at M with a series of positive and negative d's from M that are symmetrically disposed on either side of it and whose frequency decreases progressively as their size increases.

Such a distribution implies the operation in the conditions that underlie each measurement of the feature or trait under measurement, of an indefinitely large number of individual factors, each of which is as likely to be present and effective in any one measurement as in any other. When, however, there are limiting or restricting conditions, or when one or more factors are present oftener than mere chance would allow, the resultant distribution will tend to depart from the normal type.[2] Thus the chances of death at different ages are not distributed according to the normal curve, but are higher in infancy and old age than in youth and middle age. The mental ability of college students is not likely to be distributed like that of the non-college population of the same age on account of the selective influence of entrance requirement. Thus, the curve of distribution for actual marks given to more than 20,000 Cornell University students (Fig. 2) is skewed to the right,

---

[1] For a detailed discussion of these topics, consult especially Yule, Ch. xv.

[2] It is, perhaps, hardly necessary to warn the reader of the distinction between (a) the number of observations and (b) the number of chance factors affecting each observation. If the former be large, the effect is merely to 'smooth' the distribution, but not necessarily to produce a normal distribution; if the latter be large, the distribution tends to approximate the 'normal' probability surface.

perhaps partly on account of this selective factor, but also on account of the operation of other disturbing factors, like the tendency to 'mark high,' the effect of zeal and industry in transmuting ability into the accomplishment that is being marked by the instructors, etc.[1] In general, distributions that do not conform to the normal type are termed 'skewed' distributions, and may demand special mathematical treatment.

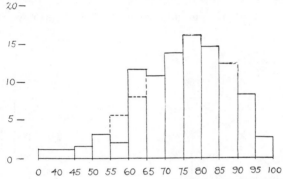

FIG. 2. DISTRIBUTION OF THE MARKS OF 20,348 CORNELL UNIVERSITY
STUDENTS. From I. E. FINKELSTEIN. *The Marking
System in Theory and Practice.*

2. *Relation of the Normal Curve to S. D. and P. E.*

The normal surface of frequency has interest still further because in it the significance of *P. E.* and of *S. D.* becomes clear. In fact, the latter bears to the curve a relation like that of a radius to its circle. If *S. D.* is small, the measurements are relatively similar and the curve is steep and compact (right-hand curve in Fig. 3), whereas, if *S. D.* is large, the curve is broad and of easy slope (left-hand curve in Fig. 3). If *M* and

---

[1]One special source of disturbance breaks the smoothness of the distribution at the 60 point, because this is the boundary between failure ("conditioned") and passing. Instructors dislike to report grades from 55 to 59. inclusive, but tend to change these to 60. This affords an excellent illustration of the manner in which a constant tendency will affect a curve of distribution. The dotted lines at this point in the diagram show what the curve theoretically should be were this constant error removed.

S. D. are known, the entire curve for a normal distribution is known. If the distribution is not of the normal form, the *S. D.* still remains a good measure of its variability, though not completely descriptive of the entire distribution.[1]

The geometrical explanation of the *P. E.* is simple. In Fig. 3 we draw the ordinates *ab* and *cd* equidistant from *OY* and at such a distance that the area *abYcd* is equal to the remainder of the total area under the curve: then the abscissa *Oa* or *Od* represents the value of *P. E., i. e.,* a deviation above and below the mean that will include one-half of the total deviations.

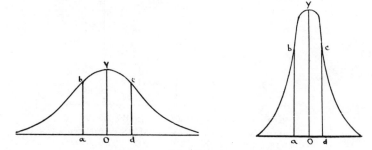

FIG. 3. TYPICAL CURVES OF NORMAL DISTRIBUTION.

The consistency of a series of measurements may also be indicated by stating the degree of probability that will attach to the appearance of an 'error' or deviation or residual, as it is often termed, of a magnitude equal to any assigned multiple of *P. E.* By definition, a deviation of the magnitude of *P. E.* is one as likely to be exceeded as not; in other words, the chances are even, or one to one, that it is exceeded. The probability of the occurrence of a deviation several times as large as *P. E.* is, however, very much smaller, as will be seen in the following

---

[1]This mathematical relation of *S. D.* to the probability curve, together with the possibility, as is shown later, of determining many other features of the distribution from the relation of *S. D.* and *M.* is one of the principal reasons why *S. D.* is preferred by many to the more-easily calculated *A. D.*

comparisons between P, the theoretical probability and $X \div$ $P. E.$, multiples of $P. E.$, from 1 to 5.[1]

$x \div P. E.$	$P.$
1	$1 \div 1.0$
2	$1 \div 5.6$
3	$1 \div 23.2$
4	$1 \div 143.3$
5	$1 \div 1342.2$

E. MEASURES OF CORRELATION

1. The Meaning of Correlation

Physical science discovers numerous uniformities or correspondences between natural phenomena which are formulated as 'natural laws:' biological science, on account of the intricacy of the factors which condition vital phenomena, can discover, for the most part, only *tendencies* toward uniformity or tendencies toward correspondence. Such a tendency of two or more traits or capacities to vary together is termed a correlation. Thus height and weight are obviously correlated because in general tall people are heavier than short people, but, of course, this tendency toward correspondence is far from absolute like the correspondence between the distance and speed of a body falling in vacuum or between the electrical constants, voltage, amperage and resistance, as expressed in Ohm's law.

---

[1] These values are computed by reference to standard tables of values of the probability integral corresponding to various multiples of $P. E.$ A condensed table of this sort is published by Thorndike (32, p. 200). The values given above were derived for the author by Prof. G. C. Comstock of the University of Wisconsin from Oppolzer's 10-figure table of the Gamma Integral, and are correct to the first place of decimals given. To illustrate from Thorndike's condensed table; the total area of the probability surface being 1000, the total area representing deviation in either direction is 500. From the table we see that a deviation or residual equal to 3 P. E. occurs in such a manner that 479 of the 500 cases are included between it and the average or median, and hence it is exceeded by 21 of 500 cases, or by 1 case in 23.8, approximately; 23.2 when more accurate integral tables are used.

From such a series of values the consistency of the determination may be stated in various ways. For example, if a correlation of .50 were accompanied by a $P. E.$ of .10, it might be said that the chances would be but 1 in more than 1300 times that such a correlation would occur by mere chance.

Since in practically every psychological test we are searching for these tendencies toward correspondence, it is important to know how they can be measured. In not a few psychological investigations correlation has been expressed merely descriptively as 'fair,' 'large,' 'poor,' etc., and these characterizations have been derived from mere inspection of arrays of data. As a matter of fact, some of these published statements of correlation are actually wrong: correlations do not exist where they have been affirmed, or do exist where they have been denied. At the present time there is no excuse for such merely descriptive statements of correlation, since, by the use of appropriate mathematical procedure, a tendency toward correspondence may be measured and expressed by a single quantitative symbol that has as much significance and definiteness as M, S. D., or any other statistical symbol. This symbol, r, which sums up the proportionality or degree of relationship between two factors or events, is known as the *index or coefficient of correlation*.

Complete positive or direct correlation between two traits is present when the existence of the one is invariably accompanied by the existence of the other, or when increase of the one is invariably accompanied by corresponding and proportional increase of the other.

Complete negative or inverse correlation is present when two traits are mutually exclusive, or when increase in the one is invariably accompanied by a corresponding and proportional decrease in the other.

A correlation is *indifferent* or *zero* if the existence or variation of one trait is totally unrelated to that of the other.

In perfect positive correlation, r is unity or 1.00; in complete negative correlation, r is -1.00; indifference or complete absence of correlation is 0. In actual psychological investigation, at least when functional correspondences are under investigation, we have commonly to deal with some intermediate degree of correlation, and r assumes, therefore, the form of a decimal lying between 0 and 1.00 for positive and between 0 and -1.00 for negative correspondence.

While the term 'correlation' is often broadly used in a generic sense to include any sort of relationship between two series of values, it is better to distinguish between it and other terms like 'dependency,' 'contingency' and 'association.'

The term 'dependency' properly applies to any functional relationship between two series, whether or not it can be expressed by the ordinary index of correlation. Such relationships may exist in so simple a form as to be readily expressed either verbally or mathematically, but whose coefficient of correlation would figure zero by the regular methods of computation. Take, for instance, the hypothetical relation that Spearman has adduced as an example of zero correlation (22, p. 77). Suppose five persons are tested for vision and hearing with the following results (in terms of feet that the test-type is read and the sound heard):

Person	A	B	C	D	E
Vision, in feet	6	7	9	11	14
Hearing, in feet	6	11	12	10	8

Here, $r = 0$, and thus there is no correlation, direct or inverse. If, however, the values are plotted graphically, there is revealed a simple dependency, viz.: hearing is good when sight is poor, reaches a maximum when sight is fairly good, and then declines when sight continues to improve. (Lehmann and Pedersen, 16, p. 16.) From this it may be seen that it is best to plot relations in graphic form whenever possible. In many cases, indeed, such a functional graph is more significant than any coefficient could possibly be, just as a curve of distribution is more significant than an M, even when coupled with its measure of deviation.

If, however, by charting or otherwise, the relationship between the two arrays of data is found to be direct, if, in other words, the values of the one array vary proportionately with those of the other, there is not only dependency, but also correlation between the two arrays.

If these arrays each form a quantitatively graded series, the relationship may then be termed a 'series-correlation.' If the gradations are expressed in numerical values, measures or magnitudes, the relationship is one of correlation in the specific sense of that term (*Masskorrelation* of the Germans). But if the gradations are expressed only in terms of rank or order in a series, the relationship is one of *rank-correlation* or *co-ordination* (to use the term proposed by Betz).

If the values do not form a quantitatively graded series, but are merely grouped into qualitative divisions, the relation is known as *contingency* (or, following Yule, as *association*, if the classification is limited to a two-fold division).

Examples of correlations, co-ordinations and contingencies appear in what follows. As already pointed out, these terms are not always distinguished, and the phrase 'degree of correlation' is often used to cover not only correlation proper, but also degree of co-ordination, of contingency and of association.[1]

---

[1] For further discussion of terminology and for the derivation of the formulas that follow, consult especially Betz, Stern and Yule.

2. *The Computation of the Index of Correlation*[1]

(a) The 'Product-Moments' Method of Pearson

The most elaborate as well as the theoretically best possible method of computing r is the standard 'product-moments' method elaborated by Bravais, Galton, and especially by Pearson.[2]

By the product-moments method

$$r = \frac{\Sigma\, xy}{n\, \sigma_1\, \sigma_2}, \tag{24}$$

in which the x's are the series of deviations from M in the first array and the y's the corresponding series of deviations in the second array, and in which σ_1 is the standard deviation of the first and σ_2 the standard deviation of the second array, and n the number of cases in either array.

The various steps of the computation may be illustrated by reference to Table 1[3] for grip of right and left hands, as follows:

(1) Arrange the original measurements in order of their standing or rank, as shown in Columns 1, 3, and 7. (While this is not absolutely necessary, it commonly facilitates computation, though for speedier determination of the xy values, it might be preferable to place the two arrays in the same order by individuals, *e. g.*, as shown by the numbers in Columns 2 and 6.)

(2) Compute M (or the median) for each series (283 and 273.)

(3) Compute and record the individual deviations (d, Columns 4 and 8) for each series, retaining the algebraic signs.[4]

---

[1]Consult Thorndike (32, chs. x and xi) for illustrations of other methods than those described here.

[2]In referring to the product-moments as the best possible method, certain qualifications must be kept in mind. It is possible, for instance, that, as Spearman contends (25), the comparison of ranks (R-method), for reasons that will be explained later, may be more reliable and satisfactory when psychological data are under treatment.

[3]For a fuller illustration of correlation arithmetic, together with suggestions for shortening the work, see E. Davenport, pp. 455-471.

[4]In Table 1, to accord better with common thinking, standings below average are considered as minus deviations, *i. e.*, the mean has been subtracted from the individual standings instead of vice versa.

(4) Multiply the d of each individual in the first series (now termed his x) by the d for the same individual in the second series (now termed his y), and record the products, observing the algebraic signs (the xy values in Column 13), e. g., boy No. 30 has for his x, — 125 and for his y, — 135, hence, for his xy, — 125 × — 135 = 16875. Again, boy No. 25 has for his corresponding values, — 21 and + 35, hence for xy, — 735.

(5) Add the products obtained in (4) (280,118, Column 13).

(6) Compute the S. D. of both series (σ_1 and σ_2 in Formula 24, illustrated in the d^2 columns, 5th and 9th, and explained in Formula 5): multiply them together, and multiply their product by the number of cases (76.6 × 79.4 × 50 = 304,102).

(7) Divide the 5th by the 6th resultant for the index desired ($r = 280{,}118 \div 304{,}102 = + 0.92$).

The arithmetic of the Pearson method is thus simple, though somewhat tedious. The work may be materially lessened by the use of Barlow's *Tables of Squares, Cubes, Square Roots*, etc., New York, 1904, of Crelle's *Rechentafeln* (procurable through G. E. Stechert & Co., New York), which show at a glance the products of all numbers up to 1000 × 1000, and by the use of an adding machine.[1] Another considerable shortening may often be effected without serious disturbance by substituting Formula 7 for Formula 5 in computing the two S. D.'s. Thus, in our illustration, this substitution (see Table 2) gives for the denominator of the fraction: 77.8 × 79.3 × 50 = 308,477, from which we find $r = 0.94$.

The *probable error of the coefficient of correlation* as obtained by the Pearson method is calculated by the formula

$$P.\ E._r = 0.6745\ \frac{1 - r^2}{\sqrt{n}}. \tag{25}$$

It is evident that the reliability of a coefficient increases with the number of cases compared and also with the magnitude of the r obtained. The actual values of $P.\ E._r$, as computed by Formula 25 for eleven values of r from 0 to 1, accompanying values of n from 25 to 1000, are indicated in Table 5, so that one can not only read at a glance the $P.\ E.$ for a given value of r

---

[1] The author has found the Gem adding machine serviceable for work in which there is no necessity for printed records such as the Burroughs, Standard, Wales and other high-priced machines afford.

and n, but also determine the value of n, i. e., the number of observations, needed to establish a given degree of correlation with any assigned degree of accuracy. In our illustrative case, since $n = 50$, and $r = .92$, we note that $P. E._r$ is less than 0.0181, that 200 observations would have reduced the error to less than .0091, etc. If our correlation had been lower, say 0.30, the error for 50 cases would have risen to 0.0868.

TABLE 5

Probable Error of r for Various Values of r and of n (*Yule*)

VALUES OF n	$r = 0$	$r = .1$	$r = .2$	$r = .3$	$r = .4$	$r = .5$	$r = .6$	$r = .7$	$r = .8$	$r = .9$	$r = 1$
25	.1349	.1335	.1295	.1228	.1133	.1012	.0863	.0688	.0486	.0256	.0000
50	.0954	.0944	.0916	.0868	.0801	.0715	.0610	.0486	.0343	.0181	.0000
75	.0779	.0771	.0748	.0709	.0654	.0584	.0498	.0397	.0280	.0148	.0000
100	.0674	.0668	.0648	.0614	.0567	.0506	.0432	.0344	.0243	.0128	.0000
200	.0478	.0473	.0459	.0435	.0402	.0359	.0306	.0244	.0172	.0091	.0000
300	.0389	.0386	.0374	.0354	.0327	.0292	.0249	.0199	.0140	.0074	.0000
400	.0337	.0334	.0324	.0307	.0283	.0253	.0216	.0172	.0121	.0064	.0000
500	.0302	.0299	.0290	.0274	.0253	.0226	.0193	.0154	.0109	.0057	.0000
600	.0275	.0273	.0264	.0251	.0231	.0207	.0176	.0140	.0099	.0052	.0000
700	.0255	.0252	.0245	.0232	.0214	.0191	.0163	.0130	.0092	.0048	.0000
800	.0238	.0236	.0229	.0217	.0200	.0179	.0153	.0122	.0086	.0045	.0000
900	.0225	.0223	.0216	.0205	.0189	.0169	.0144	.0115	.0081	.0043	.0000
1000	.0213	.0211	.0205	.0194	.0179	.0160	.0137	.0109	.0077	.0041	.0000

In general, a correlation, like any other determination, to have claim to scientific attention must be at least twice as large as its $P. E.$, and to be perfectly satisfactory, should be perhaps four to five times as large.

Since, in our illustration, r is some 51 times as large as its $P. E.$, its appearance by mere chance is practically zero and its reliability is practically absolute.

(b) The Method of Rank-Differences (Co-ordination)

The product-moments method gives full and exact weight to the d of each m from the M. If we disregard the magnitude of these d's, however, and regard only the relative order, or station, of individual m's in each array, we may yet measure correlation (co-ordination) by what is known as the method of rank-differences.

For this method, the formula, as developed by Spearman (25), is

$$\varrho = 1 - \frac{\Sigma D^2}{c}, \tag{26}$$

in which ϱ is the coefficient of co-ordination, D is the numerical difference between each corresponding pair of ranks[1] (not to be confused with d, the deviation from the mean), and in which c is the mean value of ΣD^2 by mere chance. Since

$$c = \frac{n \, (n^2 - 1)}{6}, \tag{27}$$

Formula 26 may be written:

$$\varrho = 1 - \frac{6 \, \Sigma D^2}{n \, (n^2 - 1)}. \tag{28}$$

For illustration, note in Table 1, Column 11, the series of D's which are squared and summated in Column 12. Boy No. 30 ranks first (weakest) in the distribution for right-hand grip and first in the order for left-hand grip, hence his $D = 0$. Boy No. 52[2] is 3d in the first, and 9th in the second array, hence for him $D = 6$ and $D^2 = 36$. Since $n = 50$, by Formula 27,

$$c = \frac{50 \, (2500 - 1)}{6} = 20{,}791;$$

hence, by Formula 26,

$$\varrho = 1 - \frac{2098}{20{,}791} = 1 - .10 = .90,$$

---

[1] In this and the following method, cases of 'ties' for a given rank are preferably divided in such a manner as to keep the total number of ranks equal in the two series. If, for instance, two S's rank 5th, they should both be assigned the rank 5.5 (to replace 5 and 6), or if three S's rank 5th, they should all three be assigned the rank 6 (to replace the 5th, 6th and 7th places in the series). This procedure introduces a certain amount of error, but not usually enough to be deemed serious.

On the applicability of the method in general and the relation of its index to the Pearson index of correlation, see especially Betz, Dürr, Spearman and Pearson (*Draper's Biometric Series*, 4:1907, 35).

[2] To avoid possible confusion, it may be explained that two records were discarded, so that the boys' numbers run two over the fifty.

a result in close accordance with that of the product-moments method and obtained in a small fraction of the time.

The probable error of ϱ in the method of rank-differences is somewhat larger than in the Pearson or 'cross-multiple' method. Its formula is

$$P.\,E._{\rho} = 0.706 \frac{1 - \varrho^2}{\sqrt{n}} \tag{29}$$

The chief difficulty with the rank-method is its assumption that the unit of rank is equal throughout the scale, whereas, as is evident, the units in all probability should mean less in the middle portion than in the extreme portions of the scale. If we assume that the actual frequency-distribution of each of the compared variables is of the normal or Gaussian form, Pearson has shown that the correlation of grades[1] is then functionally related to the coefficient of co-ordination, and in such a manner that

$$r = 2 \sin \left(\frac{\pi}{6} \varrho \right) \tag{30}$$

However, this formula affects only slightly (at most two units in the second decimal) the value of ϱ, so that, for most purposes, the correction that it affords may be neglected.

The $P.\,E.$ of r thus calculated by the method of rank-differences is somewhat larger than in the Pearson, or 'cross-multiple' method. Its formula is the same as that of the coefficient of co-ordination from which it is computed (Formula 29).

(c) Spearman's Correlation 'Foot-Rule,' or R-Method

Spearman's " 'foot-rule' for measuring correlation" (25) is another and still simpler method of comparison by rank, the essential features of which are the use of D, the numerical difference of station, in place of D^2, and of only those of the D's that indicate a gain in rank (since the losses must equal the gains).

---

[1] The grade of an individual is not quite identical with his rank, but is measured by the number of individuals above him. See Brown, p. 19, for illustrative diagram.

This method, it is important to note, yields an **index**, R, that is not identical with the Pearson r, though functionally related thereto, as is explained below.

The formula for Spearman's R is

$$R = 1 - \frac{\Sigma\, g}{c}, \tag{31}$$

in which g is the numerical gain in rank of an individual in the second, as compared with the first series, and in which c is the mean value of $\Sigma\, g$ by mere chance.[1]
Since

$$c = \frac{n^2 - 1}{6}, \tag{32}$$

we obtain by substitution:

$$R = 1 - \frac{6\,\Sigma\, g}{n^2 - 1}. \tag{33}$$

For illustration, note in Table 1, Column 10, the series of gains (g), which yield $\Sigma\, g = 106$. As $n = 50$, by Formula 32, $c = (2500 - 1) \div 6 = 416.5$;
hence, by Formula 31,

$$R = 1 - \frac{106}{416.5} = 1 - .25 = .75$$

To determine whether R has any claim to reliability, one may use the formula:[2]

$$P.\,E._R = \frac{0.43}{\sqrt{n}}; \tag{34}$$

---

[1] If the result turns out to be a minus quantity, the correlation is inverse, but the value of R is then to be computed by ranking one of the series in reverse order.

[2] This formula has also been called in question by Pearson. See Spearman's rejoinder (28, 282ff).

To convert R-values into r-values, Spearman has proposed the formula:

$$r = \sin\left(\frac{\pi}{2}R\right) ; \qquad (35)$$

or, for all cases in which R is less than .50, this may be simplified with little loss of accuracy into:

$$r = 1.5\,R. \qquad (36)$$

For the quick and accurate conversion of R into r, Table 6, which is based on Formula 35, may be consulted.

In the correlation under examination, since $R = .75$, $r = .93$, or practically the value obtained by the longer Pearson method.

According to Pearson (*Drapers Biom. Series,* 4 : 1907), however, the proper formula for the conversion of R-values into r-values is

$$r = 2\cos\frac{\pi}{3}(1-R)-1. \qquad (37)$$

TABLE 6

Conversion of R-Values into r-Values, in Accordance with Formula 35

R	r	R	r	R	r	R	r	R	r
.00	.00	.20	.31	.40	.59	.60	.81	.80	.95
.01	.01	.21	.32	.41	.60	.61	.82	.81	.96
.02	.03	.22	.34	.42	.61	.62	.83	.82	.96
.03	.05	.23	.35	.43	.62	.63	.84	.83	.96
.04	.06	.24	.37	.44	.64	.64	.84	.84	.97
.05	.07	.25	.38	.45	.65	.65	.85	.85	.97
.06	.08	.26	.40	.46	.66	.66	.86	.86	.98
.07	.11	.27	.41	.47	.67	.67	.87	.87	.98
.08	.13	.28	.43	.48	.69	.68	.88	.88	.98
.09	.14	.29	.44	.49	.70	.69	.88	.89	.99
.10	.16	.30	.45	.50	.71	.70	.89	.90	.99
.11	.17	.31	.47	.51	.72	.71	.90	.91	.99
.12	.19	.32	.48	.52	.73	.72	.90	.92	.99
.13	.20	.33	.50	.53	.74	.73	.91	.93	.99
.14	.22	.34	.51	.54	.75	.74	.92	.94	1.00
.15	.23	.35	.52	.55	.76	.75	.93	.95	1.00
.16	.25	.36	.54	.56	.77	.76	.93	.96	1.00
.17	.26	.37	.55	.57	.78	.77	.94	.97	1.00
.18	.28	.38	.56	.58	.79	.78	.94	.98	1.00
.19	.29	.39	.57	.59	.80	.79	.95	.99	1.00

(d)   Comparison of Distribution in Selected Groups

The following method is sometimes useful as a device for preliminary survey, but when used, as it often has been, for a final expression of correlation, it is inferior to the methods already described.

Distribute the data for both series in order as illustrated in. Table 1, and divide them into four or five groups on the basis of equal numbers of cases or of equal amounts of deviation. By inspection it is often possible to determine at this juncture whether there is sufficient evidence of a correlation to justify further calculation. For this inspection we may take the cases found in the first group of the first series and examine their distribution in the groups of the second series. Evidently, in the absence of correlation, these cases would be distributed by chance. Thus, in Table 1, let the two series be divided into 5 groups of 10 measurements each. The 10 measurements in the first group for right-hand grip would tend, by chance alone, to be distributed 2 in each of the 5 groups in the second series, but as a matter of fact they are massed in or near the first group (8 in the 1st, 2 in the 2d), hence there is evidently a high degree of correlation.

The distribution in the second series of the remaining groups of the first series may be similarly tested, though an examination of the first group is commonly sufficient.

If the grouping is made in terms of deviation, the number of measurements found in the several groups will usually be unequal; it is then necessary to calculate the distribution of the various groups of the first series into those of the second. Suppose the two series of Table 1 are each divided into five 70-hectogram groups; the right-hand series will subdivide into groups containing 16, 15, 12, 4 and 3 measurements; the left-hand series into groups containing 12, 17, 12, 6 and 3 measurements, respectively. Take the 16 cases in the first group of the first series; by chance it is clear that 12/50, or 3.84 of them, would fall in the first group of the 2d series, 17/50, or 5.44 of them, would fall in the second group, 3.84 in the third, 1.97 in the fourth, and .98 in the fifth. The actual distribution of the 16 cases into those five groups is 11, 5, 0, 0, 0, as compared with the chance distribution, 3.84, 5.44, 3.84, 1.97, .98.

If now we wish not only to explore the distribution of selected groups tentatively for the presence of relationship, but also to present the evidence of the relationship in compact form, we may, as is often done, prepare a table by comparative averages. To return again to the relationship of right and left-hand strength of grip, we may by this means secure the following tabular statement.[1]

TABLE 7
Relation of Right and Left-Hand Grip by Group Averages (*Whipple*)

Group in 1st Series	1st 10	2d 10	3d 10	4th 10	5th 10
Average Right-hand Grip	194.9	229.9	271.5	317.9	402.2
Average Left-hand Grip	183.7	226.3	269.2	291.5	394.4

The data from such a table may be thrown into graphic form very simply: let ordinates represent the values of the one series, abscissas the values of the other, so that the one series is plotted as a function of the other: if, then, the first series ranges upward for values from low to high and the second from left to right for values from low to high, a positive correlation will be indicated by a line running in a southwest-northeast direction, inverse correlation by a line running in a northwest-southeast direction, and zero correlation by a vertical or a horizontal line (depending on which series is plotted on the ordinates). In proportion as the correlation is complete the line assumes an oblique position.

(e) Relationships of Contingency

The use of such a classified distribution as Table 7 leads naturally to a consideration of cases in which the comparison of two sets of data can be undertaken in that form only, be-

---

[1] For examples of this type of presentation, consult Bagley (1), Binet and Vaschide (3). Though this method has been frequently used, a little reflection will show that it is inferior to the several methods described before, because the advantage of weighing the relation of each individual measure is lost by lumping them into averages, and because, moreover, no coefficient of correlation is computed. If the groups were made more numerous and the data presented in the form of a graph showing the entire course of the relationship, the absence of the coefficient might be less serious.

For suggestions for further treatment of what he terms *Fraktionskorrelation*, see Stern, 305ff.

cause further information is wanting. The relationship between two sets of values that can merely be classified qualitatively and not graded by magnitude or rank is termed a contingency. Thus, in Table 8[1] the problem is to determine

TABLE 8

Contingency Table for Inheritance of Temperament (Heymans and Wiersma)

FATHERS.

	MERRY	MELAN-CHOLY	ALTER-NATING	EVEN	TOTALS
Merry	122	8	81	67	278
Melancholy	10	2	7	10	29
Alternating	70	9	101	68	248
Even	58	6	66	45	175
Totals	260	25	255	190	730

whether sons tend to resemble their fathers in certain temperamental traits. The formulas for computing the coefficient of contingency from classificatory tables of this sort are too complex to be reproduced here[2]: they are designed to calculate the difference between the numbers actually found in different compartments of the table and the numbers to be expected there by mere chance. For Table 8, the resultant coefficient of mean-square contingency, as it is termed by Pearson, amounts to 0.16.

(f) Method of Association (Four-fold Tables)

The measure of a relationship of contingency is, however, relatively simple if the classification be limited to a four-fold table. The amount of correspondence revealed in such a table is termed by Yule the *degree of association*. Very often the four-fold classification pertains to two traits whose presence or absence is ascertainable, but about whose degree nothing can be said, so that the phrase 'correlation of presence and absence' has been applied to this form of contingency.

---

[1]Taken from Schuster and Elderton, and derived by them from Heymans and Wiersma (14).

[2]See for details, Brown (p. 13), Betz (29f.), Pearson.

In a typical instance, then, we have given

$a =$ number of cases in which both traits are present,

$b =$ number of cases in which the first trait is present and the second absent,

$c =$ number of cases in which the second trait is present and the first absent,

$d =$ number of cases in which both traits are absent.

On the basis of these values, several formulas have been developed by Yule for the coefficient of association, Q.

The simplest is

$$Q = \frac{ad - bc}{ad + bc}. \tag{38}$$

This formula gives values which are not identical with r, but stand roughly in the relation $4:3$ with it. The substitution of $\sqrt{ad}$ and $\sqrt{bc}$ in both numerator and denominator has been recommended more recently by the same author: the value of Q then approaches nearer Spearman's R.

A third formula devised by Yule, which has the practical merit of yielding values comparable with the ordinary r, is

$$r = \sin \frac{\pi}{2} \frac{\sqrt{ad} - \sqrt{bc}}{\sqrt{ad} + \sqrt{bc}}. \tag{39}$$

If, in this formula, we replace the sine by the cosine of its complement, we secure

$$r = \cos \left[\frac{\pi}{2} - \frac{\pi}{2} \frac{\sqrt{ad} - \sqrt{bc}}{\sqrt{ad} + \sqrt{bc}} \right],$$

which we can reduce to

$$r = \cos \frac{\sqrt{bc}}{\sqrt{ad} + \sqrt{bc}} \pi. \tag{40}$$

The probable error, provided ab is not very unequal to cd, may be taken as

$$P. E._r = \frac{1.1}{\sqrt{n}}. \tag{41}$$

Our example of four-fold classification (Table 9) is drawn by Stern (30, p. 310) from Heymans (13, p. 336). In it we find $a = 14$, $b = 17$, $c = 7$, $d = 72$. Substituting in Formula 40, we have

$$r = \cos \frac{\sqrt{7 \times 17}}{\sqrt{14 \times 72} + \sqrt{7 \times 17}} \pi = \cos 46° = 0.69\text{[1]}$$

TABLE 9

Association of Good Judgment with Phlegmatic Temperament (Heymans)

	PHLEGMATIC	NOT PHLEGMATIC	TOTALS
Good Judgment_____	14	17	31
Not Good Judgment_____	7	72	79
Totals _____	21	89	110

Now, this same formula can often be used for preliminary exploration of series in which the degree of presence of a trait is known, and which may, therefore, be treated, if desired, by the more elaborate methods. For this purpose, assume that all measurements greater than M (or the median), *i. e.*, all *plus* cases, signify the presence of the trait, and all *minus* cases its absence. In Table 1 we find, using the median, 22 cases that are plus in both series, 3 that are plus in right and minus in left-hand grip, 3 that are minus in right and plus in left-hand grip, and 22 that are minus in both. Substituting these values in Formula 40, we have

[1] Stern (p. 312) proposes other methods of treating the four-fold classification, which have the merit of revealing the direction of the association. Thus, in the example above, inspection of the table will indicate that the association tends more in one direction than the other: phlegmatic temperament is more apt to imply good judgment than good judgment is apt to imply phlegmatic temperament. According to Stern's formulas, the first association has the strength of 0.53, the second of 0.32.

$$r = \cos \frac{\sqrt{9}}{\sqrt{484} + \sqrt{9}} \pi, \text{ or } \cos 21.6° = .93,$$

which gives again almost the same value as by the standard formula.

(g) The Method of Unlike Signs

Even this procedure may be simplified by substituting for $\sqrt{bc}$ the *percentage* of cases with unlike signs (U), and for $\sqrt{ad}$ the percentage of cases with like signs (L)[1] with the result,

$$r = \cos \frac{U}{L + U} \pi, \tag{42}$$

or, since $L + U$ must always equal 100, and since $\pi = 180°$, this formula may be condensed, if desired, to

$$r = \cos U \, 1.8° \tag{43}$$

Finally, since U must lie between 50 and 0 for positive and between 50 and 100 for inverse correlations, a table may be prepared[2] from which the values of r may be read directly from any integer value of U.

By reference to the paragraph above it will be seen that in Table 1 we have 6 cases of unlike signs in the 50, hence $U = 12$ and $r = 0.93$, as by other methods.

---

[1] That is, virtually substituting the arithmetical for the geometrical mean.

[2] Reproduced from an earlier article by the author (35) in which the applicability of the method is discussed more fully.

TABLE 10

Corresponding Values of r and U for Formula 43 (*Whipple*)

If U is greater than 50, first subtract it from 100, then prefix the minus sign to the correlation indicated

U	r	U	r	U	r	U	r	U	r
0	1.000	10	.951	20	.809	30	.587	40	.309
1	.999	11	.941	21	.790	31	.562	41	.279
2	.998	12	.929	22	.770	32	.536	42	.248
3	.995	13	.917	23	.750	33	.509	43	.218
4	.992	14	.904	24	.728	34	.482	44	.187
5	.987	15	.891	25	.707	35	.454	45	.156
6	.982	16	.876	26	.684	36	.426	46	.125
7	.976	17	.860	27	.661	37	.397	47	.094
8	.968	18	.844	28	.637	38	.368	48	.062
9	.960	19	.827	29	.613	39	.338	49	.031

This method should not be used for final determinations of important correlations because the probable error is too large, but it is a useful device for quick examination of a relation.

3. *The Correction of Obtained Correlations to their True Value*

(a) Correction of the Attenuation Produced by Chance Errors

(The Coefficient of Reliability)

The real correspondence between two traits or capacities is not, as has so often been erroneously supposed, necessarily revealed by the determination of a coefficient of correlation, even by the most approved methods and with a probable error that is satisfactorily small. All measurements, as we have noted, are subject to chance errors of observation. In the determination of averages such errors tend to counterbalance one another, so that if the measurements are sufficiently numerous, the obtained M differs from the true M by an inappreciable amount. In the case of correlations, however, these errors[1] are not eliminated by increasing the number of observations, and their pres-

---

[1] The phrase 'errors of observation' is to be understood in a wide sense to include not only errors arising from technique, instrumentation, etc., but also *chance* shifts in the disposition of subjects in their attitude toward the test, etc.

ence has the effect of *decreasing* the size of the correlation, so that, in so far as these errors are concerned, the 'raw' or obtained correlation is too small, or, to use Spearman's term, the correlation is 'attenuated' by errors which constitute, from this point of view, constant or systematic errors.

This illusory attenuation of the correlation by errors of observation seems, in fact, a principal cause of the contradictory nature of results that have hitherto been obtained; in experiments in which such errors have been very large, a correlation has not appeared, even when present, and has, in consequence, been erroneously denied. The determination of a small correlation, therefore, opens two possibilities; it may indicate actual absence of correspondence, or it may indicate merely the presence of large chance errors of observation. (Krüger and Spearman, p. 55.)

In order to correct the raw and discover the true r, it is imperative to secure at least two independent series of observations. The formula for correction of attenuation, or the 'expanding' formula, as it might be termed, is then applied as follows:

$$AB_t = \frac{M \ (A_1 \ B_1, \ A_1 \ B_2, \ A_2 \ B_1, \ A_2 \ B_2)}{M \ (A_1 \ A_2, \ B_1 \ B_2)} \tag{44}$$

in which

$AB_t =$ the true correlation,

$M =$ the mean,

$A_1 =$ the 1st series of observations of the trait A,

$A_2 =$ the 2d series of observations of the trait A,

$B_1 =$ the 1st series of observations of the trait B,

$B_2 =$ the 2d series of observations of the trait B,

$A_1 \ B_1 =$ the raw correlation of A_1 and B_1,

$A_1 \ A_2 =$ the raw correlation of A_1 and A_2, etc.

Thus the numerator is the M of the four possible r's between the measurements of A and the measurements of B, while the denominator is the M of the r of the two A series and the r of the two B series.

Attention should be called to the opportunity afforded by such correlations as $A_1 A_2$ and $B_1 B_2$ to secure an objective indication of the reliability of the tests used to measure A and B. The correlation thus measured between the results of two different applications of the same test upon the same persons has been used, particularly by recent English investigators, like Spearman, Burt, Wyatt, *et al*, as a *coefficient of reliability*. The principle is simple enough. If the outcome of a test is not disturbed by chance or by constant errors, the ranks of the several S's should be the same at each trial. Constant errors must, of course, be avoided by other precautions. If, however, chance errors are too obtrusively present, this fact will be revealed by a low correlation between A_1 and A_2. In practise a test whose coefficient of reliability is less than .60 or .70 is in need of rectification—improvement of conditions, larger number of observations—or should be discarded. It should be understood that A_1 and A_2 need not be independent series of tests given by different E's at different sittings, but may be made up from the data obtained during a single sitting, though, as a rule, two sets of data are secured and the correlation is calculated between the first half of the first performance added to the last half of the second performance and the last half of the first performance added to the first half of the second performance.

The point is that, in figuring the coefficient of reliability or in using Formula 44 it is essential that the discrepancies between the two series of measurements of the same trait should really be of a 'chance' character. Suppose, for example, that A represents "memory for nonsense syllables" and has been tested by requiring the subjects to memorize a dozen sets of syllables. It would be wrong, then, to constitute A_1 of the first six sets and A_2 of the second six sets, because the latter half-dozen would be affected by a constant factor—that of practise—to an extent different from the first half-dozen. It would be better to constitute A_1 from the odd- and A_2 from the even-numbered tests.

Again, it must be remembered that a large correction by Formula 44 involves a great increase in the probable error. Hence, it is advisable, after carrying out the tests, to calculate the correlation A_1A_2 at once. If this value turns out to be less than the requisite .60 to .70, the testing should be prolonged or improved until at least this amount is reached. This precaution is particularly necessary when the subjects are few in number, because then the probable error is more dangerous.

The above formula holds for ordinary cases, but if one series of observations, say A, should be known to be much more exact and reliable than the other, then the geometrical should be substituted for the arithmetical M. In theory the denominator should always be the geometrical M, but the arithmetical M is virtually as accurate, and for short series even more desirable. For the mathematical demonstration of this and the following formulas, consult Spearman (22). The correction does not entirely eliminate the uncertainty that arises from the use of 'random samples' for investigation; that must be removed, as already intimated, by the use of more extended series.

Simpson (21a, p. 109) complains that the gain in accuracy by the use of this corrective formula is too little for the labor expended, and that the time had better be spent in getting more accurate data in the first place.

(b) Correction of the 'Constriction' or 'Dilation' Produced by Constant Errors

Attenuation is the result of the operation of chance errors— chance in the sense that the deviation of any measurement takes place independently of the deviation of any other measurement. If, however, some influence is at work which affects all the measurements of one or of both series, such a constant factor or constant error will prove a source of disturbance that may either increase or decrease the obtained correlation. Such disturbances will result from the operation of any factor which is not strictly relevant to the correspondence under examination.

If an irrelevant factor affects both of the series, it is evident that the correlation will be unduly increased or 'dilated.' Suppose, for example, that one wished to determine the correlation of pitch discrimination with the discrimination of lifted weights, and that the subjects of the experiments were of different ages. Then, since the two capacities in question both tend to improve with age, this common dependence on age will clearly tend to induce the appearance of a correlation, even if there really be none between the capacities themselves when compared under uniform conditions of age.[1]

If an irrelevant factor affects but one of the series, it is evident that the correlation will be unduly decreased or 'constricted,' i. e., the irrelevant influence will tend to reduce any proportionality that really exists between the two series. To quote an example from Spearman, a correlation of 0.49 was discovered between pitch discrimination and school standing, but it was likewise discovered that more than half the children had 'taken lessons,' and thus had the opportunity for special training in the observation of pitches.

These constant irrelevant factors may not always be excluded,

---

[1] This undiscovered or neglected influence of age has been a very common source of error in many studies of correlation. Obviously, this particular irrelevancy may be eliminated practically by proper selection of subjects for the investigation, or it may be eliminated by manipulation of the results in various ways besides that here described: see, for example, Bagley.

but their force can frequently be measured and allowed for by the following formula :[1]

$$AB_t = \frac{AB_a - AC \cdot BC}{\sqrt{(1 - AC^2)(1 - BC^2)}}, \qquad (45)$$

in which

AB_t = the true correlation between A and B,

AB_a = the apparent correlation between A and B.

AC = the direct correlation between A and any irrelevant factor, C,

BC = the direct correlation between B and C.

If, as is most often the case, the irrelevant factor affects but one series, this influence of 'constriction' may be excluded by the simpler formula :

$$AB_t = \frac{AB_a}{\sqrt{(1 - AC^2)}} \qquad (46)$$

Thus, in the example mentioned, the correlation between pitch discrimination and its disturbing factor, musical training, was found by computation, to be 0.61; hence, by Formula 46,

$$r = \frac{0.49}{\sqrt{1 - 0.61^2}} = 0.62.$$

From the above considerations, it follows that the experimenter must define with some exactness the traits that are to be examined for a possible correlation, and that he must not seek to establish the correlation until, by means of suitable preliminary exploration, he has discovered all the irrelevant

[1]AB, AC and BC must first be 'expanded' by Formula 44. The application of these formulas for the correction of irrelevant factors in correlations was first made in psychology by Spearman. The mathematical processes concerned therein were developed independently and extended further by Yule, whose theory of 'partial coefficients' may be consulted by those who are interested in the mathematics of correlation (38, Ch. 12).

factors that might disturb the correspondence. The mere mechanical computation of an index of correlation does not, then, demonstrate the existence of a real correlation, or at least, does not accurately and certainly define its nature. Hence, while, as we have seen, we may very hopefully look to correlational work for revelation of the functional disposition of mind, this is no royal road to the attainment of that end, but is a road that can itself be entered upon only after a preparatory survey and critical inspection of the problem in hand has afforded sufficient acquaintance with the traits and capacities that are therein concerned. One must be a psychologist as well as a statistician.[1]

4. Intercorrelations, Correlations of Pooled Results, etc.

Tendencies toward functional correspondence may obviously exist not only between two variables, A and B, but also between these and other variables, C, D, etc. It is possible to determine the index of various intercorrelations for groups of data like these, but the formulas are too elaborate to be reproduced here in their entirety, and attention will be called only to two relatively simple problems.[2]

The first problem is that which arises when we wish to 'pool' the results of two or more tests of the same individuals for the purpose of comparing the resultant values with other measurements, as, for example, when we have subjected a group of school children to two or more different mental tests and wish to see whether their average efficiency in these tests correlates with their school standing. It is not permissible to compute the simple correlations and take their average, for the average of several correlations is not the same as their average correlation. Nor is it feasible simply to add together the respective

---

[1] The study of the functional correlation of five well-known tests by Krüger and Spearman affords an admirable illustration of the value of such a combination of sound psychology and sound statistics. Note, however, the criticism of Stern (30, p. 304), though Stern's formula erroneously contains a radical in the numerator.

[2] For further discussion of multiple correlation, consult especially Brown (4, 9-11), Betz (2, 31-33), Yule and other treatises on correlation.

standings of the individuals in the different tests, since the data are often incommensurate (seconds, inches, grams, etc.), while, if we resort to rank order, we deliberately throw away the more exact measures that the original magnitudes obtained by testing have placed at our disposal. Again, the resort to the use of percents of the average performance as a means of indicating the respective standings in the different tests implies that the variability of any series of measures is proportionate to the average of the series, which is an unwarranted assumption.

To meet these difficulties Woodworth (37) has proposed to regard the average of any test as zero. The unit of deviation from this zero is taken directly from the measure of variability $S. D.$ (or possibly $A. D.$) of the given array, and the standings of individuals are then computed as deviations, plus or minus, of so and so many times this unit. The arithmetic, then, is simple. Divide each individual deviation (d), as afforded by the original figures, by the $S. D.$ of the series and use the resulting quotient (which we may term the 'reduced measure') to represent the individual's standing for subsequent combination or comparison with other tests similarly treated.[1]

By appropriate substitution in the Pearson formula for correlation, it can be shown that if a_1, a_2, a_3, etc., are the reduced measures for individuals 1, 2, 3, etc., in Test A, and b_1, b_2, b_3, etc., are the corresponding values in Test B, then the correlation of A and B is given by the simple formula

$$r = \frac{\Sigma\,ab}{n} \tag{47}$$

In other words, when we have computed the reduced measures of two arrays, the coefficient of correlation between them is the average of the products of the various reduced measures.

---

[1]Compare the suggestion of Weiss (34) : regard the average in any test as 50, divide 50 by the average to determine the value of one unit in the test and multiply this value into the actual number of units accomplished by the person tested. Use the resultant product to represent the new rank of the individual in terms of the average of the group. This method avoids minus quantities, but would appear to be less useful for further computations than that proposed by Woodworth.

Again, the average position (p) of an individual in two tests, A and B, is obviously the sum of his two reduced measures, a and b, divided by 2. If, for other purposes, we have been led to compute the p of each individual, we can then find r by a still shorter method, viz., square the several p's, take the average, multiply it by 2 and subtract 1 from the product.

$$r = 2 \text{ Aver. } p^2 - 1. \tag{48}$$

Formula 48 is really the simplest case falling under the following more general formula.[1] Let $t =$ the number of tests, to find the average correlation among t tests,

$$\text{Av } r = \frac{t \text{ Aver } p^2 - 1}{t - 1}. \tag{49}$$

Finally, as a second problem of intercorrelation, mention should be made of another method of dealing with intercorrelations, which has in it much of psychological interest. If three or more psychological traits show intercorrelations one with another, the question may be raised as to whether the intercorrelations are not due to the presence of some common factor to which all the capacities are functionally related, whether, in other words, these correlations may not arise from a single underlying cause. If such a common or 'central' factor be assumed to be present, we may test the validity of the assumption by mathematical procedure, leaving the exact nature of the factor out of consideration for the time being. For example, if for any given capacity, A, we have obtained two independent measurements, A_1 and A_2, and if for two other capacities, we have obtained the measurements B and C respectively, then the correlation (AF) between the capacity A and the hypothetical common or central factor, F, may be determined by the formula:

---

[1] For further formulas based upon this method and for a discussion of the advantages and disadvantages of using $A. D.$ in place of $S. D.$ as the unit of variability in calculating reduced measures, consult Woodworth (37). In Spearman (29) will be found other formulas for computing correlations of sums or differences.

$$AF = \frac{M\ (AB,\ AC)}{M\ (A_1A_2,\ BC)}, \tag{50}$$

in which A B represents the direct correlation of A and B, and the other paired symbols have like meanings, while M is the mean (15, p. 88).

In illustration, Krüger and Spearman found the following values—correlation of pitch discrimination with the Ebbinghaus completion test, 0.65, with adding, 0.66, correlation of two measurements of pitch discrimination, 0.87, correlation of the Ebbinghaus test with adding 0.71; hence the correlation of pitch discrimination with the hypothetical central factor is the M of 0.65 and 0.66 divided by the M of 0.87 and 0.71, or 0.83.[1]

REFERENCES[2]

(1) W. C. Bagley, On the correlation of mental and motor ability in school children. *AmJPs*, 12: 1901, 193-205.

(2) W. Betz, Ueber Korrelation. Beiheft zu *ZAngPs*, Leipzig, 1911. Pp. 88. (With bibliography of over 100 titles.)

(3) A. Binet and N. Vaschide, Expériences de force musculaire et de fond chez les jeunes garçons, *AnPs*, 4: 1897 (1898), 15-63.

(4) W. Brown, The use of the theory of correlation in psychology. Cambridge, Eng., 1910. Pp. 83. (Section C published separately, *BrJPs*, 3: 1910, 296-322.)

(5) C. B. Davenport, Statistical methods, with special reference to biological variation. New York, 1899. Pp. 148. (2d revised edition, 1904.)

(6) E. Davenport, Principles of breeding; a treatise on thremmatology. Boston, 1907. Pp. 713. (With an appendix on statistical methods by H. Rietz.)

(7) K. Dunlap, Obtaining the mean variation with the aid of a calculating machine. *PsR*, 20: 1913, 154-7.

(8) E. Dürr, Review of Spearman (22, 23), *ZPs*, 41: 1906, 450. Also, Erwiderung, *ZPs*, 42: 1906, 470-2.

(9) W. P. Elderton, Frequency curves and correlation. London, 1906.

(10) F. Galton, Correlations and their measurement, chiefly from anthropometric data. *Proc. Royal Soc.* London, 45: 1888, 135.

(11) F. Galton, Natural inheritance. London, 1889. Pp. 259.

[1] This central factor is tentatively ascribed by these authors to some psychophysiological condition, possibly general neural plasticity. In another article Spearman speaks of "General Discrimination" or "General Intelligence," or the "Intellectual Function," and again (12) of "General Ability." Here, again, is revealed the instructive wealth of possibilities in the application of adequate methodological treatment to psychic life.

[2] Consult the *List of Abbreviations* for the exact titles of periodicals in these and subsequent references.

(12) B. Hart and C. Spearman, General ability, its existence and nature. *BrJPs*, 5: 1912, 51-79.

(13) G. Heymans, Ueber einige psychische Korrelationen. *ZAngPs*, 1: 1908, 313-383.

(14) G. Heymans und E. Wiersma, Beiträge zur speziellen Psychologie auf Grund einer Massenuntersuchung. *ZPs*, 42: 1906, 81-127, 258-301; 43: 1906, 321-373; 45: 1907, 321-333; 51: 1909, 1-72.

(15) F. Krueger and C. Spearman, Die Korrelation zwischen verschiedenen geistigen Leistungsfähigkeiten. *ZPs*, 44: 1907, 50-114.

(16) A. Lehmann and R. Pedersen, Das Wetter und unsere Arbeit. *ArGsPs*, 10: 1907, 1-104, especially 15-26.

(17) M. Merriman, A textbook on the method of least squares. New York, 1884. Pp. 194.

(18) K. Pearson, Mathematical contributions to the theory of evolution. (A series of papers.) *PhTraRoSoc*, 1895 on. (See also *Drapers Company Research Memoirs, Biometric Series*, London, and *Biometrica*, various articles).

(19) H. Rietz: see E. Davenport.

(20) E. C. Sanford, A course in experimental psychology. Boston, 1895 and 1898. Pp. 449.

(21) E. W. Scripture, The new psychology. London, 1897. Pp. 500.

(21a) B. R. Simpson, Correlations of mental abilities. (*Columbia ConEdTSer*, No. 53.) New York, 1912.

(22) C. Spearman, The proof and measurement of association between two things. *AmJPs*, 15: 1904, 72-101.

(23) C. Spearman, General intelligence objectively determined and measured. *AmJPs*, 15: 1904, 201-293.

(24) C. Spearman, Proof and disproof of correlation. *AmJPs*, 16: 1905, 228-231.

(25) C. Spearman, 'Footrule' for measuring correlation. *BrJPs*, 2: 1906, 89-109.

(26) C. Spearman, Entgegnung. *ZPs*, 42: 1906, 467-470.

(27) C. Spearman, Demonstration of formulæ for true measurements of correlation. *AmJPs*, 18: 1907, 161-9.

(28) C. Spearman, Correlation calculated from faulty data. *BrJPs*, 3: 1910, 271-295.

(29) C. Spearman, Correlations of sums or differences. *BrJPs*, 5: 1913, 417-426.

(30) W. Stern, Die differentielle Psychologie. Leipzig, 1911. Especially chs. x to xx. (Consult also for bibliography.)

(31) E. L. Thorndike, Educational psychology. New York, 2d ed., 1910. Pp. 248.

(32) E. L. Thorndike, An introduction to the theory of mental and social measurements. New York, 2d ed., 1913. Pp. 271.

(33) E. B. Titchener, Experimental psychology. Vol. ii, Quantitative experiments, Parts I and II. New York, 1905.

(34) A. P. Weiss. On methods of mental measurement, especially in school and college. *JEdPs*, 2: 1911, 555-563.

(35) G. M. Whipple, A quick method for determining the index of correlation. *AmJPs*, 18: 1907, 322-5.

(36) C. Wissler, The correlation of mental and physical tests. *PsMon*, 3: No. 6, 1901. Pp. 62.

(37) R. S. Woodworth, Combining the results of several tests: a study in statistical method. *PsR*, 19: 1912, 97-123.

(38) G. U. Yule, An introduction to the theory of statistics. London, 2d edition, 1912. Pp. 381.

THE TESTS

CHAPTER IV

ANTHROPOMETRIC TESTS

The tests embraced in this chapter have been developed primarily as anthropometric tests. They do not include tests of physical capacity or function (Chapter V), but simply measurements of bodily size or dimension.

The number of such measurements that have been made and recorded runs well into the hundreds, and an extensive literature has appeared. The science of anthropometry has developed partly in connection with anthropology and sociology, partly in connection with the study of physical development, including bodily growth, hygiene, gymnastic and athletic training. In recent years, moreover, a not inconsiderable contribution has been made by psychologists, physicians, educators and other investigators who have been interested in the correlation between bodily and mental traits.

It is this last-mentioned phase of anthropometry that concerns us, and hence only a few important measurements that have assumed special importance in conjunction with other physical and with mental tests are here considered.

The references which follow will enable the reader to study the development of anthropometry and the application of anthropometric tests at large. Bertillon and Galton should be consulted by those who are interested in the use of anthropometric measurements in the identification of criminals: Key and Hertel have given special consideration to the relation of growth to disease and to hygienic conditions. Anthropometric charts or record-books have been published by E. Hitchcock, D. A. Sargent, J. W. Seaver, W. W. Hastings, Anna Wood, L. H. Gulick and others.

REFERENCES

(1) A. Bertillon, Signaletic instructions; including the theory and practice of anthropometrical identification. Eng. Trans., Chicago and New York. 1896. Pp. 260 + 81 plates, charts, etc.

(2) H. G. Beyer, The growth of United States naval cadets. *ProcU SNInst*, 21: No. 2, 1895.

(3) F. Boas, The correlation of anatomical or physiological measurements. *AmAnt*, 4: 1894, 313.

(4) F. Boas, The growth of children. *Sci.*, 20: 1892, 351-352.

(5) F. Boas, On Dr. W. T. Porter's investigation of the growth of the school children of St. Louis. *Sci.*, 1: 1895, 225.

(6) F. Boas, Growth of first-born children. *Sci.*, 1: 1895, 402.

(7) F. Boas, Growth of Toronto children. *RepBrAAdSci* for 1897, 1898, 443.

(8) F. Boas, Growth of American children. *RepComEd*, 1896-7, ii, 1555.

(9) H. P. Bowditch, The growth of children. *10th An. Rep. State Brd. Health*, Mass., 1879, 35-62.

(10) H. P. Bowditch, The growth of children, studied by Galton's method of percentile grades. *22d An. Rep. State Brd. Health*, Mass., 1891, 479.

(11) F. Burk, Growth of children in height and weight. *AmJPs*, 9: 1897-8, 253.

(12) A. Engelsperger und O. Ziegler, Beiträge zur Kenntnis der physischen und psychischen Natur des sechsjährigen in die Schule eintretenden Kindes. Anthropometrisches Teil. *EPd*, 1: 1905, 173-235.

(13) Lucy Ernst und E. Meumann, Das Schulkind in seiner körperlichen und geistigen Entwicklung. Part 1, by L. Ernst, Leipzig, 1906. Pp. 165.

(14) W. Farr, *et al.*, Table showing the relative statures of boys at the age of 11 to 12 years under different social and physical conditions of life. *RepBrAAdSci*, 1880, i, 127.

(15) F. Galton, Proposal to apply for anthropological statistics from schools. *JAntInst*, 3: 1873-4, 308.

(16) F. Galton, On the height and weight of boys aged 14 in town and country schools. *Nature*, 5: 1875-6, 174.

(17) F. Galton, Range in height of males at each age and in several classes. *RepBrAAdSci*, 51: 1882, 250.

(18) F. Galton, Head growth in students at the University of Cambridge. *Nature*, 38: 1888-9, 14.

(19) F. Galton, Useful anthropometry. *ProcAmAAdPhysEd*, 6: 1891, 51.

(20) F. Galton, Anthropometrical instruments. *AntJ*, 16: 2.

(21) F. Galton, Anthropometric percentiles. *Nature*, 31: 1884-5, 223.

(22) F. Galton, Finger-prints. London, 1892. Pp. 216.

(23) A. Gihon, Physical measurements. *Wood's Ref. Hand-bk. Med. Sci.*, 5: 1887, 667.

(24) N. A. Gratsianoff, Data for the study of physical development in childhood (in Russian). St. Petersburg, 1889.

(25) J. M. Greenwood, Heights and weights of children. *Public Health Ass. Rep.*, 1891, Concord, N. H., 17: 1892, 199.

(26) E. Hartwell, Anthropometry in the United States. *Amer. Statis. Ass.*, 3: 554.

(27) E. Hartwell, Rept. of the director of physical training, Boston Normal Schools. *School Doc., No. 8*, Boston, 1894.

(28) E. Hartwell, Rept. of the director of physical training. *School Doc.*, No. 4. Boston, 1895.

(29) E. Hartwell, Bowditch's law of growth and what it teaches. Reprint from 10th *Proc. Am. A. Ad. Phys. Ed.*, Concord, N. H., 1896.

(30) W. Hastings, A manual for physical measurements for use in normal schools, public and preparatory schools, etc. Springfield, Mass., 1902. Pp. 112.

(31) A. Hertel, Neuere Untersuchungen über den allgemeinen Gesundheits-Zustand der Schülerinen. *Schulgesundheitspflege*, Nos. 6 and 7, 1888, 167-183, 201-215. (Contains a review of the work of Key.)

(32) E. Hitchcock, Jr., Physical measurements, fallacies and errors. *ProcAmAAdPhysEd*, 1887, 35.

(33) E. Hitchcock, Jr., A synoptic exhibit of 15,000 physical examinations. Ithaca, 1890.

(34) E. Hitchcock, Comparative study of measurements of male and female students at Amherst, Mt. Holyoke, and Wellesley College. *ProcAmAAdPhysEd*, 6: 1891, 37.

(35) E. Hitchcock, The results of anthropometry as derived from the measurements of the students of Amherst College. Amherst, 1892.

(36) E. Hitchcock and H. Seelye, An anthropometric manual, giving the average and mean physical measurements and tests of male college students, and modes of securing them. Amherst, 1889.

(37) B. Holmes, A study of child growth, being a review of the work of Dr. Wm. T. Porter of St. Louis. *N. Y. Med. J.*, 60: 1894, 417.

(38) W. Jackson, Jr., Graphic methods in anthropometry. *Phys. Ed.*, 2: 1893, 89.

(39) A. Key, Schulhygienische Untersuchungen, trans. and edited, somewhat condensed, from the Swedish, by L. Burgerstein, Hamburg and Leipzig, 1899. (Report of the Swedish Commission of 1882 to investigate hygienic conditions of the schools.)

(40) A. MacDonald, Experimental study of children, including anthropometrical and psychophysical measurements of Washington school children. Reprint of chs. 21 and 25 of *RepComEd*, 1897-8, Washington, 1899.

(41) P. Malling-Hansen, Perioden im Gewicht der Kinder und in der Sonnenwärme. Copenhagen, 1886.

(42) S. Moon, Measurements of the boys of the McDonogh School. McDonogh, Md., 1892. Pp. 46.

(43) K. Pearson, Growth of St. Louis children. *Nature*, 51: 1894, 145-6.

(44) G. Peckham, The growth of children. *Rep. Wis. Brd. Health*, 1881, 28.

(45) G. Peckham, Various observations on growth. *Ibid.*, 1882, 185.

(46) W. T. Porter, On the application to individual school children of the mean values derived from anthropological measurements by the generalizing method. *Pub. Amer. Statis. Ass.*, n. s. 3: 1892-3, 576.

(47) W. T. Porter, The growth of St. Louis children. *Trans. Acad. Sci.*, St. Louis, 6: 1894, 263-426.

(48) W. T. Porter, Physical basis of precocity and dullness. *Ibid.*, 6: 1893-4, 161-181.

(49) W. T. Porter, The relation between growth of children and their deviation from the physical type of their sex and age. *Ibid.*, 233-250.

(50) W. T. Porter, Use of anthropometrical measurements in schools. *EdR*, 11: 1896, 126-133.

(51) C. Roberts, A manual of anthropometry.

(52)   Sack, Physical development of the children in the middle schools of Moscow, 1892.

(53)   D. Sargent, Report on anthropometric measurements. *ProcAm AAdPhysEd*, 2: 1886, 6.

(54)   D. Sargent, Anthropometric apparatus, with directions for measuring and testing the principal physical characteristics of the human body. Cambridge, Mass., 1887.

(55)   D. Sargent, The physical proportions of the typical man. *Scribner's Mag.*, 2: 1887, 3-17.

(55a) D. Sargent, The physical development of women. *Ibid.*, 5: 1889, 541.

(56)   D. Sargent, Strength-tests and strong men at Harvard. *J. Boston Soc. Med. Sci.*, No. 13, 1896-7.

(57)   G. Schultz, Some new anthropometrical data. *Yale Med. J.*, 2: 1895-6, 149.

(58)   J. Seaver, Anthropometry and physical examination. New Haven, 1896. Pp. 200.

(59)   G. Sergi, An anthropological cabinet for pedagogic purposes. *Ed.*, 7: 1886, 42-9.

(60)   C. Stratz, Der Körper des Kindes, für Eltern, Erzieher, Aerzte, u. Künstler. Stuttgart, 1904.

(61)   F. Swain, Anthropometric measurements. *ProcAmAAdPhysEd*, 3: 1887, 43.

(62)   G. Tarbell, On the height, weight and relative growth of normal and feeble-minded children. *Proc. 6th An. Session Ass. Med. Officers Amer. Inst. Idiotic and Feeble-minded Persons.* Phila., 1883, 188.

(63)   R. Thoma, Untersuchungen über die Grösse u. das Gewicht der anatomischen Bestandtheile des menschlichen Körpers. 1882.

(64)   E. B. Titchener, Anthropometry and experimental psychology. *PhR*, 2: 1893, 187-192.

(65)   F. Tuckermann, Anthropometric data based upon nearly 3000 measurements taken from students. Amherst, 1888.

(66)   G. West, Worcester school children; the growth of the body, head and face. *Sci.*, 21: 1893, 2-4.

(67)   G. West, Observations on the relation of physical development to intellectual ability, made on the school children of Toronto, Canada. *Sci.*, n. s. 4: 1896, 156.

(68)   C. Wissler, Growth of boys; correlations for the annual increments. *AmAnt*, n. s. 5: 1903, 81.

(69)   M. Wood, Anthropometric tables, arranged after the method of percentile grades, of the measurements of 1500 Wellesley students.

(70)   M. Wood, Anthropometric tables, compiled from the measurements of 1100 Wellesley College students. 1890.

(71)   M. Wood, Statistical tables concerning the class of 1891 of Wellesley College, numbering 104 women.

(72)   M. Wood, Statistical tables, showing certain measurements of forty freshmen of Wellesley College (before and after gymnasium training). 1892.

TEST I

Height, standing and sitting.—The general purpose of this test is, of course, to furnish a measurement of height as an index of physical size or growth for the sake of comparison with mental traits or with other physical traits. It is included in practically every series of tests that include any physical measurements.

APPARATUS.—Stadiometer (Fig. 4). Small calipers (Fig. 5) or millimeter rule.

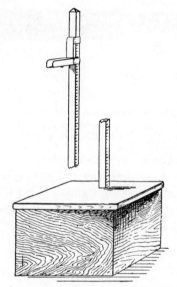

FIG. 4.   STADIOMETER, OR HEIGHT STAND.
Graduated in tenths of inches on one side and millimeters on the other.

METHOD.—(1)   For standing height, the examiner, E, should, when feasible, have the subject, S, remove his shoes, and stand on the stadiometer with the heels together and with heels, buttocks and spine between the shoulders, and the head, all in contact with the measuring rod. The chin must not be unduly raised or depressed. E then brings down the sliding arm of the instrument until it rests squarely, but without excessive pressure, upon S's head.

(2)   For sitting height, let S sit erect upon the stand of the stadiometer with spine and head in contact with the measuring rod.

RESULTS.—(1)   The best norms of stature are doubtless those calculated by Boas (4)[1] from studies by various investigators of school children (45,151 boys and 43,298 girls) in Boston, St. Louis, Milwaukee, Toronto and Oakland, Cal.[2]   For the sake of comparison with these norms and with the norms for strength

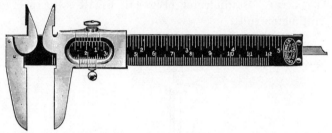

FIG. 5.   VERNIER CALIPER, FOR EXTERNAL, INTERNAL AND DEPTH MEASURING.
Fitted with both English and metric scales and verniers for each, reading to 1-128 of an inch and 1-10 of a millimeter.

of grip, vital capacity, etc., to be quoted later, there are given herewith the norms of standing and sitting height derived from the measurement of 2788 boys and 3471 girls by Director Smedley of the Department of Child-Study and Pedagogic Investigation, Chicago (25).

TABLE 11
Norms of Stature of American Children, in cm.   (Boas)[3]

Age	5.5	6.5	7.5	8.5	9.5	10.5	11.5
Boys	105.90	111.58	116.83	122.04	126.91	131.78	136.20
Girls	104.88	110.08	116.08	121.21	126.14	131.27	**136.62**

Age	12.5	13.5	14.5	15.5	16.5	17.5	18.5
Boys	140.74	146.00	152.39	159.72	164.90	168.91	171.07
Girls	**142.52**	**148.69**	**153.50**	156.50	158.03	159.14	

[1]The figures in parentheses following names refer to the reference-numbers at the end of the test in which they occur.

[2]The same averages converted into inches may be found in Burk, while these and other studies are summarized by MacDonald.   Consult Boas (4, 1555-6) for table showing the distribution of stature of American boys and girls at each age according to the frequency method.

[3]The figures in black-faced type in Tables 11-15 indicate periods in which the averages for girls exceed those for boys of the same age.   The rapid growth of puberty and early adolescence is initiated and terminated earlier in girls than in boys.

TABLE 12

Norms of Standing and Sitting Height, in cm. (*Smedley*)

AGE	STANDING HEIGHT		SITTING HEIGHT		AGE	STANDING HEIGHT		SITTING HEIGHT	
	BOYS	GIRLS	BOYS	GIRLS		BOYS	GIRLS	BOYS	GIRLS
6.0	110.69	109.66	62.40	61.72	12.5	141.89	144.32	74.70	76.29
6.5	113.25	112.51	63.54	62.90	13.0	145.54	147.68	76.24	77.91
7.0	115.82	115.37	64.67	64.07	13.5	149.09	151.04	77.79	79.54
7.5	118.39	118.22	65.78	65.25	14.0	151.92	153.64	79.21	80.99
8.0	120.93	120.49	66.75	66.34	14.5	154.74	156.24	80.64	82.43
8.5	123.48	122.75	67.72	67.43	15.0	158.07	156.83	82.18	83.21
9.0	126.14	125.24	68.79	68.32	15.5	161.41	157.42	83.68	83.99
9.5	128.80	127.74	69.85	69.21	16.0	164.03	158.30	85.43	84.54
10.0	130.91	130.07	70.56	70.05	16.5	166.65	159.18	87.17	85.09
10.5	133.03	132.41	71.26	70.89	17.0	167.85	159.26	88.16	85.20
11.0	135.11	135.35	72.10	72.23	17.5	169.04	159.34	89.14	85.30
11.5	137.19	138.30	72.93	73.58	18.0	171.23	159.42	90.30	85.51
12.0	139.54	141.31	73.80	74.93	18.5	173.41	159.50	91.46	85.72

From Smedley's data are prepared the charts (Figs. 6 and 7) showing percentiles of height for boys and girls at each age from 4 to 18. These charts show graphically the comparative rate of growth at these different ages, and they are especially valuable for locating a given child in the percentile group to which he belongs by simply following the line of his age across the chart until the point representing his measurement is reached.[1]

From these and other statistics the following important results may be gathered:

(2) There is a period of slower growth in height in boys at 11 years of age, and a similar, though less marked, retardation in girls at nine years of age.

---

[1]These charts have only an approximate accuracy because of the limited number of cases (300-400 in most years). They are reproduced here partly to show the method of displaying norms which we need to follow for quick and accurate rating of performance in various mental as well as physical tests. Evidently percentile tables of this sort necessitate the gathering of data by standardized tests from large numbers of children of both sexes and various ages. The lack of percentile tables for mental tests is one of the most serious handicaps now existing in their application.

The valuable percentile charts of Porter (20) are worthy of consultation by those particularly interested in anthropometric work.

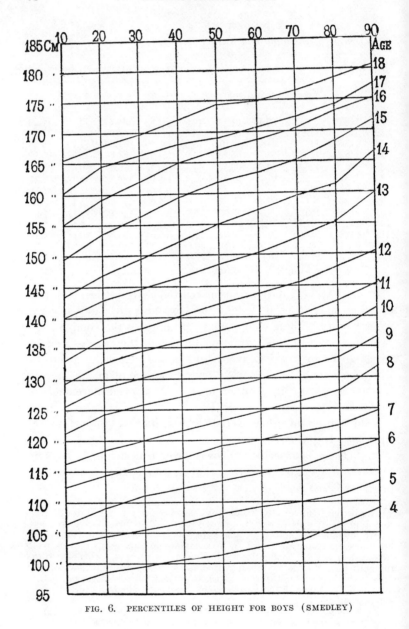

FIG. 6. PERCENTILES OF HEIGHT FOR BOYS (SMEDLEY)

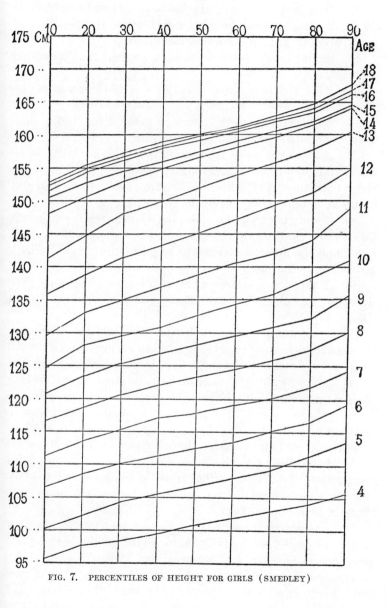

FIG. 7. PERCENTILES OF HEIGHT FOR GIRLS (SMEDLEY)

(3) During the period of approximately 11 to 14 years girls are taller than boys of the same age, because the prepubertal acceleration of growth occurs earlier in girls.

(4) Sitting-height follows the same general laws as standing-height.

(5) Boys continue their growth in height later than do girls, *i. e.,* maturity in height is not reached so early.

(6) Children of purely American descent are taller than those of foreign-born parentage (Bowditch, Peckham).

(7) Race seems to be more important than social or environmental conditions in determining absolute growth, but the latter conditions may influence the rate of growth at different stages of development (Meumann, pp. 82-3).

(8) Children of the non-laboring classes are, as a group, taller than children of the laboring classes (Bowditch, Roberts), and the difference seems to be particularly evident with girls (Pagliani).

(9) First-born are somewhat taller than later-born children, but the amount of the difference is not definitely known (Boas, 4, p. 1596).

(10) According to Bowditch, and also Baldwin, large children make their most rapid growth at an earlier age than small ones, but according to Boas (2, 3) this induction is untenable.

(11) The height of American-born children is modified by density of population. Urban life decreases stature from five years of age upward (Peckham). A similar conclusion is reached by Schmidt.

(12) According to Kline, boys in the public schools are taller than boys in truant schools, save at the age of ten. Similarly, Smedley (27) found that from the tenth year up the boys in the Chicago School for Incorrigibles and Truants were shorter than normal boys.

(13) Gratsianoff and Sack in Russia, and Porter, MacDonald and Smedley in America, have concluded that bright children are taller than dull children, and DeBusk's preliminary study in Colorado points in the same direction. West, however, found exactly the opposite to be true, while Gilbert (11, 12) found no constant relation between height and mental abil-

ity. Porter, DeBusk and Smedley determined mental ability by the relation of grade and age, Gilbert and MacDonald by the teacher's estimate.

The apparent correlation between height and mental ability raises an important question which reappears whenever we discuss the correlation between any physical trait, *c. g.*, weight, strength, vital capacity, etc. and mental ability. The trend of evidence is to the effect that all such correlations, where found, are largely explicable as phenomena of growth, *i. e.*, as correlations with relative maturity (Cf. Boas, 3; Wissler). This makes intelligible the fact that, in general, the positiveness of all such correlations lessens with age, and that many of them, indeed, become difficult or impossible of demonstration in adults. Thus, to take the correlation in question, a positive correlation is not, of course, to be interpreted as meaning that, taken individually, all tall boys, are, *ipso facto*, bright boys, but that, taken collectively, those boys whose physical condition is good, whose growth is unimpaired by ill-health, faulty nutrition, etc., and who realize to the full the possibility of physical development inherent in them (whether they will ultimately be short or tall) will be found to exhibit the best mental condition and the most rapid mental development. The assertion made by Crampton that the correlations found by Smedley and others between school grade and height, weight, strength, etc., are all due to the earlier pubescence of certain pupils would seem to be negatived by the fact that the relations in question were found in grades before pubescence could have come for any of the pupils in them. Nevertheless, there is probably some truth in Crampton's statement that "statistics for groups or individuals respecting weight, height, strength, mental or physical endurance, medical or social conditions, that are not referred to physiological age are inconsequential and misleading." In general, the whole subject of physiological age and its relations with chronological, psychological and pedagogical age is much in need of more careful and extensive investigation (cf. the author's comment, *JEdPs*, 3: 1912, 410.)

(14) From statistics gathered from 19 institutions, and including 5800 boys and 4800 girls, Goddard finds that the feeble-minded are shorter than normal children, especially at the upper ages, save that moron girls are taller than normal girls from 7 to 9 years. Furthermore, the lower the mental grade, the greater the divergence from the normal rate of growth. Sex differences of stature are less marked in low-grade defectives.

(15) Children with abnormalities are inferior in height to children in general (MacDonald).

NOTES.—The upright measuring rod should be braced in such a manner that it will not be bent out of place by the pressure of *S*'s back. Many *S*'s will be inclined to assume an unnatural position in this examination, especially to stretch themselves:

the apparent height may be increased by as much as 20 to 30 mm. in this way.

If it is not practicable to remove the shoes, height may be taken with them on, and the height of the heel may subsequently be determined by the use of the small calipers or millimeter rule, and then subtracted from the gross height; the resulting error will be very small.

Height, as is well known, decreases slightly during the day, owing to the packing of the intervertebral cartilages and the loss of muscular tone: this loss in height during the day amounts, in the case of young men, to from 10 to 18 mm. It is therefore desirable, for accurate work, to take height measurements at approximately the same period of the day. It might be possible to work out empirically a corrective formula.

REFERENCES

(1)   B. T. Baldwin, Individual differences in the correlation of physical growth of elementary and high-school pupils. *JEdPs*, 2: 1911, 150-2.

(2)   F. Boas, The growth of children. *Sci.*, 20: 1892, 351-352.

(3)   F. Boas, On Dr. W. T. Porter's investigation of the growth of the school children of St. Louis. *Sci.*, n. s. 1: 1895, 225.

(4)   F. Boas, The growth of Toronto children. *RepComEd*, 1896-7, ii, 1541-1599.

(5)   H. P. Bowditch, The growth of children. *8th An. Rep. State Board Health Mass.*, 1877.

(6)   H. P. Bowditch, The growth of children, studied by Galton's method of percentile grades. *22d An. Rep. State Brd. Health Mass.*, 1891, 479.

(7)   F. Burk, Growth of children in height and weight. *AmJPs*, 9: 1897-8, 253.

(8)   W. G. Chambers, Individual differences in grammar-grade children. *JEdP*, 1: 1910, 61-75.

(8a)   C. W. Crampton, The influence of physiological age on scholarship. *PsCl*, 1: 1907, 115-120.

(9)   B. W. DeBusk, Height, weight, vital capacity and retardation. *PdSe*, 20: 1913, 89-92.

(10)   Lucy Hoesch Ernst, Das Schulkind in seiner körperlichen und geistigen Entwicklung. I Teil, Leipzig, 1906. (Consult ch. 1 for stature of Zurich school children and comparative charts summarizing many other investigations.)

(11)   J. A. Gilbert, Researches on the mental and physical development of school children. *SdYalePsLab*, 2: 1894, 40-100.

(12)   J. A. Gilbert, Researches upon school children and college students. *UnIowaSdPs*, 1: 1897, 1-39.

(12a)   H. H. Goddard, The Height and weight of feeble-minded children in American institutions. *JNeMeDis*, 39: 1912, 217-235.

(13)   A. Key (a) Die Pubertätsentwicklung und das Verhältnis der-

selben zu den Krankheitserscheinungen der Schuljugend. Sonderabdruck aus den Verhandlungen des 10 *InCgMd.*, 1890; (b) Schulhygienische Untersuchungen. Hamburg u. Leipzig, 1889.

(14) L. W. Kline, Truancy as related to the migratory instinct. *PdSc*, 5: 1898, 381-420.

(15) A. MacDonald, Experimental study of school children, etc. *RepComEd*, 1899 (chs. 21 and 25.)

(16) E. Meumann. Vorlesungen zur Einführung in die exp. Pädagogik. Bd. I. (2d ed.). Leipzig, 1911.

(17) Pagliani, Lo sviluppo umano per atà, sesso conditione sociale ed ethica, Milano. Livelli, 1879.

(18) G. Peckham, The growth of children. *Rep. Wis. Brd. Health,* 1881, 28.

(19) G. Peckham, Various observations on growth. *Ibid.,* 1882, 185.

(20) W. T. Porter, The growth of St. Louis children. *Trans. Acad. Sci.,* St. Louis, 6: 1894, 263-426.

(21) W. T. Porter, Physical basis of precocity and dullness. *Ibid.,* 6: 1893-4, 161-181.

(22) C. Roberts, A manual of anthropometry. London, 1878.

(23) N. Sack, Physical development of the children in the middle schools of Moscow. 1892.

(24) E. Schmidt, Körpergrösse u. Gewicht der Schulkinder des Kreises Saalfeld (Meiningen). 1892.

(25) E. Schuster, First results from the Oxford anthropometric laboratory. *Biometrika*, 8: 1911, 40-51.

(26) F. W. Smedley, Rept. of the dept. of child-study and pedagogic investigation. Reprint from 46th *An. Rep. Brd. Educ.,* Chicago, 1899-1900. Also *RepComEd*, 1902, i., 1095-1115.

(27) F. W. Smedley, do., No. 3, 1900-1901; also 1902, i., 1115-1138.

(28) G. West, Observations on the relation of physical development to intellectual ability made on the school children of Toronto, Canada. *Sci.,* n. s., 4: 1896, 156.

(29) C. Wissler, The correlation of mental and physical tests. *PsMon*, 3: No. 6, 1901. Pp. 62.

TEST 2

Weight.—The general purpose of determining weight is similar to that of determining height, viz.: to furnish an index of physical size or growth as a basis for correlation with other tests or observations.

APPARATUS.—Accurate scales, preferably of the type especially devised for anthropometric work, which allow readings to be rapidly and accurately taken in the metric system, with units of 50 g. or twentieths of a kilogram (Fig. 8). If avoirdupois scales are used, they should be divided into tenths of pounds rather than into ounces.

METHOD AND TREATMENT OF RESULTS.—For accurate measurements, weight should be taken without clothes. Where this is impracticable, the weight of the clothes may be deducted by subsequent measurement. For some comparative purposes, however, the weight of the clothes may be neglected and the figures obtained from the gross weight may be taken for computation, or these figures, better yet, may be corrected by arithmetical computation based upon the weights of the clothes of a limited number of S's.

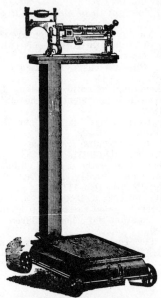

FIG 8.   ANTHROPOMETRIC SCALES.

One side of the beams is graduated metric to 100 kilos, by 50-gram divisions, and the other side avoirdupois to 200 pounds, by tenths of a pound.

We may form a tolerably accurate notion of the 'clothing error' by reference to investigations upon this point. Thus, according to W. S. Christopher, who ascertained the weight of the ordinary schoolroom clothing of 121 Chicago children, chiefly in the month of May, "the average weight of the clothing of all the pupils was 5.5 per cent. of the gross weight" (boys, 5.8 per cent.; girls, 5.2 per cent.). These figures varied little with age: obese children wore clothing lighter in proportion to their weight than that worn by others, while "the most variable

element in the clothing was found to be the shoes, especially
the shoes worn by the boys." Only a few children wear clothing that weighs more than 7 per cent., or less than 4 per cent.
of their gross weight.

RESULTS.—(1) From the data of about 68,000 children in
the cities of Boston, St. Louis and Milwaukee Burk derives the
norms reproduced in Table 13: the Chicago norms are reproduced in Table 14. For charts of percentile distribution like
Figs. 6 and 7 consult Smedley.[1] Means for English university
students will be found in Schuster.

TABLE 13

Norms of Weight, in kg. (Burk)

Approx. Age	6.5	7.5	8.5	9,5	10.5	11.5	12.5	13.5	14.5	15.5	16.5	17.5
Boys _____	20.50	22.45	24.72	27.03	29.66	32.07	34.88	38.46	43.18	48.72	54.88	—
Girls _____	19.69	21.64	23.81	26.03	28.53	31.52	35.70	40.23	44.59	48.40	50.94	52.34

TABLE 14

Norms of Weight, in kg., with Clothing (Smedley)

Age	6.0	7.0	8.0	9.0	10.0	11.0	12.0
Boys _____	19.738	21.613	23.817	26.336	28.707	31.223	34.151
Girls _____	18.870	20.974	23.010	25.257	27.795	30.662	34.373

Age	13.0	14.0	15.0	16.0	17.0	18.0
Boys _____	38.084	42.696	47.993	53.238	57.384	61.283
Girls _____	38.974	44.219	48.161	50.652	52.386	52.923

(2) As in the case of height, girls exhibit the prepubertal
increase in weight some two years earlier than boys, and are
for the years 12 to 15 heavier than boys of the same age.

(3) According to Baldwin, the period of maximal increase

---

[1]The numerical data for these distributions are reproduced without
the charts in *RepComEd*, I. 1902, pp. 1120-8.

in weight comes earlier for boys or girls who are above the median height than for those below it.

(4)   Growth in weight, as in height, is subject to some lessening of rate at 9 years for girls and at 11 for boys.

(5)   Boys continue to increase in weight after girls have practically attained their maximal normal weight. Girls grow most rapidly from 10 to 15 years, boys from 12 to 17 years.

(6)   Mean variations in weight are largest during the period of fastest growth, which shows that not all individuals participate equally or evenly in the rapid growth of adolescence.

(7)   First-born children exceed later-born children in weight, at least during the period from 6 to 15 years, though the reverse is true of the weight at birth. The difference is slight, but very regular (Boas).

(8)   Children of the non-laboring classes are as a group heavier than children of the laboring classes (Bowditch). Pagliani, in Italy, found the children of the poor especially below standard in weight.

(9)   Children of American-born parents are heavier than those of foreign-born parents.

(10)   There is, naturally, a general correlation between height and weight. Among Oxford students the correlation proved to be 0.66 (Schuster), among Cambridge students 0.49. Again, it is possible to equate growth in height and growth in weight: roughly, boys may be said to add 0.5 kg. in weight for each cm. added in height (Malling-Hansen, Ernst). However, stature is so far from being the chief conditioning factor in weight that in the tables drawn up by Ernst the lightest relative weight (*i. e.,* grams per cm. of height) was rarely found in the shortest child in each group.

(11)   The correlation between weight and mental ability or precocity is found to be positive by some investigators, negative by others, and indifferent by still others. Thus, Porter asserts very positively that "precocious children are heavier and dull children lighter than the mean child of the same age," and draws a further practical conclusion that "no child whose weight is below the average for its age should be permitted to enter a school grade beyond the average of its age, except after

such a physical examination as shall make it probable that the child's strength be equal to the strain." Porter's conclusion is confirmed by Smedley at Chicago, and, so far as his limited data suffice, by DeBusk. On the basis of the teacher's estimate of mental ability, Gilbert (8, 9), however, finds no constant relation between weight and such ability, save that from 10 to 14 years the dull children are much heavier than the bright, while West, who used a similar basis, finds a negative correlation throughout.[1]

(12)   Both Kline and Smedley find the mean weight of boys in truant schools to be less than that of boys in the public schools, save at the age of 10.

(13)   Porter concludes that the acceleration in weight preceding puberty takes place at the same age in dull, mediocre and precocious children, but investigations in New York City seem to oppose this conclusion and indicate rather that puberty and pubertal growth is distinctly earlier in precocious children, i. e., that mental and physical precocity go hand in hand.

(14)   From data from 19 institutions, including about 5800 boys and about 4800 girls, Goddard finds that feeble-minded children are distinctly heavier than normal children at birth, but below them at the age of 6, and decidedly below them at later ages, especially from 15 onward, save that moron girls are consistently heavier than normal girls. Moreover, the greater the mental defect, the greater, on the average, is the disparity between the weight of the feeble-minded and the weight of normal children. The feeble-minded also show greater variability in weight than do normals.

(15)   Children with abnormalities are below the average in weight (MacDonald).

Notes.—It is not important to have scales which render possible a very fine measurement, such as fractions of an ounce, because the normal weight of any individual varies from day to day and from hour to hour during the day: the daily variation is, in the case of young men, as high as 0.3 kg. The author, in a long series of observations conducted at the same hour daily,

---

[1]See also the discussion of correlation with mental ability in Test 1.

found gains and losses of more than 1 kg. in 24 hours. It may not be amiss in this connection to point out the absurdity of attaching any significance to small gains or losses that are observed in weighings conducted at occasional and irregular intervals. Severe exercise may reduce the weight by a large amount; *e. g.*, two hours of football practise may take off 2 or 3 kg. from a man who is not yet in training. It is well, however, for comparative purposes, to take weight measurements at approximately the same period of the day.

REFERENCES

(1) B. T. Baldwin, Individual differences in the correlation of physical growth of elementary and high-school pupils. *JEdPs*, 2 : 1911, 150-2.

(2) F. Boas, Growth of first-born children. *Sci.*, n. s. 1 : 1895, 402-4.

(3) F. Burk, Growth of children in height and weight. *AmJPs*, 9 : 1897-8, 253.

(4) W. G. Chambers, Individual differences in grammar-grade children. *JEdPs*, 1 : 1910, 61-75.

(5) W. S. Christopher, Report on child-study. Reprint from *An. Rep. Brd. Educ.* Chicago, 1898-1899.

(6) B. W. DeBusk, Height, weight, vital capacity and retardation. *PdSe*, 20 : 1913, 89-92.

(7) Lucy Hoesch Ernst, Das Schulkind in seiner körperlichen u. geistigen Entwicklung. I Teil. Leipzig, 1906. Ch. 3.

(8) J. A. Gilbert, Researches on the mental and physical development of school children. *SdYalcPsLab*, 2 : 1894, 40-100.

(9) J. A. Gilbert, Researches upon school children and college students. *UnIowaSdPs*, 1 : 1897, 1-39.

(9a) H. H. Goddard, The height and weight of feeble-minded children in American institutions. *JNeMeDis*, 39 : 1912, 217-235.

(10) L. W. Kline, Truancy as related to the migratory instinct. *PdSe*, 5 : 1898, 381-420.

(11) A. MacDonald, Experimental study of school children, etc. Reprint of chs. 21 and 25 of *RepComEd*, 1899.

(12) R. Malling-Hansen (a) Ueber Periodizität im Gewicht der Kinder. Copenhagen, 1883. (b) Perioden im Gewicht der Kinder u. in der Sonnenwärme. Copenhagen, 1886.

(13) W. T. Porter, Physical basis of precocity and dullness. *Trans. Acad. Sci. St. Louis*, 6 : 1894, 263-426.

(14) E. Schuster, First results from the Oxford anthropometric laboratory. *Biometrika*, 8 : 1911, 40-51.

(15) F. Smedley, Rept. dept. child-study and pedagogic investigation, No. 3, *Rep. Brd. Educ. Chicago*, 1900-1901 ; also *RepComEd*, 1902, i., 1115-1138.

(16) G. West, Observations on the relation of physical development to intellectual ability, made on the school children of Toronto, Canada. *Sci.*, n. s. 4 : 1896, 156.

TEST 3

Diameter of the skull.—This measurement has been commonly conducted for the purpose of investigating the correlation between size of the head and general intelligence. It forms also one of the chief measurements undertaken in the Bertillon system for the identification of criminals. The following directions are adapted from Bertillon's account (1).

A.   MEASURING THE LENGTH OF THE HEAD

INSTRUMENT.—Head calipers (Fig. 9).

METHOD.—(1)   Seat S with his right side toward a window, and stand facing his left side. Hold the left tip of the calipers firmly in place at the glabella (space between the eyebrows),

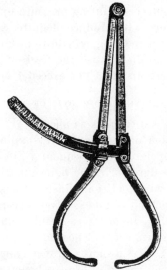

FIG 9.   HEAD CALIPERS.

with the tip of the instrument between the thumb and forefinger, and with these resting on the adjacent parts of the forehead to prevent the compass-tip from deviating.

(2)   Hold the calipers in an approximately horizontal plane so that the scale is fully lighted by the window, with the right

tip projecting about one cm. beyond the finger-tips of the right hand. Keep the eyes fixed upon the scale; then bring the right tip down over the back and middle of the head until it has passed the most projecting point; then move the tip upward again, making sure that it is well within the hair and in constant contact with the scalp; continue these exploring movements so as to pass the maximal point two or three times, keeping the eyes constantly fixed upon the scale to detect this point.

(3) Remove the calipers and set them by tightening the setscrew at the supposed length; take care to set them accurately within 0.5 mm.

(4) Replace the calipers thus set and tightened, and again execute the exploring movements described in (2). If the setting is correct, the instrument will just *touch* the skin of the head at the maximal point, but will pass over it without undue friction and without necessitating pressure upon its arms: one millimeter too short will produce definite resistance at this point; one millimeter too long, a definite lack of friction. Practise will enable E to distinguish the 'feel' of the correctly set instrument, and errors should not exceed 1 mm.

B.   MEASURING THE WIDTH OF THE HEAD

INSTRUMENT.—Head calipers as above.

METHOD.—Position of S, preliminary exploring movements, setting of the calipers, and subsequent verification follow the same general procedure as in the determination of the length of head. The following additional instructions are to be noted:

(1) E stands behind S, and is careful to preserve an erect, symmetrical position, in order to ensure equal freedom with both elbows and a symmetrical position of the calipers.

(2) Hold the calipers a short distance from each end; apply the tips first at the upper point of attachment of each ear; then raise them *vertically* and watch the scale to determine the point of greatest width, making several testing movements both upward and downward.

(3) The true maximal diameter in most cases is not yet found, but lies in the same horizontal plane as the preliminary maximal point just determined, and about 3 cm. behind it.

Hence, next move the calipers slowly back and forth two or three times in a *horizontal* plane and determine the true maximal point.

(4) Set the instrument, as in the previous measurement, and verify the setting. In this verification the caliper-points should describe a series of zig-zag movements, in order certainly to traverse the areas of maximal width (usually less than the size of a dime), which might not be traversed if the movements were circular or too coarsely executed.

TREATMENT OF RESULTS. — From the measurements of the length and width of head, the *cephalic index* may be computed readily by multiplying the width by 100 and dividing by the length. This index is considered one of the most important of those used in anthropometry. By it the type of head may be determined as follows: if the index is less than 75, *S* is long-headed (dolichocephalic); if 75-80.9, *S* is 'medium' (mesocephalic); if 81-86.9, *S* is broad-headed (brachycephalic); if 87 or over, *S* is excessively broad-headed (hyperbrachycephalic).[1]

RESULTS. — (1) *Norms.* Typical head measurements are those made by Boas, West, Chamberlain and others upon Worcester school children, and reported by West: these are reproduced in Table 15.

For comprehensive summaries of the results of various investigators, consult Ernst.

(2) It was supposed by Galton that university students, whose heads were found to continue growth after the age of 19, presented an exception to the growth of skull of the general population, but it is more probable that in all males length of head continues to increase until the age of 21; in girls, maximal length of head is practically attained at 18. The growth, both of length and width of head, is very irregular, *i. e.,* periods of growth alternate with periods of cessation of growth.

------

[1]These points of divisions are not followed precisely by all investigators. Thus, Ernst counted as hyperdolichocephalic, -69.9; as dolichocephalic, 70-76.4; as mesocephalic, 76.5-80.9; as brachycephalic, 81.0-85.9; as hyperbrachycephalic, 86.0 +.

(3) *Dependence on sex.* Boys' heads are longer and wider than those of girls throughout the whole period of growth, and consequently throughout life. The heads of males are not only absolutely larger, but also relatively larger in comparison with their stature.

TABLE 15

Diameters of the Skull, in mm., and the Cephalic Index (West)

Age	AVERAGE LENGTH		AVERAGE WIDTH		CEPHALIC INDEX	
	BOYS	GIRLS	BOYS	GIRLS	BOYS	GIRLS
5	176	174	140	138	79.56	79.40
6	177	172	142	139	78.94	79.60
7	179	175	142	140	79.42	80.02
8	180	174	143	141	78.71	80.41
9	181	176	144	140	79.63	79.71
10	182	177	145	142	80.30	79.46
11	183	180	144	142	78.80	78.90
12	183	180	145	143	79.40	79.40
13	184	181	147	145	79.50	79.60
14	187	183	147	144	78.60	79.00
15	188	184	148	146	78.59	78.99
16	191	184	149	144	77.81	78.48
17	189	185	150	146	78.34	78.50
18	192	186	151	147	78.88	79.36
19	192	183	150	145	78.33	79.68
20	195	182	152	147	77.88	79.41
21	192	186	153	145	79.29	78.36

(4) *Dependence on height.* In Oxford students Schuster found a correlation between stature and head length of 0.31, between stature and head width of 0.14. Analogous correlations reported by Pearson for Cambridge, Eng., students are 0.28 and 0.15, respectively, and for 3000 criminals 0.34 and 0.18, respectively.

(5) *Dependence on intelligence.*[1] With these measurements chief interest attaches to the question of correlation between skull size and shape and intellectual ability. The oft-quoted work of Galton comprises an investigation (assisted by Venn) of Cambridge students, who were divided on the basis

---

[1]Compare on this point the results listed in Test 4.

of intellectual ability into three groups — (a) "high-honor men," (b) "remaining honor men," (c) "poll" or "pass" men. When length, breadth and height of skull were multiplied together, Galton found that at 19 years of age the high-honor men had heads considerably larger than others, and that this difference was reduced by about one-half at the age of 25, and he concluded that high-honor men are presumably, as a class, both more precocious and more gifted throughout than others.

Vaschide and Pelletier measured 400 pupils of both sexes in the elementary schools of Paris, and, upon comparison with their teachers' estimates of ability, concluded that pupils of superior intelligence have on the average larger heads than the less intelligent, that this difference is independent of general physical development, and that height of head is the most important single cranial symptom of ability.

This last conclusion, however, does not accord with that reached by Binet in his earlier work (1900). He reports that the head of the unintelligent is smaller than that of the intelligent child in all dimensions save in vertical diameter and distance from the base of the nose to the end of the chin, though the differences are but slight and somewhat uncertain. If, however, exceptionally bright children (*enfants d'élite*) are compared with exceptionally dull children (*enfants arriérés*), differences averaging 3-4 mm. or more appear, particularly in transverse dimensions, *i. e.*, in breadth. Exceptionally bright children distinctly surpass average children, but the latter do not differ so much from dull children. In brief, then, exceptionally bright children are characterized by unusually wide heads.

The most elaborate statistical investigation by the group method is that of Karl Pearson, who collected data from 5000 school children in addition to the 1000 Cambridge undergraduates, and who classified these 6000 cases into four (or six) mental groups. From his data (Table 16) it is clear that, while there exists a sensible relationship between skull dimensions and intellectual ability, it is very small and not sufficient for any practical predictions: indeed, he discovers that the relation between color of hair and intelligence is just as good as that between size and shape of skull and intelligence (14, p. 128). Miss Lee could find no correlation between estimated cranial capacity and estimated intellectual capacity of 60 men and 30 women.

TABLE 16

Correlation Ratio Between Intelligence and Size and Shape of Head
(Pearson)

INTELLIGENCE AND	CAMBRIDGE GRADUATES			SCHOOL BOYS AGED 12 YEARS			SCHOOL GIRLS AGED 12 YEARS		
	NO.	RATIO	P. E.	NO.	RATIO	P. E.	NO.	RATIO	P. E.
Cephalic Index___	1011	—.061	.02	2345	—.041	.01	2226	.067	.01
Length of Head__	1011	.111	.02	2298	.139	.01	2188	.084	.01
Breadth of Head.	1011	.097	.02	2299	.109	.01	2165	.113	.01

On the other hand, Porter found in width of head a positive correlation with school grade. His method of arraying his data to show this principle is illustrated in Table 17, in which all the girls aged 12 and all the boys aged 10 are distributed according to their school grades. It is then seen that those children of a given age in an advanced school grade have, on the average, broader heads than those in a lower grade.

TABLE 17

Breadth of Head by School Grade (Porter)

SCHOOL GRADE	BOYS AGED 10		GIRLS AGED 12	
	CASES	AVERAGE	CASES	AVERAGE
		mm.		*mm.*
I _____	92	145.86	—	—
II _____	408	146.73	68	143.68
III _____	397	146.48	193	144.77
IV _____	170	147.21	343	144.94
V _____	—	—	217	145.50
VI _____	—	—	89	147.64

Similarly, according to MacDonald, "dolichocephaly increases in children as ability decreases. A high percentage of dolichocephaly is, to a certain extent, a concomitant of mental dullness." "Unruly boys have a large percentage of long-headedness."

(6) The extensive study of *backward and feeble-minded children* conducted by Simon confirms in a general way Binet's results with normal children of varying intelligence, and also shows that the abnormal child only rarely has a head that is average in size and shape. In other words, variability is a chief trait in such heads.

Binet (3), in 1904, sought to establish certain limiting boundaries (*frontières anthropométriques*) for abnormal children. Figures were assigned for stature, length of head, breadth of head and for the sum and the differences of these two diameters, to apply to boys at each age from 6 to 18—a scale which reminds one of his well-known metric scale of intelligence for various ages as based upon mental tests. Trial by Decroly convinced him that these boundaries were of real practical value in raising a presumption of mental inferiority.

Still later, in 1910, Binet (4) contrived yet another series of limits by adding together five cranial measures, from the use of which he concluded that children taken in groups designated as bright, medium, dull and backward will show characteristic distributions in terms of this combination index. For any individual child, however, he would predict mental inferiority only if the child's index showed a "cephalic retardation" of 6 years or more in the scale of norms, but a retardation of from 3 to 6 years, when conjoined with serious school retardation or unfavorable outcome in psychological examination, would possess a certain confirmatory value. In general, then, Binet concludes that size of head only roughly indicates size of brain, and that size of brain is but one factor determinative of intelligence—quality of brain is, of course, the other.

(7) *Cephalic index.* Norms for the cephalic index of American children are presented in Table 15. The measurements, by Engelsperger and Ziegler, of 238 boys and 238 girls of the entering classes (average age 6 years, 4.5 months) in the schools of Munich, furnish results that deviate somewhat from those just cited for American children, as is seen clearly by a comparison of Tables 15 and 18.

It is of interest to note that no cases of dolichocephaly were found, but that these children were decidedly brachycephalic.

(8) *Dependence of cephalic index on race and environment.* The general conclusion that the cephalic index tended to assume typical proportions with each race has been recently shaken by the work of Boas, who measured the heads of American immigrants and their children born in this country. Boas declares that "the head form, which has always been considered as one of the most stable and permanent characteristics of hu-

TABLE 18

Skull Dimensions and Proportions of Entering Classes at Munich
(Engelsperger and Ziegler)

	LENGTH			BREADTH			INDEX		
	Mean	Max.	Min.	Mean	Max.	Min.	Meso.	Brac'y	Hyp'b
Boys ----------	170.35	185	148	146.34	160	133	6.3	54.6	39.1
Girls ----------	165.83	186	151	142.97	159	130	6.7	45.8	47.5

man races, undergoes far-reaching changes, due to the transfer
of the races of Europe to American soil. The East European
Hebrew, who has a very round head, becomes long-headed; the
South Italian, who in Italy has an exceedingly long head, becomes more short-headed; so that both approach a uniform type
in this country." These changes "develop in early childhood
and persist throughout life," and the influence of American
life "increases with the time that the immigrants have lived in
this country before the birth of their children." But Radosavljevich criticizes severely Boas' methods of collecting and
treating these data, and declares his results meaningless.

NOTES.—Heads of unusual shape or size, irregular or de-
formed, should receive especial care in measurement, and a
descriptive note should be appended to the record.

Attempts to record the shape and size of the skull by means
of the registering 'conformateur' used by hatters have usually
been relinquished, because the hair interferes too much with
exact determination. This instrument might, however, be of
service in preserving a rough 'picture' of heads of unusual size
or proportions.

Since brain size and form are only roughly indicated by the
exterior dimensions of the head, while intelligence is conditioned primarily by the elaborateness of the finer nerve structure and not (save in pathological cases of hypertrophy or developmental arrest) by the gross size or form of the brain, it is
scarcely necessary to call attention to the absurdity, *a fortiori*,
of the claims of phrenology.

REFERENCES

(1) A. Bertillon, Signaletic instructions; including the theory and practice of anthropometrical identification. Eng. tr., Chicago and New York, 1896. Pp. 260.

(2) A. Binet, Recherches sur la technique de la mensuration de la tête vivante, and four other articles on cephalometery. *AnPs*, 7: 1900 (1901), 314-429.

(3) A. Binet, Les frontières anthropométriques des anormaux. *BuSocEtPsEnf*, 1904, p. 430.

(4) A. Binet, Les signes physiques de l'intelligence chez les enfants. *AnPs*, 16: 1910, 1-30, especially 3-12.

(5) F. Boas, Changes in bodily form of descendants of immigrants. Washington, 1910. (Immigration Commission, Senate Doc., No. 208). (Also in his book, The mind of primitive man, N. Y., 1911).

(6) O. Decroly, Les frontières anthropométriques des anormaux d'apres M. Binet appliquées a des enfants arriérés de Bruxelles. Extrait des Annales publiés par la *Société roy. des sci. méd. et nat. de Bruxelles*, 14: 1905. Pp. 35.

(7) A. Engelsperger and O. Ziegler, Beiträge zur Kenntniss der physischen und psychischen Natur des sechsjährigen in die Schule eintretenden Kindes. Anthropometrisches Teil. *EPd*, 1: 1905, 173-235.

(8) Lucy Hoesch Ernst, Das Schulkind in seiner körperlichen u. geistigen Entwicklung. I Teil. Leipzig, 1906, pp. 100-122.

(9) F. Galton, Head growth in students at the University of Cambridge. *Nature*, 38: 1888, 14-15; 40: 1889, 317-8. Also Cambridge anthropometry, *Nature*, 41: 1890, 454.

(10) ———— Historique des recherches sur les rapports de l'intelligence avec la grandeur et la forme de la tête. *AnPs*, 5: 1898 (1899), 245-298.

(11) Alice Lee, Study of the correlation of the human skull. *Sci.*, n. s. 12: 1900, 946-9.

(12) A. MacDonald, Experimental study of children, etc. Reprint of chs. 21 and 25 of *RepComEd*, 1899.

(13) E. Meumann, Intelligenzprüfungen an Kindern der Volksschule. *EPd*, 1: 1905, 35-100, especially 58 ff.

(14) K. Pearson, On the relationship of intelligence to size and shape of head, and to other physical and mental characters. *Biometrika*, 5: 1906, 105-146.

(15) W. T. Porter, The growth of St. Louis children. *Trans. Acad. Sci. St. Louis*, 6: 1894, 263-426.

(16) W. T. Porter, Physical basis of precocity and dullness. *Ibid.*, 161-181.

(17) P. R. Radosavljevich, Professor Boas' new theory of the form of the head.—A critical contribution to school anthropology. *AmAnt*, n. s. 13: 1911, 394-436 (bibliography of 80 titles).

(18) E. Schuster, First results from the Oxford anthropometric laboratory. *Biometrika*, 8: 1911, 40-51.

(19) Simon, Recherches cephalometriques sur les enfants arriérés de la colonie de Vaucluse. *AnPs*, 7: 1900 (1901), 430-489.

(19) N. Vaschide et Pelletier, Recherches sur les signes physiques de l'intelligence. *RPh*, 1903-4.

(20) G. West, Worcester school children; the growth of the body, head and face. *Sci.*, 21: 1893, 2-4.

TEST 4

Girth of the skull.—This measurement is less in favor with investigators than those just described, because of the variable factor of the hair, mentioned in the preceding test.

INSTRUMENT.—Anthropometric measuring tape (Fig. 10).

METHOD.—*E* stands at the right of *S,* who is seated. *E* holds

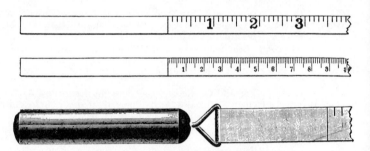

FIG. 10.   ANTHROPOMETRIC TAPE.

the tape with the thumb and forefinger of each hand at a length approximately that of the distance to be measured. He then lifts the tape over *S*'s head, keeping it horizontal, and applies it about the head at such a height as to pass around the largest part—over the frontal prominences and over the occipital prominences. The tension of the tape is regulated by observation of the spring-indicator.

RESULTS.—(1) *Norms.* Measurements by MacDonald of the circumference of the heads of 7953 boys and 8520 girls in Washington, D. C. supply the norms (converted into mm. from his original tables in inches) embodied in Table 19. Comparison with the results published by Ernst that have been obtained by Quetelet, Landsberger, Hrdlicka and herself will show that MacDonald's norms are somewhat larger than those obtained by these investigators. For ages above 18 we may refer to the results of Schuster, who found that the mean circumference of head in Cambridge undergraduates during the ages 18 to 23 and over ranged roughly from 560.76 to 565.53 mm., with a general average of 563.10 mm.

TABLE 19.

Circumference of the Head, in mm. (*MacDonald*)

AGE	BOYS	GIRLS	AGE	BOYS	GIRLS
6	513.6	506.2	13	533.7	532.1
7	519.4	506.5	14	538.7	538.0
8	520.9	511.6	15	544.8	540.5
9	523.5	515.4	16	550.4	543.0
10	526.5	518.9	17	555.5	547.4
11	528.8	521.7	18	556.5	548.6
12	531.9	527.8			

(2) *Dependence on sex.*[1] The head circumference of males is larger than that of females at all ages, both absolutely and relatively (in comparison with stature). MacDonald, however, found an exception in the case of colored children (see his Diagrams 2 and 3, pp. 1017-1018). Some investigators, notably Möbius, have argued from these facts to a general mental superiority of males over females.

(3) *Dependence on social status.* Children of the non-laboring classes have a larger head circumference than children of the laboring classes (MacDonald, Diagram 1, p. 1016).

(4) *Dependence on stature.* If the head circumference be multiplied by 100 and divided by the stature, the resultant ratio will be found to diminish as stature increases. Thus for 9-year-old boys with statures of 121 to 122 cm. the ratio is 42.3 to 42.9; for 10-year-old boys with statures of 124.8 to 127.3 cm. the ratio is 41.3 to 41.7, while with 11-year-old boys with statures 130 to 135.9 cm. the ratio is 39.0 to 39.9 (Ernst, from the data of different investigators).

(5) *Dependence on intelligence.* Möbius, as intimated above, believes that, at least in the case of normal adults, mental capacity tends to correlate with skull circumference. Mac-Donald, who related head girth with mental ability estimated by the teacher, concludes that, as the girth increases, mental ability increases, provided that one and the same race be under

---

[1] Consult MacDonald (pp. 1016ff.) for an extended discussion of the relation of circumference of head to sex, nativity, race, sociological condition and mental ability.

consideration. Dr. Ernst, however, raises the question whether this apparent correlation is not primarily determined by the relation above mentioned between size of head and social milieu.

Of special interest are the several articles by Bayerthal. In 1906 he measured the skull circumference of 234 boys and 153 girls (ages 7.5 to 8.5 years) and related these measures with school standing by classifying both sexes into five groups, as "very good" (I), "good" (II), "good on the whole" (III), "satisfactory" (IV), and "more or less unsatisfactory" (V). The results tend to confirm the existence of a positive correlation between skull circumference and general ability. Thus, the average skull circumferences were, for boys, 51.46, 50.93, 50.33, 49.60 and 49.60 cm., and for girls, 50.00, 49.83, 49.44, 49.16 and 48.84 cm., for the groups I to V, respectively.

In 1910 Bayerthal reaches the general conclusion that large heads may have all grades of intelligence from genius to idiocy, medium-sized heads may have intelligence above the average, though highly-developed intelligence is rare, while very small heads are never coupled with high-grade intelligence. There is, in other words, a one-way correspondence: very small heads exclude high intelligence, but very large heads do not guarantee it. To define more exactly what Bayerthal means by small heads we may reproduce his conclusions in tabular form as follows:

Very good intellectual capacity appears to be

	POSITIVELY EXCLUDED			ONLY RARELY PRESENT		
If at ages_____	7	10	12-14	7	10	11-12
In boys the girth is less than	48	49.5	50.5	50	52	52.5
In girls the girth is less than	47	48.5	49.5	49	51	51.5

If these boundaries (comparable to the anthropometric frontiers proposed by Binet, Test 3) are confirmed by further investigation, we may realize Bayerthal's expectation that the school physicians of the future may, at the end of the first school year, pick out by skull measurements some at least of those who are intellectually incapable of carrying the work of the public school.

(6) Children with abnormalities are inferior in head circumference to normal children.

(7) In an examination of 60 juvenile delinquents, Dawson found the average circumference of head less than that of normal children of the same age: in 64 per cent. of the cases studied the circumference was from 1.7 to 5.2 cm. less than the mean for normal children.

REFERENCES

(1) Bayerthal, Kopfumfang und Intelligenz im Kindesalter. *EPd*, 2 : 1906, 247-251.

(2) Bayerthal, Weitere Untersuchungen über Kopfumfang und Intelligenz im Kindesalter. *EPd*, 3 : 1906, 238-242.

(3) Bayerthal, Weitere Untersuchungen über die Beziehungen zwischen Schädelumfang und Intelligenz im schulpflichtigen Alter, *ZEPd*, 5 : 1907, 223-230.

(4) Bayerthal, Kopfgrösse und Intelligenz im schulpflichtigen Alter. *ZEPd*, 10 : 1910, 197-218.

(5) G. E. Dawson, A study in youthful degeneracy. *PdSe*, 4 : 1896, 221-258.

(6) Lucy Hoesch Ernst, Das Schulkind in seiner körperlichen u. geistigen Entwicklung. I Teil. Leipzig, 1906, pp. 92-99.

(7) A. MacDonald, Experimental study of school children, etc., reprint of chs. 21 and 25 of *RepComEd*, 1899.

(8) Möbius, Geschlecht und Kopfgrösse. Halle, 1903.

(9) E. Schuster, First results from the Oxford anthropometric laboratory. *Biometrika*, 8 : 1911, 40-51.

CHAPTER V.

TESTS OF PHYSICAL AND MOTOR CAPACITY.

The title 'physical and motor capacity' is here used as a convenient and practical phrase to cover a number of tests which have often been classified under diverse rubrics, such as strength tests, motor tests, physical tests, tests of physiological condition, etc. All of the tests here described differ from the anthropometric tests of Chapter IV in that they measure not mere size or dimension, but functional, especially muscular capacity. They differ from the tests of Chapter VI, many of which might equally well be said to measure physiological condition or capacity, e. g., the test of visual acuity, in that they are primarily tests of motor rather than of sensory capacity.

The first test described, that of vital capacity (often loosely termed lung capacity), is, perhaps, not so obviously a test of muscular efficiency as are the four strength tests that follow. It is, however, clearly a test of physical capacity dependent upon movement. The tests of quickness, accuracy and steadiness of movement are frequently placed in a class by themselves under the rubric 'motor tests,' but they are easily subsumed under the title here employed.

Reaction-time would by many be considered a test of quickness of movement; but it is so largely dependent upon complex psychological conditions, particularly upon the instructions, the direction of attention and the type of stimulus employed, that it belongs rather to the experimental examination of action than to the measurement of physical capacity as such.[1]

These tests of physical and motor capacity have become prominent chiefly because of their employment in the study of the correlation of physical and mental ability. For this pur-

---

[1] See an article by the writer, "Reaction-Time as a Test of Mental Ability." *AmJPs*, 15 : 1904, 489.

pose they are commonly used in conjunction with the anthropometric tests already described and with various tests of general intelligence or mental ability to be described later.

These tests have also an obvious and direct application in the study of various problems of hygiene, physical culture, etc., while some of them bid fair to serve a useful purpose in the selection of applicants for certain industrial vocations.

TEST 5

Vital capacity.—Vital capacity, also termed breathing capacity and differential capacity, is the maximal volume of air that can be expired after taking a maximal inspiration. It is not identical with lung capacity, because a certain amount of air, termed the residual air, always remains in the lungs.

Vital capacity is considered an important index of general physical condition and capacity, and has, accordingly, found a place in nearly all measurements of school children in which the physical status has been examined. It is affected by sex, age, stature, posture, occupation, amount of daily physical activity and by disease, and may be markedly increased (*e. g.,* 300 cc. in three months) by various forms of physical exercise which demand active respiration.

The ratio of vital capacity to weight is termed the *vital index,* and is held to be of extreme significance, because it expresses the balance between bodily size and the rate and completeness with which oxidization of the blood is, or may be, effected. A high vital index is undoubtedly a preventive of auto-intoxication, gives increased resistance to disease, and is the root of endurance under effort. Thus, athletic training consists primarily in the reduction of weight and the increase of breathing capacity.

APPARATUS.—Spirometer, preferably of the wet type (Fig. 11), fitted with detachable wooden mouthpiece. Extra mouthpieces.

METHOD.—See that *S*'s clothing is perfectly loose about his neck and chest. Instruct him to stand upright, to take as full an inspiration as possible, and then to blow all the air he can, not too rapidly, into the spirometer. Also caution him to take care that no air escapes about the mouthpiece.

Two or three trials may be allowed, and the best record set down.

After S's record is made, discard the mouthpiece and insert a new one into the rubber tube.

RESULTS.—(1) *Norms*. The norms of vital capacity presented in Table 20 are those established by Smedley with Chicago school children. The distribution of Smedley's data by

FIG 11. WET SPIROMETER.

Graduated in cubic inches and cubic decimeters.

percentile grades is shown in Figs. 12 and 13. For additional results Ernst's monograph may be consulted for vital capacity and chest measurements of Zurich children and summarized tables of the work of Pagliani, Kotelmann and Gilbert, while in Hastings (pp. 79-112) will be found an excellent set of anthropometric tables for vital capacity and various other physical measurements for boys and girls of each age from 5 to 20, arranged for 8 characteristic heights at each age. The average capacity reported by Vierordt for adults—3400 cc. for men and 2400 cc. for women—is noticeably lower than the Chicago norms for boys in late adolescence, and much lower than the average capacity, 4315 cc., found by Schuster in undergraduates at Cambridge University.

TABLE 20

Norms of Vital Capacity, in Cubic Centimeters (Smedley)

AGE	BOYS	GIRLS	AGE	BOYS	GIRLS
6	1023	950	13	2108	1827
7	1168	1061	14	2395	2014
8	1316	1165	15	2697	2168
9	1469	1286	16	3120	2266
10	1603	1409	17	3483	2319
11	1732	1526	18	3655	2343
12	1883	1664			

(2) *Dependence on sex.* All investigators agree that boys have a larger vital capacity than girls at all ages, and that men, similarly, have a larger capacity than women. Even if we compare men and women of the same height, the former surpass the latter by about the ratio 10 : 7.5. The increase of vital capacity in boys is slow and steady during the years 6 to 12, but very marked during the next four years, whereas the most rapid increase in girls is during the years 11 to 14. In both sexes, then, these periods of rapid increase coincide with the periods of rapid growth in height and weight.

(3) *Dependence on height.* The norm is conditioned by height. For each centimeter of increase or decrease of stature above or below the mean there is a corresponding rise or fall of the vital capacity, amounting in men to 60 cc., in women to 40 cc. This correlation with height varies somewhat at different ages. Thus, according to Wintrich, the average vital capacity for each centimeter of height is, from 8 to 10 years, 10 cc., from 16 to 18 years, 20.65 cc., and at 50 years, 21 cc.

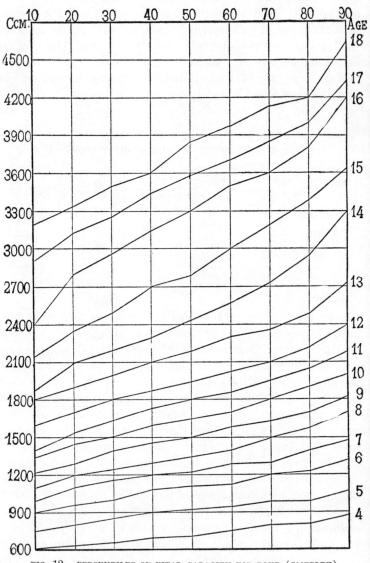

FIG. 12.   PERCENTILES OF VITAL CAPACITY FOR BOYS (SMEDLEY)

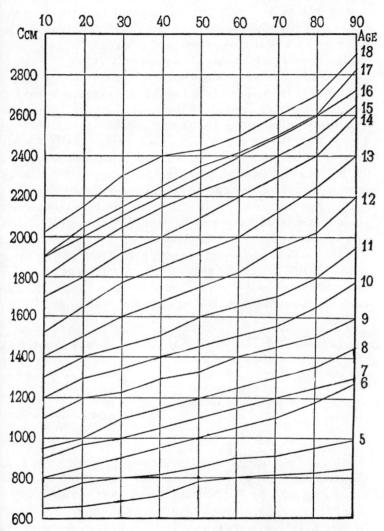

FIG. 13. PERCENTILES OF VITAL CAPACITY FOR GIRLS (SMEDLEY)

Schuster found the general correlation between vital capacity and height to be + .57, and that between the same capacity and weight to be + .59. It follows that in estimating the status of a given individual's vital capacity allowance must be made for his size of body as well as for his age.

(4) *Dependence on age.* The general dependence on age is indicated in the norms already given. It may be mentioned further that the most marked individual differences appear at the ages when the period of most rapid growth terminates (Smedley). Concerning the further development of vital capacity after the period of adolescence, Beyer, from his study of naval cadets, concludes that maximal capacity is reached at 19, but other authorities place the maximum at 35, with an annual decrease of about 32 cc. thereafter up to the age of 65.

(5) *Dependence on mode of life.* It has been pointed out above that vital capacity may be decidedly increased by forms of physical exercise that tend to induce forced respiration. Capacity is likewise proportionately reduced in men who live a sedentary life. It is also reduced by any circumstance which interferes with the free expansion of the thorax, such as tight clothing, tuberculosis of the lungs, visceral tumors, etc.

TABLE 21

Value of the Vital Index, when Weight is Taken as Unity (Kotelmann)

AGE	INDEX	AGE	INDEX	AGE	INDEX	AGE	INDEX
9	69.32	12	67.51	15	63.18	18	64.28
10	69.37	13	66.75	16	65.94	19	66.22
11	69.18	14	64.07	17	65.77	20	65.01

(6) The relation between weight and vital capacity, *i. e., the vital index,* presented in Table 21, is that found by Kotelmann, also given by MacDonald. The ratio expresses the relation in terms of kg. of weight and cc. of vital capacity. It will be seen that the weight of the body normally increases with age somewhat faster than the vital capacity. If height be similarly treated, it will be found, on the contrary, that vital capacity increases with age faster than it increases.

(6) *Relation to mental ability.*[1] Gilbert found the correlation between vital capacity and mental ability indifferent or negative: during the years 10 to 15, indeed, duller children, he found, had the larger capacity.

On the other hand, Smedley found a positive correlation between school standing and vital capacity, whether he took the distribution through the grades of all pupils of a given age, or computed the average school-grade of those who stood at various percentiles of vital capacity, or compared those at and above grade with those below grade at each age. Moreover, the same investigator found that pupils in the John Worthy School (incorrigibles, truants, etc.) were, from the age of ten up, inferior in vital capacity to children in the other schools, and that the inferiority became more noticeable with age. I am informed also by Goddard that the spirometer records of feeble-minded children are invariably below normal, and DeBusk's study of 105 Colorado pupils showed greater divergences in averages for vital capacity than for height and weight when accelerated, normal and retarded groups were compared. Almost without exception, he says, pedagogically retarded pupils show a vital capacity under the average. DeBusk also computed the vital index in terms of cc. per pound of body weight, and found the index of children pedagogically 'at grade' constant at about 25-26 cc. per pound for all ages. In the third grade, to take an instance, the general average for the index is 24.4 cc., but it falls to 23 cc. for pupils one year retarded and to 20 cc. for pupils two years retarded.

NOTES.—The dry spirometer is less expensive than the wet in first cost, and is more portable, but it has the disadvantage of getting out of repair easily. Its readings are apt to run slightly higher than those of the wet spirometer. Dr. Ernst believes that differences in apparatus are so serious that figures obtained with different types of spirometer are not directly comparable.

The mouthpiece of the ordinary spirometer forms an excellent medium for the dissemination of bacteria. For this reason

---

[1]See also the discussion of correlation with mental ability in Test 1.

the detachable mouthpieces are imperative if hygienic conditions are to be assured.

There is a certain knack in making a maximal spirometer record; some children may exhibit it; others not. In particular, to get a good record, the expiration must be neither too fast nor too slow, and an extra effort must be made just at the end of both inspiration and expiration to utilize the available lung capacity to the utmost.

REFERENCES

(1) H. G. Beyer, The growth of United States naval cadets: *Proc USNInst*, 21: No. 2, 1895.

(2) B. W. DeBusk, Height, weight, vital capacity and retardation. *PdSe*, 20: 1913, 89-92.

(3) Lucy Hoesch Ernst, Das Schulkind in seiner körperlichen und geistigen Entwicklung. I Teil. Leipzig, 1906. Pp. 67-9. (For diameters and girth of chest, see also pp. 59-67.)

(4) J. A. Gilbert, Researches on the mental and physical development of school children. *SdYalePsLab*, 2: 1894, 40-100.

(5) J. A. Gilbert, Researches upon school children and college students. *UnIowaSdPs*, 1: 1897, 1-39.

(6) W. W. Hastings, A manual for physical measurements. Springfield, Mass., 1902.

(7) ·L. Kotelmann, Die Körperverhältnisse der gelehrten Schüler des Johanneums in Hamburg. *Zeits. d. Königl. Preus. statist. Bureaus*, 1879.

(8) A. MacDonald, Experimental study of school children, etc. Reprint of chs. 21 and 25 of *RepComEd*, 1899.

(9) E. Schuster, First results from the Oxford anthropometric laboratory. *Biometrika*, 8: 1911, 40-51.

(10) F. Smedley, Rept. dept. child-study and pedagogic investigation. Reprint from 46th *An. Rep. Brd. Educ.*, Chicago, 1899-1900. Also *RepComEd*, 1902, i., 1095-1115.

(11) F. Smedley, do., No. 3, 1900-1901. Also *RepComEd*, 1902, i., 1115-1138.

TEST 6

Strength of grip.—This test has been used to secure an index of general bodily strength, to secure an index of right-handedness[1] (in conjunction with Tests 10 to 12), and for comparative purposes generally. It may be modified to secure an index of endurance or fatigue (Test 9), or combined with other forms of strength measurement (Tests 7 and 8).

---

[1]The terminology of right and left-handedness is at present somewhat confused (Cf. E. Jones. *PsBu*, 6: April, 1909). The terms 'index of unidexterity' and 'index of dextrality' have been used by some writers as equivalent to 'index of right-handedness.' 'Dextrality' is here used to indicate the superiority of one hand (whether right or left) over the other.

APPARATUS. — Improved form of Smedley's dynamometer (Fig. 14). Millimeter rule.

METHOD. — With the millimeter rule, measure the distance from where S's thumb joins his hand to the end of his fingers. Adjust the dynamometer by whirling the inner 'stirrup' until the scale on the outer stirrup indicates one-half this distance. This should bring the second phalanx to bear against the inner stirrup, and will ordinarily prove to be the optimal adjustment; if not, it may be modified to suit S's inclinations. Then set the instrument by means of the clutch, so that the inner stirrup cannot twist while in use, and record the adjustment by reference to the scale upon the stirrup.

FIG. 14. DYNAMOMETER AND DYNAMOGRAPH, AFTER SMEDLEY, IMPROVED.

Illustrate the use of the instrument to S; especially make clear that the lower pointer will register the grip, so that he does not have to continue his effort while the scale is read.

Allow three trials with each hand, right and left alternately, but introduce a brief pause, say 10 seconds, between each trial to avoid excessive fatigue. Have S exert his maximal grip, and in each trial encourage him to do his best. Record the amount registered at each trial; but, for ordinary purposes, use in subsequent computation only the highest record for each hand.

Records obtained upon the dynamometer, as nearly all investigators have pointed out, are very liable to be affected by subjective factors. Individuals who are, by assumption, exerting maximal effort, can often shove the pointer a few kilograms farther over the scale if some stimulating appeal is made to them. In order to get this last ounce of energy into the record some experimenters, *e. g.*, Binet and Vaschide, Engelsperger and Ziegler, recommend that all dynamometric records be made in the presence of other S's, so that competition shall induce the best possible efforts. For a similar purpose Wallin recommends that the Smedley instrument be held with the palm up and with the dial up, so that S may watch the movement of the pointer. Whatever be the conditions adopted by E, it is evident that the same conditions should prevail for all S's.

Engelsperger and Ziegler also recommend that this test be repeated on several different days (at about the same hour each day) in order to avoid chance errors like temporary indisposition, etc.

RESULTS.—(1) *Norms.* Tests of 2788 boys and 3471 girls at Chicago with the Smedley dynamometer yielded the norms of Table 22. The corresponding percentile distributions are shown in Figs. 15 and 16. For an extensive study of boys and girls aged 6 years, including tables of distribution, the work of Engelsperger and Ziegler should be consulted, while valuable tables, showing averages and standards for the 25th and the 75th percentile for boys and girls of each age from 5 to 20, as related to different statures, will be found in Hasting's *Manual* (pp. 79-112).

TABLE 22.
Norms of Strength of Grip, in kg. (Smedley)

	BOYS		GIRLS	
AGE	Rt. Hand	Lt. Hand	Rt. Hand	Lt. Hand
6	9.21	8.48	8.36	7.74
7	10.74	10.11	9.88	9.24
8	12.41	11.67	11.16	10.48
9	14.34	13.47	12.77	11.97
10	16.52	15.59	14.65	13.72
11	18.85	17.72	16.54	15.52
12	21.24	19.71	18.92	17.78
13	24.44	22.51	21.84	20.39
14	28.42	26.22	24.79	22.92
15	33.39	30.88	27.00	24:92
16	39.37	36.39	28.70	26.56
17	44.74	40.96	29.56	27.43
18	49.28	45.01	29.75	27.66

(2) *Dependence on age.* The general increase of strength with age is indicated in Table 22. It may be added that the

individual variation, like that for most physical traits, is more pronounced in early adolescence than at any other time.

(3) *Dependence on sex.* Boys are uniformly stronger than girls, and men than women. The difference is greater than the mere difference in bodily size, and is to be attributed partly to lesser practise, partly to intrinsically weaker muscles, and perhaps partly to the mental factor, *i. e.,* less ability or inclination to maximal exertion of actual muscular strength (Engelsperger and Ziegler). The divergence between the sexes becomes more pronounced at puberty when sex differences in general are accentuated.

(4) *Dependence on race.* According to Hrdlicka, colored children have a stronger grip than white children at all ages.

(5) *Dependence on season.* Schuyten (quoted by Engelsperger and Ziegler) took dynamometer records at several times during a year, and claims that there are seasonal variations, that muscular strength decreases from January to March, increases from April to June, probably decreases again from July to September, then increases from October to December.

(6) *Dependence on incentives.* If the test is taken under stimulating conditions, such as competition, personal encouragement, public announcement of records, etc., Binet and Vaschide found that the average grip was increased about 3 kg., or so much that the left hand surpassed the previous record of the right hand made without such incitement. Similarly, Schuyten (13) found that ennui, or loss of interest in successive tests, is sufficient to obscure the fatigue effect of a school session.

(7) *Dependence on social status.* Schuyten concludes that the children of well-to-do parents are stronger than the children of poor parents, and Hrdlicka found asylum children below average on account of their poorer circumstances and unfavorable environment in early childhood. On the other hand, the results of Engelsperger and Ziegler with 6-year-old Zurich children, and more especially of MacDonald with Washington children, suggest a contrary relation, which these authors attribute to the manual work done by poor children in partial self-support.

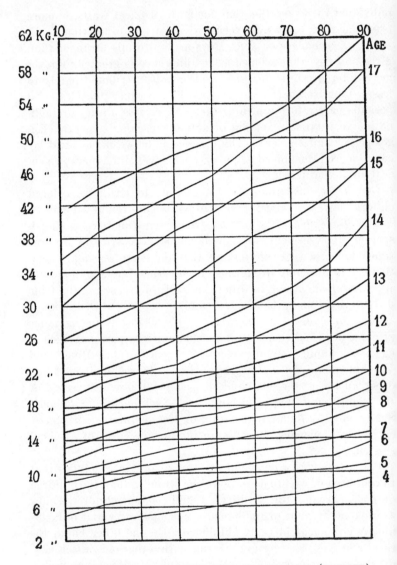

FIG. 15.   PERCENTILES OF RIGHT-HAND GRIP FOR BOYS (SMEDLEY)

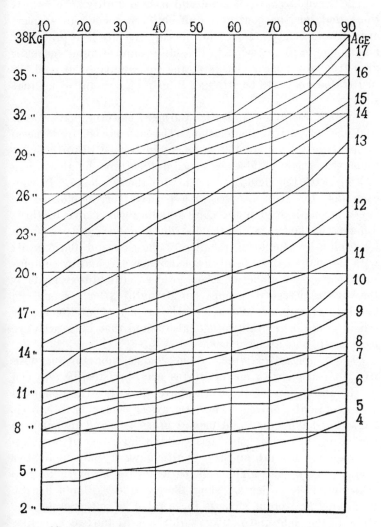

FIG. 16.   PERCENTILES OF RIGHT-HAND GRIP FOR GIRLS (SMEDLEY)

(8) *Relation to intelligence.* MacDonald found no correlation between strength of hand and mental ability: the indications that, on the contrary, dull children tended to surpass average and bright children in this capacity are interpreted by him as due to the presence in the dull groups of numerous children from the poorer classes of the community, who tend, as just stated above, to be stronger in grip on account of manual activity.

Smedley, Schuyten and Miss Carman, however, have found evidences of positive correlation. The last named, from measurements of the grip of 1507 boys and girls aged 10 to 19 years, found that bright children exceeded dull children by an average of 3 kg. with the right, and 1 kg. with the left hand. In Chicago (14, 15) the existence of a positive correspondence between strength of grip and class standing was shown by three different methods, viz.: by the distribution of 12-year-old pupils by grades, by comparing the grip of those at and above grade with the grip of those below grade at each age, and by computing the average number of school grades that had been made by the various percentile groups (in strength) after sex and age had been eliminated. Schuyten, who estimated intelligence by school grade in relation to age, also found that those who are most intelligent are strongest.

(9) *Abnormal children.* Some confirmation for the positive correlation with mental status may, perhaps, be afforded by the statements of those who have worked with subnormal and abnormal children. Thus, Barr goes so far as to say (p. 162) that hand grasp and mental grasp go hand in hand, so that a test of grip is more serviceable than a test of language to diagnose mental status. Wallin's work with epileptics shows clearly that high-grade patients are stronger in grip than low-grade patients. Thus, those at the Skillman institution rated as morons surpass those rated as imbeciles by 11.6 kg. with the right and 12.2 kg. with the left hand; there is likewise a general increase of grip with increase in rated mental ages (based on the Binet-Simon tests). Again, Dawson found that juvenile delinquents have a mean strength of grip slightly less than normal children, and that 56 per cent. of them are

inferior to the normal by from 1.32 to 11.82 kg. Similarly, boys in the school for incorrigibles and truants at Chicago are, at every age from 9 to 17 and with either hand, less strong than normal boys, and this discrepancy increases very decidedly with age, e. g., from 96.8 per cent. of the norm at the age of 9 to 63.2 per cent. of the norm at the age of 17.

(10)   The *index of right-handedness, i. e.,* the percentage of strength of the left hand compared with the right, will be found to range, for any ordinary group of school children, between 91 and 96 per cent. However, occasional right-handed children may have an index of strength exceeding 1.00, *i. e.,* grip may be stronger with their left hand. According to Hrdlicka, this tendency to have an index contrary to expectation is peculiarly evident in left-handed persons, so that he estimates that nearly one-half of *bona-fide* left-handed persons may have a stronger grip with the right hand. Dr. Ernst found 3.7 per cent. left-handed boys and 4.8 per cent. left-handed girls, and these proved not always stronger with the left hand.

It is often asserted that degenerates tend to be left-handed. Wallin's averages for epileptics show a net preponderance of 0.5 kg. for the general average in favor of the left hand, though by no means all his *S*'s had an index above 1.00.

(11)   *Dextrality, i. e.,* superiority of one hand over the other, is evident when the child enters school, but becomes increasingly evident as maturity approaches, and especially at puberty, so that a heightened difference in the strength of the hands may be regarded as one of the characteristic indications of pubertal change.

(12)   *Relation between dextrality and intelligence.* The results just cited for epileptics might be restated by saying that in strength these children tend to be ambidextrous. This agrees well with the result found by Smedley that dull pupils are more nearly ambidextrous than average, and average than bright pupils. And, again, the boys in the John Worthy School are still more nearly ambidextrous than the dull pupils of the regular Chicago schools.

(13)   *Relation between dextrality and absolute strength.* Just as mentally feeble children have less dextrality, so phys-

ically feeble children have less dextrality, so that these children may be said, as it were, to have "two left hands" (Binet and Vaschide).

(14)   The exertion of maximal strength is commonly accompanied by characteristic poses, attitudes, facial contortions, grimaces, etc., which are, in general, evidences of the escape of uncontrolled energy through various motor paths. There appears to be an inverse relation between the strength and efficiency of the subject and the number and extent of these waste movements; these are correspondingly more evident when the muscles tire and S is unable to accomplish what he is attempting. In particular, a sort of foolish laugh is characteristic of this muscular inefficiency.[1]

NOTES.—The chief objections which have been made to the employment of the dynamometer are (1) that it is painful, particularly if a series of grips is taken; (2) that some S's suffer from sweating of the hands, especially when excited, and that this causes the instrument to slip in their grasp; (3) that a wrong manner of holding the instrument may reduce the record, e. g., by as much as 10 kg.; (4) that, owing to the large number of muscles concerned, a lack of proper coördination in their contraction may lower the record.

The painfulness of the dynamometer can be largely eliminated by proper construction; the Smedley instrument is much better than the Collin elliptical form so commonly used heretofore, unless the latter be reconstructed, as was done to advantage for the tests of Engelsperger and Ziegler. Moreover, if an extended investigation is to be undertaken, inurement to the pressure is rapidly developed (Bolton and Miller).

For the ascertainment of strength of grip, excessive perspiration can be avoided by simply drying the hands with a towel whenever necessary.[2]

The proper holding of the instrument is also largely depend-

---

[1] For a description, with photographic reproductions of these motor automatisms of effort, consult Binet and Vaschide.

[2] The author has found that slipping may be obviated by winding the two grip bars with ordinary bicycle tire tape. If the fresh tape is too sticky, apply a little talcum or powdered chalk after the winding is finished.

ent on proper construction, and in this respect, again, the Smedley instrument, with its adjustable grip, is a distinct improvement over other forms.

The last objection is not to be seriously considered, first, because hand-grip is one of the most common forms of coördinated movement and is well organized early in childhood, and second, because experience shows that most S's can make their maximal record in three attempts at least.[1]

In any careful or extended investigation E must test the calibration of the dynamometer occasionally. For this purpose the instrument is held securely in a vise or other support, and a series of weights are hung upon the stirrup while the scale-readings are compared with the actual weighing (Wallin, p. 64).

For many purposes it is desirable to combine strength of grip with strength of back and strength of legs by adding the data secured in these three tests.

The advantages and disadvantages of using a series of grips in place of a single one are discussed in Test 9.

REFERENCES

(1) A. Binet and N. Vaschide, Expériences de force musculaire et de fond chez les jeunes garcons. *AnPs*, 4: 1897 (1898), 15-63. See also pp. 173-199, 236-252, 295-302.

(2) M. W. Barr, Mental defectives. Phila., 1910.

(3) T. Bolton and Eleanora Miller, On the validity of the ergograph as a measurer of work capacity. *NebraskaUnSd*, 1904. Pp. 79 + 128.

(4) Ada Carman, Pain and strength measurements of 1507 school children in Saginaw, Michigan. *AmJPs*, 10: 1899, 392-8.

(5) J. Clavière, Le travail intellectuel dans ses rapports avec la force musculaire mesurée au dynamomètre. *AnPs*, 7: 1900 (1901), 206-230.

(6) G. E. Dawson, A Study in youthful degeneracy. *PdSe*, 4: 1896, 221-258.

(7) A. Engelsperger u. O. Ziegler, Beiträge zur Kenntnis der physischen u. psychischen Natur des sechsjährigen in die Schule eintretenden Kindes. *EPd*, 1: 1905, 173-235, especially 228-235.

(8) Lucy Hoesch Ernst, Das Schulkind in seiner körperlichen u. geistigen Entwicklung. I Teil. Leipzig, 1906, pp. 78-85.

---

[1]If, for any reason, E considers these sources of error not eliminated, it may be necessary to select a number of S's and coach them in the use of the dynamometer until they can either avoid the errors, or report to E when they occur. J. Clavière asserts that to employ only those S's who are thus trained in the use of the instrument is an indispensable condition for successful dynamometry.

(9)   W. W. Hastings, A manual for physical measurements. Spring-field, Mass., 1902.

(10)   A. Hrdlicka, Anthropological investigations of 1000 white and colored children of both sexes. 47th *An. Rep. N. Y. Juvenile Asylum*, 1898.

(11)   A. MacDonald, Experimental study of school children. Reprint of chs. 21 and 25, *RepComEd*, 1899.

(12)   M. C. Schuyten, Les variations de la force musculaire et le développement intellectuel des élèves ; summarized by A. Binet. *AnPs*, 9 : 1902 (1903), 448-9, from *Pœdologisch Jaarboek*, Ghent, 1902.

(13)   M. C. Schuyten, Comment doit on mesurer la fatigue des écoliers? *ArPs*, 4 : 1904, 113-128.

(14)   F. Smedley, Rept. dept. child-study and pedagogic investigation, reprint from 46th *An. Rep. Brd. Educ. Chicago*, 1899-1900. Also *Rep ComEd*, 1902, i., 1095-1115.

(15)   F. Smedley, do., No. 3, 1900-1901. Also *RepComEd*, 1902, i., 1115-1138.

(16)   J. E. W. Wallin, Experimental studies of mental defectives. *EdPsMon*, No. 7, Baltimore, 1912.

TEST 7

Strength of back.—This test, together with the following, has been extensively used in securing an index of the general bodily strength of college students, but has not been applied in most examinations of school children. A fairer index of strength may, however, be gained by its use in combination with strength of grip.

INSTRUMENT.—Back and leg dynamometer (Fig. 17).

METHOD.—*S* stands upon the foot-rest of the instrument, which *E* should then adjust by lengthening or shortening the chain, so that *S*'s body is inclined forward at an angle of about 60 degrees (Fig. 11). *S* should then take a full breath and give a hard lift, mostly with the back and without bending the knees. Two or three trials may be recorded, and the best record used subsequently in computation.

RESULTS.—(1)   On the use of this and the succeeding test, with quantitative results as obtained in college gymnasiums, etc., consult Hastings (3), Sargent (4, 5), Seaver (6) and other authorities already cited under anthropometry in general.

(2)   Binet and Vaschide (1) found the lift (*force renale*) of 37 boys aged from 12 to 14 years to average 77 kg., with a maximum of 121 kg., and minimum of 56 kg. With 40 young men averaging 18 years of age, the same investigators (2) obtained for the average 146.64, for the maximum 187, and for the mini

mum 101.6 kg. Hastings (p. 71) publishes measurements of 5000 young men (17-30 years) whose strength of back averages 150.9 kg., *P. E.* 22.1, with a minimal record of 74.5 and a maximal record of 227.3.

FIG. 17. BACK AND LEG DYNAMOMETER. CAPACITY, 700 KG.

(3) Back lift is roughly about 3.2 times the strength of the right hand.

NOTE.—The adjustment of the chain may, with advantage, be based upon *S*'s height. For this purpose *E* may work out an empirical table of relations between height and the length of chain necessary to give the required position.

REFERENCES

(1)   A. Binet and N. Vaschide, Expériences de force musculaire et de fond chez les jeunes garçons. *AnPs*, 4 : 1897 (1898), 15-63.
(2)   A. Binet and N. Vaschide, La mesure de la force musculaire chez les jeunes gens. *Ibid.*, 173-199.

(3)   W. Hastings, A manual for physical measurements for use in normal schools, public and preparatory schools, etc.   Springfield, Mass., 1902. Pp. 112.

(4)   D. Sargent, Strength tests and strong men at Harvard.   *J. Boston Soc. Med. Sci.*, No. 13, 1896-7.

(5)   D. Sargent, Anthropometric apparatus, etc.   Cambridge, Mass., 1887. Pp. 16.

(6)   J. Seaver, Anthropometry and physical examination.   New Haven, 1890.

TEST 8

Strength of legs.—This strength test is to be used in conjunction with strength of grip and strength of back. The best records in each of these three tests may be added to secure an index of general bodily strength.

INSTRUMENT.—Back and leg dynamometer.

METHOD.—*S* stands upon the foot-rest of the instrument, with his trunk and head erect and his chest well thrown out, but

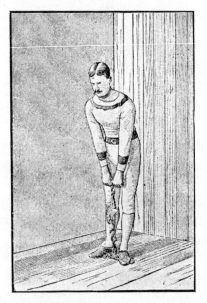

FIG. 18.   BACK AND LEG DYNAMOMETER, AS USED FOR STRENGTH OF BACK.

From D. Sargent, *Anthropometric Apparatus*.

with the knees well bent (Fig. 19). *E* then adjusts the instrument so that the handle, when grasped by *S*, rests against his thighs. *S* should then take a full breath and give a hard lift, mostly with the legs, using the hands to hold the handle in place. Allow two or three trials as before.

RESULTS.—(1) Strength of legs is commonly about 26 per cent. greater than strength of back. Thus, the 5000 men whose records are embodied in Hastings' table have a mean strength of legs of 189.5 kg., *P. E.* 35.3, with a minimal record of 102.2 kg. and a maximal record of 276.8 kg.

(2) The "strength of pull" recorded for Oxford students appears to be somewhat different as regards position of the body from either of the regular American tests with the back and leg dynamometer. Schuster's correlations and those noted in his article (Ref. 11, Test 5) from Pearson's data for Cambridge students probably apply approximately, however, for

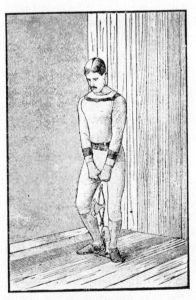

FIG. 19.   BACK AND LEG DYNAMOMETER, AS USED FOR STRENGTH OF LEGS.

From D. Sargent, *Anthropometric Apparatus*.

Test 7 or Test 8. Correlation of strength of pull with stature was found to be + .21 at Oxford, + .30 at Cambridge; correlation with weight to be + .46 at Oxford and + .56 at Cambridge. At Oxford, also, correlation with vital capacity was found to be + .37.

TEST 9

Endurance of grip.—The object is to test the capacity of S to exert maximal muscular exertion, not in a single effort, as in Tests 6, 7 and 8, but during a period of one minute: the test is thus virtually identical with the endurance tests commonly undertaken by means of the ergograph.

Since Mosso's studies of muscular fatigue (32), the ergograph has been extensively employed, not only by physiologists, but also by psychologists and by investigators of school children. The form of the apparatus and the conditions of the test have been widely varied and the numerous factors which affect the test have been exhaustively discussed. In general, the purposes for which the ergograph test has been employed may be summarized thus: (1) to study the physiology of muscular contraction; (2) to detect the presence and to examine the nature and extent of muscular fatigue; (3) like the strength tests, to gain an index of physical capacity or endurance under varying conditions, e. g., as affected by stimulants, narcotics, poisons, exercise, varying diets, etc.; (4) to secure an index of right-handedness; (5) to discover whether physical fatigue is general or local; (6) to discover how mental work affects physical capacity, and, in particular, whether mental fatigue is reflected in muscular fatigue with such clearness that its existence and degree may be ascertained by the examination of some restricted group of the muscles, and (7), on the assumption that physical capacity does measure directly the condition of mental efficiency, to determine the so-called diurnal 'course of power.'

As just intimated, the question of the applicability of the ergograph to these varied purposes raises a large number of problems, in particular that of the nature of fatigue. Since mental fatigue is reducible to physiological fatigue, the main point at issue is that of the precise nature of the latter.[1] In general, it may be said that, while the relations between mental fatigue and muscular energy are still obscure, we may hope, in principle, to secure some index of the former by our measurements of the latter. If the ergograph is to be employed for exact laboratory experimentation, there is no doubt but that the instrument must be of elaborate construction and the technique equally refined. The development of the ergograph itself from the relatively simple instrument of Mosso to such a complicated apparatus as that devised by Bergström is symptomatic of this gradual refinement of method and progressive analysis of the modifying factors.[2]

But while such problems as the merits of spring vs. weight loading, the relative capacity of a muscle working by isometric and by isotonic contractions, or the most reliable method of isolating the working muscle may be of paramount importance for laboratory investigation, it does not seem, on this account, absolutely impossible, as some writers assert, to secure valu-

[1]On the nature of general vs. local fatigue, on the relative fatiguability of muscle, nerve fiber, nerve cell and synapse, on the distinction between fatigue and exhaustion, and on the nature of other factors, like practise, habituation, readiness for work, warming-up, spurt, etc., that complicate the determination of the fatigue curve, consult Aars and Larguier, Bergström, Bettman, Ellis and Shipe, Hough, Kemsies, Kraepelin, Lee, Lindley, Loeb, Müller, Offner, Rivers, Sherrington, Thorndike, Weygandt and Yoakum. Lee, Offner and Yoakum are perhaps most useful for a preliminary survey. The discussion of these problems which the author attempted in the first edition of this *Manual*, which is here omitted for want of space, may also be consulted. It is perhaps worth repeating here, however, that to understand the nature of mental fatigue and to distinguish between general and local fatigue, it is helpful to separate the objective fatigue (*Ermüdung*), i. e., actual functional inefficiency, from 'weariness' (*Müdigkeit*) i. e., the subjective experience of ennui, loss of interest, or disinclination to work. Thus, it is weariness rather than fatigue which disappears when one's occupation is changed: weariness is fluctuating, uncertain and largely dependent upon the general conditions under which work is being done, while fatigue increases more or less steadily and progressively during our waking moments. If weariness is often specific, fatigue may be more often general and operative to reduce the available energy for work (*Leistungsfähigkeit*) in any direction.

[2]Consult also Cattell (11), Franz (15), Binet and Vaschide (5), Binet and Henri (4), Bolton and Miller (10), Hirschlaff (17), R. Müller (34).

able results for comparative purposes from large numbers of
subjects by the use of simpler apparatus and less rigorous technique—provided, of course, that the conditions of experimentation are kept as constant as possible for different subjects and
for the same subjects at different times.[1] For this reason the
test which is here described is suggested as a practical substitute for the more cumbersome and complicated ergograph.

FIG. 20.   STOP-WATCH.

Apparatus.—Smedley dynamometer (Fig. 14). Stop-watch
(Fig. 20). Metronome (Fig. 21). [If desired, a kymograph
(Fig. 22), with drum support (Fig. 23), a Marey tambour (Fig.
24) and other accessories, or the Mosso ergograph (Fig. 25).]

Two methods are described: one calls for a single, continuous
contraction, the other for a series of separate contractions.

---

[1] In general, it may be expected that minor variable errors will, in a
sufficiently long series of tests, be distributed according to the law of
chance. Possibly, some portion of the dispute concerning the value of
ergograms arises from the fact that certain experimenters have worked
upon large numbers of subjects, while others have contented themselves
with curves obtained from a single individual.

A. WITH CONTINUOUS CONTRACTION

METHOD.—Set the metronome at 60, *i. e.*, so that it beats once per second. Adjust the dynamometer to *S*'s hand, as in Test 6. Move the friction (recording) pointer of the instrument well over to the right, off the face of the scale. Instruct *S* that he is, at the signal 'now,' to grip as forcibly as possible, to maintain this grip with his utmost effort until told to stop at the end of one minute, and to keep his eyes fixed upon the pointer, so as to hold it as high as possible. (This instruction is designed to act as an incentive to maximal exertion.) Let the instrument be held in the vertical plane with the right-hand edge resting on the table before which *S* is seated.

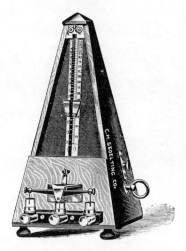

FIG. 21. METRONOME, WITH MERCURY CUPS FOR ELECTRIC CONTACT.

E starts the metronome, and, when he has caught the rhythm, starts the stop-watch, at the same instant saying 'now' for *S* to begin. *E* immediately takes the first reading, and thereafter glances at the scale at every fourth beat of the metronome. In the intervals he records, of course, the reading of the pointer just obtained, estimating to the nearest half-kilogram. If the first reading is secured promptly, *E* will have 16 readings at the end of one minute.

E must practise his work until it becomes automatic. He must take care to keep his eyes directly over the pointer to prevent the error of parallax in reading. For this reason it will be found most convenient for S and E to sit on opposite sides of the table.

If S tends to relax his effort between readings and to exert correspondingly greater effort just as E takes the reading, he must be warned against this habit, and urged to exert maximal effort continuously. Even when he does this, the pointer is apt to fall by a series of sudden drops, or even at times to rise as S makes a momentary recovery. E must take the reading precisely on the beat of the metronome, regardless of the position of the pointer just before or just after the beat.

The stop-watch is used both to test the metronome and to check up the duration of the experiment, but ought to be virtually unnecessary after E has practised the experiment sufficiently.

FIG. 22.   KYMOGRAPH, IN HORIZONTAL POSITION.

A clock-work mechanism, with regulating fans, in the base, rotates the drum at constant speed and at any desired rate from one revolution in ten seconds to one revolution in ten minutes. Used for making graphic records upon smoked paper.

VARIATIONS OF METHOD.—With the aid of the kymograph described in Test 10, E may secure a graphic record of S's work, either by the use of the pneumatic tambour (the Smedley instrument is fitted for pneumatic transmission), or by the use of a simple system of levers to magnify the movement of the handle.[1] The quantitative evaluation of the resulting curve

---

[1]For a cut showing the method of securing a dynamograph record, see MacDonald (29, p. 1184).

may then be obtained by a series of measurements of the ordinates taken at regular distances and checked by the record obtained as prescribed, or by measurement with a planimeter of the area enclosed by the curve and its base line.

FIG. 23. SUPPORT FOR KYMOGRAPH DRUM WHILE BLACKENING PAPER.

TREATMENT OF RESULTS.— (1) For some purposes the results may be treated by simply averaging the 16 readings, but (2) it will usually be more instructive also to compare the initial with the final stages, in order to secure an index of endurance, or conversely, of fatigue. For this purpose average the first four readings and the last four readings; subtract the latter from the former, and divide the remainder by the average of the first four readings. This may be expressed by the fomula

$$x = \frac{r_1 - r_2}{r_1},$$ when $x =$ the desired index of fatigue, $r_1 =$ the M of the first, and r_2 the M of the last four readings. Or (3) more simply, one may indicate endurance by the relation of the average to the maximal grip. (4) Following Binet and Vaschide (7), the records of strong, average and weak S's (judged by their maximal grip) may be collated and treated in three groups, in order to trace the presence of the three types of endurance (see below).

B. WITH SEPARATE CONTRACTIONS

METHOD.—Adjust the metronome, dynamometer handle and pointer as in the first method. Inform S that, as the word is given, he is to make a series of 16 grips, each as forcibly as possible, and that these grips will be signalled at 4-sec. intervals. E then signals 'now' on every fourth beat of the metronome, and takes the readings as previously described.

FIG. 24. MAREY TAMBOUR.

For securing tracings by pneumatic transmission. The rubber membrane is not shown.

To hasten the acquisition of skill in conducting this form of the test, E will find it helpful to accent the spoken 'now' and to get the swing of the four-beat rhythm by mentally counting the other beats, thus: "*Now,* two, three, four: *now,* two, three, four.*" As soon as the utterance becomes automatic, E can give his whole attention to the readings and the recording of them, and an accurate record can be obtained from very quick and brief excursions of the pointer. Incidentally, some S's may be found who are inclined to hold the pointer up too long: they must be cautioned against this, otherwise fatigue will set in very rapidly.

VARIATIONS OF METHOD.—Substitute the kymograph tracing as suggested above. If this is done, there is no reason why the rate of effort may not be increased, so as to secure 60 or 120 contractions per minute, with a correspondingly more rapid onset of fatigue.

If it is desired to compare results obtained by the dynamometer with those obtained by the common form of ergographic experiment, it is suggested that E repeat the experiments made upon Chicago school children. For this purpose substitute the Mosso ergograph for the dynamometer; use the kymograph for securing the graphic record, and the record furnished by the endless tape, multiplied by the weight, for the quantitative result. Adjust the weight at 7 per cent. of S's weight, and time the contractions to accord with the beats of a metronome set at 30, so as to secure 45 lifts in 90 sec.

TREATMENT OF RESULTS.—This may follow the lines already prescribed.

RESULTS.—(1) The measurement of endurance by the use of the dynamometer has been tried by Binet and Vaschide, though

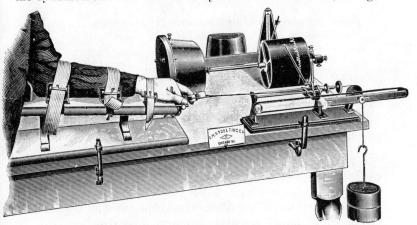

FIG. 25.   MOSSO ERGOGRAPH, MODIFIED BY LOMBARD.

under conditions somewhat dissimilar to those we have suggested, upon a group of boys aged 10-13 years (6) and upon a group of young men aged about 18 (7). When five (or ten) grips with each hand, alternately, were required, these authors made out four *types of endurance curve*, viz.: (*a*) a sudden drop, then fairly constant; (*b*) an approximately stationary or constant type, which is quite common; (*c*) a continuous, but gradual drop, and (*d*) a more or less definite rise. The last is rather infrequent (it was not found, *e. g.*, by Clavière, in tests with 15 successive grips), but is sometimes given by vigorous individuals, though the third type is more common for such subjects. Practically 90 per cent. of endurance records can, in the judgment of these writers, be classed in one of these four categories. Table 23 gives average records of five grips, made

with the right hand, by groups representing these four types of endurance curve.

(2) If we accept this hypothesis of 'types,' it is clear that the dynamometer yields a more reliable indication of the comparative muscular capacity when it is employed to test endurance in this way than when merely a single grip is taken, as in Test 6. To take an extreme, though actual, case cited by Binet and Vaschide, it will be seen (Table 24) that, if two subjects

TABLE 23

Types of Endurance in Dynamometer Trials: kilograms (Binet and Vaschide)

	TYPE *a*	TYPE *b*	TYPE *c*	TYPE *d*
1st Grip_____	23.00	18.70	24.12	17.33
2d Grip_____	18.45	18.60	22.50	17.70
3d Grip_____	19.00	19.20	21.17	18.67
4th Grip_____	18.60	19.40	21.33	18.67
5th Grip_____	18.20	17.80	19.80	20.67

belong to opposing types, their actual capacities may be completely unsuspected when but a single test is taken.

If we turn to the use of the ergograph, we find the following important, though too often conflicting results:

TABLE 24

Opposed Types of Endurance, 10 Readings (Binet and Vaschide)

NUMBER OF GRIP	1	2	3	4	5	6	7	8	9	10
Subject B_____	36	34	34	30	29	28	25	26	26	29
Subject R_____	36	27	42	43	45	42	42	45	46	45

(3) Ergograph curves are affected by *practise* improvement, which, according to Bolton and Miller (10), results (*a*) from 'inurement,' *i. e.,* a fairly rapid "process of hardening and toughening of the skin where it comes in contact with the apparatus and of habituating the muscles to the strains which the unusual effort imposes; (*b*) from improved coördination in the

movements concerned, particularly seen in the disappearance of useless movements; (c) from improvement in the rhythmic execution of the contraction, and (d) from a slow increase in endurance proper, primarily in the nerve centers. This increase of practise, as Oseretzkowsky and Kraepelin (36) have shown, affects both the height and the number of lifts, and gradually becomes less and less noticeable as maximal practise is attained.

(4) The amount of work that can be done by the muscle is increased if the *rate of lifting* is increased from 30 to 60 or 120 lifts per minute (Oseretzkowsky and Kraepelin).

(5) The work done is conditioned by the *load lifted* or tension of the spring. One cannot, without caution, compare ergograms made with different loads.

(6) The *total amount of physical work* done, as measured by weight $\times$ distance, cannot be regarded as a necessarily correct index of the physiological capacity of the muscle; thus, 100 lifts of 25 mm. each may not be assumed to be physiologically equal to 50 lifts of 50 mm. each (Binet and Henri, 4; Franz, 15).

(7) The *weight ergograph* is not adapted to the measurement of muscular capacity (Binet and Henri, 4), hence "the fatigue curves obtained by Mosso and later investigators with weights do not represent the true state of the neuro-muscular system" (Franz, 15).

(8) "The *isotonic* use of a weight or a spring for measuring muscular force is not justified, because two variable factors, extent and force, are introduced," so that an isometric spring (such as the dynamometer) should be used for all comparative experiments (Franz).

(9) With improperly contrived apparatus or inexperienced subjects the ergographic tracing is very liable to be affected by the play of *muscles* other than those under examination (Binet and Henri, 4; Bergström, 2). Müller (34) considers the failure properly to isolate the muscle a fundamental defect of the ergograph.

(10) In addition to these specific criticisms, more general *conclusions of a negative character* may be quoted. Thus, Bol-

ton (8) asserts that the ergograph is not adapted for measuring the degree of fatigue in school children; Bolton and Miller
(10) conclude that ergograph records "have slight validity
until inurement has become thorough and coördination complete; that the ergograph is quite unadapted to the obtaining
of exact statistics upon a large number of individuals, and that
records taken upon unpractised subjects, both before and after
operations whose influences are thought to affect muscular
power, are without the slightest claim to trustworthiness."
Similar conclusions are reached by Ellis and Shipe (14) after
a retrial of the methods of Keller and of Smedley, also by
Thorndike (42), and, with some qualifications, by Bergström (2).

(11) The *effect of physical work* upon ergographic curves
seems to vary with the physical condition of the individual and
with the nature and duration of the exercise. Thus, Bolton (8,
9) found his ergograms decreased by a two-hour walk, but
Oseretzkowsky and Kraepelin found that a one-hour walk
caused at first a transient improvement, then a reduction, the
first of which they attribute to the increased excitement of
central motor tracts, and the second to the damping influence
of general muscular fatigue. Smedley (39) tested Chicago children before and after a 40-minute class exercise in the gymnasium with the result that the stronger pupils were little affected, whereas weak and nervous pupils were decidedly ex-
hausted. From this study he concluded that the classes in
physical culture should be graded on a physical, instead of on
an intellectual basis.

(12) Extensive study of the *effect of mental work* on physical endurance has so far yielded but discordant results. Some
of this work, *e. g.,* that of Keller (20), may be thrown out of
court at once as careless in plan and execution and merely
illustrative of blind infatuation for the ergograph. Typical
conclusions of other investigators are as follows: Larguier (24)
reports that two hours of mathematics, and Bolton that two
hours of adding, definitely increase the ergograph record; Clavière (13), on the other hand, reports that two hours of intense
mental work produces a definite and proportionate diminution

of muscular force, whereas intellectual work of medium intensity does not produce any appreciable weakening of endurance. He further confesses his inability to determine the relative fatigue-effect of various school studies. Miss Martyn (31) found, in general, that no consistent decrease in muscular capacity accompanied the fatigue of a school day. The careful ergographic tests of Oseretzkowsky and Kraepelin show that work capacity is increased after one hour of simple addition or learning of 12-place numerals, but that it is lessened if the mental work is rendered more difficult, as by adding under distraction. In an extensively quoted study, Kemsies (21) reports the results of a long series of tests upon a selected group of average, industrious boys who had been trained to the use of the instrument, from which he concludes (a) that the ergograph is a reliable indicator of true fatigue (lowered fund of energy as distinct from weariness) ; (b) that subjective feelings of bodily or mental condition may not accord with real capacity; (c) that some of the pupils in the Berlin schools show, at least for the time being, signs of overwork; (d) that special attention should be paid to pupils who fatigue easily; (e) that one can determine for each study its special fatigue-value or 'ergographic-index,' more particularly, that the several studies range themselves, in order from highest to lowest fatigue-index, as follows: gymnastics, mathematics, foreign languages, religion, German, science and geography, history, singing and drawing.

In the attempt to explain these divergences Binet and Henri (4) suggest that we must always distinguish between mental work conducted without emotion and that conducted with emotion. They conclude that the former, if prolonged, may be expected to lessen endurance; the latter to produce a transient increase, followed by a decrease. Kraepelin (23), somewhat similarly, concludes that, while hard mental work certainly reduces muscular energy, deviating results may appear in ergograms on account of the condition of excitement (*Anregung*) that normally accompanies mental work, and that may be expected to affect, either positively or negatively, the tracing which follows such work. Kraepelin further calls attention, as do Ellis and Shipe, Bergström, Franz and others, to the very large normal variation in the curves of any individual, due to the operation of numerous constant and variable factors, often little understood. Many results are valueless (*e. g.*, in his opinion, those of Kemsies) because of the failure properly to eliminate or evaluate these factors.

(13)   The investigations of Christopher (12) and Smedley (39) at Chicago indicate a thoroughgoing correlation between *endurance and class standing,* according to the method of percentile grading, the method of distribution of 12-year-old pupils, and the method of comparison of the endurance of children at and above grade with that of children below grade at each age. Again, boys in the school for incorrigible and truant children were found to exhibit, at every age, less endurance (62 per cent. to 82 per cent.) than normal boys of the same age.

(14)   The *endurance of boys* is greater than that of girls at all ages, and the difference becomes very striking during adolescence (39).

(15)   The *development of endurance and that of vital capacity* bear a decided resemblance to one another, whether pupils are examined singly or collectively (39).

(16)   The *diurnal 'course of power'* according to the Chicago experiments may be expressed as follows: "(*a*) The extremes of endurance and fatigue in school are greater in the morning than in the afternoon; (*b*) a higher grade of power is found in the morning session in children attending two sessions daily; (*c*) while endurance is not as great, it is better sustained in the afternoon." Compilations of the ergograms of 1127 pupils place the maximum at 9 A. M. and the minimum at 12 noon. Kemsies considered the first two morning hours the best. Experiments upon adults by Lombard (28), Harley (16), Storey (41) and Marsh (30) exhibit considerable lack of agreement with one another or with the Chicago results, though Marsh summarizes them by the statement that the curve of strength efficiency seems well established for the following course: "a beginning minimum in early morning, a fairly rapid rise till 11, a level or slight decline till 1 P. M. ($\pm$ 1 hour), an increase to the maximum at 5 P. M. ($\pm$ 1 hour), thence a fall till bedtime."

(17) Kemsies concludes that Monday and Tuesday, or the first two days after any rest pause, are the *best days for general efficiency,* and he further concludes that vacations exert a powerful effect upon efficiency; but, since this effect cannot be traced for longer than four weeks, school terms should be broken up by more frequent vacations of shorter duration.

(18) If ergographic contractions are continued to the point of *exhaustion,* we have both the sum-total of the height of the lifts and their number for indexes of the neuro-muscular condition. Hoch and Kraepelin (18) are of the opinion that, in this case, the height of contraction is conditioned by the state of the muscles, but the number of contractions by the state of the central nervous system; the two factors should, therefore, be reported separately for their diagnostic value. On the other hand, Lombard (28) concludes that, at least when the contraction is not faster than once per second, the amount of fatigue experienced by the central nervous system does not correspond to the number of lifts, but rather to the strength of the motor impulses discharged, so that the sum-total of the height of lifts is the more accurate index of the state of the central nervous mechanism.

(19) According to Lombard, endurance is increased by exercise, rest (especially sleep), food, increased atmospheric pressure and by small doses of alcohol, but lessened by general and local fatigue, hunger, lessened atmospheric pressure, high temperature, especially with high humidity, and by tobacco. Oseretzkowsky and Kraepelin find that coffee increases the height of lifts, and that alcohol, in quantities from 15 to 20 g., causes at first a considerable increase, especially in the number of lifts, but that this soon disappears. On the other hand, Rivers and Webber (38) have discovered that small doses of alcohol (5-20 cc.) fail to produce any appreciable modification of the ergographic record if proper precautions are taken to keep the subject in ignorance as to when alcohol is administered. The results of previous workers are, therefore, presumably due to the influence of other factors, particularly interest and sensory stimulation, and no future work on the effects of small doses of alcohol can be acceptable unless these factors are controlled.

Harley (16) concludes that "moderate smoking, although it may have a slight influence in diminishing the power of doing voluntary muscular work, neither stops the morning rise nor, when done early in the evening, hinders the evening fall."

REFERENCES

(1) K. Aars and J. Larguier, L'effort musculaire et la fatigue des centres nerveux. *AnPs*, 7: 1900 (1901), 187-205.

(2) J. A. Bergström, A new type of ergograph, with a discussion of ergographic experimentation. *AmJPs*, 14: 1903, 510-540.

(3) S. Bettmann, Ueber die Beeinflussung einfacher psychischer Vorgänge durch körperliche u. geistige Arbeit. *PsArb*, 1: 1895, 152-208.

(4) A. Binet and V. Henri, La fatigue intellectuelle. Paris, 1898. Pp. 336.

(5) A. Binet and N. Vaschide, Examen critique de l'ergographe de Mosso. *AnPs*, 1897 (1898), 253-266. Also, Un nouvel ergographe, dit ergographe à ressort. *Ibid.*, 303-315.

(6) A. Binet and N. Vaschide, Expériences de force musculaire et de fond chez les jeunes garçons. *Ibid.*, 15-63.

(7) A. Binet and N. Vaschide, La mesure de la force musculaire chez les jeunes gens. *Ibid.*, 173-199. See also *ibid.*, 236-244, 245-252 and 295-302.

(8) T. Bolton, The reliability of certain methods for measuring the degree of fatigue in school children. *PsR*, 7: 1900, 136-7.

(9) T. Bolton, Ueber die Beziehungen zwischen Ermüdung, Raumsinn der Haut und Muskelleistung. *PsArb*, 4: 1902, 175-234.

(10) T. Bolton and Eleanora Miller, On the validity of the ergograph as a measurer of work capacity. *NebraskaUnSd*, 1904, 79 + 128.

(11) J. Cattell, An ergometer. *Sci*, n. s. 5: 1897, 909-910.

(12) W. Christopher, Rept. on child-study, reprint from *An. Rep. Brd. Educ. Chicago*, 1898-99.

(13) J. Clavière, Le travail intellectuel dans ses rapports avec la force musculaire mesurée au dynamomètre. *AnPs*, 7: 1900 (1901), 206-230.

(14) A. C. Ellis and Maud Shipe, A study of the accuracy of the present methods of testing fatigue. *AmJPs*, 14: 1903, 496-509.

(15) S. I. Franz, On the methods of estimating the force of voluntary muscular contraction and on fatigue. *AmJPhg*, 4: 1900, 348-372.

(16) V. Harley, The value of sugar and the effect of smoking on muscular work. *JPhg*, 16, 1894, 97-122.

(17) L. Hirschlaff, Zur Methode und Kritik der Ergographenmessungen. *ZPdPs*, 3: 1901, 184-198.

(18) A. Hoch and E. Kraepelin, Ueber die Wirkung der Theebestandtheile auf körperliche und geistige Arbeit. *PsArb*, 1: 1896, 378-488.

(19) T. Hough, Ergographic studies in neuro-muscular fatigue. *AmJPhg*, 5: 1901, 240-266.

(20) R. Keller, Pädagogisch-psychometrische Studien. *BiZb*, 14: 1894, 24-32, 38-53, 328-336.

(21) F. Kemsies, Zur Frage der Ueberbürdung unserer Schuljugend *DMdW*, July 2, 1896, 433. See also his Arbeitshygiene der Schule auf Grund von Ermüdungsmessungen. Berlin, 1898, and *SmAbPdPs*, 2: 1899 Heft i., pp. 64.

(22) E. Kraepelin, Zur Ueberbürdungsfrage. Jena, 1897. Pp. 49.

(23)   E. Kraepelin, Ueber Ermüdungsmessungen. *ArGsPs*, 1 : 1903, 9-30.

(24)   J. Larguier, Essai de comparison sur les différentes méthodes proposées pour la mesure de la fatigue intellectuelle. *AnPs*, 5 : 1898 (1899), 190-201.

(25)   F. S. Lee, Fatigue, in the Harvey Lectures, Phila., 1906, 169-194. Also *J. Amer. Med. Ass.*, 46 : 1906, 1491, and in *Studies in Physiology*, Columbia Univ., 1902-7.

(26)   E. H. Lindley, Ueber Arbeit und Ruhe. *PsArb*, 3 : 1900, 482-534.

(27)   J. Loeb, Muskelthätigkeit als Mass psychischer Thätigkeit. *ArGsPhg*, 39 : 1886, 592-7.

(28)   W. P. Lombard (a), The effect of fatigue on voluntary muscular contractions. *AmJPs*, 3 : 1890, 24-42.   (b) Some of the influences which affect the power of voluntary muscular contractions. *JPhg*, 13 : 1892, 1-58.

(29)   A. MacDonald, Experimental study of school children, etc., reprint of chs. 21 and 25, *RepComEd*, 1899.

(30)   H. D. Marsh, The diurnal course of efficiency, Columbia Univ. diss., N. Y., 1906. Pp. 99.

(31)   Gladys Martyn, The evidence of mental fatigue during school hours. *JEPd*, 1 : 1911, 137-147.

(32)   A. Mosso, Fatigue. Eng. tr., N. Y., 1904. Pp. 334.

(33)   G. E. Müller, Review of A. Waller's "The Sense of Effort." *ZPs*, 4 : 1893, 122-138.

(34)   R. Müller, Ueber Mosso's Ergographen, etc. *PhSd*, 17 : 1901, 1-29.

(35)   M. Offner, Mental fatigue. Eng. trans. by G. M. Whipple, Baltimore, 1911.   (Useful bibliography).

(36)   A. Oseretzkowsky and E. Kraepelin, Ueber die Beeinflussung der Muskelleistung durch verschiedene Arbeitsbedingungen. *PsArb*, 3 : 1901, 587-690.

(37)   W. Rivers and E. Kraepelin, Ueber Ermüdung u. Erholung. *PsArb*, 1 : 1896, 627-678.

(38)   W. Rivers, The influence of small doses of alcohol on muscular activity. *PsBu*, 5 : 1908, 49. See also Rivers and H. Webber, The influence of small doses of alcohol on the capacity for muscular work. *BrJPs*, 2 : 1908, 261-280.

(39)   F. Smedley, Rep. dept. child-study and pedagogic investigation, reprint from 46th *An. Rep. Brd. Educ.*, Chicago, 1899-1900. Also *Rep ComEd*, 1902, i., 1095-1115.

(40)   T. Storey, The influence of fatigue upon the speed of voluntary contraction of human muscle. *AmJPhg*, 8 : 1903, 355.

(41)   T. Storey (a), Some daily variations in height, weight and strength. *Am. Phys. Ed. Rev.*, 6 : 1901.   (b) Daily variation in the power of voluntary muscular contraction. *Ibid.*, 7 : 1902.   (c) Studies in voluntary muscular contraction, Stanford Univ. Press, 1904.

(42)   E. L. Thorndike, Mental Fatigue. *PsR*, 7 : 1900, 466-482, 547-579.

(43)   W. Weygandt, Ueber den Einfluss des Arbeitswechsels auf fortlaufende geistige Arbeit. *PsArb*, 2 : 1897, 118-202.

(44)   C. S. Yoakum, An experimental study of fatigue. *PsMon*, 11 : 1909, No. 46. Pp. 131.   (Bibliography of 108 titles).

TEST 10

Quickness or rate of movement: Tapping.—This has probably
been more frequently applied than any other 'motor test,' and
has been thought to afford a better index of motor capacity
than any other single test. Recent work with tapping, however, while not discouraging the belief that the test has value,
has shown that we cannot regard speed of voluntary movement
as an unequivocal and comprehensive 'index of voluntary motor
ability,' because a high gross rate does not necessarily go hand
in hand with high speed in other phases of motor response, and
because, moreover, we do not know precisely what may be the
ultimate neural or psychophysical factors that condition the
rate.[1]

Aside from its use in the attempt to secure this 'index of voluntary motor ability,' the tapping test has been employed to
secure an index of right-handedness (for which purpose it may
be advantageously combined with Tests 6, 9, 11 and 12), and to
secure an index of fatigue (likewise preferably in conjunction
with other tests of physical capacity). These several indexes
have been studied in various comparative investigations, more
especially in estimating sex and age factors in motor development and the relation of physical to mental ability at large.

The duration of the test has ranged from 10 sec. (Abelson),
or 15 sec. (Burt), to one minute, or to the completion of 300
taps (Dresslar), and the method from the simple making of
dots or vertical marks with pencil and paper (Binet and Vas-

---

[1]To quote from Wells (26, p. 444): "What is the precise physiological
significance of the maximum rate is by no means well made out.   *   *   *
It seems to be generally conceded that it is limited by the refractory
phase of the synapses in the motor pathways, but that does not make the
tapping test a measure of the period of this refractory phase; at least,
not in the earlier stages of practice.   *   *   *   In the beginning, as we
ordinarily have to apply the test, the factors in speed are probably those
of coördination mainly, and cannot be expected to afford information
about the condition of the motor pathways as given in the refractory
phase."

On the other hand, the correlations obtained by Abelson with 'special
class' children convince him that this test has for them a high diagnostic
value. He says: "Evidently tapping, which is quite a mechanical procedure for normal children, requires from defective children a special
effort of attention and will."

chide), or the puncturing of a small square of paper with a pointed stylus (Abelson, Burt) to the execution of difficult trilling movements upon telegraph keys.[1] The apparatus here prescribed is somewhat elaborate, but experience has shown that the tapping test cannot be conducted to the best advantage without careful control of experimental conditions and the use of a reliable device for recording a continuous and permanent record, such as the graphic method supplies.

MATERIALS.—Tapping board, 55x10 cm., with brass plates 10 cm. square on either end (Fig. 26). Tapping stylus, with flexible connecting wire attached. Kymograph (Fig. 22), with accessories—paper, smoking device, shellac solution. Double time-marker (Fig. 27). Seconds' pendulum (Fig. 28) or other

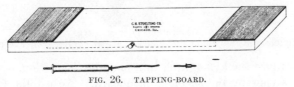

FIG. 26. TAPPING-BOARD.

noiseless instrument arranged to give electric contacts once per sec. Support with levelling screw and right-angle piece to hold time-marker. Table clamps for tapping board. Large sheet of gray or white cardboard. Suitable supports and clamps for holding cardboard. Two short-circuiting keys (Fig. 29), or simple knife switches. Stop-watch. Four dry or Leclanché cells. Flexible covered wire with connector tips or ordinary No. 18 annunciator wire. [A swivel chair, adjustable in height, and an ammeter or battery-tester are also convenient, though not absolutely essential.]

PRELIMINARIES.—(1) Clamp or screw the tapping board securely at the edge of a table in such a manner that S may

---

[1]Tests like rapid counting aloud or the rapid reading of digits or the reaction-time test are not psychologically comparable to the tapping test. Again, the form of test used at Columbia University and elsewhere to measure rate of movement (making a dot as rapidly as possible in each of 100 one-cm. squares) is not equivalent to the tapping required in most quickness tests, since a certain amount of precision is demanded of each movement, and that test therefore stands midway between Tests 10 and 11, as here prescribed. The so-called 'tapping' test used by Yoakum and by Mrs. Squire to investigate fatigue is not a test of motor coördination, but rather of attention and memory.

have free access to either end of the board for using either
right or left hand. Arrange S's chair so that he sits sidewise
to the table with his forearm resting comfortably along the
tapping board and his hand directly over the metallic plate.

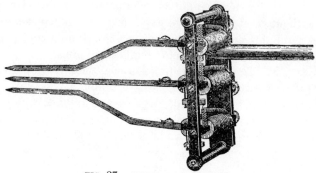

FIG. 27.   TRIPLE TIME-MARKER.
The double and the single time-marker are of similar construction.

(2)   Place the kymograph in a horizontal position, screened
from S's view by the sheet of cardboard.[1] Adjust the fans or
gear-wheels so that the drum makes (for a 30-sec. test) one revolution in about 40 sec.

(3)   Remove the drum and cover with the prepared paper by
simply moistening the gummed end, taking care to draw it
evenly and tightly around the drum. Blacken the paper by
revolving it slowly in a smoky flame.[2] Replace carefully in the
kymograph.

----

[1]The screen is to avoid the distraction of S's attention by the operation
of the apparatus. If separate tables are used for tapping board and
kymograph, this may not be necessary, but it is commonly more convenient to assemble all the apparatus on a single table.

[2]An oil stove from which the top is removed is excellent for this purpose, as the flame is very sooty and not so hot as the gas flame often
employed. A simple support (Fig. 23) is used to hold the drum, both
for the smoking and for the subsequent removal of the paper. For this
and other details in the use of the kymograph, consult Titchener, *Experimental Psychology*, Vol. I, Part II, pp. 172-180.

If an extended series of tests is to be made, cover the drum permanently with the regular kymograph paper, and, for the records, super-
pose two narrower strips, say 75 mm. wide. These strips are wide
enough to record the right and left-hand efficiency of one S: they can
then be removed promptly for fixing, and thus the danger of injury is
lessened, the ease of handling increased, and the blackening of the metal
drum is less likely to be a source of annoyance.

(4) Adjust the time-marker on the support so that the pointers bear upon the drum with just sufficient pressure to make a satisfactory tracing. The pointer must move in a plane parallel to the plane of a tangent drawn through the point of contact.

The manipulation of the apparatus may be facilitated by fastening upon the table, in front of, and parallel to the surface of the drum, a straight bit of wood somewhat longer than the drum. Let the foot of the tripod which contains the levelling screw stand away from the drum, and the other two feet bear against the wooden strip. A half turn of the levelling screw will then free the pointers from the drum, and the entire support with the time-marker may be slid along to a new position, when another half turn of the screw will quickly adjust the pointers for the next record.

(5) Wire one signal-magnet in series with the tapping board stylus, short-circuiting key and two cells of the battery. The magnet will then be set in motion by the tapping when the key is closed.

(6) Wire the second magnet in series with the pendulum, second short-circuiting key and remaining two cells of the battery. This magnet will then be set in motion by the pendulum when its controlling key is closed, and will thus beat off the time-line.

METHOD.—(1) Seat S for the use of his right hand. Instruct him to tap as rapidly as possible from the signal 'now' to the signal 'stop,' which will be given about one-half minute later. Tell him to pay attention only to his tapping. He may be allowed to exercise some latitude with regard to the type of movement used (short or wide excursion), unless he is inclined to adopt a very heavy whole-arm pounding movement. The most favorable movement for most S's is that obtained by resting the elbow on the tapping board and using both the wrist and elbow joints.

(2) Start the seconds' pendulum and close the time-line circuit.

(3) Start the kymograph, and when it is fairly in motion give S the signal 'now.'

(4) When S has had time to respond, i. e., after two or three sec., throw in the record magnet by closing its key, and at the same instant start the stop-watch.

(5)   When a clear record of 30 sec. has been inscribed, stop the watch, break the record circuit, signal 'stop' to *S*, stop the kymograph and open the time-circuit.   [*E* must practise the whole series of operations until they run smoothly and automatically.]

FIG. 28.   SECONDS' PENDULUM.

(6)   Now adjust the pointers for a new record.   Let *S* sit facing in the other direction, and test the left hand by the use of the plate at the other end of the tapping board, following the directions given for the test of the right hand.   The interval between the end of the first and the beginning of the second record is preferably kept constant at 30 sec.

VARIATIONS OF METHOD.—(1)   The duration of the test may be lengthened to 45 sec. or longer, or shortened to 10 or 20 sec.

It is, however, desirable, for the sake of comparison, that a standard duration be employed. Thirty sec. is adequate for all ordinary purposes.

FIG. 29.   SHORT-CIRCUITING KEY (DU BOIS REYMOND)

(2)   For certain types of investigation, *e. g.*, when disorders of motor innervation are suspected, it is recommended that the plan of experiment suggested by Wells and followed by him and by Strong be adopted. In Wells' terminology each 30-sec. period of continuous tapping is termed one *series*, and is regarded as composed of six 5-sec. *intervals*. Five such series constitute one *record*, and two records, the first usually with the right, the second with the left hand, constitute one standard *experiment*. The hands do not alternate from series to series, but only from record to record. The first one used is called the 'preceding,' the other the 'following' hand. Between each two series there is a rest-pause of 2.5 min., during which S should refrain from all muscular effort.

(3)   To make the test comparable to the form employed by some investigators, an ordinary 'sending' telegraph key may be substituted for the tapping board and stylus. But the key has the disadvantage of imposing a certain restriction upon the type of movement, and will be found in practise to reduce the record of many S's.

(4)   By using the key, E may compare S's rate of tapping with different fingers. For this purpose it is well to fasten down the forearm with a strap at the wrist, so as to allow movement with the fingers only.

(5)   Again, by using the key, a trilling movement, executed

by alternate movements of the index and middle fingers, may be substituted for the regulation tapping movement. Without practise this movement is quite difficult for some S's, whereas for others, notably for those who have practised trilling exercises on the piano, it is comparatively easy.[1] For this reason this form of experiment is not advised, save for some exceptional purpose, e. g., testing the effect of practise upon the acquisition of a new bit of manual dexterity. Other modifications suggest themselves, such as trilling with the 4th and 5th fingers—an exercise likely to be unfamiliar even to S's who have 'taken lessons.'

TREATMENT OF RESULTS.—(1)   When the record has been made, use any pointed article to mark it for future identification (S's name or number, date, hand used, etc.) ; then remove carefully for preservation.   A simple and satisfactory method is to pour a very thin solution of shellac and wood alcohol or of powdered resin (not over 10 per cent.) in alcohol, into a saucer or shallow dish, and to pass the strip through this, smoked side up.   Hang the record up to dry, and pour the solution back into a wide-mouthed bottle, where it should be kept tightly stoppered.   The record will dry in a few minutes and can then be trimmed and handled with impunity.

(2)   The result of the test is commonly expressed simply by the total number of taps executed, but it is quite as important, if not more important, to consider changes of speed during each trial.   The requisite data must be secured by the rather laborious process of counting the strokes made by the recording-magnet upon the blackened paper, and tabulating them by 5-sec. intervals, as illustrated below.   The 'total efficiency' of a 'record' (5 trials with the same hand) is the average of the sum of the taps per trial.   This serves as the gross index of speed : the rates for the 6 intervals within each trial afford an opportunity for studying variations in performance.

---

[1] The effect of piano practise, as the investigations of Binet and Courtier (3) and of Raif (20) show, is to improve coördination of movement, i. e., its regularity, smoothness, etc., but not to increase the natural capacity for speed or rate of movement.

The use of an electric counter, such as some investigators have employed, would eliminate this work, but the counter gives no indication of changes in speed during the trial. Moreover, the electric counter is not reliable: even with 10 or 12 cells of battery, it will miss a quick tap which the graphic method will record. It follows that all results based on the use of the counter are to be looked upon with suspicion, so that the conclusions of Bagley, Bolton, Marsh, Kelly, Smedley, and possibly those of Bryan, Davis, Gilbert and Dresslar should be accepted with reservation. If a mechanical counter of the dial type is to be used, preference should be given to the Ewald chronoscope, which, as Dunlap has shown, operates perfectly for the tapping test and is a useful instrument for many other laboratory purposes.

(3) To secure an index of fatigue, E may compare the record of the first 5 (or 10) sec. with that of the last 5 (or 10) sec. by the use of the formula for determining the relative loss of efficiency given in Test 9.

Wells has published extensive conclusions concerning fatigue in tapping that are based upon a differently computed index. The average number of taps executed in the 2d, 3d, 4th, 5th and 6th 5-sec. intervals are divided by the number of taps executed in the 1st 5-sec. interval. This index is somewhat misleading, in so far as a high index indicates a low degree of fatigue. If it is deemed worth while to relate the last five to the first of the six intervals to compute fatigue (a procedure which seems less desirable than the one above prescribed), it would be better, in the author's opinion, to subtract the average in question from the initial speed and divide the loss by the efficiency of the first interval.

TABLE 25.

Sample Record of a Tapping Test (Wells)

NUMBER OF INTERVAL	1ST	2D	3D	4TH	5TH	6TH	TOTAL
1st series_____	41	37	35	34	34	32	213
2d series_____	41	37	36	35	34	34	217
3d series_____	40	39	37	37	35	34	222
4th series_____	40	39	37	36	36	35	223
5th series_____	41	39	38	37	36	36	227
Averages _____	40.6	38.2	36.6	35.8	35.0	34.2	220.4

(4) To secure an index of right-handedness, E may compute the percentage of the left-hand to the right-hand efficiency. The fatigue-index of the right hand may also be compared with that of the left hand in a similar manner.

TYPICAL RESULTS.—Table 25 shows a sample record of the work of a normal adult with the right hand when near the limit of practise. The tabulation is in accordance with that recommended when five 30-sec. series are recorded.

GENERAL CONCLUSIONS.—Although the tapping test is one of the most objective that can be applied, and although it has been tried by a large number of investigators (see the references at the end of the test), the results have not been always accordant, and, with the exception of the recent work of Wells, have not been so treated as to afford real insight into the factors that underlie their appearance. The lack of accordance is to be attributed in large part to differences in method of procedure. Differences in apparatus, too, have been sufficient to account for some discrepancy, as has already been pointed out. As regards method, the duration of the test, to instance a single point, has varied from 5 sec. (Binet and Vaschide, Bryan, Kirkpatrick) to 2 min. (Thompson), with intermediate durations, such as 10 sec. (Bagley), 30 sec. (Smedley), 45 sec. (Gilbert), 60 sec. (Kelly), or the test has been conducted in 5 series of 5 sec. each (Bolton).[1]

In so far as these divergences of method may be neglected, we may note the chief conclusions of interest concerning the tapping test as follows:

(1) In general, the *maximal rate* of voluntary movement varies with the individual, with sex, with maturity, with the side of the body used, with practise, with the number of trials (duration of experiment), with fatigue, with mental excitement, with the time of day, but not, within wide limits, with the amplitude of the movement.[2] For practised adults the initial rate is about 8.5 taps per sec. (Dresslar), with a range from 5 to 14 taps.

(2) *Constant individual differences* in rate of tapping can be demonstrated without much difficulty, but we cannot at

---

[1]The situation here, as in most tests, shows clearly how desirable it would be to establish some standard form of test and to use it alone for all comparative purposes.

[2]For a fuller discussion of these conditions, consult Dresslar, Bryan, Strong, Abelson and Wells.

present explain them, save to say that they are conditioned in a general way by fundamental neural factors, or by these plus differences in ability to coördinate voluntary movement. Thus, in 10 adults tested by Wells (10 series for each hand), the average total efficiency (taps in 30 sec.) was approximately 194, but the fastest S averaged 225, and the slowest 153. Since the m. v. is small (here approximately 1 to 3 per cent.), these figures undoubtedly indicate persistent characteristic differences.

(3) *Dependence on age.* The rate of tapping increases with age, at least between 6 and 18 years. The slight drop at 13, upon which Gilbert comments, appears in Bryan's tables with some qualifications, but not so clearly in Smedley's results, which are reproduced herewith: it will be seen, however, that boys make no apparent gain from 13 to 14.

TABLE 24

Dependence of Rate of Tapping upon Age (Smedley)

AGE	NUMBER TESTED	BOYS		NUMBER TESTED	GIRLS	
		TAPS IN 30 SECONDS			TAPS IN 30 SECONDS	
		Rt. Hand	Lt. Hand		Rt. Hand	Lt. Hand
8 _____	31	147	117	31	146	117
9 _____	60	151	127	44	149	118
10 _____	47	161	132	48	157	129
11 _____	49	169	141	48	169	139
12 _____	44	170	145	50	169	140
13 _____	50	184	156	45	178	153
14 _____	40	184	155	67	181	157
15 _____	37	191	169	48	181	159
16 _____	21	196	170	50	188	167
17 _____	13	196	174	40	184	162
18 _____	3	197	183	24	193	169

(4) *Dependence on sex.* The results of most investigators lead to the conclusion that boys are faster than girls, and that this sex difference increases with age. Thus, Miss Thompson, who worked with a small number of adults, found that 88 per cent. of men exceeded the median speed of women. Similarly,

Burt and Moore place the median for boys at 86.5 and for girls at 80.5 taps in 15 sec., and find that 69.8 per cent. of boys exceed the median speed of girls. Bolton, however, has reported that "the girls are uniformly better than the boys," while Bryan found girls superior at 13, when they showed improvement and the boys little or none—a tendency that is apparently allied to the actual crossing of the curves of height and weight. More elaborate experiments upon adults (10 men and 10 women) by Wells (28) now seem to indicate that women surpass men in tapping with the right hand in the first experiment, whereas elsewhere they are inferior: the sex differences found by this investigator are said to be "mainly in those features of the experiment which especially involve the affective factor in the subject's attitude, and they are manifestations of the greater responsiveness of the women to this affective element."

(5)   The *index of right-handedness* (per cent. left-hand is of right-hand efficiency) was found by Wells to range from .81 to .94, average .90, for adults, and by Smedley to vary with age in the case of school children in such a manner that the average index was .82 at the age of 9, and .89 at the age of 18. It seems, therefore, as if right-handedness, so far as tapping is concerned, is more pronounced in childhood than in adult life. Wells also states (28) that "the right and left hands are farther apart in women," though the relationship is more variable in them than in men. The index is to a small extent conditioned by the order in which the records are taken. For normal *S*'s each hand tends to be relatively better when it precedes than when it follows.

(6)   *Right-handedness and intelligence.*   Smedley's conclusion that there exists a positive correlation between degree of right-handedness and school standing, *i. e.,* that the left-hand more nearly approaches the right-hand efficiency in the case of dull and backward pupils, is not confirmed by the results of Bolton.

(7)   *Warming-up.*   In practically every continuous psycho-physical activity there appears a tendency to improvement, due to what the Germans have termed *Anlauf.* This 'warming-up'

is a kind of momentum not identical with practise, and its effect is to increase or heighten the activity, and thus to retard or even to obscure the appearance of indications of fatigue. In tapping, we observe fatigue within each 30-sec. series, but a comparison of successive series within a record will show the improvement due to warming-up. With 2.5 min. rest-pauses, Wells found this factor to be clearly present (up to the 7th series at least) in right-hand records, but by no means so evident in left-hand records. The effect of warming-up appears to be primarily operative in increased immunity to fatigue, and is markedly augmented by practise, *e. g.,* in tests continued for 20 days.

(8) *Spurts.* The curve of performance in tapping, as well as any psychophysical activity, is also liable to be influenced by short periods of increased activity, which, to continue the analogy of the race-track, may be termed 'spurts' (German, *Antriebe*). Thus, Wells' discovery that the first experiment usually excels the second in women, whereas the reverse may be true in men, is referred to a special incitement of novelty (*Neuigkeitsantrieb*), which affects the women markedly. Similarly, each 'record' may be affected by an initial spurt (*Anfangsantrieb*) or by a terminal spurt (*Schlussantrieb*). These dynamogenic factors obviously tend to obscure the real effects of fatigue.

(9) *Fatigue and the fatigue-index.* (*a*) As just stated, the speed of tapping normally declines after the 1st 5-sec. interval, until it is approximately six-sevenths as great in the last as in the 1st interval (Wells). In 45-sec. series the fatigue-index (loss of last 5 sec. divided by initial 5 sec.), according to Gilbert, is highest in young children (24 per cent. at 8 years), and declines thence irregularly to 12.7 per cent. at the age of 15. Tests by the author of fifty 8th-grade grammar-school boys reveal a fatigue-index (ratio of loss in 3d 10 sec. to 1st 10 sec. in 30 sec. tapping) of .137, m. v. .048 for the right, and .15, m. v. .046, for the left hand. Wells' so-called 'fatigue-index' ranges for normal *S*'s between .85 and .95.

(*b*) According to Gilbert, the fatigue-index is higher for boys than for girls, but boys tap faster throughout each trial, so that their net efficiency is higher.[1]

(*c*) Kelly (15), who worked on a small number of children with a "fatigue-counter," found that "A"-grade pupils fatigued less than "C"-grade pupils. His index (the per cent. of the last to the 1st 10 sec. in a 60-sec. trial) was for the former, with the finger 87.2 per cent., with the arm 88.0 per cent.; for the latter, with the finger 77.0 per cent., with the arm 76.4 per cent. In the author's tests no correlation could be discovered between fatigue-index and school standing.

(*d*) The effect of fatigue is progressively to 'level up' individual differences in speed. In other words, individual differences are more evident in initial than in terminal intervals (Bliss, Wells).

(*e*) Objective fatigue (slowing in rate) persists after practise, but the subjective feeling of fatigue may be eliminated thereby.

(*f*) The fatigue induced by 30-sec. tapping is apparently completely eradicated by a 3-min. rest-pause (Wells).

(*g*) The fatigue-index of right and left hands shows only slight correlation (Wells). The author's tests, however, show a correlation in the case of 50 boys of .33. In some persons the left hand is less susceptible to fatigue than is the right hand, though the reverse is the rule.

(*h*) The subjective experience of fatigue, as has been intimated, does not accord with the objective fatigue-loss.[2]

---

[1] It is more reasonable to interpret this higher index of boys as an expression of greater zeal and enthusiasm than to follow Havelock Ellis in his inference that this is an example of the "more continuous character of woman's activity," especially since Miss Thompson, from comparative tests of adults, concludes that men surpass women both in initial rapidity and in power to sustain it, and since other tests show that high initial speed tends to be accompanied by a high fatigue loss.

[2] According to Wells: "The objective fatigue phenomena which we note in the test are in all probability either a fatigue phenomenon in the refractory phase or a lowered efficiency of coördination, especially a product of altered synaptic conditions; the sensations of fatigue, on the other hand, may with equal assurance be ascribed to tissue changes within the muscles that take place as a result of their continued effort. In this test, therefore, the fatigue sensations are absolutely no indications of the actual fatigue conditions, and any traceable correspondence between fatigue sensation and fatigue of performance must be regarded as almost wholly a product of reflex inhibition" (26, p. 473).

(10) *Practise.* (*a*) The effect of practise is to produce a gradual improvement in speed, with, of course, occasional losses.

(*b*) The rise of the curve of efficiency is not, as in most activities, more rapid at the beginning than elsewhere.

(*c*) Maximal efficiency, when two experiments are performed daily, is reached, apparently, in about 20 days.

(*d*) Practise affects the left hand no more than the right; consequently the index of right-handedness is unaffected by repetition of the test.

(*e*) Practise particularly increases the rate in the later trials, *i. e.*, it particularly affects warming-up, yet "the true practise gain is one mainly in the initial efficiency of performance, as distinguished from the warming-up gain, which shows itself chiefly in continued efficiency of performance" (Wells).

(*f*) An intermission of 10 to 14 days has no unfavorable effect upon practise gains, save that the feeling of fatigue may appear when work is resumed.

(11) *Diurnal rhythm.* Dresslar (10) found evidence of a diurnal rhythm, with a minimum at 8 A. M. and a maximum at 4 P. M. Marsh (18) also found that afternoon records generally surpassed those of the morning, though his figures do not accord very closely with those of Dresslar. Marsh also discovered that the later periods in the evening, which were not tested by Dresslar, furnished the most rapid rates of all. Similarly, Hollingworth noted a tendency toward better performance at the end of the day.

(12) *Dependence on 'general condition.'* When general well-being was ranked as good, medium, below medium and poor, Wells was unable to discern any relation between these several conditions and tapping efficiency, while there was, in the case of susceptibility to fatigue, a tendency, if anything, toward an inverse relation, *i. e.*, fatigue seemed to be greatest on 'good' days. Dresslar's observation that a vigorous walk decreases, while mental work increases speed of tapping has been generally confirmed by other investigators.

In investigating the effect of dental hygiene upon 5th-grade Cincinnati pupils Miss Kohnky found that the children who had special treatment exhibited a decided lowering of the fatigue index (1st 15 compared with last 15 sec.).

The effect upon rate of tapping induced by caffein in various amounts is summarized thus by Hollingworth: "The typical caffein effect on a motor process such as that involved in the tapping test seems to be a stimulation, which is sometimes preceded by a brief and slight initial retardation. The magnitude of the stimulation (a) varies directly with the size of the dose, and (b) is relatively slight when the caffein is taken in the forenoon." "There is no secondary or after-effect shown within the 72 hours over which the intensive doses were traced."

(13) *Correlation with mental ability and social status.* (a) The correlation between tapping ability and mental ability is found to be generally positive by Smedley, Gilbert, Bolton, Kirkpatrick, Burt ($r = .41$ to $.65$) and Abelson ($r = .28$ to $.42$), to be indifferent by Bagley (also by the author), while Binet and Vaschide report a positive correlation with 12-year-old pupils and an inverse correlation with 16 to 20-year-old pupils. While Gilbert found a very marked positive superiority of the 'bright' children in general, the relation did not appear at ages 16 and 17. Bolton found that "good children" (apparently meaning those drawn from the better social classes) were uniformly superior in tapping to children of the poorer class, both with the right and with the left hand. The fact that the divergence is greater at 9 than at 8 years he attributes to a general arrest of development in the poor-class children.

(b) Bolton also states that the "good" children showed a distinctly greater practise-improvement—a discovery which he terms "new and significant," and which he thinks is indicative of a fundamental difference in the ability of these two classes of children to take on new habits and profit quickly by experience.

(14) *Coefficient of reliability.* By repeating the test its reliability can be determined. The figures available, those of Burt and of Abelson, refer to a less desirable form of the test, and are conflicting. Burt found the coefficient of reliability to

be only .51, whereas Abelson obtained .92 for a group of girls and .91 for a group of boys. Burt reports that trials with a better form of procedure have yielded distinctly higher coefficients.

(15) *Miscellaneous correlations.* Burt found the following correlations with speed of tapping: with discrimination of pitch .48, with comparison of length of lines .36, with discrimination of lifted weights .42, with esthesiometric limen .10, with card dealing .57, with card sorting .57, with immediate memory .40, with the mirror test .74, with the spot-pattern test .57, with McDougall's dot test .78. Abelson's work with 88 girls and 43 boys in London 'special classes' afforded a somewhat similar series of correlations with eight different tests, though the results for the boys and for the girls were not always accordant. For further details the reader may consult the original article.

(16) *Epilepsy and insanity.* Smith reports inability to discern any characteristic differences between the speed of tapping in epileptic and in normal individuals. In cases of insanity that exhibit retardation, however, Wells finds three characteristic phenomena: (*a*) a reduction in the absolute rate; (*b*) 'reversal,' *i. e.*, acceleration of speed within a series, and (*c*) 'transference,' *i. e.*, superiority of 'following' over the 'preceding' hand. Strong found somewhat the same results, though he concludes that transference is not always seen in depressive states. In the manic states he finds the rate of tapping usually increased over that of the same S when normal. Inter-serial warming-up is also characteristic of manic S's.

(15) *Dependence on the type of movement.* The restriction of the tapping movement to specific joints, as has been attempted by some investigators, is difficult to accomplish in practise. However, it appears that the fastest rate is made when the movement is performed by the elbow joint, which is the one mainly concerned in the type of free movement here described. Kelly, for instance, found that the speed of tapping was faster with the forearm than with the forefinger in about the ratio of 15 to 13. From this, in connection with other tests of dexterity, especially tests of minimal movement, he argues

that children only gradually acquire dexterity and quickness of movement with the fingers, and that this passage "from fundamental to accessory," to use Burk's phrase, indicates the necessity of a general readjustment of the motor tasks required of children.

REFERENCES

(1) A. R. Abelson, (a) The measurement of mental ability of 'backward' children. *BrJPs*, 4: 1911, 268-314; (b) Tests for mental deficiency in childhood. *The Child*, 3: 1912, 1-17.

(2) W. C. Bagley, On the correlation of mental and motor ability in school children. *AmJPs*, 12: 1901, 193-205.

(3) A. Binet and J. Courtier, Recherches graphiques sur la musique. *AnPs*, 2: 1895 (1896), 201-222.

(4) A. Binet and N. Vaschide, (a) Epreuves de vitesse chez les jeunes garçons. *AnPs*, 4: 1897 (1898), 64-98. (b) Expériences de vitesse chez les jeunes gens. *Ibid.*, 200-224.

(5) C. B. Bliss, Investigations in reaction-time and attention. *Sd YalePsLab*, 1: 1893, 1-55.

(6) T. L. Bolton, The relation of motor power to intelligence. *Am JPs*, 14: 1903, 615-631.

(7) W. L. Bryan, On the development of voluntary motor ability. *AmJPs*, 5: 1892, 123-204.

(8) C. Burt, Experimental tests of general intelligence. *BrJPs*, 3: 1909, 94-177.

(9) C. Burt and R. C. Moore, The mental differences between the sexes, *JEPd*, 1: 1912, 273-284, 355-388.

(10) F. B. Dresslar, Some influences which affect the rapidity of voluntary movements. *AmJPs*, 4: 1892, 514-527.

(11) K. Dunlap, New uses for the Ewald chronoscope. *JEdPs*, 4: 1913, 99-101.

(12) J. A. Gilbert, Researches on the mental and physical development of school children. *SdYalePsLab*, 2: 1894, 40-100.

(13) J. A. Gilbert, Researches upon school children and college students. *UnIowaSdPs*, 1: 1897, 1-39.

(14) H. L. Hollingworth, The influence of caffein on mental and motor efficiency. *ArPs* (e), No. 22, 1912, N. Y. Especially ch. iv., pp. 25-43.

(15) R. L. Kelly, Psychophysical tests of normal and abnormal children; a comparative study. *PsR*, 10: 1903, 345-372.

(16) E. A. Kirkpatrick, Individual tests of school children. *PsR*, 7: 1900, 274-280.

(17) Emma Kohnky, Paper on effect of dental hygiene on physical and mental efficiency of 5th-grade children, to appear in *JEdPs*.

(18) H. D. Marsh, The diurnal course of efficiency, Columbia Univ. diss., N. Y., 1906. Pp. 99.

(19) J. M. Moore, Studies of fatigue. *SdYalePsLab*, 3: 1895, 68-95.

(20) O. Raif, Ueber Fingerfertigkeit beim Clavierspiel. *ZPs*, 24: 1900, 352.

(21) F. Smedley, *Rep. dep. child-study and pedagogic investigation.* No. 3, 1900-1901 (Chicago Public Schools). Also in *RepComEd*, 1902, i, 1115-1138.

(22) W. G. Smith, A comparison of some mental and physical tests in their application to epileptics and to normal subjects. *BrJPs*, 1: 1905, 240-260.

(23) E. K. Strong, A comparison between experimental data and clinical results in manic-depressive insanity. *AmJPs*, 24: 1913, 66-98.

(24) Helen B. Thompson, The mental traits of sex. Chicago, 1903. Pp. 188.

(25) F. L. Wells, A neglected measure of fatigue. *AmJPs*, 19: 1908, 345-358.

(26) F. L. Wells, Normal performances in the tapping test before and during practice, with special reference to fatigue phenomena. *Am JPs*, 19: 1908, 437-483.

(27) F. L. Wells, Studies in retardation as given in the fatigue phenomena of the tapping test. *AmJPs*, 20: 1909, 38-59.

(28) F. L. Wells, Sex differences in the tapping test: an interpretation. *AmJPs*, 20: 1909, 353-363.

(29) F. L. Wells, Motor retardation as a manic-depressive symptom. *AmJIns*, 66: July, 1909. (Reprint, pp. 52.)

TEST 11

Accuracy or precision of movement: Aiming.—The purposes for which tests of accuracy of movement have been employed are practically the same as those cited for the tapping test, viz.: to obtain an index of general voluntary motor ability with which to compare different children, to compare the right with the left hand, to determine the development of motor control with age, its differentiation with sex, and to test its correlation with mental ability. These tests have been only rarely used for determining the presence of fatigue, though they have been proposed as means for the diagnosis of incipient ataxia.

Tests of accuracy vary greatly in form: in fact, they virtually shade by degrees from those which prescribe a rapid, accurate movement similar to the tapping movement of Test 10, *e. g.,* the Columbia test described by Wissler (5), to those which prescribe a slow, steady movement more akin to a test for steadiness (No. 13).

Two types of precision test have been selected for consideration: the aiming, or 'target' test, and the line-drawing, or 'tracing' test (No. 12).

The common feature of all forms of aiming test is the measurement of the extent of error made by an individual when he tries in a series of discrete voluntary movements of hand or arm to hit some form of mark or target. According to the par-

ticular form of movement employed, the test has been known as
the 'probing test,' the 'target test,' the 'thrusting test,' etc.
These movements have ranged, to speak more specifically, from
a simple vertical probing movement of 6 mm. extent (Bryan, 2)
to whole-arm aiming with a pencil at a paper target at arm's
length (Thompson, 3; Whipple, 4), or making lunging thrusts
with a wand, somewhat after the fashion of a fencer, or even
throwing ordinary marbles at a bull's-eye target 2 m. distant
(Bagley, 1).

The results of any such precision test will obviously be conditioned by the position of the target with respect to S, by the
extent and rate of the aiming movement, and likewise, though
the fact seems not always to have been recognized, by the individually variable improvement in accuracy which will appear
if a series of 'shots' are taken at the same target. Hence, to be
satisfactory, an aiming test should prescribe and standardize
all these conditions; it should also admit of an exact evaluation
of each aiming movement. The form of test here described was
devised by the author several years ago to meet these conditions, and has proved satisfactory in use. Though the error
of a single stroke is large (as is certain to be the case in any
form of aiming test), the average of the 30 thrusts made by the
same S is very constant. The use of ten marks in place of a
single mark, or bull's-eye, removes to a large extent the improvement error just mentioned.

Hollingworth, in his investigation of the effect of caffein (see reference, Test 10) used a form of test known as the 'three-hole test,' which
demanded both speed and accuracy. The S's were required to thrust a
stylus as rapidly as possible into three holes arranged in a triangle, and
continue the process until 100 contacts had been registered with the
metallic insets in these holes. Here the introduction of the speed factor
makes the test different in principle from mere aiming. The same thing
is true of the 'irregular dotting' test, developed by MacDougall, and employed by him and by Burt and others in England. In it S is required
to hit with a pencil an irregularly arranged series of small circles which
are moved by clockwork past a narrow slit. The moving tape which
carries the circles is speeded up until S can just barely succeed by an
effort in hitting the marks. This test, when carried out for a prolonged
period, may be regarded more as a test of maintenance of attention than
of motor coördination.

APPARATUS.—Prepared blanks containing ten crosses irregularly arranged (Fig. 30). A base-board upon which the blanks are fastened, arranged to be secured upon the wall and adjusted to varying heights (Fig. 31). Metronome (Fig. 21). Pencil with tough and moderately hard lead.[1] Millimeter scale.

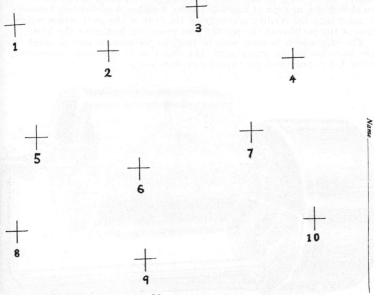

FIG. 30. TARGET BLANK.

The numbers, which are added here to show the order in which the crosses are to be struck in the first round, do not appear on the blank in use. Cut half size.

PRELIMINARIES.—Fasten the board upon the wall and arrange the counterweight properly, so that the board will remain in any position from one to two meters from the floor and will not be displaced when struck by the pencil.

Set the metronome at 138. Fasten the target-sheet upon the board, with the name-date corner in the lower right-hand corner of the board. Place a demonstration target on the wall conveniently near.

METHOD.—Make clear to S the following directions: (1) He

---

[1] By covering the base-board with a felt pad a pointed metal stylus may be substituted for the pencil.

is to stand with his right shoulder (for the right-hand test) squarely in front of the target, at such a distance that his pencil just strikes the target when his arm is fully extended.[1] (2) He is to strike in time with the beat of the metronome, following a two-beat rhythm, so that the pencil hits the target at the one beat and is drawn back at the next. (3) Each stroke is to

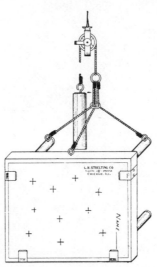

FIG. 31. ADJUSTABLE BASE-BOARD FOR TARGET TEST.

be a full, smooth stroke, not jerky or too short, and the pencil must, therefore, be brought back each time until it touches the shoulder. (4) He is to start at the first cross and make successive strokes, one at each cross in the series until the tenth is reached (see Fig. 30). This process is twice repeated, but in the second round, further to avoid practise, the order is from ten to one. S thus makes three shots at each mark, or thirty in all.

Before conducting the test proper, let S try the experiment upon the demonstration target. It will save time if E also illustrates the process at this time. E may assist S in follow-

---

[1] If the subjects are of approximately the same size, this distance may be marked upon the floor by a chalk line.

ing the rhythm of the metronome by saying: 'down, back,' 'down, back,' etc.

Place a fresh sheet upon the target-board and test the left hand.

TREATMENT OF RESULTS.—Measure the error of each thrust by the application of the millimeter scale. A pair of dividers may be helpful in this process. Average the thirty errors and compute the mean variation or standard deviation. Any 'shots' that have struck the lines of the crosses and are difficult to detect may be easily located by reversing the sheet.

RESULTS.—(1) On the basis of similar tests, other investigators have shown a gradual increase in accuracy with *age,* particularly during the years 5 to 8.

(2) *Sex* differences are slight, but, on the whole, boys are more accurate than girls, and men than women.

(3) The author, in using the test as described, has found an error of 4 to 6 mm. in university students, while in a group of fifty 8th-grade boys the following results were obtained:

Right hand, average 5.12, lowest 3.75, highest 8.34.

Left hand, average 6.39, lowest 4.15, highest 9.27.

(4) For the boys just mentioned the correlation between right and left-hand efficiency was 0.54.

REFERENCES

(1) W. C. Bagley, On the correlation of mental and motor ability in school children. *AmJPs*, 12 : 1901, 193-205.

(2) W. L. Bryan, On the development of voluntary motor ability. *AmJPs*, 5 : 1892, 123-204.

(3) Helen B. Thompson, The mental traits of sex, Chicago, 1903. Pp. 188.

(4) G. M. Whipple, The influence of forced respiration on psychical and physical activity. *AmJPs*, 9 : 1898, 560-571.

(5) C. Wissler, The correlation of mental and physical tests. *PsMon*, 3 : No. 6, 1901. Pp. 62.

TEST 12

Accuracy, precision, or steadiness of movement: Tracing.— The purposes for which tracing has been used are identical with those outlined for the preceding test, but the present test differs from the former in that the movement is continuous, analogous to that made in drawing a line—the so-called 'writing movement' of Bryan (3) or 'tracing test' of Bagley (1). Since steadiness of movement is quite as much in demand as accuracy (of the sort required in Test 11), this test is often classed as a steadiness test, rather than as an accuracy test, but it differs from steadiness tests proper in that it measures control of a voluntary movement, whereas the latter measure the extent of involuntary movement which takes place when the hand or arm is held at rest (Test 13).

The technique most commonly adopted for the tracing or line-drawing test consists in passing a metallic needle or stylus along a narrow slit between metallic strips and noting by telegraph sounder, bell, electric counter, or graphic record, the number of contacts made in passing along a given portion of the slit. This slit may be straight and bounded by parallel sides (Bolton, 2), or by slightly converging strips (Bryan, 3; Thompson, 4), or the slit may in portions be curved, as in the scrolls used by Bagley. Some tests have been made at Columbia University with an irregular printed pattern, which is to be traced by the subject with a lead pencil. In any of these tests the movement may be arranged to involve primarily either the finer muscles of the hand and fingers or the larger muscles concerned in the whole-arm movement.

FIG. 32.   TRACING-BOARD.

The test here described follows the method used by Bryan and by Thompson.

APPARATUS.—Tracing-board (Fig. 32). Metallic stylus with flexible connecting wire. Telegraph sounder (Fig. 33). Two dry or other open-circuit cells. No. 18 annunciator wire.

PRELIMINARIES.—Wire the battery in series with the tracing-board, the sounder and the stylus.

METHOD.—(1)   Seat S comfortably with the tracing-board squarely before him and the apex of the angle pointing toward him, so that the movement is directly toward the body in the median plane.   Let S hold the stylus as he chooses, place the

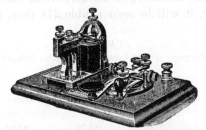

FIG. 33.   TELEGRAPH SOUNDER AND KEY.

The sounder may be purchased separately, but the key will be found useful for other experimental work, if only for opening and closing the circuit at will.   When provided with a special pointer, this sounder is used for graphic records, as in Test 13.

tip at the opening of the strips, and then attempt to draw a line on the glass between the strips of metal without touching either one.   The movement should be *continuous* from start to finish, made entirely free-arm (not a finger or wrist movement, and without supporting the hand or arm in any way).   The rate of movement must be illustrated as accurately as possible by E, and should be such that the full length of the strips is traversed in 9 sec.   Allow S two or three preliminary trials, and endeavor to secure approximately this rate before starting the records.   As soon as a click of the sounder indicates a contact, S is to stop and begin again with the left hand.   Repeat until S has made five trials with each hand, alternately. E records in each case the point on the scale at which contact is made.

(2)   Turn the apparatus around 180°, and in the same manner test movement away from the body.

(3)   Test movement from left to right and (4) from right to left with either hand by placing the test-board so that the strips lie parallel with the edge of the table nearest S.

VARIATIONS OF METHOD.—(1) If it is desired not to compare movements in different directions, but merely to compare the right and left-hand efficiency of different S's, the test may with advantage be shortened by adopting the method used by Bryan in his test of school children, viz.: set the test-board so that the strips make an angle of approximately 45° with the edge of the table, *i. e.,* with the right-hand end of the strips turned 45° away from the body for the right-hand test, and with the left-hand end of the strips turned away to the same amount for the left-hand test. Make five tests with movement inward and five with movement outward with each hand.

The conditions may be still further varied (2) by requiring S to stand and to hold the stylus at arm's length, (3) by allowing S to sit and to support his arm at the elbow, or (4) to support his hand on the base-board while executing a forearm or whole-arm movement. The last was the method followed by Miss Thompson.

TREATMENT OF RESULTS.—The simplest treatment of the data is to secure an index of precision by averaging the distances at which the several points of contact are made. For a more complex method of computing the measure of precision the reader is referred to Bryan, pp. 180 ff.

RESULTS.—(1) There is greater *variation* in the outcome of precision or steadiness of movement tests than in that of rate of movement tests.

(2) There is undoubtedly a more or less constant improvement in precision with *age,* but sufficient data are not yet at hand to determine the yearly increments clearly. There is certainly, however, a decided gain during the years 6 to 8, while Bolton also noted improvement from the 8th to the 9th year of age.

(3) *Dextrality.* In general, the right hand is, of course, distinctly superior to the left, but the amount of this superiority varies remarkably with age, and is, according to Bryan, less evident at 15 and 16 than at 6, 9 or 12 years of age.

Right-handed adults sometimes make better records with the left hand, as a rule because they perform the test relatively carelessly with the right and cautiously with the left hand.

(4) *Sex.* With either hand, boys are probably slightly superior to girls, for, while Bolton reports the superiority of the girls in his groups of children, Bryan's examination of some 700 children revealed the following relations when the results for both hands were computed together: boys were superior to girls in 51.5 per cent. of the trials, girls superior to boys in 35.3 per cent., and the sexes equal in 13.4 per cent. Moreover, in a similar test, Thompson found men superior to women.

(5) Both Bolton and Thompson found *movements inward* or toward the body uniformly steadier than movements outward or away from the body.

(6) *Correlations.* Bagley found "a decidedly inverse relation between mental ability, as indicated by class standings and motor ability, as indicated by the tracing test." But Bolton, who used a different form of test, and apparently correlated rather with the social status than with the class standing, reports that 'good' are steadier than 'poor' children.

REFERENCES

(1) W. C. Bagley, On the correlation of mental and motor ability in school children. *AmJPs*, 12: 1901, 193-205.

(2) T. L. Bolton, The relation of motor power to intelligence. *AmJPs*, 14: 1903, 615-631.

(3) W. L. Bryan, On the development of voluntary motor ability. *AmJPs*, 5: 1892, 123-204.

(4) Helen B. Thompson, The mental traits of sex. Chicago, 1903. Pp. 188.

TEST 13

Steadiness of motor control: Involuntary movement. — The general idea in this type of test is to measure the amount of involuntary movement which appears when the finger, hand, arm or body as a whole is held as nearly motionless as possible. Like the preceding tests, this has been frequently employed as a means of obtaining an index of motor ability (Bagley, 1; Bolton, 2; Hancock, 6), but it has also been employed for numerous other purposes, *e. g.*, for examining the motor tendencies accompanying ideational activity (Jastrow, 7, 8; Tucker, 15), for examining the bodily expression of affective states (Titchener, 14), for examining the nature of constant tendencies toward automatic movements, or the possibility of developing such movements by training (Thompson, 13; Solomons and Stein, 10; Stein, 12), and for detecting the presence of incipient or recent chorea (Crichton-Browne, 4).

This variety of purpose illustrates very forcibly the difficulty of so conducting the test as to examine any one phase alone—a difficulty which is aggravated by the fact that the tracings of involuntary movement are often affected, not only by the factors implied above, but also to a considerable extent by the direction of the attention, by the relative position of the body and the instrument, and by physiological processes, especially respiration. It is, therefore, not surprising that many writers, e. g., Bagley and Bolton, have incorporated records of involuntary movement only with qualifications and without placing much insistence on their worth.

The instruments most commonly employed are the ataxiagraph (described by Crichton-Browne, used by him and by Hancock, Wallin, Bolton and others for measuring the swaying of the body as a whole), the tremograph (described by Bullard and Brackett, 3, and also used by Hancock) for testing the arm or finger, the automatograph of Jastrow or that of Stein, further elaborated by Titchener, for measuring involuntary movements of the arm; the digitalgraph devised by Delabarre (5), described, together with others of the instruments just named. by MacDonald (9), and used for recording the tremor of the finger, and several instruments, as yet unnamed, for testing either the arm or hand, according to the conditions of their use.[1]

APPARATUS.—Brass plate, set at an angle of 45°, and pierced

---

[1]For some purposes it is probably quite as well to test the subject without the use of apparatus. Thus, according to Sturgis, the following constitutes an infallible test for chorea: "Bid the child hold up both hands open, with extended arms, the palms toward you. If that is done steadily, both hands upright and both alike, no finger or hand quivering, no falling back of either hand, nothing to choose between the positions of the two, then the child has not, nor is it near (either before or after) St. Vitus' dance. You may confirm this test by another. Let the child place the open hands upon yours, palm to palm. Look then at the backs of the child's hands, observe whether fingers or thumbs (especially the latter) repose without tremor and without restraint."

with a series of holes whose diameters are 32, 20, 16, 13, 11, 10, 9, 8 and 7 sixty-fourths of an inch, respectively (Fig. 34). Metallic needle of special design, with flexible connecting wire.

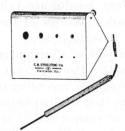

FIG. 34. STEADINESS TESTER.

Telegraph sounder (Fig. 33), with writing lever attached to the armature, and with sending key (or separate short-circuiting key). Kymograph (Fig. 22), with accessories. Stop-watch (Fig 20). Four dry or other open-circuit cells. Insulated connecting wire. [A low table, about 65 cm. high, and an adjustable chair of the typewriter chair pattern are desirable.]

PRELIMINARIES.—Wire the needle, brass plate, sounder and key in series with the battery in such a way that contact between the needle and the plate will actuate the sounder. Place smoked paper on the kymograph drum, and adjust to approximately one revolution in 40 sec. Adjust the position of the sounder so that the writing lever gives a satisfactory tracing on the drum.[1]

METHOD.—Seat S before the table in a comfortable position. Place the brass plate flush with the front edge of the table, in front of S's right shoulder for the right-hand test, and in front of his left shoulder for the left-hand test. Instruct S to hold the needle in such a way that his finger tips are in contact with the expanded flange of the holder, and, at command, to hold the tip of the needle within the largest hole, and to maintain this position, so far as possible, without touching the brass plate during the 15 sec. allowed for the trial. S's hand and arm must be entirely free from all support or contact with his

---

[1]For an account of the manipulation of the kymograph, consult Test 10.

body or other object, and his forearm should form an angle of approximately 100° with his upper arm. The needle should be inserted about 6 mm. into the hole.

Show S that the click of the sounder will serve as warning for him that the needle is making contact with the plate.

In conducting the test, allow S about 3 sec. for taking the position (since a certain amount of movement will appear when the needle is first inserted that will afterward be checked by S's control), then close the short-circuiting key and at the same time start the stop-watch. At the expiration of 15 sec. open the circuit, stop the watch and the kymograph, and at once rearrange the instruments for the left-hand test.

Allow 30 sec. rest, and then test the right hand and the left hand with the next smaller hole, and so on, until a hole is reached so small that S has reached the limit of his capacity and is clearly unable to keep the needle free from contact with the plate.

In most cases a few unrecorded preliminary trials will show approximately the degree of S's control, and the tests with the larger holes may be omitted with a consequent saving in time.

VARIATIONS OF METHOD.—The test may be modified by altering the relative position of the plate and S's body as follows: (a) by requiring S to stand and to hold the needle extended at arm's length, (b) by allowing S to rest his elbow upon the table with the forearm free, or (c) by supporting his forearm and wrist and testing the steadiness of the hand and fingers, and (d) by extending the time to 30 or 60 sec. The results will naturally differ characteristically from those obtained under the conditions prescribed as standard.

TREATMENT OF RESULTS. — By reference to the kymograph tracings, count the number of contacts for each hole. For comparative purposes, E may take the total number of contacts made in a given series of holes or the number made in that hole which most satisfactorily tests the steadiness of the subjects under investigation.

RESULTS.[1]—(1) In all tests of involuntary movement it is clearly seen that *age* is an important factor. Hancock concludes that adults have approximately 5.8 times as much control over their fingers as do children aged 5 to 7 years.

(2) Distinct *sex* differences have not been established.

(3) As measured on the ataxiagraph, involuntary swaying was found by Wallin to be clearly less for the moron than for the imbecile group of epileptics, and slightly less for males than for females.

NOTES.—In rare cases the use of the graphic method may be dispensed with, especially if E proves by practise very skillful in the correct counting of the rapid and irregular strokes made by the sounder when the test approaches the limit of S's capacity, but this simplification is not recommended, because it is exceedingly difficult to make the count under these conditions (cf. Bolton), and, moreover, there may appear very short, rapid contacts that will actuate the sounder sufficiently to produce a noticeable indication on the tracing, but not sufficiently to produce a noticeable click. Again, S will occasionally make contacts of long duration. With the graphic record it is possible for E to measure the duration of these contacts, and, if desired, to base S's record upon the proportion of the time during the 15 sec. that is occupied in contact, rather than upon the number of contacts alone.

The ordinary electric counter is not recommended as a substitute for the graphic method, because, as mentioned in Test 10, it will not operate reliably when the contact is very brief, even although a large number of cells are used in the battery. To avoid the possibility of a similar error in the use of the sounder, the excursion of the armature should be rather short, *i. e.*, the armature should be adjusted as near the fields as is possible if it is to give a clean stroke.

If involuntary tremor is to be studied with special care, *e. g.*,

---

[1] A summary of the results obtained with the automatograph is given by Jastrow (8, pp. 307-336.)

if E wishes to make an extended study of an individual case, a more sensitive instrument should be employed. For such work the tridimensional analyzer of Sommer (11), also described by Titchener (14), is recommended.

REFERENCES

(1) W. C. Bagley, On the correlation of mental and motor ability in school children. *AmJPs*, 12: 1901, 193-205.

(2) T. L. Bolton, The relation of motor power to intelligence. *AmJPs*, 14: 1903, 615-631.

(3) Bullard and Brackett, *Boston Med. and Surg. Jour.*, 2: 1888, 600.

(4) J. Crichton-Browne, The nervous system and education, being part 4 in The book of health, edited by M. Morris, London, 1883 (now out of print).

(5) E. B. Delabarre, Ueber Bewegungsempfindungen, 1891. See also *AnPs*, 1: 1894 (1895), 532.

(6) J. A. Hancock, A preliminary study of motor ability. *PdSc*, 3: 1894, 9-29.

(7) J. Jastrow, (*a*) A study of involuntary movements. *AmJPs*, 4: 1892, 398-407. (*b*) A further study of involuntary movement. *Ibid.*, 5: 1892, 223-231.

(8) J. Jastrow, Fact and fable in psychology. Boston, 1900. Pp. 370.

(9) A. MacDonald, Experimental study of school children, etc. Chs. 21 and 25, *RepComEd*, 1897-8 (1899).

(10) L. Solomons and G. Stein, Normal motor automatisms. *PsR*, 3: 1896, 492-512.

(11) R. Sommer, Lehrbuch der psychopathologischen Untersuchungs-methoden. Berlin, 1899. Pp. 399.

(12) Gertrude Stein, Cultivated motor automatisms. *PsR*, 5: 1898, 295-306.

(13) Helen Thompson, The mental traits of sex. Chicago, 1903. Pp. 188.

(14) E. B. Titchener, Experimental psychology. 2 vols., N. Y., 1901 and 1905.

(15) M. A. Tucker, Comparative observations on the involuntary movements of adults and children. *AmJPs*, 8: 1897, 394-404.

(16) J. E. Wallin, Experimental studies of mental defectives. *EdPs Mon*, No. 7, Baltimore, 1912.

CHAPTER VI

TESTS OF SENSORY CAPACITY

Psychophysical tests of sensory capacity are divisible into tests of liminal sensitivity (sensitivity proper) and tests of discriminative or differential sensitivity (sensible discrimination.) [1] In the former, we measure the bare capacity of experiencing sensations, the minimally perceptible stimulus or *stimulus limen, e. g.,* the lightest pressure that can be felt, the least intensity of tone that can be heard, etc.; in the latter, we experience different sensations and report upon their difference; we seek, in other words, to determine the minimal objective difference of stimulation that can just be mentally cognized as different, to determine the *difference limen, e. g.,* the smallest change of vibration-rate that will suffice to yield two perceptibly different tones, or the smallest difference in weight that can just be recognized as a difference.

These two measurements of sensory capacity, liminal and discriminative sensitivity, can be applied to any modality, *i. e.,* to any sense-department, and to any attribute of sensation, *i. e.,* to quality, intensity, extent, and duration. We may measure, for instance, in the case of the ear, liminal sensitivity in terms of intensity, discriminative sensitivity in terms of intensity, in terms of quality, in terms of duration, etc. We may, furthermore, determine the total number of auditory sensations that can be experienced, *i. e.,* modal sensitivity.

In the case of the two sense-departments that possess the attribute of extent, visual and cutaneous sensations, we may also measure the capacity to discriminate difference in the localization of two stimuli, or the limen for spatial discrimination. While, strictly speaking, this may be regarded as a more complex process than simple sensory discrimination, it may, for our purposes, be included as a sensory test. Indeed, with

---

[1] For a discussion of the terminology, methods, purposes, and results of psychophysical methods, consult Titchener, *Experimental Psychology*, especially, Vol. 2, part 2.

both the eye and the skin, this determination, for practical purposes of exploration of the sense-organ or of the measurement
of its functional capacity, has superseded the determination of
liminal sensitivity. Thus, in visual sensation, visual acuity
refers, not to the liminal sensitivity of the retina for stimulation, but, in principle, to the capacity to distinguish the separation of two points. Similarly, in cutaneous sensation, for a
practical test of functional capacity, the determination of the
'limen of duality,' as it may be termed, by means of the esthesiometer, has been more often employed than the simple determination of liminal sensitivity to pressure.

Now, the quantitative determination of sensitivity in the psychological laboratory has given rise to a most elaborate and refined methodology, and has, in fact, been the chief problem of
the science of psychophysics. It is not the purpose here to discuss or duplicate these exact methods, but merely to indicate
the manner in which, for comparative purposes, one may secure
an index of functional efficiency by empirical methods. It must
be clearly understood that the determination of an exact stimulus or difference limen in the psychological laboratory, with
minute introspective analysis of the factors that condition the
process and with elaborate methodological procedure, is quite
a different process from this simple determination of functional
capacity for comparative purposes. If, for convenience, the
technical terms of psychophysics are here employed, they are
employed with this qualification in mind.

To make this point clearer: the procedure for the determination of discriminative capacity as herein recommended is not
identical with any of the established psychophysical methods.
E allows S at first to try various stimulus differences ranging
from large to small, until S has acquired general familiarity
with the test, and E has obtained a general notion of his
capacity. E may next test S more formally by applying a
series of stimulus differences ranging from clear subjective difference to subjective equality. He then selects a difference
which seems likely to be just cognizable by the subject and
applies this difference ten times, with proper reversals for time
or space errors. If eight right judgments are given, he then

corroborates the result by trying similarly a slightly smaller, and finally a slightly larger difference, to see if S gives in the former case fewer, and in the latter case more correct judg ments. S knows that a difference exists, but is ignorant of its spatial or temporal position. We thus obtain an index of ca- pacity, but do not determine the mean difference limen, nor even the lower limen, in the psychophysical sense.

Sensory tests of this empirical sort have been employed, partly in connection with the psychology of individual and sex differences, partly in the objective study of general intelligence, partly in the exploration of sense organs for the determination of their working condition, *i. e.*, for hygienic and diagnostic purposes. In all of these fields the emphasis is upon the ex- amination of simple functional capacity, without particular reference to introspective examination or analysis of the ac- companying consciousness.

The use of sensory tests in correlation work is particularly interesting. In general, some writers are convinced that keen discrimination is a pre- requisite to keen intelligence, while others are equally convinced that intelligence is essentially conditioned by 'higher' processes, and only remotely by sensory capacity—barring, of course, such diminution of capacity as to interfere seriously with the experiencing of sensations, as in partial deafness or partial loss of vision.

While it is scarcely the place here to discuss the evolutionary signifi- cance of discriminative sensitivity, it may be pointed out that the normal capacity is many times in excess of the actual demands of life, and that it is consequently difficult to understand why nature has been so pro- lific and generous; to understand, in other words, what is the sanction for the seemingly hypertrophied discriminative capacity of the human sense organs. The usual 'teleological explanations' of our sensory life fail to account for this discrepancy. Again, the very fact of the existence of this surplus capacity seems to negative at the outset the notion that sensory capacity can be a conditioning factor in intelligence—with the qualification already noted.

The tests which follow are selected from a large number of theoretically possible tests, because of their prominence in such experimental studies as have been mentioned. Their classifi- cation is simply by sense-departments. Tests for the explora- tion of the organ, measurement of its defects, determination of acuity, liminal sensitivity, discriminative sensitivity, in so far as they are described, are given successively for each of the main sense departments.

TEST 14

Visual acuity.—The functional capacity of the eye is examined primarily, of course, for practical purposes in connection with hygienic investigation. Occasionally, it becomes desirable to determine the presence or absence of visual defect in connection with the administration of some mental test, *e. g.,* the cancellation test.

Visual acuity has been studied in its relation to school standing, general intelligence, occupation, habitat, race, sex, as well as to bodily disturbances, such as headache, chorea, indigestion, or other optical defects, such as strabismus, total color-blindness, etc.

Optical inefficiency, aside from color-blindness, may be due to *amblyopia* (dimness of sight not due to refractive errors or demonstrable lesion), or to *asthenopia* (general impairment of retinal efficiency due to anæmia, over-use, etc., and often yielding to proper medical treatment), but is more commonly some form of *ametropia* (defect in shape of the eye-ball, lens, or cornea, with resultant defect in refraction and in the formation of the retinal image).

Ametropia may exist as presbyopia, myopia, hyperopia, or astigmatism.

Presbyopia is the long-sightedness of old age, due to the lessened elasticity of the lens, and is not commonly present before forty.

Myopia, or short-sightedness, is commonly produced by too long an eyeball, the effect of which is to allow rays of light in distant vision to focus in front of the retina and hence to produce a blurred image when they finally impinge upon the retina. The myopic eye is thus unable by any effort clearly to see objects situated at distances of 2 m. or more away, while its 'near-point,' *i. e.,* the nearest point at which clear vision is possible, is brought correspondingly closer, so that objects may be seen clearly when 5 or 6 cm. distant—something which would be impossible for the normal (emmetropic) eye. Pure myopia, as a rule, causes no eye-strain, but it is nevertheless a serious condition, because of its tendency to increase in degree, and because of the appearance in many cases of concomitant pathological disturbances of the retina, which, in extreme cases, result in actual blindness. In practise, moreover, myopia is rarely found pure, but complicated with astigmatism and other defects. True myopia may be counteracted, and its progress checked, but not cured, by the use of properly fitted concave lenses, supplemented by the exercise of caution in the use of the eyes.

Hyperopia, hypermetropia, or long-sightedness, more exactly oversightedness, is commonly produced by too short an eye-ball, the effect of which is to intercept rays of light too soon, *i. e.,* before they are brought to a normal focus. The hyperopic eye must consequently exert an effort of accommodation in order clearly to see objects at a distance, while for near work this effort must be excessive. The result is that the hyperopic eye is under constant and abnormal strain from the incessant demands upon its ciliary muscle, and that, in consequence, numerous secondary symptoms or resultant effects appear, some of them obvious, others unexpected, many of them serious. Local symptoms appear in inflammation, redness, or soreness of the eyes, lids, or conjunctiva, and in twitching and pain within the eye-ball. Aside from these local disturbances, perhaps the most constant symptom of hyperopia is frontal or occipital headache. Characteristic also is the holding of the work at some distance from the eyes,[1] a peering or frowning expression, and dislike of near work. Eye-strain, whether hyperopic or astigmatic, may also occasion more serious physiological disturbances, such as chorea, vomiting, nervous dyspepsia, etc.[2] Since the hyperopic eye can see clearly at a distance and can read (as its possessor often boasts) with the book held at some distance, the defect is often unsuspected, because the secondary symptoms are not correctly interpreted. On this account, too, it becomes necessary to take special steps to detect its presence, and many of the simple distance tests that have been applied wholesale upon school children utterly fail to diagnose it. The oculist commonly makes use of homatropin or some other cycloplegic to paralyze temporarily the ciliary muscle and thus prevent accommodation. Hyperopia may, however, be detected, though less accurately, by the use of suitable test-lenses, as described below. The defect is counteracted by the use of properly fitted convex lenses.

Astigmatism is produced by an uneven radius of curvature, usually of the cornea; this surface, which should normally be approximately spherical in form, is, in astigmatism, more strongly curved in one axis or meridian than in another, so that the cornea is ellipsoidal in form, *e. g.*, like the bowl of a spoon, or the side, rather than the end, of an egg. Thus the eye is double-focussed, and it is impossible by any effort to focus an image clearly in both meridians simultaneously. In measuring astigmatism it is evident that one must assign both the degree of refractive error and the axis in which the error lies, and that in correcting it, a cylindrical lens of the proper curvature must be placed before the eye at exactly the proper axis to counteract the indicated deficiency. This lens only counteracts the defect, and does not cure it. Astigmatism may be in part congenital, in part a phenomenon of growth (often attributable to the pressure upon the eye-ball of the eye-lids and contracted brows, with the result that the maximal refractive index lies at or near the vertical meridian). When present in large amount it becomes a serious obstacle to vision; when present in small amounts, as is apt to be the case in many eyes, it is the occasion of the same phenomena of eye-strain that have been mentioned as accessory to hyperopia; astigmatic headache is particularly symptomatic—indeed, 60 per cent. of all headaches are said to be traceable to this source.

It must be understood that these three defects may, and commonly do, appear in combination, particularly astigmatism with hyperopia or

---

[1] In high grades of hyperopia, distinct images cannot be secured even by this process, so the child may abandon the attempt to secure clearness and seek merely to increase the size of the image by holding his book near his eyes. He may thus be falsely rated as near-sighted by the casual observer.

[2] The injurious effects of eye-strain have found a special expositor in Dr. G. M. Gould.

myopia, and that the defects may be, and commonly are, unlike in the two eyes of the same individual. Partly for this reason, the proper fitting of glasses is an art, and, like any art, requires great skill, complete familiarity with the conditions, and long practical experience. The tests which are here described make no pretence to exactitude, but are designed to determine, in so far as is possible by simple methods, the existence of defects that *should invariably be referred to a specialist for further examination and treatment.*

For the examination of refraction the chief appliances are (1) the ophthalmometer, for the exact measurement of the degree and axis of astigmatism, (2) the ophthalmoscope, for the examination of the retina, (2) the retinoscope and the skiascope, for the objective determination of refractive errors, (4) test-types and trial lenses, for actual visual tests under varying conditions. While retinoscopy is a method of great value, especially in testing young children, the test-type is, in general, the court of final appeal and constitutes the most widely used and perhaps the most valuable single means for testing visual acuity. The most varied kinds of test-type have been devised by oculists. Perhaps oldest and best known are Snellen's "Optotypi," which form the basis of the tests ordinarily used. Interesting variations are seen in Dennett's Monoyer type, Landolt's C-test, Cohn's E-test and McCallie's Vision Tests (literate and illiterate set).[1]

The first test for ametropia, which is described just below, is based upon the recommendations of the American Ophthalmological Society. The second test supplements the first by detecting astigmatism. Tests 15, 16, and 17 may be added.

A. TEST FOR MYOPIA AND HYPEROPIA

APPARATUS.—Lowell's test-type. Trial frame (Fig. 35). Two —.75 D.[2] and two + .75 D. spherical lenses, and one blank disc. Meter stick.

----

[1] The McCallie cards, purchasable of Edwin Fitzgeorge, Box 67, Trenton, N. J., are well adapted for rapid schoolroom tests, where the method of distance alone is used and no direct attempt is made to detect hyperopia or astigmatism. The illiterate set is especially ingenious.

[2] One diopter, or dioptric, D, is the amount of refraction given by a lens whose principal focal distance is 1 meter, *i. e.*, the radius of curvature of its surface has a length of 1 meter. This unit is now commonly used in place of the older system of indicating strength in inches of focal length.

PRELIMINARIES.—Place the test type on the wall or stand, on a level with S's eyes, in a strong even illumination, though not in actual sun-light.[1] Seat S comfortably at a distance of 6 m. from the chart.

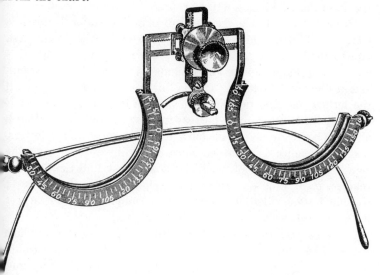

FIG. 35. TRIAL FRAME.

Holds two pairs of lenses, and has rack and pinion adjustment for pupillary distance, and for vertical, and back and forward movement of the nosepiece.

Note any indication of soreness or inflammation of the eyes, lids, or conjunctiva. Ascertain if S has ever suffered from such inflammations, from habitual headaches, or watery eyes; whether his eyes become painful, sore, or strained in doing close work; whether he has previously been examined, and if so, with what result; whether he has ever worn glasses; if they have

[1]If conditions render daylight illumination unreliable or unsatisfactory, E must arrange artificial illumination, carefully shaded from S. Excellent devices for this purpose may be purchased from dealers in optical supplies, e. g., No. 4274, catalog of E. B. Meyrowitz, New York City, price $10. Whatever the source of illumination, the light must not shine in S's eyes. An experienced E may compensate for inadequate illumination by placing S at a distance less than 6 m.—the amount of the correction being determined by E's own acuity under the prevailing conditions.

been worn and discarded, ascertain when and why. If S wears glasses, record that fact; test his vision both with and without his glasses, unless time forbids, in which case test with them.

Adjust the pupillary distance and the nose-piece of the trial frame so that the lenses will be centered before S's eyes.

METHOD.—(1) Place the solid disc in the frame before S's left eye. Instruct him always to keep both eyes open. Ask him to read the letters above the red strip[1] (line numbered 8 on the right-hand margin and designated on the chart as standard at 6 m., or 19.7 feet). If this line can be read entire, or all the letters but one, try the next smaller letters, Line 9, but if the standard line cannot be read, try some line above, like 5 or 3. When S hesitates, encourage him to guess at the letters. S's performance is recorded most easily by reference to the small figures at the left end of the smallest line that he can read, e. g., if Line 8, vision of the right eye (V. R. E.) = 1; if Line 7, then V. R. E. = 0.8. If S cannot read the largest letter, Line 1, we know that V. R. E. = — .1.

(2) *Whatever* the result of this first trial, always next place the + .75 D. lens in the trial frame. This will blur the vision if the eye is emmetropic, so that, if before, V. R. E. = 1., and if vision is now blurred, record V. R. E. = 1. Em.

If S can, with the plus lens, read the same line as before, or a smaller line than before, then the eye is hyperopic. Thus, if previously the 10-meter line was read and now the 7.5-meter line, the record will be, V. R. E. = .6 + Hy. = .8, or, if no improvement appeared, V. R. E. = .6 + Hy. = .6.

---

[1]The red and green strips placed under Lines 8 and 6, respectively, of the Lowell chart are intended to assist E in designating to S the lines to be read, and it is assumed that color-blindness may be detected in this manner by characteristic mistakes on the part of S. But, as will be understood from what is said later in Test 16, it does not necessarily follow that all color-blind S's would confuse the particular green and red that are placed on this chart. Besides these colored strips, each test-line of the Lowell chart is designated in three ways: the large figures at the right of each line simply number the lines from above downward, Nos. 1 to 11, and serve merely as convenient designations in indicating to S the line to be read; just above each test-line there is indicated in meters and in feet the standard distance at which the line should be read; at the left of each line are figures which show at a glance the rating of the line, for measuring visual acuity, in comparison with the 6-meter line (Line 8).

(3) If, in the first test, vision is less than 1.0, and if, in the second test, vision is impaired by the convex lens, then next replace the convex lens by the — .75 D. lens. If vision is now improved so that a smaller line is read, then the eye is myopic, and may be recorded thus; V. R. E. = .6 + My. = .8, or V. R. E. = .6 + My. = 1.[1]

(4) Place the solid disc before the right eye, and test the left eye similarly. Record the results for each eye separately, e. g., V. R. E. = 1. Em.   V. L. E. = .6 + My. = .8.

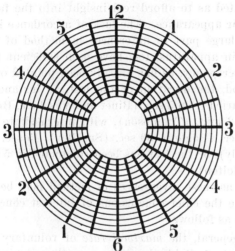

FIG. 36.   VERHOEFF'S ASTIGMATIC CHART.
About one-fifth actual size.

B.   TEST FOR ASTIGMATISM

APPARATUS.—Trial frame and lenses as above.   Verhoeff's astigmatic chart (Fig. 36).[2]

PRELIMINARIES.—Place the chart on the wall, and seat S as in the previous test.   Be sure that S's head is held squarely erect.   If S has been found to be myopic or hyperopic, place in the trial frame the lenses which correct, at least partially, this defect.

---

[1]This test may be nullified in some instances by a ciliary spasm in a hyperopic eye which may simulate myopia of almost any degree.

[2]Any standard astigmatic chart may be substituted, but Verhoeff's is, in the author's judgment, best adapted both for making evident the presence of astigmatism and for determining approximately its axis.

METHOD.—Place the solid disc in the frame before the left eye. Ask S whether one or more of the radiating lines seem to him sharper and blacker than those at right angles to them. If he answers in the affirmative, astigmatism is present. This result may be confirmed by causing S to move his head from one shoulder to the other, in which case the location of the sharpest lines should shift in a corresponding manner. The amount of astigmatism may be roughly judged by the positiveness and readiness of S's answer; its axis may be determined approximately by his designation of the blackest line or lines.

Place the disc before the right, and test similarly the left eye.

Since astigmatism may exist either alone or in combination with some form of ametropia, it should, when found, be recorded with the previous determination, e. g., V. R. E. = .6 + My. = .8 + As.

If vision is .6 or less, but no form of ametropia can be demonstrated, the defect is recorded as amblyopia, e. g., V. L. E. = .6 + Am.

To summarize the two tests : emmetropia is indicated (unless strain symptoms point to concealed hyperopia) by the reading of the line standard for the distance used and subsequent blurring by the convex lens, hyperopia by improvement or lack of impairment of vision by the plus lens, myopia by vision less than 1., which is improved by the concave lens, astigmatism by unequal clearness of the radiating lines, amblyopia by vision .6 or less without demonstrable refractive error.

RESULTS.[1]—(1) The *frequency* of defective visual acuity is somewhat difficult to state accurately owing to the differences in method and in degree of rigor and precision that have characterized the many investigations upon this point. In especial, a great many investigations in school systems have been made by simple distance tests without the aid of lenses, so that hyperopia, the most frequent defect, has gone practically unmeasured. The general outcome of these simple tests is quite uniform, viz: that one child in three in the public schools suffers

[1] For a general discussion of the examination of eyesight, with special reference to the eyesight of school children, consult Barry, Calhoun, Carter, Cohn, Gould, Hope and Browne, Kotelmann, Newsholme, Risley, Schmidt-Rimpler, Snell, Stilling and Young.

from visual defect. Typical figures are those obtained by Welch at Passaic, and Smedley at Chicago; the latter reports that 32 per cent. of the 2030 boys and 37 per cent. of the 2735 girls examined were defective in vision. While more than half of these defects are of a minor degree, yet, as already indicated, these may be productive of immediate distress and entail serious con sequences if neglected.

On the other hand, examinations that have been conducted by skilled opthalmologists with some refinement of method indicate a much larger percentage of defect.[1] Risley's figures indicate that it would be more correct to state that seven children in eight, than that one in three, are ametropic. As chairman of the Philadelphia committee that examined some 2500 children, he gives the refraction at 8½ years of age as hyperopic in 88.11 per cent. of cases, emmetropic in 7.01 per cent., and myopic in 4.27 per cent.: at 17.5 years as hyperopic in 66.84 per cent., emmetropic in 12.28 per cent. and myopic in 19.33 per cent.

(2) From the above figures we may conclude that the *eye in early childhood* is an incomplete eye, naturally underfocussed and poorly adapted for near work. But, as general bodily maturity approaches, the eye under optimal conditions apparently tends to become emmetropic. Conditions of modern life, however, are not optimal for the eye, but rather encourage overuse and neglect, with the consequence that these, at least when added to astigmatism or other congenital defects, tend to develop eye-strain, myopia, and other disturbances of vision.

(3) The relation of overuse and neglect, particularly in the form of excessive near work, to *myopia* is a matter of much dispute. The views currently held by many hygienists are typified by the position of Cohn, who contends that myopia is essentially a disease of civilization and culture; that it is infrequent in peasants and those who lead an outdoor life, and progressively more prevalent and of higher degree as persistent study and near work continue. Thus, in gymnasia, he found that the percentage of myopia increased during six years of study in the following manner: 12.5, 18.2, 23.7, 31.0, 41.3, 55.8. Similarly,

---

[1] Indeed, there are specialists who assert that an absolutely perfect pair of eyes does not exist.

of 138 pupils at the Friedrich gymnasium who were examined twice at an interval of 18 months, he found at the first test 70 normal and 54 myopic, whereas in the second test, 14 of the 70 had become myopic, 28 of the original myopes had developed a higher degree, and in 10 per cent. serious structural changes had taken place in the retina.

While statistics like these, which indicate a close relation between myopia and near work could be multiplied almost indefinitely,[1] they have not prevented other investigators, chiefly anatomists, physiologists and biologists, from attributing the causation of myopia to heredity rather than to environmental conditions (cf. Barrington and Pearson, Helmholtz). It would seem safe, at least, to conclude that the predisposing causes of myopia are frequently inherited, whatever may be the rôle of poor hygienic conditions in bringing out the defect.

(4) Smedley, on the basis of his method of correlation by grades, asserts that "a smaller per cent. of the *pupils at and above grade* have defective sight than those below grade."

(5) Smedley further demonstrates that defective vision is extremely common in *backward and troublesome children,* and that this fact may be a partial explanation of the behavior of such children. Thus, according to the tests employed at Chicago, 48 per cent of the boys of the John Worthy School were subnormal in visual acuity, as contrasted with 28 per cent of the boys of the same average age in other schools. Moreover, "many of the John Worthy boys had strabismus, hypermetropia, and astigmatism, conditions which would induce asthenopia when the eyes were used in close and long application to books, and it is easy to believe," adds Smedley, "that the strain thus set up when an attempt was made to study was a factor in producing dislike for school and subsequent truancy."

(6) Van Biervliet (22) has sought to obtain a correlation between the visual acuity test and *intelligence,* not by direct

[1]Dürr, for example, in explanation of the alarming prevalence of myopia in Germany as contrasted with other countries, has sought to show its dependence upon the excessive demands of the German school system : he estimates that, during the years 10 to 19, the typical English boy spends in study 16,500 hours, in exercise 4500 ; the French boy, in study 19,000, in exercise 1300 ; and the German boy, in study 20,000, and in exercise 650.

reference to visual acuity itself, but to the mean variation measured by a series of tests of acuity, *i. e.,* to what he terms the capacity of attention. In brief, the method was to compute a fraction, of which the denominator represented the average distance at which the test was visible, and the numerator the mean variation of the several trials. As measured by this arbitrary index, the 10 brightest and the 10 dullest of 300 university students were related, in terms of a common denominator, as 19/1000 and 62.5/1000. Binet (4), however, points out that the dull students had the better eyesight, *i. e.,* the larger denominator, and suggests that the index be taken directly from the mean variation. Abelson, who tested acuity of vision of backward children by a method which afforded five measurements of the distance from the chart moving inward and five moving outward (in each case to the point where the test-object could just be correctly reported), found little or no correlation between imputed intelligence and the average distance (acuity proper), but "the average deviation gave a correlation with the intelligence, the more capable children showing a tendency to small average deviations." He thus confirms van Biervliet.

(7) *Right-eyedness.* While both eyes are employed for binocular vision, there is some evidence that most persons 'favor' one eye, whenever, for any reason, binocular vision is not in use, *e. g.,* in looking through a microscope or telescope. Van Biervliet has measured the visual acuity of 100 persons, whose optical defects had previously been corrected, with the result that the favored eye very uniformly excels the unfavored one in visual acuity by one-ninth: he further asserts that right-handed people are right-eyed and left-handed people left-eyed, and that the same sort of sensorial asymmetry can be demonstrated in audition, cutaneous discrimination, and discrimination of lifted weights.

NOTES.—Statistics of visual defect are rendered difficult of comparison, not only by differences in the methods followed in the investigations, but also at times by failure to state whether examinations were made with or without the glasses actually worn by pupils, or, in case such statement is made, to indicate the effect upon the results of including or excluding trials made with these glasses. Cohn distinguishes between visual capacity proper (*Sehleistung*) and visual acuity (*Sehschärfe*), which is the efficiency when proper glasses are used. But since numbers of children are daily wearing improperly fitted glasses, one almost needs another term to indicate the vision that is had with these glasses.

REFERENCES

(1) A. R. Abelson, The measurement of mental ability of 'backward' children. *BrJPs*, 4: 1911, 268-314, especially 276 f.

(2) Amy Barrington and K. Pearson, A first study of the inheritance of vision and of the relative influence of heredity and environment on sight. *Eugenics Lab. Memoirs*, 5: 1909.

(3) W. F. Barry, The hygiene of the schoolroom. N. Y., 2d ed., 1904. Pp. 191.

(4) A. Binet, A propos de la mesure de l'intelligence. *AnPs*, 11: 1904 (1905), 69-82.

(5) A. M. Calhoun, Effects of student life upon eyesight. Bureau Ed., Washington, 1881. Pp. 29.

(6) R. B. Carter, Report on vision of children attending elementary schools in London. London, 1896. Pp. 16.

(7) H. Cohn, (*a*) The hygiene of the eye. Eng. tr., London, 1886. (*b*) Die Sehleistung von 50,000 Breslauer Schulkindern, nebst Anleitung zur ähnlicher Untersuchungen für Aerzte u. Lehrer. Breslau, 1899. Pp. 148. (*c*)' Was haben die Augenärzte für die Schulhygiene geleistet und was müssen sie noch leisten? Berlin, 1904. Pp. 35. (Contains bibliography of 74 titles.)

(8) G. M. Gould, The cause, nature and consequences of eyestrain. *PopSciM*, 67: 1905, 738-747.

(9) G. M. Gould, Biographic clinics. 5 vols., Phila., 1903-7.

(10) H. v. Helmholtz, Physiologische Optik. 3d. ed.

(11) E. Hope and E. Browne, A manual of school hygiene. Cambridge Eng., 1904. Pp. 207.

(12) L. Kotelmann, School hygiene. Eng. tr., Syracuse, 1889. Pp. 382.

(13) A. Newsholme, School hygiene. Boston, 1894. Pp. 140.

(14) Rep. com. on statistics of defective sight and hearing of public school children. *RepComEd*, 1902, ii., 2143-2155.

(15) S. D. Risley, Weak eyes in the public schools of Philadelphia: rep. com. on examination of the eyes of the children in the public schools of Phila. *Phila.Med.Times*, 11: 1880-1, 673-685.

(16) S. D. Risley, School hygiene, being pp. 353-418 in vol. 2 of W. Norris and C. Oliver, System of diseases of the eye. Phila., 1897.

(17) Schmidt-Rimpler, Die Schulkurzsichtigkeit u. ihre Bekämpfung. Leipzig, 1890.

(18) F. W. Smedley, Rept. dept. child-study and pedag. investigation. 46th *An.Rep.Brd.Ed.*, Chicago, 1899-1900. Also *RepComEd*, 1902, i., 1095-1115.

(19) S. Snell, Eyesight and school life. Bristol, Eng., 1895. Pp. 70.

(20) Stilling, Die Kurzsichtigkeit, ihre Entstehung und Bedeutung. *SmAbPdPs*, 7: No. 3, Berlin, 1903.

(21) J. van Biervliet, L'asymétrie sensorielle. *BuAcRoySci*, 34: Série 3: 1897, 326-366.

(22) J. van Biervliet, La mesure de l'intelligence, *JPsPa*, 1: 1904, 225-235

(23) G. T. Welch, Report on the examination of the eyes of the public school children of Passaic, N. J.   April, 1896.   Also summarized in Ref. 14.

(24) A. G. Young, 7th An. Rep. State Brd. Health, Maine.   Augusta, 1892.   Pp. 399.   See especially 128-131.

TEST 15

Balance and control of eye-muscles: Heterophoria.—Strictly speaking, the examination of the condition of the eye-muscles is a physiological test, but because this condition affects clearness of vision, it may be included here with other visual tests.

Each eye-ball is supplied with six muscles. By their action in varying combination, the eye is moved freely in its bed, somewhat after the fashion of a ball-and-socket joint. Under normal conditions, the balance and the innervation of these muscles are such that both eyes move in concert, *i. e.*, the eye-movements are automatically coördinated for purposes of single vision and the lines of regard are restricted to movements where a common fixation point is possible. In some individuals, however, there exists more or less 'imbalance,' or asymmetry of eye-movement, so that the two eyes fail to 'track,' as it were.

If we consider only the relations of the visual line to one another and neglect paralytic affections of the muscles, we may distinguish between latent tendencies toward asymmetry, or *heterophoria,* and actual or manifest asymmetry, *heterotropia* or strabismus. Following the terminology of Stevens (1), we may define the possibilities as follows: *orthophoria* is a tending of the visual lines in parallelism when the determination is made for a point not less than 6 m. distant; heterophoria is a tending of these lines in some other way under the same conditions. Heterophoria may appear (*a*) as *esophoria,* a tending of the lines inward or toward one another, (*b*) as *exophoria,* a tending of the lines outward or away from one another, (*c*) as *hyperphoria,* a tending of the right or of the left visual line in a direction above its fellow,[1] or (*d*) as tendencies in oblique directions, viz: hyperesophoria and hyperexophoria.

---

[1]The term does not imply that the line which is too high is at fault, but merely that it is higher. Hence, of course, the lack of necessity for any term to indicate that one line is lower than the other.

The tendencies just described are tendencies only, and are latent or concealed in the ordinary use of the eyes on account of the strong 'desire' for binocular vision. For their discovery, accordingly, it is necessary to resort to means for eliminating, so far as possible, this reflex or automatic correction of the latent tendency. The means most commonly employed, as illustrated in the tests that follow, is the establishment of disparate images on the two retinas.[1]

When binocular vision is not habitually attained, the tendencies above described are no longer latent, but manifest, and heterotropia (strabismus or squint) is the result. Heterotropia may appear as esotropia, converging strabismus, or deviation of the visual lines inward; as exotropia, diverging strabismus, or deviation outward; as hypertropia, strabismus sursumvergens or deorsumvergens; or as compound deviations, termed by Stevens hyperesotropia and hyperexotropia.

The most obvious immediate result of heterotropia is diplopia or double vision, a very annoying, but not usually a permanent symptom, because the person thus affected soon comes to neglect the bothersome image from the 'squinting' eye, and to take account only of that from the 'fixing' eye. In time, there results, usually, a limitation of the movements and of the retinal sensitivity of the squinting eye (exanopsic amblyopia), which is one of the most interesting instances of the loss of function through disuse.[2]

Strabismus and heterophoria are functionally associated with ametropia; in particular, divergent displacement is more apt to be associated with myopia, and convergent displacement with hyperopia, probably as a consequence of the straining after clear vision under the hyperopic handicap.

The chief instruments for the detection of muscular asymmetries are prisms of varying construction, the Maddox rod, and the stenopaic lens. Stevens' phorometer is a device for holding and rotating prisms with accuracy and under optimal conditions. The phoro-optometer is a combination of the phorometer with other instruments, such as the Maddox rod, Risley's prism, etc.

---

[1]This assumption that voluntary attempts at fusion will be renounced if the two images are sufficiently disparate, is not entirely correct, and in so far, it is not always possible to make an accurate determination of heterophoria, particularly when slight, by means of the principle of diplopia. Slight heterophoria, moreover, is not to be regarded as abnormal.

[2]As this is particularly to be feared in the case of children, whose eyes have not reached functional maturity, prompt medical attention to strabismus is highly imperative.

Two tests are here detailed, the Maddox rod and the prism test. Both are convenient, portable, and inexpensive, but possess the disadvantage common to all tests for heterophoria held close to the eye, viz: that S does not always completely renounce the fusion-impulse.

In the Maddox test, the so-called 'rod' transforms for one eye the flame of a candle into a long narrow streak of red light, while the other eye sees the candle flame naturally. Heterophoria is indicated by the lack of coincidence in these two images.

The prism test, which is essentially an auxiliary test, consists in producing artificial displacement of images by means of the prisms, and measuring S's ability to produce voluntary fusion of these displaced images.

A. THE MADDOX ROD TEST

APPARATUS.—Maddox multiple red rod (Fig. 37). Trial frame (Fig. 35). Candle. Meter stick. [A set of trial prisms may be added.]

PRELIMINARIES.—Place the lighted candle on a level with S's eyes and 6 m. distance, preferably in a darkened room. Adjust the trial frame.

FIG. 37.   MADDOX MULTIPLE ROD.

METHOD.—(1) Let S close his left eye: place the Maddox rod in the frame before the right eye with the bars set horizontally. S should then perceive a long, narrow, vertical streak of red light. Then let S open his left eye and at once state whether the red streak passes exactly through the candle flame.

(2) Turn the rod until the bars run vertically. *S* will see a horizontal red streak. Let him open his left eye and at once state whether the streak passes exactly through the candle flame.

RESULTS.—In the first test, the possible results are: (*a*) the line passes through the flame, orthophoria (Fig. 38); (*b*) the line passes to the right of the flame, esophoria or homonymous displacement (Fig. 39); (*c*) the line passes to the left of the flame, exophoria or crossed displacement (Fig. 40).

In the second test, the possible results are: (*a*) the line passes through the flame, orthophoria (Fig. 41); (*b*) the line passes below the flame, right hyperphoria (Fig. 42); (*c*) the line passes above the flame, left hyperphoria (Fig. 43).

NOTES.—Next to orthophoria, esophoria is the most common condition. Unequal vertical adjustment, hyperphoria, is not

FIGS. 38-40.   ILLUSTRATING ORTHOPHORIA, ESOPHORIA, AND EXOPHORIA, RESPECTIVELY.

As revealed by the Maddox rod when used before the right eye for horizontal deviation.   (De Schweinitz and Randall.)

common, save that an upward deviation of the squinting eye is almost always associated with high degrees of convergent strabismus.

If the latent asymmetry is but slight, there may appear a more or less rapid corrective movement: *S* will then notice lack of coincidence of the line and the flame when the left eye is opened, but the two images soon fuse together. On the other hand, if the asymmetry is larger, *E* may determine its degree by placing prisms before the left eye and ascertaining by trial how strong a prism is needed to enable fusion to occur.

If both horizontal and vertical imbalance is observed, the defect is hyperesophoria or hyperexophoria. This may be demonstrated, if desired, by placing the Maddox rod in an oblique position.

FIG. 41. MADDOX TEST FOR VERTICAL DEVIATION; ORTHOPHORIA.　　FIG. 42. MADDOX TEST FOR VERTICAL DEVIATION; RIGHT HYPERPHORIA.　　FIG. 43. MADDOX TEST FOR VERTICAL DEVIATION; LEFT HYPERPHORIA.

Stevens' stenopaic lens (Fig. 44) may be substituted for the Maddox rod. A single determination then suffices for both horizontal and vertical displacement. In orthophoria, the candle flame appears in the center of a diffused disc of light; in heterophoria, it is displaced to the right or left, above or below, or obliquely, in a manner corresponding to that of the Maddox line-and-flame test (Fig. 45). The stenopaic lens consists of a convex lens of 13 D., covered, save for a very small opening in the center. The principle is again that of disparate images.

FIG. 44.   STEVENS' STENOPAIC LENS.

B.   TEST WITH PRISMS

APPARATUS.—Trial frame.   Four prisms, one of 2, one of 8, and two of 20 prism-diopters, of the circular pattern fitted for the trial frame.[1]   Candle.   Meter stick.

FIG. 45.   HETEROPHORIA, AS REVEALED BY THE STEVENS LENS.

---

[1]These prisms permit E to test S's ability to overcome the degrees of displacement that are considered standard for the three positions: their cost is about $7. For a little more money, however, a fairly complete set of prisms may be purchased, which will permit a more flexible test. The strength of prisms is now commonly indicated in prism-diopters. One diopter is a strength of prism which will deflect a beam of light 1 cm. on a tangent plane placed at a distance of 1 m. In the smaller powers this unit is practically identical with degree of prism, or angular size of prism—the unit formerly used.

PRELIMINARIES.—Place the lighted candle on a level with S's eyes and 6 m. distant, preferably in a darkened room. Adjust the trial frame.

METHOD.—(1) To test abduction, or S's ability to overcome a standard amount of displacement by rotating the eyes outward, place the 8-D. prism before one eye with the base in, *i. e.,* toward the nose.

(2) To test S's ability in adduction, or forcible convergence, place a 20-D. prism, with the base out, *before each eye.*[1]

(3) To test S's ability in sursumduction (compensation for vertical displacement), place the 2-D. prism, with the base either up or down, before one eye.

RESULTS.—With orthophoria, S should secure fusion under the conditions imposed, if not at the first trial, at least after a few trials on different days. Failure to accomplish this, or ability to overcome larger angular displacements than those cited, is indicative of heterophoria, or of other inequalities in the set of the eye-balls, *e. g.,* declination.[2]

NOTES.—This test may, of course, be applied to cases in which either orthophoria or heterophoria is present. It may be of value in measuring S's control of his eye-muscles, not only as a matter of optical hygiene, but also in conjunction with tests and experiments of a psychological nature, *e. g.,* stereoscopy, binocular fusion, and visual space-perception in general.

REFERENCES

(1) G. T. Stevens, A treatise on the motor apparatus of the eyes. Phila., 1906. Pp. 496.

(2) W. N. Suter, The refraction and motility of the eye. Phila., 1903. Pp. 390.

TEST 16

Color-blindness.—This test continues the examination of the functional efficiency of the eye as a sense-organ. It has obvious practical import, as well as high theoretical significance in connection with the theory of vision.

---

[1]The ability to overcome prisms by convergence is about 50 D., according to Stevens, but an exact standard cannot be stated.

[2]For further details of this, and other forms of prism test, consult Suter and Stevens.

It is probably safe to say that no theory of vision has thus far been proposed that satisfactorily explains all the known facts. Certainly, in the case of color-blindness, the work of the last few years has disclosed forms and varieties of defective color-vision that offer the greatest difficulty in classification or explanation. While, then, the tests outlined below are satisfactory for most practical purposes, they need for thorough scientific examination to be supplemented by various other methods,[1] and the account of color-blindness here presented is confessedly provisional and abbreviated.

We know that the retina of the normal eye is not equally sensitive to color stimuli in all portions. If small bits of colored paper are moved inward and outward between the periphery of the field of vision and the area of clearest vision, there can be made out three fairly clearly defined zones of different sensitivity—an inner efficient zone, over which we see all colors; a middle zone, over which reds and greens are seen with difficulty or with much altered tone, and an outer zone, over which we commonly see nothing but blacks, whites and grays. If, however, the conditions are altered, especially by exposing colored stimuli of high intensity for a brief period, the boundaries of these zones are decidedly altered: green does, indeed, suffer in peripheral vision, but red, under the proper conditions, may be seen, at least as reddish, as far outward as an object may be seen at all.

It has been customary, and it is tempting, to regard color-blindness as a congenital arrest of development (or in some cases as an acquired, pathological modification) of these zones. If we accept the indication of the experiment with simple colored papers, we should expect to encounter total color-blindness (lack of both central and of intermediate zone) or partial color-blindness of a red-green type (lack of central zone). We should not expect to find blue-yellow blindness, at least as an arrest of development, if it be assumed that the red-green zone represents the latest and hence most unstable development in the structure of the retina.

---

[1] See, for example, the several methods used by Hayes (8) and by Guttmann (7) in their examination of a number of interesting cases.

As a matter of fact, *total color-blindness,* while well authenticated, is rare, and is presumably a pathological defect. It is accompanied by a distinct reduction in visual acuity, by nystagmus, photophobia, and other disorders of the visual organ.

Again, *blue-yellow blindness* (also termed violet-blindness and *tritanopia*), is in much dispute. It certainly is rare, and probably often pathological in character, though cases have been reported of late which seem to be congenital in origin.[1]

Taking, then, this interpretation of color-blindness, which accords with the hypothesis, typified in the Hering theory of vision, that the components of the retina which respond to the stimulation of light waves are arranged in three pairs—black-white, blue-yellow, and red-green—we would be left with red-green blindness as the typical and characteristic form of partial color-blindness. Deficiency in red would be accompanied by a corresponding deficiency in the complementary green, and conversely. In actual vision, certain reds and certain greens would appear neutral or gray, while stimuli that to the normal eye would be described as red or as green conjoined with blue or yellow would be seen as bluish or yellowish, and the spectrum would thus be divided into a long-waved yellow and a short-waved blue section. That many of the color-blind do conform to these theoretical expectations is not to be doubted, but recent investigations have at least raised the question whether such cases are not to be regarded as limiting and extreme, rather than as typical forms of deficiency (Hayes, 8).

The current terminology of color-blindness is, however, based upon the Helmholtz theory of color vision, wherein the three primary visual and retinal elements are assumed to be red, green and violet. In theory, on this basis, it is evident that an eye might possess all three, or but two, or but one of these visual elements; that, in other words, an eye might possess *trichromatic, dichromatic* or *monochromatic* (*achromatic*) vision. The terms red-blindness, green-blindness and violet-blindness, which would naturally be implied by this theory (on the supposition that some of the three primary components

---

[1]For examples, see Richardson.

were wanting) have, however, been discarded by all careful writers because they are misleading. In their place are employed the terms *protanopia, deuteranopia* and *tritanopia,* meaning the existence of a defect in vision allied to disturbance in the function of the first, second or third of the three components, respectively.

To comprehend the inter-correspondence of nomenclature, it must be understood that the ordinary red-green blindness of the Hering terminology appears as a rule in one of two sub-types, though the distinction is of more theoretical than practical significance. Those belonging to the first type locate the brightest part of the spectrum, as do normal persons, in the yellow; they are called deuteranopes (or rather erroneously green-blinds). Those who locate the brightest part of the spectrum in the yellow-green region and see the entire blue end of the spectrum relatively brighter than the normal person are called protanopes (or erroneously red-blinds). Protanopia is far less frequent than deuteranopia.

Of great theoretical interest and decided practical importance are those cases in which the same color qualities exist as in normal eyes, but in an unusual or anomalous form, whose vision is, therefore, trichromatic, but abnormal. These cases are known popularly *color-weaks* and technically as *anomalous trichromates.* According to Guttmann, anomalous trichromasy manifests seven characteristic symptoms—a reduced sensitivity to color stimuli, especially when the stimuli are of short duration, small area, or low intensity, decidedly heightened color contrast, difficulty in comparing color tones of unequal brightness or saturation and quick fatigue to color stimuli. While all these symptoms, taken together, constitute a characteristic symptom-complex, the reciprocal interaction of the several symptoms varies greatly in individuals, so that the defect actually shows itself in protean forms, and there exist all degrees of anomalous trichromasy, ranging from almost normal vision to practically dichromatic vision.[1]

Here, again, we meet terminological difficulties. The terms color-weak, green-weak and red-weak, which are advocated by Guttmann and employed by some investigators, are opposed by others, *e. g.* by Nagel, who prefers the term anomalous trichromasy to cover the group as a whole and protanomaly and deuteranomaly to distinguish the two main sub-types, analogous to the two main sub-types of dichromasy. The term 'anomaly,' he argues, indicates a condition of color sensitivity variant from the normal, without implying that the deficiency need be a weakness. This term is better than more specific terms like 'red-weakness' or 'green-weakness,' for the 'weakness' of both of these forms actually shows most in the greens and violets and far less strikingly in the reds

---

[1]On color-weakness, consult especially Rosmanit, Nagel and Guttmann

Holmgren contrasted total color-blindness with partial color-blindness, and divided the latter into complete partial color-blindness and incomplete partial color-blindness (confusions with the green, but not with the red test skein). This division has not been often used, but the term 'color-weakness' has been extensively employed in place of Holmgren's incomplete partial color-blindness, though not quite correctly, because this group, as determined by the Holmgren test, may embrace both von Kries's deuteranopes and the so-called color-weak.[1]

The use of confusing terminology, however, is far less serious than other errors which are exhibited in texts descriptive of color-blindness. The reader may consult, for instances, a book by Abney (1), which embodies his Tyndall lectures of 1894, and a magazine article by Ayers (2). In Abney there will be found a colored frontispiece, taken from the Report of the British Association Committee on Color Vision in 1892, which purports to show the spectrum as seen by the color-blind. The spectrum is shown in green and blue: what becomes of yellow is not explained. In Ayers' article there will be found some very pretty colored pictures of roses and Venetian scenes as observed by the color-blind,—pictures that are good examples of the illustrator's art, but absolutely false examples of color vision. Mrs. C. L. Franklin (6) has charitably applied the term "pseudo-scientific" to such writing. A more nearly correct representation of the spectrum seen by the color-blind is given by Thomson (20).

One of the best illustrations of anomalous trichromasy is afforded by the Rayleigh test-equation. Lord Rayleigh (17) discovered that when a homogeneous yellow is equated with a mixture of red and green, the proportions of red and green needed to balance the yellow show only slight variations for the great majority of persons, but that there exists a distinct type of eye that demands a distinctly different combination: most often the mixture must be made much greener, less often much redder. The first type indicates green-anomaly (green-weakness, deuteranomalous trichromasy), the second red-anomaly (red-weakness, protanomalous trichromasy).

While, in theory, the 'color-weak' are not to be identified with the color-blind, for practical purposes it is equally important to diagnose the existence of the defect. If, as seems probable, anomalous trichromasy is as prevalent as true dichromasy, then, since many of the commonly used tests for color-blindness fail to detect color-weakness, and since conditions of daily life would often demand color discrimination under unfavorable conditions, e. g., in railway and marine service,

[1]An interesting tabular summary, confessedly provisional, of the entire field of color defect has been worked out within the compass of a single page by Nagel (16c, p. 308) : this the reader is advised to consult before attempting any extensive reading on the theory of color-blindness.

it would seem very probable that some disasters may be traceable to this deficiency, which has escaped detection by medical examiners.

Thus, in Germany, among 1778 members of railway regiments, all of whom had passed the wool test and many of whom had also passed Stilling's test, 13 dichromates and 31 anomalous trichromates of various types were discovered by the use of Nagel's test in the hands of military physicians.[1]

Color-blindness may be binocular or monocular. The latter is rare, but naturally of great theoretical importance in determining the nature of color-blindness.

Color-blindness is usually congenital, and then incurable. The common form, red-green blindness (dichromasy), is regarded as an arrest of development, usually, or reversion to a more primitive form of retina. All acquired cases, variously attributed to traumatism, neuritis, atrophy of the optic nerve, hysteria, excessive fatigue, over-indulgence in tobacco, are accompanied by lessened visual acuity, are pathological, and of relatively small concern to the theory of color-vision.[2] Acquired red-green blindness, according to Köllner, is a middle stage between normal vision and total color-blindness, and indicates some grave disorder. The disturbance of function may be located either in the retina or in some part of the nervous system concerned in vision.

Color-blindness seems to have been first noted in literature in 1864, but first described accurately by Dalton, the celebrated English chemist, in 1794. The first attempt at a systematic examination of a large number of cases was made by Seebeck in Berlin in 1837 by the aid of colored papers. The first systematic examination of railway employees dates from 1875, when a serious accident in Sweden led Holmgren (11), of the University of Upsala, to devise his well-known wool test and to induce officials to adopt it.[3]

The chief devices and methods for testing color-blindness are Holmgren's, Galton's, Thomson's, Oliver's, and other assortments of colored worsteds, Stilling's pseudo-isochromatic charts, Nagel's card test, spectroscopic examination, various contrast tests, and the use of equations of mixed colors, particularly Nagel's equation-apparatus, and Hering's apparatus, which enables the examiner to adjust a color equation of transmitted light that shall appear to the color-blind as uniform gray. In addition, numerous forms of color-blindness lantern (Williams', Friedenberg's, Oliver's, etc.) have been devised for testing railroad and marine employees by simulating the con-

---

[1] For summaries of recent discussions of the practical dangers of color defects, proposals for improving tests, for altering signal lights, etc., consult Hayes (9). An annual review of the literature of color defects may be expected in the *PsBu*, March issues.

[2] For illustrative cases, consult Collin and Nagel, and Köllner.

[3] For other details of the history of color-blindness as well as a discussion of methods, though not brought down to date, consult Jennings (12) and Thomson (20).

ditions of night-signalling, and soiled signal-flags have been used for similar purposes, while Henmon has proposed a discrimination-time test.

Two forms of test are here described: the familiar and widely used Holmgren wool test, adopted by the American Ophthalmological Society, and Nagel's new card test, which is specially fitted for the diagnosis of color-weakness and of other variant types of defect. Both of these tests are inexpensive, compact, and portable. They may be employed in conjunction with one another, but the Nagel test is undoubtedly the better of the two.

It is well to point out that, by dint of daily experience, the color-blind individual develops a capacity to recognize some reds and greens by means of secondary criteria, such as brightness (tint) and saturation (chroma), and familiarity with the application of color nomenclature (grass is green, cranberries red, etc.), so that the defect may exist unrecognized, either by himself or by his acquaintances, until chance compels the recognition or discrimination of tones to which these criteria cannot be applied. Hence arises the necessity, in the administration of tests, of displaying a large number of colors of varied saturation and brightness, in order that, for any individual, some combination or series of combinations of colors may be found, in the recognition of which these criteria cannot be used. Here, too, appears in some part the explanation of the seeming individuality of defective color-vision.

A. THE HOLMGREN WOOL TEST

MATERIAL.—Holmgren's worsteds.[1] Sheet of light gray or white cardboard or a similarly colored cloth.

METHOD.—(a) *Full procedure.* (1) Remove the three large test skeins, pale green, rose and red, Nos. A, B, C. Scatter the remaining skeins over the cloth or paper in *diffuse daylight* only.[2] Hand to S the green test skein, No. A, and direct him to pick from the table all those skeins that resemble the test skein, i. e., all the tints and shades of that color. Explain that there are no two specimens alike, and that an exact match is not required. It will do no harm to illustrate the process by

---

[1] Examination of several boxes of test-worsteds supplied by different dealers in optical supplies shows that in many of them the skeins diverge widely in color-tone and saturation from the original Holmgren skeins. When this variation from standard affects the standard test-skeins, the whole set of worsteds evidently becomes valueless. The C. H. Stoelting Co. is now in a position to supply skeins in the exact original tones selected by Holmgren.

[2] When not in use the skeins must be carefully enclosed in their box, as they will fade or change color if continuously exposed to light.

selecting two or three skeins for him, provided these are afterward mixed with the pile. To save time in explanation, other S's may be allowed to watch this demonstration.

(2) If hesitation appears, or if grays, browns or reds as well as greens are selected, continue the test by the use of the rose skein, No. B. The typical color-blind will then select some blues or purples, or, less often, grays or greens.

(3) Finally, the red test skein, No. C, may be used, though many color-blinds have little difficulty with this test on account of the strong saturation of the test skein.

In all three tests, preserve a careful record of the skeins selected by S's who deviate in any particular from the normal.

(b) *Abbreviated procedure.* This test may be used for quick preliminary examination. Place irregularly on the cloth four green skeins (*e. g.,* 1, 11, 31, 65) and eight 'confusion' skeins of gray, brown, and pink (*e. g.,* 20, 98, 118, 59, 189, 199, 13, 23). Hand to S the pale green standard, No. A, and require him to pick from the cloth as rapidly as possible four skeins that match the test skein (in the sense previously described). Allow him approximately 4 sec. to make this selection. If this test can not be promptly and accurately executed, examine S further by the full procedure.

TYPICAL RESULTS.—(1) About 4 per cent. of men and less than 0.5 per cent. of women are color-blind: the most common defect is probably red-green blindness of the form known as deuteranopia.

(2) The following are actual selections of a typical red-green blind. By assembling these skeins E can gain the best idea of the nature of the confusions likely to be discovered.

Green standard: 1, 11, 51, 61, 10, 20, 17, 98, 118, 59, 119, 179, 189. (Occasionally some pink, like 12, is also selected.)

Rose standard: 32, 43, 113, 123, 104, 114, 124, 6, 46, 56, 67, 77, 87, 18.

Red standard: 33, 43, 53, 63, 73, 83, 133, 54, 49.

NOTES.—Inability to name colors rightly has sometimes been erroneously mistaken for color-blindness, but the term must be applied only to instances of actual inability to *see* colors rightly. Consequently, no color-blindness test should *hinge* upon the ability to name correctly the various colors presented, and, in the conduct of the Holmgren test at least, reference to color names should be avoided if possible.

If S works very slowly and hesitatingly, but finally makes a correct selection, this may indicate several possibilities, which should be tested by further study of the case. (*a*) The slowness may be due merely to extreme cautiousness on his part, coupled with some anxiety or uneasiness about the test, or with failure to understand clearly just what is wanted. (*b*) The slowness may be due, in the case of very young children or untutored adults, to gross ignorance of, and unfamiliarity with colors. (*c*) The slowness may be indicative of color-weakness, in which case Nagel's test should be applied for further diagnosis of the defect.

All instances in which specific color differences are at first recognized with difficulty or not at all, but in which, after coaching or instruction, an efficiency is developed adequate for passing the test in use, must be looked upon with suspicion, and it must not be assumed forthwith that color-blindness has been cured by training, for either the cautiousness or ignorance just mentioned were present at first and removed by the training, or the conditions of the test were too simple, and secondary criteria were developed by S.

If apparent cases of blue-yellow, or of total color-blindness are discovered, these should, if possible, be given most careful examination by an expert psychologist.

It is obvious that many callings are, or should be, closed to the color-blind, *e. g.*, railroading, marine and naval service, medicine, chemical analysis, painting and decorating, certain branches of botany, microscopy, mineralogy, the handling of dry goods, millinery, etc. In some phases of school work, the color-blind pupil is likewise at an evident disadvantage.[1] The test should, accordingly, be regularly instituted in the early years of school life, in order that the existence of the defect may be made known to the child as soon as possible.

---

[1] On the consequences of color-blindness for daily life, see especially Jerchel (13).

B. THE NAGEL CARD TEST

MATERIAL.—Nagel's color-blindness cards, 7th edition.[1]

METHOD.—A. Spread out the 16 cards of Section A upon a table. It is imperative that there be good daylight illumination and that *S* stand upright before the table and not bend over it or pick up the cards to examine them at close range. Provide *S* with a pen-holder or other convenient pointer by which he may indicate his responses. Ask him the following questions:

1. Can you point out to me some cards on which *red or reddish* spots are to be seen?
2. On which cards are there *red spots only?*[2]
3. On which *green spots only?*
4. On which *gray spots only?*

B. Remove the cards and show *S*, one at a time, the four cards of Section B: ask him for each card what colors he sees.

Responses of normal S's. The questions of Section A are answered rapidly and correctly, save in the case of a few timid, anxious or unintelligent persons, and these will usually reply correctly to the diagnostically more important questions, Nos. 3 and 4, once they have learned what is wanted, especially that they need not find a whole ring that is red, etc., but only single spots. A wrong answer that is afterward spontaneously corrected is not symptomatic of defective color-vision.

In dealing with Section B, *E* must remember that he is not here testing for fine discrimination in the use of color nomenclature, but merely determining whether or not *S* recognizes red and green as such, and whether he designates as red or as green some color which is neither red nor green. Thus, in Card B 1, a normal *S* readily recognizes the green, but may hesitate to name the yellow-brown, and it is indifferent whether he calls it brown, yellow, or even gray. But it would be very suspicious if he called all the spots green, or if he called the brown spots red, reddish or orange. Similarly, if the brown spots on B 2 and

---

[1] Those who desire to conduct special supplementary tests for blue-yellow blindness, or for differentiating between protanopia and deuteranopia etc., will find that the earlier editions of Nagel's test make special provision for this work. Cf. the directions printed in the first edition of thi *Manual* to accompany the 4th edition of the Nagel test.

[2] Do not ask for bluish red or rose-colored spots.

B 4 are called green, S is surely defective in color vision, and if all the spots are called red, he is certainly a color-blind, whereas, again, if the brown spots are called yellow or even gray, he need not be color-blind.

Responses of S's with defective color-vision. Errors are evident, as a rule, even in the first question of Section A. Most of the color-blind select as containing red spots Cards 6 or 11 or 12, on which they mistake the yellowish-green or the brown spots for red. Unless there be deliberate simulation, these errors are well-nigh complete evidence of color-blindness. The anomalous trichromates usually answer this question without mistake, though they may show hesitation in their responses.

With Questions 2, 3 and 4, the color-blind are reduced to sheer guess-work. The anomalous trichromates can answer Question 2 (red spots only) correctly, but with Questions 3 and 4 they will show decided uncertainty and slowness, and will, indeed, not seldom answer both incorrectly by designating cards that contain both green and gray when asked for cards containing only green and only gray. Occasionally, too, they may select cards that contain some red spots.

In Section B, color-blind S's see but a single color on each card and the color-names they select are a matter of pure guess-work. B 1 is often called green, B 2 and B 4 red, B 3 gray or green. The anomalous trichromates see as a single color only B 1 and, less often, B 3; they see B 2 and B 4 plainly in two colors, although they often call the brown green by contrast with the adjacent red.[1]

Any S, therefore, who sees the red and brown cards, B 2 and B 4, as a single color, or as red and green, is certainly defective in color-vision. But an error with B 1 only or with B 3 only merely raises a suspicion of defective color-vision, and does not permit a positive diagnosis of deficiency if *all* the other questions are correctly answered. To justify the suspicion of defect, such an S must respond incorrectly or hesitatingly to Questions 3 and 4.

---

[1] Normal S's may hesitatingly admit that the brown spots look somewhat greenish, but they never deliberately describe these two cards as composed of red and green spots.

NOTES.—The cards should not be placed under glass to prevent contact with them, since this introduces a disturbing reflection. If E wishes to put the cards in an album or otherwise arrange them to obviate spreading them out upon a table at each trial, he should take care to present them in different positions, so that it will be impossible for S's to learn their position or to communicate them to other possible examinees If anxiety or ineptitude on the part of S renders the diagnosis doubtful in the first trial, it is best to forego further trial until a later day and then to try the whole test over again.

It is imperative that E adopt a quiet, sympathetic manner free from any sign of irritation or impatience, especially when dealing with slow or stupid S's, or even with those who are plainly attempting deceit. During the test, E must avoid informing S, whether directly or by suggestion, of any mistake he has made. Discussion or criticism of S's selections is out of place, while, for the sake of future tests, it would be desirable not to explain S's errors to him in detail, even after the test.

If S has decidedly low visual acuity, this must be corrected at least approximately, by appropriate lenses, before the color blindness test is begun.

REFERENCES

(1)   W. Abney, Color vision. London, 1895. See also his Researche in colour vision and the trichromatic theory. London, 1913. Pp. 423.

(2)   E. Ayers, Color-blindness, with special reference to art and artists. *Century Mag.*, 73: 1907, 876-889.

(3)   J. W. Baird, The problems of color-blindness. *PsBu*, 5: 1908 294-300.

(4)   Collin and W. Nagel, Erworbene Tritanopie. *ZPs*, II Abt., 41 1906, 74-88.

(5)   Dalton, Extraordinary facts relating to the vision of color Trans. of the Lit. and Philos. Soc. of Manchester, 1794.

(6)   Mrs. C. L. Franklin, Magazine Science. *Sci*, n.s. 25: 1907, 746.

(7)   A. Guttmann, Untersuchungen über Farbenschwäche. *ZPs*,] Abt. 42: 1908, 24-64, 250-270; 43: 1909, 146-162, 199-223, 255-298.

(8)   S. P. Hayes, The color sensations of the partially color-blind: criticism of current teaching. *AmJPs*, 22: 1911, 369-407.

(9)   S. P. Hayes, Vision: Color defects. *PsBu*, 10: March, 1913, 10 107. (Similar annual summaries in previous years *PsBu*.)

(10.)   V. Henmon, The detection of color-blindness. *JPh*, 3: 190 341-4.

(11)   Holmgren, Die Farbenblindheit in ihrer Beziehung zum Eise bahn- und Marine-dienst. (German edition.) Leipzig, 1878.

(12)   J. E. Jennings, Color-vision and color-blindness. Phila., 189 Pp. 111.

(13)   W. Jerchel, Inwieweit wird das Medizinstudium durch Rotgrün-
blindheit beeinflusst?   ZPs, II Abt., 47: 1912, 1-33.
(14)   H. Köllner, (a) Die diagnostische Bedeutung der erworbenen
Farbensinnstörungen.   BerlinKlW, 48: 1911, 846-9, 897-900.   (b) Die
Störungen des Farbensinnes, ihre klinische Bedeutung und ihre Diagnose. Berlin, 1912. Pp. 428.
(15)   J. v. Kries, (a) Ueber Farbensysteme.   ZPs, 13: 1897, 241-324.
(Corrective note, p. 473.)   (b) Die Gesichtsempfindungen.   Nagel's
Handbuch der Physiologie des Menschen.   Braunschweig, 3: 1905, 109-
282.   (c) Normale und anomale Farbensysteme.   Helmholtz's Handbuch
der physiologischen Optik, 3te Aufl., 2: 1911, 333-378.
(16)   W. Nagel, (a) Fortgesetzte Untersuchungen zur Symptomato-
logie u. Diagnostik der angeborenen Störungen des Farbensinns.   ZPs, II
Abt., 41: 1906, 238-282, 319-337.   (b) Zur Nomenclatur der Farbensinnstörungen.   Ibid., 42: 1907, 65.   (c) Ueber typische und atypische Farbensinnstörungen.   Ibid., 43: 1908, 299-309.   (Consult also other articles by
this writer in the same periodical.)
(17)   Rayleigh, Experiments on colour.   Nature, 25: 1881, 64-66.
(18)   Florence Richardson, An unusual case of color-blindness.   PsBu,
8: 1911, 55-6.   (Also summary of another case, 214-5.)
(19)   J. Rosmanit, Zur Farbensinnprüfung im Eisenbahn- und Marine-
dienste.   Vienna and Leipzig, 1907. Pp. 59.
(20)   W. Thomson, Detection of color-blindness, being pp. 315-352 in
Norris and Oliver, System of diseases of the eye, vol. ii, Phila., 1897.

TEST 17

Discrimination of brightness.—The object of this test is to
obtain an index, for comparative purposes, of S's ability to distinguish very small differences in brightness, or more exactly,
to determine the smallest difference in brightness that S can
distinguish under simple experimental conditions. The present
test omits consideration of chromatic stimuli, and is confined
to the discrimination of brightness, first by the use of reflected,
secondly by the use of transmitted light.

Visual discrimination has been studied in the laboratory by
many competent investigators, e. g., Ament, Aubert, Bouguer,
Helmholtz, Fröbes, Kraepelin, Masson, Merkel, Schirmer,
Volkmann, and others. Tests of school children by Gilbert
(3) and Spearman (6) have followed simpler methods.

In the laboratory, use has been made of Masson's disc, both
by daylight and artificial illumination, of the episkotister, of
gray papers and of shadows. Toulouse (9) proposes solutions
of aniline colors in glass receptacles. Gilbert used a series
of ten pieces of cloth soaked in a red dye of graded intensity.
Investigations that are most comparable with the method here
proposed are those of Ament (1), Fröbes (2), and Spearman,

all of whom made use of gray papers, and of Gilbert, who examined school children, though with chromatic stimuli.

A. DISCRIMINATION OF GRAYS—REFLECTED LIGHT

APPARATUS.—Set of 10 test-cards, each composed of two gray strips, 13 x 40 mm., on a white background, 10 x 10 cm. Exposure frame, fitted with a card-holder which may be rotated

FIG. 46. APPARATUS FOR THE DISCRIMINATION OF GRAYS.

through 180°, and with a black screen, through an opening (8 x 8 cm.) in which the test-cards may be viewed (Fig. 46). Light gray cloth, about 70 x 160 cm., for a background. Two supports, with angle-pieces, and a horizontal rod 70 cm. long. Headrest.

The cards are numbered from 0 to 9, corresponding to 10 different pairs of stimuli. Each card contains one strip of the lightest or standard gray, and one strip of comparison gray. Card No. 0 represents no difference, or objective equality; Card No. 1 represents the minimal objective difference; Card No. 9 the maximal objective difference and is easily supraliminal for the normal eye. Each card is numbered on the back in such a way that, when looking at the face of the card with the number up, the right strip is the darker; there is also a small black mark on the extreme edge of the card on the side of the darker strip.

The grays used on these cards have been specially prepared, under the author's direction, by S. L. Sheldon, photographer, of Ithaca, N. Y., and have been carefully standardized. Each set of grays is printed from the same negative, on which the original series was formed by graded serial exposures before a sheet of milk glass set in a north window. They will not fade or change their tone, unless brought into contact with chemical fumes or solutions; but, for additional protection, they should be kept under cover when not in use, and never be handled in bright sunlight.

The tones, sizes, and spatial relations of the strips, cards, and background have been selected to eliminate errors that might arise from adaptation and contrast. The size of the strips is slightly smaller than that used by Ament (18x45 mm.) and slightly larger than that prescribed by Titchener (10x40 mm.) for the demonstration of Weber's law in brightnesses.

PRELIMINARIES.—Place a small table, say 65 x 90 cm., squarely before a window where good diffuse daylight may be secured (preferably a north window with full clear exposure to the sky); leave just enough space between the front of the table and the window for two chairs for S and E. Spread the gray cloth over the top of the table, and stretch it up vertically at the back edge by means of the supports, so as to form a continuous background of gray, with the vertical back at least 65 cm. high and about 65 cm. distant from S's eyes.

Place the exposure frame in the center of the table at the optimal reading distance (about 35 cm., unless S has uncorrected myopia or hyperopia), and adjust its height so that the *top* of the frame is on a level with S's eyes. Adjust the head-rest so that S may sit erect, squarely before the exposure frame and close to the table-edge, with his back, of course, to the window.

Keep the test-cards conveniently near, but out of S's sight. E will find it most convenient to sit at S's right.

METHOD.—(1) Spend 5 min. in giving S practise and familiarity with the test. For this purpose, begin with the large-numbered cards, and pass in general toward the smaller numbers, but without following any rigorous order. With each card, rotate the turn-table, so that the right strip is now the darker, now the lighter: follow an irregular order, and keep S always in ignorance of the actual location of the darker strip, and of the correctness of his judgments. In each trial, S must report his judgment *in terms of the right-hand strip,* saying either "darker," "lighter," or "equal." (Any doubtful cases may be classed as equal.)

When not observing a test-card, S should rest his eyes by directing them toward the gray background. He turns his eyes to the test-card at E's "now," and should be asked to pass a judgment *within 5 sec.* It is not necessary to record results at this point, but from this practise work, S will attain a general familiarity with the test, and E will form a fair idea of S's 'critical' region.

(2) Proceed now, more formally and exactly, to determine S's difference limen by selecting a stimulus difference which has appeared in the preliminary series to be just noticeable for him. Give this stimulus-card 10 times, 5 times with the right strip darker, 5 times with the right strip lighter, but in chance order.[1] Inform S that he will be shown the same card 10 times, but in different positions, of which he is to be ignorant. He must judge either "lighter" or "darker." S must not be informed during the series whether his judgments are right or wrong. If S gives 8 right answers in 10, the magnitude of the brightness difference then in use affords the desired index.

(3) Confirm the result by testing S 10 times with a slightly larger difference, and 10 times with a slightly smaller difference. Unless the tests are disturbed by the operation of such factors as fatigue, loss of interest, practise, fluctuations of attention, etc., S may be expected to give 9 or 10 correct judgments in the former, and fewer than 8 in the latter test.

VARIATIONS OF METHOD.—Test the discriminative capacity of each eye separately, as well as in conjunction. Employ the trial frame of Test 14, placing the solid disc before the untested eye. Care must be taken to avoid visual fatigue under these conditions. This variation of method is of interest in connection with recent work on psychophysical asymmetry and the relations between right-handedness, right-eyedness, right-earedness, etc. (See, for example, Van Biervliet.)

If means are at hand to secure effective constant illumination by artificial light, this may be tried for comparison with daylight illumination.

TREATMENT OF RESULTS.—For comparative purposes, S may be ranked in terms of the arbitrary units afforded by the card-numbers. For more exact quantitative expression, however, the results should be expressed in terms of the brightness-differences which correspond to the card-numbers. This correspondence must be worked out by E for the papers employed. Full directions for a simple and sufficiently accurate

---

[1] It is convenient to prepare on small slips, beforehand, a number of chance orders, and to follow one of these with each set of 10 trials.

photometric determination of brightness values of gray papers will be found in Titchener (Pt. I., 35 ff.).

B. DISCRIMINATION OF BRIGHTNESSES—TRANSMITTED LIGHT

APPARATUS.—Headrest. Brightness discrimination apparatus (Fig. 47). [This is a box fitted with a high power frosted tungsten lamp, the light of which is reflected from two independently adjustable white screens upon two oblong, trans-

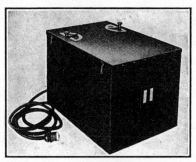

FIG. 47. APPARATUS FOR BRIGHTNESS DISCRIMINATION.

lucent windows, so placed in the face of the box as to give the same dimensions and spatial relations as obtained in the case of the gray strips.]

PRELIMINARIES.—The lamp cord is to be attached to a suitable current (106-110 volts, unless special lamps are ordered). *E* should endeavor to conduct the test in a dark or darkened room. If a brightly lighted room must be used, the effectiveness of the illumination of the 'windows' may be increased by erecting a protecting screen of cardboard or cloth around them.

METHOD.—It is extremely important to arrange the headrest so that *S* is directly in front of the apparatus, with his eyes on a level with the windows in the box. The distance is less important; 50 cm. will be found convenient. The degree of illumination is controlled by two levers, which move the reflecting screens, and which are provided with scales upon the upper surface of the box. *E* first sets the right-hand lever at the point which affords the maximal illumination of the right-hand window, and records the scale-reading exactly. In accordance with the methods just outlined for the discrimination of grays, E now determines the just discriminable difference in the setting of the two levers (when either one of them is at the maximal point). The same precautions must, of course, be taken to reverse the standards in order to correct the space error.[1]

VARIATIONS OF METHOD.—Substitute a 32 C. P. ruby lamp for the frosted lamp, and determine the discriminative capacity for reds of different brightness. Other colors may be employed similarly in this apparatus.

RESULTS.—(1) *Trained observers,* working under conditions similar to those prescribed, can discriminate a brightness difference of $\frac{1}{120}$, though this fraction is appreciably altered by changes of technique or of experimental conditions. Untrained observers have less efficiency, about $\frac{1}{80}$, according to Spearman. With the reflected light apparatus, most adults can just discriminate Card No. 3.

(2) By a different method and with colored stimuli, Gilbert found that discriminative ability increases very gradually up to the *age* of 17, but exhibits marked irregularities at the age of 7.

(3) In discrimination of shades of color, one may conclude from studies by Nichols (5), Gilbert (3), and Thompson (7) that women and girls very slightly exceed men and boys in this capacity. Luckey, however, concluded that no *sex differences* could be demonstrated in color discrimination.

(4) Individual S's are apt to possess a constant *space error, i. e.,* to tend to judge the gray on one side darker; in some cases this is the right, and in others the left, but it seems impossible to correlate this asymmetry with right and left-handedness (Spearman).

(5) Gilbert found no very decided correlation between *visual discrimination and intelligence.* Spearman's experiments upon 24 village-school children give correlations between brightness discrimination and common sense, school cleverness, and gen-

---

[1]Since the scales are identical and the entire instrument is symmetrical, a given setting of the lever will produce the same intensity of illumination for either window.

eral intelligence in the neighborhood of + 0.50. In a series
with high-class preparatory-school boys, however, school place
and brightness discrimination gave only + 0.13 for the 'raw'
correlation.

NOTES.—It is imperative that the conditions under which the
gray strips are observed should be kept as constant as possible.
Backgrounds, cards, and holder provide these conditions in
part, and relative brightness is not affected within a fairly wide
range of illumination: nevertheless, it is desirable to work in
the same place, at the same time of day, and under closely similar conditions of outdoor illumination, *e.g.*, between 9 a.m.
and 3 p.m. on sunshiny days, and at a north window. To
ensure evenness of illumination and absence of any shadows, *E*
should test the setting of the experiment by placing Card No. 0
in the holder and reversing its position several times. As this
card represents objective equality, any constant judgment of
difference may serve to indicate uneven conditions of illumination.

In working with brightness differences, and indeed, with all
small differences, *E* must be very careful to avoid suggestion of
the direction of the difference to *S*, and must keep a persistent
watch for all kinds of secondary criteria of judgment. If desired, one could experimentally determine the degree of objective brightness difference that could be overcome by suggestion.

REFERENCES

(1)   W. Ament, Ueber das Verhältniss der ebenmerklichen zu den über-
merklichen Unterschieden, etc.. *PhSd*, 16: 1900, 135-196.

(2)   J. Fröbes, Ein Beitrag über die sogenannten Vergleichungen über-
merklicher Empfindungsunterschieden. *ZPs*, 36: 1904, 344.

(3)   J. A. Gilbert, (*a*) Researches on the mental and physical development of school children. *SdYalePsLab*, 2: 1894, 40-100. (*b*) Researches
upon school children and college students. *UnIowaSdPs*, 1: 1897, 1-39.

(4)   G. Luckey, Comparative observations on the indirect color range
of children, adults and adults trained in color. *AmJPs*, 6: 1895, 489-504.

(5)   L. Nichols, On the sensitiveness of the eye to colors of a low
degree of saturation. *AmJSci*, 30: 1885, 37.

(6)   C. Spearman, General intelligence objectively determined and
measured. *AmJPs*, 15: 1904, 201-293.

(7)   Helen B. Thompson, The mental traits of sex. Chicago, 1903.
Pp. 188.

(8)   E. B. Titchener, Experimental psychology. Vol. ii, N. Y., 1905.

(9) E. Toulouse, N. Vaschide, and H. Piéron, Technique de psych. experimentale. Paris, 1904. Pp. 330.

(10) J. van Biervliet, L'asymétrie sensorielle. *BuAcRoySci*, 34: Série iii., 1897, 326-366.

TEST 18

Auditory acuity.—This test, like that of visual acuity, is primarily conducted for hygienic and practical purposes, especially in the examination of the physical condition of school children, and constitutes the chief auditory test. We may distinguish between simple acuity tests, which are designed merely to detect the existence of lessened aural efficiency and roughly to measure its degree, and more elaborate tests of a diagnostic character, which are for the most part not used in group investigations, but are confined to the work of specialists in otology or in the psychology of audition.[1] Among the latter tests may be mentioned that of binaural pitch-difference, integrity of the tonal scale, bone vs. air-conduction, determination of relative and absolute deafness, diagnostic speech-tests, etc. These tests are designed to investigate the functional efficiency of the various auditory structures, such as the tympanum, ossicles, cochlea, auditory nerve, and to determine the cause of the defect in hearing and the possibility of alleviating it by medical treatment. In particular, it is important, from this point of view, to differentiate between defect in the middle, and defect in the internal ear, because in the former case partial deafness may often be relieved, whereas in the latter medical treatment is ordinarily of no avail.

The more common and widely employed tests for acuity fall naturally into two main groups, viz: speech tests and instrumental tests. Speech tests may be conducted by either vocalized or whispered speech, and by either the method of varied range or the method of constant range. For instrumental tests use is most often made of the watch, of some form of audiometer, or acoumeter, or of a tuning fork. The relative merits of these methods and instruments deserve brief consideration.[2]

---

[1] A typical illustration is given by the interesting article of Bingham (4.)

[2] For further discussion, particularly of the difficulty of measuring the physical energy of minimal tones and noises, see Pillsbury (11).

A. Methods. In the use of both speech and instrumental tests it has been customary to employ the *method of varied range.* A range line is chalked off on the floor of the room; *S* is seated at one end of this range, while *E* moves methodically forward and backward over it, until he determines the extreme limit of auditory capacity for the voice or instrument. The assumption that is made here, viz., that the intensity of a sound decreases as the distance from its source increases (approximately as the square of the increase) turns out to be strictly valid only under ideal conditions. In practise, as the experiments of Andrews (1) have shown, serious and unsuspected errors may arise, due to varying degrees of reflection of sound waves from the floor, walls and other solid objects in the room. It follows that all tests of auditory acuity made indoors and in which the attempt is made to grade acuity in terms of distance are open to objection if anything like careful work is to be done.

The most obvious way to avoid this error is to use the *method of constant range, i. e.,* to station *E* and *S* always at the same place, to keep the position of all objects that might reflect the sound also constant, and to measure acuity in terms of the percentage of errors made in a series of tests at this selected range. For simple schoolroom diagnosis the stations of *E* and *S* may then be so chosen that all *S*'s whose acuity is known to be normal can just hear the sound used for the test.

B. Sources of Sound. (1) The primary advantage of *speech tests* is that they measure directly the most important function of the ear—the hearing of conversational speech, whereas all instrumental tests, because they test the perception of only a limited number of auditory qualities, fail to give unequivocal indication of auditory efficiency. One may hear the watch at a considerable distance and yet be relatively deaf for speech, or conversely. Speech tests should, accordingly, be given the preference where possible.

The use of speech tests is, however, rendered difficult for several reasons. (*a*) Speech involves a great variety and complex combination of pitches of varied intensity and clang-color, and these elements are further varied by changes in accent, emphasis, and inflection. To render speech tests available, therefore most careful study must be made of the elements of spoken and whispered speech, and lists of test-words must be prepared in the light of this analysis.[1]

(*b*) Examiners cannot guarantee uniformity of enunciation and intensity of stress in conducting the test, so that the results of different *E*'s, or even of the same *E* at different times, are rendered difficult of comparison. This difficulty must be met both by preliminary practise and care on *E*'s part, and by ranking *S*'s relatively, in terms of the empirically determined norms for each particular test.

(*c*) The acoustic properties of the room in which the test is held markedly affect its outcome. The method of relative ranking, coupled with the method of constant range, may be used to meet this difficulty.

(*d*) Unavoidable noises are more likely to interfere with speech tests than with tests conducted at close range, *e. g.,* by the audiometer. To offset this, tests must be conducted in as quiet a room as possible, and doubtful cases must be retested under the most favorable conditions that can be secured.

---

[1] This work has been done by Wolf (21). English number-word lists have been prepared and tested by Andrews (1). Reference to these writers will make clear why disparate words form the best speech-test material, and why numbers form the best type of words. Politzer's objection to numbers (12, p. 117) is answered by Bezold (2, p. 5; 3, p. 206).

Limits of space will usually preclude the use of vocalized or conversational speech, but *whispered speech* may be used for tests in a range of from 17 to 40 m., or about one-third that of vocalized speech. Whispering reduces the intensity of the vowels, whereas consonants are little changed. This test serves perfectly well for the practical examination of hearing and should be employed whenever feasible.

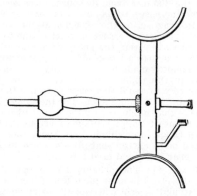

FIG. 48.   POLITZER'S ACOUMETER.
From Titchener, *Experimental Psychology.*

(2) Reverting to *instrumental tests,* we find that the *watch* is most widely used. Its advantages are its convenience and accessibility and its relatively short range. Its disadvantages are that, like any instrument, it fails adequately to test the capacity to perceive speech, that its ticking is so familiar that illusions of hearing are frequent, and that watches vary in the intensity and quality of their ticks.[1]   Proper attention to method will, however, reduce these disadvantages appreciably.

Various forms of *acoumeter* have been invented to meet the deficiencies of the watch. The instrument invented by Politzer (Fig. 48) is best

FIG. 49.   LEHMANN'S ACOUMETER.
(Improved by Titchener.)

---

[1]Statements sometimes made in books on hygiene that, if the ticking of a watch can be heard at so-and-so many inches, the subject has normal hearing, are obviously absurd. The normal range for a watch-tick is given at 2.5 to 4.5 m., but one in the author's possession has a range of 12 m.   See Bezold (3) and Sanford (14, p. 55.)

known and is extensively employed in clinical work. Its range is commonly given at 15 m., but will vary one or two meters from this, as test conditions vary. This acoumeter yields a brief tone, 512 vd., of constant intensity. It is usually employed with the method of varied range. For description, see Politzer (12, pp. 107-8). The upright is held between the thumb and forefinger, and the small hammer is dropped upon the steel cylinder from a constant height. A small disk attached to a pin, not shown in the cut, is used for bone-conduction and other diagnostic tests.

Lehmann's acoumeter (Fig. 49) has the advantage of allowing variation of intensity, and is thus better adapted to the space limits of the ordinary laboratory,[1] but it is, nevertheless, not very satisfactory for practical testing.

The acoumeter described by Toulouse, Vaschide, and Piéron (18) substitutes a drop of distilled water for the metallic ball, and an aluminum disk for the receiving plate.

Many attempts have been made to devise an instrument that will permit testing at the ear itself, in order the better to rule out disturbing noises. Commonly, these devices are electrical in nature, and are planned to utilize a telephone receiver in which clicks or tones are produced in a graded series of intensities.[2] Typical of these instruments is Seashore's

FIG. 50. SEASHORE'S AUDIOMETER.

[1]For description, see Hansen and Lehmann (7).
[2]For an extended discussion of the technique, and particularly of the calibration of this type of apparatus, consult Bruner (5).

audiometer (Fig. 50), which has been fully described by its inventor (15), and which has been extensively employed by him (16) and by others, *e. g.*, by the Child Study Bureau at Chicago (9, 17). Where its cost is not an obstacle this audiometer is to be recommended as the best device for testing hearing by the use of faint clicks or tones.

The audiometer invented by McCallie is nearly as expensive as the Seashore instrument, and is very far from being as satisfactory. It is open to objection in principle and in construction, and the author's experience with it does not confirm the favorable endorsements passed by some investigators.

Tuning forks may be employed for acuity tests in accordance with the method first suggested by Von Conta (20), in which a 512 vs. fork is struck and brought before the ear to be tested, and acuity determined by the length of time it can be heard. Blake's fork (Fig. 51) is devised especially for use by such a method, and may also be used for simple diagnostic tests as described in detail below.

A. WHISPERED SPEECH TEST

MATERIALS.—Meter stick. Telegraph snapper, for signalling. A number of small rubber stoppers, for ear plugs. List of 100 test-numbers arranged in ten series, as in the following Table.

TABLE 27.

Test-numbers for Auditory Acuity (Andrews)

I	II	III	IV	V	VI	VII	VIII	IX	X
6	84	19	90	25	14	8	52	73	24
29	69	53	7	13	31	93	35	41	95
42	17	34	39	46	9	27	64	16	62
87	92	28	62	7	65	60	81	95	49
53	33	97	84	54	98	15	6	57	80
94	26	45	21	70	76	74	19	38	71
70	50	72	56	91	40	36	78	20	16
35	75	60	75	83	23	49	40	89	3
18	48	3	43	68	52	82	23	64	58
61	1	86	18	92	87	51	97	2	37

PRELIMINARIES.—Select, if possible, an oblong room of average proportions and a length of at least 30 m. By rough preliminary tests, establish a range in this room such that not over 90 of 100 test-words can be correctly heard by a normal ear. If space will not permit this range to be established otherwise, interpose screens between *E* and *S,* or place *E* and *S* in adjoining rooms, off a straight line. The range may thus be cut down to from 18 to 20 m., or even less. Whatever may be the arrangement that affords a suitable range, make careful note of all acoustic conditions, *e.g.*, distance of range from walls, dimensions of rooms, exact position of *E* and *S,* disposition of large pieces of furniture in the rooms, number of doors or windows opened or closed, time of day, etc. Be sure always to work under precisely these conditions.

METHOD.—(1) Seat S at the end of the range selected, with his right ear toward E. Carefully close the left ear by means of a rubber stopper inserted into the meatus.

This must completely close the ear, but must not be distressingly tight. E should practise on himself beforehand. If both ears are properly stopped, the ticking of a fairly loud clock can be heard only with difficulty when 1 or 2 m. away, and an ordinary watch cannot be heard when held close to the ears. The plug of cotton often used is entirely inadequate. Inserting the moistened finger-tip into the meatus makes an effective plug, but the position is uncomfortable, and S is likely to move the finger and thus to cause distracting noises in the stopped ear. The same objection may be made to the practise of stopping the ear by pressing in the tragus, or by closing the meatus with the fleshy part of the ball of the thumb.

Direct S to close or shield his eyes during the test, and on no account to watch E's lips. His mouth must likewise be closed, since hearing is altered when the mouth is opened.

Give S a short preliminary series without recording results, until satisfied that he understands the conditions of the test and feels at ease.

(2) For the more formal test, pronounce the 100 words (or but 50, if time is limited) in groups of 10, in the following manner: at the conclusion of one expiration, snap the sounder once as a ready signal for S: at the conclusion of the next expiration, pronounce the test-number in whispered speech with the residual air in the lungs: then snap the sounder twice to indicate that the word has been pronounced, and let S either speak or write down the number that he has heard (using a dash if nothing is heard). Meantime, E interpolates three complete breaths, then gives the warning signal, then the test-number after the fourth breath, and so on until 10 test-numbers are given. After a brief rest, try the second 10 numbers, and similarly, the third, fourth, etc. To avoid possible error, let S, if he is writing his report, begin a new column with each ten.

(3) Stop S's right ear and test his left ear in the same manner.

(4) Test S's binaural hearing by letting him *face E*, but with precaution that he does not secure visual aid from E's lips. This test is important, because binaural hearing may not be related to monaural range, and it is the type of hearing actually

used in daily life. If time is very restricted, test this form of hearing alone.

TREATMENT OF RESULTS.—*S*'s acuity is determined by the percentage of test-numbers correctly heard, in relation to the normal percentage which has been ascertained by averaging the percentages of all *S*'s tested under the same conditions. Thus, if the normal percentage be 70, and *S*'s be 60, his acuity is 6/7; if *S*'s be 80, his acuity is 8/7, *i.e.,* supra-normal. Credit may be allowed for partially correct reports, *e.g.,* 62 for 65: such allowance is specially recommended if 50 or fewer test-numbers are used. If *S* can hear nothing at all at the standard range, *E* may secure an approximate idea of the degree of defectiveness either by shifting to vocalized speech and then raising the intensity of the stimulus words until *S* hears correctly or by continuing the whispered speech at lesser distances (method of varied range).

NOTES.—The sounder is used to avoid changing *E*'s vocal 'set.'

If during the test, *S* becomes restless or inattentive, defer its completion.

It is best to test but one *S* at a time: two *S*'s may, however, be placed back to back, for testing the right ear of the one and the left of the other, if precaution is taken to ensure against communication or disturbance. If the room is large, and preliminary tests warrant the belief that acoustic conditions will be identical, more *S*'s may be tested by seating them on an arc equidistant from *E*.

A very crude group test may be carried out by placing all the children in a room at the limit of the ordinary classroom distance. Let them all close their eyes; then order them in a whisper to perform some unusual movement, such as to place the right forefinger on the palm of the left hand. Repeat with similar commands. Note any children who fail to respond, or who do so in evident imitation of others. Give these more careful tests later. Or take smaller groups of 10, similarly placed across the classroom. Provide each with a block of paper and pencil. Try a series of 10 whispered number-words, and let each write them as heard. Test carefully any who make a single error.

B.   THE WATCH TEST

APPARATUS.—Ordinary watch, preferably E's own watch or one that will be available for all the experiments.   Meter stick. A number of small rubber stoppers for ear plugs.

PRELIMINARIES.—Select a room with a straight range of at least 10 m.   Chalk off upon the floor a range of 9 or 10 m. subdivided into half-meters.   (Use the meter-stick itself, held at right angles to the ear, for measuring distances less than 1 m.) Seat S at one end of the range thus marked off, preferably in a position that will not bring him within 2 m. of a reflecting wall or other surface, with his unused ear plugged and eyes and mouth closed, as in the speech test.   Remove his watch if he. carries one.

METHOD.—Hold the watch in the palm of the right hand with its face clearly exposed toward S, and on a level with his ear.[1]   Start close to S and move out along the range-line, testing at each half-meter, until a point is reached at which the ticking is no longer heard.   Do not exact continuous attention to the sound, but instruct S to reply "yes" or "no" when asked if he hears the watch.   Give a signal "now" at each point where his judgment is to be made, but at every second or third "now," cover the watch with the left hand so that S shall not consciously or unconsciously report "yes" when he should report "no."

Reverse the procedure by approaching from a point certainly beyond S's capacity to a point where the watch can certainly be heard, again by half-meter steps.

Repeat these two determinations until the results for each are consistent and average the two distances (moving outward and moving inward) to secure the range for the ear tested.

Test the other ear in the same manner, or both ears simultaneously, as directed in the speech test, if time permits but one determination.

---

[1] In this position the palm of the hand acts as a sound reflector, and any variation in the location of the watch within the hand must be avoided if the intensity of the sound thrown out is to be kept uniform. Thus, if the watch be held by its stem, free from the palm, there will result an astonishing reduction of the sound directed toward S's ear.

TREATMENT OF DATA.—The normal range for the particular watch and under the particular test conditions must be determined *empirically* by collecting data from a number of S's. It will then be found that the distance the watch is heard will be approximately the same for the majority of S's, that a few will show exceptionally keen acuity, while S's with defective hearing will range all the way from those just under the modal capacity to those who are unable to hear the watch when it is applied directly to the ear. While it is impossible to lay down rules, it may be said that with the ordinary watch having a normal range of 3-5 m., a reduction to 1 m. would signify a distinct deficiency in hearing.

C. TUNING FORK METHOD

APPARATUS.—Blake's fork (Fig. 51). Stop-watch. [Rubber tube.]

METHOD.—(1) Stand directly behind S. Sound the fork by pressing the tips of its prongs together until they touch, and then suddenly releasing them. Hold it horizontally, with its plane of vibration vertical, opposite, and close to the ear to

FIG. 51...BLAKE'S FORK.
For acuity and diagnostic tests by the temporal or 'ringing-off' method.

be tested. Lift the prongs away from the ear occasionally, so that S can state more easily when it actually ceases to be heard. Record the time by means of the stop-watch. Repeat 5 times with each ear, or until accordant times are given. Compare this time with the norm previously established empirically for the fork in use.

(2) For a simple diagnostic test, place the stem of the sounding fork between S's teeth. If both ears are normal, S will hear the tone with equal intensity in each ear, or the tone may be subjectively located in the middle of the head. If, however, one ear is defective, the tone may be heard either more loudly or less loudly in the affected ear. If the tone is heard more

loudly in the ear which previous tests have shown to be defective, we may expect that the location of the defect on that side is in the middle or external ear, and that it may yield to proper medical treatment. If, on the contrary, the tone is heard better in the good ear, we may expect that the defect on the other side lies in the internal ear, or in more deeply seated portions of the auditory mechanism, and that it will probably not yield to treatment.

GENERAL RESULTS AND CONCLUSIONS.—(1) It is difficult to state the prevalence of defective hearing in school children, because of the arbitrary and loose nature of the tests that have been used, and the varying standards that have been set for normality of hearing. Thus, in New York City, a recent report indicates only 1.1 per cent. defective hearing; but here the test consisted merely in the use of a few whispered words in the school room at *20 feet* distance. The extensive Chicago tests,[1] conducted with Seashore's audiometer upon 6729 children, show that, if a pupil is classed as defective when the audiometer record is four points or more below the norm (indicating a defect such that "he would be seriously inconvenienced in detecting sounds of medium intensity"), 1080, or 16 per cent. of the numbers were defective in one or both ears (6.64 per cent. in both, and 9.55 per cent. in one year). A defect equivalent to three or more points of the audiometer scale was found in one ear in 26.3 per cent. and in both ears in 12.3 per cent. of those examined.

Other examinations are summarized by Young (22) as follows: "Sexton, of New York, examined 575 school children, of which 13 per cent. were hard of hearing; W. von Reichard, testing with the watch 1055 pupils of the gymnasium of Riga, found 22.2 per cent. with defective hearing. Weil, of Stuttgart, tested the sense of hearing in 5905 scholars of various kinds of schools, and found it below the normal in from 10 to 30 per cent. of the children, according to their social condition. Moure, of Bordeaux, found 17 per cent.; Gellé, of Paris, 22 to 25 per cent.; Bezold, of Munich, 25.8 per cent. of pupils with hardness of hearing." See also Chrisman (6) for a summary of investigations prior to 1893.

(2) With regard to the *partially deaf,* Macmillan and Bruner (9) conclude that, in theory, there exist varying degrees of deafness, "ranging all the way from slight and tempo-

---

[1]See Smedley (17), Macmillan (8, also summarized in 13).

rary impairment of hearing due to a cold, to the stage of absolute and permanent silence." An examination of the children attending the public day-schools for the deaf in Chicago, however, showed a somewhat unequal division of these pupils into 5 classes, based upon the somewhat conventional and immediately practical test of the status of the pupil in hearing in his schoolwork. Thus, of 174 cases, 55 were classed as totally deaf, 33 as "practically deaf" (hearing only intense and continuous sounds), 53 as possessing "a degree of hearing power" (hearing loud sounds, but not understanding vocal speech),[1] 25 as "deaf for ordinary school conditions" (hearing only words spoken loudly and close to the ear), and 8 as "hearing children temporarily needing special training in articulation."

(3) *Differences between the two ears.* Seashore (16) found decided differences in the acuity of the two ears, differences that were unknown to the S's that exhibited them. Preyer, Fechner, and Bezold have concluded that the left ear tends to be the more acute: Bruner (5), however, as well as Miss Nelson (10), states that in both sexes the right ear is the more acute. Van Biervliet (19) asserts that inequality of hearing of the two ears is a universal fact, that the disparity is such that the poorer ear has a capacity ⅙ less than the better ear, but that the right ear is the better in right-handed, the left in left-handed S's.

For practical purposes in connection with schoolroom tests, the determination of this difference is significant only when the inferiority of one ear is marked; in such cases, pupils should be so seated in the classroom as to bring their 'good' ear toward the teacher.

(4) Seashore's tests (16) indicate that acuity improves with *age* up to 12 years: this improvement is due partly to the development of the ear, but is slightly affected by the growth in ability to understand and to undertake the test.

(5) There are no noticeable *sex* differences, according to Seashore. Lombroso concludes that men's hearing is keener than women's.

---

[1] This class offers hope of improvement in hearing by means of mechanical devices for the intensification of speech.

(6) Seashore says there is "no indication that the *bright children* hear better than the dull children: there may be cases of children who are dull or are accounted dull because they do not hear well, but such cases are not common enough to be revealed clearly by our method, although there may be some indication of them." Nearly every other investigator, however, has found evidence to show that defective hearing has a positively injurious effect upon school-standing.

At Chicago (17) the examination of 5706 pupils with Seashore's audiometer showed that pupils below grade have, at every age, more cases of defect than those at and above grade, and that pupils in the school for backward and troublesome boys have a greater percentage of defect than boys of the same age in other schools. At Copenhagen, Schmiegelow found that, of 79 pupils regarded by the teachers as poorly endowed mentally, 65 per cent. had defective hearing. Similarly, Gellé found 75 per cent. of the defect in the pupils classed as poorest. Permewan, at Liverpool, averaged the distance the watch could be heard by 203 pupils when divided into three groups—bright, average, and dull—and obtained the figures 51 inches, 47.3 inches, and 31.25 inches for these three groups, respectively. Shermunski, at St. Petersburg, by means of the whisper test, found that, among those of normal hearing the ratio of good to poor students was 4.19 to 1; among those whose hearing was but ½ to ⅓ normal, the ratio was 2.6 to 1; among those whose acuity was less than ⅓, the ratio was 1.7 to 1.

(7) *Racial differences.* Bruner's St. Louis Exposition tests (5) indicated that the whites were clearly superior in acuity to the other races tested. The Filipinos had the poorest hearing of those tested.

(8) The simplest disturbance of hearing, if allowed to continue, may lead to serious results. In general, those who test the hearing of school children should note the condition of the ear, as well as test its capacity. Discharge of matter from the ear should be a cause for reference to medical attention.

(9) Children who are partially deaf should be guided, in their adoption of occupation, to avoid callings for which they are unfitted, *e.g.*, medicine, law, music, school-teaching, stenography, telephone or telegraph work, railroad, marine or military service.

(10) The ears of school children should be tested carefully at least once in two years.

(11) Defective hearing, like defective vision, may exist in serious degree and yet pass unnoticed by child, teacher, par-

ents, or friends. Of the 13 per cent. found defective by Sexton, only 3 per cent. were themselves aware of any defect, and only one of them was known to be deaf by his teachers.

NOTES.—In testing the hearing of those who are known to be partially deaf, *e.g.*, such a group as is mentioned in (2) above, the ordinary speech or instrumental tests are not serviceable. Use may, however, be made of the telegraph snapper mentioned in the first method, or of Blake's fork in conjunction with a 'differential tube.'

The noise of the snapper can be heard by the average ear at a distance of some 150 m. or more. In testing the partially deaf *S*, it should be held slightly behind his ear, out of direct view, and employed like the Politzer acoumeter, *i.e.*, by asking *S* to give the number of 'clicks' (2 to 5) that he hears. In very young *S*'s, sufficient indication of hearing may be obtained by watching for reflex starts of the whole body, or of some part of it.

The differential tube, as used by Macmillan and Bruner (9) consists of a tube of soft rubber 100 cm. long, and 4 mm. internal diameter, fitted with hard rubber tips for insertion, one into *S*'s, and one into *E*'s ear. After *S* has been familiarized with the sound of the fork by hearing it with the base applied to his front teeth, his ears are tested one at a time by placing the stem of the sounding fork upon the tube. On account, presumably, of the longer duration of the sound, this device may be used to detect a grade of hearing even lower than that detected by the snapper.

REFERENCES

(1) B. R. Andrews, Auditory tests. *AmJPs*, 15: 1904, 14-56, and 16: 1905, 302-326.

(2) F. Bezold, Schuluntersuchungen über d. kindliche Gehörorgan, Wiesbaden, 1885.

(3) F. Bezold, Funktionelle Prüfung des menschlichen Gehörorgans, 1897.

(4) W. Bingham, The rôle of the tympanic mechanism in audition *PsR*, 14: 1907, 229-243.

(5) F. G. Bruner, The hearing of primitive peoples: an experimenta study of the auditory acuity and the upper limit of hearing of whites Indians, Filipinos, Ainu and African pigmies, N. Y., 1908. (Reprinted from *ArPs(E)*, No. 11.) See especially 55-108.

(6) O. Chrisman, The hearing of children. *PdSe*, 2: 1893, 397-441.

(7) F. Hansen und A. Lehmann, Ueber unwillkürliches Flüstern. Eine kritische u. exp. Untersuchung der sogenannten Gedankenübertragung *PhSd*, 11: 1895, 471-530, especially 494 ff.

(8) D. Macmillan, Some results of hearing-tests of Chicago school children. *Medicine*, April, 1902.

(9) D. Macmillan (and F. G. Bruner), A special report of the Dept. of Child-study and Pedagogic Investigation on children attending the public day-school for the deaf in Chicago. Chicago, 1908. Pp. 88.

(10) Mabel L. Nelson, The difference between men and women in the recognition of color and the perception of sound. *PsR*, 12: 1905, 271-286, especially 280 ff.

(11) W. B. Pillsbury, Methods for the determination of the intensity of sound. *PsMon*, 13: 1910, No. 53, being pp. 5-20 of Rep.Com.Amer. Psych.Assoc. on the Standardizing of Procedure in Exptl. Tests.

(12) A. Politzer, Lehrbuch d. Ohrenheilkunde. Stuttgart, 1893.

(13) Rep. com. on statistics of defective sight and hearing of public school children. *RepComEd*, 1902, ii, 2143-2155.

(14) E. C. Sanford, A course in experimental psychology. Boston, 1895 and 1898. Pp. 449.

(15) C. E. Seashore, An audiometer. *UnIowaSdPs*, 2: 1899, 158-163.

(16) C. E. Seashore, Hearing ability and discriminative sensibility for pitch. *UnIowaSdPs*, 2: 1899, 55-64.

(17) F. W. Smedley, Rept. dept. child-study and pedagogic investigation. 46th An. Rept. Brd. Educ. Chicago, 1899-1900. Also *RepComEd*, 1902, i, 1095-1115.

(18) E. Toulouse, N. Vaschide and H. Piéron, Technique de psych. expérimentale, Paris, 1904. Pp. 330.

(19) J. van Biervliet, L'asymétrie sensorielle. *BuAcRoySci*, 34: Série 3, 1897, 326-366.

(20) Von Conta, Ein neuer Hörmesser. *Archiv. f. Ohrenheilkunde*, 1: 1864, 107-111.

(21) O. Wolf, Sprache und Ohr, Braunschweig, 1871. Also various articles in otological journals, as *Arch. f. Augen u. Ohrenheilkunde*, 3: Abth. 2, 35, and Abth. 1, 125; and *Zeits. f. Ohrenheilkunde*, vol. 20.

(22) A. G. Young, School hygiene. 7th An. Rept. State Brd. Health of Maine. Augusta, 1892. Pp. 399.

TEST 19

Discrimination of pitch.—Like other forms of sensory discrimination, this has been employed to discover the relation between such sensitivity and general intelligence. It has sometimes been employed to estimate musical ability, and it has, of course, general psychological interest. With adults and with children over eight or nine years of age, the test is relatively easy to administer.

APPARATUS.—Set of 11 forks —one standard fork of 435 vd. (double vibrations), and 10 comparison forks, whose rates are 0.5, 1, 2, 3, 5, 8, 12, 17, 23, and 30 vd. above the standard. A resonance box on which the forks may be mounted as they are used (Fig. 52). Soft-tipped hammer for striking the forks.

METHOD.—(a) *Preliminary trials.* Seat S with his back to the table at which E works, and about 1 m. distant. Instruct him as follows: "When I say 'now,' close your eyes and listen carefully to the two tones you will hear; then tell me whether the second tone is higher or lower than the first. Say 'higher' if the second tone seems pitched above the first, 'lower' if below."

On the relative merits of reeds, blown bottles, vibrating strings (like the sonometer) and tuning forks for use in testing pitch discrimination, consult Seashore (8). Some of the results frequently quoted for discrimination of pitch by school children have been procured with the aid of instruments of very questionable accuracy. Thus Gilbert's tone-tester (3), which is constructed from an adjustable reed pitch-pipe, varies as much as five vd. in pitch with variation in the force with which it is blown. Stern's blown-bottles or tone-variators (10) necessitate a constant air-supply, and even then do not yield pitches which correspond to the attached scales. The sonometer (monochord or dichord) employed by Wissler (16) and Spearman (9) is rather unwieldy, not always constant in pitch and tone-color, and complicated by certain mechanical difficulties, while its pitches must be computed at each test in order to guarantee correctness of the assigned vibration-rate values. The instrument is defended, however, by Spearman (9, 243f). Wissler's method of using the monochord, in accordance with which S was obliged to manipulate the instrument, is indefensible, and his results are worthless, as far as pitch discrimination is concerned. The use of tuning forks in which the pitch of the comparison fork is varied by weights or riders (for illustration, see Titchener, 13, i, 68) also necessitates the computation of the pitch differences by counting beats, and both this and the manipulation of the riders is not easy for inexperienced E's. For these reasons, a series of carefully tuned forks, selected for uniformity of tone-color, one for each pitch desired, is here recommended. The present apparatus (Fig. 52) has been described fully by the author in conjunction with Titchener (14).

Seashore (8) objects to the wooden resonance box and to the striking of the forks while on or before a resonator. He recommends holding the fork in the hand, striking it upon a rubber-covered stick and then holding the vibrating prongs before a suspended metal resonator. I have not been able to follow his method without introducing more sources of error than those encountered by the method here proposed.

S's judgment must always be in terms of the second tone. To request him to answer merely "same" or "different," as some investigators, $e.\ g.$, Gilbert, have done, would produce different results, as it is commonly less difficult to judge a difference than to judge the direction of this difference. In this preliminary series, S may be allowed to give the answer "same," if he naturally does so when he is unable to say "higher" or "lower."

S's who are extremely unfamiliar with tones occasionally do not understand what is meant by 'higher' and 'lower,' and, like markedly unmusical or tonally-deaf S's, are apt to search for differences in intensity or duration of the tones instead of for qualitative (pitch) differences. In such an event, E must select two forks that give the maximal difference, and give S a short course of training by striking the forks in succession, and explaining after each pair that the second was higher or lower, as the case may be. If this training is futile, S's discrimination must be extremely poor, and he may be ranked 30+.

Insert firmly in the oak pedestal, with their axes at right angles to the main axis of the resonance box, two forks that afford a large stimulus difference, *e.g.,* the standard and the highest fork (marked 30). Damp one fork, *e. g.,* the nearer one,

FIG. 52.   TUNING FORKS FOR PITCH DISCRIMINATION.

by placing the left forefinger on the tip of one of its prongs: sound the other fork by striking one prong a clean light tap at a point about ¼ the distance from its tip.   Let the fork ring about 2 sec., then damp it by resting the middle finger upon it. After an interval of 2 sec., lift the forefinger, sound the second fork (while the 1st is still damped) and damp it similarly at the end of the 2 sec.   Keep these time relations—2 sec. 1st tone, 2 sec. interval, 2 sec. 2d tone—constant, and strike the forks as uniformly as possible in all tests.[1]   *S* always judges in terms of the second tone.

---

[1]Seashore (8) prescribes 1 sec. for the duration of each tone and 1 sec. for the interval.   The author does not find the argument for these durations conclusive, and has obtained better results in practise from the use of the longer periods.   Seashore's insistence of a tone of very mild intensity—just loud enough to be clearly heard by *S*—is fully justified. *E* should hold the hammer only 4-5 cm. from the forks and strike them a light tap with the thick felt tip of the hammer.

Continue the practise series, in accordance with the general plan for discrimination work described in the opening pages of this chapter, by inserting other comparison forks in place of the "30" fork, giving sometimes the standard, sometimes the comparison stimulus first. This preliminary series is to familiarize S with the general nature of the test, and to afford E a rough notion of the limits of S's discriminative capacity. For most S's, at least 4 or 5 min. should be given to this practise.

(b) *Test proper*. If S's 'critical region' is not yet evident, give a formal series of pairs of stimuli, beginning with a supraliminal difference and passing toward subjective equality, until a difference is reached which S mistakes, or recognizes with difficulty. When, through this procedure or through the practise series, two forks are found that seem to be just barely different to S, keep these forks on the resonance box, and give a series of ten pairs of stimuli—five with the standard first, five with the comparison first, but in an irregular order. In this series S must not be allowed to judge "same," but should be made to guess in case of doubt. He should know that two different forks are being used, but should not know the direction of the differences which he is judging. If he gives 10 correct judgments, select for the next series a comparison fork nearer the standard in pitch; if he gives but 5 or 6 correct answers, and these with difficulty, select a comparison fork farther from the standard. Seek a pair of forks which will yield about 8 right cases in 10. Confirm the difference limen thus secured by trying series with comparison forks just sharper and just flatter than the one in hand. S's discriminative capacity for pitch is indicated by the difference in vibrations between the standard fork and the comparison fork that yielded 80 per cent right answers.

RESULTS AND CONCLUSIONS.—(1) The *difference limen* for highly practiced S's in careful laboratory tests is, for this region of the tonal continuum, about 0.3 vd.[1]

(2) The *pattern distribution* undoubtedly follows a skewed curve like that shown in Fig. 53, which is reported by Seashore

---

[1] For a summary of the work of Delezenne, Seebeck, Preyer, Luft, Meyer and others, consult Titchener (13, Pt. ii., 235 ff).

(8), and represents the records of 781 college students, 296 men and 485 women, for the differences indicated on the abscissa only, and without previous special training. On account of the skewness of the distribution and the absence of any well-defined mode, it is difficult to state what is the average or the modal capacity, but it is evident that more than one-half of those tested had a discrimination of 3 vd. or less. Similarly, Norton's test of 276 college students furnished an average of 6 vd., M.V. 4.2, and mode 3.5 vd., while in two-thirds of the cases the discriminative limit lay between 0 and 4.5 vd.

(3) *Dependence on sex.* According to Seashore, "pitch discrimination does not vary in any constant manner with sex" (8, p. 56). This result is at variance with the conclusions of Wissler (16), Thompson (12) and Burt and Moore (2), all of whom found females superior to males. The results of Wissler and Thompson are less reliable than those of Seashore: those of Burt and Moore deserve more attention. These investigators tested English school children and found for the boys a median of 6.0 vd., for the girls a median of 4.9 vd. They compute that only 21 per cent. of boys have a discrimination exceeding the median discrimination of girls, whereas in adults about 40 per cent. of men have a discrimination exceeding the median of women. The 'sex-difference' in favor of males is, therefore, negative for this test, being—29 per cent. for children and —10 per cent. for adults.[1]

(4) *Dependence on age.* While the relation of pitch discrimination to age is not entirely clear, it would appear to be established that from the time when a child can undertake the test intelligently there is no very great improvement in discrimination with age. Certainly individual differences appear at an early stage: some very young children can discriminate 2 vd. and less with certainty,[2] while others remain virtually

---

[1]To avoid possible confusion it may be explained that the sex-difference, following Burt and Moore, is computed on the basis of the relation of male to female performance. Thus, in the above instance, the median of female performance is, of course, exceeded by 50 per cent. of women, so that male performance is 10 per cent. short of this standard.

[2]Seashore says that "in a bright child with a good ear the physiological limit can be established for all practical purposes as early as the age of five."

tone-deaf throughout life. Thus, the distribution displayed in Table 28[1] is not markedly different from that displayed in Fig. 53. The figures published by Gilbert, whose 'tone-tester' is, as has been remarked, a questionable device, show a minimum of capacity at 6, a rapid improvement to 9 and then a gradual improvement to 19, with seeming losses of capacity at 10 and 15, which are referred by Gilbert to pubertal and other disturbances.[2]

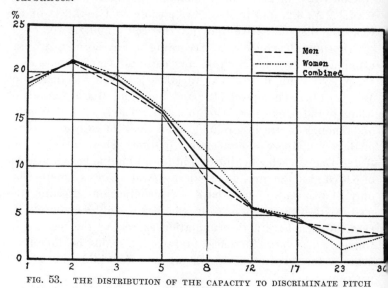

FIG. 53.　THE DISTRIBUTION OF THE CAPACITY TO DISCRIMINATE PITCH (SEASHORE).

TABLE 28

Pitch Discrimination of 167 Children, Aged 6-15 Years (Seashore)

NO.	LIMEN IN VD.	NO.	LIMEN IN VD.
20	1 to 2	21	12 to 30
63	3 " 5	14	Over 30
48	6 " 10		

[1]These results are subject to the qualifications that the figures obtained from those of the children under 9 years of age are not very reliable. In some 30 cases not here included, Seashore was unable to determine a limen within the time at his disposal. Gilbert found only 3 of 130 children who could not discriminate a half-tone, *i. e.*, about 30 vibs. in this region, but as already stated, his *S*'s were asked to judge only difference.

[2]Cf. similar disturbances found by Bryan at 10 and 15 in motor tests.

(5) Seashore found a slight positive correlation between pitch discrimination and *auditory acuity* (Test 18).

(6) (*a*) *Practise* does undoubtedly improve pitch discrimination, but investigators are not in agreement as to the extent of such improvement. It seems evident that its limits are fixed by anatomical and physiological conditions in the ear itself, and that these limiting conditions vary in different individuals. In general, the improvement is not as great as that observed in some other functional capacities, *e.g.*, the discrimination of dual cutaneous impressions (Test 23), and is reached after so short a period of training as to justify the statement that pitch discrimination is an inborn capacity.

Seashore believes that maximal capacity can be attained after very little practise. In 20 days training, he found that some *S*'s exhibited no improvement, while the maximal improvement reported was the reduction of the limen of an unmusical *S* from 30 to 5 vd., and he believes that an ingenious *E* can discover "the proximate physiological threshold to a fair degree of certainty in a well-planned half-hour individual test."

Spearman (9, p. 231) believes that 15 minutes fore-exercise will reduce the pitch-limen by an amount depending very largely upon *S*'s previous general familiarity with tonal experiences. Thus, he computes a reduction for specially practised *S*'s from a limen of 0.5 (before the 'exercise') to 0.3 (after the special exercise), for musicians from 4 to 2 vd., for non-musicians of general culture from 10 to 4 vd., and for European villagers from 30 to 8 vd. These figures would indicate that even a practised musical *S* profits by a preliminary 'warming-up,' and they emphasize the importance of giving such fore-exercise to all *S*'s.

(*b*) Aside from practise in the narrow sense, *i.e.*, special exercise in pitch-discrimination under experimental conditions, we may consider the effect upon discrimination of practise in the wider sense, *i.e.*, of general *musical training*. Seashore is, again, very emphatic in his declaration that individual differences in pitch discrimination are not due principally to musical training, and Spearman's conclusion is that, "though a correspondence really does exist, yet it is not to the smallest degree of the specific character contemplated by those who talk of 'musical sensitivity,'" *i.e.*, by those who refer to pitch discrimination as a test of "musical sensitivity."

To the author, this seems a case of one-way correspondence; an individual who cannot discriminate a half-tone cannot be musical, but an individual who is not musical *may* have a perfectly good discrimination after a little preliminary practise. Given, however, a good natural capacity for discrimination, it is unquestionably true that musical training tends to keep this capacity up to the individual's physiological limit. In testing 50 grammar-school boys for pitch discrimination, the three best discriminators were found to be "taking lessons" on the violin. The author has also shown elsewhere (15) that in the case of an unpractised, unmusical S, it may be possible to reduce the limen very decidedly by working under very constant, favorable conditions—such as duration, intensity, timbre of tones, time-intervals, etc.—but that the slightest modification of these conditions will make discrimination very difficult or impossible.

The fact that the test of pitch discrimination measures a specific capacity, apparently dependent upon the structure of the sense organ and to this extent unaffected by exercises for training, justifies the use of the test, according to Seashore (7 and 8), as a tentative classificatory device. The relation between the difference limen and the educational 'prognosis' of the child is set forth thus:

Below 2 vd. :   May become a musician;

3-8 vd. :   Should have a plain musical education (singing in school may be obligatory) ;

9-17 vd. :   Should have a plain musical education only if special inclination for some kind of music is shown (singing in school should be optional) ;

18 vd. and above: Should have nothing to do with music.

   (7)   *Correlation with intelligence.*   Seashore reported no correlation between pitch discrimination and intelligence, when general intelligence was indicated by class standing and teachers' estimates, and the correlation was worked out by the method of group-classification. Spearman terms this an "ingenious," but somewhat "disseminated" method, and by subjecting Seashore's results to his (Spearman's) methods, obtains from them a correlation index of 0.24 ± 0.07. From his own results, Spearman concludes that general intelligence is correlated with pitch discrimination by the index 0.94, or, as he states, "The [Intellectual] Function is 9 parts out of 10 responsible for success in such a simple act as Discrimination of Pitch."[1] Later, in conjunction with Krueger (4), Spearman computes a correlation of .83 between the capacity for pitch discrimination and the hypothetical "central factor," later identified with "General Ability." Another Englishman, Burt (1), has also reported results which tend to confirm the position of Spearman as against that of Seashore. Burt tested 320 normal children in elementary and preparatory schools and

------

[1]It is but fair to call attention to the fact that Spearman's formulas have been called in question.

obtained corrected coefficients of .52 and .41 for the correlation with the teachers' estimates of intelligence.[1]

The author's test of mental and physical ability in fifty 8th-grade boys included a determination of pitch discrimination, both with the Stern tone-variator and with a monochord. These two tests showed a correlation of .83. The variator test, which was, on the whole, most reliable, showed a correlation of .27 with class standing.

(8) *Other correlations.* Krueger and Spearman report 'raw' correlations between pitch discrimination and both adding and the Ebbinghaus completion test, of .67 and .59, respectively. After the application of the expanding formula (see Ch. 3), these correlations become .80 and .81, respectively. Thus it appears certain to these authors (1, p. 78) that the capacity to discriminate pitch actually exhibits a very high degree of correlation with the seemingly fundamentally different capacities requisite in adding and in the Ebbinghaus test.

Norton (5) compared discrimination of pitch with discrimination of intensity of noise and found a correlation of .39 (median ratio .67).

The author found a correlation of .27 between pitch discrimination and the discrimination of lifted weights.

NOTES.—With reference to musical ability, Stumpf (11, ii., p. 157) proposes as tests: (1) discrimination, (2) ability to sing a note struck on the piano, (3) ability to judge whether one or two tones are present in various fusions, (4) skill in determining the relative pleasantness or unpleasantness of two chords separated by a short pause. M. Meyer denies the validity of the discrimination test for musical ability, and favors a form of test in which *S* is asked to state whether a given bass note does, or does not, form the proper fundamental for a given chord (played in the treble region of the piano). Seashore regards the discrimination test as first and fundamental, and

---

[1] In commenting upon the relatively high correlation found by himself and by Spearman between discrimination of pitch and general intelligence, Burt thinks the relation is to be explained not as a manifestation "of a fundamental identity between Intelligence and General Sensory Discrimination, but rather historically, * * * by the large dependence of the development of intelligence in man upon power of speech, and of this, in turn, upon auditory acuity" (1, p. 132).

mentions as supplementary tests: "the sense of rhythm, and rhythmic action, tonal fusion (consonance and dissonance), auditory imagery, auditory memory, discrimination for intensity of sound, and vocal reproduction of a tone" (8, p. 58).

It is well to inquire of all S's, before the test is administered, whether they are musical or not, whether they play any musical instrument, or sing, or are 'fond' of music. The author has found several instances of children who were quite unable to distinguish pitches several tones apart, but who were compelled by their teachers to take systematic instruction in singing along with other children in the public-school classes.

S's that fail to discriminate the 30 vd. difference may be further tested by a piano to see whether they are absolutely tone-deaf. If time permits, it is of interest to see whether S's with very poor discrimination can be improved by systematic practise.

For best results, the discrimination test should be given individually; if necessary to undertake group tests, it is better to work with small groups of 5 or 6 S's: supply them with pencil and paper; let them number the trials and write their judgments—"H" for higher or "L" for lower—after each number.

REFERENCES

(1) C. Burt, Experimental tests of general intelligence. *BrJPs*, 3: 1909, 94-177.

(2) C. Burt and R. C. Moore, The mental differences between the sexes. *JEPd*, 1: 1912, 273-284, 355-388.

(3) J. A. Gilbert, Experiments on the musical sensitiveness of school children. *SdYalePsLab*, 1: 1893, 80-87.

(4) F. Krueger and C. Spearman, Die Korrelation zwischen verschiedenen geistigen Leistungsfähigkeiten. *ZPs*, 44: 1907, 50-114.

(5) W. W. Norton, The correlation of pitch and intensity discrimination. *PsBu*, 7: 1910, 55-56.

(6) C. E. Seashore, Hearing-ability and discriminative sensibility for pitch. *UnIowaSdPs*, 2: 1899, 55-64.

(7) C. E. Seashore, Suggestions for tests on school children. *Ed. Rev.*, 22: 1901, 59-82.

(8) C. E. Seashore, The measurement of pitch discrimination: a preliminary report. *PsMon*, 13: 1910, No. 53. (Being pp. 21-60 of Rep.Com Amer.Psych.Assoc. on the Standardizing of Procedure in Exptl. Tests.)

(9) C. Spearman, General intelligence objectively determined and measured. *AmJPs*, 15: 1904, 201-293.

(10) L. Stern, Der Tonvariator. *ZPs*, 30: 1902, 422-432.

(11) C. Stumpf, Tonpsychologie. 2 vols., Leipzig, 1883, 1890.

(12) Helen Thompson, The mental traits of sex. Chicago, 1903. Pp. 188

(13) E. B. Titchener, Experimental psychology. Vol. II, Quantitative experiments. New York, 1905.

(14) E. B. Titchener and G. M. Whipple, Tuning forks for pitch discrimination. *AmJPs*, 20: 1909, 279-281.

(15) G. M. Whipple, Studies in pitch discrimination. *AmJPs*, 14: 1903, 553-573.

(16) C. Wissler, The correlation of mental and physical tests. *PsMon*, 3: No. 6, 1901. Pp. 62.

TEST 20

Discrimination of lifted weights.—We may compare two weights either by attending passively to the pressures set up when they are laid upon the skin, or by actively lifting or 'hefting' them. In the first instance, we see illustrated the procedure employed in testing discrimination of pressure (Test 21); in the second, that employed in testing discrimination of weight (in the narrow sense). The latter form of discrimination is always the keener, since to cutaneous pressure, there are added sensations contributed from muscle, joint, and tendon, particularly from the tendon. Because it is the movement of lifting the weight that aids us in estimating its comparative amount, the determination of this form of discriminative capacity is sometimes loosely termed the measurement of the 'muscle sense,' or the 'muscle sense test.'

Of the historical development of this important experiment, this is not the place to speak.[1] Attention is given here merely to the use of the experiment as a comparative test of mental or psychophysical efficiency. The most important investigations of this type are those of Burt (2), Gilbert(5), Thompson (10) and Spearman (8). The test was also included in those administered by the author to 50 8th-grade boys.

---

[1]The stock laboratory experiment is described and its technical aspects are discussed with sufficiently full citations of its literature by Titchener (11, Pt. 1, 115 ff; Pt. II, 265 ff). As Titchener remarks: "This may be regarded as the classical experiment of quantitative psychology. On the psychophysical side, it has engaged a long line of investigators: Weber himself (13), Fechner (3) and Hering, all employed it to test the validity of Weber's Law; and a glance at the current magazines will show that the work begun by them has continued down to the present day. On the psychological side, it has been made by L. J. Martin and G. E. Müller (6) the vehicle of a qualitative analysis of the sensory judgment, the most elaborate and penetrating that we have." The recent work of Brown (1) should be cited in this connection.

Gilbert used weights of the 'cartridge' pattern, similar to those here prescribed.   Ls method was less exact than could have been desired: his school children had simply to sort out all the weights that were the same as the standard, 32 g. As there were but 9 comparison weights, yielding a maximal weight of but 100 g., Gilbert encountered numerous cases (see Table 27) in which no discrimination could be made within this range.

Miss Thompson employed cartridge weights giving a range from 80 to 100 g., and apparently found no difficulty in testing adults with this equipment.

Spearman, similarly, employed cartridge weights with a standard of 1000 grains and with a series of geometrical increments, as proposed by Galton (4, Appendix). It is to be noted that the smallest increment of the original Galton series, 1/100, proved too coarse to test the capacity of some of Spearman's S's, while the largest increment (mentioned by Galton for use with "morbid" cases) proved too fine to test the capacity of others.

A test carried on at Columbia University under the name "perception of weight" or "force of movement" consisted in lifting the handle of a spring dynamometer until it touched a stop. The 'reagent' then made 10 successive attempts to pull the handle to the same point when the stop was removed. It is evident that the results cited by Wissler (15) for this test are not comparable with those obtained by the standard form of the weight-discrimination test.

Van Biervliet (12) used weights of 500, 1000, 1500 and 2000 g. on the 'favored' side of the body in the case of 100 S's that were tested by him for asymmetry in weight. The weights were lifted by a string attached to the index finger, and a simple gradation method was employed to determine the equivalent, for the left side, of a given weight on the right side of the body. The method is too unlike the standard method to admit of comparison of results. It may be stated, however, that the fraction 1/9 which the same author claims to have established as a constant of asymmetry in all sense-departments, was also found in this test, e. g., a weight of 450 g. in the left was equal to a weight of 500 g. in the right hand, etc

APPARATUS.—Blindfold or cardboard screen. Set of dis crimination weights, comprising a standard, 80 g., and 23 com parison weights, yielding the series—80.5, 81, 81.5, 82, 82.5, 83 83.5, 84, 84.5, 85, 86, 87, 88, 89, 90, 92, 94, 96, 98, 100, 105, 110 and 120 g. The weights are of identical size, shape, and color are made of wood to avoid disturbing temperature sensations and are marked inconspicuously (with reversed numbers), so that their weight may be known to E, but not to S.

METHOD.—Follow the general plan of procedure outlined in the introductory pages of this chapter. This plan embodies (1) a preliminary series of trials between the standard and various comparison weights to familiarize S with the condi tions of the test and to indicate to E the probable 'critical region' in which S's limit of capacity will be found, (2) a mor formal determination of this region by systematic procedure from too great to too small a stimulus-difference, (3) the selection from this region of a stimulus-difference (the standard and some single comparison weight) which may be expected to yield about 8 right judgments in 10, and which is given 10 times (5 times with the standard first, 5 with the comparison weight first—the arrangement being determined by chance), and (4) the final confirmation of the difference that yields 8 correct judgments in 10 by the trial of slightly smaller or slightly larger stimulus-differences, as may be required.

In the application of this procedure to weight discrimination, the following suggestions may be made. S should take his position, standing, before the table upon which E has arranged the weights. S's view of the weights must be cut off, either by a well-arranged blindfold or by a horizontal cardboard screen so adjusted that he may lift the weights easily, but may not see them. In each trial, E selects a comparison weight, determines upon the order (standard first or comparison first); then, with a warning 'now,' places the first weight between S's thumb and his first and second fingers: S hefts this weight, replaces it upon the table, when E quickly removes it and substitutes the second weight of the pair under trial, which is, in turn, hefted and replaced by S. The judgment must then be given promptly by S and always in terms of the second weight:—"heavier," "lighter," or "equal."[1] The details of the manner of lifting the weights may, in general, be left to each S. Fechner allowed 1 sec. for raising, 1 sec. for lowering, and 1 sec. for changing the weight, so that each comparison required 5 sec. for its execution.

TREATMENT OF DATA.—The difference between the comparison weight that yields 8 right judgments in 10 and the standard weight, 80 g., affords the absolute difference limen. The fraction formed by taking this difference as the numerator and the standard weight as the denominator affords the relative difference limen, and is the common index of efficiency in the test, since relative capacity is found to be nearly constant for a

---

[1] In the final test of 10 trials with a constant stimulus-difference, it is preferable to ask S to guess in case of an equal judgment; otherwise equal judgments may be recorded as wrong. S should not be permitted to return to the first weight after the second has been lifted.

given individual within a wide range of absolute weights.[1] It is, of course, the constancy of this fraction that constitutes the essential fact of Weber's Law.[2]

RESULTS.—(1) *Normal capacity.* In one place, Weber cites as the average sensible discrimination for lifted weights for four *S's*, 3/32; in another place, he gives 1/40 as the difference just distinguishable by "quite the majority of human beings without any long preliminary practise" (13). Other authorities have placed the norm of performance at 1/17 or at 1/24 (Seashore, 7, p. 96). The author's tests with the apparatus and methods here described indicate for 8th-grade boys an average limen of 4.7 g. (standard 80 g.). The corresponding fraction, 1/17, is presumably close to the average performance for boys of this age. This result is corroborated by Spearman's series, which most nearly resemble the author's in method and apparatus; Spearman quotes 1/15 for a test made under unfavorable conditions and 1/20 for a test made upon older children under favorable conditions. The results reported by Burt for elementary school pupils (threshold 8.75 g., m.v., 1.5, extremes 6 and 16 g.) and for "high-class preparatory school" pupils (threshold 9.3 g., m.v., 1.6, extremes 5 and 11.5 g.), since they are based on a standard of 100 g., indicate a much less fine discrimination, possibly due to differences in the arrangement and execution of his tests.

(2) *Individual differences.* The work of every investigator has shown that the capacity to discriminate lifted weights differs very considerably among normal *S's*, even when age, sex, and practise factors are eliminated. The author found boys in 50 who could discriminate 80 and 81 grams, and one boy who could just discriminate 80 and 97 grams: reference has already been made to the fact that several experimenters

---

[1]Judgments of weight are to some extent affected by the height to which the weights are lifted. In case *S* shows distinct tendencies to lift the weights to unequal heights it may be necessary to arrange some device to regulate the amount of movement. Burt, for example, stretches a tape horizontally between two posts 17.5 cm. above the table.

[2]Recent work, however, raises a strong presumption of doubt as to the applicability of the law over all ranges. See especially Brown and Strong.

have found their weights inadequate to measure the wide differences in capacity that they encountered.

(3) *Dependence on age.* Spearman's tests convinced him "that the younger children were almost equal to the older ones and both were not far from adults," and also that there is no appreciable loss in weight discrimination with the coming of old age. Gilbert, however, as Table 29 shows, found a gradual improvement in discrimination from the 6th to the 13th year. Developmental disturbances appear from 12 to 14, and discrimination apparently does not improve thereafter. The method by which these results were obtained is, as already noted, open to criticism.

TABLE 29.

Dependence of the Discrimination of Lifted Weights on Age (Gilbert).

	6	7	8	9	10	11	12	13	14	15	16	17
Median Limen, Boys	13.0	13.2	12.2	10.2	8.6	10.2	7.6	6.0	5.0	6.2	6.0	6.0
Median Limen, Girls	16.8	13.2	11.0	10.0	9.2	7.6	7.6	5.6	7.2	7.2	6.8	6.4
Per cent over 18 g., Boys	26	36	35	23	12	5	0	5	0	0	2	0
Per cent over 18 g., Girls	49	40	28	17	12	6	6	0	0	0	2	2

(4) *Dependence on sex.* That boys are superior to girls and men to women in the discrimination of lifted weights is conceded by all investigators. This is indicated in most, though not in all of the groups of Table 29. Burt and Moore state (3, p. 366) that "the sex-differences in children and adults appear to be about + 40 per cent."[1] They also have computed the sex-difference discovered by Miss Thompson to amount to + 16 per cent. Miss Thompson is inclined to find the explanation for this difference in the same factors that make men superior in tests of motor ability, though this would not appear of necessity to affect a sensory capacity. Spearman, on the other hand, contends that "the fluctuating differences of sen-

---

[1]The difference, however, is given by these writers in their table, p. 369, as -48 per cent., despite the fact that the same table shows the median for boys to be 8.5 g., for girls 12.5 g. The correct excess percentage over 50 per cent. in favor of the boys is + 48. In other words, 98 per cent. of boys are better than the median girl.

sory discrimination observable in connection with sex at the various stages of growth are chiefly and perhaps altogether a mere consequence of similarly fluctuating differences in intelligence" (8, p. 261).

(5) *Dependence on practise.* The consensus of opinion is that, at least in comparison with many other mental activities, the discrimination of lifted weights is but little affected by practise. Thus, for instance, Biedermann and Loewit (quoted by Spearman) found that a difference limen of 1/21 fell only to 1/23 at the conclusion of a protracted research. It is also true that Fechner, who devoted most heroic amounts of time to weight discrimination, did not thereby attain remarkable capacity, and Brown, who made on a "faithful and devoted observer 75,100 experiments," concludes that there exists in these experiments no influence of practise. It is, nevertheless, possible that in the very early stages of this test, say in the first 15 min., there may be a decided improvement, especially for untrained and unskilled S's. Spearman says that sometimes "the improvement is enormous." In general, then, the effect of practise upon this form of discrimination is very like that for the discrimination of pitch.

(6) *Correlation with intelligence.* Spearman's 'corrected' index of correlation between discrimination of lifted weights and general intelligence (rankings both for 'common-sense' and 'school-cleverness') for 24 village-school children amounted to .43, P.E. .10. In his work with high-class preparatory school pupils, under less desirable test conditions, the correlation was only .12, P.E. .09. Burt concludes from his own tests that the "connection between weight discrimination and intelligence seems to be either zero or even slightly inverse" (about —.10); and that "boys of superior cultural status are hardly as acute in distinguishing fine differences of weight as those of lower social status."[1] The author's tests of 50 school boys showed no correlation with intelligence.

---

[1] The discrepancy between their results causes Spearman to explain his higher correlation as due to a larger amount of practise, saying: "I have found over and over again that practise may greatly increase tendencies to correlate." The reader may compare the similar conclusion reached by Hollingworth, cited in Ch. 2, and the seemingly contradictory conclusion reached by Burt that practise in *successive* sittings tends to have the reverse effect on intelligence correlations, at least in tests whose procedure is readily grasped (2, pp. 123 and 168).

(7) *The feeble-minded.* Unpublished results of tests at Vineland, N. J., show that the feeble-minded fall into three groups with respect to the discrimination of weight—those who are totally unable to perform the test, those who succeed in discriminating by the use of simultaneous, but not of successive lifting, and those who succeed with successive lifting.[1] The results seem further to indicate that when discrimination can be made at all, the difference limen is not much different from that of normal S's.

(8) *Other correlations.* The combined results for his elementary-school and preparatory-school pupils gave Burt the following values for correlations with the discrimination of lifted weights: esthesiometric limen .49, tapping .42, mirror drawing .30, pitch discrimination .29, the spot-pattern test .18, McDougall's dotting test .16, memory-span for words .14, alphabet test .10, comparison of lines .00, sorting cards —.05, dealing cards —.17. The coefficient of reliability for the discrimination test itself was .86 for the elementary and .51 for the preparatory school.

(9) Strong was unable to secure with the weight test indications of the defects clinically demonstrated in manic-depressive insanity.

(10) A *'constant error'* is exhibited by most S's, in that they tend to overestimate the second weight. This, of course, makes it doubly imperative that the procedure be so arranged as to reverse the time-order in half the trials.[2]

REFERENCES

(1) W. Brown, The judgment of difference with special reference to the doctrine of the threshold in the case of lifted weights. Berkeley, 1910. Pp. 71.

(2) C. Burt, Experimental tests of general intelligence. *BrJPs*, 3: 1909, 94-177, especially 120-3.

(3) C. Burt and R. C. Moore, The mental differences between the sexes. *JEPd*, 1: 1912, 223-284, 355-388.

(4) G. T. Fechner, Elemente der Psychophysik, esply. vol. I. (Reprint, Leipzig, 1889, 1907.)

(5) F. Galton, Inquiries into human faculty. New York and London, 1883. (Reprinted in Everyman's Library, No. 263.)

[1] Attention may be called to the fact that in the Binet-Simon scale the test of arrangement of weights, which necessitates discrimination of lifted weights, is a 9-year test.

[2] On other qualitative aspects of this test, see especially Martin and Müller and Brown.

230 SENSORY CAPACITY

(6.) J. A. Gilbert, Researches on the mental and physical development of school children. *SdYalePsLab*, 2 : 1894, 40-100.

(7) Lillie J. Martin and G. E. Müller, Zur Analyse der Unterschiedsempfindlichkeit. Leipzig. 1899.

(8) C. E. Seashore, Elementary experiments in psychology. New York, 1908. Pp. 218. See especially Ch. viii.

(9) C. Spearman, General intelligence objectively determined and measured. *AmJPs*, 15 : 1904, 201-293.

(10) E. K. Strong, Jr., A comparison between experimental data and clinical results in manic-depressive insanity. *AmJPs*, 24 : 1913, 66-98, especially 80-2.

(11) Helen B. Thompson, The mental traits of sex. Chicago, 1903.

(12) E. B. Titchener, Experimental psychology. Vol. II. Quantitative experiments. New York, 1905.

(13) J. J. van Biervliet, L'asymétrie sensorielle. *BuAcRoySci*, 34 : Série iii., 1897, 326-366, especially 330.

(14) E. H. Weber, Der Tastsinn und das Gemeingefühl, in Wagner's Handwörterbuch d. Physiol., vol. 35, 1846. (Reprinted separately 1851.)

(15) F. L. Wells, On the variability of individual judgments. Essays in Philos. and Psych. in Honor of Wm. James. 1908.

(16) C. Wissler, The correlation of mental and physical tests. *PsMon*, 3 : No. 6, 1901. Pp. 62.

TEST 21

Discrimination of pressure.—The determination of the difference limen for pressure, like that for lifted weights (Test 20), has constituted one of the standard psychophysical experiments since the time of E. H. Weber, who utilized it in connection with other tests to establish the well-known law that bears his name. By experimenting with standard weights of 32 oz. and 32 dr., respectively, Weber was able to report that "a difference of the smaller weights is not less accurately distinguished by touch than the same difference of the larger weights."

This test with 'resting weights,' sometimes termed the 'pressure sense' test, appears to have been less frequently used for functional and comparative purposes than the test with 'lifted weights.' Its feasibility depends very largely upon the type of apparatus employed. Differences between the temperature of the weights and that of the skin, variation in the temperature of the weights themselves, in the 'jar' of application, in the area and place of application, etc., must be excluded, since they inevitably produce conflicting results. To obviate these errors and to render the test more simple in execution and more reliable in outcome, the use of a 'pressure-balance,' following the principle adopted by Merkel (7, p. 255) is desirable, if not essential.

Other forms of pressure-balance have been elaborated by Jastrow (5)—figured by Sanford (8, pp. 417-8) and by Titchener (10, pt. ii.)—and by Bolton and Withey (1). The balance here prescribed has been designed by the author (11) to supply in a single relatively simple apparatus a device for determining both the capacity for pressure discrimination and sensitivity to pain (Test 22). It may be regarded as a combination of the principle of Merkel's and of Jastrow's pressure-balances and that of Gilbert's balance-algometer (3).

APPARATUS.—The author's pressure-pain balance (Fig. 54). Cardboard screen with suitable supports. Seconds' pendulum (Fig. 28), or other noiseless device for controlling the time-relations of the test.

FIG. 54. PRESSURE-PAIN BALANCE.

PRELIMINARIES.—Place the balance upon a low table. See that the beam of the instrument moves freely, but comes to rest in a horizontal position when no weights are applied: if necessary, turn the small screw in the tip of the arm inward or outward until this position of rest is secured.

To assure comfort, the instrument should be so placed that S's wrist will come just over the edge of the table; his elbow will not then be forced up into an awkward position, and his hand can lie upon the hand-rest, with the end of his forefinger projecting straight forward between the upper (stationary) and the lower (movable) tip of the balance. Adjust the upper tip so that it is in permanent contact with the center of the finger-nail, but does not touch the skin of the finger.

Arrange the screen to cut off S's view of the apparatus, or, if he be reliable, simply instruct him to close his eyes.

Place the pendulum where its oscillations will be easily visible.

METHOD.—The general plan of procedure is identical with that outlined in the introductory pages of this chapter, and recapitulated in Test 20. To apply this procedure to the test with the pressure-balance, after throwing the lever down to the right, place the weight marked *B-100 g.* on the pin marked *B*, at the outer end of the beam. This weight is not removed during the experiment, and constitutes the standard stimulus. Place upon the second pin, marked *A,* the desired increment weight— any one, or any combination, of the weights marked *A*. To apply a pressure-stimulus, move the release-lever up to the left, so as to depress the support beneath the beam of the balance. To remove the stimulus, move the same lever to the right. The increment-weights are added to the standard stimulus when they rest upon the beam at *A:* they are subtracted from the total pressure, at will, by depressing the increment-weight lever, which lifts them from the beam and allows only the standard stimulus, 100 g., to be operative. Thus, for example, to test the discrimination of 150 g. and 100 g., move the release-lever down to the right, place upon the pin *A* the 30 g. and the 20 g. weights, and upon the pin *B* the 100 g. weight. Give S a warning "now," and 2 sec. later move the release-lever smoothly up to the left: allow the pressure (150 g.) to be felt for 2 sec., then move the release-lever to the right: immediately depress the increment-weight lever, and apply the second stimulus (100 g.) in the same manner, while this lever is held down. S judges, always in terms of the second stimulus, saying "heavier," "lighter," or "equal."[1]

The exact duration of the stimuli and of the interval between them is of less importance than constancy from trial to trial.

To avoid local fatigue, at least 15 sec. should elapse between successive judgments.

E must practise the manipulation of the instrument, and take particular precaution to move the release lever so as to

---

[1]Equal judgments, as previously explained, are to be avoided, if possible, in the final trials with a constant stimulus-difference.

avoid either too sudden application, which produces a disturbing 'bump' and vibration, or too slow application, which
also renders the judgment more difficult.[1]

S must be specially instructed to receive the stimulus passively, so far as his finger is concerned. A downward movement of reaction in the finger tip converts the test, virtually,
into a test of discrimination of lifted weights.[2]

TREATMENT OF DATA.—The calculation of the difference
limen and of the discriminative sensitivity is similar to that in
the preceding test, save, of course, that the standard is now
100, instead of 80 g.

RESULTS.—(1) *Normal capacity.* The discriminative sensitivity for cutaneous pressure depends so largely upon the type
of the instrument (including especially the area of the pressure
stimulus and the manner of application) that the norms obtained with other instruments can not be assumed to hold
good for the present form of balance. Jastrow's results indicate a constant of approximately 1/15, which is nearly equal
to that for lifted weights. Merkel similarly, reports 1/14 for
his pressure balance, though Griffing believes that so fine a
capacity as this must be attributed to the presence of a "muscular reaction of the finger." With a standard of 100 g. applied
to the palm of the left hand, Miss Thompson found limens
ranging from 4 to 20 g.

(2) *Dependence on the standard pressure.* The limen for
the same S, with the same instrument and method, is constant,
at least for stimuli between 50 and 2000 g. (Weber's Law).

(3) *Dependence on the area of stimulation.* According to
Külpe (6, p. 160), the limen is 1/19 to 1/20 with an area of
contact 1 mm. in diameter, but rises to from 1/13 to 1/16 with
an area of contact 7 mm. in diameter.[3] Griffing, however, de-

---

[1] The author has found that some E's, by a curious kind of unconscious
'sympathy,' are inclined to apply the lighter pressure more gently than the
heavier pressure. S's judgments will almost certainly, even without his
knowledge of it, betray the operation of this secondary criterion by exhib-
iting an unexpected and impossible delicacy of discrimination.

[2] If it were not for the awkwardness of the position, it would, perhaps,
be better to insert the finger volar side uppermost, in order more certainly
to ensure against this movement of reaction in unreliable S's.

[3] The tips of the author's balance are 8 mm. in diameter.

clares that "the area of stimulation does not, on the whole, affect the accuracy of discrimination for weights, but individual peculiarities appear in the results obtained."

(4) *"Practise* seems to aid discrimination at places not accustomed to pressure stimuli" (Griffing).

(5) There is no constant *sex* difference (Dehn, 2, and Thompson, 9).

(6) *Dependence on length of interval.* Accuracy of discrimination does not vary appreciably when the interval between application of the two stimuli is prolonged to 10 sec. (Griffing) or even to 30 sec. (Weber).

(7) *Dependence on place stimulated.* For weights of 100 g. or more, there is no appreciable difference in the discrimination of pressure on the palm of the hand, back of the hand, and the volar side of the index finger, though the last is probably more sensitive for very light weights (Griffing).

(8) *Constant error.* Most S's show a tendency, frequently a marked tendency, to overestimate the second weight, *i.e.,* to judge it to be heavier (Griffing).

(9) *Direct judgments.* The impression of the standard stimulus not infrequently becomes so clear that it is carried over from one trial to another, so that, at least with large stimulus-differences, S may pass judgment when the first pressure is applied.

REFERENCES

(1) T. L. Bolton and Donna L. Withey, On the relation of muscle sense to pressure sense. *NebraskaUniv.Studies,* 7 : No. 2, April, 1907, 175-195.

(2) W. Dehn, Vergleichende Prüfung über den Haut- und Geschmacksinn bei Männern u. Frauen verschiedener Stände. Dorpat, 1894.

(3) J. A. Gilbert, Researches upon school children and college students. *UnIowaSdPs,* 1 : 1897, 1-39.

(4) H. Griffing, On sensations from pressure and impact. *PsMon,* 1 : 1895, No. 1, pp. 88. (Also *ColumbiaConPhPsEd,* 4.) Summarized in *PsR,* 2 : 1895, 125-130.

(5) J. Jastrow, On the pressure sense. *AmJPs,* 3 : 1890, 54-6.

(6) O. Külpe, Outlines of Psychology. Eng. tr., London, 1895.

(7) J. Merkel, Die Abhängigkeit zwischen Reiz. u. Empfindung (II). *PhSd,* 5 : 1889, 245.

(8) E. C. Sanford, A course in experimental psychology. Boston, 1895 and 1898. Pp. 449.

(9) Helen B. Thompson, The mental traits of sex. Chicago, 1903. Pp 188.

(10) E. B. Titchener, Experimental psychology. Vol. II, Quantitative experiments. New York, 1905.

(11) G. M. Whipple, New instruments for testing discrimination of brightness and of pressure and sensitivity to pain. *JEdPs*, 1: 1910, 101-106.

TEST 22

Sensitivity to pain.—The determination of the threshold or limen for pain has been conducted for the usual comparative purposes, but it has had, in addition, a peculiar interest for some investigators, because it has been assumed that the limen varies in a characteristic manner with sociological status.

For the determination of the pain limen, use has been made both of electrical and of mechanical stimulation. Electrical stimulation (induction-coil current) has been employed chiefly by the Italian criminologists: pressure stimulation (upon the temple, palm, or finger-tip) has been employed almost exclusively by more recent investigators, and to this form of test our attention will be chiefly confined.

The value of the conclusions that have been so far reached from the use of pain tests is minimized by the difficulties, not always clearly realized, which appear in their administration. These difficulties, like those of most functional tests, arise primarily from the presence of a number of variable factors. The most important of these factors are : (1) dependence of the limen upon S's ability to keep pain distinct both from strong pressure and from simple discomfort, (2) dependence upon the rate of application of the stimulus, including the length of time elapsing between successive applications, (3) dependence upon the place of stimulation, (4) dependence upon the area of the stimulus, (5) dependence upon the general condition and attitude of S, his "good-will," degree of fatigue, amount of practise, etc., (6) dependence upon individual constitutional differences in sensitivity, including sex, age, etc. This last is, of course, the particular dependence sought for in the results; the others, then, constitute disturbing factors and must, accordingly, be eliminated or at least evaluated. Proofs of these several dependences are given below in the discussion of results, but the first and second of them demand consideration here because they determine the choice of apparatus and of method.

(1) The dependence upon S's judgment as to what constitutes pain has been recognized by most investigators as the primary source of difficulty in this test. It is undoubtedly true that pain is a specific sensory quality, distinct from pressure and distinct from unpleasantness; yet it appears equally true that it is often difficult, even for a practised S, to disentangle from his experience the three elements—cutaneous pressure, cutaneous pain, and discomfort. Children, to say the least, are not always competent to make such a differentiation, at least with the method of procedure that has commonly been followed.

To meet this difficulty, some E's have instructed their S's to wait for the distinct appearance of pain; others have asked them to report the first appearance of discomfort—an affective experience that might, or might not, be accompanied by pain, and which can thus scarcely be regarded as a rational index of the real pain limen. Thus MacDonald says (14, 15) "As soon as the subject feels the pressure to be in the *least disagreeable* the amount of pressure is read from the scale . . . . The subject sometimes hesitates to say just when the pressure becomes the least disagreeable, but this is part of the experiment (!). The idea is to approximate as near as possible to the threshold of pain." Griffing, however thinks that there is little liability to error from this source: "It is very easy to tell," he says, "when the pressure begins to be uncomfortable, and the 'imagination' does not seem to be a disturbing factor. Indeed, the pain seems often to come with greater [great?] suddenness." We may wonder then, why he says in the preceding paragraph: "The observers were asked to speak when the instrument began to hurt at all or to be uncomfortable; for it was found that individuals differed as to what they called 'pain.' " Perusal of the literature makes it evident, as these instance illustrate, that some E's have been measuring a "discomfort" limen, other a "pain" limen: doubtless, in either case, some S's reported "discomfort," while others reported real "pain."

Yet again, it appears that schoolboys have sometimes understood th test to be a measure of their endurance of pain, and have manfull asserted: "It doesn't hurt yet" when the pain limen has long been exceeded.

This difficulty of identification of the pain consciousness cannot b wholly avoided, but it may be met, in part by giving S a clear account o the experience he is to report as pain, in part, especially in doubtful case by repeating the test, and in part by comparison of the results of a give S with the established norms for individuals of his age, sex, and type.

(2) Unless the rate of application of the pressure is constant from te to test, there is introduced a serious variable error. Roughly speakin the limen will be higher if the pressure is applied rapidly, lower if it applied slowly. In the use of the ordinary type of pain-tester, e. g.. Cattell's (see 15, p. 1161) or of MacDonald's (13 and 15, pp. 1155-6 algometer, the rate of application of pressure is difficult to control; more over, the rate has never been standardized, so that different investigator have followed different rates.[1] The chief merit of the pain-balance, balance-algometer, as employed by Gilbert as prescribed in the presen test, consists in the guarantee that it affords of a rate of pressure increas that shall be uniform from step to step during each trial and from trial trial.

Again, the time interval between successive trials must be standardize If a given region, say the right temple, has been tested, its sensitivity

---

[1] In illustration, Griffin applied pressure with the Cattell algometer the rate of 1.4 kg. per sec., whereas Gilbert applied pressure with his ow instrument at the rate of 50 g. per sec., or only 1-28 as fast.

increased for some time thereafter, yet some investigators have not hesitated to make a series of 5 or 6 tests upon the same spot in immediate succession. On the other hand, if a given region be subjected to daily tests for several weeks, its sensitivity becomes reduced by a process of inurement. It is clear that both of these sources of error must be avoided in the determination of the limen.

The remaining sources of error are fully illustratd below, and are intelligible without further discussion. When all precautions have been taken, it is probable, however, that the results of this test will be more variable and less reliable than those of other psychophysical tests.[1]

APPARATUS.—The author's (21) pressure-pain balance (Fig. 53). Cardboard screen with suitable supports. Seconds' pendulum (Fig. 28) or other device for time-control. A low table. [Telegraph sounder (Fig. 33), battery and wire.]

PRELIMINARIES.—Arrange the instrument and screen as in Test 21. Place the pendulum within easy range of vision, or, since the time-relations are so important, convert it into an auditory signal by the use of the telegraph sounder and battery (preferably adjusted to give a rather faint click).

METHOD.—Seat S comfortably so that his hand lies upon the hand-rest with his finger-tip between the pressure-tips of the instrument, as described in Test 21. Give him the following instructions: "I want to measure your sensitiveness to pain. There is nothing for you to be afraid of, as I will stop the moment you tell me that you notice any pain. I shall add these weights, one after the other, on the end of this bar, and I want you simply to notice what you feel in your finger-tip. The pressure will grow stronger, bit by bit. It will, perhaps, feel uncomfortable after a time, but never mind that. Wait for the first moment when it really hurts, when you feel a stinging, sore feeling, or a real ache. Do you understand what I mean? I don't want to know *how much* pain you can 'stand' without crying out; I don't want to know when it is simply *uncomfort-*

---

[1]The comments just given make it evident that MacDonald's algometer and Cattell's algometer are inadequate instruments. It follows that the results published by Griffing, Wissler, Swift, MacDonald, and Miss Carman are of doubtful value. Gilbert's results, though obtained by a better instrument, are more uneven than those of any other of the tests that he undertook and, on account of the slow rate of application that he used, are not directly comparable with those obtained by the method outlined below.

able; I want to know when you first notice what you would call *actual pain.*"

Throw the release-lever up to the left, so that the support beneath the balance-beam is permanently depressed: this makes possible a continuous, but cumulative pressure upon the finger.

Apply one of the large brass disc-weights, marked *B-200 g.,* every 2 sec. These discs are placed, *without jar,* upon the pin marked *B,* at the outer end of the beam. Continue application until *S* reports pain, then immediately remove the pressure. The total weight on the beam measures *S*'s pain limen.

Repeat the test with the left forefinger.

VARIATIONS OF METHOD.—(1) Test other fingers of both hands.

(2) Apply the stimulus weights at a slower rate, say once in 4 sec., and note the effect upon the limen.

(3) Substitute a series of pressures for the cumulative, continuous pressure, by using the release-lever as in Test 21, and applying the pressure for 1 sec. only, after each weight is added.

RESULTS.—(1) The short series of tests available with the pressure-pain balance thus far has shown that, with adults, the pain limen may be expected to lie between 1600 and 2400 g., when the method of cumulative pressure is employed.

(2) *Dependence on rate of application.* (*a*) "The rate at which pressure is added influences greatly the amount that is required to produce pain" (Gilbert).

(*b*) Immediate or close repetition of stimulation causes increased sensitivity, but continued practise for several weeks appears to reduce it (Griffing 9).

(3) *Dependence on nature of stimulus.* Sensitivity to pain produced by electrical stimulation bears no noticeable relation to that produced in the same person by pressure stimulation (Griffing, 8).

(4) *Dependence on the area of the stimulus.* "The pain threshold increases with the area of stimulation in an approximately logarithmic proportion" (Griffing, 9). Thus, when Cattell's algometer was applied to the palm of the hand, areas of 10, 30, 90 and 270 sq. mm. were correlated with limens of 1.4, 2.8, 4.4, and 6.6 kg., respectively.[1]

---

[1]The area of the pressure tip in the author's balance is approximately 50 sq. mm.

(5) *Dependence on region.* The regions of the body most sensitive to pain (from pressure stimulation) are those over the frontal and temporal bones, while the heel, the back, and the muscular regions of the leg and the hand are distinctly less sensitive. Illustrative limens obtained by Griffing are:

	KG.		KG.
Top of head	= 1.8	Right thigh, ventral surface	= 4.3
Forehead	= 1.3	Left hand, volar side	= 6.2
Right temple	= 1.0	Right heel, plantar side	= 7.0
Left temple	= 1.3	Back	= 8.0

These differences seem "to depend largely upon the thickness of the skin and the extent of the subcutaneous tissues." The left side of the body is in general somewhat more sensitive than the right. Differences of sensitivity will be found in the several fingers and frequently between corresponding fingers of the two hands.

(6) *Dependence on sex.* Gilbert (7), MacDonald, Dehn (5), Carman (3), Swift (17), and Wissler (22) agree that women are more sensitive to pain than are men. Thompson (18) agrees to this generalization, but adds that there are more men than women with very low thresholds, *i.e.*, that there is greater variability in men. Ottolenghi (16) and Lombroso (11), on the other hand, state that (with electrical stimulation) women are markedly less sensitive than men.

The latter authority believes that this result is confirmed by the experience of surgeons, who find that women possess greater endurance of pain: the popular opinion that women are more sensitive to pain is due, in his view, to the greater tendency of women to express feelings of pain by tears or otherwise; he also believes that their greater longevity may be due partly to their inferior susceptibility to pain.[1]

Typical results are those of Wissler and of Gilbert: the former publishes the following averages (Cattell algometer on the ball of the right thumb); college men, 5.9 kg.; college women, 2.4 kg. Gilbert finds that the average difference between boys and girls is about 400 g., and that this difference increases with age, until at 18 or 19 it becomes over 1 kg. (See Table 30.)

---

[1] Cf. Burt and Moore, The mental differences between the sexes. *JEPd*, 1: 1912, p. 366.

(7) *Dependence on age.* Sensitivity to pain, in general, decreases with age up to 18 or 19 years, and is thenceforth approximately stationary, but Carman and MacDonald both find
irregularities near the period of puberty, and Wissler finds
Seniors more sensitive than Freshmen (as a class). It is probable that the general result is disturbed by a tendency on the
part of younger children to shrink from the test and to report
discomfort rather than pain. Gilbert's results are embodied
in Table 30.[1].

TABLE 30.

Pain Limen, in kg., for about 50 Boys and 50 Girls of each Age (Gilbert).

AGE	6	7	8	9	10	11	12	13	14	15	16	17	18
Boys	1.26	1.38	1.70	1.69	1.67	2.07	2.00	2.05	2.13	2.35	2.70	2.75	2.85
Girls	1.15	0.93	1.18	1.36	1.45	1.56	1.46	1.70	1.82	1.77	1.85	1.93	1.80
Average	1.21	1.16	1.44	1.53	1.56	1.82	1.73	1.88	1.98	2.06	2.28	2.34	2.33

(8) The range of *individual difference* is large in the pain
test. Gilbert, for example, found that the mean variation for
his groups of children ranged from 330 to 820 g.

(9) *Dependence on fatigue.* Swift (17) concludes that
fatigue increases sensitivity to pain, especially in the case of
younger pupils and of girls, because it lowers the tone and increases the irritability of the whole system.[2] Essentially similar results are reported by Vannod (19) and by Vaschide (20).
The former employed an instrument ('algesiometer') analogous
to v. Frey's 'hair-esthesiometer,' and found that the pressure
needed to produce pain fell from 45 g. at 8 a.m. to 39 g. at 10
a.m., and to 29 g. at 12 m., under the influence of school work.
The latter concluded that pain tests warranted him in stating

---

[1]It should be remembered, again, that Gilbert used a very slow rate of
application, so that his results may not be comparable with those obtained
by the methods we have prescribed.

[2]This conclusion is based upon tests before and after a 10 day's vacation
in which the "physical condition" was determined by a dynamometer—
a method already shown to be of doubtful value (Tests 6 and 9). There
is no evidence to indicate that check-tests were made to determine the
range of variations that might have appeared under constant work-con-
ditions.

(1) that mathematics and ancient languages possess an especially high fatigue-value, (2) that written exercises in the form of tests produce intense intellectual fatigue, (3) that afternoon is much more fatiguing than forenoon instruction, and (4) that a forenoon spent outside of the school permits a return, in most cases, to normal sensitivity. On the other hand, Binet (1), who used an adaptation of Blocq's sphygmometer, has come to diametrically opposite conclusions, and asserts that the effect of fatigue is to reduce, not to heighten, pain sensitivity.

(10) *Dependence on mental ability.* Binet and Simon (2, p. 58) declare that the more intelligent children have a lower pain limen. Carman also found that bright boys (teacher's estimate) were more sensitive than dull boys. Swift comes to a similar conclusion by contrasting the best with the poorest fifth of a class, and attributes the result to the more delicate nervous organization of bright children. MacDonald, however, says "there is no necessary relation between intellectual development and pain sensitiveness." "Obtuseness to pain seems to be due more to hardihood in early life."

A curious and somewhat dubious correlation unearthed by Miss Carman is that boys and girls who are especially dull in mathematics are more sensitive on the right than on the left temple.

(11) *The feeble-minded.* Scientific tests of the sensitivity of feeble-minded children present obvious difficulty: it is hard, as we have seen, to induce even normal children to report accurately the first appearance of the pain quality. However, everyday observation, as well as cruder tests of reaction to pinching, burning, etc. (see especially Binet and Simon), would indicate that the feeble-minded, as a class, are markedly insensitive to pain.

(12) *Dependence on sociological condition.* (a) Somewhat inconvincing is the series of conclusions in which MacDonald (12, 14, 15) summarizes his correlations between pain sensitivity and sociological condition; *e.g.,* girls in private schools, who are generally of wealthy parents, are more sensitive than girls in public schools; university women are more sensitive

than washerwomen, but less sensitive than business women; self-educated women are more sensitive than business or university women (owing, perhaps, to overtaxing their nervous systems in the unequal struggle for an education); the non-laboring classes are more sensitive than the laboring classes, etc.[1]

(*b*) The study of the pain sensitivity of the *criminal* is a specific sociological problem that has attracted much attention since the concept of the 'criminal type,' or of the 'instinctive criminal,' was introduced by Lombroso and his school. It has been generally stated that the typical criminal is distinctly less sensitive to pain than the average normal man, and it has frequently been added that the moral insensibility of the criminal is to be largely attributed to this bodily insensibility. These statements are based upon certain experimental tests and upon common observations of the hardihood and general obtusity of the 'typical criminal.' Nevertheless, recent pain measurements indicate that the generalization is too sweeping, and that numerous exceptions occur. It may even be doubted whether the existence of a distinct criminal type has been satisfactorily established.

A general summary of the pain sensitivity of criminals is given by Ellis (6, Section 8). The inadequacy of the algometer test as applied to criminals is discussed briefly by Miss Kellor. A typical exception to the general belief is found in Dawson's conclusion (4) that normal children are less sensitive to pain than delinquent children, probably because many of the delinquents were of neurotic type.

(13) *Miscellaneous correlations* reported by Miss Carman are: boys with light hair and eyes are less sensitive than boys with dark hair and eyes. First-born are more sensitive than second-born boys, and the latter than later-born brothers: the same is true of girls, save on the right temple (!). These conclusions are subject to obvious criticism.

---

[1]The measurements from which these conclusions are drawn were made by different investigators, by an unreliable method, and have been assembled apparently by mere comparison of averages and with no attempt to determine the limit of error; they might, or might not, be confirmed by more exact methods.

REFERENCES

(1) A. Binet, Recherches sur la fatigue intellectuelle scolaire et la mesure qui peut en être faite au moyen de l'esthésiomètre. *AnPs*, 11: 1905, 1-37, especially 32 ff.

(2) A. Binet and T. Simon, L'intelligence des imbéciles. *AnPs*, 15: 1909, 1-147 (section on Le sens de la douleur, 52-8).

(3) Ada Carman, Pain and strength measurements of 1507 school children in Saginaw, Michigan. *AmJPs*, 10: 1899, 392-8.

(4) G. E. Dawson, A study in youthful degeneracy. *PdSe*, 4: 1896, 221-258.

(5) W. Dehn, Vergleichende Prüfung über den Haut- und Geschmacksinn bei Männern u. Frauen verschiedener Stände. Dorpat, 1894.

(6) H. Ellis, The criminal. 3d ed., London, 1907.

(7) J. A. Gilbert, Researches upon school children and college students. *UnIowaSdPs*, 1: 1897, 1-39.

(8) H. Griffing, On individual sensitivity to pain. *PsR*, 3: 1896, 412-5.

(9) H. Griffing, On sensations from pressure and impact. *PsMon*, 1: 1895, No. 1. Pp. 88. (Also *ColumbiaConPhPsEd*, 4.) Summarized in *PsR*, 2: 1895, 125-130.

(10) Frances Kellor, Experimental sociology. N. Y., 1901. Pp. 316.

(11) C. Lombroso, The sensibility of women, brief report, *Mind* n. s. 1: 1892, 582.

(12) A. MacDonald, Sensibility to pain by pressure in the hands of individuals of different classes, sexes and nationalities. *AmJPs*, 6: 1895, 621-2.

(13) A. MacDonald, A temporal algometer. *PsR*, 5: 1898, 408-9.

(14) A. MacDonald, Further measurements of pain. *PsR*, 6: 1899, 168-9.

(15) A. MacDonald, Experimental study of children, etc., reprint chs. 21 and 25, *RepComEd*, 1897-8, Washington, 1899.

(16) S. Ottolenghi, La sensibilité de la femme. *RSci*, Ser. 4, vols. 5: 395, and 6: 698.

(17) E. Swift, Sensibility to pain. *AmJPs*, 11: 1900, 312-7.

(18) Helen B. Thompson, The mental traits of sex. Chicago, 1903. Pp. 188.

(19) Th. Vannod, La fatigue intellectuelle et son influence sur la sensibilité cutanée. *RMdSuisse*, 27: 1896, 21.

(20) N. Vaschide, Les recherches expérimentelles sur la fatigue intellectuelle. *RPh*, 5: 1905, 428.

(21) G. M. Whipple, New instruments for testing discrimination of brightness and of pressure and sensitivity to pain. *JEdPs*, 1: 1910, 101-106.

(22) C. Wissler, The correlation of mental and physical tests. *PsMon*, 3: No. 6, 1901. Pp. 62.

TEST 23

Discrimination of dual cutaneous impressions: Esthesiometric index.—As long ago as 1834, E. H. Weber, a German physiologist, observed (62) that, if two punctiform pressures are applied simultaneously to adjacent points on the skin, a single impression results, whereas, if the pressure points are applied at gradually increased distances, an extent can be discovered which is just sufficient to yield a perception of two points. Weber explored many regions of the skin and published extended tables of measurements of this distance, which has since become known variously as the "limen for duality," or "doubleness," as the "esthesiometric index," the "space threshold," or even, less exactly, as the "index of delicacy of touch."

On account of Weber's explanation of the phenomenon, which was in terms of the supposedly quasi-circular distribution of the end-organs of the sensory nerves, the experiment is often referred to as the test of "sensory circles." On account of the type of instrument employed, it is sometimes termed the "compass test."

Since Weber's time the experiment has become a classic in psychology. Seemingly simple and definite, more careful examination has revealed the fact that the determination of the esthesiometric index is in reality unusually difficult, and that the factors which underlie the observer's judgment are surprisingly varied and subtle.

For differential psychology, the chief interest in the test is found in its use by criminologists to measure "general sensibility," and by several German investigators to measure the degree of fatigue of school children. Physicians, also, have employed it for diagnostic purposes, particularly in connection with pathological conditions of the spinal cord, and it has found special favor in the psychological laboratory, both for its intrinsic interest and for the illustration of various psychophysical methods.

As in the case of other tests, the chief difficulty in the use of the esthesiometric test lies in the presence of numerous sources of error, which must be fully recognized and controlled if valid results are to be secured. In general, it may be said that the esthesiometric limen will depend upon (1) the instrument employed, (2) the region of the body tested, (3) the method of procedure, including the nature of the instructions, (4) the care with which E applies the stimulus and the actual pressure employed, (5) S's degree of fatigue, (6) S's degree of practise, (7) S's ability to attend to the impressions and to make accurate reports, and his general type of judgment, especially in the 'critical region,' and (8) upon a number of other factors, such as S's sex, age, the condition of the circulation in the region tested, etc. The manner in which these factors affect the index will be discussed below.

The instrument employed may be extremely simple, *e.g.*, the set of needles thrust through bits of cardboard, used by Binet in his earlier tests (2) and subsequently improved by Buzenet (14) and by Hill (26), or it may be very complicated and elaborate.

In general, the development of the esthesiometer since Weber's time has been in the direction of greater complexity and delicacy, with a view of affording more adequate control of the separation of the points, of the simultaneity of their application, and of the degree of pressure exerted. It is doubtful whether much of this elaboration is needful: objective equalization of the pressure does not insure subjective equalization, and a careful E is better able to apply the points simultaneously if he works with a relatively simple instrument.

The instruments selected, an improved form of Jastrow's esthesiometer for one method and Hill's needles for another, possess all the requisite features. For other models, consult Blazek (7), Binet (3, 4), and Washburn (60). The models of Ebbinghaus and v. Frey are figured in Zimmermann's catalog. Spearman's instrument is described in Sommer (50) and pictured in use in Schulze (44, p. 67).

Two methods are described, each with the apparatus best adapted to it: the first, or ordinary method follows more closely the regular procedure of the laboratory and is to be considered standard for competent E's and adult or well-trained S's. The second is better adapted for less skillful E's and for use with children or untrained adults.

A. ORDINARY METHOD

APPARATUS.—Jastrow's improved esthesiometer (Fig. 55). Cardboard screen and supports. Pillow or folded towel.

METHOD.—(a) *Preliminary practise.* Seat S comfortably with his right forearm laid horizontally, volar side uppermost, upon a small pillow or folded towel, with the clothing arranged to expose the forearm from elbow to wrist, without impeding the circulation at the elbow.

With ink or pencil mark with a transverse line the region approximately midway between the wrist and the elbow.

Arrange the screen to cut off from S the view of his forearm and of the instrument.

Devote from 2 to 5 min. to a preliminary practise series in order to familiarize S with the test, particularly with the perception of one and of two points.

Instruct all S's, in the same words, substantially as follows: "I'm going to touch your arm with points, something like pencil-points. They won't hurt you at all. You are to give careful attention to what you feel, and tell me if you think I'm touching you with one point or with two points. You will have to watch very carefully. If you feel only one point, say 'one;' if you feel two, say 'two.'"

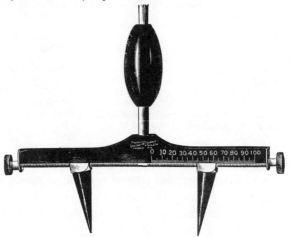

FIG. 55. JASTROW'S IMPROVED ESTHESIOMETER.

Begin with a distinctly supraliminal distance, say 80 mm. After a warning 'ready' signal, bring the instrument down perpendicularly upon the middle of the forearm, parallel with its longitudinal axis, in such a manner that both points make contact simultaneously,[1] and rest by their own weight upon the skin, as the holder is allowed to slide one or two cm. down the stem of the instrument. The several applications should be uniform in duration—about 1.5 sec.

---

[1] This is imperative because the limen for successive stimuli is only $\frac{1}{3}$ to $\frac{1}{4}$ that for simultaneous stimuli.

Next apply two points at 70 mm., then 60 mm., and so on, with occasional trials of one point. Leave an interval of 7 to 10 sec. between trials to allow the preceding sensory disturbance to die away. Keep the applications in the same general region with one point of the compasses below and the other above the transverse line, but do not seek to apply the compass upon exactly the same spots at each trial. When one point is applied, place it in the neighborhood of the spots where one or the other of the two points are being applied. Avoid contact with hairs, which set up tickling sensations, or pressure upon projecting veins or tendons, which will be of a character dissimilar to the normal contact.

This practise should help S to be familiar with, and to distinguish the 'feels' of one point and two points. It will be found that some S's will, nevertheless, occasionally answer "two" when but one point is given. This is the not uncommon *Vexirfehler*, or esthesiometric paradox, which is well recognized as a source of difficulty in esthesiometry. If it proves persistent, it will probably be impossible to determine an exact limen with that particular S unless Method B proves more successful. To avoid it, E may allow S to look at the instrument when one point is resting on the skin and he has just announced "two." Sometimes young S's, who have caught sight of the instrument, may, with childish logic, conclude that there must always be two points because there are two on the instrument. Some investigators never permit S to catch sight of the instrument on this account.

Children who display timidity must be encouraged to adopt a more favorable attitude toward the test.

(b) *Test proper.* Allow S a short rest (during which his arm should be withdrawn from the somewhat constrained position); then proceed from a distinctly supraliminal distance toward the critical region until S judges "one," and follow this with an ascending series from clearly "one" until S judges "two." Average the two determinations for the limen.

B.   METHOD OF CONTRAST

As is explained more fully in the results that follow, the esthesiometric experiment is often rendered difficult, first by the circumstance that a real illusion of two points may arise when one point is applied, and secondly, by the circumstance that there really is no abrupt transition between the clear perception of two points and the clear perception of one point. Rather there exists an intermediate region where neither clearly one nor clearly two is felt. Evidently, these intermediate experiences may be reported by some S's as "one," by others as "two;" and indeed, the same S may shift his criterion of response during the course of an experiment. Various plans have been proposed for circumventing this difficulty. It is possible, for instance, to instruct S to answer "one" unless he feels two quite clearly distinct points (Rivers, Burt). Another plan, which has been followed with some measure of success by

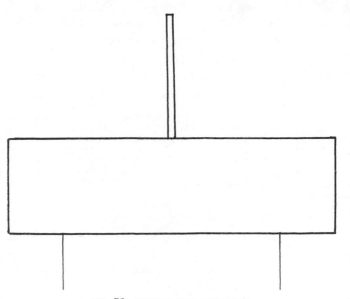

FIG. 56.   NEEDLE ESTHESIOMETER.

Wagner, Binet, Martin and others, consists in applying the stimuli in such an order as to produce as much contrast as possible between the feel of one point and the feel of two points. If, in addition, the one-point stimuli and the two-point stimuli are applied with equal frequency, any tendency of S to favor the one or the other judgment is much reduced.

To make the rapid changes that are necessitated by this method in the distances separating the compass-points it is better to use special apparatus, i.e., apparatus that will provide a series of different fixed distances, as has been recommended by Binet and Henri, Meumann, Buzenet, Hill and others.

APPARATUS.—Set of 14 needle esthesiometers (Fig. 56), after Binet and Buzenet, modified by Hill. These afford 13 separations from 10 to 70 mm. by 5 mm. steps and one single point (zero separation).

METHOD.—Preliminary arrangement of S's arm, screen, etc., and instructions to S, as in Method A.

Show S the apparatus, so that he knows that either one point or two points may be applied. Hold the esthesiometers by the metal handle; apply them gently and evenly to the skin and let them rest by their own weight, merely steadying them by the handle. Work downward from the widest separation toward the threshold, using the instruments always in pairs containing one double point and the single point, *e.g.*, 70 and 0, 65 and 0, 60 and 0, etc., in other words, so that one point is applied as often as two points, and so that clearly one and clearly two are frequently perceived in close succession. Apply each contrasting pair two or three times in irregular order, and reduce the separation of the double-point stimulus until a separation is reached at which S calls the two points "one."

This separation is now applied, together with the zero separation, in a series of 20 trials (10 zeroes and 10 doubles arranged in chance order). If S makes more than two errors with the 10 double points, try a new set of 20 applications with the next larger separation of the two points; if but one error or no errors, a set with the next smaller separation of the two points. The threshold may be taken as the distance at which two errors are first made with the ten double points, unless subsequent better records with lesser separations show that these errors were due to a temporary lapse of attention.

VARIATIONS OF METHOD.—Test other regions of the body. Use a transverse application on the forearm. Compare the sensitivity before and after periods of rest or of fatiguing work. Test the acquisition of practise and its transfer to symmetrical and adjacent portions of the body. Try the method advocated by Rivers for uncultured S's of informing S after each response whether he is right or wrong.

RESULTS AND CONCLUSIONS.[1]—(1) *Dependence on sex.* Wissler (63) could discover no sex differences in cutaneous discrimination of dual pressure, but Miss Thompson (53), despite some acknowledged difficulties in the administration of her test, concludes that "women have a somewhat finer discrimination in the crosswise direction, and a decidedly finer discrimination in the lengthwise direction." Actual figures cited are 20 and 65 mm. for women and 35 and 75 mm. for men, in the transverse and longitudinal directions, respectively.

Burt and Moore (13) figure the differences found by Miss Thompson as showing an inferiority of the men of 32 per cent. in lengthwise and 7 per cent. in the transverse direction (that is, 32 per cent. of the women surpass the median of men, etc.). Burt further cites the work of Galton, who tested over 1200 persons on the nape of the neck and found for the men an average of 14.04 (range 6 to 19) and for the women 13.70 (range 4 to 15). Again, Burt and Moore declare that the sex difference in esthesiometry is the largest they have discovered in any mental test, being so large (—47.7 per cent. in one group of school children and —37.4 per cent. in another, in terms of proportion of males exceeding the median of females) that the curves for the two sexes scarcely overlap.[2] They regard this difference, therefore, as peculiarly striking and undoubtedly innate. Lombroso seems to be the only writer of importance whose results disagree with this conclusion, and his technique was so primitive as to throw decided doubt upon the validity of his results.

(2) *Dependence on age.* There is fair agreement, especially among the earlier investigators (see *e.g.*, Czermak, 15) that children have a greater sensitivity than adults. Similarly, Wissler found Seniors inferior to themselves as Freshmen. In regions where the sensitivity is poor, the difference between

---

[1]In reporting these results, it may be stated that many of them have been obtained by methods that are open to criticism, particularly in that suitable precautions have been wanting to control or to eliminate the numerous disturbing factors already mentioned.

[2]As a matter of fact, a larger sex difference was found for lifted weights. See Test 20, Result 4.

children and adults is quite distinct, *e.g.*, a limen of 67 mm. on the thigh of an adult in contrast to 35 mm. upon the same region in a boy of 12.

The usual explanation that the child has a greater number of nerve endings within the same-sized area is probably only a partial explanation, as it has been computed that the child's sensitivity is out of all proportion to the differences in dimensions here concerned. A contributory factor is doubtless to be found in the fact that the child's skin is thinner and more tender, so that a given impact produces a sharper sensory experience.

Griesbach (20), who found no difference between children from 11 years up to 19, is practically the only investigator who has not found the child more sensitive than the adult, but Griesbach's figures can not be accepted without misgivings.

(3) *Dependence on region.* (*a*) Table 31, which is derived from Weber's original results, gives an idea of the topographic distribution of sensitivity.

TABLE 31.

Topography of Esthesiometric Sensitivity (*Weber*)

REGION	L'MEN IN MM.	REGION	LIMEN IN MM.
Tip of the tongue	1.1	Forehead	22.5
Tip of the fingers	2.2	Back of hand	31.5
Mucous membrane of the lips	4.5	Forearm	40.5
End of the nose	6.7	Back	54.1
Cheek	11.2	Thigh	67.6

An empirical generalization, known as Vierordt's Law (57, p. 298), summarizes these differences in sensitivity, especially of the limbs and head, by the statement that the delicacy of discrimination of two regions on the skin of a portion of the body that is moved as a whole is proportional to the average distance of these regions from their common axis of rotation.[1] In illustration, if the discriminative sensitivity of the tip of the shoulder (acromion) be taken at 100, then that of the upper

[1]Somewhat analogously, Krohn (32) cites an instance in which a man whose arm had been held immovable in a plaster cast for three months exhibited marked decrease of sensitivity of that arm shortly after the cast had been removed.

arm is 151, of the forearm 272, hand 659, thumb 2417, middle finger 2582.

Burt's results (11) for 13-year-old school boys on the volar side of the forearm were for an Oxford elementary school, average 36.2 mm., M.V. 9.0, range 19-58.3, and for a high-class preparatory school, average 38.9 mm., M.V. 11.0, range 12.5-63.7.

(*b*) Van Biervliet (54), who asserts that in many sense-departments the favored *side of the body* is superior to the other side by the fraction ⅑, publishes tables which indicate that the same constant applies in esthesiometry.

(4) *Dependence on time of day.* A comparison of the sensitivity at different periods of the day, in the search for a diurnal rhythm, is, of course, complicated by the presence of fatigue (see the following paragraph), and doubtless by individual differences as well. Schmey (43) believes sensitivity to be less at night than in the morning. Adsersen (1), however, asserts that sensitivity is lowest in the morning, begins to improve at about 11, reaches a maximum from 3 to 7, and thence decreases. By comparison, he shows that this rhythm coincides very closely with the diurnal curve of bodily temperature, and he therefore argues that the esthesiometric fluctuations are indices of physiological changes common to the diurnal rhythm. Tawney's work (51), on the other hand, leads one to believe that the limen undergoes, in many *S*'s, such irregular fluctuations that it is impossible to find a limen that is constant for half an hour at a time.

(5) *Dependence on fatigue.* The effect of fatigue upon the limen forms the chief source of interest in connection with the esthesiometric test. Griesbach (20) was the first to make extended use of the test in the examination of school children. His amazingly uniform and definite results, when taken at their face value, indicate unequivocally that the method is of value and importance in the detection of the fatigue induced by school work. They have, moreover, been confirmed more or less thoroughly by Binet (6b), Blazek (7), Bonoff (10), Heller, Schuyten (46), Vannod (56), and Wagner (59). On the other hand, they have been controverted with equal emphasis by Bolton (8, 9), Germann (18), Kraepelin (31), Leuba (34), and Ritter

(40), while recent work by Miss Martin has given negative results. Investigations of fatigue by means of the esthesiometric test have also been made of late by Ferrai in Italy, Sakaki (42) in Japan, Ley in Belgium, Michotte in Belgium, and Noikow (38) in Bulgaria.[1]

Griesbach argues that fatigue reduces the power of sustained attention and that this in turn reduces the cutaneous sensitivity. He appears to believe that he is the first to have discovered this relation, but it may be noted that Weber, himself, had cautioned his readers to avoid fatigue if valid results were to be secured, that Schmey, in 1884, had demonstrated that the fatigue of the arm by calisthenic exercises reduced sensitivity, and that Stanley Hall (23), in 1879, had commented on the variability of the results obtained from Laura Bridgman, and had expressed the hope that "a curve of fatigue may be obtained by which some approximate comparison with the fatigue of a nerve-muscle preparation may be made." Griesbach worked on the glabella, cheek-bone, tip of the nose, under lip, ball of the thumb, and tip of the index-finger, and tested pupils before and after various kinds of school work, on Sundays, holidays, at the end of vacations, etc. A single example will suffice: a girl of 14 had a limen on the glabella of 5 mm. at 7 a. m., but this increased to 12.5 mm. at 12, noon, after a morning at school, whereas on Sunday her limen was but 3.5 mm. Griesbach concludes his memoir with a strong plea against overwork, and asserts that no schoolboy can meet in full the demands of present-day higher education without endangering his health (20, p. 88).

So far from being silenced by the critics of his method, Griesbach has subsequently published (1910) results which, he claims, demonstrate that esthesiometrical measurements of fatigue are adequate to explain the functions and localization of brain centers employed in various activities, and adduces such conclusions as: fatigue induced by mental or bodily activity does not affect both hemispheres alike. In mental work, especially linguistic and algebraical, different values afforded by the esthesiometer show that the left hemisphere is predominantly engaged in right-handed, the right in left-handed persons, while in bodily exertion, the right hemisphere is predominantly engaged in both right and left-handed persons, etc. So far as we are aware, no other investigator has confirmed these findings, nor has anyone even attempted to use the esthesiometric method for such precise inferential work.

Blazek divides pupils into three types: (1) those who possess ability, who work industriously and attentively, and thus exhibit distinct and progressive fatigue curves, (2) those who work intermittently, and whose curve is therefore broken by recuperative periods, (3) those whose curve is approximately a straight line. The fatigue curve, therefore, depends in the main upon the type of worker, but the individuality of the teacher and the subject-matter in hand are also determining influences. He concludes that more than half the pupils work irregularly and thus save themselves in part from overwork. He would recommend 4 subjects daily, of 45 min. each, with 15 min. rest periods between each subject.

Wagner says that the Griesbach method is a valuable adjunct for the study of fatigue. Afternoon instruction is practically valueless peda-

---

[1] For further discussion of the value of the method, consult Gineff (19), Neumann (37, vol. ii., 89-94, 107-110) and the recent monograph of Offner (39, pp. 31-38). Griesbach's rejoinder to his critics (21) should also be consulted.

gogically. Play and gymnastics are sources of fatigue to many pupils, and should be relegated to the close of instruction or to the afternoon. If the fatigue-value of mathematics be placed at 100, other subjects may be rated thus: Latin 91, gymnastics 90, geography and history 85, French and German 82, nature-study 80, drawing and religion 77.

Binet summarizes the results obtained by himself, and by a group of teachers who worked under his direction, by declaring that "intellectual fatigue is manifested by a reduction of sensitivity, measurable on the back of the hand: this reduction is revealed by fewer judgments of 'two' for smaller distances (0.5 to 1.5 cm.), is more pronounced for girls than for boys, and is to be attributed to an actual reduction of tactual sensitivity itself, not to a mere relaxation of attention" (6 b, p. 29). It is to be noted, however. that this conclusion is based upon the 'lump' results obtained from groups of school children: analysis shows that, in some groups at least, less than half of the pupils (e. g., 31 of 75), gave evidence of fatigue in this way. In this investigation Binet employed an ingenious, though perhaps debatable method for measuring separately skin sensitivity and attention. The percentage of the answers "two" for separations 5, 10 and 15 mm. was used to indicate delicacy of touch, the percentage of the answers "one" for separations 20, 25 and 30 mm. to indicate relaxation of attention. His data show, after fatiguing school work, a reduction in the first, but no change in the second group of answers, and hence he argues that the fatigue of the school work reduced the sensitivity of the skin, but did not relax attention. It should be added that Binet claims no more than to have demonstrated the feasibility of the method for group tests.

Schuyten at first condemned the esthesiometric method (45), but later (46) he found to his surprise that it worked satisfactorily. He used groups of 5 selected pupils.

Ritter tested himself at intervals for two years, but could get no evidence of fatigue by the esthesiometer.

Bolton says the limen is so hard to determine that it cannot be satisfactorily accomplished in a single sitting. In his tests, severe mental work of two hours duration did not produce a measurable change in the index

Germann, after making 2450 trials on a single S, could not discover any relation between fatigue and the limen.

Leuba admits that fatigue affects the limen, but says that it is only one of a great many factors. He was unable to draw any general inductions concerning fatigue, even when the results for three days of severe mental work were contrasted with those for three days of rest.

Meumann (37, vol. 2, 90 ff), similarly, admits that the tendency of fatigue is to heighten the limen, but protests vigorously that the relation is but indirect, and so complicated by numerous little-known factors that the numerical expression of shifts in the limen can in no wise be regarded as a measure of fatigue. ("Wir haben in der Erhöhung der Raumschwelle durch die Ermüdung *nur ein objectives Symptom derselben, aber kein Messung.*")

Kraepelin, however, declares flatly that investigations that embody measurements of fatigue by the use of the esthesiometer are "all in the air" (*stehen einfach in der Luft*), and are nothing but the unintentional expression of the preconceived opinions of the investigators.

(6) *Dependence on practise.* The effect of practise was studied by Czermak (15), as early as 1855, in his investiga

tion of the sensitivity of the blind, was measured more care-fully by Volkmann (58), and confirmed later in particular by Dresslar (16). From these investigations, it would appear that the practise-effect is visible within two hours, and may be pushed to unexpected lengths by continued work; thus, Dress-lar reports one S, who started with a limen of 29 mm., re-duced this to 21 mm. in the first week, to 10 mm. the second week, 5.5 mm. the third week, and 2.8 mm. the fourth week—a net reduction, then, to approximately ¹⁄₁₀ of the original figure. This practise-effect is, however, rapidly lost, being reduced very definitely within 8 days and completely lost within a month. The practise-effect is said to appear much more rap-idly on fingers, hands, and other exposed parts, than on the back and other relatively inaccessible and immobile regions. Both Volkmann and Dresslar submit evidence to show that this 'education' is subject to *transfer to symmetrical regions,* though not to regions adjacent to the one on which it was effected.

In seeking an explanation for the effect of practise, we are met with the fact that other investigators have not confirmed the results just cited. Camerer, in his lengthy series, did not find such extensive practise-effects. Foucault (17) hesitates to commit himself on the effect of practise on the actual limen. Tawney (52) found his work so vitiated by *Vexirfehler* and by auto-suggestion in general that he was unable, for some S's, to establish any constant limen. Both Tawney and Henri (24, b) deny that the influence of practise, when established, is confined to symmetrical regions of the body. Solomons (49) asserts that the practise-effect is rapid if S is informed of his errors, but practically non-existent if he is not—a principle which, if confirmed, may explain the disagreements just cited.

The explanation of the process of 'education' in this test is found by some writers to lie in certain peripheral processes—not necessarily in anatomical, since the practise is too rapid to admit of that, but rather in local physiological processes. Others, *e. g.,* Judd (28) and Solomons, believe that the education is essentially a 'central,' or psychological, process—an improvement in judgment due to the learning of new asso-ciations.

The low *threshold of the blind,* reported by Goltz, Gärtner, Heller, Miss Washburn (60), Hall (23), Jastrow (27), and others, is to be deemed a special example of practise, and does not imply the presence of excep-tional sensitivity or special peripheral delicacy. Helen Keller (27) has a limen of 1.5 mm. on the tip of the left forefinger, and 3-4 mm. on the palm of the hand, which is smaller than that of the average S. Laura Bridgman (23) is credited with a limen of 0.7 mm. on the right forefinger, and her general sensitivity of touch, according to Hall, was "from two to three times as great as that of an ordinary person."

Foucault appears to be the only investigator who has not found the blind more sensitive.

(7) *Dependence on S's type of judgment.* Mention has already been made of the difficulty arising in esthesiometry owing to the different ways in which the perceptions intermediary between "one" and "two" may be reported.[1] Binet, for example, classified S's as *simplistes, distraits* or *interpreteurs,* according to their mode of reporting these perceptions. But the most recent and valued critique of this field, that of Foucault, goes yet farther, and distinguishes eight possible perceptions and four types of S.

The eight different possible perceptions are:

(1) a single distinct point, without area,

(2) a clean-cut small circular area, with often a center where the pressure is stronger,

(3) like the 2d, but larger, though still circular,

(4) an elongated area of pressure, like a line, an oval, an ellipse, etc.,

(5) like the 4th, but with two points within it where the pressure is greater than in the region between them,

(6) two circular areas overlapping one another,

(7) two circular areas tangent to one another,

(8) two circles of pressure separated by a between-lying area of no pressure.

According to the manner in which they 'assess' or report these eight possible perceptions, there are, according to Foucault, four different types of S's:

(1) the 'rational' S, who reports only 7 and 8 (of the perceptions) as "two," 1 and 2 as "one," and the others as "intermediate,"

(2) the 'prudent' S, who reports 1 to 6 as "one" and 7-8 as "two,"

(3) the 'bold' (*hardi*) S, who reports 1 to 4 as "one," and 5 to 8 as "two,"

(4) the 'imprudent' S, who reports anything save 1 and 2 as "two."

These types are found in actual work, and they may shift as the experiment progresses.

Foucault's way out of this complexity of issues [Binet is evidently quite right in saying that "esthesiometry ceases to be a simple little exercise"] is to train all S's into the first, or rational type by giving them frequently, with knowledge, the feel of one point and two points and by coaching them to report "intermediate" whenever they experience Perceptions 3 to 6. He assures us that even young children can submit to this training, so that it does become possible, after all, to measure the threshold. In substance, it will be seen that his plan virtually means th

---

[1]The fact is, of course, that all the conditions of the experiment, and particularly the instructions and the sight of the apparatus conspire to force upon S what the psychologist calls the "stimulus error." S is constrained to answer either "one point" or "two points." Ideally, he should perhaps, never see the apparatus, and be instructed to report accurately and in detail just precisely what sort of cutaneous experience he senses.

instruction of S to answer "two" when the two areas of contact do not seem to overlap one another. The frequent giving of two points means, of course, of two supraliminally distant points. Only series of stimuli in which such distances frequently occur can be called 'normal' or standard series, in Foucault's judgment. All other series are abnormal or misleading (*trompeuse*), and tend, in particular, to develop the paradoxical error—a statement that coincides well with the results of Solomons and of Tawney, both in the latter's own investigation (52) and in that undertaken with Henri (25). These writers have laid emphasis upon the role played by suggestion in esthesiometry. They were able, for example, by arranging conditions suitably, to induce practised and reliable S's to judge "one" when two points were given and "two" when one point was given, and with considerable uniformity.[1]

(8) *Dependence on circulation of the blood.* The condition of the circulation in the region under test affects the limen. It appears from the studies of Brown-Sequard, Schmey, and others, that arterial hyperemia increases cutaneous sensitivity, whereas anemia, or venous hyperemia, or decided cold, reduces sensitivity. Excessive stretching of the skin decreases sensitivity, as does the use of narcotics.

(9) *Corrrelation with intelligence.* Schuyten seems to be the only investigator to discover a distinct positive correlation with mental ability. His very rapid tests (one per minute) on the cheeks of Antwerp pupils led him to conclude that the intelligent group had a decidedly acuter average threshold than the unintelligent group, and again he claims by this method to have been able to detect abnormal children readily and to classify a group of 60 children approximately as to mental power. Binet (2) found his intelligent superior to his unintelligent group at the first trial, but the difference soon lessened as the boys became adapted to the test. On the other hand, the rather crude test of Wissler (63) revealed no correlation with the class standing of university students, and the more careful work of Burt with Oxford school children gave the non-significant correlations of .13 and —.06, with large probable errors.

---

[1]These observations, which might be repeated in many other fields, show how essential it is to work methodically and under constant conditions. The extent to which S's discrimination is affected by his attitude toward the experiment, and by his manner of judging in general, has led Binet to declare (5) that the "compass test" measures "tactual intelligence" rather than the fineness of touch itself.

Van Biervliet (55) used the compass test to secure a measure of intelligence, not by the limen itself, but by its mean variation, on the assumption that this latter measure is, in almost any test, the real index of intelligent work. His figures give the 10 most intelligent of 300 university students an index of 17.7, and the 10 least intelligent an index of 27.6. His index, however, as Binet (6a) has pointed out, is a rather dubious device.

(10) As might be expected, the use of the test for the examination of *abnormal children,* criminals, truants, etc., is beset with difficulty, because it exacts prolonged, sustained attention and interest (Kellor, 29; Kelly, 30). Simon (48) was unable to test the lowest grade of children in a school for the feeble-minded, but obtained results from the less defective types which indicated that their sensitivity was less than that of normal children. Whether the difference is reducible to differences in cutaneous sensitivity itself, or to differences in ability to control the attention and understand directions, is not clear. Burt found one congenital imbecile with a very low limen.

(11) *Dependence on cultural status.* Burt (11, 119-120) has assembled the results obtained by Rivers upon the Todas and by McDougall upon Papuans and Dayaks, and by joining them with other data by McDougall and himself upon various social classes in England, and making certain allowances for differences in method, has come to the conclusion that "the groups would fall in an order showing a complete inverse correspondence with that of cultural development," *i.e.,* "the least intellectual group tend in average tactile discrimination to be the more acute; while among individuals of the same cultural class, any apparent positive correlation between tactile discrimination and intelligence is probably illusory and due to the interpretative quickness of the more intelligent."

(12) *Other correlations.* Burt's tests showed a coefficient of reliability in the neighborhood of .74, but those of Krüger and Spearman of only .42, and it was partly for this reason, perhaps, that these latter investigators were unable to establish any correlation between the limen for twoness and capacity

in pitch discrimination, in addition, in committing to memory
or in the Ebbinghaus completion method.

REFERENCES

(1) H. Adsersen, Eine aesthesiometrische Untersuchung. *ZScGd*, 27:
1904, 540-3.

(2) A. Binet, Attention et adaptation. *AnPs*, 6: 1899 (1900), 248-404.

(3) A. Binet, (*a*) Un nouvel esthésiomètre. *AnPs*, 7: 1900 (1901),
231-9; (*b*) Technique de l'esthésiomètre, 240-8.

(4) A. Binet, La mesure de la sensibilité, *AnPs*, 9: 1902 (1903) 79-128.
Also five other articles on esthesiometry, pp. 129-252.

(5) A. Binet, De la sensation à l'intelligence. *RPhF*, 56: 1903, 450-
467, and 592-618.

(6) A. Binet, (*a*) A propos de la mesure de l'intelligence. *AnPs*, 11:
1905, 69-82. (*b*) Recherches sur la fatigue intellectuelle scolaire et la
mesure qui peut en être faite au moyen de l'esthésiomètre. *Ibid.*, 1-37.
(Also reported as Expériences sur la mesure de la fatigue intellectuelle
scolaire au moyen du sens du toucher. *BuSocEtPsEnf*, 5: 1905, 628-632,
644-652.)

(7) B. Blazek, Ermüdungsmessen mit dem Federaesthesiometer an
Schülern des Franz-Joseph-Gymnasiums in Lemberg. *ZPdPs*, 1: 1899,
311-325.

(8) T. Bolton, The reliability of certain methods for measuring the
degree of fatigue in school children. *PsR*, 7: 1900, 136-7.

(9) T. Bolton, Ueber die Beziehungen zwischen Ermüdung, Raumsinn
der Haut und Muskelleistung. *PsArb*, 4: 1902, 175-234.

(10) N. Bonoff, Étude médico-pédagogique sur l'esthésiométrie et la
simulation a l'école. *InMagScHyg*, 4: 1907-8, 384-394.

(11) C. Burt. Experimental tests of general intelligence. *BrJPs*, 3:
1909, 94-177.

(12) C. Burt, Experimental tests of the higher mental processes and
their relation to general intelligence. *JEPd*, 1: 1911, 93-112.

(13) C. Burt and R. C. Moore, The mental differences between the
sexes. *JEPd*, 1: 1912, 273-284, 355-388.

(14) Buzenet, Mesure de la sensibilité tactile. *BuSocEtPsEnf*, 5: 1905,
633-4.

(15) J. N. Czermak, (*a*) Beiträge zur Physiologie des Tastsinnes.
Sitzungsber. d. k. Akad. d. Wiss. (Wien), math.-nat. Kl., Abt. 1, 15: 1855,
482-521. (*b*) Weitere Beiträge, etc. *Ibid.*, 17: 1855, 577-600.

(16) F. B. Dresslar, Studies in the psychology of touch. *AmJPs*, 6:
1894, 313-368.

(17) M. Foucault, L'illusion paradoxale et la seuil de Weber. Mont-
pellier, 1910. Pp. 211. (Critical review by A. Binet. *AnPs*, 17: 1911,
420-7.)

(18) G. Germann, On the invalidity of the esthesiometric method as a
measure of mental fatigue. *PsR*, 6: 1899, 599-605.

(19) D. Gineff, Prüfung der Methoden zur Messung geistiger Ermüdung. Zürich, 1899. Pp. 68.

(20) H. Griesbach, Energetik u. Hygiene des Nerven-Systems in der
Schule. München u. Leipzig, 1895. Pp. 97. Also published as Ueber
Beziehungen zwischen geistiger Ermüdung u. Empfindungsvermögen der
Haut. *Arch. f. Hygiene*, 24: 124.

(21) H. Griesbach, Weitere Untersuchungen über Beziehungen zwischen
geistiger Ermüdung u. Hautsensibilität. *InMagScHyg*, 1: 1905, 317-417.

260   SENSORY CAPACITY

(22) H. Griesbach, Hirnlokalisation und Ermüdung. (Schlussfolgerungen des Autors aus *ArGsPhg*, 131: 1910, in *InMagScHyg*, 6: 1910, 174.)

(23) G. S. Hall, Laura Bridgman. *Mind*, 4: 1879, 149-172, especially 160 ff.

(24) V. Henri, (*a*) Revue générale sur le sens du lieu de la peau. *AnPs*, 2: 1895 (1896), 295-362 (with bibliography). (*b*) Ueber die Raumwahrnehmungen des Tastsinnes. Berlin, 1898. Pp. 228. (With extended bibliography.)

(25) V. Henri and G. Tawney, Ueber die Trugwahrnehmung zweier Punkte bei der Berührung eines Punktes der Haut. *PhSd*, 11: 1895, 394-405.

(26) D. S. Hill, Tests with a modified Binet-Buzenet esthesiometer. *PsBu*, 7: 1910, 66-7.

(27) J. Jastrow, Psychological notes on Helen Keller. *PsR*, 1: 1894, 356-362.

(28) C. Judd, Ueber Raumwahrnehmungen im Gebiete des Tastsinnes. *PhSd*, 12: 1896, 409-464. (Historical survey, 451-8.)

(29) Frances Kellor, Experimental sociology. N. Y., 1901. Pp. 316.

(30) R. L. Kelly, Psychophysical tests of normal and abnormal children; a comparative study. *PsR*, 10: 1903, 345-372.

(31) E. Kraepelin, Ueber Ermüdungsmessungen. *ArGsPs*, 1: 1903, 9-30.

(32) W. Krohn, Sensation-areas and movement. *PsR*, 1: 1894, 280-1.

(33) F. Krueger and C. Spearman, Die Korrelation zwischen verschiedenen geistigen Leistungsfähigkeiten. *ZPs*, 44: 1906, 50-114.

(34) J. Leuba, On the validity of the Griesbach method of determining fatigue. *PsR*, 6: 1899, 573-598.

(35) Gladys W. Martin, The evidence of mental fatigue during school hours. *JEPd*, 1: 1911, 39-45, 137-147.

(36) Gladys W. Martin, A study of mental fatigue. *BrJPs*, 5: 1913, 427-446.

(37) E. Meumann, Vorlesungen zur Einführung in die exp. Pädagogik. 1st ed., Leipzig, 1907.

(38) P. Noikow, Aesthesiometrische Ermüdungsmessungen. *InMagSc Hyg*, 4: 1907-8, 437-481.

(39) M. Offner, Mental fatigue. Eng. trans. Baltimore, 1911. Pp. 133.

(40) C. Ritter, Ermüdungsmessungen. *ZPs*, 24: 1900, 401-444.

(41) W. H. R. Rivers, Observations on the senses of the Todas. *BrJPs*, 1: 1905, 321-396, especially 363-371.

(42) Y. Sakaki, Ermüdungsmessungen in vier japanischen Schulen. *InMagScHyg*, 1: 1905, 53-100.

(43) Schmey, Ueber Modificationen der Tastempfindung. *DuBois-Reymond's Archiv.* (Physiol.), 1884, 309-312.

(44) R. Schulze, Aus der Werkstatt d. exp. Psych. u. Pädagogik. Leipzig, 1909. Pp. 292.

(45) M.-C. Schuyten, Sur les méthodes de mensuration de la fatigue des écoliers. *ArPs(f)*, 2: 1903, 321-6.

(46) M.-C. Schuyten, Comment doit-on mesurer la fatigue des écoliers. *ArPs(f)*, 4: 1904, 113-128.

(47) M.-C. Schuyten, Researches in the mental classification of children. (Summary from *PdlJb*, 7: 1909, 73-118, in *InMagScHyg*, 6: 1910, 179-180.) (See also Revue de psychiatrie, 1908, p. 135.)

(48) T. Simon, L'interpretation des sensations tactiles chez les enfants arrières. *AnPs*, 7: 1900 (1901), 536-558.

(49) L. Solomons, Discrimination in cutaneous sensations. *PsR*, 4: 1897, 246-250.

(50) R. Sommer, Ausstellung v. exp. psych. App. u. Methoden. 1904.

(51) G. Tawney, The perception of two points not the space-threshold. *PsR*, 2 : 1895, 585-593.

(52) G. Tawney, Ueber die Wahrnehmung zweier Punkte mittelst des Tastsinnes, mit Rücksicht auf die Frage der Uebung. *PhSd*, 13 : 1897, 163-222.

(53) Helen B. Thompson, The mental traits of sex. Chicago, 1903. Pp. 188.

(54) J. van Biervliet, L'asymétrie sensorielle. *BuAcRoySci*, 34 : Série 3, 1897, 326-366.

(55) J. van Biervliet, La mesure de l'intelligence. *JPsPa*, 1 : 1904, 225-235.

(56) T. Vannod, (*a*) La fatigue intellectuelle et son influence sur la sensibilité cutanée. *RMdSuisse*, 17 : 1897, 21. (*b*) La méthode esthésiométrique pour la mensuration de la fatigue intellectuelle. *Rep. 1st Intern. Cong. on Sch. Hygiene*, Nürnberg, 1904, vol. ii.

(57) K. Vierordt, Ueber die Ursache verschiedenen Entwickelung des Ortssinnes der Haut. *ArGsPhg*, 2 : 1869, 298-306. Also Die Abhängigkeit der Ausbildung des Raumsinnes der Haut v. d. Beweglichkeit der Körperteile. *ZBi*, 6 : 1870.

(58) A. Volkmann, Ueber den Einfluss der Uebung auf das Erkennen räumlicher Distanzen. *Ber. d. Sächs.-Ges. d. Wiss.*, 10 : 1858, *math. phys. Abth.*, 38-69.

(59) L. Wagner, Unterricht u. Ermüdungsmessungen an Schülern des neuen Gymnasiums in Darmstadt. *SmAbPdPs*, 1 : 1898, Hft. 4, Pp. 134.

(60) Margaret Washburn, Some apparatus for cutaneous stimulation (with cut). *AmJPs*, 6 : 1894, 422-3.

(61) Margaret Washburn, Ueber den Einfluss der Gesichtsassociationen auf die Raumwahrnehmungen der Haut. *PhSd*, 11 : 1895, 190-225.

(62) E. H. Weber, De pulsu, resorptione, auditu et tactu. Leipzig, 1834.

(63) C. Wissler, The correlation of mental and physical tests. *PsMon*, 3 : No. 6, 1901. Pp. 62.

CHAPTER VII

Tests of Attention and Perception

The tests included in this chapter are those commonly assumed to measure such capacities as "power of observation," "quickness of perception," "range of attention," "mental grasp," etc. They are practically confined to the sphere of visual perception, and imply that this perception takes place under active attention: thus, in general, they seek to determine the subject's capacity to perceive visual objects or symbols when the conditions of perception are limited by short temporal persistence of the stimulus, or by other difficulties or complications that are intentionally introduced.

It has been said that experimental psychology discovered attention. Whether this be strictly true or not, every psychological experiment of necessity takes account of attention. And so, in every mental test that presupposes effort or concentration, we measure the capacity under investigation, always as conditioned by the particular degree of attention manifested at the time. It follows that a fundamental presupposition for the comparison of the results of such tests is that they shall all be secured under the same condition of attention. In practise, we find that the best way to secure this constant degree of attention is always to exact the maximal degree. Yet, in so far as the capacity to attend does differ in different individuals and in the same individuals at different times, just so far our tests of various other capacities, such as discrimination, retention, and the like, are often felt to be measures of attention, quite as much as measures of these other capacities.

Despite this fact, or perhaps on account of it, a direct measure or test of degree of attention is difficult to secure. In theory, since attention is a condition of consciousness in which certain constituent processes are clear and prominent, attention is directly measurable in terms of clearness. In practise, we must, in all probability, content ourselves with an attempt to measure attention indirectly, not by any single test, but by a series of tests, all of which exact maximal effort. Even then, it must be recognized that we measure, not the process or condition of attention itself, but a product or concomitant of that condition.

A fundamental source of difficulty in these tests of attention lies in the fact that, with repetition, or even with the progress of the first trial, the task assigned becomes progressively easier; a tendency toward automatism appears, and the tax on attention diminishes proportionately.

TEST 24

Range of visual attention.—In a single 'pulse' of attention only a small number of impressions can stand out clearly: the area of span of consciousness is definitely limited. In the sphere of vision, we find that if we give but a single glance at any heterogeneous collection of objects, such as the goods displayed in a store-window, or the jumble of odds and ends in an old tool-chest, we are able to grasp and enumerate only a very few, perhaps four or five, of these objects.

For the scientific study of the area or range of visual attention, psychologists employ some form of short exposure apparatus, or tachistoscope.[1] (Greek, *tachistos,* very rapid, and *skopein,* to view). The essential idea of a tachistoscope is to furnish a field upon which S may fixate his glance and attention, and to supplant this field for a brief instant by another which contains the test-material. There is, then, a pre-exposure field (which contains a fixation-mark), an exposure-field, and a post-exposure field. The contents of the exposure-field depend, of course, upon the object of the experiment. In the main, the tachistoscope has been most used for the experimental investigation of the process of reading, and, accordingly, with an exposure field containing printed texts, isolated words, nonsense syllables, single letters, etc., but it has also been used for determining the range of attention for the visual apprehension of groups of dots, lines, geometrical drawings, objects, colors, etc.

---

[1] The name *Tachistoskop* was first employed by Volkmann (27).

As Dodge has remarked, "no psychological instrument is subject to greater modification in response to special experimental conditions than exposure apparatus," and it may be added that in no other experiment are the results more evidently conditioned by the form of apparatus and type of procedure employed.[1]

Wundt has formulated the essentials of a good tachistoscope as follows:

(1) The exposure must be short enough to preclude eye-movements.

(2) The arrangement of the fixation-mark and of the stimulus must be such that all the constituents of the exposed object can be seen with at least approximately equal distinctness, i. e., the exposure-field must coincide with the ocular field of direct vision.

(3) The exposure of all parts of the field should be simultaneous, or so nearly so that there shall be no noticeable time-differences in the illumination of the various regions.

(4) Retinal adaptation must be favorable, and sudden transitions from dark to light must be avoided.

(5) Persistent after-images must be avoided.

(6) The duration of the retinal excitation must be limited enough to preclude roving of attention over the exposure-field.

(7) A ready-signal must be given at an appropriate time before the exposure.

Further requirements given by Dodge are as follows:

(8) The relative illumination of the pre-exposure, exposure, and post-exposure fields should be capable of experimental modification.

(9) The exposure should be noiseless and free from distraction.

(10) It should be possible to arrange for monocular or binocular observation.

APPARATUS.—Disc tachistoscope (Fig. 57).[2] Frosted tubular lamp, 16 C. P. Two 4-inch clamps. Blanks of cardboard 9 cm. square. Two complete sets of Willson's gummed black letters

---

[1] For the history of the development of the tachistoscope and for the various controversies that have been waged concerning the necessity for absolutely simultaneity of exposure of the entire field, the extent to which convergence and accommodation are controlled by different forms of fixation-point, the actual and the optimal duration of the retinal excitation set up by the exposure, and the optimal conditions of general and local adaptation, the reader may consult the various references at the end of the test, especially Binet, Cattell, Dodge, Erdmann and Dodge, Goldscheider and Müller, Becher, Wundt, Huey and Zeitler. A short summary of these issues was published by the author in the first edition of this work. It may be pointed out merely that the black pre- and post-exposure fields of the disc tachistoscope here prescribed afford the most brilliant possible exposures, with longest retinal effects, so that an exposure of 50 to 75 σ will give a well "cleared-up image" (to employ Dodge's term) and at the same time eliminate eye-movement.

[2] This instrument, devised by the author and employed by him in studying the effect of practise on the range of attention does not fulfill all of the requirements of the ideal tachistoscope, but it has the merit of being relatively inexpensive, simple in operation and construction, and of answering satisfactorily for comparative tests. It has also been designed with a view for use both for these short and for much longer exposures (Test 25).

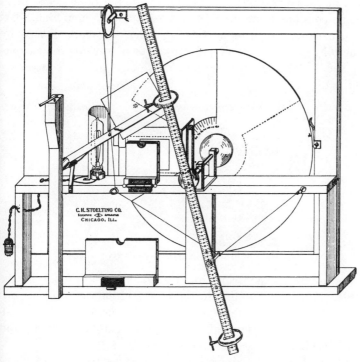

FIG. 57. DISC TACHISTOSCOPE.

and figures, Size 3. Drawing ink and ruling pen. Head-rest,[1] with suitable supports and clamps. [Fifty-vibrations dry-contact fork (Fig. 58.) Dry battery. Connecting wire.]

PRELIMINARIES.—Prepare a series of exposure-cards by use of the gummed letters and figures. Paste the letters smoothly and evenly, and center the series on each card. The test-objects should include isolated letters, groups of letters, or letters mixed with digits in nonsense arrangement, in numbers from two to eight or ten per card. Prepare other cards with short words, short sentences, or columns of digits. Prepare still others with the aid of drawing ink, so as to present regular or irregular series of spots, lines, geometrical figures, surfaces,

---

[1]Suggestions for the construction of head-rests are given by Judd.

etc., in varied fashion.[1] It is well to confine the objects, in so far as possible, to an area 50 mm. wide and 35 mm. high. Exposure cards can also be formed, after the method used by Huey, by pasting bits of printed texts of various dimensions on the blanks, or colored surfaces may be introduced *ad libitum*.

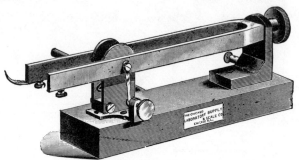

FIG. 58.   FIFTY-VIBRATIONS DRY-CONTACT FORK.

Set up the tachistoscope, and clamp or screw it firmly to the table. Connect the electric light to a circuit of proper voltage. By means of the supports and clamps, adjust the head-rest so that S's eyes shall be about 40 cm. in front of, and slightly higher than, the exposure card.

Adjust the tachistoscope for a point-exposure of 60σ.[2]

The pendulum-arm is attached with its mm. scale in view at the back of the instrument, and with the zero end of its scale lying upon the release-lever when the instrument is ready for exposure. To secure an exposure of 60σ, E should set the first weight at 5 cm. (measured at the edge of the weight nearer the lever), should set the second weight at 60 cm. and should open the sector 25 deg. He may fasten the overlapping edges of sector and disc by pushing a small paper-clip over them at the periphery. The entire disc is to be tightened up upon its axis in such a position as to bring the square opening in the disc in alignment with the

[1]For general suggestions, see Huey, 18, pp. 75 ff, and Binet, 3, p. 349. For special suggestions on the use of spots to test ability to apprehend number, see Freeman. A number of prepared cards accompany the set of material supplied by Rossolimo for his 'profile' method.

[2]The time of total exposure of several rows of objects is not the same as that of the exposure of any single point. If t is the time required for the notched portion of the disc to pass a given point on the exposure field, and L is the time of exposure of the group of objects to be determined, and if H and h are the heights of the total exposure field and of the portion of the field occupied by the objects, respectively, then $L = t \left(1 + \dfrac{h}{H}\right).$

square opening in the screen.[1] The axle must be properly oiled and its bearings in good alignment.

See that the device that lifts the fixation-card works smoothly and quietly. The movement of this card should be invisible to S, and the stimulus-object should be entirely unobstructed by it at the moment of exposure.

METHOD.—Seat S so that his head is supported in the head-rest without undue strain (Fig. 59). Set the tachistoscope for an exposure, and place a very simple exposure-card in the holder. In this position of the disc, the exposure-card is hidden by the fixation-card, which is visible through an opening in the disc. Instruct S to fixate the cross of the fixation-card as accurately and intently as possible, and, when he feels that his attention is thoroughly prepared, to signal for the release of the disc.[2] Let him then report, orally or preferably by drawing, what he has seen. Unless attention is manifestly poor, do not repeat the exposure.[3]

---

[1] If he wishes to measure the time of exposure accurately, E may attach a piece of smoked paper temporarily to the back face of the disc, connect the 50-vibs. fork with the battery, and adjust the fork so that its recording point (or the recorder of a sensitive signal-magnet, e. g., a Deprez signal with which the fork is electrically connected) leaves its curve traced upon the paper when the disc is released. He may then determine the time of exposure by counting the number of 'waves' recorded while the notched portion of the disc is passing the center of the exposure field. Or he may apply the fork directly to a smoked kymograph drum (see Test 10) and record the duration of the exposure with a signal-magnet on a parallel tracing. For this purpose, the two clips fitted with light connecting wire, with which the instrument is provided, are placed on the periphery of the disc in such a manner that, at the moment of exposure and at the moment of occlusion of the center of the field, they make electrical contact with the copper brush which is fastened to the frame of the instrument.

[2] The rather unusual procedure of allowing S to control initiation of the experiment is justified here by the fact that the signal for the release may be very simple, and that we are more likely to secure maximal attention from S. In fact, a simple mechanical release may be arranged for the disc tachistoscope by running a cord from the release-lever through two screw-eyes to a small lever convenient to S, who can then set off the exposure himself when he is quite ready. If, after several practise trials, it is evident that S is distracted by this procedure, E should revert to the usual method of giving the ready signal himself. The practise series, in any event, need be no longer than is required to accustom S to the general setting of the test.

[3] There is, however, good precedent for using repeated exposures, if desired: Cattell used a series of 5 exposures; Huey occasionally, and Binet regularly, made as many as 20 exposures; Titchener prescribes an indefinite number of exposures. This procedure is based on the assumption that no more is actually *seen* in 20 exposures than in 1, but that the series of exposures determines the limits of assimilative capacity. This method seems unnecessary, especially for comparative purposes.

Introduce more and more complex cards of the type under investigation until a limit is reached beyond which S cannot carry his observation. For the experiment proper, use in the main simple series of consonants, and drawings, but unless there is some special reason for it, do not change without notice from the one type of exposure-card to the other.

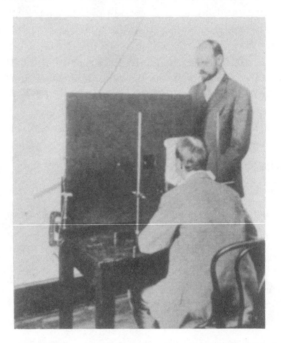

FIG. 59.   TESTING THE RANGE OF ATTENTION.

VARIATIONS OF METHOD.—Test the range of attention with other forms of material, e.g., digits, nonsense syllables, words and especially with short sentences and drawings. Test the assimilative completion of word skeletons (groups of characteristic letters, mutilated or misspelled words). Vary the time of exposure, especially toward the shorter times. Try changes in the backgrounds and fields by covering the screen and disc with white, gray and black papers in different combinations, and using gray or black blanks for exposure-cards.

Try the cumulative method of exposure. Try reading distances greater than 40 cm. Try various sizes, forms, or colors of type.

TREATMENT OF RESULTS.—S's rank is measured in general by the number of concrete objects correctly reproduced. This rank should be computed separately for different forms of exposure-card (if other than isolated letter tests are used) and for letter-series of different lengths, *e.g.,* for 6-place, 7-place, 8-place series, etc. In the case of letters or words, the simplest method of ranking is to assign one unit for each letter or word correctly reproduced, but to deduct 0.5 for errors of insertion or transposition. Thus, if the stimulus-card was FRMUTH, then FRMTUTH or FMRUTH would be ranked as 5.5, whereas FRMUT or FRMUH would be ranked 5. If desired, double errors, *e.g.,* transposition and insertion, as FMRTUTH, may be doubly discounted, but it is simpler to count this rendering also as 5.5.

In the case of more complex exposure-cards, such as drawings, it is sometimes possible to rank S on the basis of the number of lines reproduced, discounting 0.5 for lines incorrectly placed with respect to the total figure; in other cases, it is more satisfactory to assign a subjective estimate of the general fidelity of the reproduction on some arbitrary scale, *e.g.,* 10 for a perfect reproduction, 0 for absolutely nothing, and intermediate ranks in proportion.

If the method of serial exposures is followed, S's rank can often be indicated by the number of exposures necessary to obtain accurate reproduction.

RESULTS AND CONCLUSIONS.—(1) When a series of *unrelated objects* is exposed, the average number of impressions that can be grasped in a single exposure lies between four and five. While, occasionally, S's may grasp as many as seven impressions, this is usually due to a more or less well-recognized tendency to group or unify the objects in some manner. Table 32 summarizes the author's experiments (30) upon four college students with *letter-series,* 100σ exposure, and with the use of apparatus like that prescribed, save that the pre- and post-exposure fields were white. It will be seen that the average

TABLE 32.

Average Number of Letters Read Correctly in one Exposure (Whipple).

OBSERVERS	FIVE-PLACE SERIES	SIX-PLACE SERIES	SEVEN-PLACE SERIES	ALL
Mr. B_____	4.85	5.09	5.25	5.06
Mr. E_____	4.84	4.49	4.48	4.53
Mr. N_____	4.74	4.92	5.38	4.97
Mr. T_____	4.51	4.86	4.40	4.71
Average _____	4.74	4.84	4.88	4.82

performance for different S's under different conditions is quite similar, and that it lies between four and five impressions. The 6- and 7-place series are somewhat more favorable because the S's can occasionally reproduce 6 or 7 impressions.

These results are in close accord with those of other experimenters.[1] Cattell's tests (4) place the average limit for digits at 5, for letters at 3-4, and more often 3, though one S could grasp 6 letters. Erdmann and Dodge found that 6-7 letters could be read at times. Zeitler (30) points out that, while a series of consonants has an assimilative limit of 4-7, one may grasp 5-8 impressions, if vowels are interspersed. In the author's experiments, it was found, similarly, that the 7-place series that were read successfully were almost always those containing vowels which permitted the formation of nonsense syllables, e.g., WAEGZME, KMDEMBH. The statement that the first and last letters are those usually seen clearly is not so easily confirmed and does not apply to the results of all S's.

(2) S's not infrequently report that more is seen than can be remembered a moment later when the report is given. In such cases, it is still often possible to state whether or not a given character was present.

(3) Despite the meaningless character of isolated letters, a series once exposed may be sufficiently well remembered to be

---

[1] The horizontal seriatim exposure used by Hylan is so little comparable with the whole-field exposure of others that his results may not be expected to conform with theirs. Hylan found that, with an exposure of 6 letters at the rate of 3.6 σ per letter, an average of 1.9 letters was read, while a longer exposure, 42 σ for the entire card, permitted 2.6 letters to be read.

recognized if used in the experiment again, even after a lapse of several days.

(4) When familiar syllables are combined to form *nonsense words*, e.g., *lencurbilber*, 6-10 letters can be grasped in one exposure (Zeitler).

(5 In the reading of *isolated words*, i.e., collocations of words that do not make sense, the results of different investigators show a lack of accordance. As in the case of letters, Cattell's results indicate a lower range than those of other investigators. Cattell placed the limit of grasp at 2-3 short one-syllabled words. Erdmann and Dodge (8) found that, in a single exposure, 4 isolated words can almost always be read, and very often 5. Again, single words of 19-22 letters can be read in one exposure without roving of attention. Some of Zeitler's *S*'s could even read a 25-letter word, such as *Aufmerksam-keitsschwankung*. Becher read 26-letter words with a single, electric spark exposure. In general, the difficulty of grasping words does not increase in proportion to their length, while Cattell's reaction experiments showed that short words can be named more quickly than letters.

(6) When short words are combined into *simple sentences*, it is found that the average reading capacity is 4-6 words. Zeitler's *S*'s read such sentences when the total number of letters was 20-30; Erdmann and Dodge report 4-6 words of 2-10 letters each; Cattell found the average amount 4 words, occasionally 6, though *S* could read at times a 7-word sentence. One of the longest correctly read sentences contained 34 letters: *"Eine Tochter muss ihrem Vater gehorchen."*

Huey (17, 18) exposed for 15 σ lines cut from magazines. His results show clearly the striking individual differences in the reading range, which practically every investigator has noted;[1] thus, one *S* read on the average continuously and correctly 10.25 mm. of the line, another 21.33 mm., a third 23.80 mm. and a fourth 32.40 mm.[2] Under very favorable conditions (atten-

[1]Cattell concludes that there is a decided difference in the sensitiveness of the retinas in different *S*'s, but it is quite as likely that these individual differences are as much central as peripheral.

[2]In the type used, 40 mm. was equal approximately to 26 letter-spaces.

tion, subject-matter, etc.), one of Huey's S's could read a stretch of line 50 mm. long (about half a line), *e.g.*, such phrases as "condition of consciousness," or "the whole body converges," but these are not ordinary performances.

In exposures of this sort the amount read to the left and to the right of the fixation-point is not at all equal, but varies in either direction according to the subject-matter, *e.g.*, in the second phrase above, the fixation-point was at the *o* of *whole*. The tendency is, as might be anticipated, to read more to the right than to the left. "In almost every case in which a large amount is read, far more is read to the right of the fixation-point than to the left."

In these, as in other exposures, the extent of reading is curtailed in proportion as the word-groups resemble isolated words, as when divided by punctuation-marks.

There is evidence to show that the unit of reading is the word, inasmuch as S's see, or at least report, words or phrases rather than letters, even at the ends of the sections read.

(7) Freeman (11) made comparative tests of the ability of adults and of children aged 6 to 14 years to apprehend the number of objects (*spots* of light for the most part) thrown on a screen by a tachistoscope. The actual scope of attention, as estimated with the aid of introspection, was found not to differ much with age. The range averaged between 4 and 5 impressions for adults, while for children of 8 to 10 years judgments of number averaged only 4.5 per cent. poorer than those of adults when the number of objects was four or less. But for five objects children's judgments are 22 per cent. poorer than the judgments of adults—a difference due primarily to the superior ability of adults to form groups. "Not only do adults apprehend objects which are objectively grouped better than children, but they also have an advantage in dealing with objectively ungrouped objects which are beyond the scope of attention by means of subjective grouping."

Virtually the same results have been found with exposure-cards composed of series of 4 to 15 ruled perpendicular *lines,* 2 mm. apart. Cattell found that S's could give the correct number of lines exposed, up to 4-6 only. Similarly, Goldscheider and Müller (12) tried various combinations of straight and curved lines (10 σ exposure), with the result that, if the arrangement was quite irregular, only 4-5 constituents could be grasped, but in proportion as the arrangement became more symmetrical (thus facilitating grouping or unitizing), the number of constituents that could be grasped was increased. A symmetrical arrangement of simple perpendicular strokes increased the observation-limit to 7, while a combination of straight lines into squares, symmetrically arranged, permitted the apprehension of 5 squares, and hence of 20 constituent lines. Similarly, experiments with semicircles, ellipses, etc., confirmed the general principle that the number of constituent elements grasped in a short exposure is a function of the degree of combination which these elements permit.[1]

(8) The apprehension of *simple geometrical forms, e.g.,* circles, diamonds, oblongs, etc., cut from black paper and pasted on a white background, is easier than that of letters. Hylan's results, compared with his results for letters above, may serve for illustration. Six S's averaged 7 forms; his poorest S averaged 4.5, and his best S, 9.5 forms.[2] Quantz's test of requiring S's to name aloud, in order and as rapidly as possible, a series of geometrical forms, colors, or words, during an exposure of 0.5 sec. or 1.0 sec. is not strictly comparable to the short exposure tests: he found that forms could be named less rapidly than colors or words, and that, so far as forms are concerned, as many can be named with 0.5 sec. as with 1.0 sec. exposure (2.75 and 2.8, respectively).[3]

If *complex drawings* which are not clearly related to well-known geometrical figures are used, the test becomes more difficult because the visual image cannot be identified or held by the assistance of verbal associates (Binet, 3).

(9) *Practise* has a curiously small effect upon the range of attention, when once the period of preliminary habituation to the arrangement of apparatus and method is passed (Cattell, 4; Hylan, 20, p. 396). The chief feature of whatever practise

---

[1]An obvious illustration of this principle is seen in the reading of letters and digits themselves. For an account of Goldscheider and Müller's tests of the constituents of digits, etc., consult Huey (19, pp. 78 f).

[2]Some idea of the qualitative factors which influence the perception of liminal visual forms may be obtained from the experiments of Miss Hempstead, though these were conducted with different apparatus and by a different method.

[3]Huey's statement (19, p. 54) that, according to Quantz, more could be read in a short than in a long exposure, is not substantiated by Quantz's tables, which merely show that *relatively* more can be read in a half-second than in a second exposure.

can be detected is an increase in ability to group isolated impressions into combinations. "Practise tends to unite into a closer perceptive unity impressions first combined with difficulty" (Hylan). The practise effect for isolated letter series for a period of seven to ten days as found in the author's tests (30) is indicated in Table 33.[1] It is evident that, if we discount the improvement due to adaptation, there is but a small enlargement of the range through practise.

TABLE 33

Effect of Practise upon the Perception of Letters (*Whipple*)

OBSERVER	FIVE-PLACE SERIES			SIX-PLACE SERIES				SEVEN-PLACE SERIES		
	B.	N.	T.	B.	E.	N.	T.	E.	N.	T.
First period	4.87	4.44	4.50	5.03	4.75	4.38	4.73	4.25	4.90	3.83
Later period	—	4.87	—	—	—	4.85	—	4.02	5.54	—
Last period	4.78	4.77	4.50	5.25	5.08	5.06	5.08	4.90	5.40	5.80

(10) Aside from the work of Freeman already cited, the relation of the visual range of attention to *age* has been studied carefully only by Griffing (13), but by a method so peculiar[2] as to make the applicability of his results to ordinary conditions rather dubious. Table 34 presents Griffing's results in terms of the total number of letters correctly read in a series of 10 exposures of 6 letters each. Griffing concludes from these data that the number of visual impressions perceived "is a function of individual growth, reaching its maximum only when the observer is fully developed."

---

[1]The four *S*'s did not take the same series, nor work for the same length of time, so that the data are too few to permit accurate averaging into three periods, save for *N.*, and for *E.* in the 7-place series.

[2]Griffing's method was to expose with a fall-tachistoscope for 0.1 sec. or 1.0 sec., to a group of 10 to 20 *S*'s, six printed capital letters, 48 mm. high, but to vary the interval between the ready-signal and the exposure from 6 sec. to 1.5 min., or even 4 min., without the knowledge of the *S*'s, with the idea of testing "the observer's powers of prolonged attention" by keeping them waiting an indefinite time for the exposure. In view of the well-known irregularity and fluctuation of attention under such conditions, it seems clear that the degree of attention present at the moment of exposure, at least in a short series of tests, is almost a matter of chance.

TABLE 34

Relation of Visual Range of Attention to Age (Griffing)

NUMBER OF S s	AGE	LETTERS READ
39	7–9	4
77	10–12	13
73	13–15	18
132	16–18 +	27

(11)   Griffing found no difference between the *sexes*.

(12)   There is only questionable evidence of a relation between the *range of visual attention and mental ability*. Griffing divided his pupils into three groups on the basis of teachers' estimates, and found that his 'A' group had a somewhat higher average range of attention than the other groups, but that there were marked exceptions, so that "many pupils must have good powers of attention even when they show no evidence of them to their teachers." It is possible, however, that the outcome of Griffing's test is more dependent on the interest and good-will of the pupils than on their intelligence, for, as Griffing himself says: "Children of the most active minds would be most interested in novel experiences." Cattell states that in his tests "obtuse porters" required three times as long as educated persons to read a letter or word. Binet could not differentiate his bright from his dull children by the exposure of single words, but could differentiate them very clearly by the exposure of a drawing 20 times in succession.[1]

(13)   The *qualitative analysis* of the perceptive processes concerned in reading during short exposures has developed differences of opinion with regard to the following points: (*a*) Is it possible for roving of attention to occur in exposures which are sufficiently short to eliminate eye-movement? (*b*) Do we apprehend words by wholes or by parts? (*c*) Are there

---

[1]Binet's *S*'s drew what they could of the drawing after each exposure of 70σ. An interval of 5-10 sec. was interposed between the exposure and the drawing. Only three of 11 *S*'s were able to give a correct copy within the limit set to the test; these three *S*'s were all of the group selected for superior intelligence. For reproductions of the actual drawings, consult Binet, 3, pp. 351-360.

certain letters or combinations of letters which give the cue for the perception of words, and if so, what are these letters? What share does the total length and general visual contour of a printed word have in its perception? (*d*) Do different readers adopt different methods of reading?

Without going into details[1] it may be said that the seeming lack of agreement between the results of different investigators is due in part to the divergence in experimental conditions, in part to the divergence in type of the *S*'s employed. We do not always read by wholes: neither do we always read by successive apprehension. The unit of attention, of visual apprehension, in reading is a variable quantity. In normal reading, assuming equally easy subject-matter, the manner of reading will depend upon the type of the reader. Aside from differences in speed and fluency of reading, we may probably distinguish two fundamental types of readers, the subjective and the objective. The latter exhibit the following characteristics: in tachistoscopic tests, their attention is directed to the optical fixation-mark; their range is small, *e.g.*, three isolated letters or one 12-letter word, but they read accurately, are quite certain of what they do see, and seldom guess; for them there exists a distinct time-interval between the visual perception and assimilative interpretation or rise of meaning, and they seldom confuse these two phases. The subjective readers differ from the objective in every one of these points: they can read words lying in indirect vision; they have a range of five isolated letters or one 27-letter word; their attention is placed mainly on the interpretative or assimilative phase, and their reading occurs mainly by large word-wholes, or even by phrases, on the basis of relatively meager visual cues. These subjective readers are not, however, necessarily the faster.[2]

If, now, the subject-matter is difficult, the tendency for the subjective type of reader is toward the more extensive use of visual symbols, and here, doubtless, as in the case of short

---

[1]Readers who are particularly interested in these special problems will find a discussion of them in the first edition of this work, pp. 237-240, which is here omitted for want of space and because the subject-matter belongs more to the psychology of reading than to the psychology of tests.

[2]For a more detailed discussion of these types, see Meumann, ii, 250 ff.

exposures, dominating letters or complexes become more important: it will depend upon the difficulty of the passage whether these letters play their chief rôle as prominent elements in the configuration of the word, or whether they are directly the object of attention.

If the subject-matter is very difficult, *e.g.*, the reading of beginners, or of an adult in a foreign language, especially if reading unfamiliar characters, such as Greek or Hebrew, we have an extreme case in which reading may, and often does, proceed letter by letter.

The reading of children, once the primary mechanical difficulties are mastered, is almost always of the subjective or interpretative type (Messmer), though for different reasons than in the case of the subjective reading of adults. That, however, there are many exceptions to this generalization is shown by the recent work of Pintner (25a).

REFERENCES

(1) N. Baxt, Ueber d. Zeit welche nöthig ist, damit ein Gesichtseindruck zum Bewusstsein kommt, etc. *ArGsPhg*, 4: 1871, 325-336.

(2) E. Becher, Experimentelle u. kritische Beiträge zur Psychologie es Lesens bei kurzen Expositionzeiten. *ZPs*, 36: 1904, 19-73.

(3) A. Binet, Attention et adaptation. *AnPs*, 6: 1899 (1900), 248-404.

(4) J. Cattell, The inertia of the eye and brain. *Brain*, 8: 1886, 295-12; also as Ueber die Trägheit der Netzhaut u. des Sehcentrums. *PhSd*, : 1886, 94-127.

(5) R. Dodge, An improved exposure apparatus. *PsBu*, 4: January, 907, 10-13.

(6) R. Dodge, The psychology of reading. *PsR*, 8: 1901, 56-60.

(7) R. Dodge, An experimental study of visual fixation. *PsMon*, 8: o. 4, 1907, (No. 35). Pp. 95.

(8) B. Erdmann and R. Dodge, Psychologische Untersuchungen über is Lesen. Halle, 1898. Pp. 360.

(9) B. Erdmann and R. Dodge, Zur Erläuterung unserer tachistoskopihen Versuche. *ZPs*, 22: 1900, 241-267.

(10) S. Exner, Ueber die zu einer Gesichtswahrnehmung nöthige Zeit. *tz. Ber. d. Wiener Akad.*, 58: (2), 1868, 601-632.

(11) F. N. Freeman, Experiments on the perception of number in chilen and adults. *PsBu*, 8: 1911, 43-44.

(12) A. Goldscheider and R. Müller, Zur Phys. u. Path. des Lesens. *its. f. klin. Med.*, 23: 1893, 131-167. For critical summary, see Wallahek, *ZPs*, 7: 1894, 228-231.

(13) H. Griffing, On the development of visual perception and attention. *nJPs*, 7: 1896, 227-236.

(14) F. Hamilton, The perceptual processes in reading. *ArPs(e)*, No. December, 1907 (Columbia Univ. Contr., etc., 17: No. 1).

(15) H. Helmholtz, Handbuch d. physiol. Optik. Hamburg and Leipzig, 96.

(16) Louise Hempstead, The perception of visual form. *AmJPs*, 12: 01, 185-192.

(17) E. B. Huey, Preliminary experiments in the physiology and psylogy of reading. *AmJPs*, 9: 1898, 575-586.

(18) E. B. Huey, The psychology and physiology of reading. *AmJPs*, 11 : 1900, 283-302 and 12 : 1901, 292-312.

(19) E. B. Huey, The psychology and pedagogy of reading. New York, 1908. Pp. 445.

(20) J. P. Hylan, The distribution of attention. *PsR*, 10 : 1903, 373-403 and 498-533.

(21) C. Judd, (*a*) Laboratory manual of psychology. N. Y., 1907. Pp. 124. (*b*) Laboratory equipment for psychological experiments. N. Y., 1907. Pp. 257.

(22) O. Messmer, Zur Psychologie des Lesens bei Kindern u. Erwachsenen. *ArGsPs*, 2 : 1903, 190-298.

(23) E. Meumann, Vorlesungen zur Einführung in die exp. Pädagogik u. ihre psychol. Grundlagen. 2 vols. Leipzig, 1907. Pp. 555 and 446.

(24) A. Michotte, Description et fonctionnement d'un nouveau tachistoscope de comparaison. *ArPs(f)*, 12 : 1912, 1-13.

(25) W. B. Pillsbury, Attention. London and N. Y., 1908. Pp. 330.

(25a) R. Pintner, Untersuchungen über die Aufmerksamkeitsformei der Kinder beim Lesen und Reagieren. *PdPsArb*, 4 : 1913, 1-54.

(26) J. Quantz, Problems in the psychology of reading. *PsMon*, 2 No. 1, 1897.

(27) E. C. Sanford, The relative legibility of the small letters. *AmJPs* 1 : 1888, 402-435.

(28) E. B. Titchener, Experimental psychology, vol. 1, Qualitative experiments. N. Y., 1901.

(29) A. Volkmann, Das Tachistoskop, etc. *Sitz. d. k. s. Gcs. d. Wiss Leipzig (math.-phys. Cl)*, 1859, 90 ff.

(30) G. M. Whipple, The effect of practise upon the range of visua attention and of visual apprehension. *JEdPs*, 1 : 1910, 249-262.

(31) F. Wirth, Das Spiegeltachistoskop. *PhSd*, 18 : 1903, 687-700.

(32) W. Wundt, Zur Kritik tachistoskopischer Versuche. *PhSd*, 15 1899, 287-317, and 16 : 1900, 61-70. See also his *Völkerpsychologie*, vol. : Die Sprache, 1900, 530 ff, and his *Grundzüge d. physiol. Psychologie*, 5t ed., 1903, 3 : 611 f.

(33) J. Zeitler, Tachistoskopische Versuche über das Lesen. *PhS* 16 : 1900, 380-463.

TEST 25

Visual apprehension.—This test is, in many respects, simila to that of the range of visual attention (Test 24), but it diffei in certain important particulars: the period of exposure is i creased from a small fraction of a second to several second and the test-object is correspondingly more complex. Both ey movement and roving of attention take place, so that we cann speak of the range of attention;[1] we are measuring, rather, tl capacity to apprehend a number of disparate objects by visu examination during a short period.

Tests of this type have been variously designated as tests "quick perception," of "observation," of "degree of attention

---

[1] If one accepts the view of Pillsbury and Hylan that attention tachistoscopy is really successive, this test differs from the former oi in degree : we now give opportunity for a greater number of successi acts of attention.

or even as "memory tests." The term "apprehension," however, seems suited to describe the psychological processes under examination, though it is impossible to draw any hard and fast lines between tests of apprehension, tests of memory and tests of fidelity of report.

This test has long been used as a source of amusement in competitive parlor games, and it has been urged by some writers, particularly by Miss Aiken (1), as a source of mental training[1] in the form of systematic schoolroom exercises. Miss Aiken's suggestions have been subjected to experimental test in the laboratory by the author and by Foster and in the schoolroom by Dallenbach. These investigations, aside from the work of Quantz (9) in his investigation of the psychology of reading, and of Jones (6) in a study of individual differences of children, seem to be the chief instances of the study of visual apprehension under experimental conditions.

Two forms of test are described: a special variation of one form is presented in Test 25A; other variations may easily be worked out to suit special conditions.

A. THREE SECONDS' EXPOSURE WITH THE TACHISTOSCOPE

APPARATUS.—Disc tachistoscope[2] and other material as in Test 24, save that the cardboard blanks are replaced by blanks of stiff paper 12.5 × 20 cm., and that the exposure-card holder

---

[1]The famous conjurer, Robert Houdin (4) used what he termed "perception by appreciation" as a basis for certain feats of "second sight." The capacity which he and his son Emile attained is so marvellous as to be worthy of record. For preliminary tests Houdin tried the estimation of the numbers of dots on dominoes till, he says, "we at length were enabled to give instantaneously the product [sum?] of a dozen dominoes. This result obtained, we applied ourselves to a far more difficult task, over which we spent a month. My son and I passed rapidly before a toy-shop, or any other displaying a variety of wares, and cast an attentive glance upon it. A few steps further on we drew paper and pencil from our pockets, and tried which could describe the greater number of objects seen in passing. I must own that my son reached a perfection far greater than mine, for he could often write down *forty* objects, while I could scarce reach thirty. Often feeling vexed at this defeat, I would return to the shop and verify his statement, but he rarely made a mistake."

This capacity may be compared with the results obtained by adults after practise for a month in the author's experiments: here the average number of objects named was but *six*, the maximum ten.

[2]A simpler, but less efficient, substitute may be contrived after the style of the 'krypteon' described by Sanford (p. 403).

and the opening in the screen of the instrument are adjusted to corresponding dimensions. Collection of pictures of all kinds, cut from old magazines and trimmed to a size not over 12.5 × 20 cm. [Seconds' pendulum, Fig. 28, or metronome with electrical contacts (Fig. 21) and double time-marker, Fig. 27, in place of the 50-vd. fork.]

PRELIMINARIES.—Set up the tachistoscope as described in Test 24. Remove the fixation-card, or turn it off to one side. Replace the small by the large card-holder, and arrange the screen so that the rectangular replaces the square opening. Adjust the disc so that the pre-exposure section just covers the exposure-card when the instrument is set.[1] Adjust the weights and the sector of the disc to give a point-exposure of 3 sec. This will be secured approximately by setting the first weight at 10 cm., the second at 85.2 cm., and opening the sector 115 deg.[2] For rough determination of the exposure, the stop-watch (Fig. 20) may be used. For accurate determination, use the seconds' pendulum or metronome and the signal-magnet (time-marker) mentioned in Test 10; make the determination as directed in Test 24.

The following *types of exposure cards* will be found desirable; 10-20 cards should be prepared of each type selected.[3] (*a*) Groups of irregularly arranged *dots* or small circles or crosses, in number from 6 to 20.[4] These should be grouped in a space not exceeding 35 mm. square in the center of the blank and care must be taken to avoid too obvious hints of combinations in the groupings. These cards may readily be made by the use of the asterisk (*) sign of a typewriter. (*b*) Cards on which *pictures*—drawings, cuts, lithographs, etc., cut from magazines—have been pasted. (*c*) Cards containing a single line of 8-10 three-letter *nonsense syllables*. These may be prepared most easily by the typewriter. As it is important to

---

[1] Fixation is not so exact, of course, with this arrangement, but in view of the long exposures, the error may be neglected for comparative work.

[2] To get full 3 sec. exposure it is imperative that the bearings of the axle of the instrument be in perfect alignment and properly oiled.

[3] Consult Foster (pp. 13-14) and Dallenbach for suggestions on the preparation of various types of material.

[4] Cf. Aiken (1, p. 37), who terms this the test of "unconscious counting. Groups of about 14 dots prove satisfactory for testing adults.

avoid syllables that resemble words when pronounced, a selected list is given here. The last column may be used to illustrate the effect of using sense syllables. (*d*) Cards containing varied com-

tob	vap	urs	mib	kun	zib	gos	orl	ith	tas	arc
arg	ept	ibe	ong	pof	orm	eig	lin	enf	ech	ton
ime	ull	zin	acq	jek	ige	buh	spo	ipp	ume	add
arl	omb	irm	ruv	euf	gur	ite	pru	baw	ret	red
elt	ilt	smi	nen	gla	lud	rad	lel	cha	heb	eel
vid	zet	dak	ung	geg	tau	ahn	uff	teg	ruj	not
ool	euk	sef	ank	jur	rik	nuc	tef	lom	fid	rat
bli	bri	tud	ift	aum	yef	rin	orp	pud	gom	low
ild	rud	rab	urf	ked	geb	pum	gah	arb	zan	end
vel	zen	vem	eit	nis	zud	dro	wol	zig	luh	tan

binations of lines in meaningless *drawings*. Make these with pen and ink; keep the drawings within an area 75 mm. high and 130 mm. long; use combinations of arrows, circles, loops, and straight lines, with 10 to 15 of these elements in each drawing. One or two drawings with some hint of meaning, such as a conventionalized desk-telephone, a 'woodeny' disjointed horse, etc., may be introduced if *E* desires to secure light upon *S*'s use of verbal and other associations for holding the drawings in mind. (*e*) Cards containing typewritten four-line *stanzas* from some not too difficult nor too well-known poem. The object in using poetry is to secure a certain degree of equivalence in length, rhythm, style, and topic from one exposure-card to the next. (*f*) Cards containing columns of *digits,* as illustrated in Aiken, p.30. A sample column from her book is the following:

$$230$$
$$729$$
$$11$$
$$36$$
$$40000$$
$$16$$
$$40$$

METHOD.—Proceed in general as in Test 24 (save that there is no preliminary fixation-mark). Inform *S* what *type* of card is to be exposed, *i.e.,* a drawing, a stanza, etc.

S's reports may be as follows: for *dots,* a statement of their number, supplemented, if desired, by a rough pencil sketch of their position and an account of their grouping; for *nonsense syllables, poetry,* or *digits,* an oral or written report; for *drawings,* a pencil sketch; for *pictures,* a verbal description, supplemented, if *S* desires, by a pencil sketch. In the case of pictures, *E* may also quiz *S* with regard to the observation of various details which *S* has not reported, to see whether they have actually escaped his observation or have merely been neglected in his report, *e.g.,* by the use of such questions as: "Did you notice any details in the background?" "Is there any printing in the picture?" "What color was the girl's dress?" After *S*'s report is finished, *E* may often obtain further light upon *S*'s work by confronting him with the stimulus-card and asking him what features or details he had failed to note, what he had forgotten, or what he had misapprehended.

TREATMENT OF RESULTS.—Some of the material lends itself well, some but poorly, to quantitative treatment, but the latter is often most useful for qualitative analysis of the mental processes concerned. The following system, though obviously arbitrary, has been found serviceable. (*a*) *Counting dots:* assign credit for the reporting of the correct number only; consider any mistake, even of one number, a failure. (*b*) *Pictures:* estimate *S*'s grade upon a scale of 10, *i.e.,* assign the grade 10 to a report which seems to indicate complete recall of all the salient features of the picture; assign the grade 0 to complete failure, and score intermediate grades accordingly. This grading may be made fairly objective by counting up the number of features or 'points' which are adjudged essential to a satisfactory report, and comparing the number given by *S* with this standard number for the picture in question. (*c*) *Nonsense syllables:* assign one unit to each letter correctly reported (*e.g.,* 4 syllables = 12), but deduct 0.5 for each error of transposition or insertion, whether of letters within syllables or the syllables themselves.[1] (*d*) *Drawings:* as in the case of pictures, rate the reproduction on a scale of 10, by reference to

---

[1] For a somewhat more elaborate, though still simple method of scoring nonsense syllables and words with reference to the correctness of their position as well as of their composition, see Lyon (7).

the number of lines or elements correctly reproduced, in comparison with a standard number for the drawing in question. (e) *Poetry:* assign one unit for each word correctly reproduced, but deduct 0.5 for each error of transposition or insertion. (f) *Digits:* as with nonsense syllables, assign one unit for each digit correctly reported, but deduct 0.5 for each error of transposition or insertion, whether of digits within numbers or of the numbers themselves.

B.   SIX SECONDS' EXPOSURE WITHOUT THE TACHISTOSCOPE

MATERIAL.—Small table. Piece of cloth, preferably gray, large enough to cover the table-top. Seconds' pendulum (Fig. 28). A piece of cardboard about 30 × 45 cm., and a full-sized sheet (22 × 28 in.) of gray cardboard. Collection of miscellaneous small objects, familiar enough to be named by all the S's, *e.g.,* pencil, rule, spoon, tin box, leaf, cup, bunch of keys, toy animals, salt-shaker, postcard, etc. Ten different objects will be needed for each exposure.

METHOD.—Place the large sheet of gray cardboard on the table. Arrange on this as a background a group of ten objects, but avoid combinations of obviously related objects, such as pen and inkstand. Make a rough sketch of the group, with a list of the objects, so that it can be restored when desired for later tests. Cover with the gray cloth (to conceal the objects while S is taking his position and receiving instructions). Let S now stand in front of, and close to, the table, but in a position that will not interfere with its full illumination. Inform him that he will be given 6 sec. to view a group of familiar objects, after which he will be asked to enumerate as many of these objects as possible and further to describe them briefly. Let him hold the smaller sheet of cardboard so as to cut off the view of the table-top. Start the seconds' pendulum, which must be placed somewhat to one side, where it can easily be seen by E, but will not distract S. Remove the cloth and take the cardboard which S has been holding. Give S a "ready" signal, and 2 sec. later, quickly remove the cardboard screen. At the expiration of 6 sec.[1] again cut off S's view with the screen. Let

---

[1] The simplest method is to count the strokes mentally, "one, two, three," etc.: if the exposure is made at "one," the screen is to be restored, of course, at "seven."

him immediately turn his back to the table, and give a verbal description of the objects.

The chief stress should be placed on naming as many objects as possible: afterwards, *S* may be asked to describe the details of the objects or to make a rough sketch to indicate their relative positions. For qualitative purposes, *S* should be encouraged to give an account of the manner in which he observed the objects and the manner in which he has reproduced them. After *S* has enumerated as many objects as possible, exhibit the objects that were unnamed, either singly, or mingled with a number of objects not on the table, and ask *S* if he can identify any more of the objects exposed.

TREATMENT OF RESULTS.—Credit *S* with one unit for each object named.

RESULTS FOR BOTH METHODS.—(1) The author's experiments with adults brought out strikingly the very small increase in the *range of apprehension in comparison with the range of attention* (Test 24). Thus, in an exposure of 10·50σ, an average *S* can grasp 4 or 5 objects: here, with an exposure more than 100 times as long, the average *S* enumerates but 6 objects (with a mimimum of 3, and a maximum of 10). Similarly, 3 sec. exposure of nonsense syllables allows, on the average, 10.15 letters (Table 35), *i.e.*, between 3 and 4 syllables, to be read correctly, which is approximately the same as can be read with exposures of a small fraction of a second. On the other hand, the 3 sec. exposure of sense material gives an average range of nearly 12 words in contrast to the 4·6 word limit for ordinary tachistoscopy. This interesting advantage of sense material in the longer exposure is evidently due to the fact that such material can be grouped and recalled by larger and more meaningful units, whereas the heterogeneous combinations of nonsense syllables or disparate objects are more difficult to identify and recall. In the case of poetry, *S*'s feel that the limit of their performance is set simply by the amount that can be read during the exposure, whereas, even in the 6 sec. exposures, there is not time enough clearly to apprehend 10 disparate objects. The maximal reproduction of poetry with 3 sec. exposure was the first 19 words of the following:

> "Were they unhappy then? It cannot be.
> Too many tears for lovers have been shed,
> Too many sighs give we to them in fee,
> Too much of pity after they are dead."

(2) *Individual differences* in capacity for quick apprehension are clearly indicated by Table 35. Thus, V excels in the estimation of dots and in reading poetry, but is the poorest S in reading nonsense syllables, in reproducing drawings, or in describing pictures and objects. G excels in these performances, but is handicapped in reading poetry by his relative

TABLE 35

Individual Differences in Visual Apprehension (*Whipple*)

MATERIAL	DOTS*	PICTURES	NONSENSE	DRAWINGS	POETRY	OBJECTS
G _____	11/33	6.96	10.90	8.65	9.42	7.10
R _____	16/35	6.89	10.70	6.42	12.92	5.57
V _____	28/35	4.40	8.85	3.70	13.21	5.50
Average _____		6.09	10.15	6.26	11.83	6.03

*Efficiency is indicated here by the number of times the group of dots was correctly reported, *i. e.*, 11 out of 33 trials, etc. As *G.* missed two trials, the average cannot be figured exactly.

unfamiliarity with English poetry (he is of German descent): his poor capacity in estimating dots cannot be explained.

These results indicate that it is not possible to assert that an S has a given grade of general ability of apprehension, or even of visual apprehension: rather, we must state that he excels in the attentive observation of pictures, of drawings, of words, or of certain kinds of objects, etc. This confirms in an interesting way the general verdict of experimental work that mental ability is narrow and specific: here, for instance, we find that V is more than twice as efficient as G in the quick perception of groups of dots, while G is more than twice as efficient as V in the quick perception of irregular drawings.

These results obtained by the author are confirmed by subsequent investigators. Thus, Foster's three S's, all graduate students in psychology, scored .97, .85 and .80 in the apprehension of nonsense syllables and .82, .65 and .74, respectively, in the apprehension of sense material. Dallenbach discovered decided differences in the capacities of individual school children in the same school grade, and Jones' tests with cards containing 10 familiar objects gave an average reproduction of 4.98 objects,[1] but with extremes of 2.6 and 7.4 in average scores for trials with ten sets of objects exposed for 1.5 sec.

(3) *Dependence on sex.* Dallenbach's work with 2d grade pupils showed that boys surpassed girls in nearly all the tests. His supplementary trials with adults in university classes likewise indicated a superiority of men over women in visual apprehension.

(4) *Dependence on age.* Dallenbach found a direct, though small correlation with age in the work of the pupils in the 2d grade. University students without previous practise were found to surpass, on the average, the performance of the grade pupils who had had three months daily practise, though the two groups overlapped, so that the best group in the 2d grade surpassed the poorest group of university students under these conditions.

(5) *Dependence on practise.* The work of Foster and of the author was specially directed upon the possibility of improvement by practise in the case of adults, that of Dallenbach upon the possibility of improvement in the case of children. The results seem to indicate distinct differences in the practise possibilities of children and of adults. Thus, the results obtained by the author (Table 36), in which each 'period' represents the average of three exposures, usually one daily for three days, afford little warrant for the belief that systematic practise would enable an adult *S* markedly to improve his ability

TABLE 36

Effect of Practise upon Visual Apprehension. Average for Three Observers (Whipple)

PERIOD	1	2	3	4	5	6	7	8	9
Pictures	6.6	4.9	5.9	6.3	6.9	6.9	6.5	5.5	
Nonsense	9.3	10.6	8.4	10.8	11.7	10.6	10.4	8.9	9.2
Drawings	6.6	6.3	5.0	5.6	5.0	7.7	6.5	6.6	5.7
Poetry	10.7	11.5	11.3	10.8	13.0	12.5	13.0	11.7	
Objects	5.6	6.3	5.9	6.0	5.9	6.5	6.4		

[1]In the original article the average is erroneously given as 6.3.

for quick visual perception. The tests with dots do not lend themselves readily to quantitative treatment. The seeming improvement with drawings during the 6th period was due to the use of one very easy drawing in that group. There is some slight evidence of an improvement in reading poetry, which amounts roughly to the addition of one word, but this may be attributed to increased familiarity with the peculiar style of the poem in use. If any improvement can be inferred in the case of the objects-test, it must amount, on the average, to the addition of less than one object.

Foster sought to induce a direct improvement in the capacity for visualization itself. He found a net practise gain for three adults during 40 hours of practise extending over 10 weeks time of from 6 to 44 per cent., depending on the observer and on the material, but no part of this gain was ascribed to direct improvement of visualization.

The gain is, on the contrary, ascribed to these factors:
1. "Confidence and 'doing one's best' replaced discouragement and 'giving up.'
2. "Familiarity with material lessened the difficulty.
3. "The observers learned where and how to distribute attention effectively.
4. "More efficient methods of work were adopted. Tricks of counting, naming, grouping, etc., were discovered and used.
5. "Regular and definite procedure replaced hap-hazard, unorganized procedure."

Foster further found that practise-gains were large in the earlier and small in the later stages of the experiment and that they were much greater with nonsense than with sense material (28 vs. 10 per cent.).

Dallenbach's work with 5-sec. exposure of visual material before a class of children aged 7 to 10 years extended in daily exercises over a period of 17 weeks. Like Foster he found the improvement in visual apprehension rapid at first, then slow. When these pupils were divided into three groups on the basis of their ability first shown, the curve of improvement of the poorest group shows interesting divergences: these pupils had a slower initial rise in capacity, but eventually surpassed the group of medium ability (Fig. 60). When retested after 41 weeks of no drill, the children in the experiment showed them-

selves distinctly superior to classmates of their age who had
not been through the drill, so that we here have apparent evidence of a permanent improvement in capacity effected by drill
in visual apprehension.[1]

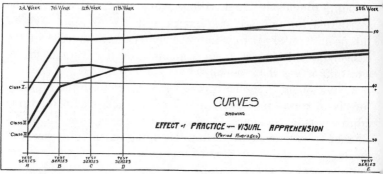

FIG. 60.　EFFECT OF PRACTISE UPON VISUAL APPREHENSION (DALLENBACH).

(6)　*Correlation with other abilities.*　Dallenbach found a
positive correlation between capacity for visual apprehension
and school standing, amounting in one group to .85, in another
to .20. Jones' tests gave a negative correlation, — 0.15, between
visual apprehension of a group of 10 objects and auditory memory for words naming common objects.

(7)　A *qualitative analysis* of the data secured in this experiment shows that the efficiency in visual apprehension exhibited
by any S will depend on the following:

(*a*)　*Native capacity* for concentrating attention in general. This is the
factor which is desired primarily to isolate and measure, but it is impossible to secure such a measurement until the other factors are measured or eliminated.

(*b*)　The *degree of attention* given at the exposure in question. In
theory, each exposure is accompanied by S's maximal attention: in practise, this is not always secured. Tests in which S reports distraction
must be thrown out. The effect of good preparedness on S's part may be
illustrated readily by exposing test-cards without warning of their type:
the consequent elimination of 'expectant attention' will reduce S's efficiency.

---

[1]Confirmation of this conclusion appears in the fact that there was a
striking improvement in the school grades of these children after the experiment and that they surpassed a group of undrilled class-mates of
their age in performance with the Binet card of objects (Test 32) when
tested nearly a year after the period of drill.

(c) *Individual capacity* of *S* to attend to, and to assimilate, the particular *type of material* in use—drawings, nonsense syllables, etc.

(d) The *ease of assimilation* of the particular test-card in use. Thus, an easy bit of poetry will increase the performance of all *S*'s; a drawing that can be *named*, however fancifully, can on this account be held longer and reproduced better by most *S*'s.

(e) *Obstruction or distraction:* Some feature in the object displayed, whether important or trivial, will often catch *S*'s attention, interfere with his exploitation of the balance of the exposure field, and thus measurably reduce his performance. Thus, a misprint in a line of poetry, or the presence of some unusual word, will induce most *S*'s to reread the line, even at the obvious expense of their record.

(f) *Ideational type:* Visually-minded *S*'s hold drawings, pictures, and objects by their visual appearance, and are inclined to use visualization for the reproduction of at least portions of the nonsense syllables and poetry. Auditory-minded *S*'s hold verbal material by auditory imagery: if decidedly auditory-minded, like the author, they may also attempt to hold even pictures, drawings, and objects in so far as possible in auditory terms by using verbal formulations, names, etc., as cues for recall. It is important to realize that this transfer from the presented sense-department to some other one more natural to *S* does not necessitate inferior performance. Thus, Foster remarks that while the work of observing visual material "may be surrogated, transferred to a given sense-department," yet "such surrogation may even be advantageous." The best *S* in his tests of visual reproduction was the one who visualized least.

(g) *Restriction:* *S*'s performance is definitely conditioned by his voluntary attempt to assimilate and reproduce either a large amount or a small amount of the material exposed. Thus, the nonsense syllables exposed are ten in number: by an effort, all ten may sometimes be read, but the result will be a poor reproduction of two or three syllables; if *S* confines his attention to the first four syllables, he may read these twice, and succeed fairly often in reporting all four. Similarly, there may be voluntary restriction of attention to other types of material.

(h) *Grouping:* As noted in Test 24, visual apprehension is greatly facilitated by any device that permits the grouping of the constituent elements in the exposure-field. This factor, more than any other, gives us the explanation both of the individual differences and of the practise-improvement above mentioned. Thus, in the dot tests, the mass of irregularly arranged dots is, by most *S*'s, arbitrarily rearranged (subjectively) into two, three, or sometimes four, groups of dots—each group containing three to six dots. Drawings are, similarly, often split up into component elements, and then recombined by a sort of analysis and synthesis. Sometimes this process is accompanied by the application of verbal symbols as tags for recall, e.g., "a rectangle, two peaks, and an arrow." For most *S*'s, this analytic-grouping method turns out to be more effective than the 'steady stare' which they are prone to employ at first.

REFERENCES

(1) Catherine Aiken, Methods of mind-training. New York, 1896. Pp. 75. For supplementary exercises, see her Exercises in mind-training. New York.

(2) K. M. Dallenbach, The effect of practise upon visual apprehension. To appear in *JEdPs*.

(3) W. S. Foster, The effect of practise upon visualizing and upon the reproduction of visual impressions. *JEdPs*, 2: 1911, 11-22.

(4)   Life of Robert Houdin, the king of conjurers, by himself.   Phila., 1859.   (Ch. 14, p. 256.)

(5)   J. P. Hylan, The distribution of attention.   *PsR*, 10: 1903, 373-403 and 498-533.

(6)   E. E. Jones, Individual differences in school children.   *PsCl*, 6: 1913, 241-251.

(7)   D. O. Lyon, A rapid and accurate method of scoring nonsense syllables and words.   *AmJPs*, 24: 1913, 525-531.

(8)   W. B. Pillsbury, Attention, London and N. Y., 1908.   Pp. 330.

(9)   J. Quantz, Problems in the psychology of reading.   *PsMon*, 2: No. 1, 1897.

(10)   E. C. Sanford, A course in experimental psychology.   Boston, 1895 and 1898.   Pp. 449.

(11)   G. M. Whipple, The effect of practise upon the range of visual attention and of visual apprehension.   *JEdPs*, 1: 1910, 249-262.

TEST 25A

Apprehension of topographic relationship: Spot-pattern test.—
It was pointed out in Tests 24 and 25 that visual apprehension is facilitated by grouping and that in the test of counting dots the irregularly arranged dots are by most S's rearranged (subjectively) into groups of dots. If we wish to test more directly this capacity for locating the components of a complex visual stimulus, we may proceed after the method developed by McDougall and used by several English investigators under the name of the 'spot-pattern test.' This test of "scope of apprehension" (McDougall) or "scope of attention" (Burt) or "power of concentration" (Schuster) or "apprehension of topographic relationship," as it has been variously termed, differs from the simpler dot-counting of Test 25 in the following particulars: (1) the dots or 'spots' are limited in number (7 to 10) ; (2) their number is known to S; (3) they are located on the exposure card in such a way as to fall at the intersections of imaginary cross-lines a quarter-inch apart and within an area 1.5 inches square; (4) S's task is to reproduce the position of these spots correctly upon a sheet of quarter-inch cross-section paper (Fig. 61) ; and (5) the exposure is repeated until this task is correctly performed.

This test has special interest on account of the tolerably high correlations it affords with estimated general intelligence.

Two methods are described, the first a more exact one for use in the laboratory, the second a simpler one for schoolroom use.

A. WITH THE DISC TACHISTOSCOPE

APPARATUS.[1]—Disc tachistoscope, with lamp, clamps and head-rest, as in Test 24. Special set of 20 9-cm. square stimulus cards, comprising 20 spot-patterns, 5 each of 7, 8, 9 and 10 spots. Prepared sheets of cross-section paper. Stop-watch.

PRELIMINARIES.—Set up the tachistoscope as directed in Test 24, using the smaller opening in the front screen, but adjusting the instrument to give a point exposure of 2 sec. This may be timed with sufficient accuracy with the aid of the stop-watch, and will be secured approximately by opening the sector to 115 deg. and setting the upper weight at 5 cm., and the lower at 87 cm. With a pencil block off a number of sheets of cross-section paper to outline a series of 1.5 inch squares, as in Fig. 61.

METHOD.—Seat S so as to bring his eyes directly in front of the exposure opening, at some 45 cm. distance and preferably slightly above its level. Give him substantially the following instructions: "About 1.5 sec. after I say 'ready,' there will appear in this opening for a brief period, 2 sec., a card containing 7 [or 8 or 9 or 10] spots. The card will look something like this one [showing another card for a moment]. You are immediately afterward to try to reproduce this arrangement of spots upon this square of cross-section paper [see Fig. 61]. The spots are so placed that each one will fall at the point of intersection of some pair of these lines, that is, at the corner of one of the small squares, but never on the outer margin of the large square. If you fail to get the pattern right at the first trial, the exposure will be repeated until you do."

---

[1] The apparatus and method employed by McDougall, Burt and Schuster are needlessly complex. A special portable tachistoscope was used. in which the exposure cards were illuminated from behind by transmitted light from a lamp shining in a darkened room. The cards were so contrived as to present a uniform 'dead' surface, save when the opening of the tachistoscope shutter illumined them for an instant (0.04 sec.), when the pattern flashed out like a tiny constellation of stars. The exposures were arranged in groups of five, separated by intervals of 1.5 sec., and S's attempt at reproduction was made only after each group of five exposures. (See Burt, 1, pp. 150-151, for further details.) As stated in our results, the rank-order for S's is virtually identical by the simpler procedure we recommend.

Use one card of the simplest patterns, inserted 180 deg. from its regular position, for a short fore-exercise to accustom *S* to the task.

S is always informed of the exact number of spots to be exposed on each stimulus card. A fresh square of cross-section paper is to be used for each attempted reproduction and all preceding attempts are to be kept covered from his sight as soon as they have been filled out.[2] Each trial is numbered in order, and *S*'s capacity is scored directly from the number of exposures required for an absolutely correct reproduction. After each trial *E* will notify *S* either 'right' or 'wrong,' but never anything more than that.

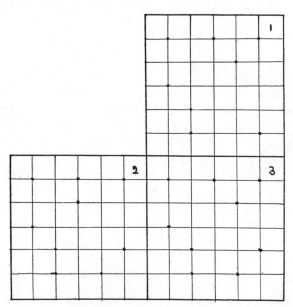

FIG. 61.   SPOT-PATTERN AND REPRODUCTIONS.
The original pattern is shown for convenience with the series of three reproductions.

If it is desired to continue the test beyond five patterns of a given number of spots, the standard set of cards may be used

---

[2] It is not clear whether the English investigators covered *S*'s attempts or not. If not, the conditions under which their results were secured are decidedly different from those here prescribed.

over again three times by turning them about to bring the other edges at the top.

Since the results vary decidedly with the individual patterns as well as with the number of spots, it is important for comparative purposes to give all *S*'s the same patterns in the same position and in the same order. It will depend on the general proficiency of the *S*'s to be examined whether 7, 8, 9 or 10-spot patterns are used. Adults can work with 10-spot patterns after a short period of practise, but 8 and 9-spot patterns are rather difficult for many school children.

B. WITH THE PORTABLE TACHISTOSCOPE

APPARATUS.—Special portable tachistoscope, consisting of a 3-inch, focal-plane photographic shutter, with wire release, mounted on a small easel adapted for holding the stimulus cards. Stimulus cards and cross-section paper as in Method A. Seconds pendulum.[3]

PRELIMINARIES.—Place the shutter on the easel with its curtain at the back, *i.e.*, next the stimulus card. Set the apparatus in such a position as to command full and uniform illumination of the cards when the shutter is open. Place the pendulum in view of *E*, but out of the range of *S*'s vision.

METHOD.—Seating of *S* (save for the head-rest), instructions, fore-exercise, choice of cards, their reproduction and the scoring as in Method A. Wind up the exposure curtain while the face of the apparatus is turned away from *S*: 1.5 sec. after a warning 'ready,' expose the stimulus card and hold the shutter open for 2 sec., using the pendulum for controlling these periods. While *S* is attempting his reproduction, *E* will find it convenient to wind the shutter half-way up, so as to leave the pattern exposed to his view for comparison with *S*'s work. If *S* makes any error, finish winding up the shutter, replace the apparatus before *S* and continue, as in Method A, until a correct reproduction is made.

RESULTS.—Working with trained college students, Miss Goudge obtained the averages given in Table 37 for the disc

---

[3] As the chief object in devising this apparatus is to secure portability for schoolroom testing, the regular laboratory pendulum may be replaced by a small weight and a cord of the proper length to swing seconds.

tachistoscope (with 1.5 sec. exposures) and for McDougall's method of groups of flashes, with 10 patterns of each type in both methods. As each one of the five flashes in each group is here scored as one exposure (not as 5, as by the English investigators), it will be seen that the 1.5 sec. exposure with the disc tachistoscope is less effective than a group of five exposures of 0.04 sec. each by the McDougall method, but more effective than one of these shorter exposures. Her results also indicate very high correlations between the rankings of the several S's in the two forms of the experiment—0.92, 0.99 and 0.87 for the 8, 9 and 10-spot patterns, respectively. Hence it follows that, at least for adults, the simpler method of single exposures with the tachistoscope furnishes an index of S's ability just as reliable as that given by the more complex method used by McDougall, Burt and Schuster.

TABLE 37.

Mean Number of Exposures Needed to Reproduce Spot-Patterns (*Goudge*)

SUBJECT	DISC TACHISTOSCOPE						M'DOUGALL'S METHOD					
	A	B	C	D	E	F	A	B	C	D	E	F
8 Spots	2.0	4.7	8.5	5.4	7.4	3.3	8.5	12.5	21.0	19.5	22.5	13.5
9 Spots	1.3	2.6	6.5	5.4	3.7	2.6	5.5	9.5	23.0	20.0	16.5	9.5
10 Spots	1.9	2.4	5.1	2.9	3.2	2.7	9.0	9.0	20.5	16.0	13.5	15.0

Burt found 8 and 9-spot patterns too difficult for many 13 year-old pupils. His test with these pupils in an elementary school, when four series of 7-spot, one series of 8-spot and one of 9-spot patterns were used, yielded for boys an average number of exposures (counting each flash) of 45.3, m.v. 21.1, extremes 10 and 157, and with pupils of the same age at a preparatory school an average for 8-spot patterns of 38.6 exposures.[4]

(2) *Dependence on sex.* Burt and Moore found boys superior to girls: median for boys 51 exposures, for girls 64 exposures; percentage of boys exceeding the median performance of girls 65.5, leaving an excess superiority for boys of 15.5 pe

---

[4]It should be pointed out again that it is not clear whether these pupi had their earlier attempts at reproduction in sight as they continued th test.

cent. This test, according to these investigators, constitutes the chief exception to the rule that sex differences are least in tests that correlate highest with intelligence, possibly because the technique proved difficult and the coefficient of reliability correspondingly low.

(3) *Dependence on practise.* Observations of adult S's all show that there is a very rapid improvement due to practise, which usually comes early in the tests. This improvement is chiefly due to the development of schemes of grouping. In Table 37 the fact that Miss Goudge's S's worked first with the 8-spot, then with the 9-spot, and lastly with the 10-spot patterns is a main reason for the result that the 9-spot required fewer exposures than the 8-spot patterns, and the 10-spot less, with one or two exceptions, than the 9-spot patterns.

(4) *Dependence on number of spots.* Taking a number of patterns and averaging the results of several S's, it will be found that the difficulty of a pattern increases with the increase in the number of spots. Thus, tests by Method A in the author's laboratory give as the mean number of exposures for adults: 8 spots, 3.93; 9 spots, 4.96; 10 spots, 6.13: in other words, the difficulty of 8, 9 and 10 spots is practically in the relation 4, 5 and 6. On the other hand, it is possible to arrange a 10-spot pattern that shall be easier than an 8-spot or even a 7-spot pattern, since much depends upon the position of the spots with reference to one another. A card that favors grouping when viewed by an S who has developed a satisfactory scheme of mental grouping may be reproduced correctly after a single exposure.

(5) *Correlation with intelligence.* The test has a high correlation with estimated intelligence. By the amalgamation of three series of trials Burt obtained in one school .76, *P.E.* .05, and in another school .75, *P. E.* .09. Again, when the boys in the elementary school were divided into three sections, clever, average and 'infra-normal,' the mean number of exposures was 19.5, 41 and 71.6, respectively, while a weak-minded boy needed 155 on one occasion and 220 on a second. It would seem, therefore, that the spot-pattern test promises to be of diagnostic value.

Schuster's results with a limited number of Oxford students, based on 9-spot patterns by the McDougall method, indicate small, but regularly positive correlations (about .20) between capacity in the test and intellectual status, as determined by a very rough classification according to the 4-fold table method.

(6) *Other relations.* Schuster reports that Oxford students specializing in science and mathematics were superior to those specializing in other subjects, and he also shows that "eyesight does not appreciably affect the results of this test."

(7) *Reliability.* The coefficient of reliability reported by Burt is rather low, about 0.50, but this is explicable by the unnecessarily complex method and apparatus he employed: the high correlations obtained by Miss Goudge between two forms of the test indicate, on the contrary, a very high degree of reliability.

(8) *Qualitative analysis.* The correct reproduction of the spot-patterns necessitates a process of analysis and synthesis. Miss Goudge's introspective records show that the patterns are always learned by a mental grouping of the spots. Usually, *S* gives up the attempt to assimilate the entire pattern as a whole and confines his attention in successive exposures to different subjectively formed groups within the total pattern. Some *S*'s continue for several seconds after the exposure to study the memory after-image of the pattern. The reproduction is assisted not only by visual imagery, but also by kinesthetic factors (movements of eye or hand, felt or imagined) and by verbal formulation. Patterns in which there are one or more rather isolated spots, even if the total number of spots be relatively small, offer special difficulty in grouping.

REFERENCES

(1) C. Burt, Experimental tests of general intelligence. *BrJPs*, 3: 1909, 94-177, especially 150 ff.

(2) C. Burt and R. C. Moore. The mental differences between the sexes. *JEPd*, 1: 1912, 273-284, 355-388.

(3) Mabel Goudge. A simplified method of conducting McDougall's 'spot-pattern test.' To appear in *JEdPs*.

(4) W. McDougall, Physiological psychology. London, 2d ed., 1908. See especially 129 ff.

(5) E. Schuster, First results from the Oxford anthropometric laboratory. *Biometrika*, 8: 1911, 40-51.

TEST 25B

The form-board.[1]—The form-board seems to have been first used by Seguin as a means of training feeble-minded children, out of recent years it has become better known as a mental test.

The task set by the form-board, that of perceiving or recognizing ten different forms, either by sight or by touch, and making a definite movement of reaction with each form (inserting it into its appropriate 'hole') is such that it is difficult to classify the test precisely. With quite young children and with feeble-minded children the perception of form is doubtless a prime factor, and with older children and adults the same thing is true when the test is carried out blindfolded, but otherwise performance in the test is for them largely conditioned by speed and coördination of movement. Yet again, repetition of the test under proper conditions may make it available as a test of learning capacity.

This complexity in the mental processes concerned in the test is reflected in the statements of those who have made most use of it. Norsworthy, for instance, called it a "test of form perception and rate of movement," and also sought to secure indication of learning capacity from her data. Jones likewise used the test to determine learning capacity, and speaks of it, too, as "a very good test of native ability." This idea that the test has diagnostic value in examining intelligence is again reflected in Norsworthy's statement that "this test seems to me to measure to a certain extent the ability of dealing quickly and well with a new situation" (which approximates Stern's definition of intelligence), and in Witmer's statement that "the form-board is one of the best tests rapidly to distinguish between the feeble-minded and the normal child," to which he adds that "it very quickly gives the experimenter a general idea of the child's powers of recognition, discrimination, memory, and coördination," while "repetition of the experiment leads to a conclusion as to his ability to learn." Wallin believes that the form-board test throws light upon the patient's ability to identify forms visually, upon his constructive capacity and his power of muscular coördination. Goddard says: "We have in our laboratory no other test that shows us so much about a child's condition in so short a time." His table of norms suggests strongly that the test can be of direct service in the examination and classification of mentally defective children.

From what has just been said it is evident that if we wish to measure perception of form and not mere capacity to make rapid movements, the test must be administered to older chil-

---

[1]The author is indebted to E. A. Doll, Research Assistant at The Training School, Vineland, N. J., for the general arrangement of this test.

dren and adults by a different method than to young or feeble-minded children. Two methods are therefore described, the one for visual, the other for tactual perception. E should use the former for children of perhaps 7 years old or less and for feeble-minded children, the latter for adults and for children above 10 or 12 years; for children between 7 and 12, E must use his judgment which method to employ. In case of doubt, the tactual should be tried first.

A. VISUAL METHOD

MATERIALS.—Form-board (either Goddard's, Fig. 62, or the new Cornell pattern).[2] Printed record-sheets. Stop-watch.

PRELIMINARIES.—E should first learn by heart a scheme of numbering of the blocks and their corresponding holes. The numbering runs from 1 to 10, beginning at the upper left-hand corner (Maltese cross) and proceeding from left to right.

METHOD.—Let S stand before a table of convenient height with the board squarely in front of him and with the blocks placed at the right side for right-handed and at the left side for left-handed S's. The standard position of the blocks for beginning the test with right-handed S's is shown by the following numbering:

	2		4		10
(Board)	7		9		6
	5	8		3	1

For left-handed persons the blocks are reversed to bring them in the same order moving outward from the board. As

---

[2]The form-board in most common use is Goddard's adaptation of the Norsworthy board. In it the Norsworthy hexagon and octagon are replaced by a Maltese cross and a 5-pointed star. The board used by Witmer is one such as would be obtained by rotating the Goddard board 180 deg. about its lengthwise axis, and is also supplied with a light rim (4, p. 249.)

Mr. D. K. Fraser has pointed out to me that for extended tests with adults by Method B it would be a great advantage to have a board in which the holes were made in a series of removable blocks of such dimensions as to permit of rather free interchange within the board as a whole which would then constitute a sort of tray, as it were, to contain these ten blocks. Such a device would permit E to make various groupings of these ten holes (or of yet others at will) and thus study S's capacity to learn new arrangements. The adjustable board recently perfected in the Cornell Educational Laboratory to meet these conditions is recommended as a useful substitute for Goddard's board.

is indicated by the arrangement of the record sheets, the blocks are picked up beginning with the lower row and working from the board outward, *i.e.*, following the sequence: 5, 8, 3, 1, 7, 9, 6, 2, 4, 10.

FIG. 62. GODDARD'S FORM-BOARD.

Instruct *S* as follows: "You see these blocks and the holes in the board into which they fit. You are to put the blocks into the holes as fast as you can. You must take the blocks with your right [left] hand, one at a time, in this order from left to right [right to left for left-handed *S*'s], beginning with the lower row [pointing to the blocks to illustrate what is wanted].³ You must place each block properly before you pick up the next one. Do you understand? Ready. Go!" At this signal *E* starts the watch and records the time taken to place all the blocks correctly.

---

³If *S* is too immature to understand these directions, *E* must push the blocks over to him, one at a time, in the prescribed order. The form-board test has usually been conducted without any attempt to standardize the position of the blocks at the outset, or the order in which they are taken, but experience shows that the outcome may be much affected by chance variations in this respect, so that the regulation order should be followed in every trial.

This quantitative record ought, however, to be supplemented by a qualitative record which shows what precisely S does with each block in his attempts to place it correctly. For this purpose E uses the printed record-sheets and sets down S's attempts in the following manner. As S attempts to place a given block, E records against the number of that block on the printed sheet the numbers of the holes into which S tries to place it. If a block is correctly placed without any false moves, no number will appear: otherwise, the series of numbers recorded against a given number indicates the full series of trials until the block is rightly placed. The following sample partial record will make the plan clear:

$$5 - 9 - 2 - 5$$
$$8 - 1 - 10 - 1 - 8$$
$$3 - 6 - 3$$
$$1$$

Here S first tried to place the rectangle in the 'oval,' then in the semi circle, then rightly in the rectangle. Again the third block, the semi circle, was tried in the hexagon before being correctly located. The fourth block, the circle, was placed at once without error, etc.

After this first trial with the 'favored' hand, place the blocks on the other side of the board (left for right-handed S's) in the positions above prescribed (reversed so as to produce the same order moving outward) and repeat the experiment as before, save that S must now use the other hand.

A third trial is made with the blocks at the top of the board (arranged in the order of their first trial), and this time is instructed to use both hands.

VARIATIONS OF METHOD.—See below, under Method B.

B. TACTUAL METHOD

MATERIALS.—As before, with the addition of a blindfold for S.[4] Large cloth to cover board and blocks.

METHOD.—Keep the material covered with the cloth when is not working with it and on no account permit him to se

[4] The blindfold must positively exclude any possibility of glancing at the board from underneath its folds. For children E will find it desirable construct a special blindfold that will guarantee perfect exclusion of the sight of the board.

the board or the blocks before or during the test, or after it if there is any likelihood of later trials. The blocks are arranged as in the visual method, but off to one side, under E's charge, who shoves them over to S, one at a time, in the order prescribed.

When S has been properly blindfolded and led to the position in front of the board, instruct him thus: "On the table before you there is a board in which are a series of ten holes of different shapes. I shall hand you, one at a time, a series of blocks of wood that just fit these ten holes. Put each block in place as quickly as you can. A new block will be placed for you just here [indicating a point on the table just at the right of the board] as soon as you have placed the one before it."

S is allowed to handle the block and examine the board with his fingers in any way that he wishes. Note whether both hands are used, and record any points of interest in S's way of accomplishing his task, particularly whether he continues to seek 'blindly' to thrust the block into some hole or uses his hands to feel the holes first. Keep both the quantitative and the qualitative records as in Method A. In the qualitative record, exploring the holes with the fingers does not, of course, constitute an error, but only the attempt to insert a block into a wrong hole.

When the last block is correctly placed, cover the board carefully with the cloth, remove S's blindfold and let him try to sketch the positions of the forms and their shapes.

Restore the blindfold and repeat the test precisely as before. Make a third similar trial or continue the test in this manner until S is able correctly to reproduce all the forms in their proper positions. Note the number of trials made and plot a curve of time taken in relation to number of trial.

VARIATIONS FOR BOTH METHODS.—(1) In either the visual or the tactual method the board may, at any point in the series of trials and without previous warning, be turned about 90 or 180 deg., and the effect of this alteration noted. (Cf. the special 'adaptation-board' devised by Goddard for a simpler, but analogous test of low-grade intelligence.)

(2)   Some indication of memory type may be obtained by
permitting S to study the board visually (without inserting
the blocks) until he has learned all the forms and their positions (as determined by a sketch made from memory).   Then
blindfold him, turn the board through 90 deg., and require him
to insert the blocks after having been notified of the alteration
made in the position of the board.   Note whether he seems to
have visual or kinesthetic memory, whether he makes errors,
whether he is forced to use the method of trial and error, etc.

(3)   In Method A the number of trials may be increased to
30, 10 for each hand and 10 for both hands, in regular alternation of 'favored' hand, other hand and both hands.   These trials
may then be separately averaged and the results taken as measures not only of learning capacity, but also of dexterity,
though for the latter purpose the first few trials, while practise is being acquired, must be excluded.

TREATMENT OF DATA.—Unless it is evident that there has
been some disturbing factor that should have been eliminated,
S's quantitative performance in the first trial may be taken as
the measure of his normal unpractised performance.[5]

The qualitative record, in terms of numbers of errors (each
attempt to place a block in a hole in which it does not belong
constitutes one error) may usually be taken as the measure of
his inability to perceive or recognize form.   In Method A persistent attempts to insert a block where it is manifestly impossible for it to go, or such absurd things as turning the blocks
upside down to make them fit, standing them on end, etc., should
be especially noted, as they are symptomatic of decided imma-
turity and are often seen in mentally defective S's.

RESULTS.—(1)   *Norms for Method A.*   Table 38 shows the
results published by Goddard from a study of 271 normal children classified by chronological and by mental age and of 420
mentally defective children classified by mental age.   The same
results are shown graphically in Fig. 63.   They are based upon
Method A, speed in seconds, best of three trials, without distinction of sex.   They are probably subject to some revision

---

[5] For direct comparison with Goddard's table and curve, E must, however, take the best of the first three trials.

TABLE 38

Mean Times for the Form-Board, Visual Method (Goddard)

	NORMAL		NORMAL			MENTALLY DEFECTIVE		
Chron. Age	No. Tested	Mean in Sec.	Mental Age	No. Tested	Mean in Sec.	Mental Age	No. Tested	Mean in Sec.
	--	----	4	7	33.8	4	53	76.12
5	17	29.5	5	7	30.3	5	52	51.25
6	26	27.5	6	13	27.5	6	54	38.24
7	25	24.5	7	47	25.4	7	85	26.39
8	28	21.8	8	43	20.7	8	87	23.80
9	47	19.3	9	46	19.2	9	48	18.30
10	49	18.2	10	69	16.6	10	29	17.50
11	38	17.6	11	25	15.9	11	8	16.40
12	20	15.9	12	14	14.3	12	4	12.09

and unfortunately furnish no clue to the amount of variation about the means for each age. From supplementary data obtained from Vineland it would appear that the mean variations range roughly from 2 to 5 sec. in the years 8 to 12 and approximate 40 or 50 sec. (for the defectives) in the mental ages 3 to 5. Children whose mental age is 1 or 2 years almost invariably fail with the test, and a certain percentage of those mentally 3 and 4 years also fail entirely. Attention should be called to the fact that in ages 4, 5 and 6 there is a marked discrepancy between the speed of normal and of feeble-minded children of the same mental age.

For data on the form-board test as applied to epileptics the elaborate tables prepared by Wallin, showing relation to age, sex and types of feeble-mindedness, should be consulted.[6]

(2) *Norms for Method B.* Data secured by the author from a small number of advanced university students give for three successive trials without sight of the board averages of 140, 120 and 69 sec., respectively. When the attempt was made to sketch the board after each trial, it was found that no S could accomplish this after the first trial, whereas about one-half located the blocks correctly and sketched their forms with but

---

[6] Wallin's averages are not entirely reliable in the totals, because some cases have been omitted entirely and none of these totals are weighted averages—a fact which would perhaps explain certain contradictions which appear in them.

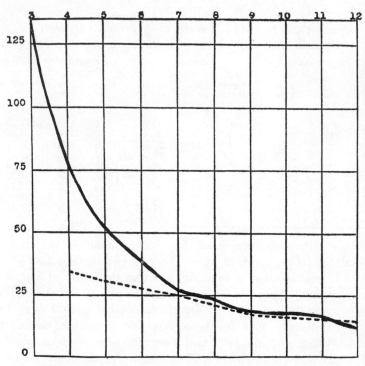

FIG. 63. MEAN TIMES FOR THE FORM-BOARD (From Goddard).

Ordinates represent seconds. abscissas mental age, solid line mental defectives, dotted line normal children.

trivial errors after the third trial. Decided individual differences are discovered in capacity to identify forms tactually. It is possible for S to learn to place the blocks rapidly by touch and yet have extremely erroneous ideas of their actual form.

(3) *Dependence on practise.* Some idea of the improvement due to repetition of the test (visual method) may be gained from Jones' figures for 15 unselected 4th-grade pupils, from which the following figures may be obtained:

	average	m. v.
1st trial,	22.3 sec.	4.4 sec.
3d trial,	19.3	3.3
10th trial,	15.5	2.7
Mean,	18.2	2.4
Best,	14.2	1.8

Jones found that the best record was made in 5 cases on the 10th trial, in 5 cases on the 9th, in 3 on the 7th, in one of the 4th, while in one both the 5th and the 10th were equally good. The maximal improvement for any pupil was a reduction from 32.4 to 10.6 sec., the minimal from 18.2 to 17.2 sec.

Norsworthy's repetition of the test after a year's interval showed the median improvement to be 1.2 sec. for defective, and 10.0 sec. for normal children.

REFERENCES

(1) H. H. Goddard, The form-board as a measure of intellectual development in children. Reprint from *The Training School*, 9: June, 1912. Pp. 4. (See also The adaptation-board. *PsBu*, 9: 1912, 79-80.)

(2) E. E. Jones, Individual differences in school children. *PsCl*, 6: 1913, 241-251.

(3) N. Norsworthy, Psychology of mentally deficient children. *ColumbiaConPhPs*, 1906. Pp. 111.

(4) J. E. Wallin, Experimental studies of mental defectives. *EdPs Mon*, No. 7, Baltimore, 1912. Pp. 155.

(5) J. E. Wallin, Human efficiency. *PdSe*, 18: 1911, 74-84.

(6) L. Witmer, A monkey with a mind. *PsCl*, 3: 1909, 179-205.

(7) L. Witmer, Courses in psychology at the summer school of the University of Pennsylvania. *PsCl*, 4: 1911, 245-273.

TEST 26

Cancellation.—There are in use several forms of mental test in which a continuous task is assigned under conditions such that maximal attention is demanded for the best work, and that any reduction of attention is reflected directly in the speed or accuracy of the work. Prominent among these tests is that which, following Miss Sharp (27), we shall term 'cancellation.' The essential principle is the crossing out of an assigned symbol or symbols (letters, words, digits, etc.) from a prepared form containing the assigned symbol in conjunction with a number of others of the same general order. The test is rather remarkable for the variety of forms it has assumed, the variety of names that have been given it, and the divergence of statement as to what it really measures.

Thus, its originator, Bourdon (6), used it with ten adults to measure "discrimination;" Oehrn (24) proposed it, under the title "search for assigned letters," as a convenient test of attention for experimentation in individual psychology; Cattell and Farrand (10) introduced it into the series of tests of Columbia University students in the form of the "*A*-test" for "rate of perception," and Thorndike employed it later, together with what may be regarded as variations of it (the "*a-t* test," the "*e-r* test," and the "misspelled-word test") for various comparative studies, particularly for his examination of the mental traits of twins (32); Binet (4, 236 ff.) called it the "correction of proof" test, and used it to contrast the ability of intelligent and unintelligent children (as did Winteler, 37), to measure fatigue (as did Ritter, 25), and incidentally, to study their capacity to break and form associations; Vogt used cancellation to examine attention and distraction; Judd (17) has classed it among tests devoted to discrimination reactions, Woodworth and Wells as an association test; Simpson speaks of it as a test of "efficiency of perception," Chambers as a test "quickness of perception," Wallin as a test of "speed and accuracy of perceptual discrimination," Franz as a test of "time of discrimination, association and movement," while Hollingworth points out that the processes depend somewhat on the subject: for some there is mere recognition of the assigned symbol without much discrimination, whereas for others there occurs deliberate discrimination of that symbol from the other symbols. Meumann objects to all these general characterizations and insists that we must discover the elementary processes at work. The primary activity demanded of the subject in the cancellation test is, he says, the holding in attention of the problem assigned him, and this means that he must keep in mind not only the particular letters to be cancelled, but also what is to be done with them (noting their presence and crossing them out). 'Discrimination' or 'quickness of apprehension' is something secondary to this primary activity. But this keeping in mind of a specific thing or attribute to be looked for in a totality of presented material is, he says, the fundamental activity in all systematic observation, so that the test can be said, if we would use a general term, to measure real capacity of observation. In the opinion of Bobertag[1] the value of the test is not very clear, since it certainly does not test pure attention, and seems particularly affected by non-intellectual factors, such as conscientiousness and good-will.

However the activity concerned in cancellation may be described in psychological terms, it is clear that the objective results of the test must vary, even for the same S, according as the test-conditions are varied with respect to (a) kind and arrangement of symbols, (b) number of symbols assigned to be cancelled and (c) the duration of the test. To secure direct comparison with the work of others for material and method other than that prescribed below, E must consult the original sources for the detailed description of test-conditions, but some idea of the methodological variations that have been used may be given at this point.

(a) *Kind and arrangement of symbols.* We may distinguish at least five kinds of material with variations in the arrangement of some of these kinds: (1) spaced prose, (2) unspaced prose, (3) disconnected words, (4) unregulated pied material, and (5) regulated pied material, with (a) unequal, or (b) equal, proportion of the symbols.

(1) *Spaced prose* is secured by taking any ordinary printed matter, but preference has been given to scientific (Binet, Lapie) or philosophical (Sharp) texts, rather than to easily grasped material (Winteler).

(2) *Unspaced prose*, as employed by Miss Sharp, is secured by having a page of concrete description, or of more abstract material, printed without capitals, spacing, or punctuation. The following lines will serve to illustrate two such texts:

---

[1] Expressed in a personal communication to the author.

theshoresoftheislandwerecompletelyfringedwithbushesand
greatcarehadbeentakentopreservethemastheyansweredasascreen

theproblemofphilosophyhasbeenineveryagetodeterminethe
relationbetweenbeingandthoughtbetweensubjectandobjecteveryphil

(3) *Disconnected words* may take the form of (*a*) sense words in non-sense arrangement (Sharp) or of (*b*) nonsense words, as in the a-test used by MacMillan and Bruner and by Mrs. Squire. Similarly, the arrangement of French words in irregular order as used by Brown with English children amounts to nonsense arrangement as does the style of form illustrated in the misspelled-words test prescribed below.

(4) *Unregulated pied material* has sometimes been formed, after the fashion of Bourdon and Vogt, by printing a page of some foreign language sure not to be known (Hungarian, Finnish) without spacing, capitals or punctuation, but the same material can be secured more simply by letting the printer set up a page of letters picked up at random from a pile of 'pied' type.

(5) *Regulated pied material, i. e.*, an arrangement of symbols in irregular order, but with precaution to secure a given number of certain of them has perfectly obvious advantages for experimental work, and this is the form of material now used by nearly all experimenters. Aside from the choice of the nature of the symbols (letters, digits, etc.) this form of material subdivides into two forms, according to the arrangement into (*a*) unequal and (*b*) equal number of each symbol.

A good example of unequal distribution is seen in the familiar A-test (reproduced herewith, and employed by Whitley, Doll, Simpson, Chambers and as one of the stock tests of Columbia freshmen), in which there are 50 A's interspersed among other letters of less frequency, and other examples in the six forms of 200 A's each used by Wallin, the B-test and geometrical form test as used by Simpson, Wyatt's form with 600 letters, Whitley's form containing 50 each of A, B, K and S (36, p. 62) and her set of hieroglyphic characters (p. 69) and in the curious rows of dots arranged in groups of 3, 4 or 5 dots, 24 groups to the line, used by Abelson.

Equal distribution of the symbols is exemplified in the number-checking tests devised by Woodworth and Wells, in an improved geometrical-form sheet described by Whitley (p. 70) and in Franz's special set of seven forms (15, pp. 130-133), each containing 25 of eight different symbols (letters, digits or other forms) so placed that a given character in the one form corresponds in location with a given character in every other form, which permits special examination to be made of ability to learn (see Kent and Boring).

THE A-TEST

```
OYKFIUDBHTAGDAACDIXAMRPAGQZTAACVAOWLYX
WABBTHJJANEEFAAMEAACBSVSKALLPHANRNPKAZF
YRQAQEAXJUDFOIMWZSAUCGVAOABMAYDYAAZJDAL
JACINEVBGAOFHARPVEJCTQZAPJLEIQWNAHRBUIAS
SNZMWAAAWHACAXHXQAXTDPUTYGSKGVKVLGKIM
FUOFAAKYFGTMBLYZIJAAVAUAACXDTVDACJSIUFMO
TXWAMQEAKHAOPXZWCAIRBRZNSOQAQLMDGUSGB
AKNAAPLPAAAHYOAEKLNVFARJAEHNPWIBAYAQRK
UPDSHAAQGGHTAMZAQGMTPNURKNXIJEOWYCREJD
UOLJCCAKSZAUAFERFAWAFZAWXBAAABHAMBATAD
KVSTBNAPLILAOXYSJUOVYIVPAAPSDNLKRQAAOJLE
GAAQYEMPAZNTIBXGAIMRUSAWZAZWXAMXBDXAJZ
ECNABAHGDVSVFTCLAYKUKCWAFRWHTQYAFAAAOH
```

The *A*-test has three disadvantages : it is not devised to permit the use of any letters other than *A ;* it does not lend itself easily to four-letter cancellation ; in many instances, two or more *A*'s are in juxtaposition, so that some *S*'s may see and cancel several at once.

To avoid these difficulties, recourse may be had to the second form of regulation, viz : the use of each of the 26 letters the same number of times each. In the two letter-forms which are prepared for this test, the printer has mixed together 100 types of each letter and set them in chance order, save where a given letter was repeated too closely.

(*b*) *Letters cancelled.* It is easily demonstrated that the ranks of a given number of *S*'s will vary somewhat according as a few (1-2) or several letters (4-6) are to be cancelled. Where but one letter has been used, this has commonly been the letter *a* (Bourdon, Cattell and Farrand, Wissler, Thorndike, Sharp, Descoeudres, Simpson, Squire, Chambers, Doll, Wallin, Whitley, MacMillan and Bruner) or occasionally *e.* In cancelling more than one letter, we find that Bourdon tried at different times, *a* and *i; a, r, i, s; a, e, l, t;* or *a, e, l, t, o, k;* Binet, *a, e, d, r, s,* also *i, o, l, f, t,* and *a, e, r, o, s, m;* Vogt, *l, n, s;* Winteler, *n, s, t,* and *l, m, r, s, t;* Burt, *o* and *c;* Lapie, *a* and *r;* Wyatt and Brown, *e* and *r,* and *a, n, o, s;* Whitley, *a, b, k, s;* Woodworth and Wells and Strong, any single digit ; Kent and Boring, various single characters ; and Whitley and Simpson different single geometrical forms.

It was Binet's contention that, when but one letter is cancelled, *S*'s tend to work with approximately equal accuracy, but with varying speed, whereas, when four or five letters are cancelled, they tend to work with approximately equal speed, but with varying accuracy ; he, accordingly, arranged the test in one or the other of these ways, as he wished to measure either speed or accuracy. As will be shown later, this assumption is not strictly justifiable.

The cancellation of one letter is so easy that some investigators have tried other devices for complicating the task : Ritter, for example, had his *S*'s cancel every *r* with a vertical stroke and every article (in German texts) with a horizontal stroke, or, again, every *s* with a vertical and every preposition with a horizontal stroke : his idea that these two assignments would be equally easy and could thus be used interchangeably was not borne out in practise. Thorndike has used still another variation : mark every *word* (in a Spanish text) containing both *e* and *r,* or both *a* and *t.* Similarly, in the "number-group checking test" of Woodworth and Wells, *S* is to cross out every combination containing both 2 and 3, or both 8 and 9. Investigators at Columbia University have also made frequent use of the misspelled-word test described below.

(*c*) *Duration.* It is preferable, whenever possible, to have all *S*'s cover the same amount of material and to secure the quantitative record in terms of elapsed time (Abelson, Boring, Kent, Descoeudres, MacMillan and Bruner, Simpson, Squire, Strong, Woodworth and Wells and others). But for group work it is necessary to use the time-limit method (unless using the special time-clock), and the actual limits used by investigators have ranged from 45 sec. to several hours. At Columbia, 1 min. is allowed for the *A*-test, 2 min. for the *a-t* test, 3 min. for the misspelled word test. When working by the individual method, the *A*-test takes, on the average, about 95 sec. Miss Sharp's tests demanded from 3 to 4 min. ; Bourdon used 6 min. ; Winteler 15 min. ; Binet found that by extending the time to 10 or 20 min., he could get signs of fatigue. When such long times are used, *E* may follow the time with the stop-watch and at expiration of each minute, check with a small horizontal underlining mark, the point at which *S* is then working. It was Oehrn's idea that the cancellation test might be extended through several hours in order to analyze such factors as praise, fatigue, ennui, spurt, warming-up, etc. This has been partially done by Vogt, who worked for an hour or more at a time, in 10 min. periods with 5 min. intermissions.

Among recent investigators we find durations for this test of 75 sec. (Chambers), 100 sec. (Wallin), 2 min. (Doll, Burt, Wyatt), 3 min. (Wyatt's *anos*-test, Brown with adults), and 5 min. (Lapie and Brown with children).

Seven forms of cancellation test are here described: the first four furnish material for the cancellation of one or more symbols, whether letters, digits or geometrical forms; the fifth reproduces the word-cancelling tests and the last two the misspelled-word tests, as administered at Columbia University.

A. Cancellation of a single letter

MATERIALS.—Four printed forms. Set of three control keys. Stop-watch. Moderately soft pencil.

The first form, beginning *hplg*, etc., contains 100 each of the 26 letters, arranged in chance order, but with precaution against the repetition of any letter within two places.

The second form, beginning *zycu*, etc., is a substitute form of similar construction.

The third form, geometrical figures, contains 8 different forms, each of which is presented 50 times, and is identical with the form used by Whitley (36, p. 70).

The fourth form, digits, resembles the 'number-checking test' of Woodworth and Wells, but has been improved in several respects. The digits are printed in 12-point instead of 8-point type, with about doubled spacing and leading, and the location of the several digits has been so arranged that by means of but three control keys the location of all 100 of any one of the digits can be rendered instantly visible, thus greatly facilitating the correction of *S*'s performance. Due care has been taken to avoid 'runs' of any digit, so that any digits may be assigned for cancelling.[2]

METHOD.—Whenever convenient, work with one *S* at a time. Place the form before *S*, printed side down. For the first form instruct him as follows: "When I say 'ready,' turn over this sheet of paper, begin at the first line, and mark every *a*[3] on the page like this." (Exhibit for an instant another sample form, already marked, to be sure that *S* understands the instructions.) "Mark as rapidly as you can, but try not to leave out

---

[2] For the construction of this form and its ingenious keys I am indebted to my assistant, Mr. D. K. Fraser.

[3] The letter *a* is chosen merely because it has commonly been used. If it is desired to repeat the test with other letters, it would doubtless be preferable to select a number which have been shown to be of nearly equal legibility. For this, one may recommend *m* and *w*, or the four letters, *q. p, b, d*. (See Sanford, 26).

any *a*'s." Give the command—"ready." Start the watch when *S* glances at the first line: stop it when he finishes the last line; record on the form the time, together with *S*'s name, the date, and other needed items.

Repeat with another letter, as *o*, on the same form, or with the letter *a* again on the second form.

Test the third form, using similar instructions and assigning the triangle for cancellation. For further testing, the circle or semi-circle will be found easier than the trapezoid.

In using the fourth form, try for the standard test the digit 7, with the digit 1 for the second test. For further testing, 0 and 4 will be found harder than 1 or 7, while 6 and 9 are the hardest to cancel.

S may be allowed to traverse alternate lines from right to left.

If necessary to follow the group method, as in conducting classroom tests, it is a good plan to write a sample line on the blackboard and show how the cancellation is to be done. Make sure that no *S* turns the paper before the signal, and that all start simultaneously. All *S*'s must cease work at the command "stop," and underscore horizontally the letter at which they were looking when this command was given. The exact time to be used must be determined by a few preliminary experiments; it should be such that the fastest *S* to be examined will not quite be able to finish: 2 min. is to be generally recommended, since very few adults can finish within that time.[4]

B. Cancellation of more than one symbol

Materials.—As in Method A.

Preliminaries.—The characters to be cancelled must first be typewritten or drawn upon each form, so as to be readily visible to *S* during the work. For letters it is recommended that *q, r, s, t* be cancelled upon either the first or second form;[5] for the

---

[4] The author's time-clock for group testing will render group testing by the work-limit method feasible with reliable *S*'s.

[5] Save for special purposes, the cancellation of four letters suffices as well as that of five or six to bring out the characteristics of the test. The letters *q, r, s, t* are selected because they form a combination fairly easily remembered, and embrace one letter projecting above, one projecting below the line, and two small letters.

third form try any two, three or four of the geometrical figures; for digits, try two or more of the digits 2, 4, 6, 8.

METHOD.—As before, with the added explanation that the letters to be marked have been placed for reference at the top of the sheet. (*E* must, of course, also state the letters verbally beforehand.) The time will naturally be longer than before: 4 min. may safely be used in most group tests, as a competent adult takes nearly 5 min.

VARIATION OF METHOD.—Omit the typewriting of the letters to be cancelled.

C. CANCELLATION OF WORDS—THE A-T AND THE E-R TEST

MATERIALS.—Printed page from a Spanish text. Stop-watch.

METHOD.—Instruct *S* to mark with a horizontal stroke each *word* containing *both a* and *t*. Exhibit a sample page, or illustrate on the blackboard. Forewarn *S* that the words are in a foreign language. If the individual method can be followed, take the time for the whole sheet; if the group method is followed, allow 2 min.

For a second test, use fresh sheets of the same text, but substitute *e* and *r* for *a* and *t*.

D. CANCELLATION OF MISSPELLED WORDS

MATERIALS.—Two printed texts containing a large number of misspelled words. Stop-watch.

METHOD.—Test each text separately. In each case, instruct *S* to mark with a horizontal stroke every word that is not spelled correctly. Take the time for the whole sheet, or allow 3 min.

TREATMENT OF DATA: SCORING.—In these cancellation tests we meet the difficulty common to many mental tests that we have two indexes of efficiency—the one quantitative (speed), the other qualitative (accuracy). There are evidently three ways of scoring under these conditions: (1) we may keep both records and try to use them independently, in which event we may find it almost impossible to make any extensive comparison of results for different individuals or different groups; (2) we may neglect either speed or accuracy and make all our comparisons in terms of the other index; or (3) we may attempt by some corrective formula to combine the two indexes into a single index that shall express fairly, though perhaps somewhat arbitrarily, S's net efficiency. Examples of these three methods will make them clearer.

(1) In Doll's tabular presentation of the work of feeble-minded children the average number of a's crossed is given for each group as a measure of speed and the average number of a's passed over (omissions within the portion of the form attempted) is likewise given for each group as a measure of inaccuracy.

(2) Under some circumstances it will be found that the errors are so few as to become virtually negligible, in which case comparison may be made directly in terms of speed (see, for example, the recommendations made by Woodworth and Wells for their number-checking tests). Similarly, MacMillan and Bruner omit their corrective formula if the accuracy is 96 per cent. or above. Binet, as noted above, also believed that the cancellation of one letter tended to produce approximately equal accuracy and that of four or five letters approximately equal speed.

(3) The conversion of speed and accuracy into a single index of efficiency has been attempted in various ways. The simplest is doubtless to select some arbitrary quantity as a penalty for each error and to use this same penalty for all S's. Thus, Simpson corrected the time for the A-test by adding 5 sec. for each A omitted, and his geometrical form test by adding 3 or 6 sec. (depending on the assigned symbol) for each omission and neglecting the few errors of wrong cancellation. The principle used is that of penalizing S for each omission by an amount slightly greater than the time found by experience to be needed on the average for cancelling one symbol. Another very simple correction is that used by Wyatt and by Brown when working by the time-limit method: give $+ 1$ to each symbol correctly marked and $- 1$ for each error of omission or of insertion within the ground covered. A similar method is used by Wallin for scoring his forms containing 200 A's: quantitative efficiency is measured by crediting 0.5 per cent. for each A cancelled, while combined quantitative and qualitative efficiency is measured by subtracting from the quantitative score 0.5 per cent. for each A missed or wrongly crossed within the ground covered.

Other investigators have used more elaborate corrective formulas. Thus Miss Sharp converted speed into accuracy on the assumption that "in a given individual maintaining a constant degree of attention while doing a piece of work the percentage of error is inversely proportional to the time taken for the work." But most investigators, following the suggestion of Cattell and Farrand, have sought to convert accuracy into speed by some formula that would add to the obtained time an amount that would be required to mark the letters omitted, with possibly some additional penalty. The first method may be illustrated by reference to MacMillan and Bruner, who divided the recorded time by the proportion of a's crossed out (unless this fraction was 96 per cent. or over), the second method by the scheme of Strong, who for each omission added to the obtained time twice the time required to mark a single letter.

The following treatment has been used by the writer. When possible, rank speed in terms of time (T), otherwise in terms of symbols examined (e), i. e., ground covered.

Let A = the index of accuracy,

E = the index of net efficiency,

T = the time in seconds for the entire form,

e = the number of symbols examined,

o = the number of letters erroneously omitted,

c = the number of letters crossed,

w = the number of letters wrongly crossed.

Then, to compute the index of accuracy, use the formula

$$A = \frac{c - w}{c + o}.$$

To compute the index of net efficiency when using the time-limit method, employ the formula

$$E = eA,$$

and when using the work-limit method, the formula

$$E = 100 \frac{A}{T}.$$

The chief defect of these formulas seems to lie in over-severe penalizing of extreme cases. Thus, an S in the $qrst$-test examined 825 letters, crossed 40 (including 2 w's) and omitted 78. Here $e = 825$, $A = .322$, $E = 266$.

While the author has not had opportunity to test it, the plan proposed by Münsterberg to meet a similar difficulty in another connection would appear likely to supply a still better correction (22, 77 ff.) and possibly to provide an adequate method of equating speed and accuracy in many tests. The idea is to ascertain the approximate range of both quantitative and qualitative performance and to equate units on the qualitative range with units on the quantitative range. To borrow the figures from Münsterberg, assume that in the cancellation test times ranged from 180 to 420 sec., and errors from 4 to 28. Then one of the 24 qualitative units is equal to 10 of the quantitative units, so that a penalty of 10 sec. may be added to the time record for each error in cancellation.

It is often of interest to keep records of the number of omissions for each letter, as in this way one may get comparative estimates of their difficulty.

For the word-cancellation, similar methods may be pursued: when the test is administered by the time-limit method, efficiency, for the sake of simplicity, may be taken in terms of the number of words marked, with a deduction of 2 for each wrongly marked word.[6]

The rank in the misspelled word test may, similarly, be best computed in terms of time, with a reduction for errors as described for the cancellation of letters.[7]

RESULTS. (1) *Average performances.* The number-checking test of Woodworth and Wells takes for adults from 100 to 200 sec., with an average of about 133 sec. The *A*-test at Columbia has yielded averages of 87.3 sec. for women and 100 sec. for men. A similar test, used by Chambers with a time-limit of 75 sec., was scored in *A*'s crossed by 7th and 8th-grade pupils, average 60.25, minimum 39, maximum 95. The misspelled word tests are of unequal difficulty: on the average the time required by adults per word cancelled ranges from 1.11 to 1.87 sec., with a mean (based on 183 students) of 1.64 sec. For further norms consult the tables that follow and those published by Whitley (p. 72).

(2) *Dependence on age.* There is undoubtedly a general improvement with age both in speed and accuracy of cancellation. Wissler's results for the *A*-test show that Columbia seniors better their records as freshmen: in 35 cases there was an average reduction in time from 105.4 to 88.9 sec., and in errors from 4.7 to 1.6. The relation of performance in this test to mental age is shown in the Vineland results published by Doll, and reproduced here in Table 39. It will be seen that defectives classed as 1 to 3 years old mentally cannot perform the test and that total failure may extend up through the 6th year. From the 4th to the 12th mental year the number of *a*'s crossed increases from an average of 11 to an average of 41 (2 min. time-limit).

---

[6] This method is followed by Thorndike, who found such errors only in one of ten papers on the average.

[7] Thorndike neglected errors in this test, though they occurred in about one-third of the papers.

TABLE 39

Results with the A-test at Vineland, Classed by Mental Age (Doll)

MEN-TAL AGE	AVER. CHRON. AGE	NO. OF CASES	NO. OF TESTS	NO. OF FAIL-URES	NO. A'S CROSSED		AV. NO. LETTERS OMITTED	EXTREMES	
					AV.	M. V.		WORST	BEST
1	16	7	7	7					
2	17	6	7	7					
3	17	13	17	17					
4	17	22	37	16	11	3	15	0	16
5	22	24	26	12	13	5	20	0	27
6	20	38	61	6	21	8	14	0	51
7	19	32	64	0	18	6	17	4	34
8	20	55	109	0	25	7	12	3	64
9	20	33	89	0	33	9	9	15	50
10	21	14	34	0	35	8	6	17	51
11	19	6	19	0	41	15	4	30	56
12	18	2	9	0	41	4	4	37	45

Mrs. Squire, using the special *a*-test devised by MacMillan and Bruner, found a fairly steady decrease of 'perception-time' with age, with two distinct points of sudden improvement, viz: at the years 7-8 and 11-12. She therefore proposes to include this test with others in a scheme of diagnostic tests, with the following standards of performance.[8] Age 6, omissions (taken to indicate degree of attention) not to exceed 11, time not to exceed 175 sec.; age 7, omissions under 11, time under 90 sec.; ages 8 to 10, omissions under 6, time under 60 sec.; age 11, omissions under 5, time under 60 sec.; ages 12 or 13, omissions not over 1 and time 49 to 50 sec.

(3) *Dependence on sex.* All investigators concur in reporting a sex difference in favor of women and girls. The results of freshmen tests at Columbia have already been quoted. Woodworth and Wells find women distinctly better in the number-checking test; Burt, with 2 min. cancellation of *o*'s and *e*'s, found that boys cancelled 99.5, girls 110.0 letters, while Doll's figures for Vineland show, for the ages where sufficient cases of both sexes are included, a superiority for the girls of from 8 to 16 per cent.

---

[8]There is at least serious doubt as to the validity of the 'perception-time' here used. It is computed as by MacMillan and Bruner, whose method is criticized below (Result 8).

(4) *Dependence on letter cancelled.* According to Bourdon, letters whose form is simplest are oftenest omitted; with the letter *o*, 6 to 10 times as many errors were made by his *S's* as with the letter *c*, but the author's comparative tests with the letters *c* and *o* do not substantiate these conclusions fully. Table 40 shows that in 40 consecutive tests, grouped by tens, *o* is distinctly easier to cancel than *c*, save in the first group; it may therefore be expected that it is easier to cancel than *e*, which, in practise, is often confused with *c*. In the *qrst*-test, 50 boys committed errors of omission as follows: *s*, 337; *t*, 561; *r*, 653; and *q*, 718. Here there is no relation whatsoever with legibility, since *s* belongs to the group of relatively illegible letters, and *q* to the group of very legible letters (Sanford, 26). We may conclude that when school children cancel these four letters in one test, it is the least often used letter that suffers most from omission.

TABLE 40

Effects of Letters and of Fatigue on Cancellation (*Whipple*)

LETTER	1ST TEN	M. V.	2ND TEN	M. V.	3RD TEN	M. V.	4TH TEN	M. V.	AVERAGE
c_____	93.12	5.36	91.04	5.73	89.86	3.0	96.64	4.69	92.66
o_____	94.06	4.93	86.28	1.42	82.64	3.4	87.52	3.46	87.62
Average_____	93.59		88.21		86.25		92.08		

In number-checking Woodworth and Wells find 1 and 7 easiest, next 0 and 4, and 6 and 9 hardest. In crossing *A*, *B*, *K* and *S* in a page of capitals, Whitley found *K* harder than *B* and *A* harder than *S*. Her monograph may be consulted for further details on the subject of this and of the following paragraph.

(5) *Dependence on the form of material.* Bourdon found that a change in size of type from one in which the small letters were 1.75 mm. high to one in which they were 1.25 high made little difference: if anything, the smaller type proved better. On the other hand, several investigators have complained against the use of small type (Strong, for instance, finds even

Woodworth and Wells number-checking form too trying on the eyes), and Whitley found the use of hieroglyphics resembling Chinese letters quite unsuited for cancellation work.

There seems no doubt that more errors are made in cancelling letters out of ordinary prose than out of 'pied' material. Sharp, for example, found that even the elimination of spacing between words altered the performance: the average time for 7 S's for a spaced text was 190 sec., for an unspaced text 219 sec., and the average percentage of errors was 9.6 and 4.58, respectively. The faster speed and poorer quality of work done with ordinary prose is plainly due to the tendency for the rise of meaning to act as a distraction to the process of cancellation; the latter requires attention to individual letters, whereas the former (ordinary reading) proceeds naturally by the assimilation of words as wholes. As will be noted below, most S's do not 'read' the text when cancelling letters in pied material.

A very good illustration of the effect of form of material upon performance is seen in the comparative results of Brown and Wyatt, both of whom used upon school children 11-12 years old what they refer to as the er-test and the anos-test. Wyatt's S's cancelled 17.75 e's and r's in 2 min., Brown's cancelled from 362 to 377 in 5 min.; in the anos-test Wyatt's S's cancelled 41.20 letters in 3 min., Brown's cancelled 161 in 5 min. The striking disparity is due, so far as one can judge, to the use by Wyatt of 600 letters with only 21 each of the letters to be crossed, and of a page of French words by Brown. All of which shows that, unless a standard procedure is followed, a test cannot surely be recognized by its name.

(6) *Dependence on number of letters to be cancelled.* According to Bourdon, an increase in the number of letters to be cancelled causes a progressive decrease in the extent of material examined, but approximately the same number of letters is cancelled in a given time. This conclusion may be accepted as generally valid, but much depends upon the arrangement of the material (cf. the above comment on Wyatt and Brown). Bourdon is of the opinion that S's that are accurate in cancelling one are also accurate in cancelling several letters. The au-

thor's tests confirm this generalization in the main, as they show a value for this correlation of + 0.38 (Table 42). With regard to speed, Bourdon merely states that some individuals slow in marking one letter prove fast in marking several; my results indicate, however, that the correlation between one- and four-letter efficiency is greater in the case of speed (+ 0.49) than in the case of accuracy (Table 42).

(7) *Relation of speed and accuracy.* Binet, as previously noted, assumes that speed tends to be equalized in marking four letters, accuracy in marking one letter. My tests with 50 boys (Table 41, last column) show that, while there is a tendency in this direction, it is not sufficiently pronounced to warrant the neglect of either speed or accuracy in estimating efficiency. In other words, the variation in speed is proportionately less in marking four letters than in marking one letter, and the variation in accuracy is proportionately less in marking one letter than in marking four letters, but there is nothing approaching equalization of either factor.

TABLE 41

Averages and Variations in Cancellation Tests (*Whipple*)

LETTERS CANCELLED	INDEX	AVERAGE	M, V.	COEFFICIENT OF VARIABILITY
e	Speed	702	193	27
q, r, s, t	Speed	811	177	22
e	Accuracy	89.6	8.0	9
q, r, s, t	Accuracy	63.1	11.4	18

Cattell and Farrand state that some S's are slow and accurate, some slow and inaccurate, some fast and accurate, some fast and inaccurate. Since, however, an S that works very fast presumably tends to work less accurately, we may expect to find indications of an inverse correlation between speed and accuracy, and this is the case. Wissler's relatively easy A-test gives an inverse correlation ($r = - 0.28$). In the author's tests, the cancellation of one letter is harder than that of the A-test, and the cancellation of four letters is still harder; i consequence, we find inverse relations of — 0.37 and — 0.64, respectively (Table 42). In the case of 30 Cornell University students, speed and accuracy were found similarly inversely related, but by a lower coefficient ($r = -0.48$, Table 42).

TABLE 42

Correlations in Cancellation Tests: 50 Grammar-School Boys (*Whipple*)

FIRST MEMBER	SECOND MEMBER	PEARSON COEFFICIENT
Speed, one letter	Accuracy, one letter	—0.37
Speed, four letters	Accuracy, four letters	—0.64
Speed, four letters	Accuracy, four letters	—0.48*
Speed, one letter	Speed, four letters	0.49
Accuracy, one letter	Accuracy, four letters	0.38
Speed, one letter	Class-standing	—0.40
Accuracy, one letter	Class-standing	none
Net efficiency, one letter	Class-standing	—0.32
Speed, four letters	Class-standing	—0.40
Accuracy, four letters	Class-standing	0.39
Net efficiency, four letters	Class-standing	—0.09
Net efficiency, one letter	Word-building (Test 47)	none

*This correlation refers to 30 University students.

(8) *Dependence on movement.* Bourdon's description of the process of cancellation seems to imply that the examination of the line is interrupted during the actual process of cancelling. The same implication is made, perhaps less baldly, in the method used by some investigators to secure a 'perception-time' or 'discrimination-time' by subtracting a 'motor-time' from the total time. The following quotation from MacMillan and Bruner (p. 52) is illustrative:

"It is readily apparent that at least two factors enter into the selection and marking of a's as called for in this test; the one a mental factor concerned in the several acts of discrimination in finding the a's, and the second, physiological, having to do with the motor task of making the marks. To disintegrate these factors and arrive at a measure of the purely mental time actually involved in perception, is the point of chief moment. . . . And this is accomplished approximately by subtracting the *motor time* gotten in the first part of the test from the total time required to perform the second part."

Now, it is perhaps true that the movement of reaction does in some case interfere with the process of perception and recognition, but it is equally true that for others, especially for adults, there is virtually no interference whatever, and that for other S's the two processes undergo a very considerable degree of 'telescoping.' In any event, the degree of interference may be investigated directly. Thus, Vogt has attempted an experimental analysis of this interference by comparing the amount of ground covered in the usual method and the amount of ground covered when the assigned letters are simply recognized but not marked.[9]

He found that, in his own case, the marking slowed the speed of the performance as a whole by at least 15.8 per cent., in the case of another, less practised S, by the astonishing amount, 42.3 per cent. If these conclusions are generally valid, we shall have to admit that the apparently 'mechanical' phase of the cancellation work may easily be the determining factor in the individual differences which the test may reveal, and this will alter radically our conception of the nature of the test.

But, in the author's opinion, Vogt's results are so warped by the intrusion of practise and warming-up (*Anregung*) as to be

TABLE 43

Effects of Different Methods of 'Reaction' in qrst-Test (Whipple)

NUM-BER	TIME ELAPSED SINCE PRECEDING TRIAL	METHOD OF REACTING	SPEED IN SEC.	OMITTED OUT OF 199*
1	————	Finger tapping	283	?
2	10 minutes	Electric key	246	3
3	10 minutes	Actual marking	207	3
4	15 hours	Electric key	220	0
5	5 minutes	Actual marking	193	4
6	5 minutes	Mere recognition	197	?
7	2 hours	Electric key	237	1
8	1 hour	Actual marking	184	4

*In the test in use there were only 49 s's, owing to a printer's error.

inconclusive. They certainly do not accord with the results in Table 43, which represent the author's tests upon himself by several variant methods.

In this work the same text and the same letters were employed in eight trials on two days. Test 6 was in accordance with Vogt's series in

[9]There is here no check upon accuracy: it would seem better to let name the letters as fast as recognized, or at least utter some simple sound or tap his finger at each recognition as suggested below.

which S merely recognizes the letters, and executes no movement of reaction. In Trial 1, the finger was lifted slightly as each letter was recognized. In Trials 2, 4, and 7, this movement was changed into a simple
tap upon an electric key, which was connected to an electric recorder:
This device enables one to record the total number of movements of reaction and hence to measure accuracy in terms of omissions, while the
movement is so familiar and simple as to be virtually negligible. In the
remaining tests, the letters were cancelled by pencil strokes in the regulation manner.

It is evident that when two or three tests are administered in
close succession, there tends to be improvement due to practise
and warming-up, especially the latter. If the process of marking delayed the performance by any appreciable amount, we
should expect Trial 6 to be shorter than Trial 5, and it would be
difficult to account for the minimal time shown in Trial 8.
Moreover, the author can testify from introspection that there
is no conscious delay introduced by the movement of cancelling
itself. It is quite possible that some S's may be delayed, however, by the cancelling, and it would be profitable, whenever
time permits, to investigate, by appropriate tests, the nature
and extent of this retardation in speed, which, if appreciable,
will evidently vitiate the test.

(9) *Dependence on practise.* Practise increases efficiency in
all cancellation tests, as is illustrated in Tables 40, 43 and 45.
Whether this practise-effect concerns only the letter used, or
extends to all letters, cannot be stated until a series of equivalent letters has been determined by preliminary tests. Continued practise with the same letters almost doubles speed, and
raises accuracy to a maximum. The letters are not held in
mind by conscious effort, but recognized quasi-automatically,
and the whole process becomes unexpectedly simplified. But
the A-test, according to Whitley, is little disturbed by practise
when a single repetition is made, e. g., time per A in the first
trial .643 sec., in the second trial .636 sec. On the contrary,
repetition of the a-t test, even after one or more weeks, "has an
effect of over 40 per cent. gain."

The cancellation test has been used by Kent and by Boring as
a test of learning, "to test the acquisition of skill in a complicated operation and the effect of skill acquired in one operation
upon the acquisition of skill in another very similar operation"
Boring). Both investigators worked at the Government Hos-

pital for the Insane on dementia praecox cases. Boring, whose work was the later and more carefully planned, found that practise under his special conditions (12 days, 5 forms a day) reduced the average time from 47.6 to 33.7 sec., but did not reduce the errors. Contrary to Miss Kent, he found no marked or unambiguous evidence of transfer of practise to new, but equivalent forms.

For a more extended analysis of practise and 'warming-up' gains in the cancellation test see Wells (35).

(10) *Dependence on fatigue.* The experiments of Bourdon, Binet, and Ritter show that cancellation is affected by fatigue which reduces accuracy, rather than speed—a result in accordance with what we know of the effects of fatigue on other form of mental activity. It follows that the cancellation of four or more letters is better adapted than the cancellation of one letter for testing fatigue. If but one letter is cancelled, practise and warming-up may easily conceal fatigue, as is shown in the author's continuous tests, extending over two hours and characterized by marked subjective fatigue (Table 40).[10]

In his examination of fatigue, Binet compared the first and second half of a 20 min. test, and found that his *S*'s had made 54 errors in the first, and 95 in the second, 10 min. Ritter was successful in 8 of 10 trials in getting indications of fatigue in school children by his form of the cancellation test: Table 4 gives a sample series of errors.

TABLE 44

Effects of Fatigue on Cancellation (Ritter)

TIME	PREVIOUS SCHOOL EXERCISE	ERROR
9 a. m.	_____	37
9.55 a. m.	_____Greek_____	94
10.10 a. m.	_____Pause for Vespers_____	78
12 m.	_____Livy and Chemistry_____	84

(11) *Reliability.* Notwithstanding the assertion of Woodworth and Wells that the function tested in number-checking

---

[10] It may be stated, however, that some three or four tests which followed the fourth group, but which are not included in the table, indicate a distinct increase in time required, *e. g.*, from 85-95 to 106-108 sec. The quality of the work showed no progressive changes.

seems "one whose expression in the test can be distorted by incidental factors that are as yet very imperfectly understood," the fact remains that in nearly all forms of cancellation coefficients of reliability have proved fairly satisfactory: samples are Wyatt for his *er*-test .72, for his *anos*-test .64; Brown for his *er*-test .60 to .97, for his *anos*-test .51 to .56; Winch (see Brown) for his simple motor test (marking all letters) .82 to .91, for his complex motor test (*anos*-test) from .87 to .93; Abelson for his dot-form test .94 to .97; Burt for his *oe*-test .75, and Simpson for the regular *A*-test .60 to .72 and for his geometrical forms test .69 to .91. Simpson believes that four trials might advantageously be used in rating *S*'s with the *A*-test. Whitley concludes that for short tests the *A*-test, *a-t* test and the geometrical forms test are significant of an individual's ability in visual perception.

(12) *Correlation with intelligence.* Earlier investigators, working for the most part by the method of contrasted groups, did not reveal consistent relationship between cancellation and intelligence: later investigators, working by more refined correlation formulas, have usually discovered a small positive correlation.

Binet's results were gained from four different series: in Series 1 (cancellation of five letters), the intelligent and unintelligent showed little difference in speed, though the former increased their speed more in the second half of the test; the unintelligent, however, made four times as many errors. In Series 2, conducted 15 days later, the unintelligent equalled the intelligent in speed, but were still inferior in accuracy. In Series 3, a sudden change was made in the letters assigned; this reduced the speed of all *S*'s more than one-half, and the intelligent, rather oddly, made more errors than the unintelligent. Binet explains this on the ground that they, the intelligent, had established their associations more strongly in previous series.[11] In Series 4 (20 min., 6 letters, two of them new),

---

[11] These results need reinvestigating. It would be interesting to see whether, in such a test, the intelligent would surpass the unintelligent, provided the latter had, by added practise, been brought to an equal state of proficiency before the change of letters. In accordance with Binet's thesis that intelligence is indicated primarily by readiness to adapt oneself to a new situation, we should then expect the unintelligent to make the greater number of errors.

the speed was about equal for the two groups, but the unintelligent made more errors.

Winteler's gross results (Table 45) indicate the superiority of his intelligent children. but when his S's are ranked individually, two of the four unintelligent are found to be superior to some of the intelligent. Similarly, the unintelligent seemed as capable as the others in adapting themselves to the change from crossing three to crossing five letters, so that Winteler concludes that one cannot, on the whole, discern any inferiority on the part of the unintelligent with respect to the numbers of letters cancelled, to their quickness of adaptation, or to the steadiness with which attention is maintained within the series. It is to be regretted that Winteler did not take any account, direct or indirect, of the number of errors.

TABLE 45

Relation of Average Number of Letters Cancelled to Intelligence
(*Winteler*)

| | N S T | | | L M R S T | | | |
	FIRST DAY	SECOND DAY	BOTH	FIRST DAY	SECOND DAY	BOTH	ALL TESTS
Intell	277	329	606	312	414	726	1326
Unintell	255	303	558	248.5	326.5	575	1133

The author's own tests are summarized in Table 42: it is evident that there is an inverse relation (— 0.40) between speed and class standing; that, when one letter is cancelled, there is no correlation, but when four letters are cancelled, there is a direct correlation (0.39) between accuracy and class standing; that, when accuracy and speed are conjoined in a single index (net efficiency), there is a definite inverse correlation for one letter, and a possible inverse correlation for four letters, between such efficiency and class standing. In other words, the best pupils work more slowly at the cancellation test; if four letters are cancelled, this slower speed has its reward in a relatively high degree of accuracy. The recent work of Lapie (19) lends confirmation to this conclusion: his advanced children worked with consistent care, his retarded children hastily and somewhat capriciously—which recalls the suggestion made above that good-will and conscientiousness may effect the test with children to an extent sufficient to obscure the rôle of the intellectual factors.

The following are the coefficients of correlation with intelligence reported by recent investigators: Wyatt, *cr*-test .37 to .40, *anos*-test .32 to .45; Burt, *oc*-test .39; Brown, *cr*-test 0 to .28. *anos*-test .10 to .13; Simpson, *A*-test with 17 highly selected adults .21; Abelson, dot-form test with 88 girls .32, and with 43 boys .28; Descoeudres, with 14 backward children .67—all cases, therefore, of positive correlation, but mostly of rather low degree.

(13) *Correlations with other tests.* Abelson found correlations ranging from .06 to .45 between cancellation and the following tests (averages for both sexes only stated here): interpretation of pictures .20, memory for sentences .23, tapping .26, memory for commissions .17, crossing rings .56, discrimination of length .34, memory of names of objects .12, all these tests combined .41. Wyatt's results, if we may average the correlations for two groups of *S*'s in both his *cr* and *anos* tests, are with analogies .32, with the Ebbinghaus test .50, with word-building .43 and with part-wholes .42. Somewhat smaller correlations are reported by the same investigator for a single group of *S*'s with memory for nonsense syllables, interpretation of fables, letter-squares, dissected pictures and Healy's cross-line test. Further work of this sort in which the correlations are less accordant and tend toward zero relationships will be found in Brown. Wissler found no correlation between cancellation and reaction-time to sound, and only a low correlation (0.21) between the *A*-test and a test of quickness in naming colors. The same investigator found that weak eye-sight was conjoined with inaccuracy in the *A*-test, but that the reverse was not true.[12] Thorndike found a correlation between twins

_____

[12] In certain series conducted by the author with a University student to test the relative values of various letters, the net result of two months' work was to indicate the probability that the student had astigmatism!—an inference which was confirmed by the oculist.

of 0.73 in the A-test, 0.75 in the a-t and e-r tests and in the misspelled word test.

The author's grammar-school boys showed no correlation between net efficiency in cancelling one letter and the word-building test.

Aikins, Thorndike and Hubbell found no correlation between quickness in the misspelled word test and quickness in the e-r test, and a correlation of 0.16 (8th-grade pupils) to 0.25 (5th-grade pupils) between accuracy in these two tests, as measured by number of words or letters marked per line. The correlation of efficiency in the e-r test and in addition and association tests was also found to be slight or none, but efficiency in misspelled words and in addition and association tests was correlated by 0.50.

Heymans and Brugman (15a) found but a low correlation (0.16) between the cancellation of numbers containing three specified digits and two other tests of 'concentration'—the McDougall dotting test and listening to faint noises made by a fall phonometer. They conclude that the lack of correspondence was due to certain difficulties in the use of the two tests that were compared with cancellation.

The cancellation test has also been used by Wallin (see his Table V, pp. 26-7) and by Kohnky, in conjunction with other tests, for measuring mental improvement due to dental inspection in public-school classes, and by Hollingworth in his investigation of the influence of caffein. In the caffein experiment the general effect is stimulation for large doses and retardation for small, and the stimulation is more evident in S's that work by recognition and without perceptual discrimination: these conclusions, however, are given with considerable reservation because the test was found not well adapted for this work.

(14) *Defectives.* Miss Norsworthy used the A-test and the a-t test upon 150 feeble-minded children. Compared with normal children at three points in the surface of distribution median, above — 1 P. E. and above — 2 P. E., corresponding 50, 75 and 91 per cent., respectively, the frequency for feeble minded children was found to be 9, 18, and 34 for the A-test and 1, 14, and 28 for the a-t test, *i. e.*, 18 per cent. of the feeble

minded reach a score attained by 75 per cent. of normal children, etc. The results with Vineland children are reported in Table 39. It will be seen that there is general improvement with mental age, but Doll remarks that the mean variation and the extremes of performance are both large; moreover, "at no age do 80 per cent. or even 75 per cent. surpass the average of 80 per cent. of the cases at the preceding age," so that the test has obvious defects as a diagnostic test. Another defect is found in the lack of correspondence between repeated examinations of the same feeble-minded child.

Tests by MacMillan and Bruner with pupils attending the public day-school for the deaf at Chicago show (1) that, taking all cases (about 140) from 7 to 16 years, an average of 82.5 per cent. of these children are slower than hearing children in perception-time, (2) that, roughly speaking, motor-time and perception-time are about the same at all ages. These authors conclude that "deaf children, on the average, are from two to three years less mature than hearing children of the same ages in the kind of ability that is called for in this test."

Strong says that it "seems very probable that both depressive and manic attacks interfere with performance in the cancellation test" (by increasing the time).

Fernald tested out and retained the cancellation test in his effort to arrange a group of diagnostic tests to use with defectives and delinquents.

(15) *Qualitative analysis.* Most S's do not pronounce the letters of the text, as is shown both by introspection and by the fact that a greater number of letters can be examined than could be read over silently in the same period, *e. g.,* 1876 and 986, respectively (Bourdon). The letters to be cancelled, however, are often mentally pronounced by S, especially if four in number, in order to keep them in mind. Attention is then arrested by the sight of the assigned letters, which are recognized either visually or by inner pronunciation. (Cf. the reference previously made to Meumann's analysis.)

The most common error is that of omission. When four letters are marked, S often temporarily forgets one or more letters. Less often, S makes no marks at all for limited parts of a line, or even for whole lines. The latter defect is, in the author's experience, characteristic of either very young, or very careless S's.

Adults may hit upon the device of traversing every other line from right to left; this seems to economize time and to insure at least as great accuracy.

REFERENCES

(1) A. R. Abelson, The measurement of mental ability of 'backward' children. *BrJPs*, 4: 1911, 268-314. (Same material in simpler form, Tests for mental deficiency in childhood. *The Child*, 3: 1912, 1-17.)

(2) H. Aikins, E. Thorndike, and E. Hubbell, Correlations among perceptive and associative processes. *PsR*, 9: 1902, 374-382.

(3) A. Binet, Attention et adaptation. *AnPs*, 6: 1900, 248-404.

(4) A. Binet, L'étude expérimentale de l'intelligence, Paris, 1903. Pp. 309.

(5) E. G. Boring, Learning in dementia praecox. *PsMon*, 15: 1913, No. 63. Pp. 101, especially 30-50.

(6) B. Bourdon, Observations comparatives sur la reconnaissance, la discrimination et l'association. *RPhF*, 40: 1895, 153-185.

(7) W. Brown, The essentials of mental measurement. Cambridge, 1911. (See also *BrJPs*, 3: 1910.)

(8) W. Brown, The effects of 'observational errors' and other factors upon correlation coefficients in psychology. *BrJPs*, 6: 1913, 223-238. (Including a section by W. H. Winch, on Description of simple motor and complex motor tests, pp. 228-230.)

(9) C. Burt, Experimental tests of higher mental processes and their relation to general intelligence. *JEPd*, 1: 1911, 93-112.

(10) J. Cattell and L. Farrand, Physical and mental measurements of the students of Columbia University. *PsR*, 3: 1896, 618-648.

(11) W. G. Chambers, Individual differences in grammar-grade children. *JEdPs*, 1: 1910, 61-75.

(12) Alice Descoeudres, Exploration de quelques tests d'intelligence chez des enfants anormaux et arriérés. *ArPs* (*f*), 11: 1911, 351-375.

(13) E. A. Doll, The A-test with the feeble-minded. *TrSc*, 10: 1913, 49-57.

(14) G. G. Fernald, The defective-delinquent class: differentiating tests. *AmJIns*, 68: 1912, 523-594.

(15) S. I. Franz, Handbook of mental examination methods. *JNeMeDisMon*, No. 10. 1912. Pp. 165, especially 129ff.

(15a) G. Heymans und H. Brugmans, Intelligenzprüfungen mit Studierenden. *ZAngPs*, 7: 1913, 317-331.

(16) H. L. Hollingworth, The influence of caffein on mental and motor efficiency. *ArPs*(*e*), No. 22, 1912. Pp. 166.

(17) C. Judd, Laboratory manual of psychology. N. Y., 1907. Pp. 12

(18) Emma Kohnky, Preliminary study of the effect of dental treatment upon the physical and mental efficiency of school children. *JEdP* 4: 1913, 571-8.

(19) P. Lapie, Avancés et retardés. *AnPs*, 18: 1912, 233-270.

(20) D. MacMillan and F. G. Bruner, Special report Dept. of Child Study and Pedagogic Investigation on children attending the public day schools for the deaf in Chicago. 1908. Pp. 88.

(21) E. Meumann, Vorlesungen zur Einführung in die experimentel Pädagogik. 2d ed., Vol. 2, Leipzig, 1913, especially 393 f.

(22) H. Münsterberg, Psychology and industrial efficiency. Boston, 1913. Pp. 321. Especially 77 ff.

(23) Naomi Norsworthy, Suggestions concerning the psychology of mentally deficient children. *JPsAsth*, 12: 1907, 3-17. (See also her Psychology of mentally deficient children, New York, 1906. Pp. 111.)

(24) A. Oehrn, Experimentelle Studien zur Individualpsychologie. *PsArb*, 1: 1896, 92-151.

(25) C. Ritter, Ermüdungsmessungen. *ZPs*, 24: 1900, 401-444.

(26) E. C. Sanford, The relative legibility of small letters. *AmJPs*, 1: 1888, 402-435.

(27) Stella Sharp, Individual psychology: a study in psychological method. *AmJPs*, 10: 1899, 329-391.

(28) B. R. Simpson, Correlations of mental abilities. *Columbia ConEd*, No. 53, 1912. Pp. 122.

(29) Carrie R. Squire, Graded mental tests. *JEdPs*, 3: 1912, 363-380, 430-443, 493-506, especially 370-374 and 500 ff.

(30) E. K. Strong, Jr. A comparison between experimental data and clinical results in manic-depressive insanity. *AmJPs*, 24: 1913, 66-98.

(31) E. L. Thorndike, An introduction to the theory of mental and social measurements, N. Y., 1904. Pp. 210.

(32) E. L. Thorndike, Measurements of twins. *ColumbiaConPhPs*, 13: No. 3. Pp. 64.

(33) R. Vogt, Ueber Ablenkbarkeit und Gewohnungsfähigkeit. *PsArb*, 3: 1901, 62-201.

(34) J. E. W. Wallin, Experimental oral euthenics. *Dental Cosmos*, April and May, 1912. Reprint, 32 pp.

(35) F. L. Wells, (*a*) The relation of practise to individual differences. *AmJPs*, 23: 1912, 75-88. (*b*) Practise and the work-curve. *AmJPs*, 24: 1913, 35-51.

(36) Mary T. Whitley, An empirical study of certain tests for individual differences. *ArPs*(*e*), No. 19, 1911. Pp. 146, especially 61-75.

(37) J. Winteler, Experimentelle Beiträge zu einer Begabungslehre. *ZPd*, 2: 1906, 1-48, 147-247.

(38) C. Wissler, The correlation of mental and physical tests. *PsMon*, 3: No. 6, 1901. Pp. 62.

(39) R. S. Woodworth and F. L. Wells, Association tests. *PsMon*, 13: 1911, No. 57. Pp. 85.

(40) S. Wyatt, The quantitative investigation of higher mental processes. *BrJPs*, 6: 1913, 109-133.

TEST 27

Counting dots.—This test was devised by Binet (1) and employed by him and later by Winteler (2) in their comparative studies of intelligent and unintelligent children in order to measure the degree of attention. The problem set before S is that of counting a number of dots which are arranged in an irregular group or in lines of varying length and spacing.[1]

---

[1] The test evidently has similarity with the dot-counting under 3 sec. exposure (Test 25), but the removal of the time restrictions and the increase in the number of dots make the conditions quite different: here it is the degree rather than the range of attention that is primarily to be measured.

When this work is attempted without the aid of pointer or pencil to keep the place, it is distinctly difficult and necessitates active concentration, but by selecting different arrangements of dots, this difficulty can be graded to suit S's of different degrees of development, and comparative scales of ability or norms for given arrangements of dots may presumably be established for each age.

MATERIAL.—Stop-watch. Two sets (in duplicate) of 27 printed test-cards.

These cards are numbered in the upper left-hand corner in accordance with the following plan: Cards A 1 to A 10 contain rows of dots with uniform spacing (for each card): Cards Ba 1 to Bd 4 contain lines with groups of 2, 3, 4 or 5 dots each in which the spacing within the groups and between the groups varies as indicated in Table 46. Cards C 1 to C 5 contain 5 arrangements of dots in irregular clusters. These three kinds of material reproduce those found to be of value by Binet and Winteler. The dots, like Winteler's, are 1.5 mm. in diam.[2] The 'A' cards were used by both experimenters, the 'B' cards by Winteler only, the 'C' cards by Binet only. The term 'points' in the Table refers to the printer's point or typographic unit: one point is 1/72 inch.

TABLE 46

Specifications for Test-Cards Used in Dot-Counting.

CARD NUMBER	A1	A2	A3	A4	A5	A6	A7	A8	A9	A10
Points in Spacing	20	19	12	10	8	5	4	3	3	3
Number of Dots	13	15	14	17	21	27	29	45	52	60

CARD NUMBER	Ba1	Ba2	Ba3	Ba4	Bb1	Bb2	Bb3	Bb4
Points within Groups	6	6	6	6	4	4	4	4
Points between Groups	18	18	18	18	12	12	12	12
Number of Dots	45	47	55	52	50	54	70	64

CARD NUMBER	Bc1	Bc2	Bc3	Bc4	Bd1	Bd2	Bd3	Bd4
Points within Groups	3	3	3	3	3	3	3	3
Points between Groups	9	9	9	9	15	15	15	15
Number of Dots	70	73	81	90	65	75	70	72

Card Number and Number of Dots: C1, 50; C2, 48; C3, 49; C4, 54; C5, 57.

---

[2] Binet found that S's with poor eye-sight had difficulty with the test when the dots were 1 mm. in diam.

METHOD.—Make the tests in the order indicated by the card-numbers. Instruct S: "Find the total number of dots on this card: count aloud, in any way you wish (that is, by ones, twos, threes, etc.): work as rapidly as you can, but try particularly to get the number right." The emphasis is thus placed on accuracy rather than upon speed. S must not use his finger, pencil or other object to keep his place. E should record S's time, but without the latter's knowledge. He should also keep before him a duplicate of the card upon which S is working and should note thereon S's method of grouping, in order to discover whether he counts always by ones, or always by twos, etc., and whether he accommodates himself to the objective grouping of the 'B' cards. (S's attention should not, of course, be called by E to the grouping in these cards.) E should also record the magnitude of the error and its nature—whether overestimation or underestimation—but should not communicate this information to S.

TREATMENT OF RESULTS.— Binet and Winteler both ranked S's merely in terms of accuracy and put no time-limit upon their performance. It would seem possible, after some experience, to discover the relation between speed and accuracy, and possibly to make use of a corrective formula as in the case of other tests where these two factors appear, e.g., the Cancellation Test (No. 26). The errors are to be counted simply by subtracting the given from the true number, e.g., 62 for 65 represents 3 errors.

RESULTS.—(1) Many S's have a *constant error*, but this may be either an error of overestimation or an error of underestimation.[3]

(2) Winteler found that some S's always counted by the same number, i.e., used the same *increment in adding*, as "one, two, three, four," etc., or "two, four, six, eight," etc. When

---

[3] No attempt has been made to analyze the conditions under which these constant errors appear; they might conceivably be due in part to illusions of filled and empty space, in part to individual differences in method of keeping the place in the line, in part to temperamental attitudes (over-cautiousness, careless haste, etc.). This test, like many others, has not been subjected to careful introspective analysis by trained adults. But critical qualitative study of this sort is as desirable for the intelligent employment of any test as is the mere accumulation of quantitative results.

the change was made to the 'B' material, he found that all three of his bright children and one of the dull adapted their counting to the objective grouping, whereas the rest of the dull children continued for the most part to employ the form of counting (almost invariably by ones or by twos) that they had adopted in the 'A' cards.

(3) In examining the *relation between dot-counting and intelligence,* Binet concludes that, although the test exacts a high degree of attention, the outcome depends more upon S's care than upon his intelligence. His results were confused by the presence of one bright child with poor eye-sight: when this case is eliminated, the intelligent children are found to make fewer errors than the unintelligent: in one series the relation is 13 to 19, in another 16 to 24; the difference, as in many other tests, tends to lessen with practise.

Winteler likewise found the bright children, as a group, more accurate, and also more rapid, than the dull children, but there were individual exceptions. The average for 10 series on each of two days were: errors, bright 8.33, dull 17.25: time in sec. per 10 dots, bright 4.97, dull 6.30—a suggestion that the tendency to inverse relation of speed and accuracy may not be so clearly evident as in many other tests. The difference in capacity of the two groups becomes striking, however, when the 'B' type of material is employed, because the unintelligent, as already noted, fail to adapt themselves to the objective grouping and make a large number of errors (79.7: to 9.00 of the intelligent).

(4) The outcome of the test is not affected by general ability in arithmetic; some of Winteler's S's who did poorly had good grades in arithmetic.

REFERENCES

(1) A. Binet, Attention et adaptation. *AnPs*, 6: 1899 (1900), 248-40.
(2) J. Winteler, Experimentelle Beiträge zu einer Begabungslehr *EPd*, 2: 1906, 1-48, 147-247.

TEST 28

Reading simple and complicated prose.—Reading, like counting, is a form of perceptual activity that has been proposed as a means for measuring attention. In reading, as in counting (Test 27), the process has been complicated in some ma

ner in order that the increased difficulty may exact a higher
degree of attention and so furnish a better opportunity for the
study of individual differences. Miss Sharp, for instance, followed this plan when she sought to test degree of attention by
requiring S's to read two texts (a page of concrete description
and a page of abstract exposition), which were printed without capitals, punctuation, or spacing.

In the present test, this plan has been extended, first by
printing the complicated text backward, as well as without
spacing, and second, by adding a test-sheet of similar subject-
matter and identical length, but of regular form, in order to
supply a check-test of maximal speed of reading under normal
conditions.

This simpler test of reading under normal conditions may
also be used with immature S's as a direct index of general
mental status. It was in this form, for example, that Binet
and Simon used reading in their 1908 scale as a differentiating
test between imbecility and moronity. Wallin's work with
epileptics shows that the test has decided value in this direction, so that its elimination from the Binet scale in 1911 seems
at least unfortunate.

MATERIALS.—Two printed texts: (a) a page of prose in regular form, (b) a page of equivalent, but 'complicated' prose.
Stop-watch.

METHOD.—The regular text (a) is used first. E gives the
following directions. "When I say 'now,' I want you to read
this aloud, just as fast as you can without making mistakes."
With older children and adults the tendency to slurring and
skipping must be checked by the further direction to "read
clearly enough so that another person who did not know the
passage could understand you." E records the time; also, if
desired, the number of errors. He does not, however, correct
S's errors in this part of the test.[1]

---

[1] With most adults the errors are few in number and trivial in nature.
To attempt to correct them would render it impossible to measure the
speed of reading. If the errors are numerous, E may, however, ask S to
reread the text, this time without making a single error, but still as fast
as possible. The advantage that S gains by knowing the subject-matter is
of little moment compared to the false advantage that he has gained by
hurrying his reading so fast as to commit many errors.

In using the reversed and unspaced text (*b*), *E*'s directions are: "When I say 'now,' read this aloud as fast as you can without making mistakes. You will find this page more difficult than the one you have just read, because you will have to begin here in the lower right-hand corner and read it backward, and because this page is printed without any punctuation or capitals and without spaces between the words. I shall not give you any help, but if you make a mistake, I shall stop you, and ask you to correct it."

E follows *S*'s reading upon a duplicate text. He records the time for the entire reading, and by glancing at the watch at every pause in the reading, he notes upon the duplicate text at the points concerned, the time in sec. consumed by *S* at these pauses. These notations should be made for every pause of 5 sec. or over. In case *S* pauses for 30 sec. at any point, *E* then supplies for him the word or phrase which he needs to continue his work.

To secure accuracy, *E* must correct every error in *S*'s reading, even slight errors, such as singular for plural forms, etc., and he must especially avoid the temptation to assist *S* whenever he halts, save for the 30 sec. halts, as just stated. He must notify *S* of each error, as it occurs, by simply interjecting 'no,' and must indicate its place by repeating the two or three words just preceding it. For example, if *S* reads: "they were all alike in tone," *E* interrupts with: "No!—all alike in?—" *S* corrects himself: "all alike in one respect," etc.

VARIATIONS IN METHOD.—In order to measure, and to be able to allow for, individual differences in maximal rapidity of articulation, *E* may require *S* to reread the normal text four or five times, or until the subject-matter is thoroughly familiar and further repetition fails to reduce the time. A brief rest pause should follow each trial to avoid cumulative fatigue. Another method is to test *S*'s time for counting aloud to 50 at maximal speed, though here it is often more difficult to check or control *S*'s tendency to gain time by slurring or otherwise mutilating the words he pronounces.

In view of the correlation mentioned below between speed of reading forward and speed of reading backward, it is of in terest to ask S after his first reading what it was that set the limit to his speed. The usual answer—inability to articulate faster—appears not wholly adequate in view of the fact that many S's can read the passage slightly faster on a second trial. To insure that this gain is not due to simple 'warming-up' of the vocal apparatus, E might give S a preliminary exercise with some other text.

RESULTS.—The results obtained by Burt with two groups of school children at Liverpool with the simple task of reading forward are shown in Table 47, those obtained by the author with the texts prescribed above are shown in Table 48. From these data the conclusions that follow are drawn.

TABLE 47

Results of Reading Tests at Liverpool (Burt and Moore).

Kind of Reading	Ages	Mean or Median for Boys	Mean or Median for Girls	Coefficient of Reliability	Correlation with Int'lig'ce	Excess Perc'tage for Boys
Aloud ___	12.5	224.2 min.	191.5 min.	--	.26	---
Silently _	12.5	181.5 min.	138.8 min.	--	.21	---
Mass test	13	231 words	315 words	.46	.00	—32.7
Silently _	13	166.0 sec.	134.6 sec.	.69	.22	—32.1
Aloud ___	13	211.8 sec.	186.4 sec.	.81	.29	—36.6

TABLE 48

Results of Reading Tests, in Sec. (Whipple).

GROUP	NUMBER	READING FORWARD				READING BACKWARD			
		Av.	M. V.	Min.	Max.	Aver.	M. V.	Min.	Max.
Dull Children_____	5	116.4	19.	101	169	1061.	291.	814	1500*
Bright Children_____	5	100.0	11.6	85	125	544.4	167.2	490	910
University Students__	26	73.3	8.5	47	100	320.	100.	125	755

*This time is estimated from the amount of the text covered in 10

(1) *Dependence on age.* Speed of reading forward increases with age. The average for five bright children aged 10.33 to 12.75 years is less than that of university students, though the fastest child excels the slowest adult. The same

relations obtain for speed in reading backward, though here the increased difficulty entails a still greater difference between children and adults.

Wallin tested epileptics at Skillman, N. J., with the aid of the passage of prose containing 53 words that formed a portion of the Binet-Simon 1908 scale. His averages (in sec.), in comparison with the standards laid down by Binet and Simon for normal children, all expressed in mental ages, may be summarized as follows:

MENTAL AGE	VII	VIII	IX	X	XI	XII
Average according to B.-S.	____	45	40	30	25	___
Average for epileptics	129.2	86.5	61.9	44.6	26.5	23.2

There is, then, a gradual increase in speed of reading with age, but epileptics of a given mental age average slower than normal children of the same mental age.

(2) *Dependence on sex.* All observers agree that as a class females read faster than males. The early study of Romanes (1887) showed a distinct superiority of women over men, while the sex differences calculated by Burt and Moore all range between 32 and 36 per cent. in favor of the girls, *i.e.*, about two-thirds of the girls exceed the median performance of boys.

(3) *Individual differences* are large in either form of test, and are specially accentuated when the reversed text is used.

The coefficient of variability, for example, in the group of adults is approximately 11 per cent. for forward, as contrasted with 33 per cent. for backward reading.

The actual range of performance is also surprisingly large. Thus, in the adult group, the quickest backward reading is 1/6 as long as the slowest backward reading. Miss Sharp's seven *S*'s showed even greater individual differences—ranging from 143 to 900 sec. for concrete, and from 125 to 405 sec. for abstract texts. When it is remembered that her *S*'s were all college students in advanced classes, the variability in performance seems unexpectedly large, and it is hard to understand Miss Sharp's declaration: "We had expected to discover individual differences of much more definite character and much greater amount."

(4) *Correlation with mental ability.* A comparison of the performance of the dull and the bright children of approxi-

mately the same school grades shows the clear superiority of the bright pupils, despite the fact that they are some two years younger than the dull pupils. Here, again, the difference is accentuated in the complicated text. The more extensive tests of Burt also reveal a direct, though slight correlation (about .25) between speed of reading forward and estimated intelligence.

(5) *Relation of speed reading forward to speed reading backward.* The author's tests show a correlation of .79, *P.E.* about .09, between the rate of reading the normal text and the rate of reading the complicated text.

This relation appears, to the author at least, unexpected, and hence of special interest. Adults who try the test are almost unanimous in their declaration that their speed in reading forward is not conditioned by the task of assimilating the substance of the text, but solely by the physiological limit to intelligible articulation: their speed in reading the reversed text, however, is quite obviously not conditioned by speed of articulation, but by a sort of 'linguistic readiness,' or ease of apperceiving the constituent words or phrases of the text. If these statements are correct, we are evidently driven to the conclusion that persons who read difficult and complicated subject-matter rapidly also tend to speak more rapidly—a conclusion that subsidiary tests appear to confirm. It is, furthermore, not unlikely that fast readers are also fast thinkers as well as fast speakers, though this generalization has at present no experimental verification.

Notes.—We have not had sufficient experience as yet with the complicated, or reversed prose test to understand fully the nature of the processes upon which it depends. The considerations just developed make it evident that these processes embrace something besides attention, if, indeed, attention plays any large share in the conditioning factors. For fast readers, in the reversed text, the proper combinations 'rise up' like the hidden faces in the puzzle picture when once they have been seen.

Since a facile apperception of printed symbols would appear, on theoretical grounds, to be a natural concomitant of good intelligence, it is possible that this test may prove to have considerable diagnostic value. To determine this point, however, it needs extended trial with control both by introspective analysis and by the statistical examination of all possible functional correlations.

REFERENCES

(1) C. Burt, Experimental tests of higher mental processes and their relation to general intelligence. *JEPd*, 1: 1911, 93-112.

(2) C. Burt and R. C. Moore, The mental differences between the sexes. *JEPd*, 1: 1912, 273-284, 355-388.

(3) G. Romanes, Mental differences between men and women. *Nineteenth Century*, May, 1887.

(4) Stella E. Sharp, Individual psychology: a study in psychological method. *AmJPs*, 10: 1899, 329-391.

(5) J. E. W. Wallin, Experimental studies of mental defectives. *EdPsMon*, No. 7: 1912. Pp. 155.

TEST 29

Simultaneous adding.—In Tests 24 and 25, the attempt was made to measure the field of consciousness or range of attention during a relatively brief period. Tests have been proposed in which attention is solicited by several claimants, not for a brief period, but continuously. These tests may be grouped as tests of simultaneous activity. Their primary purpose is to ascertain how successfully a number of activities can be carried on at the same time. Ordinarily, disparate activities are selected (Test 30). Less often, as in the present case, a single type of activity is complicated or 'spread' in such a manner as to demand simultaneous attention to more than one phase of activity.

In simultaneous adding, as devised and conducted by Binet in his comparative study of six bright and six dull children, the task is to carry on a series of additions in three columns of figures at once.

MATERIALS.—Prepared forms, ruled in series of three vertical columns, with the numbers 6, 28, 43, printed at the head of the first three columns. Stop-watch. Pencil. A piece of cardboard about 20 cm. square.

METHOD.—Explain to *S* the arrangement of the form and its three columns. Let him glance for a few seconds at a sample form which has been previously filled out. Make clear to him that he is to continue for six minutes, as fast as he can, to add *one* to each number and to write the sum directly below the line just written. Thus, he first writes: 7, 29, 44, then 8, 30, 45, etc. Inform him that the moment he has written a line (three sums), this line will be covered with the cardboard, so that he must hold the three sums in his mind from one line to the next. Make clear also that when the foot of one vertical column is reached, he must proceed without delay to fill out the next column. Finally, warn S that in case he at any time forgets entirely the sum that he has just written, he must guess at it and continue the work as well as he can.

Record the number of additions made in 6 min., and note the number and nature of the errors. A convenient method is to run the eye vertically down each column and mark a ring around each number that is not an addition of one to the number just above it.

VARIATIONS OF METHOD.—For mature S's, the addition of 1 to each sum may not be difficult enough; E may then complicate the task by requiring S to add, say, 3 to the first, 1 to the second, and 2 to the third column. If desired, repeat the test with another variation in the constants to be added, say, 2 to the first, 3 to the second, and 1 to the third column.

RESULTS.—(1) Binet found that this test excited a great deal of interest, and exacted a greater effort of attention than any he tried.[1]

(2) There are marked differences in the *amount of work* (number of additions) done by different S's, *e.g.*, in Binet's tests, from 40 to 96 numbers, *i.e.*, from 13 to 32 lines of 3 numbers each.

(3) Examinations of the *errors* shows that S's commonly center their attention upon either one or two columns: here they make few or no errors, but the neglected columns contain many errors. In other words, errors in all three columns at once are rare. Binet's pupils wrote 100 of 245 lines erroneously; of these 100 errors, 59 were found in one column only, 34 in two columns, and 7 in all three columns. Errors are more frequent in the third column than the second, and in the second than the first; by count, 76, 60 and 31, respectively.

There is often displayed a tendency toward a form of error that (unintentionally) simplifies the relation between the col-

<hr>

[1] For detailed illustrative work secured from his S's, consult his article, p. 384.

umns, *e.g.*, the difference between the second and third columns suddenly drops to 10 instead of 15. Once such an error is made, the chance is greatly increased that S guides his work by the difference from column to column, and the test is practically invalidated. Furthermore, the earlier such an error occurs, the more S's performance is facilitated and his score increased. For this reason the variant method suggested above, whereby the differences between the columns are constantly shifting, is much to be preferred for testing mature S's.

(4) Contrary to the results of many laboratory tests, says Binet, the number of errors committed tends to increase with continued work. This, we may surmise, is due in part to the fact that the later portion of the work necessarily deals with higher numbers, and in part to the confusion and loss of confidence that is felt after a number of errors have been made.

(5) *Degree of intelligence* appears to have little influence upon this test. Binet states that speed is not at all a matter of intelligence, merely an individual variation. The unintelligent make more errors than the intelligent, but the difference (17 *vs.* 13.4) is not as great as one might expect.

NOTES.—As a matter of fact, it is improbable that simultaneous adding really exacts a 'spread' of attention to all three columns. What S does is to write a given line on the basis of his memory of the preceding line: his additions are made successively; he is not really adding three columns at once. The test, therefore, really measures what is termed "immediate memory" rather than the spread of attention. The results may also be conditioned by the readiness with which S handles numbers and performs additions generally.

REFERENCE

A. Binet, Attention et adaptation. *AnPs*, 6: 1899 (1900), 248-404.

TEST 30

Simultaneous disparate activities.—In tachistoscopy and visual apprehension (Tests 24 and 25), we measure the range of attention for simultaneous *impressions*: in simultaneous adding (Test 29), we test the capacity of attention for concurrent activities of a *homogeneous* type: in the present test we employ *disparate activities,* and study what Meumann terms "heterosensory" distribution of attention (8, i., p. 503). Theoretically, the measure of the capacity of an individual to direct his attention to the execution of several activities at once should be of importance, since this capacity seems to imply the possession of such traits as keen concentration, mental alertness, quick-wittedness, and general intelligence. Gifted men, like Napoleon and Caesar, are said to have possessed this capacity in high degree. The latter, for instance, could dictate four letters while writing a fifth.

There seems to be a possibility that such a distribution of attention may take place under some circumstances, at least a distribution to two lines of activity, but strict experimental examination of the phenomenon is not easy, because, in practise, one of two things usually occurs; if both activities are difficult, attention alternates between them, and the activity not attended to at any moment is temporarily reduced, if not altogether suspended; and if one activity is relatively easy, it becomes, after short practise, reduced to automatism, so that attention can be given freely to the other. It is, then, difficult, if not impossible,[1] so to arrange experimental conditions as to secure *continuous division* of attention to disparate activities. On the other hand, it may be said that the very capacity to alternate attention quickly and successfully from one activity to another, or to reduce one activity quickly to automatism, is itself an indication of important capacities—particularly of well-trained, highly concentrated attention, quick adaptability, and general mental alertness.

The test selected, simultaneous reading and writing, is but one of a large number of possible combinations, others of which are suggested below. This test has been proposed by Paulhan (9), by Binet and Henri (2, pp. 446-7), and tried in several forms by Miss Sharp (10) as a test of "range of attention."

MATERIALS.—A selected poem—preferably one which is divided into a number of stanzas of equal length—which will be

---

[1] Cf. the remark of Titchener (12, p. 376) : "Simultaneity of two psychologically disparate 'attentions' is, in my experience, altogether impossible."

of interest to S, but which is not well-known to him.   Stop-watch.   Pencil and paper.

METHOD.—(1)   Let S read aloud at his *normal rate* a given section (about 8 lines) of the poem.

(2)   Let S read another section[2] of the same length, and while reading, write the letter a as many times as possible. Continue the test by the use of other sections of the poem combined with the writing (3) of $a\,b$, (4) of $a\,b\,c$, and (5) of the entire alphabet.

This last test is the most satisfactory and should be the one employed if time permits but a single trial.   It is important that S should *try* to maintain his reading at the normal rate.

VARIATIONS OF METHOD.—(1)   Let S read both passages at his maximal instead of at his normal rate.

(2)   Repeat the test several times with fresh texts to determine the effect of practise upon its performance.

(3)   Compare the effect of striving especially for a large number of letters written with the effect of striving especially for a normal or for a maximal rate of reading.

TREATMENT OF RESULTS.—In practise, it will rarely be found that S maintains his normal rate of reading, particularly when writing the whole alphabet.   To avoid the difficulty of working with two quantities, rate of reading and number of letters written, it is desirable to reduce these to a single "index of simultaneity."   This is done, as is illustrated for the whole alphabet test in Table 49, by subtracting the normal reading-time from the reading-time during simultaneous activity, and dividing the number of letters written by this difference.[3]   Thus, ob-

---

[2] Sharp used prose, and had her S's read the same section five times. This has the disadvantage of tending to automatic reading.   The advantage of securing identical length is practically assured here by the use of stanzas of poetry.

[3] Miss Sharp divided the difference by the number of letters.   The reverse procedure has the advantage of indicating the degree of simultaneity directly, as a large quotient means good ability.   Whichever method is used for figuring the index of simultaneity, it is difficult to avoid a certain arbitrariness by any fixed formula.   Possibly a more satisfactory formula could be worked out empirically on the basis of a considerable mass of data.   The methods employed by Simpson in another connection (Correlations of mental abilities. *Columbia Univ. Contr. to Educ.*, No. 53, 1912) may be consulted for suggestions to this end.

server *B* read normally in 28 sec., with alphabet-writing in 113 sec.—a difference of 85 sec. He wrote 91 letters, and has an index of 1.07.

RESULTS.—The results for Miss Sharp's seven *S*'s are summarized in Table 49. It will be noted, (1) that the reading-time is usually lengthened by the complication of writing, (2) that more letters can be written with three than with two letters and more with two letters than with one letter, but not fully three times and two times as many, (3) that the writing of the whole alphabet is much different; either the reading is very much slowed, or fewer letters are written than when only a

TABLE 49

Simultaneous Reading and Writing (Sharp).

S's	TIMES OF THE FIVE READINGS IN SECONDS					NUMBER OF LETTERS WRITTEN				Reduction in 5th Reading	Index of Simultaneity 5th Test
	1st	2d	3d	4th	5th	*a*	*ab*	*abc*	Alph'b't		
B. ___	28	38	42	50	113	47	62	78	91	85	1.07
G. ___	22	22	22	21	28	29	34	39	40	6	6.66
V. M._	29	30	30	30	50	40	56	57	46	21	2.19
W. M._	26	27	27	27	29	27	28	36	13	3	4.33
E. R._	27	27	29	27	31	31	40	48	20	4	5.00
L. R._	22	25	26	25	37	41	44	51	26	15	1.76
T. ____	27	29	30	31	29	36	40	45	25	2	12.50
Average_	26	28	29	30	45	36	43	51	37	19	4.78

is employed, (4) that the *S*'s differ markedly in their capacity to carry on two processes simultaneously. The rank of the *S*'s in this test did not, however, correlate with their rank in any other of Miss Sharp's tests.

(5) Paulhan noted that the simultaneous performance of two relatively easy activities did not take as long as the performance of the two in succession. He says: "I write the first four verses of *Athalie*, whilst reciting eleven of Musset. The whole performance occupies 40 sec. But reciting alone takes 22 and writing alone 31, or 53 altogether, so that there is a

difference in favor of the simultaneous operations.[4]" And again: "I multiply 421,312,212 by 2; the operation takes 6 sec.; the recitation of 4 verses also takes 6 sec. But the two operations done at once only take 6 sec., so that there is no loss of time from combining them."

NOTES.—Several *other tests* of a similar nature may be briefly described; still others may be contrived by *E* to suit conditions.

(1) As suggested by Meumann (p. 504), the *Cancellation Test* (No. 26) may be combined with other forms of activity, *e.g.*, let *S* cancel one or more letters and at the same time repeat short sentences read to him by *E*, or listen to the reading of a page of narration (Cf. Test 39) and repeat as much as possible of it after the cancellation is finished, or discriminate two points on the skin (Test 23), etc.

Vogt (13) combined the cancellation of three letters in a nonsense test with reaction to *metronome-beats* in the following manner: the metronome was set at 38, and the bell attachment set for every other stroke, so that there were 19 bell-strokes per minute; in some series *S* was required to make a slight movement of the finger at every bell-stroke, in other series also to lift two fingers at every fourth bell-stroke. Vogt found that this 'metronome-counting' retarded the total process of cancellation from 11.6 per cent. to 35.2 per cent., but that it did not affect appreciably the simple apprehension of the letters without actual cancellation (see Test 26, Result 8); in other words, he concludes that the movements of reaction to the metronome interfered with the movements of reaction in cancelling, but did not interfere with the apprehension of the letters in cancelling. This result is difficult to interpret if we do not admit Vogt's contention that the marking is in itself an appreciable factor in the cancellation test.

(2) McDougall (7) has proposed a form of 'dot tapping' to test the capacity for continuous exertion of attention in the following manner: Place upon a kymograph drum a sheet of white paper on which have been printed eight rows of 120

---

red dots; each dot is 1.5 mm. in diameter, and 5 mm. distant
vertically from the next in the row; each series of 120 dots is
arranged in an irregular line, which covers an extreme width
of 10 mm., but the displacement of adjacent dots is not more
than 5 mm. in the horizontal direction. This zigzag line of
dots is now viewed, as the drum revolves, through a horizontal
slit 10-15 mm. in the vertical dimension, and somewhat wider
than the row of dots. *S* tries to strike each dot with a blunt
soft pencil, and the drum is rotated at a speed (about one rev.
in 23 sec.) such that he can succeed in striking each dot only
by maximal effort. *S*'s work is graded as follows: for the
omission of a dot or the making of an extra mark, count 1
error; for each lateral deviation of more than 1 mm., or each
vertical deviation of more than 2 mm., count ½ error. Sample
records show 50 to 150 errors in a series of eight rows, *i.e.*, 960
dots. For simultaneous activity tests, require *S* to undertake
some other work at the same time, *e.g.*, mental arithmetic, reaction-time with the left hand, esthesiometry, etc.

In the few trials that the author has given this test, there
has appeared a decided tendency for the dot-marking to lapse
into automatism.[5]

(3) Both Binet (1) and Jastrow (6) have tested the *interference of intellectual processes with simple motor activities*.[6]

[5] For a modification and development of McDougall's method with particular reference to the determination of degrees of clearness in attention,
see Geissler (5, pp. 515 ff). For the more recent development of the apparatus by McDougall and by Rivers, together with an account of results
obtained for dot-tapping (without concurrent activities), see Burt (4,
pp. 153-6).

[6] Burnett (3) has recently suggested a test in which visual attention is
measured under conditions of visual distraction. Two mazes are employed, which are alike in every respect save one. Each maze is an ink
line drawn in an irregular, wandering way over a white paper surface
about 18 x 26 cm. In the second maze, small, embossed pictures and bits
of paper of various forms and colors are scattered thickly among the twist-
ings of the maze, though not actually covering any part of it. In use, the
maze is covered with a glass plate, *S* is instructed to trace the pattern of
the maze accurately and as rapidly as possible with a small wooden
pointer. The measure of attention is afforded by the comparison of the
time taken in Maze 1 (without distraction) with that taken in Maze 2
(with distraction). In a limited number of trials of Burnett's mazes the
author found that, for adults at least, the performance in Maze 2 does
not provide an unequivocal measure of distraction: the stimulus of the
distracting material simply induces extra effort with resulting increase,
instead of decrease in the speed of tracing.

To repeat these experiments, close one end of a relatively soft-walled rubber tube; connect the other to a Marey tambour (Fig. 24) and adjust the tambour for a graphic record upon the kymograph. Let S press or pinch the tube either (a) at an optimal rate, (b) at a maximal rate, (c) in groups of 2, 3, 4, or more pressures with stated time-intervals between the groups, e.g., 3 quick pressures per sec., (d) in alternate groups of fours and sixes, etc., (e) in time to the beat of a metronome, or (f) in time to a melody which he himself hums, or in any manner that will provide a suitably complex task.[7] Meanwhile, let him read sentences or disconnected words either silently or aloud, or let him undertake the mental addition of two-place numbers.[8]

The *general results* of such tests are: (1) the amount of interference of the two activities is proportional to their complexity and general difficulty; (2) movements that involve counting are more disturbed by adding than by reading; (3) reading or adding aloud interferes more with motor activity than does reading or adding silently; (4) the reading of disconnected words is more easily interfered with than the reading of sentences; (5) additions are slower and less accurate when performed with, than when performed without, motor activity of the 'tapping' variety; (6) concurrent intellectual processes affect the motor activities mentioned by (a) lengthening the interval between pressures, (b) diminishing their recorded height, (c) confusing their number or arrangement, or (d) causing the appearance of various motor incoördinations, tremblings, unevennesses, etc., which may amount well-nigh to a 'motor delirium;' (7) S may or may not be conscious of these disturbances in his motor activity; in general, he can give but

---

[7] One might, for instance, adopt the plan suggested by Squire (11) for measuring fatigue of attention. Use the tube and tambour; let S memorize a series of eight or ten digits, c. g., 6, 9, 2, 1, 3, 6, 4, 7, and then tap this 'pattern' as rapidly as possible. Introduce concurrent processes and study their effect upon the tapping.

[8] An excellent method is to give S two numbers to start with, and instruct him thereafter to add at each addition the larger digit in the previous sum, c. g., if 16 and 8 are assigned, the correct series will be—16, 24, 28, 36, 42, 46, etc.

obscure or fleeting attention to the pressures if the mental task is at all difficult; (8) the experiment soon induces symptoms of fatigue; (9) individual S's differ noticeably in the degree of complexity of the motor activity that they can execute successfully while engaged in intellectual activity—differences which appear to depend primarily upon the extent to which the motor activity may be reduced to automatism.

(4) Binet suggests a number of methods for testing ability to execute *concurrent motor activities,* which may, with a little ingenuity, be turned to account in the arrangement of simple tests; *e.g.,* (1) make with the right hand a circular movement parallel to the median plane of the body in a clock-wise direction and with the left hand a simultaneous movement in a parallel plane in the reverse direction; (2) duplicate the registering apparatus above described, so as to provide a tube for each hand, and require S to press regularly and rapidly with the right hand, but to press with the left hand only twice for each five pressures of the right hand; (3) take a fountain-pen or pencil in each hand; with the right hand write some familiar poem and simultaneously with the left hand describe a series of small circles, or make a series of *u*'s with the right, and a series of dashes with the left hand. In the last-named test there will be seen, as a rule, a tendency toward the production of similar movements, *i.e.,* the dashes become *u*-like, or the *u*'s spread out in a dash-like fashion. If S's attention be called to this tendency, he may inhibit it by actual control, but the tendency will usually recur the moment his attention becomes distracted—an observation that suggests the possibility of securing in this manner an index or measure of active attention.

(5) In the interesting 'psychological-profile' method of Rossolimo will be found a series of ten tests with simultaneous disparate activities. Some of these demand special materials: of the remainder the following may be mentioned: (1) Name the days of the week backward and close the eyes when saying Wednesday and Friday only; (2) Tap five times on the table with the left hand, five taps each time, and with the right hand

tap simultaneously 1, 2, 3, 4 and 5 times; (3) Count aloud from one to seven; when saying 'one,' tap 7 times, when saying 'two,' tap six times, etc. (4) Show S an irregular group of some 12 or 14 dots, which he is to count: while he is counting them to himself, tap three times on the table: when S announces his count, ask him what happened while he was counting.

REFERENCES

(1) A. Binet, La concurrence des états psychologiques. *RPhF*, 29: 1890, 138-155.

(2) A. Binet and V. Henri, La psychologie individuelle. *AnPs*, 2: 1895 (1896). 411-465.

(3) C. T. Burnett. A new test for attention against distraction. *PsBu*, 7: February, 1910, 64.

(4) C. Burt, Experimental tests of general intelligence. *BrJPs*, 3: 1909, 94-177.

(5) L. R. Geissler, The measurement of attention. *AmJPs*, 20: 1909, 473-529.

(6) J. Jastrow. The interference of mental processes,—a preliminary survey. *AmJPs*, 4: 1891, 219-223.

(7) W. McDougall, On a new method for the study of concurrent mental operations and of mental fatigue. *BrJPs*, 1: 1904-5, 435-445.

(8) E. Meumann, Vorlesungen zur Einführung in die experimentelle Pädagogik u. ihre psychol. Grundlagen. Leipzig, 1907. (2 vols.)

(9) F. Paulhan, La simultanéité des actes psychiques. *RSci*, 39: 1887, 684-9.

(9a) G. Rossolimo, Die psychologischen Profile. Zur Methodik der quantitativen Untersuchung der psychischen Vorgänge in normalen und pathologischen Fällen. *Klinik f. psychische u. nervöse Krankheiten*, 6: 1911, Heft 3.

(10) Stella Sharp, Individual psychology: a study in psychological method. *AmJPs*, 10: 1899, 329-391.

(11) Carrie R. Squire. Fatigue: suggestions for a new method of investigation. *PsR*, 10: 1903, 248-267.

(12) E. B. Titchener, Lectures on the elementary psychology of feeling and attention. New York, 1908. Pp. 391.

(13) R. Vogt, Ueber Ablenkbarkeit u. Gewöhnungsfähigkeit. *PsAr*, 3: 1901, 62-201.

APPENDIX I

Formulas for Converting Measures (English and Metric Systems)

Measures of Length
1 mm. = 0.0394 inch.
1 cm. = 0.3937 inch.
1 m. = 39.37 inches.
1 in. = 2.54 cm.
1 ft. = 0.3048 m.

Measures of Surface
1 sq. cm. = 0.155 sq. in.
1 sq. in. = 6.452 sq. cm.

Measures of Capacity
1 cu. cm. = 0.061 cu. in.
1 cu. in. = 16.4 cu. cm.

Measures of Weight
1 gram = 0.035 oz.
1 kg. = 2.204 lbs.
1 oz. = 28.35 g.
1 lb. = 453.59 g.

APPENDIX II

List of Abbreviations

The following abbreviations, save for a few additions, are identical with those recommended and employed in the *Zeitschrift für angewandte Psychologie*, V, Heft 5-6, VI, Heft 5-6.

AmAnt: American Anthropologist (Lancaster, Pa.).
AmJIns: American Journal of Insanity (Baltimore, Md.).
AmJPhg: American Journal of Physiology (Boston, Mass.).
AmJPs: American Journal of Psychology (Worcester, Mass.).
AmJSci: American Journal of Science (New Haven, Conn.).
AnPs: L'Année psychologique (Paris).
ArGsPhg: Archiv für die gesamte Physiologie des Menschen und der Tiere (Bonn).
ArGsPs: Archiv für die gesamte Psychologie (Leipzig).
ArPs(e): Archives of Psychology (New York).
ArPs(f): Archives de Psychologie (Geneva, Switzerland).
BuAcRoySci: Bulletins de l'Académie Royale des Sciences, des Lettres et des Beaux-arts de Belgique (Brussels).
BerlinKlW: Berliner Klinische Wochenschrift (Berlin).
BiZb: Biologisches Zentralblatt (Erlangen).
BrJPs: British Journal of Psychology (Cambridge, England).
BuSocEtPsEnf: Bulletin de la Société libre pour l'étude psychologique de l'enfant (Paris).
ColumbiaConEd: Columbia Contributions to Education (New York).
ColumbiaConPhPs: Columbia Contributions to Philosophy and Psychology (New York).
DMdW: Deutsche Medizinische Wochenschrift (Leipzig).
Ed: Education (Boston, Mass.).
EPd: Die experimentelle Pädagogik (Leipzig).
EdPsMon: Educational Psychology Monographs (Baltimore, Md.).
FsPs: Fortschritte der Psychologie und ihre Anwendungen (Berlin).
InMagScHyg: International Magazine of School Hygiene (Leipzig).

JAntInst: Journal of the Anthropological Institute of Great Britain and Ireland (London).
JEdPs: The Journal of Educational Psychology (Baltimore, Md.).
JEPd: Journal of Experimental Pedagogy and Training College Record (London).
JNeMeDis: Journal of Nervous and Mental Disease (New York).
JPh: Journal of Philosophy, Psychology and Scientific Methods (New York).
JPhg: Journal of Physiology (Cambridge, England).
JPsAsth: Journal of Psycho-Asthenics (Faribault, Minn.).
NeMeDisMon: Nervous and Mental Disease Monograph Series (New York).
PdPsArb: Padagogisch-psychologische Arbeiten (Leipzig).
PdSc: Pedagogical Seminary (Worcester, Mass.).
PdlJb: Paedologisch Jaarboek (Antwerp).
PhR: Philosophical Review (Lancaster, Pa.).
PhSd: Philosophische Studien (Leipzig).
PopSciM: Popular Science Monthly (Garrison, N. Y.).
PsArb: Psychologische Arbeiten (Leipzig).
PsBu: Psychological Bulletin (Lancaster, Pa.).
PsCl: Psychological Clinic (Philadelphia, Pa.).
PsMon: Psychological Monographs (Lancaster, Pa.).
PsR: Psychological Review (Lancaster, Pa.).
RepComEd: Report United States Commissioner of Education (Washington, D. C.).
RMdSuisse: Revue médicale de la Suisse Romande (Geneva, Switzerland).
RPhF: Revue philosophique de la France et de l'Etranger (Paris).
RSci: Revue scientifique (Paris).
Sci: Science (Garrison, N. Y.).
SdYalePsLab: Studies from the Yale Psychological Laboratory.
SmAbPdPs: Sammlung von Abhandlungen aus dem Gebiete der pädagogischen Psychologie und Physiologie (Berlin).
TrSc: The Training School (Vineland, N. J.).
UnIowaSdPs: University of Iowa Studies in Psychology (Iowa City, Iowa).
ZAngPs: Zeitschrift für angewandte Psychologie und psychologische Sammelforschung (Leipzig).
ZBi: Zeitschrift für Biologie (Munich).
ZEPd: Zeitschrift für experimentelle Pädagogik (Leipzig).
ZPdPs: Zeitschrift für pädagogische Psychologie und experimentelle Pädagogik (Leipzig).
ZPs: Zeitschrift für Psychologie (Leipzig).
ZScGd: Zeitschrift für Schulgesundheitspflege (Hamburg).

APPENDIX III

List of Materials

Roman numerals refer to test-numbers, italicized numerals to page-numbers. Items starred refer to materials that are recommended, but not prescribed, or to materials for the conduct of alternative or supplementary tests.

The Materials may be ordered of C. H. Stoelting Company, 121 N. Green St., Chicago, Illinois, who will quote prices on application.

I. SPECIAL APPLIANCES

Adding machine, *21**, *39**
Acoumeter. Politzer's, 18*
Analyzer, Sommer's tridimensional, 13*
Astigmatic chart. Verhoeff's, 14
Audiometer. Seashore's, 18*
Caliper, Vernier, 1
Calipers, head, 3
Color-blindness cards, Nagel's, 16
Color-blindness worsteds, Holmgren's, 16
Conformateur, 3*
Disc, blank, 14, 17*
Discrimination of brightness, Whipple's apparatus for, 17
Discrimination of grays, Whipple's apparatus for, 17
Dynamometer, back and leg, 7, 8
Dynamometer, Smedley's, 6, 9
Ergograph, Mosso's, 9*
Esthesiometer, Jastrow's, 23
Esthesiometers, needle, 23
Fork, Blake's, 18
Fork, fifty-vibration, 24*, 25*
Forks for pitch discrimination, 19
Form-board, Cornell or Goddard, 25B
Hammer, soft tipped, 19
Key, telegraph, 10*, 13
Krypteon, 25*
Kymograph, and accessories, 9, 10, 13, 24*, 30*
Lenses, trial, 14
Maddox rod, 15

Mouth-pieces for spirometer, 5
Pendulum, second's, 10, 21, 22, 25, 25A
Pressure-pain balance, Whipple's, 21, 22
Prisms, set of four, 15
Resonance box, 19
Scales, anthropometric, 2
Signal-magnet, see time-marker
Smoking stand, see kymograph
Spirometer, 5
Stadiometer, 1
Steadiness tester and stylus, Whipple's, 13
Stenopaic lens, Stevens', 15*
Tables of squares, cubes, etc., *39**
Tables, Krelle's for multiplication, *39**
Tachistoscope, portable, 25A
Tachistoscope, Whipple's disc, 24, 25, 25A
Tambour, Marey, 9*, 30*
Tape, anthropometric, 4
Tapping board and stylus, Whipple's, 10
Target board, Whipple's, 11
Test cards, McCallie's, 14*
Test-type, Lowell's, 14
Time-clock, *9**
Time-marker, 10, 24*, 25*
Tracing board and stylus, 12
Trial frame, 14, 15, 17*
Weights, for discrimination, 20

II. SPECIAL PRINTED FORMS

Cancellation tests; digits, 26; geometrical figures, 26; letters (two forms) 26, 30*; Spanish text, 26; misspelled words (two forms), 26; control keys (3), 26

Counting dots, twenty-seven forms (in duplicate), 27
Form-Board records, 25B
Reading test (two forms), 28
Simultaneous adding, 29
Spot pattern (twenty cards), 25A
Target blanks, 11.

III. GENERAL APPLIANCES AND MATERIALS

Alcohol, denatured, 10
Ammeter, 10*
Anglepieces, 17
Battery, open circuit, 10, 12, 13, 22*, 24*
Candle, 15
Cardboard, 10, 16, 17*, 24, 25, 29
Cardboard screen, 20, 21, 22, 23
Chair, typewriter, 10*, 13*
Clamps, 9, 10, 24, 25, 25A
Cloth, gray, 16*, 17, 25, 25B
Cross-section paper, *29;* (¼ in.), 25A
Curves, celluloid, *31*
Dividers, 11*
Drawing instruments, 24, 25
Felt pad, 11*
Gummed letters and figures, 24, 25
Head-rest, 17, 24, 25, 25A
Key, short-circuiting, 10, 13*
Lamp, electric; 16-C. P. tubular, 24, 25, 25A; 40-C. P. tungsten 17; ruby, 17

Meter stick, 14, 15, 18
Metronome, 9, 11, 25*, with bell attachment, 30*
Paper 12½x20 cm. blanks, 25
Pencil, 26, 28, 30; hard lead, 11
Pictures cut from magazines, 25
Pillow, 23
Resin, solution of, 10*
Rod, 70 cm., 17
Rule, millimeter, 1, 6, 11
Shellac solution, see kymograph
Snapper, telegraph, 18
Splines, *31*
Stoppers, rubber, 18
Stop-watch, 9, 10, 13, 18, 25-30
Supports, 9, 10, 17, 21, 22, 23, 24, 25
Table, low, 13*, 21*, 22*
Telegraph sounder, 12, 22*; with special pointer, 13
Tube, rubber, 18*, 30*
Watch, 18
Wire, No. 18, insulated, 10, 12, 13, 22*, 24*, 25*

INDEX OF NAMES

INDEX OF NAMES

Roman numerals refer to test-numbers, italicized numerals to page-numbers.

INDEX OF SUBJECTS

INDEX OF SUBJECTS

For authors quoted, see Index of Names; for apparatus, see List of Materials.

MANUAL OF MENTAL AND PHYSICAL TESTS
Part II: Complex Processes

[SECOND EDITION, REVISED AND ENLARGED]

MANUAL OF
MENTAL AND PHYSICAL
TESTS

In Two Parts

Part II: Complex Processes

A BOOK OF DIRECTIONS
COMPILED WITH SPECIAL REFERENCE TO THE EXPERIMENTAL STUDY
OF SCHOOL CHILDREN IN THE LABORATORY
OR CLASSROOM

BY

GUY MONTROSE WHIPPLE, PH.D.

ASSOCIATE PROFESSOR OF EDUCATION, UNIVERSITY OF ILLINOIS

AUTHOR OF "A GUIDE TO HIGH SCHOOL OBSERVATION," "QUESTIONS IN
GENERAL AND EDUCATIONAL PSYCHOLOGY"
"QUESTIONS IN SCHOOL HYGIENE"

BALTIMORE, U. S. A.
WARWICK & YORK, Inc.
1915

PREFACE TO PART II

If it be not thought bad form to preface a volume with an apology, I should like to ask the indulgence of those of my readers who have been so complimentary as to express to the publishers and to me their irritation at this delay of two years or more in the completion of the revised second edition of the *Manual*. The truth is, that the unexpected exhaustion of the first edition of the book found me quite unprepared to rewrite the text at short notice, and that the whole subject of mental tests had meanwhile so expanded as to present a task of no small magnitude to one who would seek to deal at all adequately with the material that had become available.

In this volume, then, as in Part I, the text has undergone extensive revision and alteration. In a number of instances the addition of new materials, of new methods and of new results has been sufficient to alter the complexion of the tests so decidedly as to amount to entirely new presentations of the topics with which they deal. The Kent-Rosanoff Test and the Analogies Test are introduced as totally new material.

On the other hand, I have been compelled, reluctantly, for reasons set forth in the text, to omit consideration of serial graded tests (Chapter XIII). This omission I hope to repair later on by publishing a supplementary volume dealing with Systems of Tests in general. To incorporate this material in the present volume would increase its size unduly and delay its appearance beyond reasonable limits of time.

In addition to the acknowledgments for assistance made in the preface to Part I, my thanks are extended to Miss Margaret Cobb and Dr. H. O. Rugg for valuable assistance in the reading of proof. Other special acknowledgments I have tried to make in the course of the text.

G. M. W.

University of Illinois, April, 1915.

v

TABLE OF CONTENTS

INDEX OF FIGURES

3

PART II

COMPLEX PROCESSES

CHAPTER VIII

Tests of Description and Report

The two tests which are described in this chapter have certain features in common which demarcate them, on the one hand from the tests of perception and attention of the previous chapter, and on the other hand from the memory tests of the succeeding chapter, though, in many respects, they resemble these tests.

The essential idea in both of the present tests is to determine capacity, not merely to attend and observe, or to recall what has been observed, but to put the results of this observation into linguistic form. If the observer gives his account of the experience at the time of his observation, this constitutes description; if at some time subsequent to his observation, this constitutes report.

It is evident that this giving of an account of an experience, particularly if the experience be somewhat complicated in form, is a more complex psychical process than those under discussion in the tests of attention and perception. This greater complexity makes the reduction of the observer's performance to exact quantitative terms a matter of greater difficulty, but, on the other hand, the activity called forth is more akin to that demanded in everyday life, and it is for this reason that these tests have been felt to possess a peculiar value, particularly in the study of individual differences in mental constitution and mental efficiency. Again, language occupies so strikingly prominent a place in our mental economy that tests which seek to bring out the observer's ability to cast experience into linguistic form are, on that account, well worth while. This is particularly the case in the second form of test, that of the report, which, in connection with the "psychology of testimony," has of late had a prominent place in psychological research.

TEST 31

Description of an object.—The description test first came into prominence through the work of Binet, who urged that the study of individual psychology may be best advanced by resort to the experimental examination of complex, rather than of simple mental processes, and who considered the description test of special value in this connection. Binet made preliminary tests with Henri in 1893 (3), and worked at the test later by himself (1, 2). His method has been followed, though not in exact detail, by LeClere (7), Sharp (9), Monroe (8), and Cohn and Dieffenbacher (5).

MATERIALS.—Cigarette. Cancelled 2-cent postage stamp. Lithograph, entitled "Hindoos."

The cancelled stamp was used by Monroe, the cigarette by Binet. The lithograph is substituted for the different pictures that have been used by other investigators (Binet and Henri used Neuville's "The Last Cartridge," Binet a picture representing Fontaine's "Le Laboreur et ses Enfants," Miss Sharp "The Golden Wedding" and "The Interrupted Duel"), because of the impossibility of securing these particular pictures, or of the difficulty of using them under the conditions that prevailed in the original experiments (Binet's school children were well acquainted with the fable from Fontaine, for example).

If it is desired to extend the list of materials, E may employ other objects used by Binet (2), such as a box of matches, a penny, a leaf, etc.

For group tests, there should be at least one picture for every 5 S's, one cigarette for every 2 S's, and a stamp for each S.

For group tests, it would be desirable to secure a set of stamps whose cancellation marks were approximately the same. The stamps should be trimmed off in such a manner as to show the full border of the stamp and a narrow margin of the paper upon which it was attached.

The lithograph is one of a series called Leutemann's Types of Nations, catalogued by E. Steiger & Co., New York. It may be purchased, like all other material cited in this book, of C. H. Stoelting Co., Chicago, Ill.

METHOD.—(1) For the picture-test, supply S with writing materials; place the lithograph upright before him, about 75 cm. distant. Instruct him: "Write a description of this picture so that one who had never seen it would know all about it." Allow 10 min.

(2)   For the cigarette-test, give the following instructions, and no others: "I'm going to put on this table before you a small object. I shall leave it there under your eyes. I want you to write a description of it; not to draw it, but describe it in words. You will have about 5 min. Here is the object." If S is busy at the end of the allotted time, or has written but a few lines, the time may be slightly extended.

(3)   For the stamp-test, proceed in a similar manner, save that S's are not forbidden to draw the stamp, if they wish to. The instructions may run: "Describe this postage stamp so that a person who had never seen one would know all about it." Allow 10 min., or more if needed.

VARIATIONS OF METHOD.—The problem of assigning an appropriate title to a picture or of asking appropriate questions concerning it may be regarded as a variation of the description test. For suggestions as to this test see below, under Notes.

For young children, and, indeed, for older ones under many conditions, it is better that E should write from S's dictation, perhaps stenographically.

TREATMENT OF DATA.—In general, the results of the description test are not intended to be submitted to exact quantitative treatment, but are to be inspected for the purpose of forming an opinion of S's general mental type and capacity. The papers may, however, be treated quantitatively, by (1) counting the number of words written, or (2) counting the number of lines written. E may, further (3), record in general terms the readiness and ease with which S undertakes the description, and (4) may rate his paper as a whole, with respect to its comparative merit, on a score of 10 for a satisfactory or adequate description. (5) The description may, perhaps, be classified also with respect to its general type or character, following the classification adopted by Binet, Le Clere, and others as explained below. (6) It is possible, following Cohn and Dieffenbacher, to score descriptions more formally and precisely after the manner proposed for reports (Test 32). (7) Descriptions of the postage stamp may also be catalogued with respect to the items mentioned, as was done by Monroe.

RESULTS.—(1) The description of an object is inadequate, because it is almost invariably *simplified, i. e.,* a considerable number of its features, even important features, are unmentioned. Thus, in one of Binet's photographs, of the 22 objects or features that were mentioned at all, only 9.4 were mentioned, on the average, in each description.

(2) This simplification or reduction in the description is the result of what might be termed a process of *selection.* Certain features are mentioned in practically all descriptions, others are mentioned only occasionally. By tabulating the number of times each feature is mentioned, one may discover some of the principles which condition this selective process. Thus, in Binet's picture of the "Laborer," the old man is mentioned 36 times, his sons 30, his bed 29, the seated woman 27, etc., until we come to relatively unimportant objects that may almost escape mention at all, *e. g.,* a stick in the hands of one of the children—only 4 times in 36 descriptions. When pictures are used, persons are more often mentioned than furniture or other details of the setting of the scene.

Similarly, in the stamp-test, tabulation indicates, according to Monroe, the following order of frequency of mention: (1) word-inscriptions, (2) color, (3) number-inscriptions, (4) portrait, (5) substance, (6) form, (7) use, (8) perforated edge, (9) size, (10) cancellation, (11) ornamentations. The item *use* declines with age: all others are mentioned more frequently as age increases.

(3) *Dependence on sex.* Monroe states that girls generally mention more items than boys, and *"seem* to surpass boys in their knowledge of the postage stamp." It is not clear, however, whether this seeming superiority is due to better observation, to greater industry or to greater zeal and conscientiousness. Cohn and Dieffenbacher similarly find the descriptions by girls more comprehensive than those by boys.

(4) *Dependence on age.* Cohn and Dieffenbacher tested school children 7 to 20 years of age with a colored picture ('Puss in Boots'). There was no clear augmentation of the range of description after 10.5 years in the case of the boys. At the age of 8, the description is predominantly an enumeration of objects,

though not a single color was mentioned by boys of that age. Esthetic and interpretative features are rarely noted before the 16th year, when a reflective element is first apparent. Increase of age is characterized by an increase in organization and systematization of the descriptions. Actual errors are relatively uncommon: the few that are met with (fidelity is 97.2 per cent. among boys, 98.7 per cent. among girls) are often verbal mistakes, the remainder true errors of apprehension.

(5) *Individual differences.* In 150 accounts of the photograph, Binet found no two alike. This wealth of individuality makes the description-test at once valuable and difficult—valuable as an indication of the variety of mental constitution, difficult as to quantitative or comparative treatment. As an extreme illustration, one may contrast the following descriptions of a postage-stamp—the first by a girl of 8, the second by a boy of 16.

(*a*) "The postage stamp has a picture in it. The postage stamp costs two cents. It says united states postage on it. The man has hair braided in back of his head. The Boarder is round. It has arms on it. The shape is square. The color is red. The man is White. You can get these to the postice [post-office] for two cents. There are lines around the boarder. The back of the stamp is white. It has nomber 2 on each side of it. The man has long hair."

(*b*) "COMMENTS ON THE ACCOMPANYING U. S. OF AMERICA 2 CENT POSTAGE STAMP.

"1. Its meaning: The Postage stamps have glorious history. In the past 57 years they have been more and more useful until now they are not only absolutely necessary, but constitute one of the great helps in the study of Geography, and one of the noblest pleasures for thousands and millions of people; Kings and Queens as well as children in the most miserable social condition.
"2. This Postage Stamp has the red color and is now next to the one penny stamps of Great Britain the most extensively used stamp used in the world. If I am not wrong its circulation in the past and present is the next largest of all others. The one penny stamp, I think has the first place.
"3. Its surroundings are very interesting. It is mounted on a piece of paper, remainder of an envelope, which fact easily indicates that it is used in the most cases for letter correspondence. I notice...... [Continues in this and the fourth paragraph a description of the stamp itself.]
"5. Some particular observations. I had 500-600 of them at home which my cousin had the kindness to send me. Of course they are of no special value, but yet they teach my little brothers the important lesson that such a little thing, like a stamp, will do all the necessary things for the transportation of a letter or other mail matter from the Atlantic to the Pacific. It is very interesting to me that with the march of civilization the great Postal system of the World has increased its actions more

and more until it is now one of the chief functions under the sun. How much this single stamp has done I cannot say, but I know that some stamps, precisely like this, have done great service to the country."

(6) *Types.* Notwithstanding this diversity, investigators have sought to classify descriptions into a limited number of types. Thus, Binet proposes four types—the descriptive, the observational, the emotional (poetic, imaginative), and the erudite—each present in varying shades and degrees.

(*a*) The *describer*, or enumerator, as one might term him, merely catalogs the features of the object before him, with little regard for their interrelations, or for the meaning of the object as a whole.

Example: "The cigarette has the general form of a cylinder, cut at one end by an inclined plane where the paper is folded. It is stuffed with a rather dark brown tobacco. The paper is striped lengthwise. The paper is somewhat bruised. The tobacco projects about 0.5 centimeter from one end."

(*b*) The *observer*, though not necessarily more intelligent or clever than the describer, places more emphasis upon the interrelations of the several features that he mentions, interprets what he sees, conjectures and indicates the significance of the object as a whole. This type is also mentioned by Mrs. Bryant in her 'description-of-a-room' test (4).

Example: "A long, white, round object, composed of a paper cylinder, about ½ or ¾ centimeter in diameter, filled with what is probably Oriental tobacco. It is about 7 centimeters long and must weigh about 6 grams [really 2 g.]. It is a badly rolled, uneven cigarette, and has been handled since it was pasted. In two places, to the right and left of the middle, the paper shows streaks as if it had been twisted. Other horizontal depressions indicate that there has been some pressure exerted upon the cigarette. I don't see the line where it has been stuck, but it must be badly fastened."

(*c*) The *emotional*, imaginative, or poetic S is less accurate in observation, but introduces emotion, sentiment or imaginative interpretation in his description.

Example: "It is a cigarette. It is thin, long, somewhat wrinkled. Its shape suggests a kind of elegant ease. Is it the cigarette itself or the memories that it awakes that remind me somehow of a scape-grace? This cigarette, there, all by itself on the table, makes me think of the bad student that goes off in the corner by himself to smoke. But I must write about the cigarette itself. and banish the idea of the smoker," etc.

(*d*) The *erudite* S tells what he knows, what he has been taught, or interjects bits of personal information about the object. This may indicate the presence of an unusual fund of information, or it may indicate sheer laziness, in that it is often easier to write what one knows than actually to describe from direct inspection.

Example: "We have before us here a cigarette. Let us see how it is made. In the first place, the exterior envelope is of light paper, called silk-paper. Then, inside is the tobacco. Tobacco is a product that grows almost everywhere in warm or temperate climates. The leaves of this shrub are gathered, and. after a treatment which lasts four years, are turned over to the public in the form of powder, that is, snuff, or in shreds, as in the present instance," etc.

Miss Sharp did not attempt a classification into types, but noted that *S*'s observation "may be primarily directed to the particular objects or details of the picture, to the general arrangement of the objects, that is, the composition of the picture, or to the meaning of the picture, the story which it conveys,—the details observed being such as lead up to this interpretation, or explain and apply the interpretation that is given first. The different ways in which the same picture appeals to the various individuals indicate differences in mental constitution."

The results of LeClere's test are not directly comparable with those of other investigators, because his instructions were not to describe the object (gold watch), but to "write something that comes into mind as you look at it." He distinguishes in the contributions made by 30 girls, aged 13 to 17 years, seven types, viz.: description, observation, imagination, moral reflection, erudition, pure or simple emotion, and esthetic emotion. He does not find, however, that any one of his *S*'s contributes a paper that may be classified in any one of these types, nor does any paper give evidence of a 'complete mind,' in the sense that all seven of the types are represented therein. In general, older or relatively more intelligent children write more varied or complex papers, *i. e.*, approach the theoretically 'complete' type of mental constitution.

Mention may be made here of the use of pictures in the Binet-Simon scale with the simple question: "What do you see in that picture?" or "What is that picture about?" Credit is given the child according as his replies indicate mere enumeration or a comprehension of the total meaning of the scene depicted. Mlle. Descoeudres (6) has extended the scoring of this form of description test by assigning scores to replies of different qualities and also by noting the number of ideas expressed. She gave a credit of 1 for simple enumeration, 2 if a phrase or sentence was used and 3 if the replies showed interpretation of meaning. Application of three pictures (not those used by Binet) to 14 backward children showed that rank in quality correlated distinctly with rank in quantity and also with estimated intelligence (.84, *P.E.* .02).

NOTES.—The attempt to use the description-test for classification of *S*'s into types of mental constitution is of obvious interest. The drawing, from such a classification, of inferences as to the mental make-up of the *S*'s is as obviously hazardous, for *S* may write his description in the vein that he thinks is wanted by *E*. Thus, Binet had reason to think that several *S*'s that he had classed as poetic or emotional were actually, in their everyday life, of a very matter-of-fact and unsympathetic disposition. In general, the drawing of inferences from the work of *S*'s would become safer in proportion as the descriptions were increased in number and variety, *i e.*, an *S* who wrote in an emotional vein in four descriptions of four different objects has, presumably, a real emotional constitution.

What may be regarded as a modification of the description test is the test employed by Squire (10), in which children of various school grades were shown a series of 5 pictures and asked in each case (*a*) to supply an appropriate title to the picture, and (*b*) to ask an appropriate question about the picture. The titles proffered by the children were classed under five rubrics: "mere enumeration of objects, description of pictures, unification in terms of action of principal figures, superficial unification in terms of relation to principal object and complete comprehension evidencing imaginative insight."

With regard to the first problem, Mrs. Squire concludes: (1) No six-year-old child can be expected completely to comprehend a situation presented pictorially. (2) Neither can a seven-year-old child be expected to give an adequate title. (3) The eight-year-old children are inclined to interpret meaning in terms of action, and a few are able to give superficial titles. (4) In the ninth and tenth years the titles given are mostly descriptive, but put tersely, rather than in disjointed statements. (5) By the twelfth year the majority of the names given will pass for titles, though a large proportion still deal with superficial aspects. (6) There are many cases of complete comprehension in the thirteenth year.

With regard to the second problem, replies may be classed as failures, irrelevant, minor or essential. There are no failures after the eighth year, while the percentage of 'essential' questions rises from 6 at age 7 to 58 at age 13.

It is scarcely necessary to add that these conclusions obtain only for the particular pictures employed by Mrs. Squire, whose article should be consulted by those who seek to repeat this form of test of comprehension.

REFERENCES

(1) A. Binet, Psychologie individuelle. La description d'un objet. *AnPs*, 3: 1896 (1897), 296-332.

(2) A. Binet, L'étude expérimentale de l'intelligence. Paris, 1903. Pp. 309.

(3) A. Binet and V. Henri, La psychologie individuelle. *AnPs*, 2: 1895, (1896), 411-465.

(4) Sophie Bryant, Experiments in testing the character of school children. *J. Anthrop. Inst. of Great Britain and Ireland*, 15: 1886, 338-349.

(5) J. Cohn und J. Dieffenbacher, Untersuchungen über Geschlechts-, Alters- und Begabungs-Unterschiede bei Schülern. *Beihefte zur ZAngPs*, 2: 1911, pp. 213.

(6) Alice Descoeudres, Exploration de quelques tests d'intelligence chez des enfants anormaux et arriérés. *ArPs* (*f*), 11: 1911, 351-375.

(7) A. LeClere, Description d'un objet. *AnPs*, 4: 1897 (1898), 379-389.

(8) W. Monroe, Perception of children. *PdSe*, 11: 1904, 498-507.

(9) Stella Sharp, Individual psychology: a study in psychological method. *AmJPs*, 10: 1899, 329-391.

(10) Carrie R. Squire, Graded mental tests. *JEdPs*, 3: 1912, 363-380, etc., especially 373f.

TEST 32

Fidelity of report (*Aussage* test).—Capacity to observe, or range of observation, may be tested by methods previously described (Tests 24 and 25); native retentiveness or capacity for recall may be tested by methods such as those that are described in subsequent sections; capacity to describe what is seen may be tested as has been indicated in Test 31, but there exists a type of activity, that of reporting a previous experience, which in a way combines these several activities, in that it demands both attentive observation, retention, recall, and an ability to marshal and formulate the items of experience in a verbal report (*Aussage*). In studying the 'psychology of testimony, interest has been developed of late in the direct examination by experimental methods of the capacity to report as such, and it has been found that reports may exhibit varying degrees of fidelity or reliability, more or less independently of the capacity that the reporters possess to observe or to retain experience; in other words, reports may contain discrepancies or inadequacies which are due, not only to misdirected attention, mal-observation and errors of memory, but also to lack of caution or of zeal for accurate statement, to scanty vocabulary, to injudicious phraseology, or, of course, to deliberate intent to mislead.[1]

Historically, the idea of subjecting capacity of report to test seems first to have been definitely proposed by Binet (3). Since

---

[1]It is true that no hard and fast line can be drawn between the report-test and the test of range of apprehension, or between it and the ordinary memory-test; in the main, however, range of apprehension implies a brief exposure followed by simple enumeration of the objects seen, so that what is tested is capacity to grasp or observe, rather than capacity to retain or to formulate. And the stock memory-test measures the *amount* of material that can be reproduced; in it the learning is usually by heart, and the reproduction is largely mechanical. In the report-test, the object is more complex, the time of scrutiny much longer than in the observation-test, while stress is placed as much upon quality as upon quantity of reproduction, especially upon the fidelity of reproduction as conditioned by such personal factors as timidity, cautiousness, assurance, skill in verbal formulation, etc. Again, the typical memory-test comprises a direct verbal reproduction of verbal material, while the typical *Aussage* test comprises a verbal presentation of material originally experienced as visual scenes (pictures, events, etc.), with or without some verbal features. Nevertheless, in the interrogation, the report-test does closely resemble an ordinary test of memory.

then, the study of the psychology of testimony has found its most enthusiastic and active expositor in Stern, who has written an extensive monograph (31) on the subject, and in whose periodicals (*Beiträge zur Psychologie der Aussage* and *Zeits. f. angewandte Psychologie*) most of the work of subsequent investigators has, directly or indirectly, appeared. The applicability of this line of work to many practical problems, particularly in the field of jurisprudence, is too obvious to need further comment.

GENERAL METHODOLOGY OF THE REPORT-TEST

1. *Choice of material.* Of the several types of material that have been elaborated for the study of the report, *e. g.*, the picture-test, the event-test, the rumor-test, etc., the first mentioned has many advantages for our present purposes.[2] Two types of picture-test are prescribed; the first closely patterned after that employed by Binet in his study of suggestibility in school children, the second more in accord with the stock picture-test, as developed by Stern, Borst, Wreschner, Lobsien, and others.

2. *Choice of exposure-time.* For pictures, times ranging from 5 sec. to 7 min. have been used, though 45-60 sec. is most usual. The principle which has controlled the choice of exposure-time for the two tests that follow is to select such a period as will permit an average S to examine each detail of the object once.

3. *Choice of time-interval.* For the sake of brevity, the instructions that follow prescribe a report directly after the exposure. If circumstances permit, E will find it of interest to extend the interval to several minutes, or even hours or weeks. The effect of lengthening time-interval has not as yet been satisfactorily determined.

4. *Choice of form of report.* There are two distinct forms of report, (1) the 'narrative' (*Bericht. recit*), (2) the 'interrogatory' (*Verhör* of Stern, *Prüfung* of Wreschner, *interrogatoire* of

---

[2]For a discussion of these advantages, of the several methods in detail of the chief results, and for a general review of the whole field of the psychology of testimony, the reader is referred to an earlier discussion by the author (34). Suggestions for further tests will likewise be found **therein.**

Borst, *forçage de memoire* or *questionnaire* of Binet).[3] The narrative is a free account, delivered by *S*, either orally or in writing,
without comment, question, or suggestion by *E:* the interrogatory is a series of prearranged questions; the replies to these
questions constitute the 'deposition' (*Vehörsprodukt*). The
constituent parts of the narrative or the deposition may be
termed 'statements' or 'items.' Each form of report has its advantages and its disadvantages : both should be employed whenever possible.

5. *Choice of form of interrogatory.* An interrogatory is
'complete' when its questions cover all features of the experience
exhaustively, and are propounded to all *S*'s in the same order
and manner : an interrogatory is 'incomplete' when its questions
are restricted to such as refer only to those items not mentioned
by *S* in his narrative. The interrogatories that follow are designed to be complete, but *E* may, by appropriate selection, convert them into the incomplete type.

6. *Choice of questions.* The form of questioning very materially affects *S*'s deposition, particularly if the questions are of
the type known as 'leading' or 'suggestive' questions. To some
extent any question is suggestive, in so far as it implies that its
recipient knows something. If we follow Stern, at least six
types of questions may be framed, viz.: determinative, completely disjunctive, incompletely disjunctive, expectative, implicative, and consecutive.

A *determinative* question is one that is introduced by a pronoun or
interrogative adverb, and is the least suggestive form of question, *e. g.*,
"What color is the dog?"

A *completely disjunctive* question is one that forces the reporter to
choose between two specified alternatives, *e. g.*, "Is there a dog in the
picture?"

An *incompletely disjunctive* question is one that offers the reporter a
choice between two alternatives, but does not entirely preclude a third
possibility, *e. g.*, "Is the dog white or black?" In practise, for many reporters, especially for children, this form is virtually completely disjunctive, since a certain amount of independence is demanded for the choice
of the third possibility, *c. g.*, for the answer "The dog is brown."

An *expectative* question is one that arouses a moderately strong sug-

---

[3]The terminology of the report-experiment has developed in Germany
and France. I have been obliged to coin English equivalents—a task not
always easy because the foreign terms have not been chosen with special
care to secure consistency or to accord with legal phraseology. For this
reason, the foreign equivalents are included here and elsewhere in the
discussion.

gestion of the answer, *e. g.,* "Was there not a dog in the picture?" (This is the form used by Binet to induce moderate suggestion.)

An *implicative* question is one that assumes or at least implies the presence of a feature that was not really present in the experience, *e. g.,* "What color is the cat?" In practise, it is clear that a determinative question might become implicative if the reporter had completely forgotten the item to which it referred. (The implicative question was used by Binet to induce strong suggestion.)

The *consecutive* question is any form of question that is used to augment a suggeston that has been developed by previous questions.

7. *Choice of method of grading. Treatment of data.* In general, the adequacy of a report depends both upon its quantity and its quality: quantity is measured by the number of items mentioned or the number of questions answered (in absolute or in relative terms) and is referred to as the range of report (*Umfang, étendue*); quality is measured by the fidelity of the statements made, and is referred to as the accuracy of report (*Treue, fidélité*).

We have also at our command useful indications of the positiveness or degree of assurance that S places in his report. Besides (1) complete uncertainty ("I don't know" or "I have forgotten"), we may distinguish (2) hesitancy ("I think" or "I believe"), (3) positive statement or assurance of ordinary degree, and (4) attestation or attestable assurance, *i. e.,* the highest degree of assurance, as indicated by S's willingness to take his oath that the statement is correct.

On this basis, the data may be subjected to treatment for the computation of a number of 'coefficients of report,' by the aid of the following simple formulas:

COEFFICIENTS OF REPORT[4]

Let $P =$ number of possible items,
            $n =$ number of items reported (or replies made),
            $c =$ number of items reported with certainty (including attestation),

---

[4] The fourth formula is used by many writers, in place of the fifth, for accuracy of report; as here indicated, however, the indeterminate cases ("I don't know") are omitted from the denominator in computing accuracy.

Next to range and accuracy, the most important coefficient is probably warranted assurance (8th formula), as a high ratio indicates a good witness, who reports a large number of items both correctly and with assurance.

$a =$ number of items whose correctness is attested under oath,

$n(N) =$ number of items reported in the narrative,

$n(D) =$ number of items reported in the deposition,

$n(r) =$ number of items that are rightly reported,

$c(r) =$ number of items that are certain and right,

$a(r) =$ number of items that are attested and right,

$a(w) =$ number of items that are attested and wrong

Then

(1) $\qquad n =$ range of report, absolute (*Umfang, étendue*),

(2) $\qquad n/P =$ range of report, relative,

(3) $n(N)/n(D) =$ spontaneity of report,

(4) $\qquad n(r)/n =$ range of knowledge (*Umfang des Wissens, étendue du savoir*),

(5) $\qquad n(r)/c =$ accuracy of report (*Treue, fidélité*),

(6) $\qquad c/n =$ assurance (*subjective Sicherheit, assurance*),

(7) $\qquad c(r)/c =$ reliability of assurance (*Zuverlässigkeit der S i c h e r h e i t, Sicherheitsberechtigung, fidélité de la certitude*),

(8) $\qquad c(r)/n =$ warranted assurance (*Sicherheit der Person, assurance justifiée*),

(9) $\quad c(r)/n(r) =$ assured accuracy (*Versicherte Richtigkeit, justesse certifiée*),

(10) $\qquad a/n =$ tendency to oath or attestable assurance (*tendance au serment*),

(11) $\qquad a(r)/n =$ warranted tendency to oath (*tendance au serment véridique*),

(12) $\qquad a(w)/n =$ unwarranted tendency to oath (*tendance au faux-témoignage*),

(13) $\qquad a(r)/a =$ reliability of oath (*fidélité du serment*).

The determination of P, and hence of relative range of report, is often beset with difficulty; the most practical working rule is to rank as 'one item' any combination of features that forms a single natural working group, the details of which would escape individual observation under ordinary conditions. Again, P may be taken as the number of separate items mentioned by a competent S in describing the picture or test-object by direct observation. Or, as Hegge (18) proposes, P may be computed by adding all the specific items mentioned in the reports of any one of a number of S's. Obviously, the magnitude of P will tend to increase with the number of S's until a point is reached beyond which additional reports fail to affect it appreciably.

A similar difficulty arises in deciding what items and how many should be the subject of questions in the interrogatory. In general, the coefficients computed will have value only for a given picture or event and only when obtained by a given interrogatory, and the interrogatory must be constructed empirically, on the basis of actual preliminary trials, never *a priori*.

Although different errors unquestionably have different degrees of importance (to forget a man is more serious than to forget the color of his necktie), no satisfactory plan for arbitrarily 'weighting' different items has been devised.

The psychologically best method of grading is unquestionably to classify the data statistically according to various categories—such as persons, objects, colors, sizes, etc.—and to compute range, accuracy, assurance and the other coefficients for each category separately. This will greatly increase the labor of quantitative treatment, but it will afford valuable insight into the qualitative conditions of report that could not otherwise be secured: the several coefficients can, for comparative purposes, be united subsequently into a single series of coefficients for the person or persons under consideration.

A. REPORT-TEST WITH BINET'S CARD OF OBJECTS

MATERIAL.—Rectangular sheet of orange-yellow cardboard, 33.5 × 40.5 cm., to which are attached two photographs, a label, a button, a penny, and a postage stamp.[5] Watch.

METHOD.—Give S the following instructions: "I want to try an experiment with you to see how good your memory is. I am going to show you a large card with a number of things fastened on it. You will have just half a minute to look at it. Half a minute is a pretty short time, so you must look very carefully, because afterwards I shall want you to tell me what you have seen, and I shall ask you questions about many little details, and I want you to answer these questions exactly, if you can. Do you understand?"

Place the card directly before S in a good light. At the end of 30 sec., remove it and keep it well concealed. Direct S at once: "Now tell me everything you saw: describe it so clearly that if I had never seen the card I should know all about what was on it." The narrative is given orally by S, and recorded verbatim by E, without comment, query, or suggestion. Reread the report to S, and ask him to indicate what statements he is so sure of

---

[5] These objects are not exact duplicates of the Binet group, and the card is somewhat larger. The exposure-time and the questions of the interrogatory have been correspondingly modified.

that he would swear to their accuracy. Underline these statements.

Proceed next with the interrogatory. If possible, ask *S* the following questions in the order given.[6] Record his replies by number, verbatim, and underline all attested replies.

Interrogatory for the card of objects.

(1)   Did you notice a *coin?*

(2)   What kind of a coin is it?   (What denomination?)

(3)   Does it show 'heads' or 'tails?'

(4)   Is it bright or dull?

(5)   Is it in good condition, or scratched and marred?

(6)   What is engraved on it?   (What does it say?)

(7)   How is it fastened to the cardboard?

(8)   Did you notice a *button?*

(9)   What is its shape?

(10)   What is its color?

(11)   Is it the same color all over?

(12)   Is it made of cloth or of some other substance?

(13)   How many holes are there in it?

(14)   How is it fastened to the cardboard?

(15)   Did you notice a *small picture* (*print*) near the top of the cardboard?

(16)   What shape is it?

(17)   What does it represent?   (What is it about?)

(18)   How many persons are there in it?

(19)   What is the lady doing with her right hand?

---

[6] *S* may interfere with this program, either by anticipating the answers to some questions, or by committing errors, *e. g.*, describing an essentially different scene in the larger photograph ; in such an event, *E* must devise other questions to follow up the cues thus given. Thus, if to Question 14, *S* replies "By a thread," ask further questions, *e. g.*, "Do the threads pass through the holes or around the whole button?" "Draw them." "What color are they." etc :

It is probably better to question *S* concerning objects that he fails to mention in his narrative, save that, naturally, if the first question in each group, "Did you notice ——?" is answered negatively, the remaining questions about that object are omitted. Many children fail spontaneously to recall one or more objects, but can nevertheless answer correctly questions about them, once the object is suggested.

(20)   What is the other person doing?

(21)   Where is he sitting?

(22)   What is he looking at? Describe it exactly.

(23)   Is the name of the picture printed on it?

(24)   Did you notice *another picture?* (*A photograph?*)

(25)   What shape is it?

(26)   What does it represent? (What is it about?)

(27)   How many persons are there in it?

(28)   How are they dressed?

(29)   Where are they standing?

(30)   How many animals are there in the picture?

(31)   Is the cart on wheels or not?

(32)   Are there any words printed in the picture? What are they?

(33)   What did you see in the background (in the back of the picture?)

(34)   What did you see in the foreground (in the front of the picture?)

(35)   Is the picture taken in summer or winter? How do you know?

(36)   Did you notice a *stamp?*

(37)   Is it American or foreign?

(38)   How much is it worth? (What denomination?)

(39)   What color is it?

(40)   What is on it? (What picture or printing is on it?)

(41)   On what part of the cardboard is it?

(42)   Is it a new one or has it been used? (Describe the cancellation mark.)

(43)   Did you notice a *label* (*sticker, paster?*)

(44)   What color is it?

(45)   What shape is it? (Is it perfectly rectangular? Draw it.)

(46)   Is there any printing on it? What?

(47)   Is there any border around the printing?

(48)   How is it fastened to the cardboard?

(49)   How is it placed on the cardboard—right-side up, slanting, or how?

(50)   What color is the cardboard?

VARIATIONS OF METHOD.—(1) To shorten the experiment, omit the narrative and take only the deposition, but first ask S to name the objects seen. Record the number.

(2) Mature S's may be tested in small groups, though this is not recommended. Both narrative and deposition must then be written by the S's. For comparative purposes, the same procedure must be followed for all S's, since oral and written reports cannot be assumed to be equivalent.

(3) To induce a moderate degree of suggestion, E may recast the questions of the above interrogatory into an expectative form and add others, *e. g.*, in place of No. 14: "Is not the button fastened to the cardboard by a thread?" In place of No. 30: "Isn't there a little dog besides the horse?" In place of No. 42: "Isn't the postage-stamp cancelled?" Or, for additions: "Isn't there a seventh object on the cardboard?" "Draw it." "Are there not four wheels on the cart?" etc.

(4) To induce a strong degree of suggestion, E may recast the questions given into an implicative form, and add others as desired, *e. g.,* in place of No. 9: "Draw the button so as to show the place where it is broken." In place of 30: "Are both horses of the same color?" In place of 42: "Describe the cancellation-mark on the stamp." In addition to 46: "What else does the label have on it besides 'Glass. Handle with care.'?" Or, in place of 21: "Is the little boy's mother putting her arm around him as he sits in her lap?" For additional questions, devise a number such as: "Is the lady's necktie dark brown or blue?" etc.

RESULTS.—(1) With regard to the number of objects spontaneously recalled, the following results indicate the outcome found by Binet[7] with 23 children 9 to 12 years of age and by an experimenter from the author's laboratory (12b) with 34 school children in the fourth grade of an Ithaca (N. Y.) public school:

Number of objects	6	5	4	3	Average.
French children	4	10	8	1	4.78
Ithaca children	14	10	6	4	5.00

Counting 1 for each right answer and 0.5 for each partly right

---

[7]For a detailed presentation of these results, see his book (3, pp. 255-329).

answer, the Ithaca children scored in their depositions (possible score $= 50$) an average of 30.5, with a maximum of 43.5 and a minimum of 6.5.

(2) Bearing in mind that the actual objects differed somewhat, the reader may compare Binet's results and our own with regard to the order and frequency of omission in the narrative:

Name of object.....	stamp	label	button	coin	small picture	large picture
French children....	10	9	4	3	2	0
Ithaca children.....	8	6	6	7	3	4

(3) In tests of older children with written narratives, Binet found little difference in the total number of objects mentioned, but marked differences in the wealth of details and the precision of their formulation.

(4) The objects have distinct individuality, $i.$ $e.$, though S may forget the color or the value of the stamp, yet if he recalls the object at all, it is as a stamp, not, for instance, as "some square, greenish-colored thing." In other words, S recalls a thing, not a number of meaningless attributes.[8]

(5) S's may report very precisely and with assurance objects or features of objects which are totally incorrect, $e.$ $g.$, they may draw the thread fastening the button, and take oath as to its presence. Hence, testimony given with precision and detail and with the highest degree of assurance may be absolutely false.

(6) S's may recall one feature of an object exactly, but fail entirely in their description of another feature of the same object, $e.$ $g.$, recall that the label is red, but err as to its shape. It follows that, in testimony, a witness whose assertions are verified in many details may, nevertheless, err in his statements with regard to some other detail that happens not to be susceptible of verification.

(7) If S fails to mention an object in his narrative, but recalls it immediately in the interrogatory, his further characterization of it may be quite as accurate as that of other S's who had recalled it spontaneously.

---

[8]In the author's study of range of visual apprehension. however, there appeared numerous cases of the character thus denied by Binet, for example, a nickel was recalled only as "something bright and round in the upper corner of the cardboard."

(8)   In comparing different types of questions, Binet found 26 per cent. error for indifferent, 38 per cent. for moderately suggestive, and 61 per cent. error for strongly suggestive questions.

B. REPORT-TEST WITH A COLORED PICTURE

MATERIALS.—Set of four colored pictures: "Australians," "A Disputed Case," "Washington and Sally," and "The Orphan's Prayer."[9] Watch.

METHOD.—Give S instructions analogous to those in the preceding form of report-test, but without specifying the time of exposure. Expose the picture for 20 sec. Secure an oral narrative and deposition as directed above. Suggestions for interrogatories for two of the pictures follow.

Interrogatory for "A Disputed Case."

(1)   How wide is the picture (horizontally)?
(2)   How high is the picture (vertically)?
(3)   Is there any border: if so, what color?
(4)   How many persons are there in the picture?
    Take the person on *your* right:
(5)   Is he young, middle-aged, or old?
(6)   What is his posture,—sitting, standing, or lying down?
(7)   What is he doing?
(8)   What is his facial expression?
(9)   Is he bald or has he abundant hair?
10)   What color is his hair?
11)   Is he smooth-faced or has he a moustache or a beard?
12)   What color is his beard?

---

[9]All four pictures may be procured through C. H. Stoelting Co., Chicago, Il. The "Australians" is a large lithograph, one of a series called Leutemann's Types of Nations, catalogued by E. Steiger & Co., New York City. It is recommended for use with large groups. numbering from 10 to 50 or more S's. The "Hindoos" lithograph prescribed in Test 31 may be used with this for check tests, as it is of the same dimensions and of similar character.
The "Disputed Case" (No. 1235 of the Taber-Prang Art Co.'s collection) is recommended for use save for very young children or for large groups. "Washington and Sally." and "The Orphan's Prayer" (Nos. 699 and 1207, respectively. of the same collection) may be used for subsidiary and check tests.

(13)   Does his moustache conceal his mouth?
(14)   Does he wear eye-glasses or spectacles?
(15)   Has he a hat on? What kind? What color?
(16)   Where is his right hand?
(17)   Where is his left hand?
(18)   What color is his coat?
(19)   What color is his shirt?
(20)   Has he a collar on?
(21)   What color is his necktie?
(22)   What color is his vest?
(23)   What color are his trousers?
(24)   Does he wear slippers or shoes or boots?

Take the person on *your* left :[10]

(25-44)   Repeat questions 5-24.
(45)   What kind of light or lamp is used?
(46)   Where is it placed?
(47)   Where is the ink-well?
(48)   Is there not a pen in it?
(49)   What color is the dog?
(50)   Is there a table or bench?
(51)   How long is it (really)?
(52)   What color is the table cloth or covering?
(53)   Is the fringe of the same or of a different color?
(54)   Name the objects on the table.
(55)   How many chairs are there in the room?
(56)   Is the rocking chair on your left or on your right?
(57)   Is there an umbrella?
(58)   Do you think it is jet-black or dark-blue?
(59)   In what position is it?
(60)   Name the objects in front of the table on the floor.
(61)   Is there a satchel or dress-suit case in the room? Which?
(62)   Is it open or shut?
(63)   What do the pictures on the wall represent?
(64)   How many windows are visible?
(65)   Can you see any detail of outdoor scenery through them?

---

[10]If it is desired to economize time, omit questions 25 to 44.

(66) How many hats are there in the room?
(67) Describe and locate them.
(68) Can you recall the time indicated by the clock on the wall?
(69) What object is on your extreme right?
(70) Are there any books in this part of the room?
(71) What color is the wall?
(72) Where is the newspaper?
(73) How long did you see the picture?

Interrogatory for the "Australians."

(1) How many persons are there in the picture?
(2) How many animals?
(3) What kind of animals?
(4) What is the person on *your* left doing?
(5) What is the object behind him?
(6) What is the person in the middle of the picture doing?
(7) Has this person a beard or not?
(8) Is the man who is in charge of the dog holding him by a leash (guiding rope) or by taking hold directly of the scruff of his neck?
(9) What are the persons in the background doing?
(10) Do the persons in the foreground wear anything beside the loin-cloth?
(11) What color is their skin?
(12) What color is the dog?
(13) What is the most peculiar thing that you noted in the appearance of the men in the picture?
(14) What objects lie in the immediate foreground?
(15) Is there any water represented in the picture?
(16) Is the white man standing on the left or on the right?
(17) Is the sun represented in the picture as shining from your right or from your left? How do you know?
(18) How long did you see the picture?

VARIATIONS OF METHOD.—Test the effect of varying the time of exposure, of extending the time-interval between exposure and report, of repeating the report (narrative or interrogatory), without further exposure, two or more times at intervals of several days or weeks,[11] of confronting *S* with the picture for careful criticisms of the report he has submitted. Though it is not advised as the best method, the substitution of written for oral narratives and depositions will permit an instructive class experiment.

TYPICAL RESULTS.—The following narrative by a college senior, a man of varied experience, mature, much traveled, and well trained, though of mediocre native ability, shows clearly the tendency of an adult *S* to describe a situation, a meaningful whole, rather than merely to enumerate details, as do many children. Indeed, the detail here is distinctly subordinated to the interpretative rendering. The narrative tells what the picture is about, rather than what it is.

"The picture, about 10x10 inches, represents a scene that would be typical of a rural justice of the peace and a man who has come to ask his advice on some subject. The Justice sits before his desk, an old manuscript before him, one hand on his head as if he had not yet given his decision. The office is filled with books and on one of them in the left of the picture rests his top-hat. The visitor seems to be troubled very much; his clothing denotes that he is of a different station in life. He has placed his carpet-bag on the floor and his hat near it, as a sign of great mental strain, which seems to increase as he awaits the decision. On the wall to the right is a double map of the world, showing, perhaps, that the Justice is a man of wisdom and a source of information to his neighbors. The room, furniture, the manner of dress would have denoted a time long before ours. The men seem to be about 65 or 70 years of age."

In his deposition, this student rendered an unusually full list of answers: the reply—"I don't know"—is given only twice (Questions 34 and 72). The range of report is, therefore, large, but the fidelity is relatively small, since all the statements that follow are erroneous ones from his report (those italicized are also attested statements) :

The picture is 14x14 inches. The man on the right *is bald, wears spectacles, has his right hand on a paper*, wears a collar, *a purple tie*, black trousers, and slippers. The man on the left is thinking hard, has a troubled expression, wears a sandy moustache; he has his right hand in his pocket, *his left on his knee;* he wears a light-colored vest and brown trousers. The room is lighted by a candle which stands on the pile of books. There is a pen in the ink-well. The table is 14 feet long, has a light-colored cloth top *with fringe of a different color.* There are three chairs in the room, the rocker being at the left. *The umbrella is dark blue in color, and lies on the floor. There is a coat on the floor in front of the table;* there is a basket on the table. *The satchel is shut.* One window is

[11]See Ref. 34 for further suggestions.

visible. There is a chair at the extreme right of the picture. The wall is white. (The cuspidor and the newspaper are not recalled.)

GENERAL RESULTS OF TESTS OF REPORT.—(1) *Accuracy.* The chief single result of the *Aussage* psychology is that an errorless report is not the rule, but the exception, even when the report is made by a competent *S* under favorable conditions. Thus, in 240 reports, Miss Borst found only 2 per cent. errorless narratives and 0.5 per cent. errorless depositions. These errorless reports are commonly characterized by very small range, *i. e.*, they are reports of *S*'s who are extremely cautious and state only what they are certain of. For certain types of material, particularly estimates of time, space, number, etc., not only are erroneous reports the rule, but the most common single answer is more likely wrong than right (Dauber).

The average *S*, when no suggestive questions are employed, exhibits a *coefficient of accuracy* of approximately 75 per cent.

(2) *Range and accuracy.* There is no general relation of range to accuracy, though, for a given *S*, it is doubtless true that there is an inverse relation between these two coefficients.[12]

(3) *Range and other constants.* There is no general parallelism between range of report and other coefficients which depend upon degree of assurance.

TABLE 50

Comparative Accuracy of Sworn and Unsworn Statements
(Stern and Borst)

EXPERIMENTER	STERN		STERN		STERN		BORST	
	Range	Errors	Range	Errors	Range	Errors	Range	Errors
Positive statements___	(100)	13.6	(100)	19	(100)	23	(100)	11.0
Sworn statements_____	76	11	68	7	70	14	60	8.2
Unsworn statements__	24	20	32	—	30	—	40	15.5
Certain statements____							97.5	10.1
Uncertain statements_							2.5	44.0

Note.—All figures are in per cents. The results, save those of the third and fourth columns, refer to narratives, not depositions.

---

[12]The reason for this lack of general relation between range and accuracy is presumably that there are two kinds of good witnesses—the one possesses good capacity of observation, recall and report, and hence exhibits a large range and a high degree of accuracy; the other is cautious, and therefore restricts his range, which may be poor at best.

(4) *Accuracy and attestation.* Generally speaking, attestation does not guarantee accuracy; on the contrary, though the number of errors is nearly twice as great in unsworn as in sworn testimony (according to Stern, 1.82 times, according to Borst, 1.89 times as great), there still remains as high as 10 per cent. error in sworn testimony. These relations are shown clearly in Table 50.

(5) *Dependence on sex.* In all of Stern's work, both in narratives and depositions, with pictures, or events, or estimations of times and distances, whether under oath or not, the reports of men have been more accurate (by from 20 to 33 per cent.), though less extended, than those of women, and a similar sex-difference has appeared in some tests of school children. This superior accuracy of boys becomes more evident when the report is difficult to make. Stern's conclusions, however, have not been confirmed by Wreschner, Breukink, or Miss Borst. Wreschner found that among adults women did better than men. Breukink found that men students reported slightly more than women, but with less accuracy, especially when colors were concerned. His men, however, proved more resistant to suggestive questions. Miss Borst, similarly, declares women to be superior to men, but an inspection of her results shows that the superiority of women consisted in the fact that they returned a larger number of correct statements, while the men did not make less accurate statements in their more limited reports. A recent and as yet unpublished investigation conducted by Boring (6) in the author's laboratory, in which groups of boys and girls and of men and women reported upon the events displayed in a moving picture leads to the conclusion that relatively little sex-difference exists between boys and girls (with a tendency in favor of the boys) whereas a quite marked and certain superiority of men over women exists among adult *S*'s.

More specifically, Borst found that in the narrative the range of men was 76 per cent., and in the deposition 83 per cent. of the range of women while the accuracy of men in both forms of report was approximately 90 per cent. of the accuracy of women.

There is a similar discrepancy between Stern and Borst with regard to the tendency to attestation; the former found that men swore to 71 per cent. and women to 85 per cent. of their report, whereas the latter found that men swore to 61 per cent. and women to but 59 per cent. of their report.

Boring found evidence that boys tend to exceed girls in range of report, tendency to oath and unwarranted tendency to oath, while girls undoubtedly exceed boys in reliability of oath. With adults, men apparently exceed women in range of report, and they undoubtedly exceed them in range of knowledge, assurance, warranted assurance, assured accuracy and reliability of oath. Women possess a very decidedly greater unwarranted tendency to oath. The fact that sex-differences in report are more pronounced in adults than in children accords with what we know of sex-differences in general.

(6) *Dependence on age.* Most experimenters conclude that the reports of children are in every way inferior to those of adults, that their range is smaller, their inaccuracy greater, and their warranted assurance and reliability of assurance much lower because their assurance is too great. Stern concludes that during the ages 7 to 18 the range, especially the range of knowledge, increases as much as 50 per cent., but the accuracy, save in the deposition, does not increase as rapidly (20 per cent.). This development of capacity to report is not continuous, but characterized by rapid modification at the age of puberty. Nearly all experimenters have commented upon the excessive suggestibility of children before the age of puberty. Cohn and Dieffenbacher detected improvement in fidelity up to 15 years in boys, but up to 20 in girls.

Stern has endeavored to analyze in part the development of the child's capacity to report, and has distinguished four stages : (1) the very young child enumerates only isolated objects or persons (Binet's enumerator type) ; (2) at about the eighth year, actions are reported more carefully ; (3) during the years 9-10, attention is for the first time paid to spatial, temporal and causal relations ; (4) in a still later period there appears the capacity to make a qualitative analysis of the constituent features of the objects reported. Cohn and Dieffenbacher think that there should perhaps be added a fifth period, from 16 years on, when the report shows evidence of reflective and interpretative consideration.

The question as to whether the testimony of children is so imperfect as to warrant absolute exclusion from court proceedings has given rise to much discussion. Thus, Baginsky, the German specialist in children's diseases, declares that children are the most dangerous of all witnesses and demands that their testimony be excluded wherever possible. Gross, the leading German authority on criminal law and criminal psychology, however, asserts that a healthy half-grown boy is the best possible witness for simple events, that children make different errors, but no worse ones than do adults, while, in respect to freedom from prejudice, erroneous interpretation, emotion, intoxication and the like, a child is better fitted than an adult to give an accurate report.

Lipmann contends, quite on the contrary, that the unreliability of children's testimony is due in part to an uncritical filling out of gaps in memory, and in part to an unskillful distribution of the attention (though the child's attention is well enough concentrated on what he does report). Heindl says that children are perfectly good observers, perhaps even more objective than adults, but that they cannot translate their observations into verbal reports skillfully.

The work of Boring was specially directed toward this controversy. He found men superior to boys in all coefficients, save assurance, assured accuracy and tendency to oath, in which there was no decided difference. Women exceed girls unquestionably in both range and spontaneity of report; women display a greater tendency to oath and a greater warranted tendency to oath, but they also display a greater unwarranted tendency to oath and a lesser reliability of oath, $i.\ e.$, they seem to be less cautious than girls.

(7) *Dependence on intelligence.* There is no conclusive evidence upon the relation between good report and general intelligence. Winteler found no difference in range of knowledge and fidelity of report between the three most intelligent and the four least intelligent in his classes of 10-year-old boys.

(8) *Dependence on social status.* That intelligence may, however, play a positive role is suggested by the conclusions of Breukink that physicians, professors and teachers give more extended and more accurate reports than nurses and laboring men, and that the cultured group is much less open to suggestion than the uncultured and much less liable to take oath to their answers to suggestive questions.

(9) *Defectives.* The reports of defectives, paralytics, epileptics, the insane, etc., show, as one might expect, a very high degree of inaccuracy, even when the pathological condition is not seriously developed. Such persons are also highly suggestible (de Placzek). Duprée points out that the reports of such persons are peculiarly dangerous when their deficiency is latent or concealed. Gregor found that paralytics were not very bad reporters when the conditions were all favorable, but that they fell off decidedly under less favorable conditions—long time-interval, suggestion, etc.

(10) *Dependence on time-interval.* Lengthening the interval between experience and report tends, on the whole, to reduce range and accuracy, but there is nothing like the loss in efficiency shown in typical curves of forgetting for nonsense syllables and similar material; indeed, for some S's the report may be

improved in some respects after several days have elapsed. Dallenbach's figures (Table 51) may be taken as fairly typical.

TABLE 51

Effect of Time-Interval on Report (*Dallenbach*)

INTERVAL	NARRATIVE		DEPOSITION	
	Items Recalled	Per Cent. Error	Questions Answered	Per Cent. Error
0 _____	765	10.5	880	14.1
5 Days_____	735	14.3	855	18.2
15 Days_____	750	18.0	854	20.7
45 Days_____	569	22.4	801	22.4

From his earlier tests, Stern computed a fairly constant decrease of
accuracy with time, amounting, on the average, to a loss of 0.33 per cent.
per day over the period of three weeks which he studied; similarly, Borst
computed a decrease in accuracy of 0.27 per cent. per day during a period
of six days.

Though range and accuracy seem thus to suffer with the lapse of time,
assurance, as shown by the number of certain and attested statements,
is not, it seems, equally affected, but shows either a surprising constancy,
or, if anything, a tendency to increase. From this it may be concluded
that assurance and tendency to oath are due to *S*'s 'personal equation'
rather than to the freshness of his memory. It would follow, of course,
that warranted assurance and warranted tendency to oath decline with
the lapse of time.

In explaining the improvement found in some reports after lapse of
time, Schultz contends that perseveration is one of the disturbing factors
in reports made shortly after the experience; in so far as perseveration is
a tendency that weakens with time, there would thus be less inaccuracy
from this source of error in later reports.

Jaffa asserts, more positively, that narration directly after an event by
no means gives the best result; rather the memory of the event is organized and consolidated several weeks later and then affords a far more
faithful picture of the event than an account after a brief interval. It
seems doubtful, however, whether such a view can be accepted as a generalization, however true it may be under some conditions.

That the lapse of time occasions various and complex modifications is
also indicated by the work of Cohn and Dieffenbacher, who compared
direct descriptions of one colored picture (Test 31) with narratives and
depositions upon another colored picture with an 8-day interval between
presentation and report. Here, while there was a positive correlation
between range of description and range of narration, there appeared distinct differences in the nature of the two accounts, *e. g.*, acts and interpretations are more prominent in reports than in descriptions.

(11) *Dependence on form of report.* All authorities agree
that the use of the interrogatory, whether of the complete or in-

complete form, increases the range and decreases the accuracy of the report. Thus, in comparison with the narrative, the range of the interrogatory may be 50 per cent. greater, while the inaccuracy (of the incomplete interrogatory) may be as much as 550 per cent. greater. In general terms we may say that about one-tenth of the narrative is inexact, but about one-quarter of the deposition. Typical statistics are given in Table 52. Cohn and Dieffenbacher believe that reliability should always be computed from the narrative and deposition combined, because only thus can differences in the two forms of report be eliminated.

TABLE 52

Dependence of Report on its Form (Stern and Borst)

AUTHOR	RANGE		ACCURACY	
	Narrative	Deposition	Narrative	Deposition
Stern -------------------	25.5	52.1	*Per cent.* 94	*Per cent.* 67.1
Borst -------------------	40.5	65.6	89	83.0

Note.—In comparing these figures, it should be remembered that Stern used an incomplete, and Borst a complete interrogatory.

According to Breukink, the use of written instead of oral reports apparently tends to increase the number of indefinite answers, but to decrease the number of erroneous answers.

(12) *Dependence on the type of question.* The work of Stern, Lipmann, Binet and others shows that the introduction of leading or suggestive questions decidedly decreases the accuracy of report in children and may affect seriously the testimony of uncultured adults, or even of competent adults unless the conditions are favorable. Stern (33) estimates 50 per cent. error for 7-year-old children and 20 per cent. error for 18-year-old S's in replies to suggestive questions. Most experimenters have found women less resistant to suggestive questions than men. Cohn and Dieffenbacher find relatively slight differences in the suggestibility of boys and girls, though the boys tend, on the whole, to take a somewhat more critical attitude. They find that

the decrease in suggestibility with age is more marked in girls than in boys, and that greater suggestibility in dull as compared with bright pupils is evident in girls, but not in boys. These investigators call attention to the fact that a suggestive question that is introduced too abruptly (so that its very form attracts attention) is apt to arouse immediate resistance.

(13) *Dependence on contents or features.* Not all the features of the original experience are reported with the same frequency or with the same accuracy. In general, we may say that persons and their acts, objects, things and spatial relations are reported with considerable accuracy (85-90 per cent.), whereas secondary features, especially quantities and colors, are reported with considerable inaccuracy (reports on color have an error of from 40 to 50 per cent.) In his subsidiary test with geometrical forms of different shapes, sizes and colors, Dallenbach found the errors most frequent with color, next with position, next with size, and least with shape, and this regardless of time-interval. Of the colors, errors were most frequent with green and least frequent with yellow tone. On the reliability of different classes of S's with respect to different features, see further the tables of Cohn and Dieffenbacher (11a, pp. 86f.).

(14) *Dependence on the ideational type of the reporter.* The best reports are given by observers of a mixed ideational type, *c. g.,* acoustic-motor or visual-motor (Borst) : even in a picture-test, the purely visual-minded observer is inferior, though less open to suggestion (Lobsien).

A characteristic analysis of reports, for the purpose of classifying reporters into ideational types has been given in the description-of-an-object test (No. 31), in which Binet distinguishes four types of reporter—the observer, the describer, the emotionally-minded, and the erudite. Miss Borst was unable to use this classification, however, with her S's.

Another classification of reporters according to mental type was attempted by Miss Borst, who, after a preliminary tachistoscopic test, compared the reports of 'fixating' and 'fluctuating' S's, and concluded that S's whose attention is of the 'fixating' type have uniformly the greater warranted assurance of report. There was no relationship found with extent of report.

(15) *Qualitative analysis of errors.* Stern finds four kinds of errors in the narrative: (*a*) errors of apprehension (observation), like overlooking, misapprehending, underestimating, over-

estimating, etc.; (b) real errors of memory, like forgetting, filling in of gaps, gradual amplification, etc.; (c) errors of imagination, 'retouching' the recollection, unintentional blending of imagined experiences with the one reported, or the harmless 'playing' with the report (*Fabulieren*) often seen in children, and (d) errors of judgment (will), like lack of caution or self-criticism.

Schultz (29) has also attempted a qualitative analysis of the material gathered by Aall in an event test. The following are the main points upon which stress is laid:

(a) Whether an item is reported depends both upon the mental state at the moment and also upon the objective complex in which the item occurs. Attention is attracted by novelty and by the logical significance of the impression.

(b) But there is a certain 'spread' of attention such that details that are trivial and accessory may also be included with those that *S* is aiming to observe.

(c) The novel attracts attention, but it is also difficult to observe correctly. Optimal conditions are given when a familiar thing (easy to understand) is in an unfamiliar setting (motive of novelty).

(d) An event which suddenly breaks into consciousness and disturbs the set of the moment is a source of difficulty until a new adaptation for it is secured.

(e) "Perseveration plays an important role in the mistakes of witnesses." Its falsifying effect decreases with time, and thus reports that are separated by a time-interval from the event may be better than immediately given reports.

(f) There takes place a process of logical elaboration, the effect of which is to emphasize the kernel of the episode and to minimize unessential details (principle of conscious economy).

(g) This tendency also operates to distort reports so as to make them conform to what the witness regards as the natural course of events. Portions of the episode unperceived or not understood are filled out or rearranged in accordance with this principle. Characterizations of person especially show this tendency.

(h) Many *S*'s show a distinct tendency to embellish or round out their reports into good literary form, and may thus unwittingly distort their statements.

(i) If the experience moves *S* emotionally, his reports are strongly colored and may suffer decided modification, particularly reports upon verbal items (quotations).

(j) Experiments so arranged as to cause *S* to believe that his report is serious and responsible (not a mere classroom test) produce a different conscious attitude and reveal the presence of new factors, both inciting and inhibitory; in general, the effect is to augment the value of the testimony.

(k) That a witness should be motivated by a desire to awaken a certain judgment upon a case need not be an undesirable condition.

(16) *The effect of repeating a report.* When *S* is called upon to make his report several times, the effect of this repetition is complex, for (1) it tends in part to establish in mind the items reported, whether they be true or false, and (2) it tends also to induce some departure in the later reports, because these are based more upon the memory of the verbal statements of the earlier reports than upon the original experience itself, *i. e.,* the later reports undergo distortion on account of the flexibility of verbal expression.

(17) *The effect of practise: educability.* On the basis of Miss Borst's work (Table 53), it would appear that simple prac-

TABLE 53

Effect of Practise upon Coefficients of Report (Narrative) (Borst)

NUMBER OF REPORT (TEST)	I	II	III	IV	▼
Range _____	39.0	39.0	42.3	40.3	42.0
Accuracy _____	86.6	87.7	92.9	88.2	90.0
Assurance _____	96.6	96.4	97.8	97.9	98.6
Warranted assurance_____	84.0	87.0	91.0	88.0	89.0
Reliability of assurance_____	87.5	89.4	92.6	89.8	90.3
Assured accuracy_____	97.0	98.0	98.4	98.6	99.2
Tendency to oath_____	43.0	59.8	62.8	61.9	72.1
Warranted tendency to oath__	40.2	53.2	58.5	57.5	66.5
Unwarranted tendency to oath_	2.8	6.6	4.3	4.4	5.6
Reliability of oath_____	93.0	88.8	92.5	93.0	91.7

Note.--The effect of practise in these tests is somewhat obscured by the fact that the first and third tests were made after a 3-day, the others after a 9-day interval.

tise, without special coaching or conscious effort to improve, facilitates the report. In her work it will be noted that the tendency to oath and warranted tendency to oath are both particularly improved, while there is appreciable improvement in the other coefficients, save assurance and assured accuracy. On the other hand, some doubt is cast upon generalizations from Miss Borst's work by the reports made by Baade and Lipmann for the Commission of the Institute for Applied Psychology appointed especially to investigate this problem of the educability of report. Baade shows that with regard to reports made upon verbal statements (quotations) the *S*'s (196 girls, aged 12-13 years) showed no demonstrable improvement, either as a result of the threefold repetition of each experiment (physical laboratory demonstrations) or as a result of the succession of three different experiments. There was an influence of earlier upon later experiments, but this influence was sometimes favorable and sometimes unfavorable. Lipmann, who scored the estimates of duration and size, found, on the whole, some improvement in these estimates due to the succession of experiments, but only a very slight improvement due to the repetition of given experiments.

Other experimenters have reported results more nearly in accord with Miss Borst's conclusions. Breukink, for instance, found that if *S*'s are allowed to see the picture after reporting, the practise increases fidelity of report, especially in the deposition and in resistance to suggestive questions. Again, the very interesting *Methode der Entscheidungs- und Bestimungsfragen* (questions in form of: "Do you know thus and so?" and "What is thus and so?" respectively) has led Franken to declare that such training as this method induces, causes an improved cautiousness in asserting positive knowledge.

Other experiments by Marie Dürr-Borst (1906) indicate that improvement in the capacity of children may be best secured by appeal to zeal, interest, enthusiasm and desire for improvement, whereas more formal training of an intellectual type—suggestions for systematic observation, specific training in sense-perception, etc.—is much less effective.

REFERENCES

A.   The most important single source is Stern's *Beiträge zur Psychologie der Aussage*, Leipzig, 1903-6. Lack of space forbids the itemizing of the numerous titles: besides extended reviews, communications, reports of lectures, etc., this periodical contains important articles by Stern, Jaffa, Cramer, Lobsien, Lipmann, Borst, Bogdanoff, Rodenwaldt, Oppenheim, Kosog. Wendriner, Günther, Gottschalk, and others.

B.   The following are other important references. See especially Nos. 11, 21, 32, 34 and 35 for bibliographies and general reviews. The new literature is summarized annually in *PsBu*.

(1) W. Baade, Aussage über physikalische Demonstrationen. (Mit besonderer Berücksichtigung der Frage der Erziehbarkeit der Aussage.)

1 Abh. Die Methodik der Versuche und die Inhalte der Textaussagen. *ZAngPs*, 4: 1911, 189-311.

(2) A. Baginsky, Die Kinderaussage vor Gericht. Berlin, 1910. Pp. 41.

(3) A. Binet, La suggestibilité. Paris, 1900. Pp. 391.

(4) A. Binet, La science du temoignage. *AnPs*, 11: 1904 (1905), 128-137.

(5) A. Binet, Psychologie individuelle. La description d'un objet. *AnPs*, 3: 1896 (1897), 296-332.

(6) E. G. Boring, Capacity to report upon moving pictures as conditioned by age and sex. To appear probably in *PsRev*.

(7) Marie Borst. Recherches experimentelles sur l'éducabilité et la fidélité du temoignage. *ArPs(f)*, 3: 1904, 233-314.

(8) Marie Dürr-Borst, Die Erziehung der Aussage und Anschauung des Schulkindes. *EPd*, 3: 1906, 1-30.

(9) M. Borst et E. Claparède, La fidélité et l'éducabilité du témoignage. *Arch. des sciences physiques et naturelles*, April 7, 1904.

(10) H. Breukink, Ueber die Erziehbarkeit der Aussage. *ZAngPs*, 3: 1909, 32-87.

(11) E. Claparède, Psychologie du temoignage. (General review.) *ArPs(f)*, 9: 1910, 228-232.

(11a) J. Cohn und J. Dieffenbacher, Untersuchungen über Geschlechts-, Alters- und Begabungs-Unterschiede bei Schülern. *Beihefte zur ZAngPs*, 2: 1911. Pp. 213.

(12) K. M. Dallenbach, (a) The relation of memory error to time-interval. *PsR*, 20: 1913, 323-337. (b) The effect of practise upon visual apprehension in school children. *JEdPs*, 5: 1914, 321-334, 387-404.

(13) J. Dauber, Die Gleichformigkeit des psychischen Geschehens und die Zeugenaussagen. *FsPs*, 1: 1912, 83-131.

(14) E. Duprée, Le temoignage: étude psychologique et médico-legale. *Rev. d. deux Mondes*, 55: 1910, 343-370.

(15) A. Franken, (a) Ueber die Erziehbarkeit der Erinnerungsaussage bei Schulkindern. *ZPdPs*, 12: 1911, 635-642. (b) Aussageversuche nach der Methode der Entscheidungs- und Bestimmungsfrage bei Erwachsenen und Kindern. *ZAngPs*, 6: 1912, 174-253.

(16) H. B. Gerland, Zur Frage der Zeugenaussage. *Arkr*, 39: 1910, 116-119.

(17) H. Gross, Zur Frage der Zeugenaussage. *ArKr*, 36: 1910, 372-382.

(18) T. Hegge, Zur Frage der Bewertung von Aussagen bei Bildversuchen. *ZAngPs*, 6: 1912, 51-59.

(19) R. Heindl, Die Zuverlässigkeit von Signalamentsaussage bei Schulkindern. *ArKr*, 43: 1909, 109-132.

(20) S. Jaffa, Ein psychologisches Experiment im kriminalistischen Seminar der Universität Berlin. *Beiträge zur Psych. der Aussage*, 1: 1903, 79-99.

(21) O. Lipmann, Neuere Arbeiten zur Psychologie der Aussage: Sammelbericht. *JPsN*, 3: 1904, 245-249.

(22) O. Lipmann, Die Wirkung der Suggestivfragen. *ZPdPs*, 8: 1906, 39-96.

(23) O. Lipmann, Die Wirkung v. Suggestivfragen. *ZAngPs*, 1: 1907-1908, 44-92, 382-415, 504-546; 2: 1908, 198-242. Also published separately, Leipzig, 1909.

(24) O. Lipmann, Pedagogical psychology of report. *JEdPs*, 2: 1911, 253-261.

(25) M. Lobsien, Ueber Psych. der Aussage. *ZPdPs*, 6: 1904, 161-209.

(26)   L. Maurer, Beobachtungen über das Anschauungsvermögen der Kinder. *ZPdPs*, 5 : 1903, 62-85.

(27)   H. Münsterberg, On the witness stand. N. Y., 1908. Pp. 265. (The several sections of this book have also appeared in magazine form, chiefly in McClure's Magazine.)

(28)   de Placzek, Experimentelle Untersuchungen über die Zeugenaussagen Schwachsinniger. *ArKr*, 18 : 1904, 22-63.

(29)   G. Schultz, Zur Aussagepsychologie: Prinzipielle Erörterungen im Anschluss an ein zweifaches Experiment. *ZAngPs*, 7 : 1913, 547-574.

(30)   C. und W. Stern, Erinnerung, Aussage und Lüge in der ersten Kindheit. Leipzig, 1909. Pp. 160.

(31)   W. Stern, Zur Psychologie der Aussage. Experimentelle Untersuchungen über Erinnerungstreue. *Zeits. f. d. ges. Strafrechtwissenschaft*, 22 : 1902. (Also published separately, Berlin, 1902.)

(32)   W. Stern, (*a*) Literatur zur Psychologie der Aussage. *ZAngPs*, 1 : 1907-8, 429-450. (*b*) Bibliographie zur Psychologie der Aussage, 1908-1910. *ZAngPs*, 4 : 1911, 378-381. (*c*) Psychologie der Aussage, 1911-1913. *ZAngPs*, 7 : 1913, 577-596.

(33)   W. Stern, Abstracts of lectures on the psychology of testimony. *AmJPs*, 21 : 1910, 270-275.

(34)   G. M. Whipple, The observer as reporter: a survey of the 'psychology of testimony.' *PsBu*, 6 : 1909, 153-170. (Also annual summaries of literature on the topic, *PsBu*, 1910 on.)

(35)   J. H. Wigmore, Professor Münsterberg and the psychology of evidence. *Illinois Law Review*, 3 : Feb., 1909, 399-445 (with bibliography of 127 titles).

(36)   A. Wreschner, Zur Psych. d. Aussage. *ArGesPs*, 1 : 1905, 148-183.

CHAPTER IX

TESTS OF ASSOCIATION, LEARNING, AND MEMORY

A generation ago, the members of the 'English School' of psychologists exalted 'association' as a fundamental principle or law of mind comparable in its scope and importance with the law of gravitation in the material world. Whether this extreme position be held or not, it must be admitted that the more complex phases of mental activity are more readily understood if certain basic conditions of mental elaboration are posited, particularly the conditions: attention, retention, and association. Disregarding the first of these, which we have already discussed, we find in retention the *sine qua non* of the development of human mental activity, and we find constantly at work in the conscious life of the organism a tendency for the establishment of connections between its concurrent and its successive psychophysical activities. In so far as the conscious organism acquires new capacities for response, there must be retention and organization. Learning, retaining, recalling, associating, these are terms obviously descriptive of a series of related activities, and on this account, tests which deal with them are here assembled.

Association and memory, taken together, have undoubtedly been the occasion of more numerous and more elaborate experimental investigations than any other phase of mental life. Learning, in the narrower sense, has, perhaps, received somewhat less attention, though of late the importance of its application to pedagogical problems has stimulated work upon it.

The experimental study of associative activity can be, and has been, undertaken for quite varied purposes, *e. g.*, to examine the time relations of mental phenomena, to study individual differences in thought-processes, as conditioned by age, sex, training, physical condition, and the like, to analyze the diurnal curve of psychophysical efficiency (as in Kraepelin's use of computation), to diagnose mental content, and even to reveal obscure mental tendencies and motives or intentionally withheld information (diagnostic association tests). Space forbids the exploitation of all the tests that have been developed in these fields, but a study of the more common tests of learning, association and memory that have been selected for treatment here as being most applicable to the experimental study of school children will serve to indicate the lines along which variant methods may be developed and employed.

The earlier tests in this chapter investigate the nature and efficiency of those associative connections that the subject has already established at the time of the test, either when the associative processes are allowed free rein (uncontrolled association) or when they are placed under certain restrictions (controlled association). The tests of learning that follow investigate the subject's capacity to establish new associative connections, under relatively novel conditions. The memory tests, in a somewhat different way, investigate his retentive capacity or his ability to reproduce a series of symbols or a series of related ideas. The classification of tests of association, learning and memory is, of course, somewhat rough; it is difficult to draw sharp distinctions between each type or to delimit precisely the mental processes that are brought into operation, as is illustrated, for example, in the obvious overlapping of tests of memory, of memory-span, of report, of range of attention and range of apprehension.

TEST 33

Uncontrolled association—continuous method.—The essence of this test is the requirement to write or pronounce an extended series of words not in the form of sentences. Our interest lies first, in the difference of facility exhibited by different S's in the production of such a series of terms; secondly, in the nature of the terms given by S's of different sex, age, or social condition and thirdly, in the nature of the mental processes underlying the word-naming process.

Cattell and Bryant (4) make brief mention of the test; Jastrow (6, 7), and later Miss Nevers (10), Miss Calkins (3), Miss

Tanner (11) and Miss Manchester (8), employed it for the study of the community of ideas of men and women, Flournoy (5) for the study of the effect of environment, present and immediately past, upon the course of association, and Binet (1) for the study of individual differences in intellectual processes. In a modified form (test of 60 words in 3 min.) it appears in the Binet-Simon Scale (Ch. XIII).

MATERIALS.—Stop-watch. Blank forms containing numbered spaces for 100 words. [The seconds-clock.]

METHOD.—Give S these instructions: "When I say 'now,' I want you to start in with some word, any one you like, and keep on saying words *as fast as you can* until you have given a hundred different words. You may give any words you like, but they must not be in sentences. I will tell you when to stop." E starts the stop-watch at the command 'now' and writes on the prepared form the words spoken by S. With mature S's, it may be possible to get nothing more than scant abbreviations for the more rapid portions of the series, but these may be filled out subsequently. The points at which S makes distinct pauses may be noted on the form. At the 100th word, stop the watch and record the time. If time permits, and S can do so, it is advisable at once to go over his series, not only to fill out the list of terms, but also to make marginal notes of all the intermediate links and subsidiary associative processes that he can recall.

VARIATIONS OF METHOD.—(1) For group tests, E should provide each S with a blank. He may allow 3 min. for writing, and rate speed in terms of number of words written (method followed by Pyle, 10), or each S may record his own time for writing 100 words by the aid of the seconds-clock for group tests. The latter procedure is recommended rather than the former. When S does the writing, the method resembles that of the users of it discussed below, but the standard method of oral naming is best.

(2) Instruct S to keep his eyes closed during the test. This variant is to be preferred for individual testing, at least with adults; its effect is commonly to reduce the speed of naming and to lessen the number of terms suggested by objects visible in the room where the test is administered.

(3) Vary the test by demanding short lists, say of 20 words each, referring to the several categories indicated in the table which follows, e. g., "Name words pertaining to clothing." "Name abstract terms." "Name adjectives," etc. Note the time needed for each such list.

(4) E may omit the instruction to write or to speak as rapidly as possible, and allow S to work at his leisure. This method, which was followed by Miss Nevers, is perhaps more satisfactory for the subsequent qualitative report upon the series, but deprives the test of whatever quantitative merits it possesses, besides tending to yield results of a distinctly different nature that are not comparable with those otherwise obtained.

(5) When working with younger S's, E may with advantage limit the length of the series. Thus, Flournoy demanded but 1. words, while Binet recorded the time for three series of 20 word each, and occupied the intervals in reviewing with S the term of the preceding series. This method is less fatiguing, and enables immature S's to give a more satisfactory account of their associative connections, but it does not test S's capacity a rigorously as the longer list.

(6) E may secure a very limited measure of uniformity i the earlier portion of the series by starting all S's from the sam word. For this, the words *quick* and *play* are recommende Here it is of interest to observe the lines of divergence in asso ciation taken by different S's.

(7) Another variation is that of Flournoy, who, in additio to the word test, gave 45 S's instructions to make 10 drawin of any sort.

TREATMENT OF DATA.—In the standard form of test, S's spe is indicated directly by his time for naming 100 words. In t group test, it is customary, similarly, to rate S's speed in ter of words written in 3 min. It is not possible, however, to rega the times obtained from these two forms of the test as int changeable, since the second form includes writing and this, is demonstrated below, tends, even in the case of mature S's, slow the rate of performance. In so far, too, as S's differ in th speed of writing, this fact enters as an unavoidable disturbi factor in the group test.

For qualitative comparison of the lists, *E* may, by inspection, supplemented by *S's* explanation, catalog the words, either in the 7 categories used by Binet, or in the 25 categories used by Jastrow, Miss Nevers and Miss Manchester. Both classifications are embodied in the results below.

RESULTS.—(1) Some idea of the relation between performance in the group test (words *written* in 3 min.) and *age and sex in normal S's* may be secured from the averages published by Pyle for a limited number of cases and under less precise instructions than those above recommended. These results are set forth in Table 54, where it will be observed that on the whole the number of words increases with age year by year, and that girls at nearly every age somewhat excel boys in their scores.

TABLE 54

Words Written in Three Minutes by Normal Children (Pyle)

SEX	AGE	8	9	10	11	12	13	14	15	16	17	18	ADULT
Male	Cases	33	60	66	66	77	80	57	38	36	16	21	64
Male	Aver.	23.0	26.9	29.7	33.3	34.2	33.9	33.3	40.0	33.3	42.8	48.9	42.2
Male	Av. Dev.	7.5	7.6	9.0	11.4	10.9	14.6	13.2	14.8	14.6	12.3	16.6	13.8
Fem.	Cases	37	82	88	65	90	66	61	46	46	38	29	86
Fem.	Aver.	23.7	31.0	32.2	36.8	36.6	38.3	39.1	40.2	40.9	41.6	47.1	38.3
Fem.	Av. Dev.	8.2	8.9	10.8	12.1	15.4	16.8	12.9	13.8	14.1	14.0	13.9	13.1

(2) In tests of college students the average time for writing 100 words ranges between 5 and 6 min. Jastrow reports an average of 130 sec. for oral and 308 sec. for written lists of this length. Since writing an equal number of words from dictation took 212 sec., he concludes that about 1.14 sec. was used, on the average, in thinking the association between one word and the next.

(3) Table 55, derived from Wallin's studies of *mentally defective epileptics* (12), shows that the test of uncontrolled association (here the number of words *spoken* in 3 min. under certain special instructions necessitated by the nature of the *S's*) is of some value for mental classification, since the average re-

sults show a steady increase with increase in mental age
(Binet-Simon diagnosis) when due allowance is made for the
small number of cases tested in certain ages.

TABLE 55

Words Uttered in Three Minutes by Epileptics (Wallin)

Binet-Simon Age	VI	VII	VIII	IX	X	XI	XII	XIII
Average Words Spoken	16.0	25.5	21.5	33.4	43.6	51.3	59.9	65.0

(4) Inspection of the lists printed both by Jastrow and by
Binet shows that *S*'s follow what might be termed a *series of
themes:* a number of terms are written, all of which cluster
about a common central idea; through one of these terms access
is given to a new central idea, which in turn becomes a theme
for the next series of terms. Thus, in the series *hand, face, lip,
chest, knees, calf, cow, horse, pig,* etc., the transition from the
parts-of-the-body theme to the animal theme is effected by the
common term *calf.*

(5) In some *S*'s, the controlling theme is an *auditory sequence,* which occasions long series of rimed or alliterative
terms, *e. g., run, pun, fun,* etc., or *hen, hand, head, harp,* etc.

(6) In this test, the *most common words, i. e.,* those most
easily got at, or those that lie, as it were, on the surface, are
given first. After these are delivered, the task grows more difficult; deeper and more remote-lying terms must be actively
sought for. Closely related to this is the fact that, at least in
the lists of younger *S*'s, practically all the terms are nouns.[1]
This is particularly the case in the short series conducted by
Binet, so that, as he remarks, the test, as he conducted it, is
virtually equivalent to a request to write 20 common nouns.

(7) In view of the vast number of words available, it is at
first surprising to note the *degree of community* present in lists

---

[1]Children often interpret the instructions to mean that only nouns are
wanted. If *E* stops to explain that other parts of speech are permissible,
the result is sometimes more confusing yet, as they may then seek to name
some of every part of speech.

of 100 terms given by a limited number of persons. Thus, Jastrow found that in 50 lists (5000 words), only 2024 words were different, only 1266 words occurred but once, while the 100 most frequent words made up three-tenths of the whole number.

These most frequent words are, as has just been said, names of common objects: in Jastrow's 50 lists, the following were the most frequently used words: *book* (40), *horse* (37), *girl* (35), *man* (34), *boy* (33), *table* (30); then follow *chair, tree, cow, paper, dress,* etc., in somewhat lesser frequency

(8)   For the *classification* of the words given by 20 12-year-old pupils, Binet found seven categories adequate, viz.: (*a*) names of objects in the room where the test was held, (*b*) parts of the person or clothes, (*c*) objects or persons in the school, (*d*) objects recalled from the home, (*e*) objects seen in the streets (horse, tree), (*f*) objects seen in fields or on country excursions, (*g*) unclassified nouns. Here there is no place for abstract terms, many of which were found in series given by American pupils in Jastrow's tests. Jastrow's own classification is indicated in Table 48, where it will be seen that his 25 categories are much more elaborate and extended than those employed by Binet.

(9)   *Dependence on sex.* The question as to sex difference in spontaneous trains of ideas such as are evoked in this test has been answered differently by the tests conducted at different institutions. The comparison of Wisconsin men and Wisconsin women was made by Jastrow, the 1894 test of Wellesley women by Miss Nevers and with no instruction as to speed, the 1896 test of Wellesley women by Miss Calkins but with the same instructions as those of Jastrow, the test of 75 men and 75 women at the University of California in 1905 by Miss Manchester after Jastrow's method. The categories of particular interest are those printed in italics. Jastrow's results in this and other tests led him to believe that "women repeat one another's words much more than the men." He found that "the class to which women contribute most largely is that of articles of dress, one word in every eleven belonging to this class. The inference from this that dress is the predominant category of the feminine (or of the

privy feminine) mind is valid with proper reservations." Since the women exceed the men in the enumeration also of foods, amusements, arts, and educational matters, but fall below them in naming implements and utensils, professions, and especially in abstract terms, Jastrow concludes, "that the feminine traits revealed in this study are an attention to the immediate surroundings, to the finished product, to the ornamental, the individual, and the concrete, while the masculine preference is for the more remote, the constructive, the useful, the general, and the abstract" (6; pp. 564-5). Most of these conclusions are flatly opposed by the Wellesley results of 1894, but the employment of Jastrows' methods in the 1896 test produced less marked divergencies. It is particularly to be noted that writing at a faster rate (1896 test) caused a marked decrease in the number of abstract terms, and brought the terms relating to 'interior furnishings' up even beyond those of the Wisconsin women; on the other hand, the frequency of terms for 'wearing apparel' was not affected by this change in method.

The three sets of 25 lists each (25 men and 25 women) procured by Miss Manchester at California show complete agreement with Jastrow's results in the following aspects: men lead in naming (1) verbs, (2) implements and utensils, (3) occupations; women lead in naming (1) wearing apparel, (2) buildings and building materials,[2] (3) interior furnishings, (4) educational terms, (5) arts, and (6) amusements. Miss Manchester generalizes these differences as follows: (1) "The dynamic aspect of objects is more attractive to men, while the static or completed aspect appeals more to women." (2) "Time as a factor enters more largely into the surface ideas of men; space is more often a prominent feature of the surface ideas of women." (3) "Men are interested in far-reaching relations existing between things; women give more attention to the minute analysis of things themselves." (4) "The range of the surface ideas of men, as a group, is slightly greater than that of women.

---

[2] In explanation of this seemingly unusual superiority of the women it should be said that the things named are not distinctive building materials or operations, like mortar, cement, mortising, etc., but such common terms as *floor, door, gate, church*, etc.

TABLE 56

Distribution of Terms in 'Uncontrolled' Association (Jastrow, Nevers, Calkins, Manchester)

(Each column represents 25 lists of 100 words each. Those from California are based upon 75 lists reduced to the same basis.)

CATEGORIES	WISCONSIN MEN	WISCONSIN WOMEN	CALIFORNIA MEN	CALIFORNIA WOMEN	WELLESLEY WOMEN, 1896	WELLESLEY WOMEN, 1894
1. Animal kingdom	254	178	214	187	146	223
2. Wearing apparel and fabrics	129	224	82	118	97	96
3. Proper names	194	153	84	92	81	141
4. Verbs	197	134	302	258	279	114
5. Implements and utensils	169	121	115	82	139	132
6. Interior furnishings	89	190	90	119	212	84
7. Adjectives	177	102	208	266	300	234
8. Foods	53	179	81	78	88	56
9. Vegetable kingdom	121	110	83	90	101	91
10. Abstract terms	131	97	113	101	101	280
11. Buildings and building materials	105	117	121	140	86	106
12. Parts of body	101	105	91	62	66	34
13. Miscellaneous	91	97	197	180	123	162
14. Geographical and landscape features	97	80	102	114	70	142
15. Mineral kingdom	74	96	96	58	30	54
16. Meteorological and astronomical	85	76	86	87	109	26
17. Stationery	60	86	58	54	69	26
18. Occupations and callings	71	47	60	35	24	33
19. Conveyances	62	52	44	50	19	79
20. Educational	34	76	59	74	102	167
21. Other parts of speech	96	5	108	103	164	41
22. Arts	33	61	59	79	17	44
23. Amusements	30	53	25	45	17	102
24. Mercantile terms	30	29	13	14	18	15
25. Kinship	17	32	9	12	42	18

Burt and Moore repeated Jastrow's test both with children and adults of both sexes, with results that roughly confirm Jastrow's. "The females are more personal and subjective in their interests; the males are more impersonal and objective. . . .

Women alter their themes and topics far more frequently than men; men, on the other hand, show a greater variety of associative connections between one idea and another within the same theme. The course of ideas is also more frequently disturbed in women by the various signs of 'complexes' (systems of associated ideas characterized by strong emotional colorings)."

These discrepancies raise the issue, as Miss Tanner has pointed out, whether this test can be expected to reveal fundamental native differences in mental constitution of the two sexes, or whether it reveals merely acquired traits, social traditions, individual habits, educational and other environmental influences. The lists written by college students might be expected, for example, to be considerably affected by their recent occupations, courses of study pursued at the time, etc.

The more direct comparison of the speed of the two sexes in naming terms of different kinds which we have suggested (Variation of Method, 3) does not appear to have been attempted by any of these investigators.

(10)   This *influence of environment* upon the lists of associations is indicated particularly in Flournoy's brief tests (10 words and 10 drawings), the results of which are summarized in Table 57.

TABLE 57

Influences that Affect 'Uncontrolled' Series of Words or Drawings
(Flournoy)

	DRAWINGS	WORDS
	Per cent.	*Per cent.*
Traced to present surroundings_____	13.8	29.0
Traced to the immediate past_____	1.9	8.2
Due to the milieu_____	15.7	37.2
Traced to recent personal experiences_____	2.4	3.9
Traced to personal habits_____	39.2	9.2
Expressing individuality_____	41.6	13.1
Unexplained _____	42.7	49.7

REFERENCES

(1)   A. Binet, L'étude expérimentale de l'intelligence.   Paris, 1903.
Pp. 309. Especially chs. ii to iv.

(2)   C. Burt and R. C. Moore, The mental differences between the
sexes. *JEPd*, 1: 1912, 273-284, 355-388.

(3)   Mary W. Calkins, Community of ideas of men and women. *PsR*,
3: 1896, 426-430.

(4)   J. McK. Cattell and Sophie Bryant, Mental association investigated by experiment. *Mind*, 14: 1889, 230-250.

(5)   Th. Flournoy, De l'action du milieu sur l'ideation. *AnPs*, 1: 1894
(1895), 180-190.

(6)   J. Jastrow, A study in mental statistics. *New Review*, 5: 1891,
559-568.

(7)   J. Jastrow, Community of ideas of men and women. *PsR*, 3:
1896, 68-71, 430-1.

(8)   Genevieve S. Manchester, Experiments on the unreflective ideas
of men and women. *PsR*, 12: 1905, 50-66.

(9)   Cordelia Nevers, Dr. Jastrow on community of ideas of men and
women. *PsR*, 2: 1895, 363-7.

(10)   W. H. Pyle, The examination of school children.   New York,
1913. Pp. 70, especially 24-27.

(11)   Amy Tanner, The community of ideas of men and women. *PsR*,
3: 1896, 548-550.

(12)   J. E. W. Wallin, Experimental studies of mental defectives.
EdPsMon, No. 7, Baltimore, 1912. Pp. 155.

TEST 33A

Uncontrolled association—discrete method (Kent-Rosanoff test).

—This test resembles the preceding one in that it deals
with association of the free, unrestricted or uncontrolled type,
but it differs from it in that *S* is called upon to respond with a
single term only to each of a series of words presented by *E*.
This form of response has been, of course, the object of an extraordinary amount of investigation, particularly with reference to its time-relations. But in the special arrangement of
the test developed by Kent and Rosanoff no attempt is made to
measure the time-relations, and the search for devices for the
logical classification of the responses (a decidedly prominent
feature of many laboratory and clinical studies in association)
is limited to a simple empirical sorting of them into 'common,'
'doubtful,' and 'individual' responses, on the basis of prepared
frequency tables.

Tabulated lists of the frequency with which different responses are made to the stimuli presented in association tests

were constructed by Cattell and Bryant (4) as early as 1889, and since then have been developed to some extent by Gertrud Saling (20) in 1908, and by Reinhold (16) in 1910, while Bovet (1) has outlined several methods by which such tables might be handled in figuring a 'coefficient of banality.' Nevertheless, the frequency tables published by Grace Kent and A. J. Rosanoff (10) in 1910, taken in conjunction with the supplementary reports upon their applicability made by Rosanoff with the assistance of Eastman (5) in 1912 and of Isabel Rosanoff (18) in 1913 and the recent study by Miss Otis (15), constitute so important and well-standardized a development of the idea of measuring commonplaceness, or normality of response by means of empirical tables of distribution, as to warrant the introduction of their test as a special and specific method of testing association.

Whether the Kent-Rosanoff test merits the rather extravagant encomiums that have been awarded it by some writers[1] appears to me extremely doubtful; it has certainly discarded whatever advantages might be secured by resort to introspection and to the making of time measurements; it sets up an arbitrary standard of normality, valid at best only in the gross and when the test is conducted by certain fixed and probably far from ideal conditions for exploring individuality in mental connections.

MATERIALS.—Prepared forms comprising a printed list of 100 stimulus words[2] with spaces for recording responses, their times and their indexes. The Kent-Rosanoff frequency tables. [Stop-watch.]

---

[1]Woodworth and Wells (25), for example, talk of the free association test as having achieved, and being likely to retain, a place "in the foremost rank among the methods of individual psychology," and assert that the form of it developed by Kent and Rosanoff gives "perhaps the best objective correlate of temperament at present to hand," and that it has "established a definite standard of normality"—statements that are hard to understand in the light of the results established to date.

[2]Sixty-six of these terms are taken from the series published by Sommer in his *Diagnostik der Geisteskrankheiten;* the remainder have been selected on the basis of preliminary experimentation in such a manner as to cover a variety of situations without being especially liable to call up personal experiences.

METHOD.—Seat S in a room free from distracting influences and with his back to E. Instruct him as follows: "I am going to read to you, one at a time, a series of 100 words. Just before each word I shall call out 'ready.' As soon as you hear the word that follows the 'ready' signal, you are to respond by saying the first word that comes to your mind other than the word that I have just spoken. Your response must be a single word, and you must say it just as quickly as you can."

If S, despite these instructions, repeats the stimulus word, he is cautioned not to do so, and the same stimulus is given again after several other stimuli have been used. If he continues to repeat the stimulus word during some 25 trials, E should forego further attempts to prevent this form of response. If S responds by a sentence or phrase, a compound word or a grammatical variation of the stimulus-word, he is similarly warned of this infringement of the instructions, and the stimulus words are similarly repeated later in the testing. In any event, the original response as well as the subsequent one had best be noted in the record, though the second ones should be used in computing the results.[3]

If any response seems incoherent, devoid of any apparent connection with the stimulus, ask S why he responded as he did, and make a note of his explanation.

As the test is somewhat wearisome with children, it is advisable to introduce a rest-pause of a minute or so after the 50th word, or even after the 25th, 50th and 75th words.

VARIATIONS OF METHOD.—(1) Use the stop-watch to measure the time elapsing between the stimulus and the response. Start the watch just as the stimulus is uttered; stop it when S utters his response; record the time in tenths of a second. This variation of method is strongly advised, despite the reasons advanced by Kent and Rosanoff for neglecting the measurement of the association time. The experience of other users of the Kent-Rosanoff test shows that the times are frequently valuable adjuncts in diagnosis. E must remember, of course, that the time

---

[3]With quite young children, say 4 or 5 years old, it will be impossible to follow these instructions precisely. Thus the Rosanoffs (18) were obliged in such cases to permit responses of a sentence form and to take the main word in the sentence as the desired single word.

does not always measure the speed of the association that is recorded, since between stimulus and response more than one mental process may intervene which is not reported by S and which may be quite unrevealed in the word he utters.

(2) Make the test without instructions for speed, but with explicit instructions to adopt a quiet, leisurely attitude in which the association is allowed to develop in whatever way it may. This method of conducting the association test yields responses that often differ widely from those obtained under instructions for speed, and it must be understood that the coefficients obtained from the frequency tables then possess no necessary correspondence with those obtained when the standard method is followed.

(3) Follow the suggestions just cited in Variation 2, with the additional proviso that S may respond by a phrase or compound word in case that be the first verbal association that rises in his mind. It is instructive to compare the responses obtained under this *Aufgabe* with those obtained by the standard method. Here, again, the calculated coefficients are not directly comparable with those established by Rosanoff with his tables and his instructions, though the method is, in the author's opinion, a better one for determining the degree of individuality in associative tendencies.

TREATMENT OF DATA.—To determine the coefficient of commonplaceness compare the responses for each one of the 100 terms with the responses listed in the Kent-Rosanoff frequency tables; record the several 'index-values,' then average them to obtain the coefficient. Thus, if to *table S* responds *chair,* the index is recorded as 267, because 267 of the 1000 persons tested by Kent and Rosanoff gave this response: if the association be *table-hard,* its index is 9; if it be *table-black,* the index is 0 because no one of the 1000 persons chanced to give that response. The association *table-black* and any other association which is not found in the frequency tables is termed an *individual* response, while any association found in the tables whatever its index may be, is termed a *common* response. Any response that is a grammatical variant of a term listed in the tables is classed as a *doubtful* response, *e. g.,* the association *table-inky* is doubtful since only *table-ink* is found in the list for that stimulus word.

The percentage of common, individual and doubtful responses are then computed. If no response is obtained (*e. g.*, "nothing," "don't know"), *E* may find it necessary to add a fourth class ("failures") to the three classes just mentioned.

The term *common response* is not entirely synonymous with the term *normal response*, because, obviously, the responses gathered from 1000 persons do not exhaust the possibilities of perfectly 'natural' associations. To meet this difficulty Kent and Rosanoff have given in their appendix statements that cover in a general way the responses that are to be deemed 'normal' for each of the 100 stimulus words and also still more general rules to cover associations to any stimulus word. These explanations (10, pp. 126-142) must be kept in mind whenever the question arises whether the responses of a given *S*, however individual they may be, are yet within the bounds of normality.

In certain of the words in their list this restriction of the indexes to those responses actually secured from the 1000 persons occasions a perfectly obvious and rather unfortunate artificiality. Take, for example, the word *city* (No. 79). As a response to it, 12 different cities have been named, and with the most divers frequencies, *e. g.*, *New York*, 99 ; Cleveland, 1. If *S* chanced to respond *Indianapolis*, he would have to be credited with an individual response, index 0. I would suggest that in this case all names of cities be counted together and the name of any city be given the resultant index, 124. Similar situations arise with other stimulus words, like *doctor*, *square*, *child*, *ocean*, etc., and with respect to the grammatical variants of many of the responses. Thus, for instance, the association *man-woman* has an index of 394, that *man-women* an index of 0. There are numerous such cases in which a very slight modification of the response alters enormously its index value, so that changes in the association which would appear psychologically indifferent remove responses from the realm of the commonplace and credit them with individuality.

Another criticism that might be raised against the use of the frequency tables in the manner prescribed is that the tendency toward commonplaceness may be abnormally raised by the chance giving of a very few responses whose index value is unusually high. To give the three responses *table-chair*, *dark-light*, *soft-hard*, alone, will give *S* 1059 points of commonplaceness, even if he should happen to give an entirely individual response to every one of the 97 remaining terms. To meet this difficulty, *S*'s may be compared simply with respect to the number of common and of individual responses they have given, or, as suggested by Bovet, by computing as an index of banality the number of terms to which the *most common* response is given and as an index of originality the number of unique responses. Still other methods have been suggested by Bovet.

In addition to computing the coefficient of commonplaceness, and the percentage of common, doubtful and individual responses and failures, E may attempt a further classification of the responses, and, indeed, he will find it quite desirable to do so whenever the number of individual responses distinctly exceeds the ordinary number, or whenever other features of the responses indicate the possibility of some anomaly in the associative processes. For this purpose the classification and analysis published by Kent and Rosanoff in conjunction with their frequency tables will serve satisfactorily.[4]

The following explanation may serve to assist in the use of this classification.

(a) While common responses are as a rule also normal responses, there are certain ones of them that may be termed *non-specific responses*, which, if present to an unusual degree, may have some pathological significance. A non-specific response is one which has so wide an application as to be a possible associate for almost any stimulus word, *e. g.*, such nouns as *thing, article, object*, or such adjectives as *good, small, useful, pleasant*.

Within the individual responses, in addition to individual non-specific responses (like those just mentioned, but not in the frequency tables), there may be distinguished:

(b) *Responses by sound*, that lead to neologisms, *i. e.*, construction of new words, *c. g.*, *man-manion, anger-Angoria*.

(c) *Neologisms without sound relation*, as *dark-unbright, deep-deptableness*.

(d) *Repetition of the preceding response*.

(e) *Repetition of a response* five times or over (stereotypy), as the response *parent* to the stimuli *man, mountain, mutton, short, woman, cold*, etc.

(f) *Repetition of the preceding stimulus*.

(g) Response by derivatives, *i. e.*, grammatical variants of the stimulus word, *e. g.*, *short-shortness, sweet-sweetened*.

(h) *Individual non-specific responses*.

(i) *Responses by sound*, but with actual words, *c. g.*, *man-manners, short-shorthand*.

(j) *Word complements*, *i. e.*, responses in which an addition to the stimulus word forms a word, name or compound term in common use, *e. g.*, *baby-hood, thirsty-blood, green-Paris*.

(k) *Responses by particles of speech*, as articles, numerals, pronouns, auxiliary verbs, adverbs of time, place and degree, conjunctions, prepositions and interjections, *e. g.*, *chair-down, eating-sometimes, soldier-yours, whiskey-no*.

(l) *Association to preceding stimulus*, meaning a response not found

---

[4]The prolonged discussion concerning the most feasible and psychologically justifiable system of classifying responses in association tests is too lengthy for consideration here. For some account of recent classifications the reader may consult Wells (22) and Kelley (9). The idea of Kent and Rosanoff has been to forego logical classification in favor of a strictly empirical and objective system.

in the frequency tables for the word that it follows, but found in them as a response for the preceding stimulus, as in the pair of responses, *thief-night, lion-pocketbook*.

(*m*) *Association to preceding response*, meaning a response not found in the tables for the word that it follows, but found in them as a response to the response given for the preceding stimulus (whether in direct or reverse order), as in the pair of responses, *eating-table, mountain-floor*.

(*n*) *Repetition of a previous response* (distinguished from repetition of preceding response).

(*o*) *Repetition of a previous stimulus.*

(*p*) *Individual, but normal responses*, according to rules given in the appendix.

(*q*) *Association to a preceding response* (so judged by *E*, though neither response chances to be one of the 100 stimulus words), as in the pairs *priest-father, ocean-mother.*

(*r*) *Unclassified responses*—a rather large group in some types of pathological *S*'s, because of the presence of numerous incoherent responses, but also found with normal *S*'s when the response is affected by distracting circumstances, by purely personal experiences, etc.

In using this classification, responses that might be listed in two or more categories are to be assigned to the one of them cited earliest in the above list.

When times are obtained, the speed of each *S* is best indicated by the median, rather than by the average time of his 100 responses. Similarly, the best indication of variability is found in the quartile variation, *i. e.,* one-half of the difference between the 25th and the 75th time, when the times are arranged in order from fastest to slowest.

RESULTS.—(1) *Normal distribution* into the three fundamental categories of the Kent-Rosanoff system—common, doubtful, and individual—is best indicated by the results obtained by these workers for the 1000 *S*'s on which their frequency tables have been based. Their results are summarized in Table 58, wherein the distribution obtained by them and by other workers for other types of *S*'s has also been given to facilitate comparison. The point upon which most emphasis has been placed is the relatively small percentage of individual responses (6.8) given by normal *S*'s.

(2) *Normal times* for free association with the Kent-Rosanoff series have been reported by few experimenters. Miss Otis merely states that the times proved significant and valuable and that defective children were both slower and more variable than normal children. Goett (6), who used Jung's list, found that with normal children the mode was in the 2d second and

TABLE 58

Average Distributions for the Kent-Rosanoff Test (Compiled from Eastman, Kent, Rosanoff and Strong)

EXPERIMENTERS	S's	AGES	COMMON	DOUBTFUL	INDIVID'AL
Kent and Rosanoff	1000 normals	8–80	91.7	1.5	6.8
Kent and Rosanoff	247 insane	adults	70.7	2.5	26.8
Kent and Rosanoff	32 man.-dep.	adults	75.8	3.0	21.5
Strong	16 man.-dep.	adults	78.6	1.0	19.7
Eastman and Rosanoff	253 delinq't	11–17	84.0	2.2	13.2

was not much affected by age, while with mental defectives the mode was in the 3d second. Kelley's tests of 12 college students, with a list of 100 terms decidedly more difficult than the Kent-Rosanoff list, revealed a skewed curve with the mean slightly higher than the median, the median slightly higher than the mode; the mode was 1.0 sec., the minimal time 0.5 sec., the maximal time 3.5 sec. The author has found the average times for college students with the Kent-Rosanoff list to lie between 1.00 and 2.75 sec. An *average* less than 1.5 sec. may be construed as a fast association time.

(3) *Dependence on age.* That children give distinctly fewer common associations (and hence more individual associations) than adults is the general conclusion of all experimenters (Reinhold, Saling, Wreschner, Ziehen and the Rosanoffs), though Reinhold did not find the number of common responses to increase steadily from year to year, and the Rosanoffs believe that the differences between children and adults are practically obliterated after the age of 11.

Their results, expressed in per cents., are shown in Table 59. Graphs of these distributions will be found in the original text (p. 49). The increase in the frequency of individual responses at the age of 15 is attributed to the presence of a number of retarded pupils who were still members of a grammar school at this age. Failures to respond (sixth column), which include replies of "don't know," are found to be due usually to lack of familiarity with the stimulus words. While this conclusion is borne out by their detailed table of failures (18, p. 47), it

TABLE 59

Dependence of Distribution in the Kent-Rosanoff Test on Age
(*Isabel Rosanoff and A. J. Rosanoff*)

AGE	COMMON RESPONSES		DOUBTFUL RESPONSES	INDIVIDUAL RESPONSES	FAILURES TO RESPOND
	Specific	Non-Specific			
4	40.4	1.1	3.8	25.3	29.4
5	55.1	2.0	4.4	21.4	17.1
6	62.2	2.7	3.2	18.6	13.3
7	64.9	4.0	3.5	20.0	7.6
8	68.4	5.8	3.1	18.0	4.7
9	75.1	5.5	1.7	14.2	3.5
10	72.9	8.4	2.3	14.3	2.1
11	82.0	7.1	1.7	8.6	0.6
12	83.8	6.6	1.3	7.6	0.7
13	81.1	8.4	1.8	8.5	0.2
14	84.1	6.3	1.4	7.7	0.5
15	78.7	7.6	2.0	10.8	0.9
Adults	85.5	6.2	1.5	6.8	——

must be borne in mind that occasionally even normal adults reply "nothing," and again that young children often make no reply and yet subsequent questioning shows that they have had numerous visual and even verbal associates in consciousness to which for one reason or another they have given no expression.

A further analysis of these writers sheds some light upon the relative preponderance in children (300 cases, 4-15 years old) as compared with adults (86 normal cases, selected records containing not over 10 per cent. individual responses) of certain types of individual responses. Reference to this analysis, reproduced in Table 60, shows that the greater part of the excess individual responses given by children fall in the categories 'partial dissociation' and 'perseveration,' while the individual, but normal responses (by appendix to the frequency tables) are actually fewer with children.[5]

[5]In this analysis the term 'partial dissociation' embraces what have been described above as non-specific responses, responses by sound (including neologisms), word complements and particles of speech, while the term 'perseveration' embraces all varieties of responses to earlier stimuli or to earlier responses and repetitions of responses more than five times.

These experimenters argue that "it would seem, then, that the tendency of children to respond with individual reactions more

TABLE 60

Individual Responses of Children and Adults in the Kent-Rosanoff Test
(Isabel Rosanoff and A. J. Rosanoff)

TYPES OF RESPONSE	86 NORMAL ADULTS	300 CHILDREN
Normal (by appendix)_____	41.8	20.0
Derivatives of stimulus words_____	0.3	0.1
Partial dissociation_____	8.0	11.1
Perseveration _____	6.1	27.8
Neologisms (without sound relation)_	—	0.6
Unclassified _____	43.8	40.4

often than adults rests in a large measure upon a certain lack of mobility of attention which results in an inability to quickly dismiss from the mind previous stimulus or reaction words and to turn the mind wholly toward the new stimulus word."

The author is inclined to believe that here, as in not a few other instances in which children differ from adults in psychological tests, what we are really bringing to light is an inability of the children to understand the instructions or disinclination to follow them if they are understood. In other words, the regular instructions of the Kent-Rosanoff test constitute an artificial restriction of the natural associative tendencies, as will be shown further on. Adults are able and willing to maintain the proper attitude and follow the rules of the game; many children are unable or unwilling to do so.

Again, as regards the perseverative tendencies, no instructions are given to the child to avoid repetition of association, while it is common for cultured adults to avoid repetition from some preconceived notion that they are called upon so to do.

Moreover, while data are lacking to prove this contention, it seems very likely that the amount of 'perseveration' witnessed in responses to an association test is much influenced by the speed with which the entire test is conducted, because the faster the succession of stimuli, the greater the 'hang-over' effects of the words, whether stimuli or responses, that have been in consciousness. Although precise statements are wanting, Rosanoff and his co-workers appear to have conducted their tests at a fast pace. It goes without saying that for purposes of comparison between any groups of S's, the speed of giving the stimuli should be constant and that pauses for rest introduced with one group should be introduced likewise with the others.

A closely similar opinion is expressed by Kakise (8), when he says: "To sum up, these so-called characteristic forms in children and the abnormal can all be found in normal adults in their natural associations, *i. e.*, when they react according to natural and spontaneous suggestions,

as was the case with our experiment, and do not react according to artificial and 'sophisticated' associations, *i. e.*, by mere verbal associations, as
is the case in the customary experiment with normal observers who are
expert enough to obey the 'rules.'"

Another attempt to establish relations between age and associative type has been made by Miss Otis, who tested 200 normal
children, aged 4 to 8 years, 40 in each of the 5 ages, and compared the results with those for 130 children in the Vineland,
N. J., Training School for the Feeble-Minded, classified for
mental age by the Binet-Simon tests.

TABLE 61

*Types of Associative Response in Normal and Feeble-Minded
Children (Otis)*

Normals.

AGE	FAILURE	TYPE I	TYPE II	TYPE III	TYPE IV	TYPE V	TOTAL
4	1	21	4	0	11	3	40
5		6	13	1	14	9	43
6			2	6	13	18	39
7			2	1	8	29	40
8		1	1	3	5	30	40
All	1	28	22	11	51	89	202

Defectives.

AGE	FAILURE	TYPE I	TYPE II	TYPE III	TYPE IV	TYPE V	TOTAL
2		4					4
3		5	1			1	7
4		3	1		1		5
5		1			5	1	7
6	2	3	1		9	1	16
7			1		11	6	18
8				1	7	19	27
9		1			7	15	23
10					3	14	17
11						4	4
12						4	4
All	2	17	4	1	43	65	132

In Table 61, Type I signifies repetition of the stimulus, Type II non-logical responses (no apparent connection between stimulus and response), Type III responses by sound (whether by a real word or by a neologism), Type IV multiverbal responses (like *whistle—when you whistle, doctor—to make you better, table—there's a table*), and Type V normal responses (meaning here responses by one word, of which at least 50 per cent. must be found in the frequency tables). A child is classed as belonging clearly to one of these five types only when at least 50 per cent. of his responses are of the kind indicated, but the figures given in Table 61 include cases of 'mixed' types, which have been classed by the preponderant tendency. So far as normal children are concerned, it appears (1) that at 4 years more than half belong to the types characterized by repetition of the stimulus, (2) that non-logical responses (Type II) are characteristic of 5 years, (3) that multiverbal responses (Type IV) are very prevalent from 4 to 6 years, (4) that a normal type of response, in the sense here used, is established in 75 per cent. of children by the age of 8 years, though these children by no means respond like adults, or even like children of 12 when their detailed responses are taken into consideration.

The relation of speed of association to age is not so clearly made out as one might expect. Nearly all experimenters find that work with the Kent-Rosanoff lists takes longer with children than with adults. Ziehen concluded that free association times decreased markedly year by year and Wreschner reached a similar conclusion, but both Goett and Rusk report that there is no definite relation between speed and age, while Meumann calls attention to the fact that, though work progresses more rapidly with older children, the more intelligent not infrequently respond more slowly, and the less intelligent, by reason, seemingly, of their relatively less originality and paucity of imagery, frequently respond more rapidly. In the limited number of tests made by the author, children (of about the age of 9) have invariably been distinctly slower than adults.

(3) *Dependence on sex.* The results reported by Burt and by Burt and Moore show a number of inconsistencies: in one group at least (65 children in the Holt School, Liverpool) the

girls slightly exceeded the boys in number of associations written, while in another group (130 children, aged 13 years, in the Wallasey School) 35 per cent. of the boys exceeded the median of girls. Burt and Moore, in any event, conclude that "the males are far quicker than the females."

In their compilation of data from 1000 normal S's Kent and Rosanoff did not find any considerable differences between the sexes in the nature of the distribution of the responses.

(4) *Dependence on practise.* Both Rusk and Wells (23) find that practise in giving free associations reduces the time. Since this practise is not gained by actual repetition of the same series of stimulus words, the gain in time must lie in facilitation of general factors that condition the process of associating. Wells finds that the responses become less emotional, that the number of supraordinate relations is diminished and that of simple language-motor responses is increased, while at the same time there is greater 'particularization' in the responses. Verbal connections appear to become 'loosened up,' and general linguistic readiness is augmented. The effect of practise, then, is to develop an easier, simpler and more superficial type of response. Practise also decreases the times, so that the median speed is reduced to about 1.2 sec. from any amount above that up to 3.0 sec., with the consequence that individual differences in speed are less after practise than before it.

(5) *Dependence on intelligence.* The original data collected by Kent and Rosanoff permit them to compare the responses of 100 persons of collegiate education with those of 100 persons of common school education. The comparison indicates (see their Table I, p. 9) more individuality in the responses of those of collegiate education, but the authors deem it unsafe to risk definite generalization to this effect on account of the wide variability in individual records of both groups.

In the case of children Isabel and A. J. Rosanoff compared 21 'bright,' 21 'average' and 21 'dull' children (teachers' estimates) and secured the results shown in Table 62.

The same investigators contrasted 38 pupils who were pedagogically advanced with 38 pupils of the same ages who were pedagogically retarded, and found, similarly, that the retarded

TABLE 62

Distribution of Responses as Conditioned by Intelligence (Isabel and A. J. Rosanoff)

GROUP	COMMON	DOUBTFUL	INDIVIDUAL	FAILURES
Bright ---	79.0	3.4	12.0	5.6
Average--	75.3	2.7	12.6	9.4
Dull------	66.9	2.3	22.0	8.8

pupils gave more individual responses (13.7 vs. 9.8 per cent.) and the advanced pupils more common responses (86.9 vs. 81.6 per cent.). They believe that extreme departure from the distribution which is average for the age of the child in question is an indication of a fundamental difference in mental ability; that 'plus-variations' [exceptionally high percentage of common responses?] characterize cases of precocity, while "minus-variations border on the pathological."

These conclusions are distinctly at variance with those reached by Ziehen, by Wreschner and by Meumann, all of whom find a greater degree of originality, *i. e.,* more individuality in the associations given by more intelligent children. Other differences cited by Meumann (14, 89-101) are the following (1) the unintelligent more often misunderstand or misinterpre the stimulus word; (2) they more often fail to respond; (3) they give a greater number of incoherent and seemingly sense less associations; (4) they more often use very 'superficial' con nections, such as grammatical variants of the stimulus, rimes simple opposites; (5) they often give responses derived from phrases or verbal connections that they have learned in some school exercise; (6) they often exhibit an apparent precocit. by giving responses like adults rather than the more concret and pictorial associations that are characteristic of most chi dren of their years; (7) they tend to stick to certain forms o response once they have begun to use them (perseveration). Reinhold, on the other hand, found that in two of four classe the better children showed more, and in the other two less ori; inality than the poorer children: he also argues that no differe tiation between intelligent and unintelligent children can b made on the basis of the tendency toward responses by sound, as this tendency is found on repetition of the test to be quite variable and a mere matter of chance attitude or 'set.' Similarly, Winteler, who sought to distinguish two types of response (the one termed the perceptual or describing, the other the comparing or relating type), could discern no relation between intelligence and propensity to use these types.

(6) *Dependence on family relationship.* Fürst, who tested 100 persons in 24 families with Jung's test words (7) and classified the responses under various categories, concluded that persons related to one another tend to exhibit more similarity in the use of these types than do persons not related. He also concluded that the associative type of children resembles that of their mother more than that of their father.

(7) *The feeble-minded.* Miss Otis' results with Vineland children have been presented in Table 61, where it is shown that repetition of the stimulus (Type I) is a common tendency with low-grade mental defectives, that multiverbal responses (Type IV) are encountered more often and persist till a later age in feeble-minded than in normal children, and that normal responses (Type V) appear later and less regularly in the feeble-minded. Goett deems the test of diagnostic value for examining abnormal children. He states that imbeciles have slower association times, tend to repeat responses and to give an unusually large number of multiverbal and non-specific responses and responses of the 'predicative' type (*wood—burn, glass—breaking*). The 253 children examined by Eastman and Rosanoff seem to have been at least two years or more pedagogically retarded. The results accord quite closely with those of Miss Otis and of Goett in that they reveal an unusual number of non-specific responses, of repetitions of response, and of the use of particles. In addition, these investigators found a relatively large proportion of failures to respond, and a percentage of individual responses much above the average for normal persons, though not so great as in the insane (Table 58). On the other hand, really incoherent responses, senseless neologisms, etc., so frequent in the insane, were almost never given by the feeble-minded. These authors point out that the conclusions

just cited are true only for the group as a whole; a good many of the children rated as feeble-minded or delinquent gave normal associations. When to this admission is added the demonstration of Kakise, to which we have alluded, that multiverbal responses, repetition of the stimulus and other tendencies supposed to be characteristic of abnormal minds can also be found in normal adults, the value of the Kent-Rosanoff test as a device for diagnosis of individual cases is certainly much less evident than some of its friends would have us believe.

(8) *The insane.* That the insane show a relatively high frequency of individual responses is shown by the work of Kent and Rosanoff and of Strong (Table 58). Kent and Rosanoff have also shown by further analysis of their material (10, p. 29) that there are characteristic differences in the distribution of the various forms of individual responses in the several different forms of insanity, such as dementia praecox, paranoia, epilepsy, general paresis, manic-depressive insanity. A similar conclusion is reached by Ley and Menzerath (12). The results obtained by Strong with 16 cases of manic-depressive insanity show good agreement with those obtained by Kent and Rosanoff for 32 cases of the same sort. To what extent inferences may safely be drawn from peculiarities in the times of responses, particularly from excessive slowness of reply, with respect to the presence of hidded emotional complexes is a matter of much dispute.[6]

(9) *Dependence on instructions.* Attention has already been called to the difference in the outcome of the association test according as S is set to respond as *quickly* as possible or as *well* as possible.[7] It should be repeated that the conclusions drawn from the Kent-Rosanoff test with its frequency tables hold only when the instructions to respond by a single word as quickly as possible are strictly followed. In illustration reference may be made to the author's own responses, taken under Varia-

---

[6]A general idea of this problem may be gained from the references here cited from Jung, Ley and Menzerath and Levy-Sühl.

[7]Consult Meumann (13, 420 ff.) for further analysis of possible instructions for this test. Roels (17) has also called attention to the fact that S's, despite uniformity of instructions, do adopt different attitudes toward the test and thus give different times and responses.

tion of Method No. 3 (leisurely response with permission to use phrases when such did appear first in consciousness). Three alterations are prominent when the responses are compared with those by the standard instructions. (*a*) The number of individual responses is decidedly increased, so that the coefficient of commonplaceness falls from 12.8 to 10.5 (reckoned in terms of the mean) or from 7.0 to 3.0 (reckoned in terms of the median). Striking examples are the following:

STIMULUS	QUICK RESPONSE	COEFFICIENT	LEISURELY RESPONSE	COEFFICIENT
soft	hard	365	pedal	0
needle	thread	160	stickpin	0
religion	faith	47	ecstasy	0
whiskey	rye	9	rotten	0
city	town	258	voleur[8]	0

(*b*) There are numerous responses by phrases, and, furthermore, comparison of these phrases with the single-term responses under standard instruction shows that the single terms were really picked out from the phrase that was rising in consciousness. That young children may not always stop to make this selection is the evident explanation of the tendency seen in them to respond by phrases, even despite repeated instructions to the contrary by *E*. The following examples will make this point clear:

STIMULUS	QUICK RESPONSE	LEISURELY RESPONSE
lion	beast	king of beasts
command	order	yours to command
justice	peace	justice, peace and mercy
child	father	child is father to the man

(*c*) There are numerous indications of 'perseverative' tendencies, especially in the use of the same response for a number

---

[8]By way of the phrase: "the city is full of thieves" and thence to the French for thief—an excellent illustration of the complexity of the process that may intervene before it is possible to ejaculate an oral response, and of the fact that the dropping of all introspective reports must rob the test of much of its interest.

of different stimuli, as *soft—pedal, smooth—soft, hard—soft, loud—soft pedal, quiet—soft pedal.*

REFERENCES

(1)   P. Bovet, L'originalité et la banalité dans les expériences collectives d'association. *ArPs(f)*, 10:1910, 79-83.

(2)   C. Burt, Experimental tests of higher mental processes and their relation to general intelligence. *JEPd*, 1:1911, 93-112.

(3)   C. Burt and R. C. Moore, The mental differences between the sexes. *JEPd*, 1:1912, 273-284, 355-388.

(4)   J. M. Cattell and Sophie Bryant, Mental association investigated by experiment. *Mind*, 14:1889, 230-250.

(5)   F. C. Eastman and A. J. Rosanoff, Association in feeble-minded and delinquent children. *AmJIns*, 69: 1912, 125-141.

(6)   T. Goett, Associationsversuche an Kindern. *Z. f. Kinderheilkunde:* 1911. (Reprint, Pp. 105.) For detailed review, see *ArPs(f)*, 12: 1912, 192-193.

(7)   C. G. Jung, The association method. *AmJPs*, 21: 1910, 219-269.

(8)   H. Kakise, A preliminary study of the conscious concomitants of understanding. *AmJPs*, 22: 1911, 14-64.

(9)   T. L. Kelley, The association experiment: individual differences and correlations. *PsR*, 20: 1913, 479-504.

(10)   Grace H. Kent and A. J. Rosanoff, A study of association in insanity. *AmJIns*, 67: 1910. (Reprint. Pp. 142.)

(11)   M. Levy-Sühl, Ueber experimentelle Beeinflussung des Vorstellungsverlaufs bei Geisteskranken. Leipzig, 1911. Pp. 142.

(12)   Ley et Menzerath, Les associations des idées dans les maladies mentales. Gand, 1911. Pp. 200.

(13)   E. Meumann, Vorlesungen zur Einführung in die exp. Pädagogik. Vol. II. Leipzig, 1913. (2d ed.)

(14)   E. Meumann, Intelligenzprüfungen an Kindern der Volksschule *EPd*, 1: 1905, 35-101.

(15)   Margaret Otis, A study of association in defectives. To appear in *JEdPs* (?).

(16)   F. Reinhold, Beiträge zur Associationslehre auf Grund von Massenversuchen. *ZPs*, 54: 1910, 183-214.

(17)   F. Roels, La recherche du mot de réaction dans les expériences d'association. Extrait, *Annales de l'Institut Superieur de Philosophi* (Louvain), 3: 1914, 553-573.

(18)   Isabel Rosanoff and A. J. Rosanoff, A study of association in children. *PsR*, 20: 1913, 43-89.

(19)   R. R. Rusk, Experiments on mental association in children. *BrJPs*, 3: 1910, 349-385.

(20)   Gertrud Saling, Associative Massenversuche. *ZPs*, 49: 1905, 238-253.

(21)   E. K. Strong, Jr., A comparison between experimental data and clinical results in manic-depressive insanity. *AmJPs*, 24: 1913, 66-98.

(22)   F. L. Wells, (*a*) A preliminary note on the categories of association reactions. *PsR*, 18: 1911, 229-233. (*b*) The question of association types. *PsR*, 19: 1912, 253-270.

(23)   F. L. Wells, Practise effects in free association. *AmJPs*, 22: 1911, 1-13.

(24)   J. Winteler, Experimentelle Beiträge zu einer Begabungslehr *EPd*, 2: 1906, 1-48, 147-247.

(25) R. S. Woodworth and F. L. Wells, Association tests. *PsMon*, 13 : 1911 (No. 57). Pp. 85.
(26) A. Wreschner, Die Reproduktion und Assoziation von Vorstellungen. Leipzig. *Ergänzungsband, ZPs*, 3 : 1907.
(27) T. Ziehen, Die Ideenassoziation des Kindes. Berlin, 1898 and 1900.

TEST 34

Controlled association: logical relations.—These tests differ from the preceding test of association in that they demand the giving of a response which is so restricted that only a very limited number of terms may be deemed correct associates. There are, of course, numerous forms of controlled association, since numerous logical relations may be demanded between the stimulus words and the responses. The relations that have received most attention in the literature of mental tests are part-whole, genus-species (subordinate) and opposites. Other less often used relations are whole-part, agent-action (subject-verb), action-agent (verb-subject), attribute-substance (adjective-noun), substance-attribute (noun-adjective), cause-effect, effect-cause, species-genus (supraordinate), co-ordinate and mixed relations.

Just precisely what mental capacities are measured by these tests is not always clear. Of course, it may be said roughly that they call forth the "ability to appreciate relationships and to control associations." It is also evident that the skill in handling these various relations is based upon what is known in psychology as a "determining tendency," or "adjustment to react according to instructions," and that "the more completely this adjustment dominates the performance, facilitating the right responses and inhibiting other, interfering associations and perseverations, the less hesitation and confusion will occur and the more prompt will be the reaction."

On the other hand, an obstacle both to designating the capacities measured and to evaluating the results of these tests lies in the selection of the stimulus words themselves, for, if the terms are too difficult, failures appear due to lack of familiarity with their meaning or with the meaning of the terms connected with them in various logical relations; while, if they are too simple, no 'thinking' is demanded and the responses are given well-nigh automatically. Moreover, the inclusion in a list of terms of one or more stimuli that are markedly different from the others in this respect introduces a source of difficulty in administering the test that is hard to meet, especially in group tests. The only solution of these difficulties is to discover by comprehensive testing what might be termed the 'association value' of each stimulus word for S's of a given sex, age, intelligence, etc., and then to prepare standardized lists of stimuli suited by their like association values to the measure of controlled association in specified types of S's. Much has been accomplished in this direction, but much still remains to be done.

Consideration of the various possible forms of controlled association is limited in what follows mainly to the most-used relations, part-whole, genus-species, and opposites.

A. THE PART-WHOLE TEST

MATERIALS.—(1) For individual tests: Split-second stop-watch. Set of 20 cards (and 3 samples), each containing a stimulus word. Paper for recording times, responses and remarks. (2) For group test: Stop-watch or special seconds clock. Printed form containing the same stimuli and provided with spaces for the recording of the 20 associates.

The terms incorporated in these cards and in the form are those recommended by Woodworth and Wells as the result of numerous efforts at standardization. Cards are used, however, instead of the narrow cardboard strip of these authors in order that the time of each response may be measured by itself. The paper form is used to admit of written group tests.

The terms proposed by Pyle for this test are: window, leaf, pillow, button, nose, smokestack, cogwheel, cover, letter, petal, page, cob, axle, lever, blade, sail, coach, cylinder, beak, stamen. His supplementary list is the same as that of Woodworth and Wells.

The 10-word lists used by Rusk were: ear, wheel, beak, inch, platform, mast, branch, kernel, funnel, buckle: *alternatives*, mouth, handle, claw, ounce, pavement, sail, stem, core, boiler, knob.

The ten terms employed by Miss Norsworthy were: door, pillow, letter, leaf, button, nose, cover, page, engine, glass.

The ten terms employed by Wyatt are not specified by him.

---

[1]The mixed relations or analogies test is dealt with separately as Test 34A. For further details concerning other tests of logical relationship, consult Rusk (15), Watt (20) and Woodworth and Wells (22).

METHOD.—Instruct S as follows: "Each one of these cards has printed on it a word. As soon as I uncover a card I want you to look at the word on it and then, as quickly as you can, say aloud the name of the whole thing of which that word is a part. The word you read is a part: you are to name the whole. For example, if the card should have the word *fur* on it, you might say *cat* or *seal* or *fox*. We will try these sample cards first to make sure you understand."

After a warning 'now' remove the cover-card from the top of the pile and take S's time for the first sample—*button*. Follow with the other samples, *leaf* and *drawer*. These cards are displayed and the time taken just as in the test proper, in order to accustom S to the regular procedure. Misunderstandings are, of course, corrected and cleared away.

Proceed with the 20 standard test cards. Record on the blank sheet of paper the times, in tenths of a second, together with S's responses and any comments that suggest themselves. Each card is provided with its own cover-card. They are best removed with the left hand and the watch started simultaneously with the right. It is recommended that the split-second watch be used, so that one hand may be stopped when S first responds; then, if his response chances to be wrong, say 'No, give me another,' and take the time of his second attempt with the other hand of the watch. In this event, both times and both responses are recorded.

VARIATIONS OF METHOD.—(1) Individual testing may also be carried out, especially if none of the terms is likely to cause unusual delay, by giving S the printed form provided for group tests and taking his total time for naming *orally* the entire series of responses.

(2) For a group test by the work-limit method[2] (which is recommended for S's who are competent to record their own time) use the printed forms and the special seconds clock, after the samples above mentioned have been displayed on a blackboard and discussed with the S's. The clock is started at the signal for turning over the forms. Each S, of course, makes his own written record.

---

[2]See Vol. I, p. 8, Section (7).

(3) For a group test by the time-limit method use the same forms and stop all S's at a time-limit so chosen on the basis of preliminary trials with S's of that grade of ability that the fastest S. shall reach about the 16th term on the list.[3] It is hardly necessary to state that the scores obtained by either group test are not directly comparable with those obtained by the individual method.

TREATMENT OF DATA.—(1) In the individual test the best indication of speed is furnished by the median. For a measure of variability the semi-quartile variation may be used, *i. e.,* one-half the difference between the 5th and 15th time, when the series of times is arranged in order from fastest to slowest. If the S's are competent, the errors will ordinarily be negligible, so that performance may be measured in terms of speed alone. If it should happen that differences in speed are slight, while qualitative differences are well-marked, speed may be neglected and performance rated in terms of quality, as by scoring 1 for each well-chosen associate, 0.5 for each 'partly right' associate, and 0 for wrong associates or omissions. If both speed and correctness need to be considered, some of the methods suggested in the cancellation test (No. 26) or in the opposites test (below) may be employed.

(2) When individuals are tested by recording the total time for the entire list (Variation 1), errors may again be neglected if few and of slight moment; if more serious, the time may be increased by adding to it a penalty figured on the basis of the average time taken to utter a correct response to each stimulus omitted or responded to wrongly.

(3) In group tests by the work-limit method, performance may, similarly, be taken in terms of total time, or of correctness, or of some combination of time and correctness.

(4) In group tests by the time-limit method, the simplest method of scoring is that of crediting 1, 0.5 or 0 for each re-

---

[3]The lists of terms in these tests of controlled association have been so arranged by Woodworth and Wells that the terms lying between the 8th and the 16th represent as nearly as possible stimuli of equal difficulty. Thirty sec. will suffice for testing competent adults. Pyle recommends 60 sec. for Grades 2, 3 and 4: 45 sec. for other grades (and 30 sec. for adults?).

sponse, as above explained. If necessary to compare the performances of groups that have had different time-limits, they may be related by computing them all as if 60 sec. had been assigned, *e. g.,* by multiplying the score of adults by 2, etc.

RESULTS.—(1) Norms of performance in the part-whole test are supplied chiefly in the data published by Woodworth and Wells, by Miss Norsworthy and by Pyle. Tests of adult college students by the first-named authors show that the average association time for this variety of controlled association (Variation of Method No. 1) may be taken as 1.53 sec., P.E. .06, with a range for different individuals of from 1.03 to 2.50 sec. The median times reported by Rusk for 22 children, aged 7 years 6 months to 14 years 9 months, under Meumann's 'B' instructions (emphasizing quality rather than speed) range from 1.6 to 5.0 sec. Miss Norsworthy's norms, based on 504 cases, represent results with her list of 10 words, no time-limit, scored in terms of number of correct associates. Pyle's norms are based upon his list of 20 words, scored in number correctly written in a group test, computed on a basis of 60 sec. time-limit.

TABLE 63

Performance in the Part-Whole Test (Norsworthy)

AGE	8	9	10	11	12	13	14	15	16	ADULTS
Median	6.5	7.8	7.8	8.7	8.7	9.0	9.0	9.0	9.0	10.0
P. E.	2.3	1.3	1.9	1.1	1.2	0.7	0.7	0.7	0.7	0.5

TABLE 64

Correct Associates Written in 60 Sec. Part-Whole Test (Pyle)

SEX	AGE	8	9	10	11	12	13	14	15	16	17	18	ADULT
Male	Cases	31	67	70	65	76	77	62	42	35	12	23	66
	Aver.	5.5	6.5	7.3	8.9	8.9	11.1	12.2	14.8	15.9	15.8	19.3	18.5
	A. D.	3.6	2.9	2.5	2.8	3.4	4.3	4.1	5.5	5.3	4.0	5.6	3.6
Female	Cases	43	64	88	67	87	71	63	48	51	38	28	87
	Aver.	4.6	5.9	7.8	10.0	10.0	10.8	12.5	14.0	16.9	16.2	19.7	19.7
	A. D.	2.6	2.4	2.9	3.5	3.7	3.5	3.2	4.5	4.5	4.8	4.6	3.4

(2) *Dependence on age.* The results obtained by both Pyle and Miss Norsworthy show that performance in this test undergoes a fairly steady improvement from 8 to 18 years. The lack of any correspondence between speed and age reported by Rusk is probably due to the small number of cases examined by him.

(3) *Dependence on sex.* Sex-differences are not sufficiently evident to warrant conclusions, though it may be surmised that girls and women tend to be slightly superior to boys and men.

(4) *Dependence on intelligence.* Wyatt found a fair degree of correlation with intelligence (0.67, P.E. .07 in one group using teachers' estimates, and 0.56, P.E. .08 in another group, using class examinations as the basis for intelligence).

(5) *Feeble-minded.* The work of Miss Norsworthy shows that mentally defective children are distinctly inferior to normal children in this test: thus the percentage of normal children with a record above the median, above —1 P.E., and above —2 P.E., would, of course, be 50, 75, and 91, respectively, but the percentages of feeble-minded children obtaining these three grades of efficiency were but 9, 17, and 27, respectively. That is, only 9 per cent. of the feeble-minded children reached the degree of efficiency attained by one-half of the normal children, etc.

(6) *Other correlations.* Wyatt obtained with his Group I a moderately satisfactory coefficient of reliability, 0.65. His correlations with other tests range from 0.09 to 0.77. The lowest correlation was with the letter-squares test; the higher correlations appeared with analogies (0.67), the completion test (0.75) and word-building (0.77).

B. THE GENUS-SPECIES TEST

MATERIALS.—(1) For individual tests: Split-second stop-watch. Set of 20 cards (and three samples) each containing a stimulus word. Paper for recording times, responses and remarks. (2) For group tests: Stop-watch or special seconds clock. Printed form containing the same stimuli and provided with space for recording the 20 associates.

These 20 terms are those recommended by Woodworth and Wells.

The 10 terms used by Miss Norsworthy are: book, tree, room, toy, name, dish, boat, game, plant, fish.

The 20 terms proposed by Pyle are: mountain, city, weed, metal, furniture, machine, author, planet, river, book, ocean, fruit, country, animal, bird, food, lake, tool, fish, money. His supplementary list is the same as Woodworth and Wells.

The 10-word lists used by Rusk were: tree, fish, college, battle, picture, tool, hero, lesson, taste, wrong: *alternatives*, bird, leaf, game, poem, song, toy, hobby, book, smell, virtue.

METHOD.—Instruct S as follows: "Each one of these cards has printed on it a word. As soon as I uncover a card, look at the word on it and then, as quickly as you can, say aloud the name of some particular thing that belongs in the class that is given on the card. The word you read is the name of a class or genus; you are to name an example of that class, a species of that genus. For example, if the card should have on it the word *taste*, you might say *sweet* or *salt*, or if the word *verb*, you might name any verb like *run* or *go*. We will try three sample cards first to make sure you understand." Follow the procedure outlined for the part-whole test in regard to the use of the sample cards, timing, etc.

VARIATIONS OF METHOD.—Follow the suggestions given for part-whole test, save that here the samples will be *bird, dish* and *game*.

TREATMENT OF DATA.—Follow the suggestions given for the part-whole test.

RESULTS.—(1) Tests of adult college students by Woodworth and Wells (Variant Method No. 1) show for the genus-species test an average association time of 1.84 sec., P.E. .07, with a range for different individuals of from 1.20 to 2.63 sec. The medians reported by Rusk for 22 children from about 7 to 15 years of age, with quality emphasized more than speed, range from 1.6 to 11.4 sec. The norms reproduced here from Miss Norsworthy are based on 511 cases and represent performances made with her list of 10 words, no time-limit, scored in terms of number of correct associates. The norms reproduced from Pyle are based on his list of 20 words, scored in terms of number correctly written in a group test, computed on a basis of 50 sec. time-limit.

TABLE 65

Performance in the Genus-Species Test (Norsworthy)

AGE	8	9	10	11	12	13	14	15	16	ADULTS
Median___	5.0	5.0	7.0	9.2	9.2	9.3	9.3	9.5	9.5	10.0
P. E. _____	2.0	2.7	2.9	1.9	0.7	0.4	0.5	0.5	0.5	0.0

TABLE 66

Correct Associates Written in 60 Sec. Genus-Species Test (Pyle)

SEX	AGE	8	9	10	11	12	13	14	15	16	17	18	ADULT
Male _____	Cases	29	67	66	62	69	68	64	41	33	18	16	65
	Aver.	4.6	5.7	6.5	7.2	7.1	10.0	10.5	11.1	15.2	14.0	17.3	15.1
	A. D.	3.4	3.4	3.7	3.3	2.5	3.8	3.8	5.4	4.3	4.1	6.0	4.0
Female _____	Cases	34	65	84	63	81	64	55	40	45	32	25	86
	Aver.	5.5	5.4	7.8	8.2	9.3	9.5	11.8	14.0	16.4	16.0	18.3	15.5
	A. D.	3.6	2.5	3.2	3.7	2.9	3.2	3.2	4.2	5.4	4.9	5.3	3.8

(2) *Dependence on age.* Though Rusk can find no definite relation between speed and age in the genus-species test, the figures reported by both Pyle and Miss Norsworthy show a general improvement with age, despite certain exceptions. Miss Norsworthy's test was obviously too easy for ages of 1. and above, so that any tendency toward improvement beyond 11 was obscured. Rusk's negative result is explicable partly by his instructions against haste and partly by the small number of cases he tested.

(3) *Dependence on sex.* Pyle's averages make it reasonable to assume a slight superiority of girls over boys, since they show this superiority in ten of the age groups.

(4) *Feeble-minded children,* according to Miss Norsworthy's results, are distinctly inferior in this test to normal children of the same age: only 9 per cent. reach the median of the normal children; only 16 per cent. reach —1 P.E.; only 17 per cent reach —2 P.E. of normal children of their age.

C. THE OPPOSITES TEST

MATERIALS.—(1) For individual tests: Split-second stop-watch. Two sets of 20 cards each (exclusive of samples), one set of easy, and one of moderately difficult stimulus words. Paper for recording times, responses and remarks. (2) For group tests: Stop-watch or special seconds clock. Printed forms containing the same stimuli (one for easy and one for difficult words) and provided with spaces for recording the 20 associates.

The opposites test has been extensively used and has appeared in a variety of forms. The most common lists are printed herewith. They demand a few words of explanation.

Lists I, II and III represent the standardized lists for easy opposites prepared by Woodworth and Wells: Lists I and II, which are those used by Briggs (his Tests 43 and 44) are presumed to be of equal difficulty and to be so arranged that the last half is just as difficult as the first half; List III, which is the set of easy opposites here recommended, is a selection of the 20 easiest opposites in Lists I and II.

MATERIAL USED BY VARIOUS INVESTIGATORS IN THE OPPOSITES TEST.

I	II	III	IV	V
long	north	high	good	best
soft	sour	summer	outside	weary
white	out	out	quick	cloudy
far	weak	white	tall	patient
up	good	slow	big	careful
smooth	after	yes	loud	stale
early	above	above	white	tender
dead	sick	north	light	ignorant
hot	slow	top	happy	doubtful
asleep	large	wet	false	serious
lost	rich	good	like	reckless
wet	dark	rich	rich	join
high	front	up	sick	advance
dirty	love	front	glad	honest
east	tall	long	thin	gay
day	open	hot	empty	forget
yes	summer	east	war	calm
wrong	new	day	many	rare
empty	come	big	above	dim
top	male	love	friend	difficult

VI	VII	VIII	IX
day	great	succeed	tender
asleep	hot	strict	animated
absent	dirty	tardy	proficient
brother	heavy	sleepy	impoverish
best	late	suspicious	cruel
above	first	rigid	generous
big	left	suave	haughty
backwards	morning	sinful	silly
buy	much	conservative	insignificant
come	near	refined	disastrous
cheap	north	pride	miser
broad	open	despondent	result
dead	round	imaginary	hindrance
land	sharp	beautiful	strength
country	east	injurious	innocent
tall	known	diligent	busy
son	something	sell	remember
here	stay	sure	increase
less	push	active	preserve
mine	nowhere	venturesome	belief

List IV, one of the oldest and most employed, appears in several published articles and texts by Thorndike; it forms one of Simpson's easy opposites, has been used by Miss Norsworthy in an extensive study, and constitutes the regular test list prescribed by Pyle. The opposite of this list, *i. e.*, bad, inside, etc., has been used by Bonser, by Miss Norsworthy and by Mrs. Squire.

List V is proposed by Pyle as harder opposites for use with adults.

List VI has been used by Bonser, by Mrs. Squire and (with two changes) by Simpson.

List VII has been used by Bonser, by Mrs. Squire and (with some changes) by Simpson and by Carpenter. It also appears in Thorndike's tests.

Lists VIII and IX are two of four hard opposites used by Simpson.

The easy opposites test may be regarded as fairly well standardized so far as choice of material is concerned. But List III, which has been selected as best for younger children, will prove too easy for most S's of 10 years or over, and we have no lists of moderately difficult and very difficult opposites that have been tested by very extensive experimentation. The set proposed by the author has been selected from the 50 terms used by Hollingworth, who, in turn, selected them from a list of 200 tested by Woodworth and Wells and showing association times of from 2 to 5 sec. The attempt has been made on the basis of the author's trials with college students and with the assistance of Dr. Hollingworth to select 20 hard opposites that shall be relatively easy to score and that shall be of closely similar difficulty.

METHOD.—Use the easy opposites for younger children, the more difficult ones for children over 10 or thereabouts and for adults. Instruct S as follows: "Each one of these cards has printed on it a word. As soon as I uncover a card, look at the word on it and then, quickly as you can, say aloud a word that means just the opposite to it. For instance, if the card should have on it the word *dirty,* you would say *clean.* We will try three sample cards first to make sure you understand." With the hard opposites follow the procedure outlined for the part-whole test with regard to the use of the sample cards, timing, recording responses, etc.

VARIATIONS OF METHOD.—Follow the suggestions given for variations of method in the part-whole test, with due regard for changes in sample terms, etc.

When the harder opposites are used, particularly with adults, the instructions may be altered to put special stress upon the giving of an exact opposite, *i. e.,* the emphasis may be placed upon quality rather than upon speed of performance. Further, it is well to instruct S that opposites formed by the use of the prefixes *un* or *in,* or of the suffix *less,* will not be allowed, save when the root of the stimulus word is changed; thus, for instance, *inharmonious* would not be accepted for *harmonious,* nor *unsafe* for *safe,* but *harmless* would be accepted for *dangerous.* The split-second watch may then be used to advantage by rejecting responses that are incorrect, and recording the time of various responses made before the proper one is given.

To test the effect of practise, the cards may be shuffled and the series repeated any desired number of times, as in the procedure adopted by Hollingworth in his tests of the effect of caffein.

TREATMENT OF DATA.—This may follow the directions given for the part-whole test. With older children and adults, however, when the instructions have emphasized quality rather than speed, the scoring of responses should be decidedly rigorous, and it may be well for many purposes to permit only a single correct opposite and allow nothing for 'partly correct' responses.[4]

---

[4]Mrs. Squire counted as errors all responses that were not accurate and gave no credit for adverbs when adjectives were correct, nor even for approximate opposites, urging that "there is no mental test in which an approximate is less permissible."

The important thing is, of course, that E should settle upon the type of mental activity that is to be demanded (speedy approximate responses or rigorous precision) and then adjust instructions and scoring to measure this aspect of the associative process. In using the cards

RESULTS.—(1) *Norms*. The average time of response of adult college students is given by Woodworth and Wells as 1.11 sec., P.E. .04, range 0.85 to 1.40, for the easy list. The norms obtained by Pyle, Miss Norsworthy, Mrs. Squire and Carpenter are reproduced in Tables 67, 68, 69 and 70, respectively: these figures may not be compared directly with one another on account of differences in materials, scoring and other conditions, but they will serve as bases for conclusions with regard to the dependence of performance in the test upon age, sex and other factors.

Pyle's norms represent the average number of opposites that could be written in 60 sec. in a group test, using a list formed of the opposites of List IV, above.

Miss Norsworthy's figures refer to the number of correct associates to the opposites of List IV (her First List) and to List IV itself (her Second List), given by about 611 normal children of both sexes. Here the maximal possible score is evidently 20.

Mrs. Squire's figures show the average time in sec. and the average number of correct responses (rigid scoring) for small groups of pedagogically unretarded children for three separate lists (our Lists VI, VII and the opposites of IV, respectively). For the standards proposed by her for each age, see the original article, pp. 500-506.

Carpenter's results are based upon what he describes as practically the same terms as our List VII. The figures show the errors and the

TABLE 67

Correct Associates Written in 60 Sec.   Opposites Test (Pyle)

SEX	AGE	8	9	10	11	12	13	14	15	16	17	18	ADULT
Male	Cases	33	65	60	61	72	65	61	40	33	17	22	62
	Aver.	9.0	8.4	7.5	10.9	11.5	14.5	14.5	16.0	18.6	17.6	22.4	22.1
	A. D.	3.3	3.0	3.1	2.9	2.9	4.5	4.3	5.2	5.3	3.3	3.2	3.3
Female	Cases	33	56	77	65	74	73	58	49	48	27	26	85
	Aver.	8.0	7.6	10.9	11.2	13.9	14.9	17.4	17.3	19.3	21.4	23.4	23.4
	A. D.	4.0	2.9	3.1	3.0	3.6	4.3	3.9	5.1	4.2	4.9	3.1	4.0

for individual testing it will be found convenient to list upon the back of each card the different words that are given by S's, together with the score previously determined upon for each word.

For a more elaborate system of equating speed and quality of work the reader may consult Simpson (16, pp. 14, 16).

The work of Woolley and Fischer contains many valuable suggestions for the evaluation of various responses in the opposites test (see 22, pp. 216-221).

time in sec. obtained in individual tests in which the terms were read by *E* and responded to orally by *S*. His records are confessedly "of little value below age 9." Since the times were taken with an ordinary watch and merely express the total time occupied by the test for each child, it is impossible, of course, to derive from them any precise idea of the association time, strictly speaking.

TABLE 68

Correct Associates of a Possible 20. Opposites Test (Norsworthy)

LIST	AGE	8	9	10	11	12	13	14	15	16	ADULTS
Opp. of IV.._ _____	Median	7.4	9.0	9.9	12.5	13.5	14.0	14.5	15.0	15.5	20.0
	P. E.	2.0	2.0	3.0	3.0	2.6	2.5	2.3	2.3	2.3	1.0
IV._____	Median	8.7	9.5	11.5	13.1	14.7	16.4	17.8	18.5	19.0	20.0
	P. E.	1.4	1.7	2.2	2.9	3.6	2.4	2.0	2.0	2.0	1.0

TABLE 69

Correct Associates and Times. Opposites Test (Squire)

AGE	LIST VI		LIST VII		LIST IV (OPP.)		AVER. FOR ALL	
	Words	Time	Words	Time	Words	Time	Words	Time
6	8.5	192.3	11.3	143.3	11.6	120.0	10.5	151.8
7	13.1	155.6	15.0	137.7	14.5	117.6	14.2	136.9
8	16.1	110.3	17.1	98.2	16.7	104.9	16.6	104.8
9	17.6	103.7	16.5	101.1	17.7	98.4	17.2	101.7
10	17.1	87.1	17.7	87.0	18.2	76.2	17.6	83.4
11	19.3	79.3	19.0	102.0	19.6	68.3	19.3	83.2
12	19.5	81.2	19.2	85.5	19.2	63.2	19.3	63.2
13	19.4	72.5	19.2	61.5	19.2	65.0	19.3	66.3

TABLE 70

Errors and Times. Opposites Test (Carpenter)

AGE	7	8	9	10	11	12	13	14
Cases _____	7	19	46	50	41	44	58	49
Aver. Time_____	118	118	108	101	98	82	79	71
Aver. Errors ___	4.1	4.2	4.5	4.7	4.8	3.8	3.6	3.2

(2) *Dependence on age.* The evidence from these four tables, as well as from the results of Woolley and Fischer, though not guaranteeing in every instance a uniform increase in quantity or quality of performance from year to year, undoubtedly justifies the generalization that both speed of finding opposites and accuracy of the responses made, improve with age. The failure of this tendency to appear in the tables published by Bonser is apparently due to the inadequacy of his test material for bringing out the abilities of the older pupils.

(3) *Dependence on sex.* In all comparisons of groups the superiority of females over males is readily noted. Thus, girls surpass boys in 10 of Pyle's 12 age-groups; Hollingworth (9) found women faster than men in naming opposites both before and after practise; Burt and Moore report that in one group only 29.2 and in another only 42.2 per cent. of the boys reached the median mark of girls; Bonser found girls superior to boys in every school grade, though it is significant that in most of his groups more boys than girls were found in the highest quartile. Woolley and Fischer report a slight superiority of girls, but add that "it is too small to be considered very significant."

(4) *Dependence on school grade.* Bonser found a general progress from grade to grade, coupled with a decrease of variability; his results are somewhat affected by the fact that his test was too easy for use much beyond the 6A grade. On the other hand, the curves of distribution published by Chambers show that it is impossible to distinguish 7th grade and 8th grade pupils by their curves of distribution in this test.

(5) *Dependence on intelligence.* With the exception of Winteler's conclusion (based on the study of only 8 boys, divided into two contrasted groups) that the opposites test is less well adapted than other forms of controlled association to reveal differences in intelligence, the general opinion of experimenters is decidedly favorable to its use for this purpose. Mrs. Squire found that pedagogically retarded pupils show a distinctly lower general average performance with more irregularity in speed and quality of work than the unretarded. Bonser ob-

tained a correlation of 0.85 between opposites and the average standing in all the tests used by him to measure ability to reason, and declares that "the opposites test seems to be a test of rather superior merit as a single test for this general form of mental ability." In Simpson's interesting study of two contrasted groups of adults (17 of superior, and 20 of quite inferior general ability) the two groups were completely separated by both the easy and the hard opposites test, i. e., no person in the poorer group did as well as the poorest in the good group. Simpson estimates the true correlation with the intelligence of people in general to be as high as 0.82 for the easy, and 0.96 for the hard opposites test.

At Bedford Hills Reformatory, Miss Weidensall reports a correlation of 0.79, P.E. .03, between rank-order in opposites and the estimate of intelligence of the women made by the director of the Industrial School of the institution. The correlation would have been higher under more favorable conditions for the testing and the estimating. Again, the institutional women who had received the most schooling showed almost exactly the same ability as the Cincinnati 15-year-old working girls tested by Woolley and Fischer, whereas the Bedford Below-Grade Group (schooling less than Grade 5B) were decidedly inferior to the Bedford Grade Group and to the Cincinnati girls.

(6) *The feeble-minded and delinquent.* No feeble-minded child, according to Miss Norsworthy's figures, reached the median performance of normal children; only about one in a hundred were better than —1 P.E. and only about six in a hundred were better than —2 P.E. of normal children of their age.

Reference has just been made to the comparison of delinquent women and school girls. Dr. Weidensall's results show also that the Bedford women, taken as a group, are slightly inferior to the Cincinnati 15-year-old working girls at the upper quartile, 7.5 per cent. less accurate at the median and 26.2 per cent. less accurate at the lower quartile. It is of interest to note that the opposites test proved somewhat difficult of comprehension for these S's, so that special explanations had to be contrived and repeated as well before the testing could proceed.

(7) *Dependence on practise.* Hollingworth (9) put 11 men and 8 women through 100 trials with opposites, and also tested their speed in reading the stimuli and the responses from a typewritten sheet. The results were:

Initial naming (average of trials 2-6),   men 113.5 sec., women 99.7 sec.
Final naming (average of trials 96-100),   "   36.3 "   "   31.2 "
Reading directly (average of 5 trials),   "   18.5 "   "   16.1 "

It is seen that extensive practise increases the speed of the associative process markedly, but that even after 95 trials a considerable part of the time taken in the test is occupied by the process of association as over against the time needed in reading and uttering the words. The speed attained by individuals in the test by reading correlates with the speed obtained in the regular test of naming the opposites by approximately 0.60.

(8) *Dependence on fatigue.* In the course of his experiments upon the effects of caffein Hollingworth (8a) was able to observe the effects of time of day upon the opposites test under unusually favorable conditions as regards elimination of the practise error. In preliminary experiments (tests made at intervals of two or three hours) and also in more intensive experiments (15 trials between 10.30 A. M. and 10.30 P. M.) there appeared a distinct reduction in speed of naming opposites as the day passed, and the fatigue effect was more pronounced in this test than in any others that were tried. After the second trial the initial records of the day were never surpassed.

(9) *Dependence on race.* In opposites, and also in other controlled association tests (genus-species, part-whole), Pyle (13a) found negro children of both sexes less than half as efficient as white children.

(10) *Reliability.* Simpson found internal correlations between his various lists amounting to from 0.53 to 0.93 for his easy and to from 0.60 to 0.97 for his hard list. The test may, therefore, be regarded as possessing a good degree of reliability, particularly since Simpson's lists contained some words of unequal difficulty and are presumably less well

adapted for testing than the lists which have here been proposed for standard use.

(11) *Various correlations.* In the case of the women at Bedford Hills Reformatory, whose work was decidedly slow on the whole, the correlation between speed and accuracy was so high (0.83, P.E. .03, for those who needed no help in reading or writing) that the scoring was finally done in terms of accuracy alone.

Correlations determined by Simpson between the easy and the hard opposites and other tests were as follows: with the Ebbinghaus completion test 0.72 and 0.85, with memory for words 0.65 and 0.84, with the A-test 0.50 and 0.58, with memory for passages 0.50 and 0.70, with adding 0.56 and 0.70, respectively. These figures represent "estimated true correlations for people in general," as based upon raw correlations figured for his own adult S's, corrected for attenuation and other probable sources of error.[5]

Thorndike found a very high correlation, 0.90, P.E. about .05, between the capacities of twins in this test.

Notes.—Special comparisons of different forms of controlled association have been made, among others, by Watt, Rusk and Winteler. The average association times reported by Watt are 1.364 sec. for part-whole, 1.454 for whole-part, 1.418 for co-ordinate, 1.548 for superordinate and 1.859 for subordinate relations. General agreement appears in the conclusions reached by Rusk, who lists the several varieties of association tested by him in the following order, passing from the easiest to the hardest: whole-part and part-whole, co-ordination, free concretes, superordination, subordination, free abstracts, causal. Winteler concludes that when superordinate, subordinate, co-ordinate, species-genus and opposite relations are tried with school children, the first takes the most and the last the least logical power.

The so-called 'B-method' of Ries, a test in which S is given a number of nouns representing causes and asked to name an-

---

[5] See the original article for the raw correlations and for correlations with other tests than those here cited. For Bonser's correlations, which refer to various special tests, see his monograph, p. 96.

other noun representing a related effect, yielded in his hands extraordinarily high correlations with estimated intelligence, 0.85, 0.86, 0.91 and 0.94 in different groups. The method is endorsed by Meumann (11, 432f.), who also reports excellent results achieved with it by Oksala, in Finland. Meumann declares that the capacity to seek out causes or effects affords a decisive index of degree of intelligence in children of from about 10 to 14 years, and perhaps older. We have made attempts to use this test in the educational laboratory, both at Cornell University and at the University of Illinois, and have encountered so many difficulties in the preparation of material, and especially in scoring, as to render the method unsatisfactory, even for mature college students.

Another relatively easy, though strictly controlled association test is that known as the backward-alphabet test. This has usually been conducted by asking S to name, or to write, as rapidly as possible, the letters that precede f, k, s, p, w, l, e, r, d, o, v, j, n, t, and h. For comparison, and to obtain a rough notion of S's familiarity with the sequence of the alphabet in general, this test might be supplemented by another in which S was required to state the letters that follow another series of 15 letters.[6]

REFERENCES

(1)   A. R. Abelson, Tests for mental deficiency in childhood. *The Child*, No. 3 : 1912, 1-17. See also : The measurement of mental ability of 'backward' children. *BrJPs*, 4 : 1911, 268-314.

(2)   H. A. Aikins, E. L. Thorndike and Elizabeth Hubbell. Correlation among perceptive and associative processes. *PsR*, 9 : 1902, 374-38.

(3)   F. G. Bonser, The reasoning ability of children of the fourth, fifth and sixth school grades. *ColumbiaConEd*, No. 37. New York, 1910. Pp. 113.

(4)   T. H. Briggs, Formal English grammar as a discipline. *Teachers College Record*, 14 : 1913, 251-343.

(5)   C. Burt and R. C. Moore, The mental differences between the sexes. *JEPd*, 1 : 1912, 273-284, 355-388.

(6)   D. F. Carpenter, Mental age tests. *JEdPs*, 4 : 1913, 538-544.

(7)   W. G. Chambers, Individual differences in grammar grade children. *JEdPs*, 1 : 1910, 61-75.

(8)   H. L. Hollingworth, The influence of caffein on mental and motor efficiency. *ArPs(e)*, No. 22 (*ColumbiaConPhPs*, 20 : No. 4). New York, 1912. Pp. 166.

(8a)   H. L. Hollingworth, Variations in efficiency during the working day. *PsR*, 21 : 1914, 473-491.

---

[6]On the use of this test, see Aikins, Thorndike and Hubbell.

(9) H. L. Hollingworth, Articulation and association. *JEdPs*, 6: 1915, 99-105.

(10)· E. Jones, Some results of association tests among delinquent girls. *PsB*, 10: 1913, 78-79.

(11) E. Meumann, Vorlesungen zur Einführung in die exp. Päda-gogik, 2d ed., Vol. II. Leipzig, 1913, especially 418-433.

(12) Naomi Norsworthy, The psychology of mentally deficient chil-dren. New York, 1906. Pp. 111. (Much of this material is also given in *JPsAsth*, 12: 1907-08, 3-17.)

(13) W. H. Pyle, The examination of school children. New York, 1913. Pp. 70.

(13a) W. H. Pyle, The mind of the negro child. *School and Society*, 1: 1915, 357-360.

(14) G. Ries, Beiträge zur Methodik der Intelligenzprüfung. *ZPs*, 56: 1910, 321-343.

(15) R. R. Rusk, Experiments on mental association in children. *BrJPs*, 3: 1910, 349-385.

(16) B. R. Simpson, Correlations of mental abilities. *ColumbiaCon Ed*, No. 53. New York, 1912. Pp. 122.

(17) Carrie R. Squire, Graded mental tests. *JEdPs*, 3: 1912, 363-380, 430-443, 493-506, especially 430-443 and 500-506.

(18) E. L. Thorndike, Measurements of twins. *ColumbiaConPhPs*, 1905. Pp. 64.

(19) E. L. Thorndike, Educational psychology, 2d ed., New York, 1910. Pp. 248. See also his Principles of teaching. New York, 1906, and his Introduction to the theory of social and mental measurements, 2d ed. New York, 1913. Pp. 277.

(20) H. J. Watt, Exp. Beiträge zu einer Theorie des Denkens. *ArGsPs*, 4: 1905, 289-436.

(20a) Jean Weidensall, The mentality of the criminal woman. To appear in *EdPsMon*.

(21) J. Winteler, Exp. Beiträge zu einer Begabungslehre. *EPd*, 2: 1-48, 147-247, especially 207-239.

(22) R. S. Woodworth and F. L. Wells, Association tests. *PsMon*, 13: 1911, Whole No. 57. Pp. 85.

(22a) Helen T. Woolley and Charlotte R. Fischer, Mental and physical measurements of working children. *PsMon*, No. 77, 18: 1914. Pp. 247. Especially 213-227.

(23) S. Wyatt, The quantitative investigation of higher mental processes. *BrJPs*, 6: 1913, 109-133.

TEST 34A

Analogies.[1]—In Test 33 the associations to be formed are left entirely to *S*'s choice, are unrestricted; in Test 34 the associa-tion is restricted to a single form of relationship throughout any one series. In the analogies test there exists restriction, but the kind of restriction varies from one stimulus to another

---

[1] The author is indebted to Professor D. Kennedy Fraser, of Cornell University, for the arrangement of this test.

within the series of terms. The kind of restriction, moreover, is not indicated to S in the instructions, but is supplied to him by the test material itself, and must be apprehended by him from that material. Each stimulus in the series consists of three terms; the first and second terms illustrate the relation in question; the third term is the first of a pair which are to stand in the same relation one to another as the first and second terms. S's problem, then, is to find the appropriate fourth term. Because the relation varies from stimulus to stimulus, the test is sometimes referred to as the 'mixed relations test,' as, for example, by Woodworth and Wells (6), who say that it tests 'flexibility of mental performance' and also 'skill in handling associations.' Burt (2), from whom the term 'analogies' is borrowed, holds that the test involves "perception, implicit or explicit, of the relation and reconstruction of the analogous one by so-called relative suggestion." The test is recommended by these authors, as well as by Wyatt (7), and it needs little trial to show that it has many possibilities, particularly in view of the chance that it affords of constructing series of stimuli of varying difficulty.

MATERIALS.—(1) For individual tests: Split-second stop-watch. Three sets of 20 cards each, affording tests of three grades of difficulty. Sample set of 7 cards for preliminary trials. Prepared blank for registering times and incorrect answers. (2) For group tests or variant form of individual tests stop-watch or special seconds-clock. Printed forms for each of the three sets of stimuli, provided with spaces for recording the responses.

The stimuli chosen for these series are taken from a large number of stimuli originally employed by Burt in work with the analogies test in England. They have been selected on the basis of fairly extensive trial with children and high-school and college students. If further material are desired, E will find it more profitable to turn to the two lists of 2- stimuli each that are published by Woodworth and Wells (also reproduced by Briggs (1)) than to construct lists of his own, as only by actual trial can the feasibility of a given set of terms for use in this test be demonstrated.

METHOD.—Show S one of the sample cards and instruct him as follows: "On each of these cards there are three words, as on this one. As you see, there is relation between the first and the second word. You are also given a third word, and I want you to find a fourth word which shall have the same relation to the third as the second has to the first. Work as rapidly as you can, and say the fourth word aloud as soon as you know what it should be. Thus, in this first card the fourth word is what? In the cards that follow the relation does not remain the same as this one, but varies from one card to another." If this explanation seems sufficient, proceed with the other sample cards, saying: "I will try these sample cards now to make sure that you understand."

Follow the instructions given in Test 34, part-whole test, including the use of the warning 'now,' the taking of times during the sample set, the correction of wrong responses, etc., save that it is unnecessary to record S's response unless it be a word which is not provided for upon the prepared form. In ordinary testing E should pass to the next card whenever S is unable to give a response within 30 sec. Whether List A, List B, or List C, or some combination of them shall be used will depend upon S's age and ability and upon the time at E's disposal.

VARIATIONS OF METHOD.—Follow the suggestions for variant methods given for the part-whole test.

TREATMENT OF DATA.—This may be based, in general, upon the instructions already given for the part-whole test and for the opposites test.

The English investigators have attempted a somewhat finer scoring of quality of response than we have recommended. Thus, Burt scored 1 for each correct response, ⅔ for fair and ⅓ for poor responses, and 0 for omissions. Wyatt gave 4, 3, 2, 1 or 0 for responses grading from fully correct to omissions. This elaborate scoring is not needed for most of the terms in our lists, for in quite the majority of cases there is but one single correct response. In the other cases the use of the split-second watch in individual testing permits E to wait until the correct response is given and secure a direct measure of the time needed for this response, while the time at which the first (erroneous) response is made can also be put on record as an indirect measure of S's general accuracy.

RESULTS.—(1) A general idea of the times that may be expected by the use of these three lists may be gained from the

results that have been obtained by their use in a limited number of cases (Table 71). The averages exceed the medians on
account of the occasional very long association times which
appear with nearly all S's. The average time reported for their
lists by Woodworth and Wells (about a dozen college and
graduate students, using the method of exposing the entire
list) is 3.14 sec., P.E. .13, with a range for individual averages
of from 2.33 to 4.40 sec.

TABLE 71

Speed in Sec. for Correct Responses in the Analogics Test (*Fraser*)

Group	Cases	LIST A*		LIST B*		LIST C	
		Median	Aver.	Median	Aver.	Median	Aver.
College ____	8	1.8	2.36	3.0	4.38	3.4	6.51
Adults_____	19	2.0	2.64	—	———	——	———
High-school Girls_____	30	2.4	3.16	—	———	—	———

*Lists A and B, at the time these figures were secured, contained 25
stimuli each. The omitted ones do not alter the conditions enough, however, to invalidate these records as norms.

More extended use of the Woodworth and Wells tests by
W. V. Bingham, to whom I am indebted for advance figures
from the results secured with 200 freshmen at Dartmouth College, has yielded the following percentile distribution for the
analogies test (average time in sec. per response, based on two
trials of 10 responses each) :

Poorest	10	20	30	40	50	60	70	80	90	Best
5.49	3.98	3.69	3.31	3.03	2.85	2.67	2.52	2.36	2.06	1.35

(2) *Dependence on age.* While sufficient data are lacking
to present figures for various ages, there is a clear difference in
the speed of S's of grammar-school, high-school and college

standing when List A is used. Similarly, List B, and more especially List C, proves too difficult for younger S's.

(3) *Dependence on sex.* Burt found an advantage of 15 per cent. in favor of the girls at the Wallasley School, Liverpool, *i. e.,* only 35 per cent. of the boys reached the median performance of girls. In other tests at the Holt Secondary School, however, the average performances of the two sexes were virtually identical. No sex difference appeared in our tests of Cornell University students.

(4) *Dependence on intelligence.* Wyatt, working with the time-limit method on groups, found that the analogies test afforded the highest correlations with intelligence of any of the tests he tried, save the completion test. His correlations amount to 0.62 in one and 0.80 in another group. Burt's tests at the Holt School gave a correlation between the results of analogies and intelligence of 0.50 in the individual test and 0.52 in the group test; his tests at the Wallasey School gave again a correlation of 0.50 (see Burt and Moore).

(5) *Reliability.* Burt's figures show that the analogies test possesses a good degree of reliability, as its coefficient of internal correlation figured in different trials 0.58, 0.71 and 0.92.

NOTES.—The analogies test appears to be better suited than other tests of association to bring out individual differences in quickness of adaptation to the task demanded. Thus, in the case of one high-school girl, the average association time for the first half of the list was 4.83 sec., for the second half only 2.19 sec. The inference that this S was naturally slow in adapting herself to new situations, but was able to work efficiently when once adapted, was afterward confirmed by the reports secured from her teachers of her performance in her school tasks, especially in geometry.

When S's are tested by the standard method of securing the time for each response, it is often instructive to plot a rough frequency curve, with the second as a unit. A comparison of the distribution of the times for different S's, as in the following example, shows clearly individual differences in steadiness and consistency of performance as well as differences in general tendency toward fast or slow rates of mental activity.

Sample Distribution for Two College Students, List C

SECONDS	1	2	3	4	5	6	7	8	9	10+	MEDIAN	AVER.
Subject D __	1	9	3	4	0	1	1	0	0	1	2.9	3.91
Subject G __	0	4	3	1	3	2	2	1	1	3	5.6	5.67

It is also instructive to make notes of *S*'s general attitude toward the test, whether confident or hesitating, hurried or tranquil, etc., and to compare these attitudes with the quantitative results.

REFERENCES

(1)   T. H. Briggs, Formal English grammar as a discipline. *Teachers College Record*, 14: 1913, 251-343.

(2)   C. Burt, Experimental tests of higher mental processes and their relation to general intelligence. *JEPd*, 1: 1911, 93 112.

(3)   C. Burt, The experimental study of general intelligence. *Child Study*, 4: 1911, 14-15.

(4)   C. Burt and R. C. Moore, The mental differences between the sexes. *JEPd*, 1: 1912, 273-284, 355-388.

(5)   R. S. Woodworth, The consciousness of relation. *Essays, philosophical and psychological, in honor of William James*, 1908, 485-507.

(6)   R. S. Woodworth and F. L. Wells, Association tests. *PsMon*, 13: 1911, Whole Number 57. Pp. 85.

(7)   S. Wyatt, The quantitative investigation of higher mental processes. *BrJPs*, 6: 1913, 109-133.

TEST 35

Controlled association: Computation.—The solution of simple arithmetical problems in addition, subtraction, multiplication, and division may be considered as essentially dependent upon the accuracy and rapidity with which the appropriate associative processes are executed. Computation is, therefore, a test of controlled association in which the restriction of the associative sequence is complete, in which only a single outcome is correct. But numerous subsidiary activities are, of course, involved. Thus, the solution of arithmetical problems with the aid of paper and pencil demands, besides associative activity, both visual perception and motor activity, while mental computation imposes an additional tax by necessitating the holding in mind of the problem itself and of the various steps in its solution.

Because of this implication of perception, movement, attention, retention, and perhaps other forms of mental activity, as well as simple associative activity, the computation test has been employed not merely for the special purpose of studying the nature and course of associative processes, but also for the more general purpose of investigating mental efficiency at large (*geistige Leistungsfähigkeit*). Oehrn, for example, who was one of the first to use computation as a mental test, sought to study individual differences in the nature of associative processes; Aikins, Thorndike, and Hubbell, Brown, Burt, Simpson, Hollingworth, and Krueger and Spearman to study the correlation of specific mental functions; Thorndike to determine the relative influence of heredity and environment upon mental efficiency; Reis to compare the ability of normal, paralytic, and hebephrenic children; Jones to investigate the effect of bodily posture, Vogt the effect of distraction, and Hollingworth the effect of caffein upon mental efficiency; Winch and Starch to investigate the transfer of special drill. But the commonest application of the computation test has been made in the formulation of the curve of mental efficiency, or the work-curve (*Arbeitskurve*), with special reference to the influence of practise, rest-pauses, exercise, and similar factors upon the mental efficiency of adults, and especially of children, during a school day. This use of the test is illustrated in the work of Arai, Bellei, Bischoff, Bolton, Burgerstein, Ebbinghaus, Friedrich, Heck, Heüman, Holmes, Katzen-Ellenbogen, Kafemann, Keller, Kemsies, Laser, Lindley, Marsh, Martin, Ordahl, Robinson, Schultze, Specht, Teljatnik, Thorndike, Wells, Weygandt, Winch and others.[1]

Addition, multiplication, and both in alternation, have been more popular forms of computation than subtraction or division. With all four forms varied types of problems have been used. These variations in the arrangement of the test naturally affect its outcome. The most important types of test are illustrated herewith. Beside the types that are shown, Winch

---

[1] A major portion of these studies are the direct or indirect developments of the special technique of the adding experiment as formulated by Kraepelin and his followers (see the various volumes of the *Psychologische Arbeiten* and Kraepelin's summary (27).

and others have employed miscellaneous arithmetical problems,[2] Reis had his S's add mentally for 1 min. by 7's or by 12's, while Hollingworth has used a form of test, also recommended by Woodworth and Wells, in which a constant number is added (or subtracted) from a given list of numbers.

Examples of Material Used in Computation Tests

A	B	C	4 2 8 3 2 9 9 5 4 6 5 4 3 1 7	E 42	F 492
2	4		7 9 2 9 3 8 3 8 2 6 5 5 1 3 9	+79	+763
6	1		1 1 0 2 etc.		
9	3				

A	B	D	G				
7	5			H 64293643194831457627	I 982	J 64	K 28
4	2	95799	93	+38682725423585791858	—469	—27	× 8
8	6	86967	68				
9	4	32687	41	L 363	M 47	N 948	O 7986 R 4)799
5	3	84799	25	×6	×89	× 579	× 4523
1	4	95976	52				
7	6	34797					
5	1	97864		P 42842399547925331 4325		Q 254)4659234(	
2	5	98945		× 4			
6	4	87824					
3	2	68792					
5	1	79867					
1	2	88896					
3	3	97745					
9	6	39799					
2	5	48970					
1	3	89043					
3	6	67354					
6	5	54628					
9	1	91176					
8	2	90253					
3							
5							
2							
7							
6							
2							

[2]It is hardly necessary to allude to the development and use, particu larly by Courtis, of special sets of tests for measuring the abilities of school children in the fundamental operations of arithmetic, the solving of arithmetical problems, copying figures and the like. Similar tests for algebra and geometry have been announced recently by other investi gators. Tests of this variety are, of course, aimed at the determination of specific pedagogical attainments and differ, therefore, in scope and method from those here under consideration. For an account of the Courtis tests, with results of their application to a large group of school children, see Courtis (12).

Addition

A. Vertical series of 1-place numbers, arranged to avoid repetitions and pairs adding to 10. *S*'s add continuously and drop back to units when each hundred is reached, or add by pairs, either orally or writing down the unit figure of each sum. The pairs are sometimes taken so that each digit is used twice, thus *S* adds 1 and 2, 2 and 3, 3 and 4, etc., and sometimes so that each digit is used once, as 1 and 2, 3 and 4, etc. Oehrn, Vogt, and others working under Kraepelin used columns of as many as 7,000 of such digits. Krueger and Spearman used 70, grouped by 10's as illustrated. Marsh used similar columns of 15 or 25 digits.

B. Vertical column of 24 1-place numbers, using 1 to 6 only. Used by Jones, who had *S* add aloud while he himself followed with a check list.

C. Horizontal series of 1-place pairs of digits. A modification of the Kraepelin 1-place series in order to make possible the examination of the accuracy of each addition. The unit figure of the sum is the only one recorded, as illustrated in the first four problems. Used by Schulze, and apparently also by Ebbinghaus and by Vogt.

D. Twenty 5-place numbers. Used by Thorndike.

E. Two 2-place numbers. Used by Teljatnik.

F. Two 3-place numbers. Used by Kemsies for mental addition.

G. Five 2-place numbers. Twenty such problems were given and 2 min. allowed for computation. Used by Thorndike and by Aikins, Thorndike and Hubbell. Four longer columns (25 numbers in each) are used in the Woodworth and Wells constant-increment test.

H. Two 20-place numbers. Used by Burgerstein, Laser, Friedrich, and Holmes. The last-named investigator published elaborate rules for the construction of these problems in such a way as to avoid the extension of errors in 'carrying.' She used 4 blanks with 16 such problems on each blank.

Subtraction

I. Two 3-place numbers. Used by Kemsies for mental subtraction.

J. Two 2-place numbers, to be written on the blackboard (Teljatnik).

Multiplication

K. Two-place multiplicand, 1-place multiplier. Used by Kemsies for mental computation, and by Ebbinghaus for written group tests.

L. Three-place multiplicand, 1-place multiplier. Used by Kemsies.

M. Two-place multiplicand, 2-place multiplier. Used by Keller, and by Marsh with the digits 1, 2, 5, and 9 excluded.

N. Three-place multiplicand, 3-place multiplier. Used by Keller for written, and by Thorndike for mental computation.

O. Four-place multiplicand and multiplier. Used by Thorndike and others both for written and for mental computation. The multiplicand is usually a combination of 6, 7, 8, and 9; the multiplier of 2, 3, 4, and 5.

P. Twenty-place multiplicand, 1-place multiplier. Used by Burgerstein, Laser, and Friedrich, with the restriction of the multiplier, in most tests, to 2, 3, 4, 5, or 6.

Division

Q. Three-place divisor, 7-place dividend. Four blanks of 10 problems each were used by Bellei for an hour's work.

R. One-place divisor, 3-place dividend. Used by Kemsies for mental computation.

There are certain advantages and certain disadvantages in each of these forms of material. In general, E must select that form of test that best suits the conditions under which he works.

MATERIALS.—Stop-watch, preferably split-second. Printed forms, containing problems in addition and multiplication. For group tests, the special seconds clock.

Five forms have been prepared for this test: others may be prepared by E as desired.

A.   Addition test: several thousand digits in vertical columns with a line separating each 10 digits, after Model A. This form may be used with children or with adults, and either for short series or for continuous adding, after the Kraepelin method, after the plan of Krueger and Spearman, or after the method of adding pairs.

B.   Addition test with 36 problems, patterned after Model G, but containing 10, in place of 5 numbers each. This can be used also for tests in which a constant number is added or subtracted.

C.   Addition test, patterned after Model C (Schulze's method), and specially recommended for younger S's.

D.   Addition test, patterned after Holmes, Model H, and virtually identical with the material used by Burgerstein, Laser, and Friedrich.

E.   Multiplication test, after Model P, as used by Burgerstein, Laser, and Friedrich.

METHOD.—(1) *General determination of S's ability* may be carried on with any one of the forms. The following general principles should be kept in mind: (*a*) Individual tests are usually more satisfactory than group tests. (*b*) Any computation work that is so easy that the mental operations can proceed as fast as the results can be written (as Form C for adults) would better be given individually and arranged so that S may announce the results orally and E check them off upon a prepared key; and in general, care must be taken that the recording of results shall not fall to S unless it is certain that his associations will neither be delayed nor disturbed by the process of recording. (*c*) Group tests with competent S's may be most satisfactorily carried on by the work-limit method with the aid of the seconds clock. (*d*) Group tests by the time limit method should, as a rule, be terminated at such a time that the fastest S in the group can no more than complete the task.

In accordance with these general principles, Forms B, D and E will be found adapted for group tests or for individual test with the recording of the figuring done by S himself. E can take the time for performing any specified number of the problems, or he may also, especially by using a split-second stop-watch, secure the exact time for solving each problem without interrupting S's work until the entire test form is finished.

For the *constant-increment test* S is given Form B, printed side down. He is instructed at the signal 'now' to add a specified number to each number found in the columns when he turns over the form. The numbers commonly used have been either 4 or 17. The test may be repeated with other increments, and these may be so chosen as to secure wide variations in difficulty, as by assigning easy constants, like 1 or 2, or more difficult ones than 17. Again, the assignment may be to subtract a given number.[2]

Form C affords a particularly good test of skill and accuracy in the addition of units, especially when conducted orally. Record the time for each row horizontally. Adults will make but few errors, and these they may be allowed to pass over or to correct, whichever way they may prefer.

Form A may be given by a variety of methods. In particular, S may write down the sums for each section of 10 digits and E record the time for each section until one page of the material has been covered: or S may add orally by pairs while E watches for errors upon a prepared check sheet, and also notes upon it the place reached by S at given time-intervals, as at each minute or each half-minute; the adding in this case may be done by either of the methods of grouping the pairs mentioned above (Explanatory, Addition, A).

(2) For those who wish to arrange an experiment for the *special determination of S's susceptibility to practise, fatigue, etc.,* some suggestions may be found in the following development of the method of Kraepelin illustrated in the work of Specht and of Bischoff. To carry out this experiment fully, S adds by pairs, 10 min. per day, on each of 12 successive days.[3]

---

[2] For timing work by columns a convenient arrangement is to cut them out of the form and paste them singly upon small stiff cards.

[3] It would seem possible to condense this time, either by taking fewer days or by adding during several sittings on a given day, though it is impossible to predict whether the results would then be comparable to those reported below from Specht and Bischoff.

The pairs are added by the 1 and 2, 2 and 3 method and the unit figure only of each sum is written down by S.[4] A bell-stroke or other signal is given at the end of each minute, and S marks by a horizontal stroke the point he has reached at the signal. On the 1st, 3d, 5th, 7th, 9th and 11th days there is introduced between the 5th and the 6th minute of the adding a rest-pause of 5 min.: on even-numbered days S adds directly through the 10 min. without pause.

In carrying out this special form of addition test, or in fact, in carrying out any test which is designed to measure efficiency under various conditions—different periods of the day, after recesses, after gymnastics, after eating, etc.—it is evident that E must bear in mind the possibility that a number of different factors may enter to affect the performance, and that to measure any single factor, like fatigue, the influence of these other factors must be excluded or allowed for. The most serious of these disturbing factors are practise, excitement, ennui and carelessness.

A common method for cancelling out practise is to divide S's into two equivalent groups on the basis of a preliminary test, and to administer one set of problems early to the first, and late to the second group (if, for instance, fatigue is to be investigated), the other set late to the first, and early to the second group.

In studying the work curve, some E's have used computation both as the test and as the work to induce fatigue, practise, etc.; others have used computation as a test of efficiency, but have allowed S to follow in the main the regular work of the school session. In the first procedure, computation (usually addition) is pursued more or less continuously for an hour, or even for several hours; in the second procedure, the computation itself occupies but a short time, relatively, say from 1 to 10 min., and is repeated at intervals of an hour or more, while S meantime takes up his regular tasks, indulges in physical activity, or rests, as E may direct.

In illustration, Vogt, Oehrn, and other disciples of Kraepelin, have kept their S's adding continuously for several hours; Holmes used 4 periods of adding of 9 min. each, with 4-min. rest-pauses, Burgerstein 4 periods of 10 min. each, with 5-min. pauses. Typical illustrations of the second procedure are supplied by the investigations of Laser and of Ebbinghaus, who introduced 10-min. computation tests at the beginning of the school day and once an hour thereafter, and also by the studies of Heck and of Robinson. Ebbinghaus is inclined, however, to recommend 5-min. tests as being equally serviceable for the determination of efficiency and less likely to develop ennui and carelessness. Offner (35, p. 48) favors short tests for similar reasons and also for the partial avoidance of the practise-error.

TREATMENT OF DATA.—Computation tests yield two measures of efficiency—speed (or quantity of work) and accuracy (or

---

[4]It would seem to the author much preferable to use oral adding, but here, again, it is not possible to predict what effect such an alteration of method might have upon the results.

quality of work). Many investigators, particularly when examining the effect of practise, fatigue and similar factors upon performance, have found it best to keep the two measures separate. Some investigators, like Teljatnik, have considered quality of work only; more often, qualitative differences, being relatively small, have been disregarded and performance has been ranked by speed of work only. The combining of speed and accuracy into a single score representing net efficiency may be attempted by some of the methods proposed in Test 26. Or, an arbitrary penalty may be contrived for each error and the time consumed may be increased by these penalties. Thus, Simpson, who used material like our Example G, computed the final score of his S's by adding to their actual time 10 sec. for each error. An S who added 10 examples in 55 sec. and got seven answers right and three wrong would then be given a final score of 85 sec.

Quantity of work is indicated by elapsed time when using the individual method, and by the number of problems solved (sometimes by the number of figures written in the results) in the time-limit method.

Quality of work is generally regarded as directly proportional to the percentage of correct solutions. Inaccuracy is most often taken in terms of the number of errors committed, less often in terms of the number of errors plus the number of corrections made by S. The simplest, but the least desirable way to compute errors is to score one error for every wrong figure in the result. In the case of certain problems, however, a single error in computation may affect more than one figure in the result.[5] For reliable results, these complex errors must be examined and the score adjusted to indicate exactly the number of real errors of computation.

For the special experiment patterned after Specht and Bischoff more elaborate treatment of data is called for. (1) The gain in sums added the 6th min. as compared with the 5th min., in its relation to the sums added the 5th min. (i. e., the per cent. of gain) is computed both for all the days with pause

---

[5] The problems in Form D (Example H) are intentionally arranged to reduce this error.

and for all the days without pause, and the difference between
these two relative gains is found. (2) The number of sums
added in the first five and in the second five minutes, both on
days with and on days without pause, is treated in the same
manner. (3) The difference between the sums added on the 2d
and the 6th minute on days with pause, taken as a per cent. of
gain over the 2d minute, forms the coefficient of practise. (4)
To find the coefficient of fatigue

let F = the required coefficient of fatigue,
$\quad$ P = the coefficient of practise,
$\quad$ A = the sums added the first 5 min. without pause,
$\quad$ B = the sums added the second 5 min. without pause, and
$\quad$ b = the sums theoretically added the second 5 min. under
$\qquad$ practise, but not under fatigue.

$$\text{Then } b = \frac{A \times (100 + P)}{100} \quad \text{and} \quad F = \frac{100 \times (b - B)}{b}.$$

Thus, if P = 8.8, A = 1226, B = 1141, then b = 1333.9 and
F = 14.46. (5) The difference between the sums added in the
2d min. and in the 10th min. of days without pause, taken as a
ratio to the 2d min., affords another, and in some respects, a
better index of fatigue. (6) The total number of sums added
the 1st 5 min. of all days gives T (total performance), which
affords an approximate notion of S's ability to add. T is also
made the denominator of a fraction, the numerator of which is
the total number of additions made the very first 5 min. The
fraction gives some indication of S's susceptibility to practise. (7) Another index of susceptibility to practise is secured by taking the average of the gains in the first 5 min.
from day to day as against the first day and figuring the difference as a ratio to the first 5 min. (1st day). Characteristic
results for all these values are given below.

RESULTS.—(1) Woodworth and Wells report the average time
of college students in the Kraepelin form of adding as 107.2
sec., range 65 to 164 sec. The same authors report for the constant increment test (one column of 25 numbers) adding 4:
average 33.9, range 24 to 49 sec.; subtracting 4, average 41.1,
range 25 to 67 sec.; adding 17, average 97.4, range 62 to 158

sec., with an average of 2.4 errors in the last form of test. These figures are based upon a very limited number of S's (7 to 10). In the author's laboratory, tests with college students in adding 50 sections of 10 digits on the Kraepelin form have yielded individual averages per section of from 5.8 to 13.7 sec., while the number of correct sections has ranged from 34 to 46.

(2) In all computation tests, and particularly in those embodying mental multiplication, there are marked *individual differences* in speed and accuracy, even among S's of the same age and same school grade. Thus, Schulze's best pupil added more than 5 times as fast as the slowest pupil in the same class.

(3) *Dependence on sex.* There is evidently no decided sex difference in computation, since the results of various investigators are conflicting. Burt found girls slightly slower in multiplication; Burt and Moore reckon that 65 per cent. of boys exceed the 50 per cent. record of girls in adding and 63 per cent. exceed the 50 per cent. record of girls in multiplication. On the other hand, Courtis' New York results show that girls are slightly better than boys in the fundamental operations of arithmetic. Again, Miss Holmes found girls slightly better than boys, and the conclusion of Fox and Thorndike is that the girls in the high school they studied were about 5 per cent. better than boys, though here there may have been a better grade of girls selected by the school. In the solving of arithmetical problems, however, where something more than knowledge of the fundamental operations is involved, the work of Courtis and of Thorndike (52) shows a superiority of boys amounting to an excess of some 10 per cent. in the distribution above the median of the girls. "Roughly, boys are about half as far ahead of the girls in the same grade as they are of the boys in the preceding grade." Heck found that boys fell off more in quality of work in the afternoon session than did girls (4.25 vs. 1.96 per cent.)—a result possibly due to a greater carelessness on the part of the boys.

(4) *Dependence on school grade.* When sufficiently large groups are compared, there is, of course, a perceptible differ-

ence between the performance of one grade and that of the grades above or below it, but this difference is small in comparison with the range of variation within any grade, and may, on that account, disappear when small groups are compared. Thus, the curves of distribution in adding reported by Chambers for 22 seventh and 22 eighth grade pupils cannot be distinguished, while Courtis generalizes results for his multiplication test by saying that "35 per cent. of any grade membership will exceed the average score of the next higher grade: also, that 35 per cent. of the grade membership will fall below the average of the next lower grade" (12, p. 450).

(5) *Dependence on practise.* All investigators agree that practise produces a considerable improvement in all forms of computation, despite the fact that the associative connections concerned have been long established and often used. Hollingworth, who used the constant-increment test (adding 17 to 50 2-place numbers) found that, even after 35 preliminary trials, one of his groups reduced their average time from 102.7 to 61.2 sec. during 17 further trials, a reduction of some 40 per cent. Similarly, the 19 university students reported by Thorndike, who added daily for a week 48 columns of ten numbers, effected a median reduction in time of about 31 per cent., and in accuracy of about 29 per cent., although the total amount of time spent in the work was only about one hour for each S. Not all these S's showed such practise effects; for one or two there was no improvement, while one improved as much as 50 per cent. It is worth noting that practise-improvement is shown by those who stand high at the beginning of the work as well as by those who stand low then. The same result has been found also in tests of 29 boys in a New York City 4th grade school, where, according to Donovan and Thorndike, those most efficient at the beginning gained on the average as much or more (in gross gains) as did those least efficient at the beginning. Wells' tests of adults (56) lead to a similar conclusion. On the whole, however, practise in adding tends to reduce somewhat the initial differences between the S's, whereas practise in mental multiplication seems not to affect much the relative differences between S's, from which Thorndike con-

cludes that the abilities demanded in mental multiplication
are more dependent upon original capacity than are those demanded in adding. Mrs. Ordahl found that practise in mental
multiplication produced a decided gain in speed without much
improvement in accuracy, and she believes that the improvement in this operation resides more in the methods of handling
the task than in the facilitation of the numerical associations
themselves.[6]

The question of the transfer of practise-effects in computation to other forms of mental activity has been studied by
Winch and by Starch. Winch was unable to decide whether
special drill in computation produced an increase of skill in
solving arithmetical problems; there appeared to be a transfer
in some of the classes, but not in others. Starch found that a
14-day drill in mental multiplication developed an improvement of from 20 to 40 per cent. in other arithmetical operations,
but had little effect upon auditory memory span.

(6) *Dependence on intelligence.* Burt tested English school
children, aged 12, to determine the number of additions or mul-
tiplications correctly made in 10 min., and found a correlation
with intelligence of 0.25 in addition and of 0.41 in multiplication. Brown's results for a group of 39 girls, aged 11 to 12,
show no correlation between school grades and speed or accuracy of adding and a correlation of only 0.10 between speed
of adding and estimated general intelligence: his results for another group of 40 boys of the same age show correlations of
.28 between speed of adding and school marks, of 0.24 between
speed of adding and estimated intelligence, and of 0.11 between accuracy of adding and marks, with absence of correlation
between accuracy and estimated intelligence. Simpson used
adding in his study of two sharply-contrasted groups of adults;
the test separated the groups fairly clearly—only 10 per cent.
of the poor group reached the median performance of the good
group. Within the good group the results of the adding test
correlated by 0.72 with estimated intelligence.

(7) *Reliability.* Save for Burt's figures (0.50 for adding
and 0.55 for multiplication), the internal correlations for com-

---

[6]Consult her article for detailed tables and introspective reports.

putation tests show a good degree of reliability. Krueger and Spearman, for instance, obtained a reliability of 0.76, Simpson of 0.76 for his good group, 0.90 for his poor group, 0.91 for both together. Brown, who worked with several different groups, reckons the reliability for speed of adding at 0.68 to 0.98 and for accuracy of adding at 0.30 when one application of the test is made, and reliability for speed at 0.81 to 0.99 and for accuracy at 0.36 to 0.74 when the scores represent amalgamated results of two applications.

(8) *Correlations.* Aikins, Thorndike, and Hubbell compared efficiency in adding with efficiency in the other 'association' tests (misspelled words, cancellation of two letters, and opposites), and (by a special method of estimating the index) found the quality of work in adding and quantity of work in associating correlated to a degree of 50 per cent. in 8th-grade, and 20 per cent. in 5th-grade pupils, and net efficiency in adding and net efficiency in associating correlated to a degree of 48 per cent. On the other hand, the percentage of error in adding and in the other association tests exhibited no correlation or one of but slight degree.

Thorndike's study of mental resemblances in twins (47) showed a much higher correlation of ability in computation between twins than between siblings; thus, twins aged 9-11 years revealed a correlation of 0.90 in adding, and 0.91 in multiplication, and twins aged 12-14 years a correlation of 0.54 in adding and 0.69 in multiplication: taken collectively, the index of correlation amounted to 0.75 for the adding, and 0.84 for the multiplication test.

Fox and Thorndike found that ability to add correlated to a fairly high degree, 0.75, with ability to multiply, but only to a small degree, 0.20 to 0.44, with ability to solve fractions or to perform other arithmetical problems. They conclude that "ability in arithmetic is thus but an abstract name for a number of partially independent abilities."

These results do not agree well with those reached by Winch in his two studies of the transfer of drill in numerical accuracy, since he found high correlations (0.68, 0.69 and 0.74) between accuracy in computation and in arithmetical reasoning

Burris found that school grades in algebra and in geometry, as recorded in 19 representative high schools, showed, for nearly 1000 pupils, a correlation of 0.45.

Simpson publishes the following "estimated true correlations for people in general" with efficiency in adding: Ebbinghaus completion test 0.65, hard opposites 0.70, easy opposites 0.56, a-test 0.58, memory for passages 0.42, estimation of lengths 0.00. The extended series of intercorrelations found by Brown, which are in general much lower than those of Simpson, will be found reproduced in Simpson (41, 107f.) as well as in the original text (5, 309-313, 316).

Krueger and Spearman found a good degree of correlation between adding and pitch discrimination (raw correlation 0.67, 'corrected' correlation 0.68, 'completed' correlation 0.80) and between adding and the Ebbinghaus test (raw correlation 0.79, 'corrected' correlation 0.68, 'completed' correlation 0.93).

Hollingworth (20) has studied the effect of a long series of trials (over 200) upon the correlations between adding and various tests; the following are typical results:

	TAPPING	CO-ORDINATION	DISCRIM. REACTION	COLOR NAMING	OPPOSITES
1st trial	.45	.21	.23	.26	.23
205th trial	.57	.16	.15	.76	.76

(9) *Relation of speed and accuracy.* While it is doubtless true that, for a given individual working under constant conditions, an increase of speed tends to produce an increase of errors, it is equally true that under actual working conditions a given individual may show an increase of speed coupled with a decrease in number of errors. When individuals are compared, it is found that the faster S's are, on the whole, also the more accurate S's. In six of his groups Brown found correlations between speed and accuracy of adding ranging from 0.13 to 0.43, P.E.'s from .07 to .12. With small groups of college students I have obtained similar positive correlations of 0.19 in the case of adding and as high as 0.86 for mental multiplication.

(10) *Mental defectives*. Reis found that with paralytics and hebephrenics the average performance was less and the variability greater than with normals. Similarly, Specht says that, though there appear decided individual differences in fatiguableness as shown by the adding test applied to normal individuals, a still greater amount of fatiguableness appears when it is applied to patients in an insane hospital selected for their tendency toward easy fatiguableness in general. I have combined the data furnished by Bischoff for 12 normal S's and by Specht for 17 normal and 6 insane S's when tested by their special form of the Kraepelin addition test and scored according to the directions given above for that experiment. The results are given in Table 72. The differences between the two groups are readily obvious in Factors 8 and 9, which reveal tendency toward fatigue, and in Factors 10 and 11, which show the total amount of work done. Analogous results have been reported by Katzen-Ellenbogen, who concludes that "the average curve of epileptics is decidedly different from the normal [curve and characteristic of epilepsy."

TABLE 72

Average Scores of 29 Normal and 6 Insane Subjects in the Addition Test (After Specht and Bischoff).

		Normals.	Patient
(1)	Per cent. gain 6th over 5th min., with pause..	14.7	20.6
(2)	Per cent. gain 6th over 5th min., no pause.....	—1.0	—3.9
(3)	Difference between (1) and (2)..............	15.7	24.5
(4)	Per cent. gain 2d over 1st 5 min., with pause..	4.4	—0.3
(5)	Per cent. gain 2d over 1st 5 min., no pause....	—5.0	—11.4
(6)	Difference between (4) and (5)..............	9.9	11.1
(7)	Coefficient of practise......................	9.9	13.3
(8)	Coefficient of fatigue.......................	—12.6	—21.3
(9)	Per cent. gain 10th over 2d min., no pause.....	—5.6	—14.3
(10)	Additions 1st 5 min. in 1st trial..............	172.3	87.5
(11)	Total additions 1st 5 min. of all trials........	3406.8	1157.6
(12)	Progress of practise........................	11.1	2.0

(11) *Miscellaneous influences.* Hollingworth (19) used adding among other tests in his study of the *effects of caffein* and found that this drug produces pronounced stimulation in the processes of adding.

Posture was found by Jones to affect the speed of adding; both children and college students could add somewhat fast (approximately 3 to 8 per cent.) with the body in a horizontal, than with the body in a vertical position.

The *effect of distraction by concomitant* activities, *e. g.,* the reciting of a poem, was found by Vogt to reduce very materially (58.5 per cent.) the number of additions made by the continuous (Kraepelin) method, but to have relatively little effect upon the simpler process of adding pairs of digits.

(12) *Fatigue and other factors of the work curve.* The use of computation tests to determine general mental efficiency at different hours of the day, with special reference to the performance of school children under classroom conditions, represents a special form of experiment that oversteps the boundaries of mental tests in their diagnostic use. In what follows, therefore, I have limited the treatment to presenting typical results and to pointing out certain important general principles that have been established in this field.[7]

(*a*) *General analysis of the work curve.* In other tests (especially Nos. 10 and 26) we have had occasion to refer to the fact that attempts to isolate fatigue from other influences affecting a curve of work are rendered difficult because of the presence of other complicating factors. Of these, practise is perhaps the most obvious and influential. Investigators have added, however, numerous other factors, such as recuperation, adaptation, momentum, swing, or fitness for work, warming-up, and spurts of various kinds. Extended accounts of these factors will be found in Meumann (33, II, 8ff. and elsewhere), Schulze (40, 320ff.), and particularly in the writings of Kraepelin (26, 27) and his students. However patent and plausible these factors may appear from observation of our daily activities, it seems probable that they have sometimes been invoked in explanation of work curves when actual demonstration of their existence is difficult, if not impossible.[8] In work curves obtained from school children it is certain that loss of interest,

[7] For a comprehensive critique of the experimental literature upon work and fatigue the reader is referred to Thorndike (53). In my translation of Offner (35) there will also be found a more general discussion of the whole topic of mental fatigue.
[8] Thorndike is especially severe in his criticism of the numerous lesser factors exploited by the Kraepelinian school.

or ennui, and resultant carelessness complicate the performance seriously, and are often mistaken for the effects of true fatigue, in the sense of actual inability to work at a sustained level of efficiency.

(b) *Individual differences in the work curve.* We have noted the presence of clear-cut individual differences in the speed and accuracy of computation; there are also individual differences in the course of the performance. Thus, both Kemsies and Keller conclude that mass results should be subjected to scrutiny to detect individual curves of performance if reliable information is to be secured concerning fatigue and overpressure in the schools. The recent work of Miss Martyn (32) similarly, has shown that the introduction of a rest pause may be favorable to some S's and unfavorable to others, and also that the effect of fatigue may be met and masked in some S's by the presence in them of a strong permanent 'set' for accurate work. "We may conclude," she says, "that fatigue cannot be invariably estimated by diminution either in speed or in accuracy of work, since habit and method of working bear an important relation to its manifestations" (32, p. 434). Again the results obtained by Miss Arai and confirmed by numerous investigators make it fairly certain that the most competent workers are the ones least affected by fatigue.

These individual differences in susceptibility to fatigue have tempted some investigators to sort S's into certain groups or 'types' of workers. If by 'types' is implied that individuals can be sorted into 'water-tight compartments,' the hypothesis must be regarded as of doubtful utility. Illustrations are seen in the work of Kemsies, who distinguishes between persistent workers who fatigue slowly and profit much by practise and feeble workers who fatigue quickly and do not profit much by practise. Meumann's own investigations lead him (33: vol. pp. 10-11) to posit three types of workers (quantitatively regarded) : the first type attains maximal efficiency at the start and thence decreases with many fluctuations: the second attains maximal efficiency only after an interval (of a length depending upon the kind of work) ; the third attains maximum efficiency only after a long period, perhaps several hours, work. The first type, then, is characterized by rapid adaptation and rapid fatigue, the second by slower adaptation and slower fatigue, the third by very slow adaptation and very great re-sistance to fatigue. The third type, he thinks, is probably more common in adult males, the first in women and children.

(c) *The work curve for continued computation.* 1. Work without interruption. Oehrn found that when adults added continuously for 2 hours or more, maximal speed was attained on the average at about 28 min. from the start. Schulze finds, however, that with school girls aged 12.5 years, signs of fatigue appear even in the first 5 min. The total number of additions made per minute by 37 girls was 1850, 1871, 1863, 1785, and 1772 for the 1st to the 5th minute, respectively.

Schulze's results with the same pupils for longer periods (50 min. without pause) show a progressive decrease both of quan-tity and of quality of work (Table 73). These figures, which are selected from the 6th of a series of experiments, are based upon the very easy process of adding two 1-place digits, so that practise has relatively little effect, but fatigue diminishes effi-ciency.

TABLE 73

Efficiency in Addition: Five 10-Minute Periods (Schulze)

PERIOD OF TEN MINUTES	TOTAL NUMBER OF ADDITIONS	PERCENTAGE OF DE-CREASE OF QUANTITY OVER THE PREVIOUS PERIOD	PERCENTAGE OF DE-CREASE OF QUALITY OVER THE PREVIOUS PERIOD
I.	17,740	—	—
II.	16,726	5.7	.09
III.	15,855	5.2	.03
IV.	15,485	2.3	.17
V.	15,134	2.3	.01

The effect of continuous work upon a very difficult task de-pends upon the degree of practise previously attained, the actual length of the work and the general condition of S when it is begun. Thus, Thorndike (51) induced 72 college students to multiply 3-place numbers mentally for about two hours,

with the net result that the work improved somewhat both in
speed and accuracy; nevertheless, a rest of 30 min. effected an
increase of about 5 per cent. in speed and a rest over night a
still further increase in speed of about 7 per cent. But when
the same investigator had 16 S's mentally multiply a 3-place
by a 2-place number continuously for from 3 to 8 hours, or
(with pauses for meals) from 4 to 12 hours, only 3 S's did
as well at the end of their work period as when they had
rested; the results showed, as might be expected, a compound
of gradually lessening practise and gradually increasing fatigue. Miss Arai, who mentally multiplied 4-place numbers
for 11 or 12 hours at a stretch after practise-effects had been
largely eliminated, found that the time needed to work such
examples was practically doubled at the end of eleven hours.[9]

2. Work with interruptions. When repeated computation
tests are made within an hour, the usual result is a progressive
increase in the quantity, but a progressive decrease in the quality of the work. Burgerstein's figures (Table 74) furnish a
typical example of the results for four 10-min. periods with 5
min. rest-intervals between periods.

TABLE 74

Efficiency in Addition and Multiplication within an Hour (*Burgerstein*)

PERIOD	NUMBER OF FIGURES IN RESULTS	NUMBER OF ERRORS	PERCENTAGE OF ERROR
I.	28,267	851	3.01
II.	32,477	1292	3.98
III.	35,443	2011	5.67
IV.	39,450	2360	5.98

Miss Holmes' results are similar, though, on account of computing errors of a different plan ('serial' errors counting but

---

[9] In a test conducted under my direction and as yet unpublished, Mr.
Painter, after preliminary trials to remove most of the effect of practise,
worked at difficult mental multiplication, beginning late in the evening
after a day's university work and continuing until the task became impossible. The cessation of work was not gradual (with ability, for example,
to multiply 2-place numbers when 4-place were impossible), but appeared
as a sudden collapse such that mental work of any sort was quite impossible.

as one error), her percentage of error averaged but 1.3, as against Burgerstein's 3.[10]

The common interpretation of results like Burgerstein's has been that practise increases the speed of the work, while fatigue increases its inaccuracy. But Ebbinghaus (14, pp. 406f.) denies that practise could produce such marked increase of speed, and ascribes both the increase of speed and the decrease of accuracy primarily to increased haste and carelessness.

(d) *Effect of rest-pauses.* When, either from ennui or fatigue, efficiency tends to decline, a period of rest generally exerts a favorable effect. With school children, as would be expected, such a pause is favorable even after relatively short work, as is illustrated by the data of Table 75, which are derived by Burgerstein from Schulze. The effect of rest upon efficiency in mental multiplication after some two hours' work has already been mentioned with reference to experiments with college students. The tests made by Friedrich upon 10-year-old pupils and by Kraepelin upon adults (26, pp. 16-17) furnish similar evidence of the effect of rest-pauses.

TABLE 75

Additions per Pupil, with and without a Rest-Pause (Burgerstein-Schulze)

	FIRST 25 MINUTES	REST-PAUSE	SECOND 25 MINUTES
First test_____	1067	5 min.	1088
Second test_____	1146	None	1042

(e) *Efficiency at different periods of the day.* Typical instances of the use of computation as a test for the fatigue-effects of the regular school program are afforded by the experiments of Friedrich, of Laser, and of Ebbinghaus. This method has been adopted in part to avoid the entrance of ennui and carelessness previously mentioned.

---

[10]Miss Holmes' analysis of the errors showed that their increase during the hour was due primarily to increased inaccuracy in associative processes, rather than to increased frequency of 'slips of the pen.' In general, errors of transcription were about one-third as numerous as errors of association.

Laser's tests, at hourly intervals, of 226 pupils (aged 9-13 years) in a Königsberg *Bürgerschule* are summarized in Table 76. Inspection shows that, save for the 5th period, the outcome is the same as that of the tests for an hour's time by Burgerstein, viz.: a progressive increase in speed and decrease in accuracy of computation.

TABLE 76

Efficiency in Computation within a School Session (Laser)

TEST AFTER SCHOOL PERIOD	TOTAL NUMBER OF FIGURES ADDED	TOTAL NUMBER OF ERRORS	PERCENTAGE OF ERROR
I	34,900	1147	3.28
II	40,661	1460	3.59
III	43,124	1713	3.79
IV	43,999	1796	4.08
V	45,890	1668	3.63

Ebbinghaus, who sought to determine the desirability or undesirability of a 5-hour continuous school session in a *Gymnasium* and higher girls' school at Breslau, obtained results identical with those of Laser so far as the qualitative aspects are concerned, but differing somewhat as regards the quantitative aspects, more particularly in that speed of computation reached a maximum at the close of the 2d school period, to remain thereafter almost constant or to fall off slightly toward the close of the session. Friedrich's results lead him to advise lighter work in the afternoon session. Bellei found that boys and girls aged 12 solved problems in division more slowly and less accurately in the afternoon than in the morning. Marsh tested but a few individuals, so that it is probably unsafe to make inductions from his data, which seemed to indicate a greater efficiency in adding at noon than later in the day, and in multiplication at between 1.30 and 3 p. m. than at 6 or at 10.30 p. m. Miss Martin had 6 *S*'s add for 15 min. at 10, 12 and 4 o'clock, with the result that slightly more sums were completed at 12 and somewhat fewer at 4 than at 10; the differences are, however, inside the probable error. The work of the first 5 min. was relatively poorer in the afternoon, due, she thinks, to a later entrance of *Anregung* at that time. The most authoritative laboratory study of efficiency in calculation at different periods of the day, however, is that of Hollingworth (20a), who had opportunity during his experiments upon the effects of caffein to watch the daily curves of *S*'s whose work was done under exceptionally good conditions as regards elimination of practise error. In the use of the constant-increment test (adding 17 to 50 2-place numbers) at 8, 10, 12, 3 and 5.30 o'clock there appeared progressive fatigue amounting to about a 2 per cent. lengthening of the time at each trial, with a total lengthening of 7.50 per cent. in the case of 5 women and 10.5 per cent. in the case of 5 men. In further use of the same test in a more intensive experiment (15 trials between 10.30 A. M. and 10.30 P. M.) there appeared, again, a lengthening of about 10 per cent. toward the end of the day.

Heck tested 1153 New York school children (18) and 573 Lynchburg, Va., children (17) with a modification of the Courtis tests for the fundamental arithmetical operations. The New York tests lasted 10 min., those at Lynchburg 25 min., and they were distributed over various periods of the school session, particularly at 9, 11, 1 and 2.30 o'clock. The general result was an increase in quantity and a decrease in quality toward the close of the day; at New York, for instance, quantity increased by 1.57, 1.64 and 2.36 per cent. in the 2d, 3d and 4th periods, while quality decreased by 1.51, 1.41 and 2.28 per cent. in the corresponding periods. These differences are so slight as to be pedagogically negligible, in the opinion of Heck. The inferior quality of the later periods is, he thinks, more likely a sign of lessened interest than of consumption of energy or any sort of fatigue-poisoning. Rather elaborate tests with computation and other forms of school work by Robinson in South Carolina show in general little evidence of actual loss of ability toward the close of the school session.[11] The same conclusion has been reached by Thorndike (45) from schoolroom tests at Cleveland, Ohio, and Scranton, Pa. He emphasizes the statement that

---

[11]Consult the original for a discussion of the effects of recesses, lunches, gymnastics, singing, special incitement, etc., upon performance in such tests. The main conclusions are also summarized in *JEdPs*, 3: 1912, 93-595.

"incompetence, mental fatigue, does not come in regular proportion to the work done," that feelings of fatigue are not measures of mental inability, that disinclination to work does not
signify inability to work. It may be questioned, however,
whether this demonstration that pupils *can* work nearly as well
at the end of school session as at its beginning is equivalent,
as some writers have thought, to a demonstration that they
should be expected to work as well at the later periods.

A special study of *fatigue in evening schools* by Winch leads
him to the conclusion "that evening work is comparatively
unprofitable, and that a short time in class in the evening is
sufficient, *plus* the labors of the day, to induce a low condition
of mental energy."

NOTES.—Those who have used computation tests have not
sought, as a rule, to examine the mental processes involved in
them. Oehrn, however, calls attention to the fact that practise
in adding (by the Kraepelin method) tends to induce quasi-
automatic addition. This circumstance, taken in conjunction
with the relatively small correlations between different forms
of computation themselves, and between them and other abilities, including general intelligence, lends countenance to Wells'
objection (55) to accepting the computation test, without further qualification, as a measure of general mental efficiency.

Wyatt's 'missing digit' test forms an interesting modification
of the computation test. In it examples in addition, subtraction, multiplication and division are given in which one or
more figures, both in the answer and in the body of the example, are replaced by dots: the task is to restore the figures
correctly. The following will serve to illustrate his material:

$$
\begin{array}{r}
2.94 \\
.867 \\
781. \\
\hline
.42.6
\end{array}
$$

REFERENCES

(1) H. Aikins, E. L. Thorndike and Elizabeth Hubbell, Correlations among perceptive and associative processes. *PsR*, 9: 1902, 374-382.

(2) Tsuru Arai, Mental fatigue. *ColumbiaConEd*, No. 54. New York, 1912. Pp. 115.

(3) Bellei, Ulteriore contributo allo studio della fatiga mentale nei fanciulli. *Revista sperim, di freniatria*, 30: May, 1904. See summary by Binet, *AnPs*, 11: (1904) 1905, 369.

(4) E. Bischoff, Untersuchungen über Uebungsfähigkeit und Ermüdbarkeit bei 'geistiger' und 'körperlicher' Arbeit. *ArGesPs*, 22: 1912, 423-452.

(5) W. Brown, Some experimental results in the correlation of mental abilities. *BrJPs*, 3: 1910, 296-322. (Forms 3d part of his Use of the theory of correlation in psychology. Cambridge, 1910. Pp. 83.)

(6) L. Burgerstein, Die Arbeitskurve einer Schulstunde. *ZScGd*, 4: 1891, 543-564, 607-627. Also published separately in German, and in condensed form in English as: The working curve of an hour.

(7) L. Burgerstein und A. Netolitzky, Handbuch der Schulhygiene, 2d ed. Jena, 1902. Pp. 997.

(8) W. P. Burris, The correlations of the abilities involved in secondary school work. *ColumbiaConPhPs*, 11: 1903, 16-28.

(9) C. Burt, Experimental tests of higher mental processes and their relation to intelligence. *JEPd*, 1: 1911, 93-112.

(10) C. Burt and R. C. Moore, The mental differences between the sexes. *JEPd*, 1: 1912, 273-284, 355-388.

(11) W. G. Chambers, Individual differences in grammar-grade children. *JEdPs*, 1: 1910, 61-75.

(12) S. A. Courtis, The Courtis tests in arithmetic. *Final Rept. Educational Investigation Committee on School Inquiry, City of New York*. Vol. I, New York. 1911-1913. Pp. 397-546.

(13) M. E. Donovan and E. L. Thorndike, Improvement in a practise experiment under school conditions. *AmJPs*, 24: 1913, 426-8.

(14) H. Ebbinghaus, Ueber eine neue Methode zur Prüfung geistiger Fähigkeiten in ihre Anwendung bei Schulkindern. *ZPs*, 13: 1897, 401-457.

(15) W. S. Fox and E. L. Thorndike, The relationships between the different abilities involved in the study of arithmetic. Sex differences in arithmetical ability. *ColumbiaConPhPs*, 11: Feb., 1903, 32-40.

(16) J. Friedrich, Untersuchungen über die Einflusse der Arbeitsdauer und der Arbeitspausen auf die geistige Leistungsfähigkeit der Schulkinder. *ZPs*, 13: 1897, 1-53.

(17) W. H. Heck, A study of mental fatigue in relation to the daily school program. Lynchburg, Va., 1913. Pp. 28.

(18) W. H. Heck, A second study of mental fatigue in relation to the daily school program. *PsCl*, 7: 1913, 29-34.

(19) H. L. Hollingworth, The influence of caffein on mental and motor efficiency. *ArPs(e)*, No. 22 (*ColumbiaConPhPs*, 20, No. 4). New York, 1912. Pp. 166.

(20) H. L. Hollingworth, Correlation of abilities as affected by practise. *JEdPs*, 4: 1913, 405-414.

(20a) H. L. Hollingworth, Variations in efficiency during the working day. *PsR*, 21: 1914, 473-491.

(21) Marion E. Holmes, The fatigue of a school hour. *PdSe*, 3: 1895, 213-324.

(22) E. E. Jones, The influence of bodily posture on mental activities, N. Y., 1907. Pp. 60. (Reprinted from ArPs(e), No. 6.)

(23) E. Katzen-Ellenbogen, The mental efficiency in epileptics. Epilepsia, vol. 3, 504-546.

(24) R. Keller, Ueber den 40-Minutenunterrichtsbetrieb des Gymnasiums u. der Industrieschule in Winterthur. InMagScHyg, 2: 1906, 298-330, especially 307-318.

(25) F. Kemsies, Arbeitshygiene der Schule auf Grund von Ermüdungsmessungen. SmAbPdPs, 2: 1898. Pp. 64.

(26) E. Kraepelin, Ueber geistige Arbeit, 2d ed. Jena, 1897. Pp. 29.

(27) E. Kraepelin, Die Arbeitscurve. PhSd, 19: 1902, 459-507.

(28) F. Krueger und C. Spearman, Die Korrelation zwischen verschiedenen geistigen Leistungsfähigkeiten. ZPs, 44: 1907, 50-114.

(29) H. Laser, Ueber geistige Ermüdung beim Schulunterrichte. ZScGd, 7: 1894, 2-22.

(30) H. D. Marsh, The diurnal course of efficiency (Columbia Univ. thesis), N. Y., 1906. Pp. 99.

(31) Gladys W. Martin, The evidence of mental fatigue during school hours. JEPd, 1: 1911, 39-45, 137-147.

(32) Gladys W. Martyn, A study of mental fatigue. BrJPs, 5: 1913, 427-446.

(33) E. Meumann, Vorlesungen zur Einführung in die exp. Pädagogik, 1st ed., 2 vols., Leipzig, 1907. Pp. 555 and 467.

(34) A. Oehrn. Exp. Studien zur Individualpsychologie. PsArb, 1: 1896, 92-151.

(35) M. Offner, Mental fatigue. (Eng. trans.) EdPsMon. Baltimore, 1911. Pp. 133.

(36) Louise E. Ordahl, Consciousness in relation to learning. AmJPs, 22: 1911, 158-213, especially 194-202.

(37) J. Reis, Ueber einfache psychologische Versuche an Gesunden u. Geisteskranken. PsArb, 2: 1899, 587-694.

(38) L. A. Robinson, Mental fatigue and school efficiency. Bull. Winthrop Normal and Industrial College of South Carolina, 5: 1911. Pp. 56.

(39) R. Schulze, 500,000 Rechenaufgaben. Eine exp. Untersuchung. Praktische Schulmann, 44: 1895, 340.

(40) R. Schulze, Experimental psychology and pedagogy. (Eng. trans.) New York, 1912. Pp. 364.

(41) B. R. Simpson, Correlations of mental abilities. ColumbiaConEd, No. 53. New York, 1912. Pp. 122.

(42) W. Specht, Ueber klinische Ermüdungsmessungen. ArGesPs, 3: 1904, 245-339.

(43) D. Starch, Transfer of training in arithmetical operations. JEdPs, 2: 1911, 306-310.

(44) Teljatnik, article in Russian. See for details, Burgerstein u. Netolitzky, 4; especially pp. 462-5.

(45) E. L. Thorndike, Mental fatigue. PsR, 7: 1900, 466-482, 547-579.

(46) E. L. Thorndike, Educational psychology, 2d ed., N. Y., 1910. Pp. 248.

(47) E. L. Thorndike, Measurements of twins. Archives of Phil., Psych. etc., No. 1, Sept., 1905. Pp. 64.

(48) E. L. Thorndike, The effect of practise in the case of a purely intellectual function. AmJPs, 19: 1908. 374-384.

(49) E. L. Thorndike, Practise in the case of addition. AmJPs, 21: 1910, 483-486.

(50) E. L. Thorndike, Mental fatigue. JEdPs, 2: 1911, 61-80.

(51) E. L. Thorndike, The effect of continuous exercise and of rest upon difficult mental multiplication. *JEdPs*, 5: 1914, 597-599.

(52) E. L. Thorndike, Measurements of ability to solve arithmetical problems. *PdSe*, 21: 1914, 495-503.

(53) E. L. Thorndike, Educational Psychology, Vol. III. (Mental work and fatigue, etc.) New York, 1914. Pp. 408, especially Chs. 2 and 3.

(54) R. Vogt, Ueber Ablenkbarkeit und Gewöhnungsfähigkeit. *PsArb*, 3: 1901, 62-201, especially 80-118, 131-135.

(55) F. L. Wells, Technical aspects of experimental psycho-pathology. *AmJIns*, 64: 1908, 477-512.

(56) F. L. Wells, The relation of practise to individual differences. *AmJPs*, 23: 1912, 75-88.

(57) F. L. Wells, Standard tests of arithmetical associations. *JPh*, 4: 1907, 510-512.

(58) W. H. Winch, Some measurements of mental fatigue in adolescent pupils in evening school. *JEdPs*, 1: 1910, 13-23, 83-100.

(59) W. H. Winch, Accuracy in school children. Does improvement in numerical accuracy 'transfer?' *JEdPs*, 1: 1910, 557-589.

(60) W. H. Winch, Further work on numerical accuracy in school children. Does improvement in numerical accuracy transfer? *JEdPs*, 2: 1911, 262-271.

(61) R. S. Woodworth and F. L. Wells, Association tests. *PsMon*, No. 57, 1911. Pp. 85, especially 44-48.

(62) S. Wyatt, The quantitative investigation of higher mental processes. *BrJPs*, 6: 1913, 109-133.

TEST 36

Mirror-drawing.—The preceding tests of association deal with S's facility in producing unrestricted series, or in reproducing restricted series that have already been learned. The present test compels S to form a new series of associations that are opposed to associations stereotyped by several years of daily experience.

More particularly, in tracing an ordinary drawing the movements of the hand are guided by the visual perception of the drawing, plus kinesthetic sensations set up by the movement of the pencil. If the drawing is seen not directly, but in a mirror, the natural relations are reversed in certain respects, so that a new series of associative connections must be established between eye and hand. The rapidity and ease with which these new connections are established may be taken as an index of learning-capacity.

Learning is often said to take place either by practise (trial and error), by imitation, or by some form of ideational control (instruction, reasoning, etc.). In the mirror-drawing test, the conditions preclude the use of imitation, and there is but relatively little opportunity to employ ideational control; whatever improvement appears is due primarily to a process of trial and error.

The interesting phenomena of mirror-writing are mentioned in psychological literature as early as the 90's, if not before, but the first use of mirror-drawing as a psychological experiment appears to be found in Henri's article on the muscular sense (9) and in his monograph on tactual space perception of the same year, 1898. W. F. Dearborn (7), independently, experimented with mirror-drawing in 1905, though his work was not reported until after other writers, likewise independently, had hit upon a similar idea. In addition to Dearborn, Judd (11, p. 99) Starch (16) and Hill (10) have called attention to the usefulness of mirror-drawing as a demonstration experiment to illustrate the acquisition of motor habits, the trial and error method of learning, the cross-transfer of practise-effects, and the like. Burt, Yoakum and Calfee, Miss Weidensall and others have used mirror-drawing to test quickness of learning,[1] and its correlation with sex, intelligence and other factors.

APPARATUS.—Mirror.   Cardboard screen about 17x24 cm. Suitable supports for holding the cardboard. Thumb tacks. Stop-watch. Two kinds of diagrams, printed in red ink, for tracing: (a) a 6-pointed star, (b) a set of 6 patterns, each based upon a group of 12 points arranged at equidistant intervals in a circle about its central point, with guiding lines joining the 13 points in irregular fashion. [Mechanical counter A strong prism (about 20 D.).]

The six patterns resemble those used by Miss Calfee and Yoakum, but differ from them in eliminating the numbering of the points. S is directed from one point to the next by means of arrows and broken red lines, and does not have, therefore, to spend a portion of his time in hunting for the numbering to discern the order in which the points are connected. These patterns are somewhat more difficult than the star in so far as the direction of the movement of the hand is not the same in the various trials— a matter of advantage, however, since the series of trials does not develop a specific memory for a given set of hand movements. On the other hand these patterns are less difficult than the star in so far as S is not required to follow the directing lines exactly. The patterns also more nearly resemble than does the star test the mirror test used by Burt, in which

---

[1] For a discussion of prolonged adaptation to mirror-vision, see Stratton (18).

was required to punch with a stylus through 8 or more orifices arranged in a circle about an orifice at the center. They are superior to Burt's material in several respects.

Whether the stars or the patterns are used will depend upon circumstances. Either form of material may be used as supplementary to the other; thus, the star test may be used before and after drill work with the 6 patterns for an experiment to test the effect of practise.

PRELIMINARIES.—Pin the diagram out flat upon a table, directly in front of S. If the patterns are used, they should be taken in the order of their numbering. If the star is used, it should be placed with the cross-line that indicates the starting-point at the back (away from S) and with the card square with the edge of the table. (This brings the star slightly 'out of true,' as is intended.) Set up the mirror inclined slightly (about 5 deg.) from the vertical, just beyond the diagram. Arrange the screen (see Fig. 64) so that it will cut off S's direct view of the diagram, but will allow him to see it clearly in the mirror, and will not interfere with his hand in drawing.

METHOD.—(a) *With the patterns.* Place the point of a lead pencil at the center of the diagram. Assist S to grasp the pencil (permitting him to look only in the mirror). Instruct him: "When I say 'now,' move your pencil along the paper in the direction indicated by the red arrow till you reach the point at the end of the broken line; then follow the red line from that point to the next one, and so on till you have touched all 12 of the points on the paper and come to the end of the red dashes. You don't have to keep on the lines; they are put there simply to show you where to look for the points, but you must keep your pencil on the paper, and you must bring your pencil to each point before you go on to the next one. Work as rapidly as you can. Don't stop to figure out what you ought to do, but keep your pencil moving all the time." Start the watch at the signal, and record the time for the entire diagram. Pin down the second pattern and continue until all six patterns have been traced.

(b) *With the star.* Place the point of a lead pencil upon the cross-line of the star, and assist S to grasp the pencil (permitting him to look only in the mirror). Instruct S: "Trace the outline of the star, starting in this direction [indicating, *by pointing*, the tip of the star at the right of the cross-line].

FIG. 64.   THE MIRROR-DRAWING TEST.

Work as rapidly as you can, but *try to keep on the line.* Don'
stop to figure out what you ought to do, but keep your penci
going in some direction, and keep its point on the paper al
the time." Start the watch, and record the time for the entir
drawing.

E may also note the time for each sixth of the pattern. Bu
it is, perhaps, more desirable to supplement the total time b;
a record of the total number of corrective movements made b;
S. Since these movements are often rapid, and of short exten
it is necessary to use a mechanical or other form of counter t
obtain the record. Press the counter every time *S* moves tc
ward the line.[2]

For a standard test, make 6 trials with the right hand, usin
a fresh star for each trial.

VARIATIONS OF METHOD.—Make tests with the star before an
after a drill series with the patterns, as suggested above, o

---

[2]Every 'error,' or movement away from the line must, of course, be con
pensated for by a return movement. The idea is to register the numbe
of these errors, or corrective movements. Changes of direction necess
tated by the pattern itself are, obviously, to be neglected.

with either form of material make a first trial with the left hand; follow with a series of 5 to 50 trials with the right hand,[3] then return to the left hand for a final test. Note how much practise effect has been 'transferred' from the one hand to the other. Plot a graph to show the effect of practise, both upon the time and upon the corrective movements.

TREATMENT OF DATA.—In the standard form of test E has available 6 records. Several possibilities appear: S's may be compared with respect to (1) their 1st trial, (2) their 6th trial, (3) all 6 trials taken collectively (sum or average), or with respect to their rate of improvement, by computing the per cent. of gain either (4) in the 6th, compared with the 1st trial, or (5) in the average of the last three, compared with the average of the first three trials. The third method was found by Burt to yield the best correlation with intelligence. On the other hand, the 2d method would seem to have some merit, since Yoakum and Calfee conclude that "the time consumed in the first trial is an individual variation; that of the last [6th] more nearly represents the individual's place in the group." Until we have more investigations on this point it would be better for E to try more than one method of ranking S's and to select the one which gave the most favorable results.

RESULTS.— (1) The best *norms* for the patterns are supplied by the results of Yoakum and Calfee, embodied in Table 78; results from a more limited number of college students with the star test are shown in Table 77, and for other groups in Tables 79 and 80.

TABLE 77

Effect of Practise on Speed in Mirror-Drawing. College Students
(*Whipple*)

	NUMBER	1ST LEFT	1ST RIGHT	2D RIGHT	3D RIGHT	4TH RIGHT	5TH RIGHT	2D LEFT
Men_____	11	169	127	108	96	80	67	88
Women __	23	149	127	87	76	67	67	74

[3]If desired, the 6 patterns may be used, turned to bring the other edges at the back, in order to provide drill without direct repetition of the same diagram.

(2) *Individual differences* in performance are striking; thus, in the star test the time consumed in making the first tracing ranged, in the author's tests of 34 students, from about 50 sec. to more than 8 min. In the larger group of students examined

TABLE 78

Times, in Sec., for Mirror-Drawing (Yoakum and Calfee)

GROUP	TRIAL	I	II	III	IV	V	VI	AVER.
I	Median	243.0	121.0	93.0	82.0	68.0	50.0	110.33
	M. V.	94.9	45.5	28.1	34.7	24.7	17.1	36.57
	Slowest	517.0	245.0	205.0	180.0	158.0	113.0	210.00
	Fastest	69.0	51.0	41.0	43.0	40.0	32.0	53.66
II	Median	92.0	65.0	48.0	41.0	35.0	28.0	54.70
	M. V.	64.1	33.9	26.6	19.3	21.9	14.2	27.40
	Slowest	700.5	337.5	303.5	153.5	201.8	171.0	242.37
	Fastest	31.5	23.5	19.3	18.3	17.8	17.0	23.95
III	Median	167.5	105.0	80.0	68.0	56.0	48.0	97.83
	M. V.	104.2	39.3	30.3	19.7	19.9	13.5	33.38
	Slowest	752.0	277.0	270.0	175.0	121.0	105.0	193.33
	Fastest	72.0	49.0	40.0	34.0	33.0	23.0	46.87

Group I comprised 30 elementary school boys. Group II, 52 women, and Group III, 51 men in the freshman class of the University of Texas. The averages for each group in each trial are not here reproduced.

at Texas differences range from 31.5 to 752 sec., while the fastest college girl tested by Miss Weidensall had a record of 18 sec., as compared with 2072 sec. for the slowest reformatory woman (Table 79). These differences, as inspection of the tables will show, are greatly reduced after a little practise.

(3) *Dependence on sex.* That girls decidedly surpass boys and that women decidedly surpass men is shown in all the published results in mirror-drawing, with the exception of two groups reported by Burt and Moore, and in them certain divergencies in method and in other test conditions offer a sufficient explanation of the apparent exception. Miss Calfee's averages for six trials give for the freshmen women 64.4 sec., P.E. 22.3, for the freshmen men 101 sec., P.E. 28.5. She finds that only 6 per cent. of the men reach the women's median, while 90.4

per cent. of the women reach the men's median. It is not only possible, but probable, that this sex-difference is in some part due to greater familiarity of women with the use of the mirror. Burt believes that there is also an innate sex difference at work.

(4) *Dependence on practise.* (*a*) *General practise-effects.* The tables given above show that even a single trial produces a decided reduction in time: the median time for elementary school boys, for example, is cut in halves in the pattern test, while that for men and women is reduced one-third by the first trial. (See Fig. 65.) The long practise experiment conducted by Starch with the star test shows (Fig. 66) that the reduction is rapid at first, then slower, and that maximal speed is not attained for a long time, apparently not until some 90 trials (Starch's curve represents a series of 100 trials, one per day).

(*b*) *Individual differences in practise-effects.* Practise curves compounded of the performances of a group of *S*'s show a smooth drop (see Fig. 65), but the curves of individual *S*'s are not necessarily of this form: on the contrary, it is possible, as Yoakum and Calfee have shown (22, p. 290), to separate *S*'s into groups that show the 2d trial slower than the 1st, or the 3d slower than the 2d, etc. These investigators summarize these facts by saying: "Some *S*'s gain control of the situation by a fairly regular procedure; others temporarily lose control at some point in the series. The majority of the latter lose control at the fourth or fifth trial in a series of six tests." It follows that the rank-order of *S*'s in any one trial does not correlate perfectly with their rank-order in any other trial; actual correlations computed by Yoakum and Calfee between the first and subsequent trials are 0.79, 0.76, 0.74, 0.64 and 0.59 for the 2d, 3d, 4th, 5th and 6th trial, respectively. The correlation between the first trial and the average of all 6 trials is given by them as 0.93.

(*c*) *Cross-education.* A considerable amount of practise gained with the one hand is transferred to the other (unpractised) hand. Thus, Starch's 100-day practise with the right hand effected an improvement in it of 92 per cent. in accuracy and of 84 per cent. in speed. A single left-hand record, made

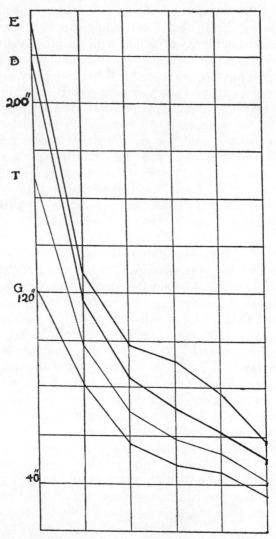

FIG. 65. THE EFFECT OF PRACTISE DURING SIX TRIALS UPON THE AVERAGE SPEED OF MIRROR-DRAWING. (From Yoakum and Calfee)

The abscissas represent the six trials, running from left to right. The ordinates represent time in sec. 'E' is the curve for the 30 elementary school boys, 'B' for the 51 freshmen men, 'G' for the 52 freshmen women, 'T' for the 103 freshmen collectively.

at the expiration of this period, showed, in comparison with a single left-hand record made before practise began, an improvement of 81 per cent. in accuracy and of 85 per cent. in speed. There is, however, nothing surprising in this so-called 'cross-

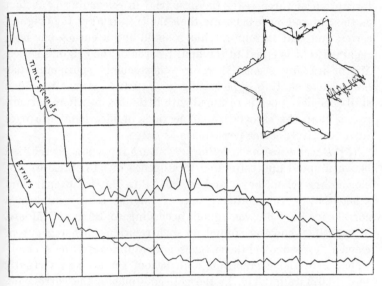

FIG. 66.   THE EFFECT OF LONG PRACTISE UPON MIRROR-DRAWING.
(From Starch)

education,' since the tracing of the star in the mirror depends primarily upon co-ordinations established in the central nervous system: in other words, the transfer is only an outwardly apparent transfer; in reality, the same factors are at work in the control of either hand.

(*d*) *Persistence of practise.* The effect of even a short period of practise in mirror-drawing is very persistent. Thus, Burt administered 6 tests in succession, during which the average speed fell from 103 to 39.5 sec. Twelve weeks later, two tests were given in succession; the average speed developed was 34.5 sec. in the first, and 27.4 sec. in the second: in other words, the 7th test surpassed the 6th, made 12 weeks previously—a condition found in the records of 16 out of 26 boys. The extent to which this persistence of practise-effect was shared by Burt's

S's is further indicated by the correlation of 0.52 between their standing before, and their standing after the 12-week interval.

Hill's work (10b) shows that the skill developed by one trial a day, continued for 50 days, is so persistent that after an interruption of three years the first trial in relearning is as fast as the 32d and more accurate than the 50th trial of the original series, and that in four retrials a speed and accuracy has been regained that is equal to the final records of the original series. Mirror-drawing seems, therefore, to resemble neuro-muscular habits, like skating, typewriting, etc., in the manner in which skill once developed is retained with little loss over long periods, rather than the associative connections of ideational life with their relatively lesser persistence.

(5) *Dependence on intelligence.* Burt reports a correlation between speed and estimated intelligence of 0.67, P.E. .07, for elementary school boys, and of 0.54, P.E. .14, for preparatory school boys. In another group of English school children a correlation of 0.60 was found, according to Burt and Moore. Miss Calfee, however, found no such relations in her group of elementary school children chosen to duplicate Burt's conditions: here the correlation with school grades was virtually zero (0.07); similarly, in the college students the correlation with grades was —.07 in the case of the men and 0.19 in the case of the women. The author was able to discern no constant differences between the work of five dull and five bright boys.

(6) *Delinquents.* Comparative study of the star-test (5 successive trials) with college girls, maids in college dormitories and girls at Bedford Hills, N. Y., Reformatory, conducted by Miss Weidensall, reveals a number of interesting results. From advance sheets of her manuscript, for which I am indebted to Dr. Weidensall, I have selected data referring primarily to the time records only[4] (Tables 79 and 80). The first of these tables shows that, both in the first and in the last trial, and whether

---

[4]Dr. Weidensall expects to publish also data for the number of errors (corrective movements) and for the degree of 'precision' with which the line is followed. Precision has been measured by ascertaining the total number of cm. in the contour of the star in which, for distances of 3 or more consecutive mm., the tracing remained within 2 mm. either way from the red line.

maximal, minimal, median, average or upper or lower quartile is considered, the three groups are invariably arranged in the same order—students best, Bedford women last and the maids intermediate. The second of these tables shows that there

TABLE 79

Times, in Sec., Used in the Star Test by 36 College Girls, 16 College Maids and 69 Bedford Reformatory Women (Weidensall)

	COLLEGE GIRLS		COLLEGE MAIDS		REFORMATORY WOMEN	
	1st Star	5th Star	1st Star	5th Star	1st Star	5th Star
Fastest	18.	7.	36.	21.	59.	36.
Upper Q.	41.	17.5	54.	29.5	203.6	80.
Median	66.	28.7	127.5	44.5	420.	117.2
Average	82.6	31.3	133.6	48.6	473.1	124.
Lower Q.	110.	39.	161.	69.	627.	148.
Slowest	252.	76.	409.	85.	2072.	436.*

*With two failures in addition.

exists a good correspondence between both the time and errors for the star test and the classification made by the institution into three groups depending on outlook for reformation: the differences are more striking in the first than in the fifth tracing.

TABLE 80

Scores in the Star Test for Three Groups of Bedford Reformatory Women (Weidensall)

INSTITUTIONAL CLASSIFICATION	FIRST STAR		FIFTH STAR	
	Time	Errors	Time	Errors
Most capable and promising	320.9	117.7	105.4	36.0
Women with illegitimate children under 2 yrs. of age	562.9	211.3	123.1	45.6
Backward and mentally feeble. Unpromising	610.5	264.4	127.2	55.1

In addition to these quantitative results, the star test has proved to possess a value in a perhaps unexpected direction, viz.: as a device for sorting out S's of the unstable and less tractable type.

On this point Dr. Weidensall writes: "This test isolates better than any we have tried at Bedford those who are incapable of sustained effort under difficulties. It isolated, of course, the low-grade feeble-minded, for, no matter how hard they try, they do not succeed in tracing a precise star. The epileptics have a characteristically bad time and their stars are all 'knotted up' with 'blind spots' where they were caught and held indefinitely. Chiefly, however, is the test of interest in the case of those who are bright enough to trace the star well, but too unstable to do so. These are invariably the girls who are difficult to manage in the institution. The tracing goes well enough until suddenly the pencil at some hard point starts off in the wrong direction. The subject then tugs and pulls, grows more and more irritated, disturbed and excited, makes big black circles and finally throws down the pencil and gives up. When calmed, praised and urged to try again, she will continue and usually in the end draw a fairly good fifth star. This behavior in tracing the star is typical of their behavior in the institution when the pressure of discipline or responsibility becomes the least bit too exacting."

(7) *Relation of speed and accuracy.* The curves reproduced from Starch show that practise produces a reduction in the number of corrective movements that parallels fairly closely the reduction in time. Correlations between time and errors obtained by Miss Weidensall are for the students 0.63, for the maids 0.87, for the reformatory women 0.61. My own work with college students has given a correlation of 0.86, P.E. .04.

(8) *Reliability.* Burt and Moore give this coefficient as 0.52. The method used at Texas is evidently superior, since the coefficient of relation between the first and second test, as above stated, amounts to 0.79, and thus assures satisfactory reliability.

(9) *Various correlations.* Miss Calfee's tests of Texas freshmen included three tests previously used by Burt, viz.: card dealing, card sorting and alphabet sorting. Correlations found by Burt between mirror-drawing and these three tests when applied to school children were 0.40, 0.34 and 0.29, respectively those found by Miss Calfee for school children were only 0.11 0.26 and 0.06, for freshmen men 0.19, 0.11 and 0.22, and for freshmen women 0.37, 0.20 and 0.29, respectively. Save, then for the last mentioned correlation, her figures are invariably lower than those of Burt. Other 'corrected' correlations re

ported by Burt for mirror-drawing (average correlations for various groups) are: tapping 0.74, dotting apparatus 0.92, spot-pattern test 0.75, immediate memory 0.38, discrimination of pitch 0.66, comparison of line lengths 0.55, esthesiometer 0.38, discrimination of lifted weights 0.30.

(10) *Qualitative aspects.* Efficiency in mirror-drawing may result from the actual formation of new visual-motor co-ordinations (indeed, some *S*'s after executing a number of drawings, find that, for a short time immediately thereafter, these new co-ordinations interfere with normal drawing or writing); but efficiency may also result, at least in the star test, from the voluntary inhibition of visual control in favor of kinesthetic control, *i. e.,* by thinking the drawing of a star in motor terms, as if working with the eyes shut. Or, the hand-movements may be started in this manner and then carried out by visual control from the mirror. Finally, adults occasionally control the drawing ideationally, *i. e.,* by applying inferred properties of reflection by mirrors.

It is evident that the existence of these qualitative differences may affect the test in such a way that the quantitative data for different *S*'s may 'measure' different mental processes.

Very slow *S*'s get 'caught' at certain difficult points of the drawing, where they make a long series of futile attempts to start in the right direction. Here the normal visual-motor control is too persistent to be readily broken or ignored.

NOTES.—A further study of the associative connections involved in mirror-drawing may be made by the use of dot-tapping through a prism or of the various forms of mirror-writing.[5]

For the first test, let *S* shut his left eye, and strike repeatedly with his right forefinger at a mark on the wall or table-top,

[5]On mirror-writing, consult Abt, Allen, Downey, Laprade, Lochte, Ordahl, Rowe, Strack, Weber, and Wegener. The most elaborate statistical study is that of Lochte, who examined 2804 pupils in Berlin, and found, for children aged 6-7 years, 13.2 per cent. of spontaneous left-hand mirror-writing in boys and 25.4 per cent. in girls, but for children aged 13-14 years, only 0.7 per cent. in boys and 35 per cent. in girls. The tendency toward this type of writing appears, therefore, to decrease with age, and to be more evident in girls than in boys.

The most elaborate qualitative analysis of the various 'controls' used in writing is that of Miss Downey.

making about one stroke per second, after the manner pre-scribed in the test of precision of aiming (No. 11). After this rhythmic movement has become well established, and *without interrupting it in the least,* place suddenly before his eye a 20 D. prism, with the base toward his nose. The mark is thereby apparently displaced some 10 cm. to the left. Count the number of strokes that S makes before he hits the mark again (with the prism kept before the eye). Similarly, count the number of strokes necessary to hit the mark again when the prism is removed.

For the second test, try any or all of the following:

(1) Close the eyes and write with both hands simultaneously. Cases will then appear, particularly in young children, of spontaneous mirror-writing (writing which reads correctly when held before a mirror) with the left hand. If this appears, see if S can write normally with the left hand when his eyes are closed.

(2) Show S a sample of mirror-writing. Explain its nature. Ask him to write in a similar manner, first with his left, then with his right hand.

(3) Write with both hands simultaneously, but with the left intentionally in mirror-writing.

(4) Read normal writing when seen only as reflected in a mirror.

(5) Write normally while watching the writing in the mirror, *i. e.,* with hand and paper hidden from direct observation as in the star test.

REFERENCES

(1)   G. Abt, L'écriture en miroir. *AnPs*, 8: 1901 (1902), 221-225.

(2)   F. J. Allen, Mirror-writing. *Brain*, 19: 1896, 385-7.

(3)   C. Burt, Experimental tests of general intelligence. *BrJPs*, 3: December, 1909, 94-177, especially 145-9.

(4)   C. Burt, Experimental tests of higher mental processes and their relation to general intelligence. *JEPd*, 1: 1911, 93-112.

(5)   C. Burt and R. C. Moore, The mental differences between the sexes. *JEPd*, 1: 1912, 273-284, 355-388.

(6)   Marguerite Calfee, College freshmen and four general intelligence tests. *JEdPs*, 4: 1913, 223-231.

(7)   W. F. Dearborn, Experiments in learning. *JEdPs*, 1: 1910, 373-388.

(8)   June E. Downey. (*a*) Control processes in modified hand-writi

ing: an experimental study. *PsMon*, 9: April, 1908, No. 37. Pp. 158.
(*b*) On the reading and writing of mirror-script. *PsR*, 21: 1914, 408-441.
(9) V. Henri, Revue générale sur le sens musculaire. *AnPs*, 5: 1898 (1899), 399-513, especially 504-508. (Also Ueber die Raumwahrnehmungen des Tastsinnes. Berlin, 1898. Pp. 228, especially p. 140.)
(10) D. S. Hill (*a*) Class and practise experiments upon the learning process. *PsB*, 8: 1911, 70-71. (*b*) Minor studies in learning and relearning. *JEdPs*, 5: 1914, 375-386.
(11) C. H. Judd, Laboratory manual of psychology. New York, 1907.
(12) A. Laprade, Contributions a l'étude de l'écriture en miroir. 1902.
(13) Lochte, Beitrag zur Kenntnis des Vorkommens u. der Bedeutung der Spiegelschrift. *Arch. f. Psychiatrie u. Nervenkrankheiten*, 28: 1896, 379-410.
(14) Louise E. Ordahl, Consciousness in relation to learning. *AmJPs*, 22: 1911, 158-213, especially 193f.
(15) E. C. Rowe, Voluntary movement. *AmJPs*, 21: 1910, 513-562, especially 537ff.
(16) D. Starch, A demonstration of the trial and error method of learning. *PsB*, 7: January, 1910, 20-23.
(17) M. Strack, Mirror writing and left-handedness. *PdSe*, 2: 1893, 236-244.
(18) G. M. Stratton, The spatial harmony of touch and sight. *Mind*, n. s. 7: 1899, 492-505.
(19) H. Weber, Spiegelschrift u. Lenkschrift. *Zeits. f. klin. Med.*, 27.
(20) H. Wegener, Die Spiegelschrift. *ZPs*, 1: 1899, 254-269.
(21) Jean Weidensall, The mentality of the criminal woman. To appear in *EdPsMon*.
(22) C. S. Yoakum and Marguerite Calfee, An analysis of the mirror-drawing experiment. *JEdPs*, 4: 1913, 283-292.

TEST 37

Substitution.—This test is one of many that may be devised to measure the rapidity with which new associations are formed by repetition. The name commonly applied to the test arises from the process that it involves, in which S is called upon to substitute for one set of characters (letters, digits, familiar geometrical forms, etc.) another set of characters in accordance with a plan set before him in a printed key. The procedure differs from most memory tests or exercises of memorizing in that the connections indicated by the key are not committed to memory at the outset, but acquired gradually by use as the test proceeds.

The principle embodied in such a test obviously admits of numerous variations in detail of application. One form of substitution, the replacement of a set of letters by another set of letters, was used by Lough (7) in 1902 for a class exercise in learning. Another and more elaborate form in which letters distributed like those of a typewriter keyboard are to be associated to numerals is reported by Starch and Dearborn to have been devised by Jastrow and used several years ago in the Wisconsin University Laboratory. In recent years several variations, some simpler, some more difficult, have appeared.

The substitution test seems primarily to have been developed as a useful demonstration and class experiment for the study of the psychology of learning and of the practise curve (Dearborn, Starch, Lough, Munn, Kline). It has also been used to study racial differences (Baldwin, Pyle), to trace the effect of dental treatment on general ability (Kohnky), to compare delinquent and normal individuals (Baldwin, Weidensall) and as one test of the capacity of working children (Woolley and Fischer). Incidentally, of course, the relation of learning ability to age, sex and school training has been the object of investigation.

Three forms of test material are here presented: the first and second, which are modifications of a form devised by W. F Dearborn (3), may be used with adults or older children; the third, which has been devised by Mrs. Woolley and used by Miss Kohnky and Miss Weidensall as well as Mrs. Woolley is much simpler and better adapted for younger or less capable children.[1]

A.   STANDARD FORM FOR INDIVIDUAL PROCEDURE (SYMBOL-DIGIT TEST)

MATERIALS.—Stop-watch, preferably split-second.   Cover board with key.   Test strips.

The cover-board, about 18 x 36 cm., is so constructed as to furnish a sort of 'tunnel' through which the test-strips may slide as fast as they are written: it also carries a printed key consisting of 9 circles, within each one of which is a digit (from 1 to 9) and a symbol (square, asterisk, etc.)

The test-strips, about 11.5 x 50 cm., contain forty 5-place series of symbols like those of the key, together with forty 5-place empty squares.

---

[1]If a test more difficult than any of those described here is desired reference may be had to the form proposed by Gray (4) and used with some modification by Baldwin (1). The Maltese Cross test arranged by Mrs. Squire, and also tried by Carpenter, proved undesirable, apparently in part because it was too easy. Much the same thing may be said of he Colored Forms test, which represents still another quite simple variety of substitution test.

METHOD.—Lay the cover-board upon the table. Insert a test-strip in such a manner that the first (top) line of characters comes just below the lower edge of the cover and hence just beneath the key.

Cover the key and do not allow S to examine it before the test, save as specified below.

Give S the following explanation: "You will find before you on the table a card on which there are nine circles. In each circle you will find one of the numbers from 1 to 9, and a symbol, *i. e.*, a small character or drawing. Then, you will find a strip of paper with rows of the same characters, and with empty squares beside them. What you are to do is to write in these empty squares the numbers that correspond with the characters. Keep at work continuously, as fast as you can, until you have filled in all the empty squares on the paper. Of course, you will have to look back and forth from the paper to the circles to find out what number to use, unless you can, after a while, remember some of the numbers without looking at them."

With young S's, this verbal explanation will be insufficient to make the task clear. It will do no harm, in such cases, to show S, for a brief instant, the card of circles and a test-strip that has already been filled out. Let him see them just long enough to make the instructions clear, but not long enough to permit him to learn any of the combinations.

Start the watch when S starts the first line: keep the watch in view, but out of S's sight: record, without stopping the watch, the position of the second-hand when S completes every 5th line (indicated, for this purpose, by a heavier division-line in the test-strip).

As fast as S finishes a line (or two lines), push the strip forward to bring a fresh line of symbols into position at the lower edge of the cover.

When the 40th line is written, conceal the key; immediately turn over the test-strip, write on it the digits 1 to 9, and ask S to place above each digit the character that accompanies it. Ascertain, if possible, whether S relied upon visual, auditory, visual-auditory, or some other type of associative imagery.

TREATMENT OF DATA.—Check up the test-strip for errors. Compare S's with respect to (1) their time for the whole test, (2) their gain in the last, as related to their speed in the first 5-line section, (3) their accuracy, and (4) their knowledge of the symbols (crediting 1 for each symbol correctly reproduced, and 1 for each pair of transposed symbols). Plot graphs showing the variation in speed for the eight sections.

B. FORM FOR GROUP TESTS, OR FOR SUPPLEMENTARY INDIVIDUAL TESTS (DIGIT-SYMBOL TEST)

MATERIALS.—Printed form, at the top of which are shown 9 circles, as in Form A (save that different symbols are used), and in the body of which is provided, in two columns, a series of forty 5-place numbers and forty 5-place blank squares in which the appropriate symbols are to be placed. Stop-watch.

METHOD.—For individual tests, give instructions similar to those for Form A, with such modifications as the altered arrangement of the material necessitates. Make clear, especially, that the second column is to be filled out the moment that the first is completed.

For group tests, supplement the instructions by an adequate blackboard explanation, preferably with an illustration so devised as not to give information concerning the symbols to be used. Have the papers distributed, face down, to be turned over only at the command to start. Work by the time-limit method, allowing 4 min. for the test. Instruct S's to place an oblique mark at the point reached when the command "mark" is heard. Give this signal every 30 sec., so that the work is divided into 8 periods of 30 sec. each. Conclude with the symbol-test as in the individual method. Plot curves for 30 sec. intervals.

VARIATIONS OF METHOD.—(1) Cut off the top of the form and glue the pattern of circles on a sheet of cardboard, as in Form A. Cut and paste the two test-columns to form a single long column, as in Form A. This will permit check-tests, comparable with the standard method, save that here symbols, there digits are written.

(2) Repeat either Form A or Form B after an interval of several hours, days, or weeks, to compare the permanence, in different *S*'s, of the associative connections established in a single trial.

(3) Repeat Form A until the associations are firmly established, and the digits can be written rapidly without seeing the pattern. Ascertain whether the use of Form B will then develop interference of associations.

(4) Cover up the key in either Form A or Form B when the last section (last quarter or last eighth) of the test is reached so as to produce a test of *S*'s ability to continue the work from memory, like that described for Form C.

C. CINCINNATI SYMBOL-DIGIT TEST

MATERIALS.—Four test sheets of geometrical forms, each containing ten rows, 5 units per row, of nine different forms. Cardboard with printed key. Cardboard cover. Stop-watch.

METHOD.—Put before *S* the first test sheet and set the key where it can be seen easily. The following are the instructions then given by Woolley and Fischer:

"You see this page of figures [forms]. Now on this card I have the same figures, but each figure has a number in it. What I want you to do is to write in each figure on this page the number that you see in the same figure on that card. For instance, what figure would you put in here? [*E* points to one of the figures which might easily be confused with another one—the inverted triangle or the U, and corrects *S* if he makes a mistake.] And in here [pointing to one of the 'unique' figures]? I want you to begin here at the top of the page and fill the figures in, in rows, just as you come to them. As you finish each row, I will cover it up with this piece of cardboard, this way. Now begin, and see how fast you can get the whole page done."

The time is taken from the moment *S* begins to look on the key for his first number to the moment he writes the last one. The second test sheet is then given with the instruction: "Now fill in this page the same way, and see if you can do it faster this time."

The third test sheet follows, with the instruction: "Fill in this page and try to do it still faster. When you finish this page, I will take the card away, and then I want you to try to fill in the last page just from memory."

S is allowed to correct any errors that he may note before the line is covered. The covering is done to insure that each line in the first three sheets is done from the key and each line in the last sheet from memory, never from the previous records.

VARIATION OF METHOD.—If *S* scores less than 98 per cent. accuracy on Sheet 4, it is instructive to give another drill sheet, followed by a second test of substitution from memory, and to continue alternating sheets filled in with the key and without the key until this degree of accuracy is secured. The number of extra trials needed forms a useful indication of relative learning capacity, especially in the case of rather incompetent *S*'s.

TREATMENT OF DATA.—For each test sheet, taken separately, is figured the time, the accuracy and an index of efficiency computed from the time and the accuracy. Accuracy is calculated by subtracting from 100 per cent. 2 per cent. for each error or omission. The index is found by dividing the obtained time by the accuracy. In the first three sheets this index may be regarded as indicating approximately the time needed to make the substitutions without error. In the fourth sheet the index is evidently a more arbitrary measure, since an error in substituting from memory might not be remedied by any amount of extension of the time.

Speaking generally, the learning capacity of a given *S* is indicated not alone by his performance with the 4th sheet, but also by his index for the first three sheets, *i. e.,* while the 4th sheet shows whether the associative connections have been made correctly or not, the work with the other sheets shows how long a time was used in establishing these connections.[2]

RESULTS.—(1) *Norms* for the three substitution tests are now available in sufficiently satisfactory form for most purposes

---

[2] It would seem possible that some measure of learning capacity might be calculated from the relation between performance with the 4th and with the other sheets, though the Cincinnati investigators have contented themselves with the treatment quoted.

Tables 81 and 82 give results for college students with Form B.
Tables 83 and 84 give Pyle's results with Form B and Form A,
respectively, for both sexes and ages from 8 years upward.
Table 85 gives some of the more important norms compiled
at Cincinnati for 753 children 14, and 679 children 15 years old

TABLE 81

Substitution Test. Number of Symbols Written. Form B. Group Method
(Whipple)

THIRTY-SEC. PERIOD	1ST	2D	3D	4TH	5TH	6TH	7TH	8TH	TOTAL	SYMBOL SCORE
Average, 12 men	13.7	16.1	14.6	16.3	14.8	17.2	16.7	17.9	127.3	8
Average, 28 women	13.9	15.4	16.0	17.9	16.0	17.0	16.8	19.0	132.0	8.2
Fastest individual	10.0	21.0	22.0	18.0	23.0	20.0	25.0	26.0	165.0	9
Slowest individual	11.0	13.0	8.0	10.0	12.0	10.0	11.0	13.0	95.0	3

TABLE 82

Substitution Test. Speed in Seconds. Form B. Individual Method
(Whipple)

SECTION OF 5 LINES	1ST	2D	3D	4TH	5TH	6TH	7TH	8TH	TOTAL
Average, 13 men	54.0	46.0	45.8	44.8	46.1	44.4	47.7	44.3	373.1
Average, 5 women	45.8	41.2	40.6	38.6	43.4	37.6	36.6	35.0	318.8
Total, 18 cases	51.8	44.7	44.3	43.1	45.4	42.5	44.6	41.7	358.1
Fastest individual	42.0	35.0	23.0	30.0	36.0	29.0	31.0	34.0	270.0
Slowest individual	63.0	58.0	59.0	61.0	62.0	53.0	60.0	65.0	481.0

TABLE 83

Correct Substitutions Made in 60 Sec. Digit-Symbol Test (Pyle).

SEX	AGE	8	9	10	11	12	13	14	15	16	17	18	ADULT
Male	Cases	34	58	50	49	56	62	48	35	31	14	17	67
	Aver.	10.3	12.6	15.4	16.3	19.1	22.6	21.1	24.7	24.8	23.8	28.7	29.3
	A. D.	3.5	4.1	3.9	3.6	5.1	5.8	4.5	4.6	5.4	4.3	3.5	8.7
Female	Cases	37	61	58	49	68	49	46	34	46	38	29	88
	Aver.	13.0	15.7	18.8	18.5	22.7	23.4	26.8	26.8	27.5	28.5	25.9	32.2
	A. D.	3.2	4.1	4.4	4.1	4.9	5.2	5.0	4.7	5.3	5.7	7.0	4.2

TABLE 84

Correct Substitutions Made in 60 Sec.   Symbol-Digit Test (Pyle).

SEX	AGE	8	9	10	11	12	13	14	15	16	17	18	ADULT
Male	Cases	37	72	76	62	75	78	59	45	38	20	17	56
	Aver.	10.0	13.2	16.5	17.7	19.3	20.7	23.3	25.8	27.8	26.1	28.0	33.0
	A. D.	5.3	5.0	5.8	5.4	5.4	5.7	5.4	5.9	6.3	7.4	5.1	9.3
Female	Cases	41	82	82	63	89	66	62	44	55	43	29	89
	Aver.	10.9	16.0	19.9	19.6	23.1	25.6	27.4	29.7	29.1	32.0	33.1	31.3
	A. D.	5.3	5.2	6.4	6.3	6.6	6.4	6.1	6.7	5.3	6.3	4.4	5.4

applying for working certificates.[3]   From data kindly supplied me by Mrs. Woolley I have constructed also the percentile curves, Figs. 67 and 68, for the same groups of children.

(2) *Dependence on age.*   Pyle's averages, with two exceptions, show that the capacity in the substitution test improves every year from 8 to 18, both in boys and in girls.   The Cincinnati children at 15 surpass their 14-year-old records, with every page and in both speed and accuracy: the difference is too pronounced to be due to the repetition of the test, since different keys were employed in the two trials.

(3) *Dependence on sex.*   Pyle's averages show that the girls make more correct substitutions than the boys at every age from 8 to 18, with a single exception (age 18, digit-symbol test). In the three test sheets the Cincinnati girls are slightly superior to boys in index, while the sex differences in accuracy are too small and inconsistent to be significant, so that speed is the important factor in the better index of the girls.   With the 4th (memory) sheet, there is no difference in index at 14, but the girls are superior at 15.   Girls at 15 also slightly surpass boys in accuracy on the 4th sheet.

(4) *Dependence on race.*   B. T. Baldwin tested 37 white and 30 negro girls at a Pennsylvania Reform School for 16 practise days, 5 min. per day, after eliminating 3 whites and 1 negroes who failed to attain 50 per cent. accuracy.   Table 8

---

[3] Consult Woolley and Fischer for table showing norms of accuracy an for numerous graphs of distribution for the substitution index in rela tion to school grade.

TABLE 85

Substitution Index, in Sec., Cincinnati Working Children (Woolley and Fischer).

AGE	RANK	SHEET 1		SHEET 2		SHEET 3		SHEET 4	
		Boys	Girls	Boys	Girls	Boys	Girls	Boys	Girls
14	Best	71.0	83.3	68.5	68.0	59.4	59.8	53.0	52.3
	75th Perc.	147.0	142.0	115.7	108.7	97.4	94.0	89.6	88.5
	50th Perc.	172.7	162.6	133.2	130.4	115.9	112.7	111.2	112.6
	25th Perc.	200.9	185.6	157.6	154.0	138.4	134.8	148.3	150.5
	Worst	400.0	419.5	378.0	298.4	276.4	242.9	1,257.6	525.4*
15	Best	82.2	98.4	55.0	67.4	54.0	59.2	52.6	50.6
	75th Perc.	137.3	130.4	104.6	103.6	92.0	91.9	84.4	85.3
	50th Perc.	157.3	148.6	123.7	119.0	110.7	108.7	104.9	103.9
	25th Perc.	179.0	171.6	145.7	138.1	133.4	128.7	145.7	139.3
	Worst	286.6	307.8	241.3	295.1	355.5	248.6	906.5	19,875.0

*To which should be added one case of complete failure—accuracy only 6 per cent. and index 60,000. In comparing this table with the original text it should be noted that I have reversed the designations of the percentiles, so that 100 per cent. here would represent the quickest performance (smallest index).

shows clearly the superiority of the whites. In general, the negroes make only 62.4 per cent. as many substitutions and 245.3 per cent. as many errors as the whites. The fact that the

TABLE 86

Average Number of Substitutions Made by 37 White and 30 Negro Girls in a Pennsylvania Reformatory (Baldwin)

TRIAL	1	2	3	4	5	6	7	8	9
Whites	23.8	42.6	46.7	54.2	61.7	64.9	67.8	78.3	79.6
Negroes	22.6	27.6	31.2	35.8	46.9	48.0	53.9	57.7	61.5

TRIAL	10	11	12	13	14	15	16	AVER.
Whites	86.9	85.9	89.5	94.1	93.7	100.1	116.5	72.3
Negroes	64.7	76.6	71.6	76.0	78.1	72.3	89.0	55.8

average age of the whites is somewhat greater (16.7 vs. 15.1 years) by no means accounts for these differences. Baldwin notes that there are also distinct qualitative differences in the work of the two races: negro girls are slower to warm up to the task, and first to drop back and lose interest: they cannot be forced or stimulated easily, except temporarily through flattery: their work is more irregular, more subject to moods, less accurate and less neat. "They are partially occupied with the task in hand and partially with a random activity, which consists in mumbling, grumbling, humming or saying original and funny things. This second attitude seems a common trait with the race unless consciously inhibited." [4]

(5) *Dependence on practise.* (a) Practise-effects within the single trial of the substitution test are revealed, of course, by comparison of the rate and accuracy of the work in the different sections or sheets into which the material is divided. With Form A or Form B the increase in speed in the 8th as over the 1st section amounts to some 10 to 20 per cent. This improvement is not acquired uniformly, however, from section to section. On the contrary, as Tables 81 and 82 show, there is a tendency toward a decrease of efficiency at about the middle of the work. Thus, in the individual tests both men and women, taken collectively, show a reduction of speed in the 5th section: similarly, in the group tests both men and women write fewer symbols in the 5th than in the 4th 30-sec. period.

In the individual tests, the 4th section comes at the bottom of the first column, the 5th at the top of the second column. The brief delay occasioned by the necessary readjustment (of paper, pencil, attention, etc.) may explain a part, but only a part of the reduction in time.

A plausible explanation is that reported by one S, who noted that, Section 4, being so far from the circles, she relied upon her memory whereas in Section 5, the very proximity of the circles tempted her glance at them to make sure of her work, and thus to work more slowly

[4]Since the above was written, Pyle (9a) has published the results of an investigation in the public schools of Missouri which discloses a similar inferiority of negroes to whites in the substitution test. Speaking in general terms, the negroes are less than half as efficient as the whites in the test.

[5]Form A has been devised especially to avoid the variation in distance of test-blanks from the pattern at different periods of the work.

To test this hypothesis, trials were made with 10 college students, using material of Form B, but rearranged (as suggested above) to resemble Form A (the test-blank in one long column sliding beneath the cardboard). The average scores, in sec., per 5-line section, were 55.7, 48.6, 44.0, 40.9, 43.0, 40.3, 41.5, and 40.8, for the Sections 1 to 8, respectively. (Total time, 354.8 sec.; symbol score, 8.2). There is, then, still a loss of more than 2 sec. at Section 5.

It would appear, therefore, either that the test-material of Section 5 happens to be more difficult than that of Sections 4 and 6, or that, as a final possibility, the slower rate in Section 5 is merely an expression of a mental condition—fatigue, weariness, loss of initial enthusiasm. That this explanation may be entertained is shown in Table 87, where it will be seen that, although more S's lose speed in the 5th than in any other section, there are, nevertheless, numerous instances of loss of speed in other portions of the work, especially in Section 7. The S's of Table 87 are the 10 just mentioned, and the 18 of Table 82.

TABLE 87

Substitution Test. Distribution of Gains and Losses in Speed (Whipple)

SECTIONS	1-2	2-3	3-4	4-5	5-6	6-7	7-8
Number gaining speed	24	17	16	9	19	12	16
Number losing speed	4	7	8	16	8	15	8
Number maintaining speed	0	4	4	3	1	1	4

(b) Special investigations upon practise in this test have been made by Starch, Lough, Kline and Miss Munn. Starch's work, which is confirmed by Miss Munn's, shows that relatively short, distributed practise periods are the most effective (Fig. 69); from 10 to 20 min. seems to be best, at least for adults. Lough found no evidence of plateaus in the curve of improvement in tests lasting from 20 to 90 days. Miss Munn found the typical curve of improvement to be rapid in rise at first, then slower. Children were slower at the start, but gained more, absolutely, than did adults. Curves from two aged S's were similar to those obtained from the young. Retrials showed that fairly strong practise-effects persisted for at least as long as 5 mos.

Kline tested the effect of practise in one form of substitution upon performance in other forms of substitution and found that "practise in writing digits for letters is transferred with favorable effect to subsequent work in writing symbols for digits, but is transferred with unfavorable effect to subsequent work

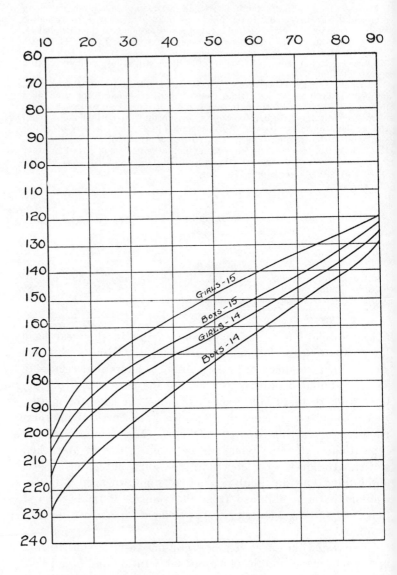

FIG. 67. PERCENTILES FOR THE SUBSTITUTION INDEX FOR CINCINNATI WORK-
ING CHILDREN 14 AND 15 YEARS OLD—SHEET 1
(After Woolley and Fischer)

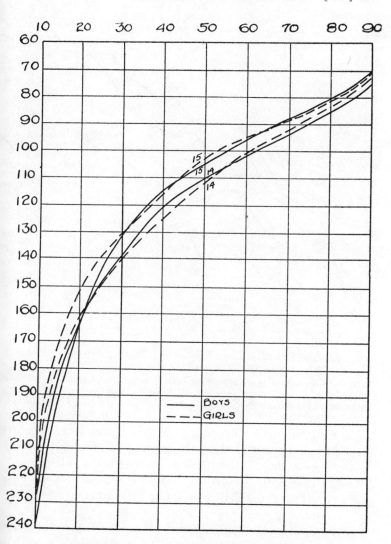

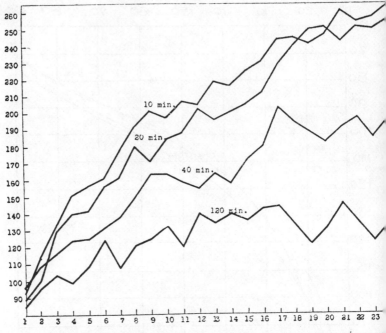

FIG. 69.   EFFECT OF PRACTISE PERIODS OF DIFFERENT LENGTHS UPON PÉRFORM-
ANCE IN THE SUBSTITUTION TEST (From Starch)

Results based on the work of 42 college students.   Units on the base
line represent number of successive 5-min. periods: ordinates represen
number of substitutions made in 5 min.   Designations attached to eac
curve indicate the length of the work periods of each group.

in writing digits for symbols."   Moreover, the more the dril
work is spread out in time, the greater, on the whole, is thi
interference effect.   Here the interference is due, of course, t
the fact that in the second test-series the same characters mus
be written as in the drill series, but with different associativ
connections.

(6) *Dependence on intelligence.*   If we admit that the scho
grade reached by children 14 or 15 years old affords a good i
dication of their general intelligence, it follows that the su
stitution test correlates well with general intelligence, sin
there was found at Cincinnati a "positive correlation wi
school grade for all four pages of the test, for both sexes, a
at both ages" (15, p. 153).   This correlation is less evident wi

the 4th (memory) sheet, where individual differences are most manifest. It follows that children who have reached higher school grades exhibit a somewhat higher performance in the memory test after having spent a decidedly shorter time in the process of learning. The above results pertain to the substitution index (Form C): as to accuracy, that is also positively correlated with school grade, though not so markedly nor so consistently as the index. Similarly, Woolley and Fischer report that some of the S's sent to them under suspicion of mental deficiency were able to attain fair success with the 4th sheet, but "required a far longer time, often more than twice the time, to reach the result" (p. 244).

The author has compared 6 dull and 5 bright grammar-school boys and obtained the results shown in Table 88. Since, with a single exception, all the dull boys are older than the bright boys—on the average about 3 years older—the actual difference in capacity between the two groups that is ascribable to intelligence is much greater than appears from the averages obtained.

TABLE 88

Substitution Test. *Bright and Dull Boys. Form B. Individual Method* (Whipple)

	BOY	AGE	SCHOOL GRADE	TIME IN SEC.	SYMBOL SCORE
Dull Group	H.	16:9	7, II	700	6
	K.	13:1	5, II	742	8
	N.	14:9	6, I	422	9
	M.	12:8	6, I	975	1
	B.	12:6	7, II	707	4
	S.	15:2	6, I	660	9
Average		14:2		701	6.17
Bright Group	Br.	11:11	8, I	677	9
	Hu.	12:8	6, II	597	5
	Id.	10:9	6, II	566	9
	Tr.	10:4	6, II	648	4
	Fe.	10:8	6, II	591	9
Average		11:1		615:8	7.2

(7) *Dependence on physical condition.* Miss Kohnky used the Cincinnati substitution test among other tests with pupils of two 5th grade classes in that city in her study of the effects of dental treatment upon physical and mental efficiency. The test was given in October to pupils in Room 18 and Room 21, two comparable groups. The pupils in Room 21 were then given elaborate dental treatment, those in Room 18 were given none. Both groups were retested in the following May. The score for the untreated room was 201.6 for the 1st sheet in October and 110.5 for the 4th sheet in May, a total gain of 91.1: the score for the treated room was 206.6 for the 1st sheet in October and 104.9 for the 4th sheet in May, a gain of 101.6, from which it is argued that the pupils subject to dental treatment developed greater 'learning power.'

(8) *Delinquents.* Miss Weidensall tested 88 Bedford Reformatory women and also a group of Vassar College dormitory maids with the material of Form C. She found that the various reformatory groups differed more from one another in speed than in accuracy, that both the college maids and the reformatory women differed from the Cincinnati working girls more widely on Sheet 1 and Sheet 4 than on Sheets 2 and 3, from which it may be inferred that the working girls make a quicker adjustment to the task and reach a higher accomplishment in distinctly less time. The work with the first and fourth pages divided the reformatory women into two distinct groups which correspond with, and confirm the school's estimate of their intelligence: thus, when the women are divided into two groups, 55 per cent. of the below-grade (schooling less than Grade 5B) are as poor in index of substitution for Sheet 4 as the poorest quarter of the grade group. Again. when the women are divided into smaller groups on the basis of years of schooling, there appears a positive correlation with amount of schooling that is as close as that found at Cincinnati. Reformatory women that had reached the 8th grade in schools were better than 15-year-old Cincinnati working girls in both accuracy and time on Sheet 4, but elsewhere the reformatory women were quite generally inferior to the working girls, and the inferiority becomes increasingly great as the grade at which the reformatory women

left school becomes lower. A general idea of the inferiority is given by Table 89. Finally, the correspondence between the results of the test and general ability is further indicated by a correlation of 0.48, P.E. .06, between rank on Sheet 4 and native ability as estimated by the principal of the Reformatory Industrial School.

TABLE 89

Differences, in Sec., Index of Substitution, Form C, between Bedford Hills Reformatory Women and Cincinnati Working Girls 14 and 15 Years Old (After Weidensall)

PERCENTILE	SHEET 1			SHEET 4		
	25th	50th	75th	25th	50th	75th
14 Years	−59.4	−10.5	+6.0	−184.5	−44.9	− 8.1
15 Years	−73.4	−24.5	−6.5	−195.7	−53.6	−11.3

Plus sign indicates that the Bedford group is faster, minus sign slower han the Cincinnati group with which it is compared. The order of per-centiles is here reversed from that used in the original tables: here the 75th is better than the 50th percentile.

NOTE.—*S*'s who make the fastest records commonly employ he scheme of holding in mind the entire 5-place number (in Form B), and writing down the symbols while keeping the eyes directed upon the circles. The material in Form A lends itself ess easily to this scheme.

REFERENCES

(1) B. T. Baldwin, The learning of delinquent adolescent girls as hown by a substitution test. *JEdPs*, 4: 1913, 317-332.

(2) D. F. Carpenter, Mental age tests. *JEdPs*, 4: 1913, 538-544.

(3) W. F. Dearborn, Experiments in learning. *JEdPs*, 1: 1910, 373-38.

(4) C. T. Gray, A new form of the substitution test. *JEdPs*, 4: 1913, 83-297.

(5) L. W. Kline, Some experimental evidence in regard to formal dis-pline. *JEdPs.* 5: 1914, 259-266.

(6) Emma Kohnky, Preliminary study of the effect of a dental treat-ent upon the physical and mental efficiency of school children. *JEdPs*, : 1913, 569-578.

(7) J. E. Lough, Plateaus in simple learning. *PsBu*, 9: 1912, 87-88.

(8) Abbie F. Munn, The curve of learning. *ArPs(e)*, 2: 1909, 36-52.

(9) W. H. Pyle, The examination of school children. New York, 1913. . 70, especially 18-22.

(9a)   W. H. Pyle, The mind of the negro child. *School and Society*, 1 : 1915, 357-360.

(10)   Carrie R. Squire, Graded mental tests. *JEdPs*, 3 : 1912, 363-380, 430-443, 493-506, especially 432-4.

(11)   D. Starch, Periods of work in learning. *JEdPs*, 3 : 1912, 209-213.

(12)   D. Starch, Experiments in educational psychology. New York, 1911.   Pp. 183, especially ch. 7.

(13)   Jean Weidensall, The mentality of the criminal woman.   To appear in *EdPsMon*.

(14)   R. S. Woodworth and F. L. Wells, Association tests. *PsMon*, 13 : 1911 (No. 57).   Pp. 75, especially 53-55.

(15)   Helen T. Woolley and Charlotte R. Fischer, Mental and physical measurements of working children (Studies from the laboratory of the Vocation Bureau, Cincinnati, Ohio). *PsMon*, 18 : 1914 (No. 77).   Pp. 247, especially 148-184.

TEST 38

Memory for serial impressions: 'Rote' memory.[1]—The essential idea in the several forms of memory test treated under this title is to present a series of discrete impressions (*e. g.,* letters, digits, words), which is, if possible, to be reproduced in correct order and exactly as presented.   These tests are to be contrasted with the so-called tests of 'logical' memory, in which the material presented is a logically connected whole, and in which the requirement is to reproduce the substance, or the meaning, of what has been presented.   In either test, the reproduction may be immediate or delayed, and the mode of presentation and method of measuring efficiency may be varied in many ways.

Memory for a series of discrete impressions has been used to study individual differences, as conditioned by sex, age, mental ability; to detect fatigue; to investigate the nature of practise, the possibility of training retention and recall, the most economical methods of learning, etc.

To understand the results and conclusions of the small army of investigators of memory, it is convenient to classify the methods and the materials that have been most commonly used.[2]

[1] The author desires to acknowledge the assistance of Dr. L. R. Geissler in the collation and sifting of the literature bearing upon this test.

[2] For more extended discussion of the historical development of the several experimental methods, together with accounts of the results that have been attained, the reader should consult Bentley, Binet (9), Burnham, Ebbinghaus, Gamble, Henri, Offner and Pohlmann.   The last-named gives a particularly valuable summary of the methods.

CLASSIFICATION OF METHODS FOR MEMORY TESTS

(1)   The *method of complete memorization*, or method of complete mastery (*Erlernungsmethode*), developed in the classic work of Ebbinghaus (*Ueber das Gedächtnis*) in 1885, and refined by Müller and Schumann, demands that S repeat the series of impressions again and again until he can reproduce it without error, without hesitation, and with certainty of correctness. Efficiency is measured by the number of presentations required for this complete learning.

In practise, this method is frequently supplemented by testing the number of presentations of the same series that is needed to relearn it at any assigned time after the first learning (*Ersparnisverfahren* or *Ersparnismethode*), in which case the saving in number of repetitions in the relearning, as compared with the learning, measures the amount of retention, or the degree to which the first impression has persisted.

(2)   The *memory-span method* (*Methode der Gedächtnis-Spanne*), first devised by Jacobs, elaborated by Ebert and Meumann, and extensively used in England and America, consists in the determination of the maximal length of a series of impressions that can be reproduced with a given degree of accuracy (usually complete accuracy) after a given number of presentations (usually, though not necessarily, one presentation).   Ordinarily, E begins with a series that is easily within S's limit, and increases the length of the series, keeping other factors constant, until errors appear.

(3)   The *method of retained members* (*Methode der behaltenen Glieder*), first so designated by Ebbinghaus, but more carefully studied by Pohlmann, consists in the determination of the degree of mastery (proportion of elements correctly reproduced) of a series of a given length, after a given number of repetitions.   The method is somewhat like the span method, but the length of the series is so chosen that S cannot attain complete mastery.   In practise, many span tests actually become tests of degree of mastery.

(4)   The *method of right associates* (*Treffermethode*), proposed by Jost and developed by Müller and Pilzecker, consists in presenting a series of impressions (typically, nonsense syllables in trochaic rhythm), and of subsequently testing S's ability to name the member that follows any given member.   Usually the accented member is given, and S tries to designate the 'right associate' for it.   (When his time of response is measured, the method is known, in full, as the *Treffer- und Zeitmethode*).   Its special value is to afford opportunity for analyzing the nature of the associative connections; it has not been proposed as a test of efficiency.

(5)   The *method of prompting* (*Methode der Hilfen*), somewhat similarly, tests the nature and strength of the individual associative connections in the series, and is of questionable usefulness for practical testing. As illustrated in the work of Ephrussi, the method consists in an attempt by S to reproduce the series before it has been fully learned, and in promptings by E at each point of hesitation or error.   Efficiency is inversely related to the number of promptings required.

(6)   The *method of interference of associations* is exemplified in Bergström's study of card-sorting (5).   Here 80 cards are sorted by E into 10 piles, and subsequently, at a given interval, into another 10 piles differently arranged.   The second sorting is slower because of the persistence of associative connections developed in the first trial.   Analogous tests can be fashioned with other forms of material, as has been suggested in the Substitution Test.

(7)   The *method of reconstruction*, used by Münsterberg and Bigham with colors, and by Miss Gamble with odors, consists in presenting a series of stimuli in a definite order, and then, after a predetermined interval, in presenting the same stimuli in chance order. *S* attempts to rearrange them in the original order.

(8)   The *method of recognition* consists in the presentation of a limited number of impressions, which are subsequently presented again, in conjunction with other stimuli, to see how many of the first series *S* can recognize in the second series. Examples will be found in the work of Smith and of Henri.

(9)   The *method of identical series*, as employed by Reuther is a modification of the method of recognition, in which the original series is always actually presented intact, though, of course, this fact is concealed from *S*.

(10)   The *method of continuous lists* (*Methode des fortlaufenden Niederschreibens oder Aufzählens*), employed by Kræpelin, is identical with the procedure described in Test 33, though sometimes *S* is required to write words that belong to specified categories.

(11)   The *method of chance verbal reactions* (*Methode der zufälligen Wortreactionen*), well illustrated by the investigations of Aschaffenburg and G. E. Müller, is the stock association experiment, with emphasis upon the qualitative as well as the quantitative study of the associative sequences. (See Test 33A.)

(12)   The *method of description or report* (*Aussage*) is a form of memory investigation with peculiar problems of its own, as has been shown in Test 32. In it, the terms in which the reproduction takes place are not restricted to a direct equivalence with the material presented, but are merely indicative or descriptive of this material.

The tests which follow are primarily intended to test capacity for immediate reproduction after a single presentation, either by the memory-span method or by the method of retained members (degree of mastery). The capacity which is tested corresponds to what the Germans call *Merkfähigkeit*—a term which is perhaps best rendered in English as *immediate memory.* Tests of capacity to recall or to recognize after an interval of greater or less duration would doubtless more nearly measure memory in the more exact sense of that term, but, unfortunately, little attention has been paid to this phase of mental testing, owing presumably to the desire to complete observations in a single sitting.

CLASSIFICATION OF MATERIAL FOR MEMORY TESTS

The material used in tests of serial memory may be classed according to the sense-department to which it is presented (visual, auditory, visual-auditory, etc.), and according to it nature or form. Again, visual material of different forms may be presented either simultaneously or successively.

(1) *Actual objects* were used by Netschajeff, Lobsien and Kirkpatrick. Thus, Lobsien showed 9 objects at the rate of 1 per sec., *e. g.*, newspaper, key, handkerchief, glass, slate, box, book, glove, chalk. Netschajeff used 12, Kirkpatrick 10 objects.

(2) *Pictures of objects*, 10 in number, were used by Miss Calkins; groups of 20 pictures by Mrs. Squire and by Carpenter, following the suggestion of the earlier Binet-Simon tests.

(3) *Sentences* also form a portion of the Binet-Simon tests, and have been tried by Ritter, Miss Sharp, Mrs. Squire, Carpenter and Abelson. Directions for their use will be found below.

(4) *Words* may be used in the most varied kinds of series. Thus, series of Latin-German, or English-German, or other pairs of nouns, have been used to produce a 'vocabulary' form of test, as by Wessely. A distinction may be made between 'related' or 'associable' terms and 'unrelated' or 'dissociable' terms (Norsworthy: Bergström, 6). For example, *paper, writing, compose,* etc., *vs. horse, bricks, soldier, acorns,* etc. Meumann (51), Burt (16) and Pyle have compared the span (3 to 8-term series) for concrete nouns, *e. g., stove, ink, lamp, street,* etc., with the span for abstract nouns, *e. g., influence,* etc. Netschajeff and Lobsien tested the relative reproducibility of words (12 and 9-term series) that connoted visual, auditory, tactual and emotional ideas, respectively. (Examples: *lightning, dial, sunbeam; thunder, crash, whistle; cold, soft, smooth; hope, doubt, regret.*) Kirkpatrick and Calkins also used 10-term series of words that related to objects, as did Pohlmann. Hawkins compared simultaneous and successive exposure of 15 nouns. Binet, Ritter, Simpson, Abelson, Lapie and Sharp also employed lists of words of varied length and complexity.

(5) *Nonsense syllables* were tried but discarded by Jacobs, likewise by Cohn and Dieffenbacher. They formed, however, the stock material in Ebbinghaus' pioneer work, and were subsequently made more serviceable by the precise rules that Müller and Schumann formulated for their construction. Bergström, Burt, Smith, Müller and Pilzecker, Pohlmann, van Biervliet, and others have found them of value: indeed, Pohlmann contends that, on account of their equivalence one to another and their relative freedom from varying associations in different *S*'s, nonsense syllables form the best and most reliable material for memory tests. Series specially adapted for English readers will be found in Test 25.

(6) *Letters* (usually consonants only, to avoid the formation of syllables or words) have been used by Jacobs, Binet (8), Cohn, Pohlmann, Sharp, Finzi, Smith (71, 73), and Winch (80). An idea of the great variety of procedure that may be developed with a single form of material may be gained by noting that Binet used 15 consonants exposed visually and simultaneously, for 20 sec.; Cohn exposed 12 consonants arranged in the form of a square for 25 sec.; Pohlmann read 10 consonants to his *S*'s 3 times over; Sharp exposed 12 letters successively with the Jastrow drop-apparatus, at the rate of 1 per sec., and repeated until the series was learned; Smith exposed 12 consonants simultaneously for 10 sec., and read other series of 4, 5, 6, 7, and 9-term consonants; Winch repeated 12 consonants auditorily in 25 sec., and also used the letter-square method (described below), as did Wyatt and Anderson.

(7) *Two-place numbers*, administered orally, were used by Schuyten (8 numbers repeated by *S*'s in concert), Lobsien (9 numbers), Pohlmann (10 numbers given three times), and Netschajeff (12 numbers).

(8) *Digits*,[3] *i. e.*, one-place numbers, have been employed by Jacobs, Johnson, Bolton, Binet, Ebbinghaus, Hawkins, Ritter, Chambers, Kohnky, Lapie, Sharp, Smedley, Krueger and Spearman, Wissler, and many others, in the most varied manner (4 to 10-place series, given auditorily, visually —either simultaneously or successively—or in combined appeal to vision and audition, to vision, audition and 'hand' memory, or to vision, audition, and 'articulatory' memory). Abelson appears to be the only investigator to have discarded digits as inappropriate for mental tests.

(9) *Geometrical drawings* have been used by Münsterberg and Bigham, and by Bernstein and Bogdanoff, who selected forms that would be unfamiliar to their *S*'s.

(10) *Lines* of varied lengths have been employed by Toulouse and by Binet (9).

(11) *Miscellaneous visual characters*, symbols, combinations of dots, lines, etc., formed a portion of the material in the investigation of Ebert and Meumann.

(12) *Sounds*, such as those produced by tearing paper, whistling, stamping, ringing a bell, etc., were arranged in 9-element series by Lobsien, and in 12-element series by Netschajeff.

(13) *Memory for commissions* forms a well-known part of the Binet-Simon tests. An extension of this idea into a sort of memory-span test of memory for commissions has been used by Abelson in the study of backward children.

Aside from these wide differences in general method and in form of material, attention should be called to differences in rate or tempo at which the series is first presented, to differences in the number of times the series is presented, and to differences in the time-interval elapsing between presentation and reproduction.

As a rule, the rate of presentation has been not slower than 1 impression in 2 sec., and not faster than 2 impressions in 1 sec. A rate of 1 impression in 0.75 sec. has been found well adapted for adults.

The typical span test is one in which the series is presented but once from the point of view of functional testing, therefore, the repetition of the stimulus series may be regarded as a variant method, not to be introduced save for the special purpose of studying its effect.

Similarly, as has already been said, the greater portion of the tests here reported have been made with no interval between presentation and reproduction. It is to be noted, however, that Smedley, in his tests of Chicago school children, separated presentation and reproduction by an interval of 5 sec. Wyatt caused his *S*'s to count backward from 20 before writing

---

[3]Reuther has formulated rules for the construction of test-series of digits, analogous to the rules of Müller and Schumann for test-series of nonsense syllables. The following are the most important of Reuther' principles: (1) Do not repeat a digit in the same series (impossible to avoid, of course, in 10-place series). (2) Do not begin a series with the number 1. (3) Avoid the use of zero. (4) Do not place any two digits in their natural relations with one another. (5) Do not use sequences that suggest historical dates. (6) Do not use in immediate succession two series that have the same digit in the same place at any point in the series.

nonsense syllables and introduced an interval of 5 sec. in his tests with letter-squares. Kirkpatrick, and Calkins in her repetition of his tests, secured a reproduction both immediately after, and 3 days after the presentation, in order to contrast 'immediate' with 'delayed' memory or recall. Somewhat similarly, Binet, and Sharp in her repetition of his tests, secured a reproduction of each of seven 7-place word-lists directly after its presentation, and a 'recapitulation,' in so far as it was possible, of the 49 terms at the close of the whole test, *i. e.*, about 3 min. after the first presentation. Binet contrasts, in this way, immediate memory with what he terms 'memory of conservation.'

Since, as the results that follow show, even minor variations in the conduct of a memory test affect its outcome, it follows that the results of different investigators may not be expected to exhibit complete accordance with respect to the relative influence of sex, age, mental ability, etc.

Five chief forms of test have been selected and are recommended as standard for this field of investigation; variant methods are suggested in each case. By reference to the classification of methods and materials just given, *E* can devise furher modifications to suit special requirements. These five forms are (1) tests with digits, resembling in scope Smedey's Chicago tests, but with several differences in procedure, (2) tests with letters, after Cohn's method, (3) tests with lists of words, after the methods of Meumann and of Burt, (4) tests with sentences of graded difficulty, and (5) tests with pictures of objects.

A.   MEMORY SPAN FOR DIGITS

MATERIALS.—Printed test-cards, 42 in number, arranged in hree sets of 14 cards each, for presentation by 3 different nethods. (Each set contains 2 cards each of 4, 5, 6, 7, 8, 9, nd 10 digits.) Metronome. [For serial visual exposure, in ddition, Jastrow's memory apparatus (Fig. 70). Cardboard. Villson's gummed figures, black, Size 5. For letter tests, full ts of gummed letters, Sizes 5 and 10.]

PRELIMINARIES.—On the back of each card write the digits hat are printed on its face: this enables *E*, when the test deands it, to pronounce the test numbers while displaying the rd to *S*. The purely auditory and the auditory-visual-handotor series are not included in the printed cards, but should prepared by *E*, preferably, for convenience, on a single piece cardboard, the size of the printed cards. For the auditory ries, use the following numbers, in the order given: 6135,

2947, 36814, 57296, 241637, 935816, 8537142, 9412837, 47293815, 71836245, 924738615, 475296318, 8697132504, 2146073859. For the visual-auditory-hand-motor series, use these numbers, reversed, *e. g.*, 5316, etc.

METHOD.—If only a single test can be made, employ the visual-auditory-articulatory form of presentation, since this is most likely to produce uniform conditions of ideational imagery for all S's. But if the tests can be taken in full, follow the order of presentation outlined herewith.[4] In any event, preface each form of presentation with a special, short sample-series, without demanding reproduction, in order that S may be perfectly clear as to the nature of the test. Within each form of test, also, preface each presentation with a statement of the number of members in the coming series, *e. g.*: "This will be a series of 5 digits." The metronome should be set at 60, *i. e.*, one stroke per sec., for all tests.[5]

(1) *Auditory presentation.* Explain the test by a simple illustrative series. Require S to close his lips firmly, and to press his tongue against the roof of his mouth—this to reduce the tendency to articulation, and in group tests (all of the memory tests lend themselves well to group presentation) to avert communication between S's. Start the metronome.[6] Pronounce the digits, one at a time, with the utmost care to ensure

---

[4] It goes without explanation that the longer series may be omitted with very young, the shorter with mature S's. Use, for the shortest series, one that is easily within the span of the poorest S to be tested, for the longest series, one that is too difficult for the best S to reproduce without error.

[5] It may be well at this place to point out the differences between this procedure and that followed by Smedley at Chicago. Smedley used no series longer than 8. He gave no warning of the length of the coming series. He set the metronome at 90. He did not present the several series in regular order, but irregularly, though beginning with an easy series. He inserted an interval of 5 sec. between presentation and reproduction. He distributed his tests, seven in all, at hourly intervals. Finally, he gives no clear statement of his method of computing results, save that the "percentage correctly recorded constituted the grade."

[6] If he finds it necessary, E may substitute a silent metronome, made by swinging a small weight on a string, but the fact that the regular metronome is somewhat noisy should not be taken as evidence that it disturbs S; on the contrary, a noise of moderate intensity is not infrequently found to be a stimulus to better attention. Moreover, the ticking metronome is much more serviceable when S is asked to pronounce the digits in conjunction with E, and it probably operates to some extent to break up tendencies to learn the digits by grouping.

even tempo, clear articulation, and entire absence of rhythm.[7] Directly at the conclusion of the series, let S repeat as much as possible of it. Although, under some circumstances (with very young or backward S's), an oral reproduction may be imperative, a written reproduction should be considered standard, both because the proper placing of the digits furnishes E with data for scoring S's performance (and the placing must indicate possible omissions), and because experiment shows that, at least for maturer S's, written reproduction is preferred, and is more successful than oral reproduction. S's recall should, therefore, be entered upon a prepared blank, with the caution to indicate every omission by a dash or a blank space.[8]

(2) *Visual presentation.* Use Cards V-4a, V-4b, etc., to V-10b. Follow the directions for auditory presentation, but in place of pronunciation, exhibit the entire card for a length of time identical with that for auditory presentation, *i. e.*, with an allowance of 1 sec. per digit. The metronome should be used here, as in all phases of this test, in order to keep the conditions of presentation comparable. It probably also tends to induce S's to apprehend the digits successively and in the same tempo as that used for auditory presentation. Note to what extent S articulates the digits: even with lips and tongue placed as directed, they will often be seen to move, and contractions of throat muscles may also indicate partial articulation.

---

[7]The difficulty of speaking without accent, or without grouping the digits, has led Binet to reject oral, in favor of visual presentation. Even if E pronounces without accent or rhythm, there is no guarantee that S may not mentally cast the digits into a strongly accented and grouped series, and, in fact, mature S's, working with the longer series, are almost certain to catch this 'trick' in time. Ritter advocates that E should give a decided objective rhythm to every series on just this account; this factor will then form a constant, rather than a variable 'error.' One difficulty with this plan lies in the fact that, in using series of varying lengths, it is impossible to use any constant metrical phrasing.

[8]For group work, the class should be provided with blank forms, so numbered and arranged that no misunderstandings may occur on the part of S in entering the data, or on the part of E in interpreting it. Allow ample time for writing. Netschajeff, Pohlmann and Schuyten all found 2 min. desirable in classroom tests. In group tests, care must be taken to prevent audible repetition of the digits during the reproduction.

(3) *Auditory-visual presentation.* *E* presents the cards, as in the purely visual procedure, but also pronounces the digits, as in the auditory procedure, by reading them from the back of the card. *S* sees and hears the digits. Cards AV-4a to AV-10b are used.

(4) *Auditory-visual-articulatory presentation.* *E* presents the cards as in (2). *E* and *S* pronounce them in concert, in time with the metronome. *S* sees, hears, and pronounces the digits. Cards AVA-4a to AVA-10b are used.

(5) *Auditory-visual-hand-motor presentation.* *E* pronounces the digits as in (1) : *S* writes them, as fast as pronounced by *E*, upon scrap paper: when the series is finished, *S* at once discards the scrap paper, and reproduces the series. *S* hears, sees, and writes the digits. Use the same numbers as in (1), but reverse the order of the digits. In this test, it will ordinarily be necessary to devote one or two preliminary trials to fore-exercise.

VARIATIONS OF METHOD.—(1) Meet the bothersome tendency toward grouping and rhythmizing—bothersome because exhibited by some *S*'s and not by others—by presenting the digits in trochaic rhythm: this device is perhaps favored by selecting series of 4, 6, 8, and 10 digits only.

(2) Introduce a time-interval between presentation and reproduction. If this interval is short, it may with advantage be occupied with some form of distraction, like saying the alphabet in concert, since the effect will be more like that of a much longer 'empty' interval. The disadvantage of an unoccupied interval is that some *S*'s will mentally rehearse the series just presented.

(3) Substitute successive for simultaneous visual presentation in Forms 2, 3, and 4. For this purpose, *E* must prepare cards for insertion in the Jastrow memory apparatus,[9] so that

---

[9] Jastrow's instrument is adequate if *E* is careful to make the exposures regularly, in time with the metronome; it is especially useful for group tests. If *E* desires a more accurate exposure apparatus, for individual tests, he may employ the Ranschburg memory-apparatus (now improved by Wirth), Kuhlmann's memory-apparatus, Bergström's rather elaborate exposure apparatus, or G. E. Müller's modification of the kymograph for 'step-fashion' exposure, as described, in improved form, by McDougall. Burt, however, contends that the distraction produced in immature and inexperienced *S*'s by the sight of unfamiliar apparatus more than counterbalances the advantage of greater precision, mechanical regulation of rate

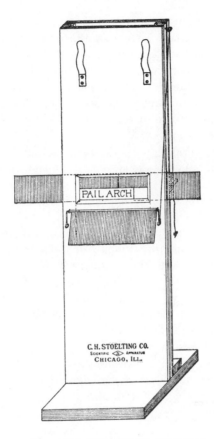

FIG. 70.—JASTROW'S MEMORY APPARATUS.

the numbers used in Forms 2, 3, and 4 (above) may now be exposed in vertical columns. In order to secure sufficiently long series, the exposure-lever of the instrument is so inserted

---

and duration of exposure, etc.; he used, for successive exposure, a slotted piece of cardboard, which was shoved along the column of impressions by E (apparently at no uniform or constant rate, but as fast as proved convenient to S).

Kuhlman arranges to have each exposure followed by a blank section of perhaps a different duration from that of the exposure. The idea is to control the amount of time that S can spend in re-imaging or recalling the impression just received. According to Kuhlmann, S's use from one-half to two-thirds of the total time at their command in ordinary presentations of material for memory tests (whether simultaneous or successive) in this process of re-imaging. The importance of the process, he thinks, varies much with individuals.

as to articulate with the pegs that provide a drop of 1 in. at each exposure. Black letters $\frac{7}{8}$ in. high (Willson's, Size 5) may then be used. These are visible to the normal eye at 50 ft., but E should take the precaution, in classroom tests, to seat myopic S's near the front of the room.

(4) Test the effect, upon a series too long for S to reproduce in one presentation, of two, three, or more presentations in immediate succession.

(5) Give repeated tests by the same method, with a series of a given length (in excess of S's span), to test the effect of practise.

(6) Change the rate of exposure from one impression per sec. to one impression in 2 sec.

(7) Keeping other conditions (form of presentation, length of series, etc.) constant, compare S's efficiency under normal conditions with that under different forms of distraction. Smith (71) used for this purpose three different concomitant activities: his S's were required during the presentation (a) to tap in time with the beat of a metronome, (b) to repeat the syllable *la,* or (c) to add mentally by 2's or by 3's.

(8) Prepare cards with letters[10] in place of digits, for use by any of the procedures above described. Use only consonants. Avoid alphabetical sequences, or suggestions of words or abbreviations.

TREATMENT OF DATA.—(1) If it is desired only to determine S's memory span, *sensu stricto,* this is indicated simply by the maximal number of digits that can be reproduced without error of any kind.

(2) If, as is more usual in comparative tests, it is desired to determine the degree of correctness with which series longer than the span are reproduced, the simplest plan is to assign arbitrary scores to the various forms of error. Ebbinghaus, for example, scored every omission as 1 error, every displacement from the correct position in the series by 2 or 3 places as 0.5 error, and every displacement by 4 or more places as 1

---

[10]Use Willson's black gummed letters, Size 5, for the Jastrow apparatus, or Size 10 to duplicate the regular printed test-cards.

error. S's should then be compared with respect to their error-score in series of each length separately.

(3) A more scientific method of determining efficiency is that of computing the degree of correlation between the order of impressions as reproduced by S and their order as presented. This is accomplished, following the example of Krueger and Spearman, by applying Spearman's 'footrule' formula for correlation (see Ch. III), though, in this connection, it is better to modify this formula by counting the sum of *all* the deviations between the two series, rather than the sum of all the positive, or of all of the negative deviations.

For treating the data of these memory tests, therefore, the formula may be written :

$$R = 1 - \frac{\Sigma d}{(n^2 - 1)/3}$$

The computation of Σd needs a little explanation. The following cases may be considered :[11]

(a) Suppose that S reproduces all the terms of the original series, but not in the correct order. The sum of the deviations is then easily computed. In Case A, Table 90, for instance, the sum of the deviations is 6, and since $n = 10$, by the formula just given, $R = 0.82$.

TABLE 90

Use of the 'Footrule' Method in Scoring the Memory Test (Spearman)

ORIGINAL SERIES	CASE A		CASE B		CASE C	
	Reproduced	Deviations	Reproduced	Deviations	Reproduced	Deviations
3	3	0	3	0	3	0
7	7	0	7	0	7	0
9	2	2	–	?	2	2
4	9	1	9	1	9	1
2	4	1	4	1	4	1
1	1	0	1	0	2	?
0	0	0	–	?	0	0
8	5	1	–	?	5	1
5	8	1	8	1	8	1
6	6	0	6	0	6	0
Sum of deviations		6		12.9		9.3

---

[11]The author is indebted for these illustrations to a personal communication from Professor Spearman.

(b) Suppose, Case B, that certain terms have been omitted. The deviations of the terms given are figured as before. There is then added the amount of deviation to be expected for the omitted terms, on the assumption that they are distributed by mere chance. The chance deviation for each term is $(n^2-1) \div 3n$. In Case B, then, there are three omitted terms, each of which deviates by chance 3.3 places. Hence, the Case C, the total deviation $= 6 + 3.3 = 9.3$.

(c) Suppose that S reproduces certain terms more than once, e. g., the digit 2 in Case C. In this case, the nearer of the two digits is considered as the correct one. The other, or duplicated, term should be regarded as an omission, and treated by the formula just given. Thus, in Case C, the total deviation $= 6 + 3.3 = 9.3$.

(d) Suppose that more than the correct number of terms are reproduced: here the superfluous numbers may be ignored, since, save in exceptional cases, they bring about their own penalty by disturbing the correspondence of order.

B.   THE METHOD OF LETTER SQUARES

The idea of displaying simultaneously a series of consonants in a simple spatial pattern appears first to have been suggested by Binet and Henri (11) : the method was extended by Cohn, who used it to compare the relative values, for a given S, of visual and of auditory-motor learning; and it has since been frequently used with modifications (see, for example, Titchener, 77, 396 ff.) as a method of studying ideational types. Winch used the method to compare immediate with delayed reproduction, Smith to compare various forms of distraction, Anderson and Winch to note the relation to sex and age, Wyatt to compare with school standing.

MATERIALS.—A set of 10 printed test-cards. Prepared forms upon which the reproduction is entered. Stop-watch. [The letter-square cards are printed in large type to make the test available for group procedure. The arrangements avoid, so far as can be foreseen, the use of collocations that might serve as aids to memory. Only consonants are used. The blank forms are ruled in sets of 12 squares.]

METHOD.—Explain to S the general nature of the test. Inform him of the duration of exposure, but give him no directions as to how he shall attempt to learn the arrangement of the letters. Expose the stimulus card for 25 sec. Let him fill out the blank form immediately after the exposure. Allow 30 sec. for writing. Repeat with other cards, until 4 to 10 trials have been made.

VARIATIONS OF METHOD.—(1) Defer the reproduction for 20 sec. (or 10 sec., to follow Cohn) after the exposure. Direct S to count aloud during this interval, from 1 to 20, 1 number per sec., in time with E (who may follow a silent metronome swinging once per sec.). The object is to subdue or eliminate the 'memory after-image,' and to secure true recall—in the strict sense of recalling an experience which had not been just previously in consciousness.

(2) Direct S to read the letters aloud, twice over, in concert with E, at the rate of 1 letter per sec. Read by horizontal lines. Reproduce with or without the 20 sec. interval.

(3) Direct S to repeat aloud, continuously and rapidly, during the exposure, the syllable 'Ah.' Reproduce preferably after the 20 sec. interval filled with the counting. This form of procedure obviously favors the visual memory. If more than one trial is made, use other syllables, such as 'La,' 'Oh,' etc., to avoid the lapse of articulation to automatism.

(4) Direct S to count aloud by 2's during the exposure (e. g., 2, 4, 6, or 3, 5, 7, etc.) or to count backwards from 20.

(5) After exposure by any of the methods just outlined, point to one square after another of the blank forms, in irregular order, asking S to name or to write the appropriate letters as rapidly as possible. Or, without previous warning, ask S to fill in the blank squares in vertical rows, or in horizontal rows from right to left. In theory, visual-minded S's can accomplish this without effort, whereas purely auditory-minded S's must retrace their verbal associations to find the necessary letters.

TREATMENT OF DATA.—(1) Following Winch, assign 3 for each letter in its right position, 2 for each letter one remove to the right, or left, or above, or below its right position, 1 for each letter two removes to the right, or left, or above, or below.[12]

---

[12]This method of scoring possibly puts somewhat too much stress upon right position; at least, in cases like the letter L in the specimen it may be felt that it should not go without credit because it is both in the wrong row and in the wrong column. However, the method above described is the one that has been followed by all who have worked with letter-squares as a mental test.

Specimen of test given				*Specimen of a marked paper*			
M	T	D	X	M(3)	T(3)	L(0)	R(1)
V	L	Y	N	L(2)	V(2)	Y(3)	N(3)
S	Z	B	R	Z(2)	B(2)	S(1)	X(1)

Score: 23 out of a possible 36.

(2) If *S* be competent to render introspective accounts of the manner in which each letter was recalled and placed, *E* may, for qualitative purposes, compute separately the score for letters recalled visually, auditorily, or in other ways.

C.   MEMORY FOR CONCRETE AND FOR ABSTRACT WORDS

The essential idea of this test of memory, as devised by Meumann, and followed, with some modifications, by Burt and by Pyle, is to compare *S*'s reproduction of a list of concrete, with his reproduction of a list of abstract terms, given under identical conditions. The comparison is based not only upon the simple quantitative efficiency in the two forms of test, but also, and more particularly, upon the qualitative analysis of the errors in the reproduced lists. Moreover, the test aims to determine not only *S*'s capacity for immediate memory, but also his degree of intelligence, or grade of mental development. The test rests in principle upon two propositions; first, that words whose meaning is understood are more easily retained and reproduced than words whose meaning is not understood; secondly, that progressive mental development implies progressive comprehension of abstract words.

MATERIAL.—For auditory presentation, use the following lists. For visual-auditory presentation, use the same lists printed upon sheets of cardboard with Willson's gummed letters. For visual presentation, serial exposure with the aid of the Jastrow or other exposure apparatus is recommended.

Three-term lists		*Four-term lists*		*Five-term lists*	
Concrete	*Abstract*	*Concrete*	*Abstract*	*Concrete*	*Abstract*
Street	Time	Spoon	Phase	Ground	Tact
Ink	Art	Horse	Work	Pen	Scope
Lamp	Route	Chair	Truth	Clock	Proof
		Stone	Thing	Boy	Scheme
				Chalk	Form

Six-term lists		Seven-term lists		Eight-term lists	
Concrete	Abstract	Concrete	Abstract	Concrete	Abstract
Desk	Space	Ball	Craft	Coat	Law
Milk	Creed	Sponge	Myth	Girl	Thought
Hand	Pride	Glass	Rate	House	Plot
Card	Guile	Hat	Cause	Salt	Glee
Floor	Pledge	Fork	Style	Glove	Life
Cat	Cue	Stove	Youth	Watch	Rhythm
		Post	Mood	Box	Faith
				Mat	Mirth

The above lists are prepared with the idea of confining the abstract terms to words of one syllable, as done by Burt and by Pyle (whose lists are quite similar to the above). This restriction materially lessens the difference in difficulty between the concrete and abstract lists. To duplicate Meumann's conditions the following abstract lists may be substituted for those given above:

Four-term list	Five-term list	Six-term list	Seven-term list
Selection	Society	Conscience	Assumption
Analysis	Symbol	Investigation	Recognition
Explanation	Arrangement	Symptom	Origin
Character	Humanity	Formation	Influence
	Theory	Complexity	Development
		Experiment	Organism
			Value

Eight-term list
Behavior
Tendency
Interpretation
Condition
Opinion
Capacity
Profession
Connection

METHOD.—For group tests, follow Meumann's procedure. Explain the nature of the test and give a sample exercise. Provide each S with blanks so arranged that his reproductions may be properly recorded, the lists carefully separated, and dashes inserted for all words omitted. Make clear that the lists are to preserve the order of presentation so far as possible. Before each presentation, notify the S's of the number of words to be spoken. Enunciate with great care, and without grouping, at the rate of one word per sec. Instruct the S's to write their lists immediately after the presentation, and as rapidly as possible, without trying to 'write their very best.' Guard against interruption, intercommunication, or other possible disturbances. Give the series in order, as above, *i. e.*, 3-term concrete, 3-term abstract, 4-term concrete, etc., save for mature *S*'s, for whom the beginning is to be made at the shortest list that all can accomplish, and for whom lists of more than 8 terms may be arranged by combining some of the shorter unused lists.

VARIATIONS OF METHOD.—Consult suggestions for the memory span for digits (Variations of Method, 2 to 7).

TREATMENT OF DATA.—(1) The simplest method is to disregard the question of order and simply to credit *S* one for each word correctly recalled. This scoring was used by Simpson with lists of 16 words, but is not recommended by him on account of its failure to penalize for erroneous insertions.

(2) Another very simple device is that adopted by Pyle of crediting one for each word correctly reproduced, plus one more for each word placed in the right order. It is evident that this scoring is not specific enough to deal adequately with the various possibilities of insertion, substitution, transposition, etc.

(3) Memory for words may be scored by any one of the three methods already proposed for memory span (Treatment of Data).

(4) The second method proposed for the memory span (arbitrary scores for various forms of error) is followed in principle by Burt in his special system of scoring memory for words: each correct word correctly placed counts 4; each correct word misplaced by one move counts 3; each correct word misplaced by more than one move counts 2; omissions or substitutions count 0. Other rules which he followed concern words with slight alterations; these, in the author's judgment, are not important enough to justify their use unless nonsense syllables are used.

(5) A very elaborate analysis of memory for words was employed by Meumann. For a careful scrutiny of the performance in this test *E* may prefer to adopt such a method, following as

a suggestive pattern the schema below, which has been transcribed from Meumann with a few minor modifications.

ILLUSTRATION OF THE TREATMENT OF DATA IN MEMORY FOR WORDS

Subject: Adolph L. Age, 8 years.

	Types of Error	Number
1.	Memory errors (omissions and displacements) concrete lists.	5⅔
2.	Memory errors (omissions and displacements), abstract lists..	7⅓
3.	Insertions......	4
4.	Insertions of nonsense words......	1
5.	Fusions......	0
6.	Perseverations......	3
7.	Regressive inhibitions......	1
8.	Complete reversals......	1
9.	Substitution of synonyms......	0
10.	Substitution of concrete for abstract......	1
11.	Wrong formations......	4
12.	Misunderstood abstract terms......	5
13.	Spelling......Very bad
14.	Handwriting......Undeveloped and ugly

(1) and (2) *Omissions* are represented by the integers, *i. e.*, Adolph L. omitted five words from the concrete lists. 7 from the abstract (the test was carried to the 7-term list only). *Displacements* from the correct order count ⅓ error when the displacement is by one remove only, ⅔ error, when more than one remove (save that with younger children, as in the case above, all displacements count ⅓.) Hence Adolph L. made 2 displacements in the concrete, 7 in the abstract series.

(3) *Insertions* are the total number of words added. These are counted as 1 error each, unless the added word has some similarity of sound to a word actually presented, in which case it counts ⅔ error.

(4) This rubric embraces the relatively infrequent addition of a *meaningless word* that has no similarity in sound or spelling to any of those presented.

(5) *Fusions* of two or more totally independent, successive terms into a single meaningless term are a very significant form of error, which appears in abstract lists written by *S*'s of poor intelligence, *e. g.*, *Organ* and *Gattung* are reproduced as *Orgattung*. Mostly found in children 8 and 9 years old.

(6) *Perseverations* are indicated by the recording by *S* in a given series of a word that had already been reproduced in an earlier series. If frequent, this is a sign of a low intelligence, lack of self-control and of critical judgment.

(7) *Regressive inhibitions.* Failure to reproduce at least one-half of the terms given is. as a rule. to be interpreted as regressive inhibition. This condition is commonly attributable to a state of confusion into which a child is thrown, when he is suddenly 'overwhelmed' by the task, when everything 'flies out of his mind,' he 'loses his wits,' and is unable to accomplish even a fraction of his normal performance. The same thing is seen in adults under conditions which are difficult for them. Since, Meumann argues, this is essentially due to inability to force attention, lack of this ability is a token of poor general ability, and hence of low intelligence. Failure due to absolute lack of intent to succeed must, of course, be distinguished from the lack of ability to succeed.

(8) *Complete reversal* of word order, either in a large portion, or in the whole of a list is "a peculiarly puzzling phenomenon." There are occasionally met, for instance, cases in which a series of 8 words are all written in the reverse of the order presented.[13]

(9) The *substitution of synonyms* refers to the easily intelligible cases in which a word of like meaning, but different sound, replaces the word given, *e. g.*, *road* for *street*.

(10) The *substitution of concrete for abstract words* refers to the use of concrete terms of similar sound, whether of similar meaning or not, *e. g.*, *cows* for *cause*, *simple* for *symbol*. *E* must use his judgment here in making allowances for faulty spelling.

(11) Wrong formations, especially the use of wrong endings, constituted a prolific source of error in the German tests, particularly with abstract words, *e. g.*, *Glaubheit* for *Glaube*. Errors of this type may be expected to be less frequent in the less highly inflected and compounded English language, but occasional instances will be found, *e. g.*, *selectness* for *selection*.

(12) *Misunderstood abstract terms* is to be regarded (as the author understands it) as expressing the sum total of misapprehended abstract terms, whether the misunderstanding is indicated by substitutions, faulty endings, fusions, very faulty misspellings, or in other ways.

(13) *Orthography* constitutes a secondary symptom of intelligence. In order to estimate spelling fairly, papers are ranked as 'poor' in spelling only when the sum of misspelled words is 50 per cent. or more greater than the average number of misspellings for *S*'s class.

(14) *Handwriting* constitutes another secondary symptom of intelligence, and is merely rated, as fairly as possible by comparison of numerous papers, as good, average, or poor.

These 14 rubrics are filled out for each *S*. For the estimation of memory capacity, pure and simple, Meumann takes Nos. 1 and 2; for the estimation of intellectual ability, he divides the rubrics into three groups, (1) those that serve as indirect indexes of intelligence (Nos. 1, 2, and 3), (2) those that serve as direct evidence of intelligence (Nos. 4 to 12, including a statement of the relation of Nos. 1 and 2), and (3) those that serve as secondary symptoms of degree of mental development (Nos. 13 and 14). Now, for each of these condensed indexes, the grade of each *S* is indicated as (1) above average, (2) average, or (3) below average, and final comparisons and correlations are based upon these grades.

---

[13]The author is inclined to regard this phenomenon as a simple case of attempt on the part of a few *S*'s to get the series right by beginning with the last word heard and working back to the first section. *S* may have intentionally disregarded instructions to reproduce in the order given, or may have interpreted these instructions to include the reverse order as acceptable. In other words, it scarcely seems probable that the child does not know that he has reversed the order of presentation.

D. MEMORY FOR SENTENCES

In the first (1905) series of tests proposed by Binet and Simon there was included a test of memory for sentences; in the second (1908) series, sentences of 6, 16 and 26 syllables were inserted in the tests for 3, 6 and 12 years, respectively; in the third (1911) series a test of memory for sentences is used at 5 and 15 years. In my previous account of the 1908 series I inserted a provisional set of 21 sentences ranging in length from 2 to 42 syllables. These were subsequently tried out by Mrs. Squire, and another analogous set of 21 sentences was arranged by Carpenter when he repeated Mrs. Squire's test. Abelson also used a set of sentences of progressive length in his test of backward children.

MATERIAL.—Two printed slips each containing 21 test sentences (2 to 42 syllables). [For visual presentation, two pieces of cardboard.]

Set I is the same as that published by the author as an adjunct to the Binet-Simon tests (1908 series), save that the 11th sentence has been made easier and the 12th and 17th sentences have been made harder to remedy the discrepancies found by Mrs. Squire in the original set (74, p. 379).

Set II is the same as that published by Carpenter, save that the 7th and 9th sentences have been simplified to remedy the discrepancies that he pointed out and that the 10th sentence has been replaced by another, because, in my judgment, it differed markedly from the others in content and meaningfulness for children.

No attempt has been made to equate the two sets in respect to difficulty of corresponding sentences. Set II is probably less well-arranged than Set I.

METHOD.—Explain to S that he is to repeat, after once hearing, a number of sentences; that these will be given one at a time, beginning with an easy sentence and becoming more and more difficult. Make clear that he must try to repeat the sentence exactly, word for word. Let S sit with his back to E. Begin with a sentence well within S's grasp—say, with the second sentence for 6-year-old children, or with the fourth or fifth sentence for older ones. Read each sentence but once, slowly and distinctly. Proceed until positive that no more sentences could be correctly repeated, until, say, S has failed with three sentences in succession. Failure is recorded for any alteration, even for a single substitution, insertion or omission. Repeat, if desired, with Set II.

VARIATION OF METHOD.—For auditory-visual presentation, arrange the two pieces of cardboard to display the material, one sentence at a time. Let S read them aloud, once over, and immediately repeat what he has read.

For the many other possible variations of method, such as increasing the number of presentations, introducing an interval between presentation and reproduction, see under Variations of Method in the preceding tests of rote memory.

TREATMENT OF DATA.—The simplest plan is to treat the test as one of memory span for sentences. S's score would then be the longest sentence that he could repeat without error.

The difficulty which may then arise from missing one sentence and succeeding with the next is perhaps, however, best resolved by using for the score the total number of sentences correctly repeated; thus, if the first 8 are correct, the 9th missed, the 10th accomplished and the remainder missed, the score is 9 sentences, not 8 or 10.

On account of the individual differences in the difficulty presented by the same sentences to different S's, the unreliability of the test should be lessened by using both sets of sentences whenever time permits; in this case the average score secured by the two trials may be taken as S's final record.

E.   MEMORY FOR PICTURES OF OBJECTS

The first Binet-Simon series (1905) contained one test (No 17) in which a card of 13 pictures of objects was shown. Decroly and Degand used 3 sets of 8 pictures each. Mrs. Squire and Carpenter used a card of 30 such pictures, while Lapie presented a series of 8 pictures, successively, at the rate of one per second.

This test, which has an obviously close relation to the test of visual apprehension (No. 25) and to Binet's card of objects (No. 32A), would appear to have some advantages over more formal material, like digits and letters, for use with younger children.

MATERIAL.—Cardboard on which is pasted small colored pictures of 13 familiar objects. Stop-watch.

METHOD.—Explain the nature of the test to *S;* inform him that he is to have half a minute to look at the pictures, and that directly afterward he is to name as many of the objects as he can. For adults or older children it may be found desirable to reduce the time of exposure to 15 sec.

VARIATIONS OF METHOD.—The mere enumeration of the objects may be supplemented by a demand for further description of them, especially of their colors, or of their location on the cardboard. Mature *S*'s may be quizzed concerning their method of memorizing and recalling the pictures. They may also be tested for recognition by presenting the cardboard, after they have named as many items as possible, to see whether the omitted items can be readily recognized, or they may be given a typewritten list of 30 or 40 objects (including those on the card) from which they are to pick those presented. (Cf. Test 25, B and Test 32, A.)

TREATMENT OF DATA.—Score one for each object correctly named. Make record of insertions and substitutions. Note which objects are most often, which least often recalled.

RESULTS.—(1) *Norms of performance* for memory span for digits will be found in Tables 91 to 94, for letter squares in Tables 95 and 96, for words in Tables 97 and 98, for sentences in Table 99 and for pictures of objects in Table 100.

TABLE 91

Norms of Memory Span for Digits, as Conditioned by Age (Smedley)

AGE	AUDITORY SPAN	VISUAL SPAN	AGE	AUDITORY SPAN	VISUAL SPAN
7	5	5	14	6	7
8	5	5	15	6	7
9	5	6	16	6	7
10	6	6	17	7	8
11	6	6	18	6	7
12	6	7	19	7	8
13	6	7			

TABLE 92
Development of Memory for Digits (Smedley)

AVERAGE AGE		NUMBER TESTED	PER CENT. REPRODUCED	
Years	Months		Auditory	Visual
7	8	19	36.4	35.2
8	8	58	44.6	42.8
9	6	100	45.0	47.4
10	5	89	49.4	54.6
11	6	91	55.4	64.7
12	6	93	55.7	72.3
13	7	109	57.9	76.8
14	6	114	66.2	80.5
15	6	94	65.6	78.2
16	6	77	66.9	81.3
17	6	56	65.5	84.1
18	5	25	67.2	77.5
19	5	12	70.0	85.3

TABLE 93
Dependence of Memory Span for Auditory Digits on Age (Jacobs)

AGE	8	9	10	11	12	13	14	15	16	17	18	19
Number tested	8	13	19	36	41	42	42	72	66	50	3ʋ	14
Average Span	6.6	6.7	6.8	7.2	7.4	7.3	7.3	7.7	8.0	8.0	8.6	8.0

TABLE 94
Dependence of Memory for Auditory Digits on Age (Ebbinghaus)
(Average Number of Errors per Pupil in Two Series)

AVERAGE AGE	8-DIGIT SERIES	9-DIGIT SERIES	10-DIGIT SERIES	6 TO 10 DIGITS
10.7	3.1	5.1	7.4	17.8
12.2	2.9	4.7	7.9	17.5
13.2	1.5	2.6	4.2	9.1
14.4	1.6	3.0	4.9	10.5
15.5	1.0	2.1	3.7	7.6
17.1	0.8	1.4	3.9	6.5
18.0	0.9	1.4	3.4	6.1

TABLE 95

Memory for Letter Squares, in Relation to Age and Practise (*Winch*)

SCHOOL GRADE	NUMBER TESTED	AVERAGE AGE	AVERAGE SCORE			Average for 3 Sets
			1st 10 Tests	2d 10 Tests	3d 10 Tests	
Ex-vii.	5	14 yrs. 3 mos.	23.8	29.0	31.7	28.1
vii.	5	13 " 5 "	26.3	27.9	31.1	28.4
vi.	5	12 " 3 "	26.8	32.0	34.6	31.1*
v.	5	11 " 4 "	18.4	22.9	26.3	22.5
iv.	6	10 " 5 "	21.3	24.8	26.6	24.2
iii.	6	9 " 0 "	14.1	17.7	19.7	17.1
ii.	6	8 " 2 "	13.2	16.8	17.2	15.7

*The girls of this group proved to have special ability.

TABLE 96

Memory for Letter Squares, Score for 10 Trials (*Anderson*)

AGE	CASES	MEAN	MINIMUM	MAXIMUM
8	52	108.2	47	198
9	92	109.7	36	182
10	115	127.7	35	213
11	126	139.8	60	264
12	139	157.8	76	272
13	125	156.9	52	298
14	96	165.6	74	283
15	58	170.8	67	323
16	25	181.6	104	318

TABLE 97

Memory for Concrete Words in Relation to Age and Sex (*Pyle*)

SEX	AGE	8	9	10	11	12	13	14	15	16	17	18	ADULTS
Male	Cases	34	58	64	55	60	60	35	25	14	7	5	64
	Mean	31.2	32.4	35.8	37.7	37.7	38.3	40.0	40.2	43.4	45.7	49.0	44.3
Female	Cases	37	68	69	52	70	51	34	13	17	8	2	88
	Mean	32.9	32.7	39.6	37.7	38.7	40.4	44.2	42.0	42.5	40.5	52.0	47.6

TABLE 98

Memory for Abstract Words in Relation to Age and Sex (Pyle)

SEX	AGE	8	9	10	11	12	13	14	15	16	17	18	ADULTS
Male	Cases	34	58	63	55	60	60	35	25	14	7	5	62
	Mean	22.9	26.3	26.8	31.7	31.0	32.4	37.3	34.1	40.0	41.1	40.8	42.3
Female	Cases	37?	68	69	52	69	52	34	13	17	9	2	88
	Mean	20.5	24.0	31.0	31.8	34.0	36.0	39.0	37.8	41.0	37.0	49.0	39.8

TABLE 99

Average Number of Sentences Correctly Repeated (After Squire and Carpenter)

AGE	6	7	8	9	10	11	12	13	14
Squire _____	7.8	8.4	9.8	10.1	10.9	10.9	13.5	14.5	--
Carpenter _____	5.3	6.0	6.2	7.2	7.4	7.7	8.0	8.3	8.?

TABLE 100

Memory for Pictures of Objects (After Squire and Carpenter)

AGE	6	7	8	9	10	11	12	13	14
Squire _____	5.3	6.5	9.5	9.8	9.1	11.4	10.5	10.0	--
Carpenter _____	5.3	6.1	6.0	7.3	7.5	7.5	8.4	9.2	10.

In comparing new data with these results, differences
method must always be kept in mind. The differences betwee
Smedley's conduct of the memory-span test and that prescrib
above has already been described. The data of Table 92 a
shown graphically in Fig. 71. It will be noted that Table
deals with averages, Table 91 with standards of performane
Table 94 with number of errors. Supplementing Tables 91 a
93, W. V. Bingham has reported to me the following resu
for auditory memory span for digits, secured from some 2
Dartmouth freshmen: median 7, P. E. 0.34, range from 5
less to 12.

I am not able to explain the differences between the averages
for letter-squares reported by Winch and by Anderson, save on
the basis of selection of S's: Anderson's results were obtained
under my direction at Ithaca, N. Y., and include children in
the public schools with no attempt at selection.

With reference to Table 99, the discrepancies between the
results of the investigators are due primarily to two causes:
Mrs. Squires' data refer to unretarded children only, and are
based, as already explained, upon a different set of sentences.
That the first of these factors is the more important seems indicated by similar divergencies in Table 100, where the experimental conditions must have been nearly identical. Other
norms for sentences based upon results with the Binet tests
include as standards: capacity to repeat a sentence of 6
syllables at 3 years, of 10 syllables at 5 years, of 16 syllables at
6 years and of 26 syllables at 12 years. It is unnecessary to
add that much depends upon the sentences.

With regard to Table 100, it must be remembered that the
averages given are based upon a presentation of a group of 30
objects: the use of 13 objects as specified in the directions
above will yield somewhat smaller averages; competent adults
usually get but 11 objects after an exposure of 15 sec. For the
exposure of 13 pictures Binet reported the following average
performances: at 7 years, 4.3 pictures; at 9 years, 6.2 pictures;
at 11 years, 7.2 pictures.

(2) *Dependence on age.* That memory capacity increases in
general from the early to the late school years is illustrated in
Tables 91 to 101. The general evidence is fairly clear that this
improvement is steady up to puberty, but that it suffers fluctuations after that period (see Tables 92, 94, 96, 97, 98). Several
investigators adduce evidence that corroborates the popular
notion that there exists a special 'memory period,' or stage of
maximal efficiency somewhere in the 'teens,' when memory is
stronger than it is later. For example, the very careful work
of Pohlmann, with varied materials and varied forms of presentation, yields the net results (method of retained members)
shown in Table 101, in which maximal efficiency is indicated at
14, followed by fluctuations, without real improvement through

the adolescent period. Bourdon could discern progress from 8 to 13, but not from 14 to 20. Bernstein and Bogdanoff, in testing memory for geometrical figures by the method of recogni-

TABLE 101

Net Efficiency of Various Memories, in Relation to Age (*Pohlmann*)

AGE	9	10	11	12	13	14	15	16	17	18	19	20
Average Capacity	39.4	41.4	55.7	59.1	62.1	68.9	55.3	62.9	58.6	58.0	65.4	68.3

tion, found that 23 *S*'s aged 14 to 15 averaged better than the 55 adults that they tested. Wessely, who tested retention during a long period (1 and 2 years), was convinced that ability to retain and reproduce poems is maximal at the years 12 to 14, and that vocabularies (Latin-German) are reproduced more accurately at the expiration of 1 to 4 weeks, when learned by 12-year-old, than when learned by 15-year-old *S*'s. Similar assertions concerning the relative amount of retentive capacity for poems by children and by adults are made by Larguier (48, 185 ff.), while Binet (8, 259 ff.) believes that children have the better retentive capacity, and adults the better attentive capacity.

Over against this evidence for a decline of efficiency after 14 we have the figures of Jacobs (Table 93) and the emphatic statement of Smedley (70, p. 49), based upon his Chicago results (Table 92), that "there is no 'memory period,' no period in early school life when the memory is stronger than it is at any later portion of the child's life." Smedley's records do, indeed, show that "auditory memory develops rapidly up to about 14 years of age, and but slowly after this period. The visual memory seems to develop rapidly up to about 15 or 16 years of age." . . . "It will be noted [Fig. 71] that, in the early life of the child, the auditory memory is stronger than the visual memory; after about 9 years of age, the visual memory of most of the children becomes stronger than the auditory

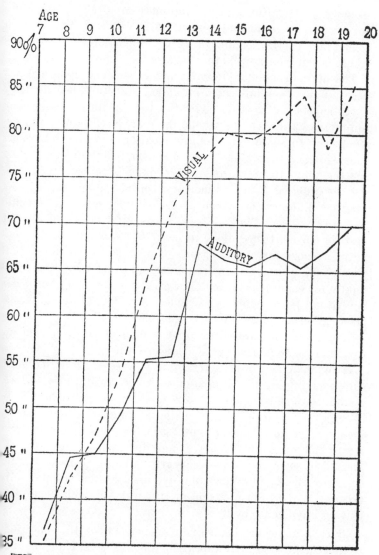

FIG. 71. DEVELOPMENT OF MEMORY FOR DIGITS (From Smedley).

memory, and continues to develop more rapidly than the auditory memory throughout school life. Yet, even in the high school, there still remains a small proportion of the pupils whose hearing memory is the stronger."

The dependence of different types of memory upon age has been studied especially by Netschajeff and by Lobsien. They agree substantially that, while the various forms of memory improve with age on the whole, there are periods of rapid development, followed by no improvement or even by a reduction; that while, on the whole, the greatest improvement occurs during the years 10 to 12, and development is retarded after 14, yet the different forms of memory, considered specifically, develop at different rates, and at periods that may not coincide in the two sexes. Thus, in boys, memory for objects is at first best developed, then follow, in order of chronological development, memory for visual terms, for acoustic terms, for actual sounds, for tactual terms, for numbers, for abstract terms, and finally for emotional terms. For girls, the chronological order is: visual terms, objects, sounds, numbers, abstract terms, acoustic terms, tactual terms, emotional terms. Special stress is laid upon the parallelism of development between memory for numbers and memory for abstract terms.

In Meumann's word-list tests, those types of error that indicate poor intelligence decreased with age, until, at 14 and 15, instances of misunderstood abstract terms were limited to about 10 per cent. of his S's, while meaningless fusions, meaningless insertions, and the substitution of concrete for abstract terms had nearly disappeared, and the memory for abstract terms had so increased as frequently to be superior to that for concrete terms. It follows that age must always be taken into account in the interpretation of this test, particularly in estimating intelligence by it.

Since in a memory test so much depends upon the condition of presentation, as will appear in what follows, I am inclined to regard many of these generalizations as of significance only under the particular conditions of the testing. The one safe generalization as to dependence on age would appear to be that made at the outset, viz.: capacity for immediate verbatim reproduction increases decidedly from early life to puberty, particularly during the period between 10 and 12, and increases more slowly and with fluctuations from puberty to maturity. The results of Cohn and Dieffenbacher, not here reproduced in detail, also accord entirely with this conclusion, as do the position of the medians in Anderson's percentile curves (Figs. 72 and 73).

(3) *Dependence on sex.* In general, girls pretty certainly surpass boys in immediate memory, but the differences are not always marked and perhaps do not extend to all forms of material. Investigations that agree in showing a general superiority of girls and women over boys and men are those of Anderson, Burt, Bolton, Calkins, Kirkpatrick, Pohlmann and Schuyten. Burt and Moore state that only 12.6 per cent. of boys exceed the median of girls, and add that "feminine superiority is a constant phenomenon in memory tests of every kind. It matters little what the age or training of the subjects may be. Hence, it is one of the best attested sex-differences and one of the most likely to be innate." [14]

The results of Anderson's extensive tests with letter squares have been summarized in Table 96. From Anderson's original data there have been arranged, after a preliminary process of numerical 'smoothing,' the percentile curves shown in Figs. 72 and 73.

Curves of this construction are so valuable for diagnosing the station of any individual's performance that these curves are here reproduced, despite the fact that they exhibit a number of irregularities due to the small number of cases available at certain ages. I have also calculated from Anderson's data the tables of distribution (102 and 103). It is therefore possible for any E to use these data by adding to them further scores and then recasting the percentile curves to accord with the combined data. For this purpose the scores may be considered as if they were the middle points within the ranges here indicated; for example, the distribution for 9-year-old boys may be read, 3 scores of 65, 4 scores of 55, etc.

By inspection of the medians (50th percentiles) in these charts it will be seen that girls are inferior to boys at 9 years

---

[14] I find, however, some difficulty in identifying the figures upon which this conclusion is based, as they appear in Burt's different articles not to refer to the same groups.

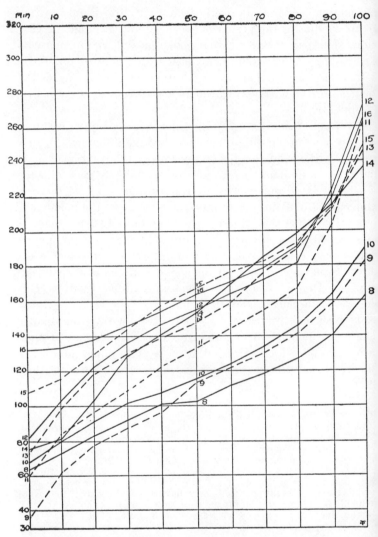

FIG. 72. PERCENTILES OF MEMORY FOR LETTER SQUARES, BOYS   (Anderson)

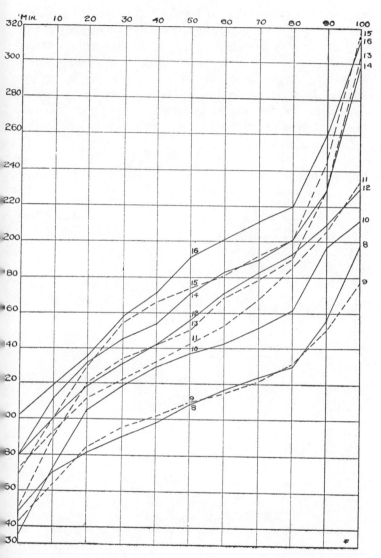

IG. 73. PERCENTILES OF MEMORY FOR LETTER SQUARES, GIRLS (Anderson).

and practically the same as boys at 12 years, but that else-where the girls are superior and that their superiority is especially striking in the higher percentiles. The curves are undoubtedly affected by a poor group of girls at 9 years and an unusually good group of boys at 12 years, since the progress with age is decidedly broken at these points in the manner mentioned. On the whole, Anderson figures, girls are some 27 per cent. better than the boys in letter squares.

TABLE 102

Distribution of Boys' Scores in Letter Squares (After Anderson)

AGE	8	9	10	11	12	13	14	15	16
60- 69	1	3	1	1					
70- 79	1	4	4	3		1	2		
80- 89	2	5	2	3	3	2	1		
90- 99	5	5	7	9	2	2	2		
100-109	5	3	10	2	3	6	1	2	
110-119	0	4	9	5	3	3	1	2	
120-129	5	6	4	4	4	3	7	1	3
130-139	1	4	3	5	9	9	2	3	1
140-149	0	3	6	9	6	9	4	3	1
150-159	0	4	3	5	11	8	3	2	1
160-169	1	1	3	4	7	4	3	2	1
170-179		0	1	4	9	3	2	5	2
180-189		1	0	3	3	4	3	5	1
190-199			1	2	1	5	4	2	1
200-209				0	2	2	3	2	1
210-219				0	3	1	3	0	0
220-229				0	1	3	1	1	0
230-239				0	2	2	1	0	0
240-249				1	1	1		0	0
250-259				0	0			1	0
260-269					1	1	•		1
270-279					1				
Total__	21	43	54	61	72	68	43	31	12

In other investigations the superiority of girls is either less clearly evident or exhibited in some aspects of the tests only. Thus Lobsien's tests with varied materials (Table 106) likewise showed that girls reproduced more, but that boys were more

TABLE 103

Distribution of Girls' Scores in Letter Squares (After Anderson)

AGE	8	9	10	11	12	13	14	15	16
30- 39			1						
40- 49	1	2	0						
50- 59	0	0	0			1			
60- 69	1	1	1			1		1	
70- 79	2	3	2	2	1	0	1	0	
80- 89	5	4	3	1	1	2	2	0	
90- 99	4	5	1	3	2	2	1	1	
100-109	4	9	4	5	5	2	0	1	1
110-119	2	11	4	3	4	0	1	0	0
120-129	6	2	7	10	4	5	2	0	1
130-139	3	4	10	6	7	6	5	2	0
140-149	1	5	10	7	8	9	6	0	1
150-159	0	1	2	6	5	3	3	4	1
160-169	0	1	4	6	3	3	6	3	1
170-179	0		2	3	7	5	5	2	2
180-189	1		0	2	4	6	6	1	0
190-199			1	4	6	3	3	7	1
200-209			1	2	4	0	3	0	1
210-219				1	3	0	3	0	3
220-229				1		2	1	0	0
230-239						0	1	0	0
240-249						0	0	0	0
250-259						1	0	0	0
260-269						1	0	0	0
270-279						1	0	0	0
280-289						0	1	0	0
290-299						1		0	0
300-309								0	0
310-319								0	1
320-329								1	
Total__	31	48	61	65	67	57	53	26	13

apt to get the order right.[15] Netschajeff also concluded that girls made more illusory errors (especially at ages 9 to 11). He also found that boys had the better memory for real objects, girls for numbers and words, in which they surpassed boys, particularly during the years 11 to 14. Wissler's tabulation

---

[15] Note analogous results in the Test of Report (No. 32).

of the freshmen tests at Columbia University and Barnard College reveals sex differences in memory span for digits that are less than the P.E. of the averages, and that favor the men for auditory, and the women for visual series (Table 105).

TABLE 104

Percentage of Accuracy in Memory for 2-place Numbers (Schuyten)

		MORNING	AFTERNOON
First test (Afternoon first)	Boys Girls	58.1 69.6	64.0 77.5
Second test (Morning first)	Boys Girls	57.9 62.6	35.0 55.1

TABLE 105

Sex Differences in Memory Span for Digits in College Freshmen (Wissler)

	AUDITORY PRESENTATION			VISUAL PRESENTATION		
	Number	Average	P. E.	Number	Average	P. E.
Men	266	7.6	0.4	142	6.9	0.5
Women	42	7.3	0.5	42	7.3	0.4

Pyle's averages for memory for words show possibly an advan tage for the girls, but the differences are only slight. Cohn and Dieffenbacher, similarly, find that girls surpass boys only when groups of the same school grade and same social status are com pared, and that when the results are plotted by age the curve cross each other six times, so that the sex-difference which ap pears in lump comparisons turns out to be practically a accident.

(4) *Dependence on practise.* (a) *General.* Practise produce a measurable increase in the memory span (Bolton). In th use of nonsense syllables, indeed, the practise effect can be dis

cerned even at the expiration of 60 days of experimental work (Müller and Schumann).

Winch, from his use of the letter-square, as well as of auditory letter series, not only declares that there is a "marked and almost invariable improvement," but "that 'pure memory' is markedly improvable by practise" (80, p. 134). Thus, 38 S's, ages 8 to over 14, obtained, in 3 sets of 10 tests each (1 week between the 1st and 2d, and 2 weeks between the 2d and 3d), the average scores 20.6, 24.4, and 26.6 (averages of the scores of Table 95).

(b) The *transfer of practise* from the specially trained form of memory to other forms of memory would appear, from theoretical grounds, to be limited to those cases in which the material, content, or method of procedure of the other forms were related to the material, content, or method of procedure of the trained form. This is essentially the conclusion reached by Ebert and Meumann (25, p. 200), who say: "The objective results of our experiment show that special memory practise is accompanied by a general improvement of memory. This concomitant improvement does not, however, extend equally to the other 'memories,' but appears to follow the law that the specific memories participate in the improvement directly in proportion as they are related in content, or in media and method of learning to the specific memory that was trained."

Winch has been led, by experiments in memorization of poetry and historical prose (81a), to take the more radical stand that "improvement, gained in practise in memorizing one subject of instruction, is transferred to memory work in other subjects whose nature is certainly diverse from that in which the improvement was gained, . . . at least so far as children of these ages and attainments are concerned." Again, in his second paper (81b) he concludes that "improvement through practise in rote memory for things with and without meaning is followed by improvement in substance memory for stories," and this even though the correlation between the two functions is very low and even doubtful.

On the other hand, Starch found no improvement in auditory

memory span after 14 days of drill in mental multiplication, and Sleight found no general improvement in his drilled sections, save that *S*'s drilled in memorizing poetry or tables showed subsequent improvement in memory for nonsense syllables, on account, he thinks, of the use of rhythm in these types of memorizing. Drill in memory for 'prose substance' improved that sort of memory, but no other, and even worked disastrously for subsequent memorizing of nonsense syllables. The conclusions reached by Ebert and Meumann have been criticized by several writers and directly controverted by Wessely, who says that for memory there seems to be no formal practise effect.[16]

(5) *Dependence on fatigue.* Though fatigue may affect immediate memory and undoubtedly does so when severe, it is difficult to arrange memory tests that will serve as useful indexes of fatigue, particularly because either practise or ennui affects the results more than does true fatigue. On this point we find Bolton, Ebbinghaus, Schuyten and Smedley in agreement. Two investigators, however, have secured results worth mentioning. Winch (82) divided pupils into two equivalent sections and practised them with letter-squares until the rank-orders were 'steady.' He then continued the tests with one group in the morning, with the other in the afternoon. Both groups showed improvement, but the morning workers improved from 2 to 6 per cent. more than the afternoon workers. Ritter gave up the determination of fatigue by span tests with numerals, but he did achieve results which he considers of special value by the use of 6-term series of two-syllabled nouns. With this material, he finds that errors increase with fatigue, and he goes so far as to assert that this test is the best one available for the investigation of fatigue.

---

[16]Allusion may be made in this connection to the evidence for transfer found by Dallenbach with experiments in the analogous field of visual apprehension (Test 25). Aside from the fact that Sleight worked with pupils as well as adults, it is possible that the discrepancies noted here concerning the transfer of practise may be due to the ages of the *S*'s studied. I have suggested elsewhere (*JEdPs*, 5: 1914, 362) that, particularly in the case of transfer, experimentation with children has been neglected and that results secured with adults may not necessarily apply to the mental processes of children.

(6) *Dependence on physical capacity.* Both Netschajeff and Smedley find that pupils that are larger, stronger, and better developed physically have better memories than those of the contrary type. "This suggests," says Smedley, "that the immediate sense memory is dependent upon good brain formation and nutrition." (See 70, pp. 58-59, for numerical evidence.)

Miss Kohnky used memory span for digits among other tests in an investigation of the effect of dental treatment upon pupils in a 5th-grade Cincinnati school. The series with 6 digits proved too easy for this work; the series with 8 digits yielded virtually the same results for treated and untreated pupils, but the series with 7 digits yielded a gain of 10.8 per cent. between tests made in October and in the following May in the case of the pupils having dental treatment, as contrasted with no gain in the pupils without treatment.

(7) *Dependence on the nature of the material.* (*a*) When *digits and consonants* are given under the same conditions, digits are easier to reproduce (Jacobs, Sharp), especially during the years 8 to 13 (Bourdon). But, if 10-place series are presented auditorily, thrice, the order of excellence for recall is (1) consonants, (2) names of objects, (3) 2-place numbers, (4) nonsense syllables (Pohlmann).

(*b*) Netschajeff, Lobsien, Pohlmann, and less elaborately Kirkpatrick and Calkins, have compared memory for series made up of real objects, of numbers, of sounds, and of words

TABLE 106

Memory for 9-term Series of Different Kinds (Lobsien)

KIND OF SERIES	SCORE IN PER CENT. CORRECT	
	Boys	Girls
Real objects	82.2	91.4
Auditory numbers	64.8	71.8
Sounds	59.6	62.2
Tactual terms	64.2	71.0
Visual terms	60.6	67.2
Auditory terms	59.4	60.2
Emotional terms	31.2	59.4
Foreign terms	24.0	23.8

having characteristically visual, auditory, tactual, or emotional associative meanings. Table 106 gives illustrative results from Lobsien. Pohlmann, however, concluded that the assumption of Netschajeff and Lobsien that the presentation of visual, auditory, and other terms arouses the visual, auditory, and other imagery that their meaning implies, is erroneous, so that the results of these investigations are of little real significance.

Kirkpatrick, and after him Miss Calkins, found, like Netschajeff and Lobsien, that memory for objects (or pictures of objects) was superior to that for words, both for immediate and for delayed reproduction; in the latter, for example, there were recalled seven times as many objects as words. The same investigators determined the order of excellence for recall of different kinds of words to be:—visual terms, auditory terms, names of objects.

(c) Up to the 12th year, *concrete words* are reproduced better than abstract words, but 14 and 15-year-old *S*'s frequently make better records with the latter, according to Meumann; but according to Pyle, concrete words are reproduced better at every age. The average difference amounts in Pyle and in

TABLE 107

Memory for Related and for Unrelated Words (Norsworthy)

AGE	RELATED WORDS, 288 CASES				UNRELATED WORDS, 270 CASES			
	BOYS		GIRLS		BOYS		GIRLS	
	Median	P. E.	Median	P. E.	Median	P. E.	Median	P. E.
8	13.0	1.0	13.0	1.6	11.1	1.6	11.5	1.3
9	14.0	2.0	14.0	1.7	12.2	1.7	12.4	1.4
10	15.0	1.7	15.3	1.9	12.2	1.7	14.4	1.4
11	15.0	1.7	16.5	1.7	12.5	1.8	14.3	1.4
12	16.4	1.8	16.0	1.6	12.8	1.8	14.0	1.5
13	16.5	1.8	17.0	1.5	13.5	2.1	13.5	1.5
14	16.9	1.3	17.5	1.5	13.7	2.2	14.0	1.5
15	16.0	1.3	17.5	1.5	13.7	2.2	14.0	1.5
16	17.0	1.3	17.8	1.5	14.0	2.2	14.5	1.5
Adults	16.5	1.5	17.0	1.9	12.8	1.2	13.0	1.4

Burt (16) to 20 per cent., roughly, *i. e.*, most *S*'s recall about one-fifth more concrete than abstract words.

(*d*) *Related terms, i. e., a series of words not in a sentence, but readily associated with one another,* are more easily recalled than unrelated words. For data, see Table 107 from Miss Norsworthy.

(*e*) Material so arranged as to aid *localization* is more easily remembered, especially by children. For example, 12 consonants in the letter-square form are easier to recall than 12 consonants in a single line; similarly, digits pronounced in rhythm are easier to recall than digits pronounced in even tempo (Müller and Schumann). Pohlmann found grouped series to be easier in 133 of 144 trials.

(8) *Dependence on sense-department directly stimulated.* It is evident that a complete isolation of the different modalities cannot be accomplished by different forms of presentation: *e. g.*, auditory-minded *S*'s may actually retain and reproduce impressions presented to the eye in auditory, or mainly in auditory terms, and so on (cf. Abbott and Finzi). It is also evident that what seem like minor variations in the manner of conducting the test may occasion considerable variations in the performance of *S*'s. These facts account for much of the divergence and seeming contradiction in the results of various investigators with regard to the relative advantage of addressing stimuli to different senses.[17]

With regard to the relative advantage of auditory over visual presentation Kemsies found presentation by ear the better for Latin words and for nonsense syllables; von Sybel found auditory presentation better than visual for both auditory and visual types of *S*'s; Henmon found as his most striking result a marked superiority of auditory over visual presentation for all of his *S*'s and for all forms of material. Hawkins reported that ten nouns heard are recalled better than ten nouns successively seen in the case of younger *S*'s, but that the reverse

---

[17]These divergencies have been well summarized by Henmon, to whose account the reader is referred for details of the conclusions reached by Meumann, Münsterberg and Bigham, Quantz, Lay, Itschner, Füchs and Haggenmüller, Cohn, Kemsies, Finzi, Fränkl, Segal, von Sybel, Schuyten, Pohlmann and others. together with his own conclusions.

holds true for above 15 years. Pohlmann's extensive experiments, which are criticized by Henmon because of being conducted by the group method, show that auditory presentation is better for meaningful material (words), while the reverse is true with non-significant material (digits and nonsense syllables). On the other hand, the superiority of visual over auditory presentation appears in the tables and charts of Smedley and in Chambers' results for 7th and 8th grade pupils.

With regard to the advantage of combined appeal to eye and ear or to eye, ear and motor memory (articulation or writing), there are similar discrepancies. The work of Pohlmann (Table 108) indicates a superiority of auditory-visual presentation over either auditory or visual presentation, alone—a result in accordance with Smedley's. Pohlmann also investigated the effect of these three forms of presentation upon numerals and nonsense syllables, with the result that for 230 *Volksschule* girls, using 10-term series, given thrice, the percentage of accuracy was, for visual-auditory 53 per cent., for visual 52 per cent., and for auditory 42 per cent., which agrees in substance, so far as it goes, with Smedley's results for digits. This investigator found the order of superiority to be: (1) auditory-visual-articulatory, (2) auditory-visual, (3) auditory-visual-hand-motor, (4 and 5) visual or auditory (depending on age). Illustrative figures for *S*'s aged 16 years are, for the five forms just

TABLE 108

Dependence of Memory upon Form of Presentation (Pohlmann)
(Percentage of Retained Members, 10-Term Series, 350 Pupils, 9-14 Years)

NATURE OF MATERIAL	FORM OF PRESENTATION	PERCENTAGE RETAINED
1. Actual objects.....	Shown and named by *E*..	72⅛
2. Actual objects..................	Shown, only, successively	70
3. Names of objects...............	Seen and heard by *S*....	
4. Names of objects...............	Heard, only, by *S*.......	55⅙
5. Names of objects...............	Seen, only, by *S*.........	50⅔
6. Names of objects...............	Seen, heard, and pronounced by *S*.........	49½

In the upper classes, 5 becomes superior to 4.

mentioned, 88.4, 86.9, 82.4 (circa), 80.0, and 66 per cent., respectively. Combined appeal is, then, most powerful, but the task of writing proves somewhat distracting. Münsterberg and Bigham conclude, similarly, that "a series of impressions offered to two senses at the same time is much more easily reproduced than if given only to sight or only to hearing." Thus, in the case of 10 numbers the per cent. of error for numbers heard, seen, and both seen and heard were 14.1, 10.5, and 3.9, respectively. On the other hand, Henmon concludes that visual-auditory-motor presentation is slightly inferior to the auditory and to the auditory-visual, but superior to the visual alone, and that visual-auditory presentation is slightly inferior to the auditory alone, while decidedly superior to the visual alone. In general, he found the advantage of combined presentation much less than that reported in earlier investigations. Kemsies discovered that visual-auditory presentation usually gave poorer results than visual or auditory alone in tests with Latin words and nonsense words.

The question as to whether articulation does or does not assist in subsequent recall is also answered differently by different investigators. Thus, Cohn found that in memorizing consonants all his *S*'s did best when they read aloud, less well when speech movements were suppressed, least well when numbers or vowels were pronounced as distractors during the reading of the consonants. Quite similar results which were reached by Lay in his investigation of the teaching of spelling have been contested by Itschner and by Fuchs and Haggenmüller. Henmon also declares that articulation or vocalization is of little value for immediate memory.

A closely related question concerns the possibility of determining *S*'s *ideational type* by scrutiny of his performance under different sorts of presentation. Fränkl and also Segal believe that visual presentation gives better results with visual types, auditory with auditory types, and Meumann concludes from such tests that in learning, better reliance can be placed upon *S*'s type than upon an appeal to several sense departments. But the evidence is fairly clear that, as Angell says, while memory tests "may certainly be so administered as to show over what sensory arcs the best results may be achieved in assimilating information of various kinds . . . as objective tests of imagery apart from introspection, they have few virtues and no reliability."

(9) *Successive vs. simultaneous presentation.* If 15 words are exposed simultaneously or successively for equivalent lengths of time, successive presentation is easier for young, but simultaneous for older children, according to Hawkins.

(10) *Dependence on number of presentations: repetition.* Pohlmann, Lipmann, Smedley, and others have found that hearing a series thrice or twice, instead of once, improves its recall. However, Hawkins found two hearings less effective than one or three. It is certain that more is accomplished in the first hearing than in a large number of repetitions, and that the effect of repeated presentation is different in different S's, so that individual differences are more marked after many hearings than after one hearing (Smith). Smedley's test of 38 10-year pupils, with auditory digits, gave, for the first hearing 47 per cent., for the second 55 per cent., and for the third 59 per cent. correct reproduction. In some of Smith's tests, 12 presentations did not double the efficiency attained in one presentation.

(11) *Dependence on rate and duration of exposure.* Bergström's tests indicate that nonsense syllables exposed at the rate of one in 0.77 sec., with durations of exposure of .041, .082, .164, and .318 sec. yield practically the same results, though there is a slight preference for .082 sec.

The same investigator found that, both with auditory letter and word series and with visual nonsense-syllables series, a relatively slow rate of exposure (1.5 to 2 sec. per term) yielded more accurate results than a faster rate (one term in a fraction of a second). The slower rate is especially helpful in lists of words, and for those S's that try to develop associations between the terms as they are presented. Bergström summarizes by saying: "The acquisition and retention of a series of familiar associable words varies approximately as the logarithm of the interval at which the words are spoken" (6, p. 221).

(12) *Dependence on interval between presentation and repro-*

duction. Relatively short intervals make, apparently, but little change in reproduction. Thus, Winch could discern no clear differences in the reproduction by school children of letter-squares, with or without a 25-sec. empty interval between presentation and reproduction.

Binet and Miss Sharp compared immediate memory with 'recapitulatory' memory (memory of conservation) ; they both noted that the word lists in immediate reproduction seemed to be held largely by sound (so that, for example, such errors as *flower* for *floor* were common), whereas lists reproduced 3 min. later appear to be held more often by meaning, since "the errors are usually additional words suggested from analogy of sense" (*e. g., dog* suggested by *cat, cold* by *winter,* etc.).[19]

Attention has already been called (7, *b,* above) to the demonstration by Kirkpatrick and by Calkins that the reproducibility of different forms of material is not equally affected by a 3-day interval.

(13) *Effect of distraction.* Smith's use of the method of letter squares (71), with and without the distraction of concomitant activities, shows the order of efficiency under these conditions to be, from best to worst:—(1) without distraction, (2) with tapping to the beat of a metronome, (3) with repetition of a vowel, and (4) with counting by 2's or 3's. Cohn, with the same test, found that an auditory-motor *S* was more seriously disturbed by auditory-motor distractors than a visually minded *S,* and that, when such distraction is used, visual memory steps in to aid, provided *S's* constitutional make-up (*Anlage*) will at all permit (22, p. 182).

(14) *Reliability.* With the exception of Brown, whose co-efficients were only .50 to .68, investigators have found tests of immediate memory to yield a satisfactory degree of reliability. Examples are: Burt, .70 for one group of *S's,* .93 for another; Wyatt, .75 for one group, .76 for another; Abelson, .74 to .81; Simpson, .73 for all *S's* collectively.

---

[19] The tendency of adults is away from rote memorizing in favor of a memory of meanings. It would, then, be interesting to see whether children exhibited these same tendencies that Sharp's university students did, or exhibited them in as marked a degree.

(15) *Correlation with mental ability.* Bolton, Ebbinghaus (Table 109) and Wissler (who found a correlation of but 0.16 between class standing and the memory capacity of 121 Columbia freshmen) seem to be the only investigators to deny a relationship between immediate memory and intelligence. Jacobs, at the other extreme, asserts that there is a "notable concomitance" between school standing and "span of prehension." The truth would appear to lie, as usual, between these extremes. The more careful correlational work of the past few years demonstrates at least a fairly good degree of correspondence between immediate memory and either school standing or estimated general intelligence. The several investigators who have found correspondence of this sort have expressed their conclusions with certain restrictions or explanations, as will appear in what follows. There is some evidence, for example, to indicate that the correspondence between immediate memory and school standing is closer in the lower than in the higher grades, and that the correspondence with general intelligence is closer with tests of delayed than of immediate recall.

TABLE 109

Relation of Memory for Auditory Digits and Intelligence (Ebbinghaus)

	AVERAGE NUMBER OF ERRORS PER PUPIL		
	Bright Group	Average Group	Dull Group
9-digit test_____	84	87	84
10-digit test_____	147	147	135
6-10 digit tests, collectively_____	318	319	303

With backward children Abelson found rather low correlations, 0.18 and 0.19, between memory for names and imputed practical intelligence (competence to perform errands), but higher correlations with school performances (0.20 and 0.24 with estimated ability in reading and 0.30 and 0.32 with estimated ability in arithmetic).

Binet (8) contrasted 6 dull and 5 bright boys, and found that, on the whole, the latter surpassed the former in memory: the difference, as in his tests of other traits, was, however, more evident at the first, than at any subsequent trial.

Brown found correlations of 0.40 to 0.59 with school marks and 0.49 to 0.55 with estimated general intelligence.

Burt estimated intelligence in various ways and measured memory for concrete words, abstract words and nonsense syllables. The corrected correlations for estimated intelligence and general standing in the memory tests were 0.60 for Elementary School, and 0.82 for Preparatory School boys. The uncorrected correlations were higher for memory for concrete words (0.58 and 0.84) than for memory for abstract words (0.48 and 0.78) ; those for nonsense syllables were 0.43 and 0.75, while the amalgamated memory tests correlated by 0.67 and 0.69 with examinations in mathematics and by 0.82 with examinations in literary subjects (in the Preparatory School). Burt argues from these figures that the current examination system stresses ability to remember. Meumann's conclusion that bright children display a relatively superior ability in memory for abstract terms was not substantiated by Burt.

Cohn and Dieffenbacher divided their S's into two groups—the better and the poorer intellectually. The former excelled the latter in the memory tests in 11 of his 14 groups ; the superiority amounted to about 10 per cent., and turned out to be less in the higher than in the lower school grades.

Lapie contrasted pedagogically advanced with pedagogically retarded pupils, and concluded that these groups differed little in retentive power as such, but that the retarded pupils frequently reproduced the material in bizarre and contradictory combinations, c. g., as in speaking of "a young peasant 54 years old."

Meumann says that the quantity of material reproduced is not in itself a reliable index of intelligence, yet the average results of mass experiments will always show that the more intelligent S's have the better memory efficiency. His own experiments, he declares, were so extensive and so carefully executed as to leave no doubt at all upon this point (51, p. 78). More reliable, however, are the qualitative results attained from memory tests of the form used in his own experiments. Here, he says, virtually complete coincidence is found between the several indexes of intelligence, and between them and the school marks and the estimate of mental ability by teachers. Certain characteristic indexes of poor intelligence, however, such as the fusion of abstract terms into meaningless collocations, may not be shown by all of the stupid children ; if they are shown, they form a reliable index of poor intelligence, while if frequent, they indicate not only poor intelligence, but also the lack of moral qualities, such as self-control and carefulness. Incidentally, Meumann points out that, in theory, we should distinguish carefully between natural ability and actual ability as shown in school performance ; these, nevertheless, tend to coincide in practise.

Pohlmann, like Binet, dealt with contrasted groups. He concludes that, while in general the better pupils have better memories, there are numerous exceptions, particularly in that poor pupils may do as well as bright pupils in the memory tests.

The two contrasted groups of adults tested by Simpson were fairly well separated by his tests of memory for words ; none of the poor group reached the median performance of the good group, and only 10 per cent. of the poor group were as good as the lowest 6 per cent. of the good group. The correlation with the estimated intelligence of the good group was 0.93.

Smedley declares that the "parallelism between school standing and memory power holds good throughout school life" (70, p. 54), and demonstrates this by reference to mass results distributed to show the memory capacity of pupils of a given age in different grades (Fig. 74), or the capacity of pupils at and above grade as compared with the capacity of pupils below grade at different ages (Table 110).

Winch's letter-square tests convince him that "general mental ability [rank in examinations in reading, arithmetic, dictation, and English composition] is accompanied by 'good memory.'" "With two exceptions, no girl whose memory mark is relatively low has a high place in class." "'Good memory,' though usually accompanied by general efficiency, is not invariably so." Again, Winch contrasted six 13-year-old girls, who stood between Number 1 and Number 11 in a class of 35, with 6 girls of the same age, who stood 25th to 30th in a class of 30, and found the average score of the bright girls to be 26.9, as compared with an average score of 19 for the dull girls (80, p. 133).

Wessely believes that the correlation between memory and class standing is more evident in lower than in higher grades—a view expressed also by Cohn and Dieffenbacher and which, if confirmed, might be explicable by the tendency to put a premium upon memorization in the lower grades.

Wyatt's tests with nonsense syllables gave as a correlation with intelligence 0.59, P.E. .07, for immediate and 0.74, P.E. .06, for delayed (2 days) reproduction; his tests with letter squares gave a negligible correlation 0.18, P.E. .11.

(16) *Memory of defectives.* Galton applied Jacobs' tests to imbeciles, and found that most S's of this type failed to repeat more than 4 digits, while several imbeciles who had remarkable memories for dates or for passages in books showed complete failure (span not over 3) in memory for digits. Johnson computes the average span for feeble-minded (selected S's of the so-called 'school-case' group) at 5.3, or approximately 1.3 digits less than the normal span of an 8-year child. The distribution of efficiency, as he found it, is shown in Table 111. Johnson comments upon the fact that the difference between the memory

TABLE 110

Relation of Memory for Digits and School Standing (Smedley)

AGE	NUMBER TESTED	AUDITORY		VISUAL	
		Average Standing of Pupils At and Above Grade.	Average Standing of Pupils Below Grade	Average Standing of Pupils At and Above Grade	Average Standing of Pupils Below Grade
9	99	47.8	39.7	50.3	41.9
10	88	54.4	42.7	61.6	46.2
11	91	59.0	48.6	69.4	53.3
12	92	62.6	52.2	76.7	66.0
13	110	70.4	64.3	80.7	72.3
14	116	68.9	62.6	87.6	74.9
15	94	68.9	62.4	80.9	75.0
16	75	70.1	65.8	83.3	78.8
17	56	67.5	62.7	87.8	81.2

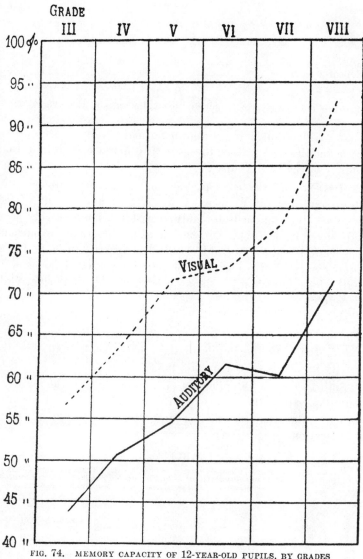

FIG. 74. MEMORY CAPACITY OF 12-YEAR-OLD PUPILS, BY GRADES
(From Smedley).

TABLE 111

Memory Span for Digits in the Feeble-Minded (Johnson)

Number of digits	3	4	5	6	7	8
Repeated correctly by	70	66	51	27	14	4

NOTE—The larger groups include the smaller ones at their right.

span of the feeble-minded and of normal children seems to be of a smaller order than the general difference in intellectual ability of the two groups.

Miss Norsworthy compared normal and feeble-minded children with respect to memory for related and for unrelated words. Her standards for normal children have already been reported (Table 107): the relation of feeble-minded to normal efficiency is shown in Table 112. The figures are to be interpreted simply: five per cent. of the feeble-minded do as well with the related-word test as do 50 per cent. of normal children, etc.

Smedley states "that the boys of the John Worthy School [incorrigibles, defectives, truants, etc.] are lower in memory power than are the pupils of the other schools, and this disparity increases with age" (70, p. 59).

Smith's tests with epileptics (73) show that, in the auditory letter-span test, they are generally inferior to normal *S*'s, and in particular, that they make nearly three times as many errors of insertion.

TABLE 112

Comparative Memory Capacity of Normal and Feeble-Minded Children
(Norsworthy)

	ABOVE MEDIAN	ABOVE —1 P. E.	ABOVE —2 P. E.
Normal (both tests)	50	75	91
Feeble-minded, in related words	5	19	30
Feeble-minded, in unrelated words	6	18	27

(17) *Other correlations.* Krueger and Spearman found no correlation between memory for digits (serial visual exposure) and either ability to add, to discriminate pitch, or to discriminate dual cutaneous impressions.

Memory for digits and memory for letters were correlated to a high degree in Miss Sharp's *S*'s, while memory for short sentences correlated best with memory for letters.

Smedley studied the relation of memory for digits and ability to spell, and concluded that "while, on the whole, the good spellers have decidedly better memory power than the bad spellers, yet there are individuals among the poor spellers who are superior in memory power, and individuals among the best spellers whose memory power is scarcely up to the average of their age. While this native power of sense-memory plays an important rôle, it is by no means the only factor in learning to spell" (70, p. 61).

Abelson found the following correlations with memory for words in his study of 88 backward boys and 43 backward girls: interpretation of pictures, boys 0.30, girls 0.33; memory for sentences, boys 0.66, girls 0.42; tapping, boys —0.08, girls 0.30; memory for commissions, boys 0.38, girls 0.34.

Brown tested several groups, mainly pupils 11 to 12 years old, and found the following correlations with his test of learning nonsense syllables: completion test, 0.28, 0.37, 0.52; memory for poetry, 0.38, 0.49; speed in addition, —0.13, 0, 0.27; accuracy in addition, —0.23, 0, 0.31; drawing, 0.39.

Burt's correlations, so far as they apply to tests mentioned in this work, are displayed in Table 113, Wyatt's in Table 114.

Simpson publishes the following as estimated true correlations with memory for words for people in general: completion test, 0.82; hard opposites, 0.84; easy opposites, 0.65; the a-test, 0.54; memory for passages, 0.80; adding, 0.39.

In the half dozen rather varied tests classed together by Heymans and Brugmans the intercorrelations for the several tests ranged from —0.34 to +0.71. The pooling together of the results of tests classed as tests of memory, imagination, etc., yielded correlations of 0.75 between memory and imagination,

TABLE 113

Correlations with Amalgamated Results of Immediate Memory Tests
(After Burt)

RELATED TEST	RAW CORRELATIONS		CORRECTED CORRELATIONS	
	Elem. Sch.	Prep. Sch.	Elem. Sch.	Prep. Sch.
Spot pattern_____	.25	.55	.41	.84
Mirror drawing____	.08	.44	.13	.64
Tapping _____	.01	.52	.01	.80
Pitch discrim._____	.13	.20	.19	.27
Lifted weights ____	.05	.15	.07	.22

TABLE 114

Correlations Between Memory Tests and Other Tests (After Wyatt)

	DELAYED MEMORY	IMMEDIATE MEMORY	LETTER SQUARES
Analogies _____	.70	.64	.28
Completion _____	.72	.61	.03
Word-building _____	.66	.57	.00
Part-wholes _____	.51	.52	.09
Fables _____	.43	.41	.31
Immediate mem._____	.71	--	.25
Letter squares_____	.15	.25	--

TABLE 115

Recall of Different Members of a 7-Term Series (Binet and Henri)

Place in series_____	1	2	3	4	5	6	7
Times recalled correctly__	143	139	115	111	122	117	140

0.73 between memory and concentration, 0.54 between memory
and intellect.

(18) *Dependence on race.* From studies conducted in several
Missouri cities Pyle (61a) concludes that "in rote memory the
negroes have a much better memory for concrete than for
abstract words, but are greatly inferior to whites in both."

(19) *Miscellaneous observations.* (*a*) Reproduction in correct order is more difficult than mere reproduction; reproduction is more difficult than recognition.

(*b*) The first and the last terms of a series are more liable to be recalled than are the middle terms (Table 115).

(*c*) In word tests, certain terms are often found to have a special reproducibility, evidently by attracting special attention in some way. Thus, Binet and Henri found that the word *pupitre* (desk), though in the middle of a series, and hence unfavorably placed, was recalled in an unusually large number of cases.

(*d*) Errors of omission are more common than errors of insertion or errors of substitution—in word tests with school children, 4 times more frequent (Binet and Henri).

(*e*) Wissler calls attention to the perseverative tendency mentioned by Meumann and others: this is evinced by the introduction, in the recall of a given series, of impressions that had been used in an earlier series. Wissler found this type of error especially common in college seniors and mature *S*'s when trying the digit test. Meumann, it will be remembered, considered perseveration in the word test as an index of poor intelligence—when the *S*'s knew that no series was like a previous one.

REFERENCES

(1) Edwina E. Abbott, Memory consciousness in orthography. *Ps Mon*, 11: 1909 (No. 44), 127-158.

(2) A. R. Abelson, The measurement of mental ability of 'backward' children. *BrJPs*, 4: 1911, 268-314. (Same condensed as Tests for mental deficiency in childhood. *The Child*, 3: 1912, 1-17.)

(2a) E. J. Anderson, Standardization of the Heilbronner, rote memory and word-building tests. (Not yet published.)

(3) J. R. Angell, Methods for the determination of mental imagery, being pp. 61-107 in Rept. Com. Amer. Psychol. Assoc. on the Standardization of procedure in experimental tests. *PsMon*, 13: 1910. No. 53.

(4) I. M. Bentley, The memory image and its qualitative fidelity. *AmJPs*, 11: 1899, 1-48.

(5) J. A. Bergström, Experiments on physiological memory by means of the interference of associations. *AmJPs*, 5: 1893, 356-369. See also An experimental study of some of the conditions of mental activity, *ibid.*, 6: 1894, 267-273, and Relation of the interference and the practise effect of an association, *ibid.*, 6: 1894, 433-442.

(6) J. A. Bergström, Effect of changes in the time variables in memorizing, together with some discussion of the technique of memory experimentation. *AmJPs*, 18: 1907, 206-238.

(7)   A. Bernstein and T. Bogdanoff, Experimente über das Verhalten der Merkfähigkeit bei Schulkindern. *Beiträge z. Psych. d. Aussage*, 2: 1905, 115-131.

(8)   A. Binet, Attention et adaptation. *AnPs*, 6: 1899 (1900), 248-404.

(9)   A. Binet, Introduction à la psychologie expérimentale. Paris, 1894. Especially ch. V.

(10)   A. Binet and V. Henri, La mémoire des mots. *AnPs*, 1: 1894 (1895), 1-23.

(11)   A. Binet and V. Henri, La psychologie individuelle. *AnPs*, 2: 1895 (1896), 411-465, especially 436-443.

(12)   T. L. Bolton, The growth of memory in school children. *AmJPs*, 4: 1892, 362-380.

(13)   B. Bourdon, Influence de l'âge sur la mémoire immédiate. *RPhF*, 38: 1894, 148-167.

(14)   W. Brown, Some experimental results in the correlation of mental abilities. *BrJPs*, 3: 1910, 296-322. (Also embodied in his Use of the theory of correlation in psychology. Cambridge, Eng., 1910. Pp. 83.)

(15)   W. H. Burnham, Memory historically and experimentally considered. *AmJPs*, 2: 1888-89, 39-90, 225-270, 431-464, 568-622.

(16)   C. Burt, Experimental tests of general intelligence. *BrJPs*, 3: 1909, 94-177.

(17)   C. Burt, Experimental tests of higher mental processes. *JEPd*, 1: 1911, 93-112.

(18)   C. Burt and R. C. Moore, The mental differences between the sexes. *JEPd*, 1: 1912, 273-284, 355-388.

(19)   Mary W. Calkins, A study of immediate and of delayed recall of the concrete and of the verbal. *PsR*, 5: 1898, 451-6.

(20)   D. F. Carpenter, Mental age tests. *JEdPs*, 4: 1913, 538-544.

(21)   W. G. Chambers, Individual differences in grammar grade children. *JEdPs*, 1: 1910, 61-75.

(22)   J. Cohn, Experimentelle Untersuchungen über das Zusammenwirken des akustisch-motorischen u. des visuellen Gedächtnisses. *ZPs* 15: 1897, 161-183.

(23)   J. Cohn und J. Dieffenbacher, Untersuchungen über Geschlechts-, Alters- und Begabungs-Unterschiede bei Schülern. *Beihefte zur ZAngPs*, No. 2, 1911. Pp. 213.

(24)   H. Ebbinghaus, (*a*) Ueber eine neue Methode zur Prüfung geistiger Fähigkeiten in ihrer Anwendung bei Schulkindern. *ZPs*, 13: 1897, 401-457. (*b*) For review of the literature, see *Grundzüge der Psychologie*, I, 2d ed., 1905, 633-707.

(25)   E. Ebert and E. Meumann, Ueber einige Grundfragen der Psych. der Uebungsphänomene im Bereiche des Gedächtnisses. *ArGsPs*, 4: 1905, 1-232.

(26)   P. Ephrussi, Experimentelle Beiträge zur Lehre vom Gedächtnis. Berlin, 1906. Pp. 191.

(27)   J. Finzi, Zur Untersuchung der Auffassungsfähigkeit und Merkfähigkeit. *PsArb*, 3: 1900, 289-384.

(28)   E. Fränkl, Ueber Vorstellungselemente und Aufmerksamkeit. Augsburg, 1905.

(29)   H. Fuchs und A. Haggenmüller, Studien und Versuche über die Erlernung der Orthographie. *SmAbPdPs*, 2: 1898.

(30)   F. Galton, Supplementary notes on 'prehension' in idiots. *Mind* 12: 1887, 79-82.

(31)   Eleanor Gamble, A study in memorizing various materials by the reconstruction method. *PsMon*, No. 43, Sept., 1909. Pp. 210.

(32)   C. J. Hawkins, Experiments on memory types. *PsR*, 4: 1897, 289-294.

(33) V. Henmon, The relation between mode of presentation and retention. *PsR*, 19: 1912, 79-96.

(34) V. Henri, Éducation de la mémoire. *AnPs*, 8: 1901 (1902), 1-48.

(35) G. Heymans und H. Brugmans, Intelligenzprüfungen mit Studierenden. *ZAngPs*, 7: 1913, 317-331.

(36) H. Itscnner, Lay's Rechtschrieb-Reform. *Jahrbuch des Vereins f. wissensch. Pädagogik*, 32: 1900.

(37) J. Jacobs, Experiments on 'prehension.' *Mind*, 12: 1887, 75-9.

(38) G. E. Johnson, Contrioution to the psychology and pedagogy of feeble-minded children. *PdSe*, 3: 1895, 245-301, especially 268-273.

(39) W. F. Jones, An experimental-critical study of the problem of grading and promotion. *PsCl*, 5: 1911, 63-96, 99-120, especially 102-113.

(40) A. Jost, Die Associationsfestigkeit in ihrer Abhängigkeit von der Verteilung der Wiederholungen. *ZPs*, 14: 1897, 436-472.

(41) F. Kemsies, Gedächtnisuntersuchungen an Schülern. *ZPdPs*, 2: 1900, 21-30, 84-95.

(42) E. A. Kirkpatrick, An experimental study of memory. *PsR*, 1: 1894, 602-9.

(43) Emma Kohnky, Preliminary study of the effect of dental treatment upon the physical and mental efficiency of school children. *JEdPs*, 4: 1913, 569-578.

(44) E. Kraepelin, Der psychologische Versuch in der Psychiatrie. *PsArb*, 1: 1896, 1-91, especially pp. 73 ff. (See also G. Aschaffenburg, *ibid.*, 209-299.)

(45) F. Krueger and C. Spearman, Die Korrelation zwischen verschiedenen geistigen Leistungsfähigkeiten. *ZPs*, 44: 1907, 50-114.

(46) F. Kuhlmann, A new memory apparatus. *PsR*, 19: 1912, 74-78.

(47) P. Lapie, Avancés et retardés. *AnPs*, 18: 1912, 233-270, especially 238-240.

(48) J. Larguier des Bancels, Sur les méthodes de mémorisation. *AnPs*, 8: 1901 (1902), 185-204.

(49) W. A. Lay, Experimentelle Didaktik. 3d ed., 1910, especially 297-305, 351-370.

(50) M. Lobsien, Experimentelle Untersuchungen über die Gedächtnissentwickelung bei Schulkindern. *ZPs*, 27: 1901, 34-76.

(51) E. Meumann, Intelligenzprüfungen an Kindern der Volksschule. *EPd*, 1: 1905, 35-101.

(52) E. Meumann, The psychology of learning. Eng. transl. New York, 1913. Pp. 393.

(53) W. McDougall, On a new method for the study of concurrent mental operations and of mental fatigue. *BrJPs*, 1: 1905, 435-445, especially 436 f.

(54) G. Müller and A. Pilzecker, Experimentelle Beiträge zur Lehre vom Gedächtniss. *ZPs, Ergänzungsband*, 1: 1900, 1-288.

(55) G. Müller and F. Schumann, Experimentelle Beiträge zur Untersuchung des Gedächtnisses. *ZPs*, 6: 1894, 81-190, 257-339.

(56) H. Münsterberg and J. Bigham, Memory. *PsR*, 1: 1904, 34-38.

(57) A. Netschajeff, Experimentelle Untersuchungen über die Gedächtnissentwickelung bei Schulkindern. *ZPs*, 24: 1900, 321-351.

(58) Naomi Norsworthy, The psychology of mentally deficient children (Columbia University thesis). New York, 1906. Pp. 111.

(59) M. Offner, Das Gedächtnis, Berlin, 1909. Pp. 238.

(60) A. Pohlmann, Experimentelle Beiträge zur Lehre vom Gedächtniss. Berlin, 1906. Pp. 191. (For full review, see *ZPs*, 44: 1907, 134-140.)

(61) W. H. Pyle, The examination of school children. New York, 1913. Pp. 70, especially 14-17.

(61a)   W. H. Pyle, The mind of the negro child. *School and Society,*
1 : 1915, 357-360.

(62)   J. O. Quantz, Problems in the psychology of reading. *PsMon,*
2 : 1897 (No. 5). Pp. 51.

(63)   F. Reuther, Beiträge zur Gedächtnisforschung. *Psych. Studien,*
1 : 1906, 4-101.

(64)   C. Ritter, Ermüdungsmessungen. *ZPs,* 24 : 1900, 401-444.

(65)   M. C. Schuyten, Sur les méthodes de mensuration de la fatigue
des écoliers. *ArPs(f),* 4 : 1904, 113-128.

(66)   J. Segal, Ueber den Reproduktionstypus und das Reprodukzieren
von Vorstellungen. *ArGsPs,* 12 : 1908, 124-235.

(67)   Stella E. Sharp, Individual psychology : a study in psychological
method. *AmJPs,* 10 : 1899, 329-391.

(68)   B. R. Simpson, Correlations of mental abilities. *Columbia
ConEd,* No. 53. New York, 1912. Pp. 122.

(69)   W. G. Sleight, Memory training ; is it general or specific? *JEPd,*
1 : 1911, 51-54.

(70)   F. Smedley, Report dept. child-study and pedagogic investigation (Chicago Public Schools).   No. 3, 1900-1901, also in *RepComEd,*
1902, i., 1115-1138.

(71)   W. G. Smith, The relation of attention to memory. *Mind,* n. s.
4 : 1895, 47-73.

(72)   W. G. Smith, The place of repetition in memory. *PsR,* 3 :
1896, 21-31.

(73)   W. G. Smith, A comparison of some mental and physical tests
in their relation to epileptic and to normal subjects. *BrJPs,* 1 : 1905,
240-260.

(74)   Carrie R. Squire, Graded mental tests. *JEdPs,* 3 : 1912, 363-380,
430-443, 493-506, especially 377-380.

(75)   D. Starch, Transfer of training in arithmetical operations.
JEdPs, 2 : 1911, 306-310.

(76)   A. v. Sybel, Ueber das Zusammenwirken verschiedener Sinnes-
gebiete bei Gedächtnisleistungen. *ZPs,* 53 : 1909, 258-353. (For summary see *PsBu,* 7 : 1910, 386-7.)

(77)   E. B. Titchener, Experimental psychology, Vol. I., New York,
1901.

(78)   J. J. van Biervliet, L'éducation de la mémoire à l'école. *RPhF,*
57 : 1904, 569-586.

(79)   R. Wessely, Zur Frage des Auswendiglernens. *Neue Jahr-
bücher f. Pädagogik,* 8 : 1905, 297-309, 373-386.

(80)   W. H. Winch, Immediate memory in school children. *BrJPs,* 1 :
1904, 127-134, and 2 : 1906, 52-57.

(81)   W. H. Winch, (*a*) The transfer of improvement in memory in
school children. *BrJPs,* 2 : 1908, 284-293. (*b*) Same, continued, 3 : 1910,
386-405.

(82)   W. H. Winch, Mental fatigue in day-school children as measured
by immediate memory. *JEdPs,* 3 : 1912, 18-28, 74-82.

(83)   C. Wissler, The correlation of mental and physical tests. *Ps
Mon,* 3 : 1901, No. 6. Pp. 62.

(84)   S. Wyatt, The quantitative investigation of higher mental
processes. *BrJPs,* 6 : 1913, 109-133.

(85)   C. S. Yoakum, An experimental study of fatigue. *PsMon,* 11 :
1909, No. 46. Pp. 131.

TEST 39

Memory for ideas: 'Logical' memory.—This test differs from the preceding tests of memory in two respects: in the first place, connected, meaningful material is used instead of a series of disparate impressions; in the second place, the reproduction that is demanded is primarily a reproduction of ideas, not an exact, verbatim reproduction of the original presentation. In other words, this test, to use current phraseology, measures 'logical,' or 'substance' memory, instead of 'rote,' or 'mechanical' memory.

While, in principle, the attitude taken by *S* toward the test of memory for ideas is distinctly different from that taken toward the test of memory for discrete impressions, yet, in practise, it is not always possible to differentiate these attitudes in the tests as actually administered. Thus, Binet and Henri, and after them, Miss Sharp, conducted tests of "memory for sentences." In these tests, the sentences ranged from short to long, and from easy to difficult. A short, easy sentence, *e. g.*, a sentence of 11 words, is almost invariably interpreted by *S* as a straightforward test of verbal memory, and the reproduction is at bottom a recall in verbal (mainly auditory verbal) terms. On the other hand, a long, difficult sentence, *e. g.*, a sentence of 86 words, when heard or read but once, must be reproduced in substance, not verbatim, and the recall, for most *S*'s at least, is a recall by meaning, a reproduction of the 'gist' of the material presented.

It is evidently better to keep separate these two different forms of memory test, with their two correspondingly different attitudes. The material of the present tests is, accordingly, sufficiently lengthy to preclude verbatim recall. Memory for sentences of progressive length has been treated in Test 38.

The purposes of the test are similar to those of other memory tests, viz.: to determine individual differences in memory efficiency as related to sex, age, training, native ability, etc. As in those tests, too, the effect of different methods of presenting the material, or of different forms of material, may be studied, and immediate may be compared with deferred reproduction. The results of the test may also be correlated with the results of other tests, particularly with the tests of rote memory just described. Among others, the following examples are characteristic of these various uses of the logical memory test. In the Binet-Simon series of 1908 the Story of the Fire was introduced at the 8th and 9th years. Wissler used a logical memory test in his series applied to Columbia freshmen, Terman in his comparative study of bright and dull boys, Winch in the investigation of fatigue and of transfer of training, Simpson in his comparison of competent and incompetent adults. The Marble Statue test, which the author derived from Shaw's study of memory in school children, has been applied by Pyle to several hundred children and adults for the purpose of establishing age and sex norms. Aall used an anecdote, much longer than those here prescribed, as the material for an interesting study of sex and individual difference, particularly as affected by immediate or deferred reproduction. Perhaps the most elaborate investigation of "memory for connected trains of thought" is, however, that of Henderson, who administered a series of tests to over 200 S's, ranging from 10-year-old 5th-grade children to adult students in the university. Henderson's work forms the basis of the tests which are here prescribed, with some modifications suggested by the use of the test by the author for several years as a class exercise.

MATERIALS.—Watch.   Three printed forms—The Marble Statue, Cicero, and The Dutch Homestead.

The first of these is taken from the appendix of Shaw's article, and was apparently used by him for subsidiary tests. The second and third are Nos. 2 and 4 of the five texts used by Henderson. If E wishes to extend the test by using more difficult material, he may employ Henderson's No. 5—a selection entitled "The Stages in the Development of Human Theory," from Comte's *Positive Philosophy*. If the Marble Statue proves too difficult or uninteresting for very young S's, E may employ to advantage the text proposed by Binet and Simon (Wallin's arrangement) or the story of Mr. Lincoln and the Pig (from Clyde and Wallace, *Through the Year*, Book 2, Silver, Burdett & Co.).

THREE HOUSES BURNED

(From the 1908 Binet-Simon tests, revised by Wallin)

(51 words, 20 ideas)

New York, | September 5th. | A fire | last night | burned three houses | in Water Street. | It took some time | to put it out. | The loss | was fifty thousand dollars, | and seventeen families | lost their homes. | In saving | a girl | who was asleep | in a bed, | a fireman | was burned | on the hands.

How Mr. Lincoln Helped the Pig
(131 words, 42 ideas)

"One day | Mr. Lincoln | was out riding. | As he passed
along the road, | he saw a pig | sinking | into a mud-hole. |
Poor | piggy would climb | part way | up the slippery | bank, |
then down he would fall again. |

'I suppose I should get down | and help | that pig,' | thought
Mr. Lincoln. 'But I have on my new suit, | and it will be quite
spoiled if I do so. | I think I'll let him get out | the best way
he can.' |

He rode on. | When nearly | two | miles away, | he turned |
and came back. | Not minding the new | clothes, | he stooped, |
and taking piggy in his arms, | he dragged him | out | of the
mud. |

The new | suit | was quite | spoiled, | but Mr. Lincoln | said |
he had taken a pain | out of his mind." |

METHOD.—Provide *S* with paper and pencil. Explain the
nature of the test, as follows: "I am going to read you something to see how well you can remember it afterward. You
must pay careful attention, as I shall read it but once. As
soon as I have finished, take your pencil and write as
much of the story as you can remember. If you can remember
it in just the words you heard, use those words, but if you can't
do that, tell in your own words, as well as you can, what it was
that I read to you."

Read the passage, including the title, with most careful
enunciation, and with proper attention to expression. The rate
of reading should be somewhat slower than in ordinary reading—say a full minute for the Cicero test. Allow *S* ample
time for writing, then ask him to underline each word in his
reproduction that he feels sure is exactly the same as the
original passage.[1]

---

[1]This test lends itself easily to the group method. The usual precautions should be taken to avoid disturbance and communication. *E* may
save himself much labor by asking each *S* to count the total number of
words he has written, then the total number of words he has underlined.
With mature *S*'s, *E* may also reread very slowly the original text, and
let each *S* check up the total number of ideas correctly reproduced, *i. e.*,
represented, whether verbatim or by equivalent phrases, in his reproduction. The division of each text into its constituent 'ideas' is indicated
below.

VARIATIONS OF METHOD.—(1) Supply *S* with the printed text. Inform him that he is to have 2 min. to read the passage. Assure him that this time is ample to read it over carefully more than once. Direct him to read the passage straight through twice, and then use any time that remains in studying it as he wishes.

(2) Defer the reproduction to any desired time after the reading, *e. g.*, 10 min., 24 hours, 1 week, 4 weeks. Or require an immediate reproduction, followed later, at one or more of the intervals just suggested, by a second or by a third reproduction.[2] Conduct these deferred trials in the same manner, as far as directions to underline, etc., are concerned, as in the first trial.

TREATMENT OF DATA.—The simplest plan for scoring the data of this test is that used by Terman and by Wissler, who merely graded the papers on a scale of 5 (or of 10) for a perfect reproduction—perfect in the sense of a reproduction of all the ideas of the original text, whether in terms identical with, or merely equivalent to, the original.

For ordinary purposes, the author has found it serviceable to score the papers for the following points: (1) number of words written, (2) number of words underlined, (3) percentage of underlined words that are correctly underlined, (4) number of ideas ('details' in Henderson's terminology) that have been reproduced, whether exactly or in equivalent phrases. To these may be added, if desired, (5) number of ideas wrongly inserted. If but a single score is to be made, the fourth is obviously the one to be used, since the task assigned to *S* is to give as many as possible of the ideas of the text.[3]

The second and subsequent reproductions are scored in the same manner as the first. Retention is then measured, follow-

---

[2] It is better, on the whole, to give no intimation of the intent to demand a second reproduction. Some *S*'s may compare notes after the first reproduction, but if the subsequent trial is announced beforehand, coupled, as it ought to be, with the request not to think of the test in the interim, the request is more apt to work as a counter-suggestion, so that many *S*'s will test their recall of the passage, and otherwise furbish up the memories during the interval.

[3] Consult Aall, Sharp or Henderson for more elaborate methods of treating data, particularly for devices for qualitative analysis.

ing Shaw and Henderson, by computing the percentage of loss between these and the first reproduction. Occasional cases of improvement in the later reproductions are rated as a negative loss.

To ascertain the 'idea-score,' S's reproduction must be compared, step by step, with the standard divisions of the original text into ideas.[4]

The Marble Statue

(166 words, 67 ideas)

A young | man | worked | years | to carve | a white | marble | statue.| of a beautiful | girl. | She grew prettier | day by day. | He began to love the statue | so well that | one day | he said to it: | "I would give | everything | in the world | if you would be alive | and be my wife." | Just then | the clock struck | twelve,| and the cold | stone began to grow warm, | the cheeks red, | the hair brown, | the lips to move. | She stepped down, | and he had his wish. | They lived happily | together | for years, | and three | beautiful | children were born. | One day | he was very tired,| and grew | so angry,| without cause,| that he struck her.| She wept, | kissed | each child | and her husband, | stepped back | upon the pedestal, | and slowly | grew cold, | pale | and stiff, | closed her eyes, | and when the clock | struck | midnight,| she was a statue | of pure | white | marble | as she had been | years before, | and could not hear | the sobs | of her husband | and children.

Cicero

(125 words, 64 ideas)

"Cicero, | the greatest | of the Roman | orators, | was born | at Arpinum, | an obscure | country | town. | His family | was of the middle class | only, | and without wealth, | yet he rose | rapidly | through the ranks | of Roman | official service | until at the age | of forty-six | he became | consul. | In oratory | he

---

[4]The scoring for ideas for these three passages is taken, with a few minor changes, from Shaw and from Henderson. For a division of the second and third texts into topics and sub-topics as well as into ideas, the reader may consult Henderson (6, pp. 29-30).

is | by universal consent | placed side by side | with Demos-
thenes, | or at least | close after him. | He surpassed | the
great | Attic | orator | in brilliancy | and variety, | but lacked |
his moral | earnestness | and consequent | impressiveness. |
He could be | humorous, | sarcastic, | pathetic, | ironical, |
satirical, | and when he was malignant | his mouth was | most |
foul | and his bite | most | venomous. | His delivery | was im-
passioned | and fiery, | his voice | strong, | full, | and sweet, |
his figure | tall, | graceful, | and impressive."

The Dutch Homestead

(180 words, 94 ideas)

"It was | one | of those spacious | farm- | houses, | with high- |
ridged, | but lowly | sloping | roofs, | built | in the style |
handed down from | the first | Dutch | settlers, | the low | pro-
jecting | eaves | forming a piazza | along the front | capable |
of being closed up | in bad weather. | Under this | were hung |
flails, | harness, | various | utensils | of husbandry, | and nets |
for fishing | in the neighboring | river. | Benches | were built |
along the side | for summer use; | and a great | spinning wheel |
at one end, | and a churn | at the other, | showed | the various |
uses | to which this | important | porch | might be devoted. |
From this piazza | one might enter | the hall, | which formed |
the center | of the mansion | and the usual | place of residence. |
Here | rows | of resplendent | pewter | ranged | on a long |
dresser | dazzled | his eyes. | In one corner | stood a huge |
bag | of wool, | ready | to be spun; | in another | a quantity | of
linsey-woolsey, | just | from the loom; | ears | of Indian | corn
and strings | of dried | apples | and peaches | hung | in gay
festoons | along the walls, | mingled | with the gaud | of red
peppers."

RESULTS.—(1) *Norms.* Performance with the Marble Statue
selection has been investigated by Pyle (group method, written
reproduction) with the results shown in Table 116. The author's results for college students with the Dutch Homestead
selection are shown in Table 117, while some idea of the dis-

tribution of performance for the Cicero selection with college students (mostly Sophomores) is given by Table 118. In all of these tables, and particularly in those referring to college students, evidence is given to show the unexpectedly large individual variation in memory for ideas that prevails even within a group of S's of apparently similar attainments.

TABLE 116

Marble Statue Test, Scores by Age and Sex (Pyle)

SEX		8	9	10	11	12	13	14	15	16	17	18	ADULT
Male	Cases	102	148	142	149	156	163	129	89	60	45	32	65
	Aver.	24.3	28.7	30.0	32.9	35.1	36.8	36.1	36.5	34.4	34.6	36.9	38.3
	A. D.	6.7	9.1	6.7	5.6	7.4	6.3	7.0	6.7	5.6	8.7	6.0	7.0
Female	Cases	89	158	138	156	191	164	146	99	94	81	48	86
	Aver.	28.5	31.0	33.5	36.4	38.1	38.5	39.0	39.1	37.3	36.6	37.8	40.1
	A. D.	11.3	9.4	6.8	7.7	7.2	7.1	7.5	6.3	5.1	6.9	4.4	5.9

TABLE 117

Dutch Homestead Test. Words Written and Underlined (Whipple)

	FIRST TRIAL, NO INTERVAL		SECOND TRIAL, 24 HOURS LATER	
	Total Words	Words Underlined	Total Words	Words Underlined
Average, 9 men	80.4	48.0	83.0	38.4
Average, 22 women	95.5	38.8	99.6	34.1
Maximal records	127.0	102.0	138.0	66.0
Minimal records	45.0	4.0	52.0	9.0

TABLE 118

Cicero Test. Distribution of 36 College Students (Whipple)

	BEST SIX	2D SIX	3D SIX	4TH SIX	5TH SIX	WORST SIX
Words written	115-96	95-88	84-75	74-66	65-60	56-25
Correct ideas	46-37	36-34	32-28	28-25	25-21	20-7

(2) *Dependence on age.* Binet and Simon put the reproduction of 2 items from the Story of the Fire as standard for 8 years, 6 items as standard for 9 years. The results reported by Vos, who read to boys and girls 9 to 14 years old a story containing 40 'ideas' and called for reproductions 3 days later, show rather unusual variations from year to year, despite the fact that some 800 *S*'s are represented: report is declared to be good at 9, best at 10, thence deteriorating decidedly to 13, but improving at 14 years. The elaborate studies of Shaw and of Henderson are also somewhat difficult to interpret. It appears evident, however, that a distinction must be made between efficiency in the first reproduction and efficiency in subsequent reproductions. If the first be termed learning capacity, and the second retentive capacity, and if the latter be measured in terms of the proportion of the first reproduction that is retained in the second (or later) reproduction, then adults may be shown to surpass children in learning capacity, but not in retentive capacity.

Thus, in Shaw's rather difficult 324-word story, the learning capacity of boys increased, from the 3d to the 9th grade, from 17 to 42 per cent., that of girls from 18 to 43 per cent. High-school boys averaged only 40 per cent., high-school girls about 47 per cent. Shaw's university students did no better, while Henderson's summer session students were inferior to his 15 and 16-year-old school children. In short, then, logical, like rote memory appears, when measured by the first reproduction, to be at its best near puberty. This conclusion agrees entirely with the averages secured by Pyle for children 8 to 18 years old and for adults (Table 116). His boys reached their maximal ability at 13, his girls at 12 years.

TABLE 119

Average Percentage of Loss in Third Reproduction (After 4 Weeks)
(Henderson)

AGE	ADULTS	16	15	14	13	12	11	10
Percentage of loss_____	14	8	13	15	14	12	10	10

Turning to the later reproductions, Shaw and Henderson (Table 119) agree that younger S's have as good retentive capacity as do adults.

(3) *Sex differences* in this test, as in the rote-memory test, are in favor of girls. The difference is indicated clearly in the author's data for college students (Table 117), and similar differences are reported by Shaw, who found the growth of memory for ideas to be faster in girls than in boys, and the average performance of girls to be some 4 per cent. better than that of boys. Wissler's records for Columbia freshmen show an average of 44.5 per cent., P.E. 11.1, for men, and 48.2 per cent., P.E. 13.2, for women. Pyle's averages reveal the superiority of girls at every age from 8 to maturity. Schramm's comparison of 16 men and 16 women (students at Freiburg University) shows a slight superiority for the women, though the differences do not exceed their probable error. The only exceptions to this trend in favor of superiority of females seem to appear in the work of Vos and of Aall. The latter states that the reproductions of women are usually fuller, but those of men are more compact, 'meatier,' and betray greater plastic power, greater originality in formulation.

(4) *Dependence on time-interval.* The insertion of a time-interval between presentation and reproduction has much less effect upon memory for ideas than upon memory for discrete impressions. Table 117 shows that, if a second reproduction is called for one day after the first, the average S actually writes more words. The words in the later reproduction are, however, less exact copies of the original text, and there is a tendency to insert extraneous material, so that fewer words are underlined, and there is a slight net reduction in the number of ideas reproduced. In the author's tests, this reduction was but 3 per cent. at the end of one week. Table 119 shows that an interval of 4 weeks produces a loss of but 8 to 15 per cent.

Similar conclusions are reached by Aall, who compared the reproductions of a lengthy story directly after hearing it and 48 hours later. The latter reports were on the whole poorer—more omissions and more 'falsification.' They are shown to 'lean' strongly on the first reports, often to become more verbose and less precise, and sometimes matters that were correctly left rather vague in the first report become erroneously 'logicized' into explicit and particularized statements, which are actually possible, but incorrect as reports. On the other hand, as Aall points out, there exists a sort of 'after-memory' such that certain details which are forgotten or at least unmentioned in the immediate reproduction come to light correctly in the delayed one. The influence of time-interval also appears to operate differently on different forms of material; for instance, names of places are lost sooner than memories of objects.

It is a matter of special interest to note that the relative standing of *S*'s remains practically the same in tests conducted with immediate, and with deferred recall. Similarly, those who memorize a passage of a given length in quick time are not found to be at a disadvantage in subsequent recall (see Ogden and Pyle, 12), though the individual differences are usually found to be less in subsequent recall than in original speed of learning. It follows that, so far as this test goes at least, the popular notion "easy come, easy go" is not borne out by experimental evidence. Henderson found that this correlation between learning capacity and retentive capacity was brought out better in scoring for ideas than in scoring for words.

(5) *Dependence on method of presentation.* When a single hearing is compared with reading done by *S* (3 min.), the former is found to be nearly as good as the latter for immediate reproduction, but the latter to be much more effective than the former for deferred reproduction.

(6) *Dependence on practise.* Baade, who scored the reports made by 196 girls, aged 12-13 years, upon what was said by an instructor in the course of a series of demonstrations in physics, found that under those conditions there was no demonstrable improvement in their work, either from the succession of the three sets of demonstrations or from the repetition of the demonstrations. Nevertheless, the work of other investigators gives little doubt that practise will improve memory for ideas, as it will improve nearly every form of psychophysical activity. Special training thus accounts, in all probability, for the high

scores (52 as over against 40 to 47 per cent.) reached by the pupils of Miss Aiken's school[5] in comparison with the work of Worcester high-school children.

Winch (21) has investigated the possibility of transfer of practise, and concludes that "improvement through practise in rote memory for things with and without meaning is followed by improvement in substance for stories." He argues that this transfer may take place despite the circumstance that correlations between rote and substance memory are sometimes, as in his own work, of a low or even doubtful character. Winch (23) has also investigated the transfer of practise in substance memory to efficiency in productive imagination. He concludes that "children practised in substance memory for stories become thereby more proficient in the invention of stories. The improvement is not due to the insertion of parts of the content of the memorized stories within the invented stories, but to some community of function less atomistic." An exception appeared, however, in portions of his experimental work, which leads him to add that "children practised in substance memory up to the fatigue point, which is taken here to mean the point at which consecutive exercises cease to produce improvement, are thereby prejudicially affected so far as their power to invent stories is concerned." These 'fatigue-effects,' he says, "appear to be temporary, whilst practise effect (improvement through practise) appears to have considerable duration."

(7) *Dependence on fatigue.* Although it is generally conceded that one of the commoner symptoms of mental fatigue is slowness or uncertainty of recall of ideas, no one but Winch (22) appears to have used the logical memory test in this connection. Winch's test was limited to a group of boys who were studying at an evening school. They were given 10 minutes to memorize the substance of passages of some 150 words and tested by the method of equivalent groups at 9 and at about 9.30 P. M., with the result that some 28 per cent. of difference was revealed. Since tests in day schools had shown prac-

---

[5] For an account of the special training given to Miss Aiken's pupils, see Test 25 and references thereto.

tically no difference between children working at noon and at 4.30 P. M., Winch argues that children who take evening school work after a day's work at various occupations exhibit a very rapid and pronounced susceptibility to mental fatigue.

(8) *Dependence on length of text.* The number of words reproduced after one hearing increases, though not in direct proportion, with the length of the passage heard (Binet and Henri).

(9) *Dependence on portion of text.* If the original passage be divided into 3ds or 4ths (or even, if long, into 8ths), it will be found that, on the average, the reproduction of any one of these portions is inferior to the one that precedes it and superior to the one that follows it. Thus, Shaw's story, on division into 4 parts, was found to be reproduced in the amounts 52, 34, 31, and 28 per cent., respectively.

What may be regarded as a test of logical memory was made by Dell with 30 boys who listened to an hour-and-a-half lecture upon material in *Punch,* which was illustrated by 80 lantern slides. The boys were asked 8 days later to indicate which slides they recalled. The first 15 slides were, on the average recalled by 11.2 boys, slides 47-59 by 3.8, slides 60-74 by 3.5 and slides 75-80 by 4.8 boys. These figures certainly seem to demonstrate a decidedly better recall of slides in the first portion of the lecture, with a questionable slight rise at the end of the lecture. Dell, however, believes that there were at work other causes than simply the dependency of memory on different positions in the lecture.

(10) *Reliability.* The work of Simpson, Winch and others shows that the logical memory test has an acceptable degree of reliability. Winch obtained coefficients of 0.65 and 0.68 between single trials; Simpson, coefficients of 0.78, 0.83 and 0.90 (for different groups) between scores in his first two and his last two trials. It follows that the amalgamated results from two, or at most three trials of this test afford quite reliable indications of ability in the capacities tested.

(11) *Dependence on intelligence.* The relation between logical memory and intelligence has been studied mainly by rating intelligence on the basis of scholarship. The resulting correla

tions are somewhat unexpectedly low. Thus, in 86 cases, Wissler found a correlation of only 0.19 with class standing, of 0.11 with standing in mathematics, and of 0.22 with standing in Latin. Henderson found but a slight correlation with class standing in the lower grades, but a closer correlation in the higher grades. He is of the opinion that, at least in the lower grades, the school marks put a premium upon industry and good conduct, rather than upon native ability, and thus obscure the existing correlation. Pyle estimates the relation with class standing in college at about 0.30, and says: . "If a slow learner has the habit of going over a lesson or task several times, and a fast learner the habit of giving a lesson but one hasty reading, other things being equal, the slow learner will have the better scholarship" (12, p. 319). The very best students have both good memory and good habits of study. If performance in tests of reasoning be taken as a measure of intelligence, then Peterson's work confirms the general statement given above, for of 30 students classed as good in reasoning, 20 ranked good, 5 medium and 5 poor in memory, while of the 17 classed as poor in reasoning 3 ranked good, 6 medium and 8 poor in memory. Again, in Simpson's investigation the correlation between logical memory and estimated intelligence of his 'good' group was but 0.35, after correction for attenuation. However, his good and his poor group were fairly well separated by the test, since none of the poor group reached the median of the good group and only 15 per cent. of the poor group excelled the lowest 12 per cent. of the good group.

(12) *Mental defectives.* Wallin tested epileptics by means of Binet's Story of the Fire, though without warning them when reading that a reproduction would be called for. Table

TABLE 120

Story of the Fire. Scores for Epileptics by Mental Age (After Wallin)

BINET-SIMON AGE	VII	VIII	IX	X	XI	XII	XIII
Cases	13	42	27	70	28	11	17
Aver. Ideas	2.1	3.7	4.8	5.3	6.5	6.8	7.4

120 shows the average number of ideas reproduced by his patients as classified for mental age by the Binet-Simon tests. It is evident that there exists a general progress in efficiency with mental age, but that the average performance of these mental defectives is not as good as would be expected of normal children in the ages from 9 to 13.

(13) *Miscellaneous correlations.* Peterson, by the method of unlike signs, using the pooled results of several tests of each 'function,' concluded that memory was correlated with reasoning by 0.40, with abstract thought by 0.64; with generalizing ability by 0.40 and with accuracy by 0.31. Simpson publishes as estimated true correlations (holding for people in general) with memory for passages the following: completion test 0.71, hard opposites 0.70, memory for words 0.80, easy opposites 0.50, a-test 0.46, adding 0.42. The high correlation with memory for words permits us, he concludes, to class substance memory with it as virtually the same capacity. Winch found correlations between substance memory and productive imagination (inventing stories) which appear to be higher in the more proficient classes (the r's secured in various classes were 0.28, 0.43, 0.48, 0.62, 0.75). Heymans and Brugmans found a correlation of only 0.08 between reproduction of a somewhat elaborate story at various time-intervals and the learning of nonsense syllables, but a correlation of 0.55 between the memory test and a test involving memory for details of a picture. They also report a correlation of 0.56 between the completion test and written reproduction of a difficult passage from Höffding's Ethics. Wissler found a correlation of 0.21 between logical memory and length of head, but no correlation between logical memory and rote memory, speed of naming colors, reaction time, or breadth of head.

(14) *Qualitative aspects.*[6] Inspection of the work of children and introspective examination by adults of their own mental

---

[6] Consult especially Balaban, Michotte and Ransy, and Michotte and Portych for further study of the qualitative aspects of logical memory, particularly of the difference between mechanical and logical memory under simple test conditions, like the method of right associates. The work of Aall has also numerous suggestive features in addition to those here mentioned.

processes reveal a number of interesting principles. In the first place, there is a process of selection · words or ideas that are logically or psychologically important ₂ best retained. Or, as Henderson expresses it, there is, especially during a long time-interval, a process of condensation and gener.ºization. The main ideas, the important topics, the brunt of the passage may remain fairly constant, but the minor details tend to be forgotten, and the original phrasing to become less and less clear.

When, then, the reproduction is demanded, most S's first recall these main ideas or larger topics, and then develop the details, as best they may, from them. There is a strong tendency, in this filling out of the details, toward what Binet and Henri speak of as "verbal assimilation," *i. e.,* a tendency to express the ideas in one's own terms, rather than in those employed in the original passage. Thus, adults often use synonyms or other forms of substitution, while children replace the words of the original by words from their ordinary vocabulary (*e. g., played* for *amused themselves, fire* for *conflagration*), and at the same time tend to simplify the syntax. In general, Binet and Henri found that the number of times that synonyms are used in the recall is, in short passages greater, and in long passages less than the number of ideas completely omitted.

Finally, the substitution of terms for those of the original tends, especially in younger S's and with longer time-intervals, to become inexact; in other words, the sense of the original becomes more or less distorted. Thus, for instance, Binet and Henri discovered that, in all sentences containing more than 20 words, more than half of their S's had made some change in the meaning of the original. Of these alterations of sense, the most conspicuous are: (1) change of proper names or of numbers, (2) replacement of an object by an analogous object that might fit the sentence equally well, (3) insertion of details not inconsistent with the original, but still not in the original, and (4) alterations apparently due to emotional reaction, especially to exaggeration, *e. g., a frightful snake* for *a snake.*

Aall thinks that two sorts of S's can be distinguished—the 'reporters,' who make every effort to get the reproduction exact, and the 'describers,' who introduce various modifications and embellishments for the sake of literary or rhetorical effect. He found the typical error in recounting a story to be omission rather than falsification. Mention has been made already of the changes found by Aall in deferred reproductions.

(15) *Miscellaneous points.* In the case of college students, from 50 to 90 per cent. of the words underlined are actually correct. A certain type of *S* may be recognized, who is extremely cautious about underlining words, but who usually has these few nearly all correct.

Binet and Henri estimate that memory for connected sentences is approximately 25 times as good as memory for discrete terms.

REFERENCES

(1) A. Aall, Zur Psychologie der Wiedererzählung. *ZAngPs*, 7: 1912-13, 185-210.

(2) W. Baade, Aussage über physikalische Demonstrationen. I. Abh. Die Methodik der Versuche über die Inhalte der Textaussagen. *ZAngPs*, 4: 1911, 189-311.

(3) A. Balaban, Ueber den Unterschied des logischen und des mechanischen Gedächtnisses. *ZPs*, 56: 1910, 356-377.

(4) A. Binet et V. Henri, La mémoire des phrases. *AnPs*, 1: 1894 (1895), 24-59.

(5) J. A. Dell, Some observations on the learning of sensible material. *JEdPs*, 3: 1912, 401-406.

(6) E. N. Henderson, A study of memory for connected trains of thought. New York. Pp. 94. (Columbia Univ. Thesis.)

(7) G. Heymans und H. Brugmans, Intelligenzprüfungen mit Studierenden. *ZAngPs*, 7: 1913, 317-331.

(8) A. Michotte et C. Ransy, Contribution a l'étude de la mémoire logique. *Extrait des Annales de l'institut supérieur de philosophie.* Louvain, 1912. Pp. 95.

(9) A. Michotte et Th. Portych, Deuxième étude sur la mémoire logique. *Ibid.*, 2: 1913, 533-657.

(10) R. M. Ogden, Untersuchungen über den Einfluss der Geschwindigkeit des lauten Lesens auf das Erlernen und Behalten von sinnlosen und sinnvollen Stoffen. *ArGesPs*, 2: 1903-4, 93-189.

(11) H. A. Peterson, Correlation of certain mental traits in normal school students. *PsR*, 15: 1908, 323-338.

(12) W. H. Pyle, Retention as related to repetition. *JEdPs*, 2: 1911, 311-321.

(13) W. H. Pyle, The examination of school children. New York, 1913. Pp. 70, especially 8-14.

(14) F. Schramm, Zur Aussagetreue der Geschlechter. *ZAngPs*, 5: 1911, 355-357.

(15) Stella E. Sharp, Individual psychology: a study in psychological method. *AmJPs*, 10: 1899, 329-391.

(16) J. C. Shaw, A test of memory in school children. *PdSc*, 4: 1896, 61-78.

(17)   B. R. Simpson, Correlations of mental abilities.   *Columbia ConEd*, No. 53. New York, 1912. Pp. 122.

(18)   L. W. Terman, Genius and stupidity. *PdSe*, 13 : 1906, 307-373.

(19)   H. B. L. Vos, Beiträge zur Psychologie der Aussage bei Schulkindern. Analyse der Aussage über eine gehörte Erzählung. Amsterdam, 1909.   (Eigenbericht, *ZAngPs*, 4 : 1911, 375-378.)

(20)   J. E. W. Wallin, Experimental studies of mental defectives. *EdPsMon*, No. 7, 1912. Pp. 155.

(21)   W. H. Winch, The transfer of improvement in memory in school children, II. *BrJPs*, 3 : 1910, 386-405.

(22)   W. H. Winch, Some measurements of mental fatigue in adolescent pupils in evening schools. *JEdPs*, 1 : 1910, 13-23, 83-100.

(23)   W. H. Winch, Some relations between substance memory and productive imagination in school children. *BrJPs*, 4 : 1911, 95-125.

(24)   C. Wissler, The correlation of mental and physical tests. *Ps Mon*, 3 : 1901. Pp. 62.

CHAPTER X

Tests of Suggestibility

The term 'suggestion' has found different usages in psychology; four at least may be readily distinguished. (1) Suggestion is equivalent to association, *e. g.*, the idea 'horse' suggests the idea 'Black Beauty.' (2) Suggestion is the conveyance of an idea by hint, intimation, or insinuation, *e. g.*, the orator suggests an idea by an appropriate gesture. (3) Suggestion is a method of creating and controlling hypnosis. (4) Suggestion is a process of creating belief or affecting judgment, usually an erroneous belief or false judgment, in the normal consciousness. Here emphasis is placed upon uncritical acceptance of a notion usually with the implication that the suggested individual is unaware that his ideas have been thus affected. From his point of view, suggestion is, then, to follow Stern's definition (6), "the imitative assumption of a mental attitude under the illusion of assuming it spontaneously."

The tests which follow all purport to measure susceptibility to suggestion in this last-named sense. In them, the experimenter seeks, by suitable arrangement of the test-material or of the instructions, to induce the subject to judge otherwise than he naturally would—to induce him, for example, to judge equal lines or equal weights to be unequal, or to perceive warmth when there is no warmth, etc. If the attempt is successful, the subject is said to have 'yielded,' or to have 'accepted' the suggestion; if unsuccessful, he is said to have 'resisted' the suggestion. The degree of his suggestibility is indicated by the quickness or frequency of his 'yields.'

Just as efficiency in observation, attention, memory, and the like has been shown to be specific, not general, in character, so is it probable that suggestibility is specific, not general, in character. For this reason, suggestibility must be tested by more than one method.

Many of the tests in other portions of this book, *e. g.,* Nos. 17, 23, and especially 32, afford opportunity for noting the suggestibility of subjects. The serial graded tests of Binet and Simon also contain directions for testing the suggestibility of young or of feeble-minded children.

The tests which follow deal with suggestibility aroused by the volume-weight illusion, the length of lines, judgments of weights under special conditions, and illusory warmth. Other experimental methods of inducing suggestibility, which have not as yet been arranged for test work, may be briefly cited.

H. J. Pearce (3) had S's sit in a chair with a circle of 3.5 ft. radius drawn about it. S fixated a small bit of paper directly in front of him. A test square was exposed briefly at a point somewhere to the right of the fixation-point, and S located its position afterward by moving his eyes to the right. Suggestion was introduced by displaying at times a third bit of paper near or farther than the test square. There was at first a tendency to resist this suggestion, but eventually there was developed a tendency to locate the test square in a direction corresponding to the location of the suggestive paper. Auditory and tactual stimuli were also tried.

J. C. Bell (1) displayed triangles of different shapes and heights, also vertical distances between points or between a point and a line. The S's reproduced the distances and were given verbal suggestions or visual suggestions to "make high" or "make low," etc. In general, the suggestions did affect the test with triangles, but there were decided individual differences, and in many cases the constant errors were greater than the errors induced by suggestion.

The work of E. K. Strong (7) was similar in character, save that his S's exerted maximal strength of grip while exposed to such suggestions as "Now you can make it stronger than usual," etc., but with the proviso not voluntarily to interfere with the suggestion. The results showed that grips following both suggestions of 'weak' and 'strong' were stronger than those intended to produce 'neutral,' while there was no difference between two first kinds.

W. D. Scott (5) produced suggestion with some success by inducing S's to think that the flight of colors following an exposure to white light corresponded in order to the arrangement of colors in the spectrum.

Inez Powelson and M. F. Washburn (4) showed colors with comments upon them, such as 'delicate,' 'crude,' etc., and influenced in this way the affective reactions of 19 S's, but failed with 16 others.

Giroud (2) showed 34 children, aged 7 to 12 years, a series of 10 colors, with the instructions to name each color and then, when the color was withdrawn, to write the name. At the 3d. 7th and 10th terms, a wrong color-name was uttered by the experimenter to try to induce S to write it. The average number of 'yields' was reduced gradually from 2.8 at 7 years to 1.7 at 12 years.

REFERENCES

(1)   J. C. Bell, The effect of suggestion upon the reproduction of triangles and of point distances. *AmJPs*, 19: 1908, 504-598.

(2)   A. Giroud, La suggestibilité chez des enfants d'école de sept à douze ans. *AnPs*, 18: 1912, 362-388.

(3)   H. J. Pearce, Normal motor suggestibility. *PsRev.*, 9: 1902, 348-355.

(4)   Inez Powelson and M. F. Washburn, The effect of verbal suggestion on judgment of the affective value of colors. *AmJPs*, 24: 1913, 267-9.

(5)   W. D. Scott, Personal differences in suggestibility. *PsRev*, 17: 1910, 147-154.

(6)   W. Stern, Abstracts of lectures on the psychology of testimony. *AmJPs*, 21: 1910, 270-275.

(7)   E. K. Strong, The effect of various types of suggestion upon muscular activity. *PsRev*, 17: 1910, 279-293.

TEST 40

Suggestion by the size-weight illusion.—Big things are ordinarily heavier than small things of the same kind. When we lift two weights of apparently the same material, but of different sizes, we more or less unconsciously put forth more energy or expect to meet with more resistance in lifting the larger. If, as in the case of the so-called 'suggestion-blocks,' the weights are really the same, we almost inevitably judge the larger weight to be the lighter; in other words, the visual appearance of the weight has given us a suggestion—or, as it turns out, rather, a disappointed suggestion—of weight.[1]

This error of judgment is undoubtedly due to an association built up by long experience in handling and lifting various articles and objects.[2] One might, therefore, suppose that younger children, or less intelligent children, who would, presumably, have had less of this discriminative association of size and weight, would be less affected by the suggestion. For this reason, the size-weight test has been applied by several investigators to determine or to measure, at least relatively, the degree of suggestibility exhibited by school children under various conditions. But it is to be noted that the having of the illusion is normal, so that this test is not on the same order as those that follow it, and it has probably no particular value as a measure of suggestibility in older children and adults; its primary value lies in its use with young or mentally defective children.

APPARATUS.—Low table. Soft black cloth. Set of 'suggestion-blocks,' patterned after Gilbert, but modified by extending the comparison series in both directions.

This set consists of two standard blocks and 20 comparison blocks. Both standards weigh 55 grams; both are 28 mm. thick, but the larger is 82 and the smaller 22 mm. in diameter. The 20 comparison blocks are all 28 mm. thick and 35 mm. in diameter, but their weights range from 5 to 100 g. by 5 g. increments.[3] All are painted dead black.

If it is desired merely to make a quick determination of the presence or absence of the illusion, simpler material may be employed, preferably the 'Demoor blocks' as used at the Vineland (N. J.) Training School. These blocks are of poplar wood, and both weigh 1.5 lbs.; the one is 1.75x 3x4 in., the other 1.75x4x12 in. They are set before S with the simple instruction: "Tell me which block seems the heavier."

METHOD.—Arrange the table at such a height that S's fore-

---

[1] As Scripture remarks, the poor fellow who has been laughed at for centuries for saying that a pound of lead is heavier than a pound of feathers is perfectly right, so long as he speaks psychologically, and looks at the pillow and the bit of lead pipe. A concrete demonstration of the truth of this statement is afforded by several experiments reported by Wolfe.

[2] Some writers, however, e. g., Flournoy, attribute the illusion to an inborn nervous connection. For a discussion of the psychological factors concerned in this experiment, particularly in its relation to the 'innervation-sense,' consult Flournoy, Müller and Schumann, Seashore, Bolton, Loomis, and van Biervliet.

[3] Gilbert's comparison blocks were but 14 in number, with a range from 15 to 80 g. This range proved inadequate for younger S's.

arm will be parallel with the floor when lifting a weight. Spread over the table the black cloth, which should be large enough to cover at least the portion of the table occupied by the weights, and thick enough to deaden the sounds incident to their replacement.

Arrange the twenty comparison blocks on the cloth, in the order of their weight from left to right, and in such a manner that any one of them may be reached by S without materially changing the angle of his arm. Place before S the larger standard block, and say: "Here is a block. I want you to find a block in this series of 20 blocks that seems to you just as heavy as this one. Lift it by picking it up edgewise with your thumb and finger, like this. [Illustrate.] Then try the first of these weights [at the left]. If that doesn't suit, try the next, then the third, and so on, till you find a block that seems equal to this one. Each time you must lift this block first, then the one you are trying in the series. Keep your eyes constantly directed at the weight you are lifting." When S has selected an equivalent weight, the same procedure is followed with the second, or smaller, standard block.

The work of investigators in the psychological laboratory, particularly Martin and Müller, and Müller and Schumann, has shown that our estimate of the absolute or relative weight of a body is conditioned by an unsuspectedly large number of factors, so that, while it may be true, as Fourche (8) asserts, that voluntary modifications in the speed of grasping and lifting the weights do not modify the size-weight illusion, it seems desirable that the conditions under which S lifts the blocks should be kept as uniform as possible.

S should pick up each block in the same manner, lift it at the same tempo and to the same height. Again, since the memory image for weight changes rapidly, S's judgment, in so far as it is based upon the image of the first weight, would be appreciably altered if the second weight were lifted at varying intervals after the first: the interval should, accordingly, be made as constant as possible, and fairly short, say not over 3 sec., and the arrangement of the weights must be such as to permit this procedure. Finally, in this test, since the suggestion hinges upon the visual perception of the block, E must be sure that S looks directly at each block as he lifts it.

TREATMENT OF DATA.—Following Gilbert, Scripture, and Seashore, the force of suggestion produced by the difference in size of the two standard blocks may be indicated by the difference in weight, in grams, between the two comparison blocks that are selected by S as the equivalents of the two standards.

The force of the size-weight illusion has been expressed by
Scripture, on the basis of the more elaborate suggestion-blocks
used by Seashore, in the form of a special law.[4]

RESULTS.—(1) *Dependence on age.* Sample results for normal children are those of Gilbert (Table 121) : it will be seen
from them that the illusion is well developed at the age of 6
years, increases gradually till 9 years, and thence declines
slowly with age.[5] Dresslar (6), however, whose method was
undoubtedly less satisfactory, judged the effect of age to be
indifferent for 7 years and above. Philippe and Clavière, who
tested children from 3 years up, declare that the illusion decreases progressively below the age of 7, that it is obtained by

TABLE 121

Force of Suggestion (Gilbert)

AGE	6	7	8	9	10	11	12	13	14	15	16	17
NB _____	45	50	46	47	49	43	54	45	47	49	47	43
NG _____	47	45	46	47	42	48	49	58	53	51	39	41
F _____	42.0	45.0	47.5	50.0	43.5	40.0	40.5	38.0	34.5	35.0	34.5	27.0
P _____	36	37	27	36	23	22	15	8	7	12	6	5
MV _____	17.0	15.5	13.5	10.5	12.5	11.5	9.0	9.0	9.5	10.5	10.0	12.0
FB _____	43.5	43.5	45.0	50.0	40.0	38.5	38.0	37.0	31.0	33.0	32.0	25.0
FG _____	42.0	43.5	49.5	49.5	44.0	40.0	41.0	38.0	33.5	38.0	38.5	31.0

NB == number of boys
NG = number of girls
F = force of suggestion, in grams, for both sexes (median values)
P = per cent. of cases in which F exceeded 65 g., the limit used
MV = statistical mean variation
FB = force of suggestion, in grams for boys (median values)
FG = force of suggestion, in grams, for girls (median values)

[4]For the data from which this law is derived, see Scripture (19, p. 276f),
also Seashore (15, pp. 3-14). For a striking demonstration of the force
of the illusion, reference may be made to Wolfe's statements that "about
one woman in 7 finds 1 g. of lead equal in weight to 60 g. of inflated paper
bag," and not "one woman in 7 will find a gram of inflated paper bag half
as heavy as a gram of lead" (21, p. 460).
[5]Gilbert's explanation is given in the following terms : "At 6 he has not
yet learned to compare. As he learns gradually to judge a thing from
more aspects than one, or in other words, learns to interpret one sense by
another. the force of suggestion given by the eye to the muscle increases
until at 9 he has come to the age of experience enough to see that things
are not always what they seem. Consequently at this age he begins to
correct misleading influences bearing upon him."

only a third of the children 3 to 6 years old, that it would perhaps disappear entirely if the test could be carried below the
age of 3. They also found that the illusion is sometimes reversed in children of these ages.

(2) *Dependence on mental age* (*defective children*). In 1900
Demoor and Daniel (4) used the size-weight illusion, together
with other tests, in an examination of 380 'abnormal' children,
6 to 15 years of age, in the city of Brussels. Ten of these children, all of them ranked as idiots or 'simple-minded,' either
failed to get the normal illusion or had the illusion reversed.
Three years later Claparède (3) obtained similar results with
18 mentally defective children at Geneva, and proposed that
'Demoor's sign' (failure to get the normal illusion) should be
regarded as indicative of a diagnosis of medical (mental) retardation. In 1913 Doll (5) reported upon the examination at
the Vineland Training School of 345 feeble-minded, of chronological ages 5 to 60, and mental ages 1 to 12 years. The results
(Table 122 and Fig. 75) show that ability to perform the test at
all (with or without getting the illusion) indicates a mental
age of 4 years or over, while getting the normal illusion indicates a mental age of 7 years or over, since 84 per cent. succeed
at 7 years and 100 per cent. at 8 years and above.

TABLE 122

Reactions of Feeble-Minded Children to the Size-Weight Illusion (*Doll*)

MENTAL AGE	NUMBER TESTED	COMPLETE FAILURE		NO ILLUSION		ILLUSION	
			%		%		%
1	35	34	97.1	1	2.9	0	0.0
2	37	28	75.7	3	8.1	4	10.8
3	38	17	44.8	8	21.6	12	31.6
4	32	5	15.6	14	43.7	13	40.7
5	35	5	14.3	9	25.7	21	60.0
6	36	2	5.6	12	33.3	22	61.2
7	45	3	6.7	4	8.9	38	84.4
8	41	0	0	0	0	41	100.0
9	25	0	0	0	0	25	100.0
10	12	0	0	0	0	12	100.0
11	4	0	0	0	0	4	100.0
12	5	0	0	0	0	5	100.0
Total	345	94		51		197	

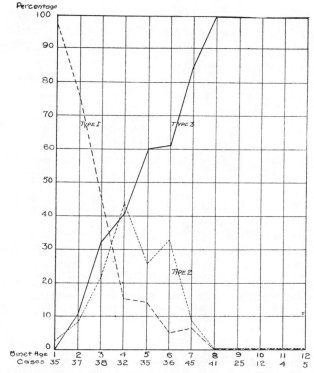

FIG. 75.   SIZE-WEIGHT ILLUSION IN THE FEEBLE-MINDED.   (Doll).

(3) *Dependence on sex.* The relation of sex to suggestion by the size-weight illusion has been differently stated by different investigators. Dresslar, for example, concludes that boys are more suggestible than girls. Wolfe, on the contrary, states that "men are less prone than women to illusions of weight," and that, in comparing wooden with lead weights, "the women overestimate the lead nearly twice as much as the men." Gilbert and Seashore find females more suggestible than males, but in nothing like the degree stated by Wolfe. Thus, inspection of his table shows that, according to Gilbert's method, after the age of 9, girls are, on the average, more influenced by the illusion than are boys. Seashore (16) tested 17 women and 28 men with two test-weights quite different in size, and found, similarly, that on the average the women showed the stronger illusion.

(4) The *relation of intelligence* to suggestibility among normal children has not been treated as carefully as the problem warrants. Gilbert made no correlations with intelligence. Dresslar concluded that bright children exhibit a stronger illusion, but Seashore (15) contends that Dresslar's method (arrangement in serial order) did not afford a real measure of the strength of the illusion.

(5) *Practise,* even if regular and persistent, does not dispel the illusion. It may, on the contrary, increase in amount (Hollingworth). If *S* be told the nature of the illusion, it still persists, though its intensity is thereby somewhat reduced (Seashore).

(6) If the method of procedure be modified, the strength of the illusion will be altered.

The more important of the relations thus revealed are the following :[a]

(*a*) "The illusion of weight dependent on size is greatest when size is estimated mainly by muscle-sense, and the weights have not previously been seen." Fourche says it is then three times as strong.

(*b*) "The illusion is more fluctuating and on the whole not quite so strong when size is estimated by the area of pressure in the flat palm, including a memory of the third dimension."

(*c*) "In these variations, the illusion is weakest when size is estimated by direct sight."

(*d*) "When size is estimated by the combined effect of all the spatial senses, the illusion is weaker than when depending on muscle-sense or touch, and stronger than when dependent on sight alone."

(*e*) The illusion is weaker when the blocks are viewed in indirect vision, and still weaker when judged by visual memory.

(*f*) A knowledge, or supposed knowledge, of the material of which weights are made may affect the estimate of their weight.

(*g*) The illusion does not necessarily vary directly with the volume of the compared weights, but depends in part upon the manner in which the difference in volume is brought about.

(*h*) The illusion obtains among the blind, where it follows the same general law as for the seeing, though it is not so strong, either for lifted or merely 'touched' weights, as for the seeing under the same conditions (Rice).

NOTES.—The outcome of any test of weight-comparison is somewhat affected by the tendency felt by all *S*'s, though differing in degree between different individuals and in the same individual at different times, to overestimate the second of two lifted weights.

---

[a]See, especially, Seashore (15).

If blocks of different material, *e. g.*, cork and lead, or wood and iron, be constructed in such a manner as to have the same dimensions and the same weight, the knowledge of the actual differences in the weight of the two materials produces an illusion similar to the size-weight illusion. Seashore (16) tested school children with this *material-weight illusion,* and found that the overestimation of the metal blocks amounted to from 7 to 11 grams (or from 13 to 20 per cent. of their actual weight, 55 g.). For this illusion, it is of interest to note, there was found virtually no variation with age, sex, or intellectual ability.

REFERENCES

(1)   F. E. Bolton, A contribution to the study of illusions, etc. *AmJPs,* 9: 1898, 167-182, especially 167-178.

(2)   A. Charpentier, Analyse expérimentale de quelques éléments de la sensation de poids. *Archives de physiologie normale et pathologique,* 5th ser., 3: 1891, 122-135, especially 126ff.

(3)   E. Claparède, L'illusion de poids chez les anormaux et le 'signe de Demoor.' *ArPs (f),* 2: 1903, 22-32.

(4)   Demoor et Daniel, Les enfants anormaux à Bruxelles. *AnPs,* 7: 1900 (1901), 296-313, especially 307-8.

(5)   E. A. Doll, The Demoor size-weight illusion. *TrSc,* 9: 1913, 145-149.

(6)   F. B. Dresslar, Studies in the psychology of touch. *AmJPs,* 6: 1894, 313-368, especially 343-360.

(7)   Th. Flournoy, De l'influence de la perception visuelle des corps sur leur poids apparent. *AnPs,* 1: 1894 (1895), 198-208.

(8)   J. A. Fourche, L'illusion de poids chez l'homme normal et le tabétique. Nancy, 1911.

(9)   J. A. Gilbert, Researches on the mental and physical development of school children. *SdYalePsLab,* 2: 1894, 40-100, especially 43-5, and 59-63.

(9a)   H. L. Hollingworth, The influence of caffein on mental and motor efficiency. *ColumbiaConPhPs* 20, and *ArPs(e),* No. 22: 1912, pp. 166, especially p. 20.

(10)   H. N. Loomis, Reactions to equal weights of unequal size. *Sd YalePsLab,* n. s. 1: No. 2, June, 1907, 334-348. (Same as *PsMon,* 8: No. 3, whole No. 34.)

(11)   L. Martin und G. E. Müller, Zur Analyse der Unterschiedsempfindlichkeit. Leipzig, 1899. Pp. 233.

(12)   G. E. Müller und F. Schumann, Ueber die psychologischen Grundlagen der Vergleichung gehobener Gewichte. *ArGsPhg,* 45: 1889, 37-112.

(13)   J. Phillipe et J. Clavière, Sur une illusion musculaire. *RPhF,* 40: 1895, 672-682.

(14)   J. F. Rice, The size-weight illusion among the blind. *SdYalePs Lab,* 5: 1897, 81-87.

(15) C. E. Seashore, Measurements of illusions and hallucinations in normal life. *SdYalePsLab*, 3: 1895, 1-67, especially 1-29.

(16) C. E. Seashore, The material-weight illusion. *UnIowaSdPs*, 2: 1899, 36-46.

(17) E. W. Scripture, Remarks on Dr. Gilbert's article. *SdYalePs Lab*, 2: 1894, 101-4.

(18) E. W. Scripture, The law of size-weight suggestion. *Sci*, n. s. 5: February 5, 1896, 227.

(19) E. W. Scripture, The new psychology. London, 1897. See ch. xix.

(20) J. van Biervliet, La mesure des illusions de poids. *AnPs*, 2: 1895, 79-86.

(21) H. K. Wolfe, Some effects of size on judgments of weight. *PsR*, 5: 1898, 25-54.

TEST 41

Suggestion by progressive weights.—This test, like that which follows it, is one of several devised by Binet for the purpose of securing a quantitative measure of the degree of suggestibility of children or adults when the suggestion is 'depersonalized,' in the sense that it is derived by *S* himself from the objective conditions of the experiment, rather than from the attitude, tone, instructions, or personality of *E*. The principle embodied in this test is, in other words, the arousal, by auto-suggestion, of a "directive idea," or the rapid development of an attitude of expectation. Suggestibility is measured, at least approximately, by the ease with which this suggestion, or habit, of judgment, is aroused and by the persistence that it displays under conditions which tend gradually to counteract it.

MATERIALS.—A set of 15 weights, of identical size and appearance, numbered conspicuously from 1 to 15. The first four weigh 20, 40, 60, and 80 grams, respectively; the remaining 11 weigh 100 grams each. Table of such a height that *S* can stand in front of it and lift the weights readily. A thick gray or black cloth.

PRELIMINARIES.—Spread the cloth over the table. Place the 15 weights in a line as numbered, with the lightest on the left and the 11 heaviest on the right, and with about 2 cm. between each weight. No. 1 is then at the left, No. 15 at the right of the row.

METHOD.—Give *S* the following instructions: "Here is a series of weights, 15 of them. I want you to lift them, one after the other, like this. [Illustrate by taking a weight between

thumb and finger and lifting some 10 cm. from the table.] As
you lift each weight, I want you to tell me whether it is heavier,
lighter, or the same as the one just before it. All you have to
say is either 'heavier,' or 'lighter,' or 'the same.' Remember
you are to compare each weight with the one you lifted just before. For instance, when you lift the 8th, you are to say
whether it is heavier, lighter, or the same as the 7th. Here is
the first weight, number one, at the left end of the row."

Watch S to see that he follows these instructions, particularly that he lifts the weights successively, without relifting
earlier ones. Record his judgments verbatim; be careful, also,
to note any secondary evidences that might throw light on his
judgments, e. g., attitudes or expressions of hesitancy, assurance, surprise, embarrassment, cautiousness, etc.

VARIATIONS OF METHOD.—(1) In the second method followed
by Binet, S is instructed to lift, in each trial, the preceding
weight as well as the one that is being judged, e. g., he lifts the
8th, then the 7th, then the 8th again: next the 9th, then the
8th, then the 9th again, etc. The lifting is all done, as before,
with the one hand.

(2) In the third method followed by Binet, S is asked to estimate the first weight lifted. He usually gives too small an
estimate. He is then told that its weight is 20 grams (about
0.7 ounce). The series is now compared, using either of the
methods of lifting above described, according to S's preference,[1]
but S is required to estimate or guess the heaviness of each
weight, basing his judgment, of course, merely on the knowledge
that the first weight is 20 grams.

TREATMENT OF DATA.—From the tabulated results, E may
easily determine in how many cases the objective progression
of the first 5 weights was correctly noted. For a measure of
suggestibility, E must take the number of times 'heavier' is
judged in the last 10 judgments (when 'same' is the correct
judgment). This measure is admittedly somewhat crude, but

---

[1]It would, obviously, be better to prescribe either the one or the other
method for all S's. The first method has the merit of taking less time,
and it is the method that is for the most part naturally adopted by
younger S's.

it affords a fairly reliable index for determining the relative order of rank of a group of S's. Thus, an S that judges 'heavier' 10 times is unquestionably more suggestible than one who answers 'heavier' but 5 times, though not necessarily twice as suggestible.

If all three methods are employed, E may determine S's suggestibility by adding the number of false 'heavier' judgments in all three tests. In the third method, the quantitative estimate given by S for the 15th weight (or the maximal estimate for weights 6 to 15) might be taken, in comparison with his estimate of the 5th weight, as an index of suggestibility, but this method is not regarded by Binet as so reliable as the one already described.

RESULTS.—(1) The general outcome of the test as conducted by the first, or standard, method is indicated in Table 123, which embodies the results obtained by Binet upon 24 elementary-school children, aged 8-10 years.

(2) It is evident that, in children of this age (8-10), not all judge correctly the actual objective increase in the *first five weights*. Since the differences are supraliminal, the exceptions

TABLE 123

The Progressive-Weight Suggestion. 24 Cases (Binet)

NO. OF WEIGHT	1	2	3	4	5	6	7	8	9	10	11	12	13	14	15
Actual weight	20	40	60	80	100	100	100	100	100	100	100	100	100	100	100
Times estimated +		24	19	19	23	13	18	18	18	12	19	19	17	15	12
Times estimated −		0	1	1	0	9	1	4	1	7	2	2	3	3	5
Times estimated =		0	4	4	1	2	5	2	5	5	3	3	4	6	7

must be ascribed to faulty attention, though, possibly, the fact that the weights are of equal size may have clouded the direct perception of weight by lifting.

(3) In general, the suggestion is still working, though less powerfully, at the 15th trial: in other words, it has persisted, for most S's, through the successive lifting of 10 equal weights.

(4) There is a marked drop in the judgment 'heavier' at *the 6th weight, i. e.*, at the first 'trick' weight—a drop which is,

obviously, due to a 'disappointed suggestion,' analogous to that which conditions the size-weight illusion of the preceding test. In the present instance, *S* is, in most cases at least, prepared to find the 6th weight heavier than the 5th: he puts forth more effort; the weight rises with unexpected ease, and is, therefore, often judged 'lighter.' If, however, *S* is more influenced by his expectation of 'heavier' than by the unexpected lightness of the weight, he still judges 'heavier,' or he may, from the conflict of these two tendencies, judge 'equal.'

(5) *Practise* has very little effect upon the suggestibility of *S*'s: at least Binet found that, when 12 older children (16 years) repeated the test by the first method five times in immediate succession, there was no alteration in the average number of times that suggestion appeared (the average number of suggestions in the five trials was 5.1, 4.9, 5.4, 5.0 and 5.5, respectively).

(6) Binet's tentative experiments indicated that *age* apparently has less effect upon suggestion by progressive weights than upon suggestion by progressive lines (see the following test). In trials by the first method, 12 children aged 16 years responded, on the average, with 5.1 suggestions, whereas 24 children aged 8-10 years, responded, on the average, with 6.75 suggestions. The later experiments conducted under Binet's direction by Giroud show a distinct lessening of suggestibility after 9 years when only those *S*'s are considered who made no errors in the first four judgments (objective increase of weight), as is indicated in the last column of Table 124.

TABLE 124

Averages for Progressive-Weight Suggestion by Age (Giroud)

AGE	HEAVIER JUDGMENTS	CONSECUTIVE HEAVIER JUDGMENTS	EQUAL JUDGMENTS	HEAVIER JUDGMENTS OF S'S MAKING NO ERROR WITH OBJECTIVE INCREASES
7	6.5	5.5	2.3	8.4
8	6.6	5.3	1.6	7.0
9	5.2	2.4	2.0	8.0
10	7.0	4.8	1.2	4.5
12	5.0	3.6	5.0	5.0

(7) According to Binet, comparison of the results of this test with *other tests of suggestibility,* especially the line-test, indicates a fair degree of correlation, so that, while the sense-department under examination may in part determine the extent of suggestion, very suggestible *S*'s may be expected to prove noticeably suggestible in all tests. On the other hand, tests undertaken in the Educational Laboratory at Cornell University[2] do not confirm Binet's statement, and lead one to believe that Scott's conclusions (Test 44) are correct, when he asserts that there is no such thing as general suggestibility.

(8) Procedure by the *second method* (compulsory lifting of the antecedent weight) makes the real progression (1st five weights) more uniformly evident, but reduces the illusory progression.

(9) Procedure by the *third method* (estimates of each weight) produces less suggestion than the first, but more than the second method. Inspection of the estimated weights (grams) show (*a*) that *S*'s have a decided preference for the use of numbers terminating in 0 or 5, (*b*) that no one of the 24 *S*'s overestimated the 5th weight (100 g.), but that they commonly greatly underestimated it (30 to 50 g.), and (*c*) that those *S*'s that showed the greater number of suggestions also gave, on the average, the largest quantitative estimations for the illusory increments. The correlation of suggestibility under these two methods of treatment (first and third) was found by Okabe and Whipple to be 0.53.

REFERENCES

(1) A. Binet, La suggestibilité. Paris, 1900. Ch. iv. (pp. 161-208).
(2) A. Giroud, La suggestibilité chez des enfants d'école de sept a douze ans. *AnPs*, 18: 1912, 362-388.

TEST 42

Suggestion by progressive lines.—The purpose and genera plan of this test are the same as in the preceding test of sugges

---

[2]These tests, which were conducted by T. Okabe, under the author's directions, included all the suggestibility tests of Binet, together with the warmth tests (No. 44). The results of their application to 29 *S*'s indicate almost total lack of correlation of suggestibility in the several tests.

tion by progressive weights, and the details are again derived from the work of Binet.

APPARATUS.—A sheet of cross-section paper, ruled in millimeter squares. Kymograph drum, with kymograph or some form of supporting stand. Cardboard. Strip of white paper, 15×15 cm. Drawing materials.

PRELIMINARIES.—Arrange the kymograph drum so that it may lie horizontally and be revolved freely by hand. It may conveniently be left in the kymograph with the driving 'step' loosened, or be placed in the smoking stand. Across the strip of white paper, draw with a ruling pen 20 parallel, straight, black lines, 2 cm. apart and each 1 mm. wide. The lines must begin at varying distances from the left-hand margin: the first four are to be 12, 24, 36, and 48 mm. long, respectively; the remaining 16 are to be each 60 mm. long. Support the sheet of cardboard vertically in front of and close to the kymograph drum, and cut a horizontal slit 1×12 cm. through the cardboard in such a position as to expose the ruled lines, one by one, as they are turned past the slit.[1]

METHOD.—Seat S 50 cm. from the screen and provide him with a sheet of cross-section paper. The instructions should take the following form: "I want to try a test to see how good your 'eye' is. I'll show you a line, say an inch or two long, and I want you to reproduce it right afterwards from memory. Some persons make bad mistakes; they make a line 2 inches long when I show them one 3 inches long; others make one 4 or 5 inches long. Let's see how well you can do. I shall show the line to you through this slit. Take just one look at it, then make a mark on this paper [cross-section paper] just the distance from this edge [left-hand margin] that the line is long. When that is done, I shall show you the second line, then the

---

[1] In default of the kymograph, the strip of ruled lines may be laid flat upon the table and exposed through a 1 × 12 cm. slit cut in the center of a sheet of cardboard 55 cm. square.

Or, the test-lines may be drawn as sections of radii upon a cardboard disc which is supported vertically just behind the screen and rotated to bring them into view successively.

third, and so on. Make the marks for the second on the line below the first, the third on the next line, and so on." [2]

E then turns the drum to bring the first, or shortest, line into view. As soon as *S* turns his attention to the recording of his estimate on the paper, the drum is moved forward slightly to conceal the line, so that further comparison is impossible. As soon as *S* has placed his mark, then, and not before, the next line is exposed. This precaution serves to maintain the impression that a new, and hence probably a longer line is exposed. Slow *S*'s may need to be hurried; too quick ones may need to be checked, so that the interval between successive exposures shall be approximately 7 sec. To keep *S*'s attention alive, *E* may accompany the exposures with non-suggestive remarks, *e. g.,* "Here is the second line." "Here is the third," etc.

If *S* has ceased to respond to the suggestion of progressive augmentation at the 20th exposure, the test ends at that point: if not, *E* should, without *S*'s knowledge, bring the drum back to the 5th line, and continue the exposures of the series of 60 mm. lines as before, until *S* does cease to respond to the suggestion.

E should note and record any significant features in *S*'s manner, *e. g.,* signs of embarrassment, hesitancy,. automatic response, etc.

When the test is completed, and provided no further tests of suggestibility are to be undertaken at the time, *E* will find it advantageous to quiz *S* with regard to his attitude toward the test. This interrogation must be very tactfully conducted. *E* may, for example, begin by saying: "Are you entirely satisfied with what you have done"? If *S* answers in the affirmative, let *E* continue with such inquiries as: "Do you think you have made any mistakes"? "Did you make any lines too short or too long"? "At what moment did you notice that your lines were too long"? "Why didn't you make them shorter"? etc.

---

[2] These directions should be followed with some care. In tests of suggestion, the slightest change in the setting of the test, or in the manner or content of the instructions, may materially affect *S*'s attitude toward the experiment. The object is to convey the idea of a straightforward test of accuracy of line-reproduction, and to avoid arousing any suspicion of snares or tricks.

If S confesses that he made some mistakes, let him take his record-sheet and make the changes that he thinks ought to be made to produce a correct record, using small circles for his corrections to avoid confusion with his first estimates.

VARIATIONS OF METHOD.—E may, if desired, adopt the arrangement first used by Binet, according to which there are 12 successive stimulus-lines, all of which begin at the same distance from the left-hand margin, and which have the following lengths: 12, 24, 36, 48, 60, *60*, 72, *72*, 84, *84*, 96, *96* mm. It is evident that numbers 6, 8, 10, and 12 constitute four 'trap-lines,' since the arrangement suggests progressive augmentation, whereas each of these four lines is equal to that which immediately precedes it.

TREATMENT OF DATA.—(1) For a measure of suggestibility, E may take the number of lines out of the last 15 lines that are drawn longer than the 5th line was drawn.

(2) A coefficient of suggestibility may also be calculated, following Binet's method, by the formula

$$x : 100 = max. L : 5th L,$$

in which
$x =$ the required coefficient,
$max. L =$ the length of the maximal line recorded by S,
$5th L =$ the length of the 5th line as recorded by S.

Absence of suggestibility is, then, indicated by a coefficient of 100: presence of suggestibility by a coefficient of over 100.

(3) When the variant method is used, the degree of suggestibility may be determined roughly in terms of the number of 'traps' in which S is 'caught,' or more exactly, by the formula

$$x : 100 = c : r,$$

in which
$x =$ the required coefficient,
$c =$ the average recorded increment of the four trap lines,
$r =$ the average recorded increment of the four lines immediately preceding the four trap-lines.

RESULTS.—(1) In his examination of pupils in the elementary schools, aged 8-10 years, Binet found that *the coefficient of suggestibility* ranged from 109 to 625. In 16 of 42 pupils, the coefficient was 200 or over, *i. e.,* the maximal line was double or more than double the 5th line.[3]

With the variant form of test, Binet found the coefficient lying between 7.6 and 120. No one of 45 children avoided all four 'traps,' and 36 children avoided none of them. Occasionally, the trap-line, presumably on account of the contrast between the stimulus and the child's expectation, was actually recorded as shorter than the preceding line. *S*'s whose coefficient in this form of test is 100, *i. e.,* whose average increment for the trap-lines is the same as for the objectively progressive lines, are termed 'automatic.'

(2) The point at which *maximal suggestion* is registered is commonly between the 19th and the 25th line, but may lie anywhere between the 7th and the 36th (this being the limit tested by Binet).

(3) Inspection of the records of individual pupils shows that in some cases the force of suggestion was steady and persistent, while in others it reached a maximum, and then declined.

(4) *Extremely suggestible S*'s may make their 'estimate' of the line without even looking at it when exposed; their minds are so completely dominated by the suggestion of uniform augmentation that they do not trouble to observe the stimulus.

(5) The degree of suggestion induced by this test declines markedly with *age:* Binet found, for instance, that the coefficients of suggestibility, in the case of 12 pupils whose age averaged 16 years, ranged only from 103 to 146. Binet's work was continued by Giroud, who tested 38 children and obtained for averages, on the basis of a possible score of 15, the following averages for the number of times any line beyond the 5th exceeded the length assigned to the line just before it:

YEARS	7	8	9	10	12
Cases tested	10	10	5	5	8
Score	10.7	8.2	4.2	4.8	1.0

That it is difficult to induce the suggestion with adults was shown in scattered tests made by the author upon college students. On the other hand, Chojecki, who tested 30 men and 30

[3]For detailed records of number of individual cases, consult Binet, 124ff.

women students of the University of Geneva, had better success, and found, indeed, 36 persons (22 men and 14 women)
susceptible of suggestion by this method.

(6) In either form of test, the *1st line* is apt to be over-esti-
mated. The *5th line* is almost invariably underestimated. Generally speaking, this underestimation is less pronounced in
those *S*'s that prove least suggestible.

(7) In many instances, the records bear witness to a struggle
between the directive idea of progressive increments and the
impressions which are actually received from the lines as they
are exposed. Especially characteristic is the appearance of a
number of estimates in which the directive idea is effective,
followed by a sudden reduction in estimation, which is again
followed by another series of progressive increments. In other
words, the idea of progression is operative until a point is
reached when the recorded length is manifestly too long. *S*
makes, then, a more or less marked correction, but does not,
curiously, relinquish the notion of progression, and this again
becomes manifest.

(8) The corrections made by young *S*'s during the inquiry
that follows the test cannot, of course, be taken as exact indications of the extent of the suggestion or of their consciousness
of error. It will be found that many *S*'s are conscious that they
have made the lines too long; some can also explain why they
made them too long; but it is rare that any one gives a satisfactory explanation of why he continued to make them too long,
after he realized that he had been overestimating.

(9) *Correlations.* Tests of school children and of adults by
Okabe and Whipple afforded the following correlations (footrule method): Suggestibility for progressive lines (number of
'yields') and suggestibility for progressive lines (maximal divided by the 5th line) 0.38; correlation, by either treatment,
with contradictory suggestion, (Test 43) about 0.25, with
directive suggestion (Test 43) about 0.20, with suggestion for
warmth 0.17, with the size-weight illusion (Test 40) 0.10 by the
first, and —0.14 by the second method of computing suggestion
for progressive lines.

REFERENCES

(1)   A. Binet, La suggestibilité. Paris, 1900. Pp. 83-160.
(2)   A. Chojecki, Contribution a l'étude de la suggestibilité. *ArPs(f)*, 11 : 1911, 182-186.
(3)   A. Giroud, La suggestibilité chez des enfants d'école de sept à douze ans. *AnPs*, 18 : 1912, 362-388.

TEST 43

Suggestion of line-lengths by personal influence.—In the three preceding tests suggestion is produced by the objective conditions of the test: in everyday life, however, suggestion is often produced by personal influence, by authoritative statement or command, or merely by what Binet terms 'moral influence.' Two forms of line-test have been utilized by Binet to study this variety of personal suggestion: the first he terms 'contradictory suggestion,' the second 'directive suggestion' (*suggestion directrice*) : in the former E makes certain statements that are intended to interrupt or modify a judgment that S has just made; in the latter, statements that are intended to control or influence a judgment that S is just about to make.

A.   CONTRADICTORY SUGGESTION

MATERIALS.—Drawing materials. A sheet of cardboard upon which are drawn in ink 24 parallel, straight, black lines, ranging in length from 12 to 104 mm., by increments of 4 mm. The lines all begin at the same distance from the left-hand margin, are 7 mm. apart, and are numbered in order of their length, from 1 to 24. Three rectangular pieces of cardboard, about 12x20 cm., on each of which is drawn a single straight line. These three stimulus-lines correspond to numbers 6, 12, and 18 of the 24 comparison-lines, and are, accordingly, 32, 56, and 80 mm. long, respectively.

METHOD.—Show S the card of comparison-lines, and explain their numbering. Replace this by the first stimulus-line (32 mm.), saying: "Look carefully at this line." After 4 sec., remove the stimulus-card, present the comparison-card, and say: "Tell me the number of the line that is just the length of the one I showed you." At the moment that S gives his judgment, E says: "Are you sure? Isn't is the —th"?—indicating always the next longer line. If S answers "No," E repeats the question in exactly the same form. If S still answers "No," the attempt to produce suggestion is suspended, and the case is recorded as one 'resistance.' The second and the third stimulus-lines are presented and the same procedure is followed in each case. If, in any of the trials S answers "Yes," E then inquires: "Isn't it this one"?—indicating the next longer line, and this inquiry is carried on from line to line until S has twice resisted the suggestion, i. e., has twice answered "No" to the same question.[1]

VARIATIONS OF METHOD.—For many S's, particularly for adults, more success will attend the use of a second method tried by Binet in preliminary tests, viz.: the introduction of an interval of 12 sec. between removal of the stimulus-line and presentation of the comparison-card.

TREATMENT OF DATA.—Following Binet, S's suggestibility may be rated in terms of the total number of 'advances' in lines that he makes, under inquiry, in all three trials. Thus, if he 'yields' two lines the first time, three the second, and none the third, his suggestibility is rated as 5.

RESULTS.—(1) Children tend to select for their first line one that is shorter than the stimulus-line.[2]

(2) Of 25 children, aged 8-10 years, Binet found 6 who resisted suggestion completely, 6 who 'yielded' once, 5 twice, 2 three times, 2 four times, and one each six, seven, and more than seven times.

(3) Preliminary experiments conducted by Binet and Henri upon 240 pupils, with some slight changes in method (particularly, giving an opportunity both for direct comparison and for selection by memory after a 12 sec. interval), yielded the results (2: p. 343) indicated in Table 125.

Here it is evident that E's suggestion is less effective when S can make direct comparison of the lines, and that suggestibility,

---

[1] Once more it should be said that it is highly important to follow the same form of inquiry, to use the same tone, the same attitude, in every question for every S, since the suggestion which we seek to measure is conditioned by the character of the inquiries.

[2] E is almost always, therefore, in a position to demonstrate to S, if need be, after the test, that his suggestion would have been a sound one to follow.

TABLE 125

Percentage of 'Yields' to Contradictory Suggestion (*Binet and Henri*)

AVERAGE AGE	MEMORY TEST	COMPARISON TEST	MEAN
7–9	89	74	81.5
9–11	80	73	76.5
11–13	54	48	51.0

under either direct comparison or comparison from memory, declines with *age*.

(4) S's who have selected the correct line are less apt to change their designation under suggestion than are S's who have selected the wrong line: thus Binet and Henri found that 56 per cent. changed their selection when it was actually right, but 88 per cent. when it was wrong. Moreover, of the latter, 81 per cent. made the change in the proper direction.

B. DIRECTIVE SUGGESTION

APPARATUS.—As in Test 42, save that only the 60 mm. lines are used.

METHOD.—Seat S 50 cm. from the cardboard screen and provide him with a sheet of cross-section paper. Instruct him as follows: "I'm going to show you a number of lines. You will see them appear through this slit, one at a time. When I show you a line, take a good look at it; then make a mark on this paper at just the distance from this edge [left-hand] that the line is long. When that is done, I shall show you the second, then the third, and so on. You will make the mark for the length of the second line on the second line of your paper, for the third on the next line, and so on."

E now displays the 5th, *i. e.,* the first 60 mm. line of the series, with the remark: "Here is the first one." When S is ready for the second line, *i. e.,* 7-10 sec. later, E remarks, as he exposes it: "Here is a longer one." When the third is exposed, he remarks "Here is a shorter one;" and he continues to use these remarks, alternately, at the moment of exposure of each line, until 15 lines have been exposed, the first without suggestion, the remainder coupled with 14 suggestions—7 of shorter, 7 of longer.

These suggestions must be given just before the line is exposed, in a quiet tone, without looking at S. S should see the disc turn and the new line appear at the moment that he receives the suggestion.

If desired, S may be questioned afterward, as indicated in Test 42, with regard to his attitude toward the suggestions.

TREATMENT OF DATA.—When S accepts the suggestion, record a 'plus' case; when he resists the suggestion, either by making the length equal to that of the preceding line, or by altering the length in a direction contrary to the intent of the suggestion, record a 'minus' case. The number of the plus cases may serve as an index of S's suggestibility. Record should also be kept of the extent of modification (in mm.) made by S in each trial.

RESULTS.—(1) The verbal directive suggestion used in this test is more potent, at least for children 8-10 years old, than the auto-suggestion induced in Test 42. Sixteen of 23 pupils tested by Binet submitted completely to the suggestion,[3] and no one resisted every suggestion.

(2) The suggestion is, in general, stronger at the outset than toward the end of the series, as is indicated by the fact that the extent of modification of line-length decreases, and the number of complete resistances increases, as the series progresses.

(3) Verbal suggestion is commonly more effective in producing augmentation than in producing reduction in line-length, in the proportion of about 5 to 4.

(4) There are marked *individual differences* in the suggestibility of school children under the conditions of this test. Binet found that in 18 trials the number of resistances to suggestion ranged from 0 to 14. (See Binet, 1, pp. 228-9, for a detailed table.)

(5) The *first line* is practically invariably underestimated.

(6) Tests upon 10 children, whose average *age* was 17 years, showed less suggestibility than in the case of younger children; still, 4 of the 17 accepted every suggestion, and 3 others resisted suggestion only once. The average extent of modification produced by suggestion is, however, less than in the case of

---

[3]This statement is made in the text, but does not appear to be borne out by Binet's table (1, pp. 228-9).

younger S's. Again, the extent of modification is practically constant throughout in the series with the older S's, but large at first and then progressively less in the series with the younger S's.

NOTES.—The experiments of Bell, Brand and Jones, in which the estimates or judgments of spatial magnitudes or extents were subjected to verbal suggestions, such as "make high," "make low," "you are now able," "you are now unable," etc., cannot be directly compared with the work of Binet, because in all of them the S's were well aware of the intentional and artificial character of the suggestions and were instructed to avoid voluntary resistance to them. In general, the suggestions in these experiments had some effect upon the work of the S's, but not upon all of them, nor always in the direction in which they were supposed to influence the outcome.

REFERENCES

(1)   A. Binet, La suggestibilité. Paris, 1900, especially 219-243.
(2)   A. Binet et V. Henri, De la suggestibilité naturelle. *RPhF*, 38: 1894, 337-347.
(3)   J. C. Bell, The effect of suggestion upon the reproduction of triangles and of point distances. *AmJPs*, 19: 1908, 504-598.
(4)   J. E. Brand, The effect of verbal suggestion upon the estimation of linear magnitudes. *PsRev.* 12: 1905, 41-49.
(5)   Grace M. Jones, Experiments on the reproduction of distance as influenced by suggestions of ability and inability. *PsRev*, 17: 1910, 269-278.

TEST 44

Suggestion by illusion of warmth.—In measuring either discriminative or liminal sensitivity, difficulty is not infrequently caused by the interference of auto-suggestion (see various tests of Chapter VI). In the immediately preceding tests (Nos. 40 to 43), a process of discrimination (of weights and line-lengths) was, accordingly, made the basis for testing suggestibility. In the present test, a (supposed) measurement of liminal sensitivity is made the basis for testing suggestibility. The plan is to arrange experimental conditions in such a way as to suggest warmth, when no warmth is present.

This idea seems to have originated in the Yale laboratory, when Seashore (5), in 1895, worked out a proposal made two years earlier by Scripture (4). Small's varied tests of suggestibility (6), which appeared in the following year, embodied two very simple 'heat' tests. More recently, Guidi in 1908, Scott in 1910, and Chojecki in 1911, have reported tests of suggestibility to warmth, the former with a simple 'warmth box,' the latter with apparatus somewhat similar to the original device of Seashore. Four methods are described herewith; the resistance-wire method of Seashore and Scott, the heated box method of Guidi, and the two simple methods employed by Small.

A. ILLUSORY WARMTH—RESISTANCE-WIRE METHOD

APPARATUS.—Stop-watch. Special warmth-tester.

The warmth-tester consists of a wooden box, open at the end facing E, and provided, on the top, with porcelain sockets for four electric lamps, wired in multiple, and with a snap switch by which the current (105-110 volt, D. C.) may be turned on or off. The wiring is purposely left visible, and leads conspicuously from the lamps to a coil of No. 24 German-silver wire, 1 m. long, which is wound, without covering, about a flat piece of hard rubber, 3 x 10 cm. This resistance coil is fastened to the front of the box, in such a manner that it máy be easily reached by S, without exposing his fingers to the warmth of the lamps on the top of the box. A concealed circuit leads to a noiseless switch, underneath the box, which can be operated by E without S's knowledge. By means of this switch, E may shunt the current through the coil, or cut the coil out entirely, without affecting the illumination of the lamps.[1]

PRELIMINARIES.—Find an arrangement of lamps such that, when the current passes through the coil, warmth becomes perceptible in 8 to 10 sec. Four 25-watt tungsten lamps generally prove satisfactory. If necessary, use one or more 40-watt lamps.

METHOD.—Give S the following instructions: "I want to test your ability to perceive warmth. Hold this coil of wire gently between your thumb and two fingers, like this [illustrating]. You will see that the coil is connected with these electric lamps, so that, when I light them, a current of electricity can flow through the coil and warm it—it is made of German-silver wire, and offers a slight resistance to the current. There is nothing at all to be afraid of. You can't feel any shock from

---

[1] In default of a 110-volt circuit, a resistance-wire apparatus may be contrived with a battery, after the plan described by Seashore, though the absence of the illuminated lamps alters the experimental conditions.

the current, nothing but a slight warmth. Watch carefully, and, the moment that you feel warmth, say 'now.'"

Without attracting S's attention, close the secret coil-switch, so that no current passes through the coil. After a preliminary 'ready,' snap the lamp-switch rather ostentatiously; start the stop-watch at the same instant, and lean forward in an attitude of expectancy, keeping one hand on the lamp-switch, as if awaiting S's 'now.' Snap the lamps off as soon as the 'now' is spoken. Record the time. Feel of the coil, or solicitously blow upon it, as if to cool it. Repeat the test 5 times with each hand, alternately.

If S, at any trial, fails to get the illusion of warmth within 60 sec., open the coil switch (without S's knowledge), so that warmth is actually felt, but record the trial as one 'resistance,' or failure.

VARIATIONS OF METHOD.—Following the plan of Seashore and of Scott, tell S that 20 trials will be made. Give a preliminary series of 5 trials with each hand, with objective warmth from the start, in each trial. Without interruption, continue with an equal number of trials in which the coil is not warmed unless S fails to report warmth within a period of some 10 sec. longer than the average time at which he had reported warmth in the first 10 trials.

TREATMENT OF DATA.—In either method, suggestibility is measured by the absolute or relative number of trials (without objective warmth) in which S reports warmth.

S may also be rated in terms of the quickness (number of seconds) with which the illusion is reported.

B. ILLUSORY WARMTH—GUIDI'S METHOD

APPARATUS.—Stop-watch. Matches. Alcohol lamp, fitted with hinged extinguishing cap. Cubical wooden box, with a chimney-like metal top, a circular hole in the front face, and a hinged door in the back face (Fig. 76).

METHOD.—E's instructions are analogous to those in the resistance-wire method. "I want to test your ability to perceive warmth. I want you to thrust your forefinger into this box through the hole in front. I shall put this lamp into the box.

It won't burn you at all. Just watch very carefully, and say 'now' the moment that you notice any warmth in the box." *E* then lights the alcohol lamp, opens the door of the box, sets in the lamps extinguishing the flame as he does so, starts the watch, closes the door, and expectantly awaits *S*'s judgments.[2]

MATERIALS.—Alcohol lamp. A pin thrust through the rubber tip of a pencil, or through a small bit of soft wood. Toothpick, or other bit of wood with a blunt point. Matches. Piece of cardboard, about 15x15 cm. Blindfold.

METHOD.—(1) Let *S* see the lighted lamp and the pin in its holder. Instruct him as follows: "I am going to warm this pin in this flame, then touch it to the back of your hand to see if you can notice the warmth it makes. Don't be afraid of being burned, as it will not be hot enough for that, and I shall try it on my own hand first. Say 'now' when you feel its warmth." Blindfold *S* carefully. Go through the operation of heating the pin; say 'ready,' but do not touch *S*'s hand at all. If *S* reports warmth, ask him to describe the feeling: if he does not report warmth, repeat the test, but touch him on the back of the hand with the pointed piece of wood, to see if the contact is reported as 'warm' or 'hot.'

(2) Light a match and move it around about 1 cm. above the back of *S*'s hand. Call his attention to the 'waves of heat' that he feels. Blindfold him carefully. Ask him to see if he can detect the heat waves every time. Strike a match, and move it about over his hand, but hold the cardboard between the match and the hand. Repeat several times with either hand. Note the number of times the suggestion is 'accepted,' and any indications of the readiness or degree of suggestibility.

RESULTS FOR ALL METHODS.—(1) In general, the results of the warmth-illusion test appear to be conditioned primarily by the success of the investigator in creating a proper atmos-

---

[2] Guidi's method deviated somewhat from the above, in that *S* was instructed to push his finger slowly into the box against a metal disc, and degree of suggestibility was measured by the extent to which the finger had been inserted when warmth was reported. This procedure presents difficulty in governing the rate of movement, and has, so far as the author's experience goes, no advantage over the procedure that has been recommended.

phere of suggestibility, rather than upon the particular apparatus employed. Thus, Seashore met with amazing success.
Of his 8 college students, only 3 resisted at all, and these but
once or twice each, so that, in 420 trials, there were only 5
failures to perceive heat. Small tested boys and girls from the
7th grade and the high school: in 21 trials, 5 reported heat,
with no contact at all, 19 reported heat from the wooden point,
while in 19 trials with the "heat-waves," 17 proved suggestible.

FIG. 76. GUIDI'S APPARATUS FOR THE WARMTH ILLUSION.
(Modified by Whipple.)

C.   ILLUSORY WARMTH—SMALL'S METHOD

Of Scott's 20 college students, 9 'yielded' 10 times (of a possible 10); 5 yielded 9 times; 2 yielded 4 times, and 1 each 8, 7,
5, and 3 times. No one of the 20 S's resisted in every trial.
Chojecki, who tested 30 men and 30 women students at the
University of Geneva, got positive results from 19 (31.8 per
cent.) with the use of Guidi's method. Okabe, who worked with
school children and adults in the Cornell laboratory under the
author's direction, obtained positive results in 70.7 per cent. of

the trials, and with 22 of 29 S's (Table 126). The Italian
children tested by Guidi were less suggestible (at least for his
method), as Table 127 shows.

TABLE 126

Suggestibility to Warmth. Resistance-Coil Method (Okabe and Whipple)

GROUP	NUMBER	TRIALS	YIELDS	PERCENTAGE OF SUGGESTIBILITY	CASES WITH NO YIELDS
Men	12	59	43	73	1
Women	7	29	20	69	2
Bright boys	5	36	27	75	1
Dull boys	5	33	21	64	1
Totals	29	157	111	70.7	5

(2) The *relation to sex and to age* cannot be stated with assurance. Guidi's results indicate maximal suggestibility at the
age of 9, but the Cornell tests, perhaps from being too few in number, failed to show characteristic differences between grammar-
school boys and adults. It is likewise unsafe to generalize from
the indications there given of the greater suggestibility of men.

(3) The *degree of suggestibility*, as indicated by the readiness
with which warmth is felt, differs, as might be expected, in
different S's, *i. e.*, even of those who invariably perceive warmth,
some report only "faint warmth," others "sudden heat," etc.
Guidi classed his pupils into three groups, according as they
took the suggestion quickly (in 1 to 2 sec.), moderately (2 to 3
sec.), or slowly (after 3 sec.), and found 33 per cent., 63.7 per
cent., and 3.3 per cent. of his S's in these three classes, respectively.

(4) Scott found no *correlation* between suggestibility as
measured by the warmth illusion and suggestibility as measured by his flight-of-colors test, Chojecki no correlations between the results of his three methods, viz.: Guidi's 'stove,'
Ochorowicz's 'hypnoscope' and Binet's progressive lines.
Okabe's tests afforded the following low correlations with other
forms of suggestibility tests: with progressive lines (Test 42)

0.17, with contradictory suggestion (Test 43) 0.21, with directive suggestion (Test 43) 0.29, with the weight illusions (Tests 40 and 41) none.

TABLE 127

Suggestibility to Warmth, as Related to Age. 187 Cases (Guidi)

Age	6	7	8	9	10	11	12	13	14	15
Per cent. suggestible	50	40.9	51.8	62.5	50	40	33.3	21.4	27.3	33.3

REFERENCES

(1) A. Chojecki, Contribution a l'étude de la suggestibilité. *ArPs(f)*, 11: 1911, 182-186.

(2) G. Guidi, Recherches expérimentales sur la suggestibilité. *ArPs (f)*, 8: 1908, 49-54.

(3) W. D. Scott, Personal differences in suggestibility. *PsR*, 17: 1910, 147-154.

(4) E. W. Scripture, Tests on school children. *EdR*, 5: 1893, 52-61.

(5) C. E. Seashore, Measurements of illusions and hallucinations in normal life. *SdYalePsLab*, 3: 1895, 1-67, especially 30-32.

(6) M. H. Small, The suggestibility of children. *PdSe*, 4: 1896, 176-220, especially 183-186.

CHAPTER XI

Tests of Imagination and Invention

Imagination, like most of the stock psychological terms, has the misfortune to be used in several different ways. In popular usage, imagination commonly implies something fanciful and unreal; we condemn a rumor, for example, by dubbing it "a mere figment of the imagination." In psychology, imagination has both a general and a specific meaning. Broadly speaking, imagination is equivalent to imaging, or thinking in images, as over against perceiving—re-presentation as contrasted with presentation. But the psychologist also differentiates between imaging which refers to some part of one's past experience (memory) and imaging, which, though necessarily based upon this same material, presents the material in new forms or patterns, and which is not felt to refer definitely to some part of one's past experience. This latter is imagination in the specific, or narrower meaning of the term.

A further distinction is made between imagination which occurs under passive attention, as illustrated in reverie, musing, or dreaming, and imagination which occurs under active attention, and which is marked by persistent, purposeful effort to dissociate former combinations of experience and to reorganize them into some new plan. We have, then, a distinction between passive imagination and active, creative, or productive imagination.

The tests of this chapter are designed both to secure indications of the wealth of spontaneous imagery in phantasy, and to measure capacity for creative or inventive thinking.

In so far as intelligence denotes not merely good attention and good memory, but also inventive capacity, ability to plan and organize, to anticipate, or to "put two and two together" (Ebbinghaus' *kombinierende Tätigkeit*), in so far must the attempt to measure intelligence employ tests of productive imagination and invention. It goes without saying that the tests here described do not exhaust the possibilities of investigation in this important field of mental activity. Undoubtedly, new tests will be devised which will prove of value in supplementing those heretofore employed. We need especially a series of tests of inventive capacity, of graded difficulty, which shall put less emphasis upon linguistic attainments.

TEST 45

Ink-blots.—In their discussion of a proposed series of tests for the examination of individual differences in mental traits, Binet and Henri, in 1895, suggested that fertility of visual imagination might be investigated by means of a series of ink-blots. Two years later, but independently, G. Dearborn published brief suggestions for making a series of blots, and in the following year described the results of the use of 120 blots in the case of 16 Harvard students and professors. Since then Kirkpatrick has tried the ink-blot test with public school children of 8 elementary grades; Miss Sharp has followed the suggestion of Binet and Henri in a study of individual psychology upon graduate students in Cornell University, and Pyle has published preliminary averages for different ages.

The ink-blot test is commonly classed as a test of passive imagination, under the assumption that S simply looks at the blot and allows his associative processes to suggest to him whatever 'pictures' they may. In practise, however, S is quite likely to search actively for these associations, so that the mental activity concerned is, perhaps, more allied to active than to passive imagination.

MATERIALS.—Standard series of ink-blots, numbered from 1 to 20. Stop-watch. Paper properly prepared for recording S's statements.

The primary difficulty heretofore existing in the application of the ink-blot test has been the lack of standardized material. To meet this difficulty, the author has prepared the series of blots just mentioned by using zinc-block prints, so that investigators may now apply the same series of blots, and thus secure strictly comparable data. Unfortunately, this series has not yet been applied upon a sufficiently extensive scale to render it possible to publish norms of performance for the test.

METHOD.—(a) *Full procedure.* Instruct S as follows: "I have here a series of 20 odd-shaped ink-blots. I want you to take them in order from 1 to 20, one at a time, to look them over at your leisure, and to tell me (or write down on a numbered blank) what things you can see in each blot. Try them in different positions. Of course, these blots are not really intended to be pictures of anything, but I want to see whether your imagination will suggest pictures of things in them, just as you sometimes try to see what objects you can make out of clouds." Let S take his own time. Especially with younger S's, it is better for E to record the results, so that S may be perfectly free to enumerate as many things as are suggested to him.

Kirkpatrick used only four blots, and allowed each pupil one minute to name as many associations as possible for each blot. Miss Sharp used 10 blots, and allowed only 5 minutes for the (whole?) test.

The test may be conducted with a group of S's by distributing the cards, and having them passed successively from member to member of the group until each S has written his associations for each card, but this method has obvious disadvantages.

(*b*) *Shorter procedure.* Following the method used by Dearborn, arrange the 20 cards face down in a pile, with the 20th card at the bottom, the 1st at the top, and the numbered edges toward S. Instruct S as follows: "Each of these 20 cards has on it an odd-shaped ink-blot. When I say 'now,' turn over the first card in this way [illustrating the movement that will expose the face of card No. 1 with the numbered edge toward S]. Look at the ink-blot, without turning the card in any other position, and say 'now' (or tap on the table) as soon as you have thought of something that the blot resembles. Of course, the blot is not really intended to be a picture of anything, but I want to see whether your imagination will suggest some 'picture' in it, just as you sometimes try to see what object you can make out of a cloud." Give the command 'now'; start the stop-watch at the same time. When S gives his signal, stop the watch, record the time and the object or association given by S. Continue in the same manner with the remaining cards.[1]

---

[1]The method proposed by Pyle (allowing 3 min. for writing the first thing suggested by each card in the order 1 to 20) is a modification of Dearborn's method for the purpose of making group tests. It suffers from the defects already pointed out (Ch. II, pp. 8-11) as characteristic of tests in which speed is made a measure of performance, in which written responses are introduced and in which a time-limit instead of a work-limit is employed.

TREATMENT OF DATA.—In the full procedure, the score is based upon the average or total number of associations; in the shorter procedure, upon the average speed of the single associations. It is also possible to form some estimate, in either case, of the type, richness and variety of S's imagery by classifying the associations after some such plan as that illustrated below from Miss Sharp's results.

TYPICAL RESULTS.—The following associations for the 20 cards of the standard series are taken from the records of several adults, and will serve to indicate the variety that may be expected when the records of several S's are compared. Note the frequent reference to animals.

(1) A lady seated on a couch. A witch riding on a new moon across the sky. A moose's head. A woman, sitting on a bank of shrubs, waving a handkerchief. Fir tree. Dragon in woods.

(2) Child, crouching in fear. Man with grotesque features. Ugly old colored woman. Old man seated. Back of bear. Lion crouching. Tree uprooted.

(3) A banner. A right-angled triangle. The God Billiken. An Egyptian idol. A jade-stone idol. A foot. Dog sitting on hind legs. Man shooting.

(4) A large beetle. A boat load of excursionists. A lobster. A spider. Potatoes. A dirigible balloon of the Zeppelin type, with a cloud of steam or smoke overhead, and a grappling-anchor trailing below. Two trees and roots. Stockings on clothes-line.

(5) A pig. A woman with a big head of hair. A butterfly. A hole through the ice. A girl wearing a tam-o-shanter cap. Human liver and heart. A rock. An oyster shell.

(6) Woman running and holding her skirt. Woman with a muff in her left hand, and her hat almost blown off. A broken bellows. Merry Widow waltz. A dog on a post. An island and lake.

(7) Large caterpillar on a horse's shoulders. A devil bending over something. An old man. A dream monster. A woman with flowers. Unicorn. Pig.

(8) Human torso. Hot and cold water faucet in a bath tub. Person with head bent forward, holding sticks in her hand.

Heads of two birds trying to swallow what is between them. A frog. A vase. Vertebra of back bone.

(9) A goat with a pack on his back. A turkey with drooping wings trailing on the ground. A tree. A goose's head.

(10) Ugly man's head. Head and arm of a woman with a lighted candle in her hand. A dachshund running off with some one's cape. A mosquito pupa. A tree.

(11) Map of Scotland and Ireland. Owl that has just placed a fish before him on the branch of a tree. Some specimen in geology. A tree blown in a heavy gale. A tiger under a tree. A conch shell.

(12) Map of United States and part of Canada. A chicken lying on its back. An Indian head. A woman sitting on a cliff under a tree, reading a novel. A buffalo running. Hydroids.

(13) A flying squirrel. The skin of a bear. A hen sitting on a nest. A dog running.

(14) A crab. A bat with outspread wings. A moth. A neurological slide. A flower. An insulator.

(15) Section of medulla oblongata. Two nuns bowing their heads together. A tulip. A false mask. A crab. Head of a fish. A plate of false teeth. A design-unit of two bears with heads together.

(16) Closed hand with thumb and little finger, or a sixth finger, projecting. A loving cup. A tea-pot. A head.

(17) A root. A porcupine. An Indian head. A nerve cell. Sponge dropping water.

(18) A Chinese dragon, as seen on packages of fire-crackers. Branch of a gnarled oak. A lizard. An old woman and child. A man with knees bent.

(19) Bird alighting on a nest. A flying squirrel. Rear of a cat in rapid motion. A lamb. A duck.

(20) Man pulling off his sweater. Runner leaning forward to start a foot-race. Photographer, with focussing cloth over his head. Crocodile suspended by the head. Bear with the grandmother's night-cap and gown, as illustrated in Little Red Riding Hood. An elephant seated.

GENERAL RESULTS.—(1) *Speed of association.* In 1920 trials, Dearborn found the average time for making a single association to a blot to be 10.3 sec. This seemingly long time may be due to the difficult nature of some of the blots in his series.

The children aged 8 to 14 tested by Pyle with the author's blots, but with the written response, averaged from 6.4 to 12.0 responses in 3 min. His adults averaged 10.6 for the men and 9.8 for the women.

(2) *Dependence on age.* Kirkpatrick states that "younger children seemed more suggestible or imaginative, as they named more spots" (Table 128). Pyle's tables show a similar tendency.

TABLE 128

Average Number of 'Names' Given to Ink-Blots (Kirkpatrick)

GRADE	I	II	III		V	VI	VII	VIII
Average	2.9	2.5	2.6	1.8	1.9	1.7	2.1	2.2

It is evident that something besides a simple decline of 'imagination' with age is exhibited in this table. In explanation, Kirkpatrick says: "The younger children seemed to have no doubt whatever of the spot being a picture of the object they named, while the older children simply said 'it is some like' or 'it looks a little like,' 'a dog,' 'cloud,' or whatever else was suggested. This superiority of the small children is striking when we consider that the number of mental images that they have is much smaller than that possessed by older children, who may name a part of the body or the map of a country or something else that the younger children know nothing about.

"The smaller number of objects seen in the spots by the children of the 4th, 5th, and 6th grades is probably to be explained by the fact that children of those ages have become more critical in their sense-perception, as their ideas have become more definite, and as they have learned from life's experiences and from training to be more careful in their judgments. The older pupils of the 7th and 8th grades, on the other hand, have passed into another stage in which they realize that a picture is not necessarily this or that, but may resemble any one of several things, hence they are not afraid to say what it looks like."

(3) *Dependence on occupation.* Dearborn believes that, at least in maturer *S*'s, the results of the ink-blot test are conditioned, not so much by age or sex directly, as by habits of living, occupation, and other environmental factors: thus, we should

expect characteristically different results from the test when applied, for example, to artists, farmers, laborers, professional men, to the city-bred or the country-bred, etc.

(4) *Dependence on race.* Pyle's averages (5b) show that negroes are nearly as good as whites in the ink-blot test.

(5) *Individual differences,* both in speed, number and type of association seem to have been been clearly marked and fairly constant, whenever the test has been applied. Thus, in Dearborn's single-association method, the highest agreement in the answers of his *S*'s for any one card was but 40 per cent., while for several cards, no two *S*'s gave the same answer.

As regards fertility of imagination, Miss Sharp noted that the most imaginative *S* in her group saw 81 objects, the least imaginative but 27 objects in the same 10 blots. The same investigator believes, however, that all *S*'s might be roughly divided into two groups, (*a*) the constructive or imaginative, who put together concrete details "in such a way as to form a significant whole," and (*b*) the matter-of-fact, or scientific type, given more to analysis than to creative synthesis.[2]

As examples of this difference, the following reports from two of Miss Sharp's *S*'s may be quoted: both refer to the same blot.
(1) *Associations few and non-constructive.* "An eagle. Stuffed turkey. Head and neck of a musk-rat."
(2) *Associations numerous and constructive.* "Giraffe. Prehistoric bird in flight. Fairy riding on a bumble-bee. Bit of tropical jungle, with trailing gray mosses and pools of water. Japanese lady. Bit of landscape with two hills and a valley between—an army encamped under one hill. Moss-grown log floating in water. Fabulous monster (griffin perhaps) walking off on his hind legs with a small Hottentot under his arm."

(6) *Qualitative classification.* It is often possible to classify the associations peculiar to a given *S*. Thus, Miss Sharp mentions as classificatory groups: (*a*) common-place, every-day objects, such as domestic utensils, tools, plants, and particularly animals, (*b*) scientific objects, such as geometric figures, schematic drawings, (*c*) objects suggested by literary reminiscence, and (*d*) objects from fable and mythology, such as

---

[2]It is tempting to regard this classification as identical with the common classification of laboratory *S*'s into 'subjective' and 'objective' observers.

centaurs, dragons, witches, fairies, etc. Some S's exhibit variety of association, in that they cite objects that belong to several of these groups; others are much less fertile in imagination and confine themselves largely to a single type of imagery.

REFERENCES

(1) A. Binet et V. Henri, La psychologie individuelle. *AnPs*, 2: 1895 (1896), 411-465, especially 444.

(2) G. Dearborn, Blots of ink in experimental psychology. *PsR*, 4: 1897, 390-1.

(3) G. Dearborn, A study of imaginations. *AmJPs*, 9: 1898, 183-190.

(4) E. Kirkpatrick, Individual tests of school children. *PsR*, 7: 1900, 274-280.

(5) W. H. Pyle, (a) The examination of school children. New York, 1913, pp. 33-35. (b) The mind of the negro child. *School and Society*, 1: 1915, 357-360.

(6) Stella E. Sharp, Individual psychology: a study in psychological method. *AmJPs*, 10: April, 1899, 329-391.

TEST 46

Linguistic invention.—The ink-blot test serves primarily as a test of visual imagery. But an even more fruitful source of individual differences in creative ability may be found in linguistic invention. Miss Sharp, acting upon the suggestions of Binet and Henri, tested what she terms 'literary imagination,' in three ways, viz.: by the development of sentences, by the development of a given theme, and by the choice of a topic for composition.

The idea of presenting a number of words to be joined into a sentence has been elaborated in various ways. The assignment of three words was employed by Masselon in 1902, and this test has, on that account, been referred to by some writers as the "Masselon method." It forms one test in the well-known Binet-Simon series, and was one of the tests used by Miss Sharp in her investigation of the mental types of adult S's. The reduction of the number of terms supplied, to two has been strongly recommended by Meumann, who selected the two terms in a special manner (see below), while another variation of the two-word test has been tried by Burt and by Wyatt, in which S is given a series of 10 words to be joined together successively, by pairs, in a series of sentences. On the other hand, the number of terms has been increased to 5, 8 or 10 with the in-

struction to invent a story containing the prescribed words
(invention of stories). This method evidently stands midway
between the method of sentence-formation and the method of
development of a theme, while by a little further extension the
well-known Ebbinghaus completion method (Test 48) is
reached. It needs little reflection to understand that the
nature of these various tests becomes decidedly varied as the
number and nature of the supplied terms is varied.

The method of completing a prose passage in which a large
amount of the original text is supplied is embodied in Test 48.
The present test includes the method of sentence-formation
known as Masselon's method, the method of sentence-formation
devised by Meumann, the completion of sentences used by Binet,
the invention of stories, and the development of a theme.

Before undertaking these formal tests, however, it is desirable, if the purpose in mind is to make a qualitative study of
the mental type of individual S's, to institute a preliminary
inquiry concerning the general literary tastes and habits of
each S. The exact nature of this inquiry must, naturally, be
adapted to the age and training of the S's: the following are
some of the points that have been covered by investigators: (1)
list of favorite books, (2) statement of favorite type of reading,
(3) statement of the magazines, periodicals, newspapers, etc.,
ordinarily read, (4) list of books (outside of classroom or professional work) read during the last year, (5) statement of
favorite games and evidence of enjoyment of games, like chess
and checkers, that demand creative activity and foresight, (6)
fondness for the theater, drama, music, painting and other
forms of art, etc., (7) experience in creative literary work.

A.   SENTENCE-FORMATION (MASSELON METHOD)

METHOD.—Ask S to write as many sentences as possible containing the three nouns: *citizen, horse, decree.* Each sentence
must contain all three nouns, though it may contain others as
well. The sentences are to be as varied as possible. Five minutes are allowed. Continue the test with four more sets of
nouns, and afterward make similar tests with five sets of verbs.

For the noun tests, use as additional sets: (2) *bell, ground, owner,* (3) *skill, modification, picture,* (4) *cup, fraction, money,* (5) *letter, law, summer.* For verbs use (1) *bless, destroy, write,* (2) *make, correspond, remain,* (3) *require, choose, run,* (4) *see, find, throw,* (5) *remember, put, depart.* In the noun tests, *S* is permitted to use either singular or plural forms, and possessive as well as nominative or objective cases; in the verb tests, he may use any form of the given verb, *e. g., blessed, to bless, will bless,* etc., as well as *bless.*

The tests may be conducted with individuals or with groups; but it is preferable, especially with young *S*'s, to work individually and to let *S* dictate the sentences instead of writing them.

TREATMENT OF DATA.—The quantitative score is determined by averaging the number of sentences written by *S.* The quality of work may be graded upon any convenient scale, *e. g.,* 1 to 5, corresponding to five degrees of excellence. Miss Sharp used the symbols *A, B,* and *C,* and indicated intermediate grades by the use of — and +. For purposes of computation, she then assigned numerical values to these symbols, as follows: $A-$ = 40, $A = 50$, $A + = 60$, $B- = 80$, $B = 100$, $B+ = 120$, $C-$ = 160, $C = 200$, $C + = 240$. In practise, this scoring is virtually equivalent to estimating quality of work in terms of average number of words per sentence, and that simpler method may be used for the qualitative score.

TYPICAL RESULTS.—(1) The following are selected single sentences reported by Miss Sharp for the first test:

1. "Decrees are made for citizens, not for horses." (The connection of the words here is simple and mechanical.)
2. "That stalwart citizen on the great gray horse is a man to be trusted with the decree." (This implies a concrete situation.)
3. "All the well-to-do citizens of the village, each mounted on a horse, rode through the streets, proclaiming their dissatisfaction with the new decree." (A situation is here more fully outlined.)

(2) The following is a full set of sentences written by a graduate student, in 5 min., for the first assignment:

1. A decree was posted that the citizen should not abuse the horse.
2. The horse of the citizen was sold by official decree.
3. "Here," said the citizen, "is the horse mentioned in the decree."

4. Early in Arabian history, a decree raised to a higher caste, a citizen who owned a horse, but later, possession was sufficient for better standing, and the law was not needed.

5. If a citizen keep a horse, it is a decree that he use it kindly.

6. "What a funny decree," exclaimed the citizen, when he read of the horse sun-bonnet law.

7. The decree was signed that the horse had kicked the citizen, and therefore the injured man could collect damages from the owner of the animal.

8. "Time is up," cried the citizen, stop-watch in hand, "I hereby decree that you write the word horse and stop at once." [Faulty on account of the use of 'decree' as a verb.]

(3) The following represent groups of sentences written for the author by two college students (selected at random from a number of papers) for the fourth set of verbs. The relatively greater variety of the second group is clear.

A. 1. "I saw the book and tried to find a place in which to throw it."

2. "I threw the cat in the creek and turned to see if anyone had found me out."

3. "I see that I can find nothing to throw at him."

4. "You see, it was this way, I simply found the hatchet and threw it."

B. 1. "The child saw a horse, found a stone and threw it at him."

2. "When you find a clover, see if it has four leaves: if not, throw it away."

3. "Throw the paper out of the window and see if it will find a good landing place."

4. "Find me a pencil, then I will see if I can find out the solution to the problem which is on the paper that you threw into the basket."

5. "The boy found an apple, but when he saw it was decayed, he threw it away."

CONCLUSIONS.[1]—(1) *Dependence on part of speech assigned.* All *S*'s tend to write fewer, but better sentences with verbs than with nouns.

TABLE 129

Scores of Seven Adults in Developing Sentences (*Sharp*)

FORM OF TEST	QUANTITY OF WORK			QUALITY OF WORK		
	Average	Maximum	Minimum	Average	Maximum	Minimum
Nouns 'given'___	4.6	6.6	3.2	79	113	55
Verbs 'given'___	8.8	5.8	2.5	93	133	54

[1]These are all drawn from the work of Miss Sharp.

(2) The rank of S's, both in quality and quantity of work, is the same when nouns and when verbs are assigned.

(3) "In general, the subjects who made the most sentences made the most elaborate, and those who made the fewest sentences made also the simplest and most unimaginative."

(4) This test correlates with the ink-blot test, in so far as those S's who show most constructive capacity with the blots also show most constructive capacity in the development of sentences.

B.   SENTENCE-FORMATION (MEUMANN'S METHOD)

The Masselon method, according to Meumann, is less well fitted to bring out differences in intelligence than his own method of presenting but two words, so selected that a number of different relations can be worked out between them, only one of which, or at least only a few of which, can be regarded as being really appropriate, pertinent and sufficiently definite as to evince good sense and a real appreciation of the relation. This appropriate combination of the two words into a sentence is accomplished only when S introduces a third relational element that supplies the 'point' needed to round out the thought.

METHOD.—Explain to S that he is to make a sentence with each pair of words. By the aid of illustrative examples make it clear that there are two ways in which any pair could be joined, the one correct enough, perhaps, but banal and loose, the other logical, sensible and specific, and that the latter form is the one desired. For example, the words *snow—melts* could be rendered as "The snow melts" or as "Snow melts when the warm sun shines on it." Again, the words *square—sides* could be rendered as "A square has sides" or as "A square has four sides of equal length." Similarly, from the pair *automobiles—tires* could be obtained "Automobiles have tires" or "Automobiles have pneumatic tires to make them ride easily."

When these instructions have been grasped, give S the following 10 pairs of terms and allow him all the time he desires to write one sentence of the 'pointed' type for each pair: (1) donkey—beatings, (2) soldiers—country, (3) city—streets, (4) sun—noon, (5) pine—winter, (6) drink—poverty, (7) cat—punished, (8) sky—red, (9) water—hill, (10) teacher—pleased.[2]

RESULTS.—The following types of answers may be readily distinguished:[3]

(*a*) The dictated words are written, but nothing else.

(*b*) The given words are joined in a nonsense statement, *e. g.*, "The city is a street."

(*c*) A number of successive sentences are cast in a very simple form which is the same in each, *e. g.*, "A donkey has beatings." "Soldiers have a country." "A city has streets."

(*d*) The written statement is incorrect, but such as to suggest that *S* had the glimmerings of an idea that failed of expression, possibly on account of some difficulty in the use of language, *e. g.*, "To drink is poverty."

(*e*) The sentence is logically correct, but indefinite, too loose, general and banal, *e. g.*, "A city has streets."

(*f*) The words are combined into a specific statement, but one that is imaginative and not expressive of the correct connection, *e. g.*, "Once upon a time there were three soldiers who lived in a beautiful country."

(*g*) The sentence is definite, logical, correct and pertinent, embodying the right causal connection, *e. g.*, "In the city the streets are wide and paved with brick." "Good soldiers are ready to die for their country."

NOTES.—The 'sentence-construction' or 'sentence-formation' test used by Wyatt and by Burt consists in presenting a series of 10 words such as *circle, moon, night, sleep,* etc., each one of which is fairly obviously connected with the next and then allowing each *S* 2.5 min. to write a series of sentences connecting the successive terms by pairs, *e. g.*, "The full moon has the form of a circle." "The moon shines at night," etc. Particular stress is laid upon the condition that the various sentences

---

[2] The last two have been supplied by the author to replace less useful or more complex combinations in Meumann's list.

[3] Although Meumann concludes that any attempt to score this test quantitatively must be arbitrary, it would seem possible to attempt some numerical comparison of the work of different *S*'s by assigning a scale of marks, like 0, 1, 2, etc., for these several qualitative degrees of performance.

must show the "closest possible connection." In practise this instruction is difficult to make clear, and the performance of S's is quite difficult to score precisely or fairly. The time consumed in writing also enters as a disturbing factor. Burt found for this test a coefficient of reliability of only .61, but a fairly high correlation with intelligence, 0.62.

C.   COMPLETION OF SENTENCES

MATERIALS.—Printed forms containing beginnings of 25 sentences,[4] with spaces for the completion of each sentence. Piece of white cardboard. Stop-watch.

METHOD.—Give S the following instructions: "On this paper there are printed the beginnings of a number of sentences. I am going to show these to you, one at a time. As soon as I show you one, I want you to finish out the sentence. You may say anything you want to, as long as the whole sentence will make sense when you have finished it. Take an easy attitude toward the test. Don't try to hurry. Let the completion of the sentence develop naturally and freely, whether it is long or short." If S fails to understand what is wanted, supply him with an extra paper on which a few trial sentences have been written in pen and ink, and show him how they might be completed. For the test proper, cover the entire test-blank with the cardboard: after a warning 'ready,' expose the first incomplete sentence.[5] Start the watch at the same time. Record as nearly as possible the time used by S in starting to complete the sentence, i. e., the time he takes, after he reads the sentence, to 'get an idea.' The timing should be done without S's knowledge.

VARIATION OF METHOD.—The printed forms are arranged to permit written tests, either of individuals or of groups. With groups the timing may be omitted without serious detriment.

---

[4]The first 20 sentences are taken, with such slight modifications as translation has suggested, from Binet. The last five (since Binet prints but 20 of the 25 he recommends) have been supplied by the author. Other sets of incomplete sentences will be found in Weidensall or in Woolley and Fischer.

[5]The sentences have purposely been numbered from the bottom of the page, so that the cardboard will not interfere with S's writing.

Some S's give shorter, others longer sentences when they are written.

TREATMENT OF DATA.—Compute the average, or determine the distribution, of the times needed by S to start the 25 sentences. For a qualitative index, estimate as well as possible (preferably by using some such system of scoring as that described in the development-of-sentences test) the general value of the completed sentences. S's sentences may also, if desired, be classified in regard to type, e. g., vague or meaningless, commonplace, reminiscential, imaginative, aphoristic, etc.

A more elaborate system of scoring was attempted by Woolley and Fischer and followed by Weidensall in part. Records were kept of (1) number of sentences attempted, (2) number of sentences correct (in the sense of constituting a real sentence, even though there might be some mistakes of grammar), (3) number of simple and of complex sentences, (4) average number of words written per sentence, (5) number of ideas expressed in the sentences, taken collectively (scored by a somewhat complex set of rules), (6) total time used in the test, (7) time used to start each sentence (classed in five groups, 0-2, 3-5, 6-10, 11-20 and 21-60 sec.), and (8) 'index' of ideas, obtained by dividing (6) by (5). Use is made in the published results, however, of only the 2d, 5th, 7th and 8th of these scores.

RESULTS.—(1) Binet found characteristic differences in the *speed of work* of his two daughters, Armande and Marguerite. Thus Armande's records show 12 sentences started in less than 5 sec., 4 sentences in from 5 to 10 sec., 6 in from 10 to 20 sec., 1 in 28 sec., and 1 in 70 sec. Marguerite's records, on the other hand, show but 1 sentence started in less than 5 sec., but 7 sentences in less than 10 sec., and the remainder in much longer times, e. g., 20, 50, and 70 sec.

(2) Binet's two S's also showed characteristic differences in the *type of sentence-completion:* Armande is poetic and imaginative; Marguerite's sentences are more precise, more practical, more in accord with real life, less emotional. For example, for Sentence 1, Armande writes: "I entered the field by a covered footpath." Marguerite writes: "I entered the grocery and bought two cents worth of chocolate."

(3) The study of school children at Cincinnati by Woolley and Fischer brings out the following points: (a) *age* is a factor of some moment, since 15-year-old pupils, when compared with 14-year-old, show a decided improvement in number of correct sentences, a large increase in number of ideas expressed and a slight increase in the speed of beginning the sentences; (b) *sex differences* seem to favor the boys, who are somewhat superior to girls in correctness and somewhat quicker than girls in speed of beginning (there was no definite sex difference in number of ideas); (c) the test shows a large positive *correlation with school grade* attained by both sexes at both years, when performance is scored by any of the three measures—number of correct sentences, number of ideas or speed of response.

(4) *Delinquents.* The results obtained by Weidensall with Bedford Reformatory women show that they are slower to respond than the Cincinnati girls, slower even than the Cincinnati retarded girls. On the other hand, the number of correct sentences and the number of ideas expressed were, contrary to expectation, greater in the Bedford group; this outcome may be due to the conditions under which the Bedford women were tested, or it may be connected, one may surmise, with the longer time taken in starting the sentences. At Bedford the ability to make correct sentences did not correlate with school grade attained before entering the institution, but the speed with which the sentences were started did correlate with the school grade; in fact, the poorest *S*'s took five times as long to start their sentences as did the more intelligent ones.

D.   INVENTION OF STORIES

Test No. 26 of the Binet-Simon 1905 series called for the construction of a sentence containing three specified words. This test has been elaborated by Mrs. Squire by asking not for a sentence, but for a *story* about three words. The same test, with 5, 8 or 10 words given, has been used by Winch in his comparative study of memory for ideas and productive imagination.

Meumann's somewhat similar test consists in dictating a series of 'cue-words' or phrases, carefully selected as to nature and number, with the instructions to make a story from them. In this test the principles involved in selecting the words make the problem of a different sort from that involved in Winch's test; the conditions are rather more rigorously drawn, so that the number of satisfactory solutions is smaller. In some respects, in fact, Meumann's test more nearly resembles the Ebbinghaus completion method (Test 48).

METHOD.—(1) For young S's, ask for a story about a *boy*, a *river* and a *ball* (Squire test). For children younger than 10, and better for yet older children, the story should be given orally and taken down verbatim by E.

(2) Winch's instructions, as given in writing to a group of 13-year-old S's, were as follows (8, p. 102):

"Write a story containing the following words: *thief, landlord, crab, shake, hotel, basket, cries, provisions, escape, custody.*

"You are to write the longest story you can, because the longer the story is, the more marks you will get, provided that everything you write has something to do with the story. You will get no marks at all for them and only be wasting your time if you write sentences which have no connection with the rest. Try and think out the story you are going to write before you start, and see that the progress of the story will enable you to fit all the words in properly."

It is desirable to make more than one test of this sort. For this purpose, use may be made of one or more of the other lists of terms used by Winch[6] with the same instructions as above. These lists are: (1) *Orphan, garden, hungry, station, parents, clothing, visitor, cottage, train, country.* (2) *Snowstorm, children, ticket, clock, dog, screams, church, basket, river, ice.* (3) *Army, hill, artillery, victory, cavalry, fight, captured, brave.* (4) For younger children (8-9 years): *dog, clock, basket, man, children.*

(3) For Meumann's test E must take a simple connected bit

---

[6]It should be said that Winch's invention tests were applied to children who were also being tested in 'substance memory' with the aid of passages containing terms quite similar to those given as material for the invention. This had undoubtedly an effect upon the invented stories, though Winch asserts that "the invented stories are, almost invariably, on a much lower plane" (p. 101).

of prose depicting a total situation and reduce it to a series of salient cue-words. After giving one or more preliminary illustrations, *S*'s are requested to write a story based on the cue-words selected. The following is the set most successfully used by Meumann: *house took fire—child alone—clever monkey—parents thankful—reward.*

No time limit is set in any of these tests. *S*'s should not be hurried.

TREATMENT OF DATA.—Mrs. Squire contented herself with recording four degrees of performance in her three-word test: (*a*) complete failure, (*b*) separate sentence given for each word, (*c*) three words in one sentence, but the sentences [of the rest of the story?] unconnected, and (*d*) complete narrative. The outcome of this scoring is indicated below.

Winch scored performance on the general basis of number of meaningful 'units' in the story, giving no allowance for any sentences or parts of sentences which did not arise connectedly from preceding sentences, but yet no penalizing for lack of esthetic unity (making every element in the story converge to a point). The aim is to rank the performance with regard to the "fertility of continuous and connected imagination" displayed in it.[7]

RESULTS.—(1) *Dependence on age* is shown in Mrs. Squires' results in the form of (*a*) "a development from the crude sentence strung together by 'ands' to a closely knit sentence," while (*b*) "another characteristic change is the transition from the fantastic type of story related by the 6, 7 and 8-year-old children to the extremely realistic, matter-of-fact style employed by the 9th, 10th and 11th year groups," and (*c*) "another plan of invention, more flexible in style is evident in the stories of the 12th and 13th year groups."

As applied in her mental age series, this test becomes roughly diagnostic as follows: the normal 6-year-old can give orally sentences containing the three words; ability to get all three words into one sentence, though with a disconnected story, would appear typical of 8 and 9-year-old children (though given by Binet as a 10-year test); ability to construct a complete

---

[7]See his discussion, pp. 102-105, for further details.

narrative as a realistic type is seen in the 9th and succeeding years, with a final level of flexibility and superiority of style appearing at 12 and 13 years.

(2) *Correlations.* Winch found moderately high correlations, .55 to .75, between substance memory and the invention of stories, and that practise in substance memory, unless carried to the 'fatigue-point' (limit of training), tends to augment proficiency in invention.

(3) *Reliability.* The reliability of the test, as might be anticipated, is not very high, about .50, so that more than one trial is demanded for significant results.

(4) *Qualitative differences.* Meumann found it somewhat difficult to score the work of school children in such a way as to distinguish fine degrees of intellectual ability, but he considers the elaboration of the story from the cue-words a good test for revealing larger differences in general mental ability and also for revealing various mental types. In general, he finds eight fairly distinct types of story.

(*a*) Zero performance; connections between the cue-words lacking or nonsensical.

(*b*) The cue-words are connected in a number of separate and independent sentences. Here the grade of mental ability is sufficient to join together pairs of terms, but not to make the larger synthesis of all the terms into a whole.

(*c*) Attempts are made to produce a whole, but the connections between the various cue-words are not rightly arranged and the point of the whole story is not grasped.

(*d*) The connections between the cue-words are rightly arranged, but the point of whole series of words is missed and the result is a story of a totally wrong 'turn.'

Types *a-d* may be regarded as all indicative of lower stages of intellectual ability: the following four types, however, may be regarded as solutions of the problem, though of different kinds.

(*e*) The *pure imaginative type* is illustrated by a story of astonishing richness of detail, with decided linguistic fluency, but with the real point either quite lost or badly distorted. *S*'s of this type evince, then, little intelligence, but a rich imagination; their endowment is perhaps exclusively linguistic.

(*f*) The *pure intellectual type* is illustrated by a story in which the connections of the cue-words are correct and the point of the whole is correctly grasped, but its elaboration into a story is accomplished in the scantiest manner possible. *S* is content to present the logical and factually correct connection of the cue-words in the shortest possible manner.

(*g*) The *imaginative-emotional type* is illustrated in stories that show evident presence of feeling, to give due expression to which *S* indulges in active imagination. He introduces invented details to express his emotional reaction.

(*h*) The *intellectual-imaginative type* is illustrated by stories that show clear grasp of the meaning of the whole supplemented by imaginative and pictorial additions, which are, however, always pertinent and subdued to the salient points in the development of the story.

For examples of these several types, consult Meumann (pp. 158-9) : a single one of them, that of Type f, may be repeated here:

Story of Arthur W., 7th school year, age 12 years 9 months:

"There was a house in the village: it took fire. The parents had just gone away. The child was all alone in the house. The people also had a clever monkey. He saved the child from the flames. And when the parents came home and saw that the monkey had saved the child, they were thankful and gave him a reward."

E. DEVELOPMENT OF A THEME

METHOD.—Supply S with writing materials, and give him 10 min. (or perhaps longer if working with young S's) to write upon some theme selected from the following: (1) *The Death of a Dog,* (2) *The Capture of a Fortress,* (3) *The Escape of a Prisoner,* (4) *A Forest Fire,* (5) *The Mission of Music,* (6) *The Influence of Newspapers,* (7) *The Delays of Justice,* (8) *A Trip in a Flying Machine.*[8]

TREATMENT OF DATA.—Quantity or speed of work may be reckoned with approximate accuracy by counting the number of words written in the assigned time; quality of work, which is really important, especially in the treatment of imaginative themes, must be estimated by E after a trial has shown what may be deemed poor, and what good work for S's of the age under investigation. Quality may be recorded in the manner already described, or upon the basis of 100, as in grading school compositions.

RESULTS.—(1) The relative number of ideas elaborated by different S's is indicated with fair approximation by the relative number of words written, so that number of words may stand as a fair index of fluency of ideation and general linguistic readiness.

---

[8]The first of these themes was used by Binet in his comparative study of the mental processes of his two daughters; the next six were used for a similar purpose in Miss Sharp's study of university students—the first three of them being designed to involve imaginative, the second three expository treatment; the last theme is suggested by the author as more suitable for younger S's. To secure a more reliable estimate of S's efficiency it is desirable that more than one theme should be developed.

This test lends itself readily to group treatment, since it involves a familiar type of school activity.

(2) As a rule, more words are written upon imaginative than upon expository themes. Sharp's best *S* wrote in 10 min., on an average, 259 words upon imaginative, and 222 upon expository themes; her poorest *S* wrote, on the average, 124 and 94 words, respectively, for the same types of themes.

(3) Those *S*'s that show constructive ability in the ink-blot test, and in the development of sentences, also exhibit the same superiority here in the development of themes.

NOTES.—These tests of linguistic invention might, without great difficulty, be paralleled in other fields of constructive effort. A test of musical ability (of the creative sort) might, for example, be devised by asking *S*'s to finish a partially given musical theme, or to construct a simple melody from a given series of notes. Similarly, certain forms of artistic invention might be tested by asking *S*'s to sketch designs for wall-paper or patterns for Venetian iron-work.

Miss Sharp's test of the choice of a theme was conducted by asking *S*'s to select, from the following 10 themes, those five upon which they would prefer to write, if asked to do so: A. Imaginative themes, (1) *In a Snowstorm*, (2) *A Polar Landscape*, (3) *A Puritan Sabbath*, (4) *My Opposite Neighbor*, (5) *Man Endowed with the Power of Flight:* B. Expository themes, (6) *Civilization not Regeneration*, (7) *Wisdom in Charity*, (8) *Friendship of Books*, (9) *Fiction as a Vehicle of Truth*, (10) *The Eloquence of the Bar and that of the Pulpit*. The expository themes were generally preferred, but some *S*'s, who, as other tests showed, had little capacity to handle imaginative themes, did select several from the latter division.

REFERENCES

(1)   A. Binet et V. Henri, La psychologie individuelle. *AnPs*, 2: 1895 (1896), 411-465, especially 444.
(2)   A. Binet, L'étude expérimentale de l'intelligence.   Paris, 1902. Pp. 309.   Especially ch. x.
(3)   C. Burt, Experimental tests of higher mental processes and their relation to general intelligence. *JEPd*, 1: 1911, 93-112.
(4)   R. Masselon, Psychologie des déments précoces.   Paris, 1902.
(5)   E. Meumann, Ueber eine neue Methode der Intelligenzprüfung und über den Wert der Kombinationsmethoden. *ZPdPs*, 13: 1912, 145-163.   (Also Vorlesungen zur Einführungen in die experimentelle Pädagogik, 2d ed., Vol. 2: 1913, 445-452.)

(6)   Stella E. Sharp, Individual psychology: a study in psychological method. *AmJPs*, 10: 1899, 329-391.

(7)   Carrie R. Squire, Graded mental tests. *JEdPs*, 3: 1912, 363-380, 430-443, 493-506, especially 439-441.

(7a)   Jean Weidensall, The mentality of the criminal woman. To appear in *EdPsMon*.

(8)   W. H. Winch, Some relations between substance memory and productive imagination in school children. *BrJPs*, 4: 1911, 95-125.

(8a)   Helen T. Woolley and Charlotte R. Fischer, Mental and physical measurements of working children. *PsMon*, 18: 1914, No. 77. Pp. 247, especially 185-212.

(9)   S. Wyatt, The quantitative investigation of higher mental processes. *BrJPs*, 6: 1913, 109-133.

TEST 47

Word-building.—The word-building test was suggested by the familiar game of anagrams, as well as by the advertisements often seen in magazines in which a prize is offered to the person who can make the most words from a given word or series of letters. This test is easily administered and evaluated; it is one that calls for ingenuity and active attention; it might fairly be said to demand that ability to combine isolated fragments into a whole, which Ebbinghaus has declared to be the essence of intelligence and for the measurement of which he devised his well-known 'completion method' (Test 48); and finally, its execution is conditioned to a certain extent by the richness and readiness of the examinee's word-vocabulary. One may expect, therefore, to find a correlation between this test and the vocabulary test (No. 50), and possibly between it and school standing or general intelligence, and other tests of creative literary ability.

In addition to the preliminary reports made by the author, the two tests proposed by him have been tried out by Pyle, Squire, Wyatt (with some modification) and most recently by Anderson, in an extended application to several hundred public school children at Ithaca carried out under the author's direction for the purpose of supplying curves of percentile distribution for performance in several tests. Heymans and Brugmans have used a similar test (making as many words as possible in 10 min. from a given 10-letter word) in their study of the intercorrelations of various tests of intelligence.

MATERIALS.—Two specially prepared blanks, the first of which calls for combination of words from the letters *a, e, o, b, m, t,* the second from the letters *e, a, i, r, l, p.*

METHOD.—Provide *S* with the first test blank, and give him the following instructions: "Make as many words as you can from the six letters given on this blank. You may use any number of letters from one to six, but no letter may be used twice in the same word, and no other letters than these six are to be used. You will have five minutes." Conclude the test by use of the second blank under the same conditions. For comparison with the curves of distribution given here, both tests must be applied and in the order just mentioned.

TREATMENT OF DATA.—Each word written in accordance with the rules counts one. To determine just what shall be termed a 'word,' the data secured by Anderson, upon which the curves that follow are based, was scored by following the division made upon each page of the 1910 edition of Webster's New International Dictionary, *i. e.*, any word found above the line was admitted; any word found below the line (and hence rare, obsolete, dialectic, etc.) was excluded. No discount was attempted for possible instances in which legitimate words were hit on by mere accident. As a guide to scoring these tests, the lists of admitted words are reproduced here.

aeobmt-test

a	bam	ea	ma	o	tab
ab	bat	eat	Mab	oat	tambo
Abe	bate	eta	Mae	om	tame
abet	be		mao		tea
am	beam		mat		team
ambo	beat		mate		to
at	bema		me		toe
ate	bet		meat		Tom
atom	beta		met		tomb
	bo		meta		tome
	boa		moa		
	boat		Moab		
	bot		moat		
	bote		mob		
			mot		
			mote		

eairlp-test

a	ea	I	la	pa	Ra
ai	ear	Ira	lair	pail	Rae
ail	earl	ire	lap	pair	rail
air	ela		lea	pal	rale
al	Eli		leap	pale	rap
ale	epi		Lear	paler	rape
alp	era		lepra	pali	re
ape	eria		lerp	par	Rea
April			liar	pare	real
ar			lie	parel	reap
are			lier	pea	rei
Ariel			lip	peal	rep
aril			lira	pear	rial
				pearl	rip
				per	ripe
				peril	rile
				pi	
				pia	
				pie	
				pier	
				pile	
				plea	
				plier	

RESULTS.—(1) *Norms* are given in Tables 130 and 131 for the two forms of the test separately and so distributed as to show the average performance for each sex at each age. These norms have been compiled by combining the data obtained by Anderson and by Pyle. Percentile distributions for the scores of the two tests added together are shown in Figs. 77 and 78. These curves have been derived from Anderson's data by subjecting the raw data to the process of numerical smoothing and by further smoothing the curves in the process of drafting them.[1]

TABLE 130

Averages by Age and Sex, aeobmt-Test (After Anderson and Pyle)

SEX	AGE	8	9	10	11	12	13	14	15	16	17	18	ADULTS
Boys	Cases	38	86	103	112	124	134	109	85	59	49	37	70
	Aver	5.9	9.0	8.7	10.5	11.4	11.5	13.2	15.3	19.3	17.0	16.9	18.4
Girls	Cases	48	101	128	115	141	99	118	96	94	70	53	93
	Aver.	7.5	8.0	10.8	11.8	13.2	14.9	15.0	15.8	15.8	15.9	18.4	20.9

[1] See Ch. 3, p. 31, for these methods.

On account of the relatively small number of cases available for each curve, its topography must be regarded as somewhat provisional, though the error is presumably within one or two points. It will be understood that the minimal and maximal scores do not afford permanent standards of comparison.

TABLE 131·

Averages by Age and Sex, aeirlp-Test (After Anderson and Pyle)

SEX	AGE	8	9	10	11	12	13	14	15	16	17	18	ADULTS
Boys____	Cases	39	88	102	112	130	144	111	87	63	52	39	30
	Aver.	5.5	7.3	8.3	10.6	11.5	12.6	13.9	16.2	17.0	19.3	16.4	21.8
Girls____	Cases	41	97	124	114	138	94	121	98	94	71	54	45
	Aver.	6.5	7.7	10.2	11.5	13.3	14.7	16.2	17.4	17.7	18.0	19.3	21.4

(2) *Dependence on age.* Mrs. Squire's conclusion that the correlation "between efficiency and maturity is not so complete as in many of the other tests" would seem to be based upon the examination of too few cases (10 of each age), for the averages of Tables 130 and 131, with the single exception of that for the 9-year-old boys in the *aeobmt*-test, show a progressive rise with age from 8 to 17 years, while adults are uniformly superior to the boys and girls of 17. The same thing is brought out in the combined results set forth in the curves: that for 9-year boys lies for the most part above that for 10-year boys. There is also a drop in the upper percentiles of 15-year-old girls that is difficult of explanation unless there has been some accidental selection of poor *S*'s in this group.

(3) *Dependence on sex.* Comparison of the two tables and of the two charts makes it easily evident that girls, at least up to the age of puberty, are consistently superior to boys and by an amount approximately equal to one year's advance. It follows that this sex difference must always be had in mind in the use of the norms and distributions for this test.

(4) *Dependence on race.* Pyle's comparative study of whites and negroes (3a) shows clearly the inferiority of the latter in this test. In terms of general averages for all ages (in which there is, unfortunately, a certain element of unreliability owing

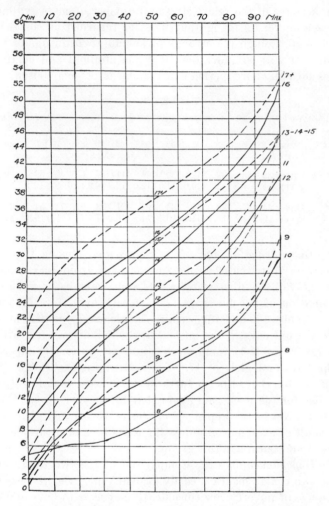

FIG. 77. PERCENTILES OF WORD BUILDING FOR BOYS. (Anderson)

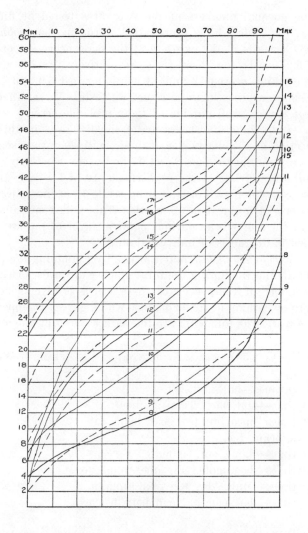

FIG. 78. PERCENTILES OF WORD BUILDING FOR GIRLS. (Anderson)

to the unequal numbers of the two races tested at different ages), the male whites scored 10.8 words in the *aeobmt*-test and 11.3 words in the *aeirlp*-test; the male negroes scored 5.2 and 6.0 words for these tests, respectively. Similarly, the female whites scored 12 and 13 words against 5.9 and 5.1 for the female negroes in these same two tests. These differences are, of course, well outside of their probable error.

(5) *Individual differences* are decidedly large in this test. Inspection of the charts, for example, will show that some *S*'s at 9 are superior to some *S*'s at 17 and over. Similarly, in the author's first trials of the *aeobmt*-test, 10 of his 36 grammar-school *S*'s scored 15 words or over, while 13 of his college students scored fewer than 15 words. This wide-range distribution of the scores is an obvious point in favor of the use of the method in diagnosis of individual status.

(6) *Frequency of different words.* By examining the papers in detail, and tabulating the total number of words formed and the number of times each of these words is given, one may discern something of the principles which govern the operation of the test. The following are the data secured by the author:

TEST NO. 1.   58 COLLEGE STUDENTS.   (43 DIFFERENT WORDS.)

Over 50 times—bat, mat, bet.
40-49 times—eat, met, Tom, at, boat.
30-39 times—meat, to, tea, beat, team, tab, ate, am, moat, mob, me, beam, toe.
20-29 times—tame, oat, be, mate.
10-19 times—boa, mote, bate, abet, tomb, tome.
 5- 9 times—Mab, Abe, Mae, ma, atom, a.
 1- 4 times—bot, mot, o, Moab, beta, bema.

TEST NO. 1.   50 GRAMMAR-GRADE BOYS.   (38 DIFFERENT WORDS.)

Over 40 times—mat, bat.
30-39 times—bet, at, met.
20-29 times—to, eat, Tom, beat, tea, meat, be, am, boat.
10-19 times—toe, mob, beam, me, ate, team, tab, boa, oat.

5- 9 times—ma, bate, a, moat, mot, tame, mate, bot.

1- 4 times—tam, tomb, Abe, mote, Moab, Mae, o.

Not given—those not given by college students, plus abet, atom, bema, beta, Mab, tome.

TEST No. 2.   69 COLLEGE STUDENTS.   (59 DIFFERENT WORDS.)

Over 60 times—lip, lap.

50-59 times—rip, rap, pear, ear, real, pie, leap, rail, pale, reap.

40-49 times—pail, pile, ale, pair, are, ape, lie, pea, peal.

30-39 times—pare, earl, pearl, air, par, lair, ripe, liar.

20-29 times—ail, Lear, rape, ire, pal.

10-19 times—lea, pa, rile, pire, era, pier.

5- 9 times—per, a, alp, Eli, plea.

1- 4 times—I, paler, peril, lira, rep, rale, ra, April, Ira, la, pi, Rea, Rae.

Inspection of these lists shows (*a*) that three-letter words are in every instance those most frequently formed, (*b*) that two-letter words and the one-letter words, which one might expect to be most frequent since most simple, stand relatively low, *e. g., ma, be, am, pa, me, a, o, I*,[2] (*c*) that grammar-school boys give all the words given by college students save a few rather unusual terms such as *atom* and *tome,* (*d*) that usage and ordinary speaking vocabulary condition the formation of words, in as much as the most ordinary words have the greatest frequency, *e. g., bat, mat, bet, eat, lip, lap,* whereas words that are less frequently used in every-day speech, although their meaning is doubtless perfectly well known, do not suggest themselves so readily under the conditions of the test, *e. g., tomb, tome, era, plea, paler,* (*e*) that the words not given by any one are, with one or two exceptions, *e. g., plier,* words of extremely rare usage or unusual form, alternative spellings, etc.

(7) *Reliability.* Wyatt found a coefficient of reliability of .88 between the results for two different arrangements of the

---

[2]It appeared, upon inquiry, that some of the college students had omitted words like *pa, ma, a, o,* and *I* on the ground that they were 'not real words,' or 'didn't count,' but, oftener, they seem to have been passed over because the attention was concentrated upon the making of *combinations.*

letters *aeobmt*. A sample group of 46 cases from Anderson's data gave a reliability of .74, P.E. .07, when the *aeobmt*-test and the *eairlp*-test were compared. The word-building test is seen, therefore, to possess a good degree of reliability.

(8) *Correlations.* Heymans and Brugmans found positive correlations of from .12 to .76 between word-building and five other tests of imagination (puzzle picture, .35, solving riddles .24, arrangement of syllables .76, jig-saw puzzles .12, Binet's paper-cutting test .47). Wyatt's corrected correlations with word-building gave with analogies .93, with the completion test .97, with the part-wholes test .99. The raw correlations for his two groups of *S*'s were for analogies .54 and .65, for the completion test .36 and .70, and for the part-whole test .36 and .77. He also found raw correlations of .39 and .52 for a test of sentence-construction, a correlation of .47 with interpretation of fables, but no correlation with the letter-square test.

The author found no correlations between word-building and class standing in the case of grammar-school pupils and the insignificant correlation of .13, P.E., .08, in the case of 58 college students. Terman, however, found his stupid boys generally inferior to his bright boys.

(9) *Conditioning factors.* Age, sex and general intelligence are not the only factors that affect the outcome of this test. Thus Terman remarks: "Much depends, of course, upon the vocabulary at command, and this in turn depends largely upon home training and amount of habitual reading as well as upon native retentiveness. A second factor is ability to spell, and habits of word analysis generally. Very important, also, is the use of a rational plan; some skipped about and made combinations at random, while others took the letters one by one and joined them in as many different ways as possible with the others. Lastly, the rate of shifting of attention, and the degree of mental inertia as opposed to spontaneity, also contribute to the result" (5, p. 342).

REFERENCES

(1) E. J. Anderson, Standardization of some mental tests. (Study from the Cornell University Educational Laboratory, as yet unpublished.)

(2)   G. Heymans und H. Brugmans, Intelligenzprüfungen mit Studierenden. *ZAngPs*, 7: 1913, 317-331.

(3)   W. H. Pyle, The examination of school children. New York, 1913. Pp. 70. Especially 22-24.

(3a)   W. H. Pyle, The mind of the negro child. *School and Society*, 1: 1915, 357-360.

(4)   Carrie R. Squire, Graded mental tests. *JEdPs*, 3: 1912, 363-380, 430-443, 493-506, especially 441-442.

(5)   L. M. Terman, Genius and stupidity: a study of some of the intellectual processes of seven 'bright' and seven 'stupid' boys. *PdSc*, 13: 1906, 307-373.

(6)   G. M. Whipple, Vocabulary and word-building tests. *PsR*, 15: 1908, 94-105.

(7)   S. Wyatt, The quantitative investigation of higher mental processes. *BrJPs*, 6: 1913, 109-133.

TEST 48

Ebbinghaus' completion method.—In July, 1905, the school authorities of Breslau requested certain persons, among them Professor H. Ebbinghaus, to undertake a scientific investigation of the fatigue-effects of the continuous five-hour session then in vogue in that city. In the course of this investigation Ebbinghaus devised and applied, in conjunction with other tests, what he termed the *'Combinationsmethode'* (since referred to by Elsenhans as the 'completion-method' and by others as the mutilated text or missing-words test).[1]

The author of the method says in substance: Mental ability demands not merely retentive capacity, readiness of recall, or facile association of specific past experiences; it demands all this and something more, something more complex and, as it were, creative; namely, the ability to combine, into a coherent and significant whole, mutually independent and even seemingly contradictory impressions. In short, intelligence is essentially a combinative activity. To measure intelligence, there-

---

[1]Meyer has pointed out the inaccuracy of the translation "combination-method," which has been current for some time. The German *Combinationsgabe* is not a talent for combination, but an ability to "put two and two together," or, to use Meyer's explanation, "a talent for drawing conclusions from premises which do not very readily present themselves to a man's consciousness as items of a unitary logical thought, but which, *as soon as they are combined*, suggest the conclusion very forcibly." This is quite true, but the author can not see that Meyer has improved matters by advocating the translation "conjectural method." To conjecture is to surmise, to guess, to form a tentative opinion, inferentially. Technically, the activity in the Ebbinghaus test might be labelled 'redintegration,' but, as this term is somewhat clumsy, the designation 'completion method' seems entirely adequate.

fore, we must employ a test that demands ability to combine fragments or isolated sections into a meaningful whole. Such a test may be afforded by mutilated prose, *i. e.*, by eliding letters, syllables, words, or even phrases, from a prose passage and requiring the examinee to restore the passage, if not to its exact original form, at least to a satisfactory equivalent of it.

On account of the enthusiastic statements of Ebbinghaus, who characterizes this method as "a real test of intelligence," and as "a simple, easily applied device for testing those intellectual activities that are fundamentally important and significant both in the school and in life," the test has assumed some prominence.

The classification of this method in a system of tests is not always easy, for the simple reason that what mental processes it demands depends almost entirely upon the number and kind of elisions that are made in the text. To take extreme cases, if the elisions are numerous and sweeping, it may become really a linguistic puzzle of a very difficult variety, and it then belongs rather in the group of tests of active or creative imagination of the literary type; if, on the other hand, the elisions are but few and simple, it may degenerate into a simple test of controlled association of any desired degree of ease. Again, if the original text be first read to the examinee, as some, *c. g.*, Elsenhans, suggest, the test becomes in the main a test of associative recall, *i. e.*, a form of memory test.

Since the elision of a single letter may, in some circumstances, very considerably increase the difficulty of the test, it follows that, without extensive preliminary trials, it is well-nigh impossible to prepare a series of texts of equivalent difficulty, or to insure that the several sections within a given text present equivalent difficulty.

That these difficulties in the preparation of the text are real and serious is attested by the unanimity with which they are expressed by all investigators. They have led some experimenters to question whether the method did, after all, get at the mental activity it was designed to call forth, but the trend of opinion has been on the whole distinctly and even enthusiastically in favor of the test.

The following is a sample section of text as used by Ebbinghaus and other German investigators: the dotted lines indicate the position and approximate length of the omissions.

Belagerung Kolbergs. 1807.

"Da der Feind fortf......an....neuen Schanze am Sandwege.... angestr.......Eifer zu...............so hatte unser neuer Kommandant gleich........ersten Nacht........Hierseins einen Aus........dieselbe angeordnet," etc.

Terman elided, in the main, whole words, instead of syllables, on the ground that the word is a more natural unit of language than the syllable, and that ability to supply missing syllables will, in the case of school children, depend largely on the extent to which word-analysis has been taught in the schools: this varies in different school systems and even in different classes of the same system.

MATERIALS.—Stop-watch, or for group work, the special seconds clock is recommended. Four printed texts. [If all four texts are to be used for the test, *E* should prepare a short sample piece of mutilated text, say three or four lines, which may be typewritten, or placed on the blackboard for group work, and used for demonstration and preliminary trial. If one of the texts is not used, this may serve the purpose.]

Text No. 1, prepared by the author, has been used by him in tests upon college students and by Mrs. Squire in tests upon school children. It contains 100 elisions, including some in which, in accordance with Ebbinghaus' plan, portions of words as well as entire words are elided.

Text No. 2, taken from Terman (18), has been used by Wyatt in tests upon English school children; it contains 93 elisions.

Text No. 3 is designed especially for use after a preliminary reading of the entire completed form. It is taken from Terman and contains 100 elisions.

Text No. 4, taken from Terman and Childs (19), and not here reproduced, is substantially the same passage as No. 2, but the elisions are made upon a new plan, such that there are four sections representing four different degrees of elision. In the first section 33, in the second 45, in the third 54 and in the fourth 66 per cent. of the original material is elided. This text demands a special system of scoring. In use in the author's laboratory it has been found that the second and third blanks are peculiarly unfortunate: they are too difficult and tend to produce discouragement and confusion at the outset. Many adults also find the fourth section easier than the third, despite the greater amount of elision in it. However, the text has been retained as presented by its authors on account of the norms published for it by them.

The reader who desires to try yet other texts will find eight of them in Simpson (16, pp. 119-121).

In the reproductions here given, italics indicate the elisions in the printed text.

Text No. 1.
Where the Dandelions Went.

When Willy *was* two *years* old, he *lived in a* red farm-ho*use* w*i*th *a* yard *in* front *of it*. The dand*elions* were *very* th*ick* there; so that *the yard* loo*ked* yellow instea*d* of *green*.

One bright *day* Willy's m*amma* put *on his* straw *hat and* sent him *out into the* yard to *play*. She knew *the yard* had *a* high *fence;* and *he* could not *open the* gate; so he *was safe*. W*hen* it *was* time *for* him *to have a* nap and *she* went *to call* him, she noticed that *a* gr*eat* m*any* of the d*andelions were gone*. She won*dered* where *they were;* but, as *Willy* could not talk much, *she* did not *ask* him *about* them.

A short *time* after, while *he* was *asleep in* his crib, *his* mamma went *out to draw some* w*ater*. When *the* buck*et* cam*e up* full *of water, the* top was all *yellow* with *dandelions*. Look*ing* down into *the well, she* could *see* no *water* at all, on*ly dandelions*.

It was no wonder, then, where *the* blos*soms* had *gone*. Willy *had* been *very* busy, try*ing to* fill *up the well*.

Text No. 2.
The Strength of the Eagle.

One *day the* eagle *went* with the *other* birds *to* see *which* could *fly the* highest. *They* agreed *that* he who *could* fly *the highest* should *be* called *the* strongest *bird*. All started *at the* same *time* and *flew* away among *the* clouds. One by one they gr*ew* weary *and* re*turned*, but *the* eagle *flew* upward and *upward* until *he* was *a* mere speck *in the* hea*vens*. When he *came* back, *the* others were *waiting* for him; and *when he* touched *the* ground a linnet *flew* off *his* back where *he had been* hidden and *said* that *he* himself *was the* strongest *bird*. "I am stronger *than the eagle*," said the *linnet*, "for not *only* did I *fly* as high, but *when* he began *his* downward *flight*, I *left my* hiding *place* and *flew* up *a* little *higher*." *At* this boastful *speech* the *others shook* their heads and *called a* council to *decide* the matter. After *a* long *debate they* decided *that* the *eagle was* the *strongest* bird, *for* not only *did* he *fly* so high, but *he carried* the *linnet* as well.

To *this* day *the* plumes *of the eagle* are emblems of *strength* and coura*ge*.

Text No. 3.
Why the Mole Is Blind.

An *Indian* once *chased a squirrel* into cloud*land*. Then *he* set *a* trap *for him*, laughing to *think* how *he* would *catch him*. The *squirrel* did *not come* back, but *alas!* the *sun* on *his* daily *rounds fell* right *into the trap.*

When *the* bright *sunlight did not* come, the *Indian* began *to* be *uneasy,* and when *he* found *his trap* had *the sun* fast he *did not* know *what to* do.

He tried *to get* near enough *to loosen* the cords, but *the heat* from the *sun scorched* him and he gave *it up.*

Then *he coaxed* many *animals* to try *it,* but *they* all found *the sun* too *hot.* At *last* the *mole said:* "I will *dig* through *the ground* under the *trap* and so get at *the cords."*

This *he did* and the *sun leaped* up *into the heavens.*

But it *went* so *quickly* that *the* poor *mole could* not *get away,* and the *heat of the sun put* out *his eyes.*

Since then the *moles* have had *to live in* dark *places,* and unless one *looks* very *closely* he *can not* find *their eyes.*

METHOD.—Provide S with a demonstration or practise text (either one of the three regular texts not to be used subsequently—except that Text 2 should not be used if 4 is to follow—or the special sample prepared by E). Explain the nature of the test, in accordance with the directions printed on the test-blanks. It is well, in addition, to suggest that, in case a certain elision offers special difficulty, it may be temporarily passed by, since the correct interpretation of the context further on will often give the necessary cue for the omitted elision.

When it is clear that S understands the conditions, proceed with the test proper. If but one trial is to be made, use Text 2 or 4 with a 10-min. limit. If more than one, follow with Text 1, using the work-limit method.

Record the time and make notes of the manner in which S undertakes the test. Does he read it all over first? Does he work systematically? Attentively? With confidence or hesitation? Does he grasp the general thread of the story?

VARIATIONS OF METHOD.—(1) To conduct the test with the memory feature, employ Text No. 3, which is specially devised for that purpose. After the preliminary trial, read the unmutilated text for No. 3, entire, to S. Then supply him with the No. 3 test-blank and proceed as before. The text may be read more than once, or any desired time-interval may be introduced between the reading and the execution of the completion. Other variations will suggest themselves, *e. g.,* auditory, visual, or auditory-visual reading, etc.

(2) To approximate the conditions observed by Brown, Wyatt and others, give S opportunity (say three to five minutes) to examine the text before filling it out. This variation of method obviously changes the character of the test considerably: it tends to greater uniformity in the mental processes of the S's, but it removes the differentiation which the standard method conserves in that some S's are quick to see the necessity of looking over the text ahead of their work while others are not.

(3) The Ebbinghaus test lends itself rather well to group tests. With Texts 1, 2 and 3 the use of the author's seconds-clock[2] is recommended. If, however, the time-limit method is followed, the limit must be so chosen that the fastest S in the groups under comparison can but just complete the work. For adults, 7 min. may be employed for Texts 1 and 2, a shorter time for Text 3. Text 4, it should be noted, is devised to be scored by the time-limit method only. For it Terman and Childs specify 15 min. Unfortunately, this time is too long for some high-school students, as investigations in the author's laboratory have shown; in fact, even when the time is shortened to 10 min., a few pupils (about 2 per cent.) will finish before that time is up.

TREATMENT OF DATA.—Text 4, as already mentioned, is used with a constant time-limit (15 min., according to its originators, but preferably 10 min., according to the author's experience). It is scored by assigning for each correctly filled blank 6 units in Section I, 8 units in Section II, 10 units in Section III and 13 units in Section IV. The total score is then divided by 10 and amounts to 100 (exactly, 100.2). One-half the above credits are given if the inserted words "make a well-connected story," but are "related in only a moderate degree to the thought that should have been given." No credit is given for inserted words that make no sense in their setting nor for words that make a continued story which is "purely literary invention, having no connection with the thought given by the printed words." Thought is "considered rather than elegance in diction." [3]

---

[2] See Vol. I, p. 9.

[3] For samples, see Terman and Childs, pp. 201-202.

For Texts 1, 2 and 3 there are three possible methods of scoring. For adults, working individually with these texts, the quality of the work is usually so good that speed alone may be used as an index of efficiency.

Secondly, speed may be neglected and attention given only to quality (in which case the instructions should be modified to indicate that S may 'take his time'). An example of this method may be seen in the work of Burt, who graded the worth of each inserted word on a system of 6 points, 0 to 5.

Thirdly, speed may be combined with quality, and in one of two ways. The quality may be determined and related to speed by means of formulas like those developed for the cancellation test (No. 26). Or, again, the time-limit method may be followed and the work scored by the plan proposed by Ebbinghaus himself and used by Krueger and Spearman, Brown, Wyatt and others. Here quantity and quality of work are computed as follows: (1) Give a credit of 1.0 for each elision filled in in any manner. (2) Give a debit of 0.5 for each elision unfilled in any manner. (3) Give a debit of 1.0 for each elision filled in such a manner as not to make sense, or for each word introduced in excess of the number called for by the lines that indicate elisions (or, if desired, also for each word that is quite obviously too short or to long for the space assigned for completion, even though the passage 'makes sense').[4] For quantity of work done, add (2) and (3) and subtract the sum from (1). For quality of work done, compute the relation in per cent. of the same sum to (1).

TYPICAL RESULTS.—The following is a sample of the work of a boy, 11 years old, one of Terman's "bright" group, who 'completed' Text 2, with the exception of three elisions, in 26 minutes. He was quick, steady, and looked ahead.

"One day an eagle went with the other birds to see who could fly the highest . . . (Next three sentences correct) . . . When he came back the others were waiting for him; and when he touched the ground a linnet flew off his back where the thief had hidden and said that he himself was the strongest bird. "I am stronger than you are," said the linnet, "for not alone did I fly as high, but as he began flying downward, then I left my hiding place and flew up a little higher," etc.

[4]Cohn and Dieffenbacher penalized only 0.5 for errors in the length of the inserted word.

The following is a sample of the work of a boy of the same age, one of Terman's "stupid" group, who worked for 25 minutes at the same text. Save in one or two easy sections, his 'completions' make no sense at all. He worked by phrases only.

"One with the eagle and with the small birds and see who could fly the highest, and agreed and he who will fly the highest should be called the strongest they All started in the same place and whent away among the clouds. . . . After a while he decided that the king of the little bird and not only and not he was so high, but he did the thing as well," etc.

RESULTS.—(1) *Norms and dependence on age.* The results gained by Terman and Childs with Text 4 are shown in Table 132, in which the last column is presented as a basis for the use of the test diagnostically; *i. e.,* the score reached by 66 per cent. of the children of a given age is taken as the limiting standard of efficiency for that age. Tables 133 and 134 show the results

TABLE 132

Completion Text No. 4.   15-Minute Limit (Terman and Childs)

AGE	CASES	MEDIAN	P. E.	REACHED BY 66%
9	32	18.4	8.5	14.9
10	39	29.2	11.8	20.4
11	52	32.2	11.1	25.2
12	56	34.2	11.7	25.6
13	57	45.9	15.2	36.6
14	33	48.5	9.4	42.8

for boys and for girls, respectively, obtained by Mr. Fraser, of the Cornell Laboratory, with Text 4, but with a 10-minute time-limit. In these two tables the number of cases for every group is given in parenthesis just above the group average, and the groups are sorted to differentiate age and school grade as well as sex.

It will be seen that at 13 and 14 (when the sexes are combined), the Ithaca children have the better scores despite the fact that they worked but 10 min. This difference is partly due to the inclusion of high-school pupils in these ages, whereas the table of Terman and Childs is limited to children from the 4th to the 8th grades at Palo Alto, California.

Cohn and Dieffenbacher's tests show progress with age, even up to the 20th year.

(2) *Dependence on school training.* Wiersma called attention to the fact that the relation between performance in this test and age is far less evident than that between performance and scholastic status. This fact is illustrated clearly in the tables prepared by Fraser: taking, for instance, the results for girls, averages by ages, 13-19, run 70.9, 63.2, 57.3, 61.8, 65.8, 63.2, 70.4, and show no definite correspondence, whereas the averages by school grades, 8th to fourth year in the high school, run 38.9, 56.5, 67.7, 64.5, 80.7. Since there exists a distinct positive correlation between standing in this test and general intelligence, and since the higher the grade of pupils of a given age, the more intelligent, on the whole, they must be, it follows

TABLE 133

Completion Text No. 4. 10-Minute Limit. Results for Boys (Fraser)

AGE	GRADES					
	8	H. S. I	H. S. II	H. S. III	H. S. IV	All
13_____	(7) 46.3	(6) 54.1	(2) 32.6			(15) 46.9
14_____	(9) 36.5	(18) 54.1	(9) 46.3	(1) 54.6		(37) 48.2
15_____	(7) 39.5	(22) 48.5	(7) 61.9	(3) 44.1	(1) 92.6	(40) 50.0
16_____	(2) 42.1	(5) 38.7	(7) 55.9	(11) 73.3	(3) 73.9	(28) 60.6
17_____	(1) 34.0	(3) 42.5	(11) 61.5	(13) 58.0	(8) 62.5	(36) 58.1
18_____		(1) 33.2	(4) 51.1	(8) 43.7	(7) 56.5	(20) 49.1
19_____			(1) 32.0		(8) 61.9	(9) 58.6
All _____	(26) 40.3	(55) 49.4	(41) 54.1	(36) 58.2	(27) 63.2	(185) 52.9

TABLE 134

Completion Text No. 4. 10-Minute Limit. Results for Girls (Fraser)

AGE	GRADES					
	8	H. S. I	H. S. II	H. S. III	H. S. IV	All
13 ----------	(4) 66.3	(4) 75.3				(8) 70.9
14 ----------	(5) 37.3	(26) 62.4	(7) 83.2	(1) 71.0		(39) 63.2
15 ----------	(8) 46.9	(28) 50.4	(11) 74.1	(6) 72.7		(53) 57.3
16 ----------	(2) 34.4	(6) 45.0	(19) 66.9	(13) 61.8	(2) 89.9	(42) 61.8
17 ----------		(1) 49.0	(10) 57.3	(17) 65.7	(5) 86.6	(33) 65.8
18 ----------		(3) 54.3	(2) 30.0	(12) 63.9	(8) 75.1	(25) 63.2
19 ----------		(1) 79.5	(1) 82.0	(2) 46.4	(2) 84.2	(6) 70.4
All --------	(19) 38.9	(69) 56.5	(50) 67.7	(51) 64.5	(17) 80.7	(206) 61.1

that some part of this correspondence between school status and the results is due to the correlation with intelligence. The effect of the school training itself undoubtedly contributes another portion of the correspondence—just how much cannot be said.

(3) *Dependence on sex.* Although Wiersma could not make out sex differences with certainty, the subsequent work of Burt and of Fraser leaves little doubt that girls are superior to boys in this, as in most tests with verbal material. Burt found girls distinctly better than boys in his text *The Two Matches* (means 84 and 70, respectively) and slightly better in another test of a more argumentative character (53.2 to 50.4). Inspection of Fraser's tables will show that, with the exception of the 8th-year averages, the girls excel in every group,

whether comparison is made by ages or by school grades. The superiority of boys found by Burt and Moore in one test is attributed by them to the nature of the text, which was such as to appeal more strongly to the interests and knowledge of the boys. It is difficult to reconcile, however, the results reported by Cohn and Dieffenbacher, who found girls inferior to boys at all grades and regardless of equivalence in ages. These sex-differences were greater in the upper than in the lower classes and sufficient to bring the better girls on a level with the poorer boys of their age and grade. It is possible that this striking opposition to the results found by others may be due to some differences in the organization of the schools at Freiburg.

It is unfortunate that Terman and Childs have made no distinction between the sexes in reporting their averages and establishing their age standards.

(4) *Individual differences.* Distribution of the data obtained from the completion method reveals large individual differences. This is demonstrated by the large size of the P.E. in the data of Terman and Childs and even more definitely by the percentile curves of distribution for each sex prepared from Fraser's combined results for pupils from 14 to 17 years of age (Fig. 79).

(5) *Practise,* according to Wiersma, may effect an improvement in efficiency in the completion test that may be easily discerned after the lapse of 10 days, and even after an interval of 6 weeks. As a consequence, it is evident that, in making use of this test for comparative work at different periods, steps must be taken to eliminate or compute the practise-effect.

(6) *Dependence on fatigue.* In Ebbinghaus' Breslau investigation no fatigue effects could be made out as the result of the five-hour session in the tests with the upper classes, or at least, if fatigue were present. it was masked by practise. In the lower classes (10-12 years) there appeared to be a decrease in the quantity and quality of work toward the end of the session.

These conclusions have been criticized by several experimenters. Binet and Henri contend that the several texts were of too unequal difficulty and that the method of scoring was arbitrary and crude. Lobsien has also criticized the general

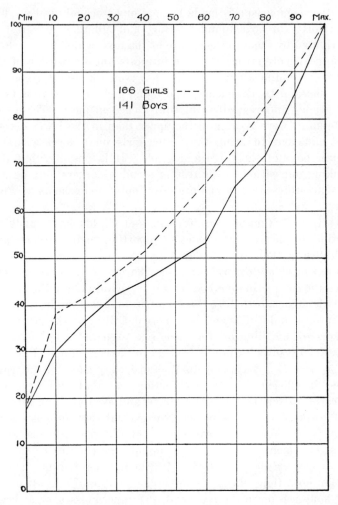

FIG. 79. PERCENTILES FOR COMPLETION TEST NO. 4. AGES 14 TO 17 COMBINED
(Fraser).

plan of administration of the tests in the Breslau investigation. It is admitted that the material used was too easy for the upper classes, and that this circumstance tended to obscure the influence of fatigue and other factors.

In the opinion of Kraepelin, the Ebbinghaus test is to be regarded more as a device for exploration than as a decisive and accurate device for measuring fatigue, for, in the first place, no systematic study has yet been made of the relations between mental fatigue and the complex activities concerned in this test, and secondly, the evaluation of the errors is so difficult and their scoring so arbitrary that the test is not well designed for single applications (*Stichprobe*) and statistical treatment.

Wiersma compared performance before and after a 10-days vacation, but he expresses his belief that the marked improvement cited above as exhibited by the pupils at the second test was largely due to practice. It is unfortunate that proper measures have been not taken to eliminate the practice error in these, and in other applications of the completion test.

(7) *Dependence on intelligence.* It has already been intimated that the relation demonstrated between performance in the completion test and scholastic standing is partially conditioned by a direct correlation with intelligence. Such a relationship was found by Ebbinghaus, most clearly in the lower and progressively less clearly in the higher grades, by sectioning the Breslau pupils into three groups—best, average, poorest—on the basis of their class standing: these three sections scored 56, 48 and 43, respectively, in quantity of work, and 17.3, 20.8 and 26.3, respectively in quality of work (percentage of errors). Similar results were reached by Cohn and Dieffenbacher. Wiersma found a positive correlation between capacity in this test and native ability (*Begabung*), both in tests at a teachers' seminary (ages 14.5 to 19.5) and at a continuation school (ages 12 to 15).

Since then, statistical treatment by the more accurate correlation methods has continued to reveal positive correlations of good magnitude between the completion test and intelligence. Brown, for example, found a correlation of .43 with one group (66 boys, aged 11-12 years) and of .69 with another group (39 girls, aged 11-12 years), and he declares that the Ebbinghaus test "is a good measure of intellectual ability. It correlates with 'general intelligence' almost as closely as 'scholastic intelligence' (school marks) does." Burt reports correlations of .48 and .53, Wyatt of .85, P.E. .04, with one group and of .61, P.E. .07, with another group. Simpson, who compared the capacities of two contrasting groups of adults in numerous tests, found that the Ebbinghaus method almost completely separated his two groups, and that there was a correlation of .89 between results with his 'good' group and the estimated intelligence of the members of that group alone.

Wyatt applied the analogies and the completion tests to seven children who were candidates for admission to the Fielden School, Manchester, England, and was able not only to advise which of the candidates should be admitted and which not, but also to predict successfully the approximate position that these pupils would take in their class at the end of the term.

Ebbinghaus believed that the correlation between the completion test and school ability might become obscured (1) because the test puts a premium upon speed of work, whereas the school grade is based on work that permits of a slower pace; (2) because, in some part, standing in the test might depend upon purely formal linguistic skill or verbal dexterity—a form of ability which he thought had but a limited scope in school work; and (3) because the text selected for the test might be too easy.

In the author's opinion, these reservations are scarcely in order, in so far as Ebbinghaus implies that school grades are inferior to his test as a measure of intellectual ability and asserts that linguistic readiness plays no part in the determination of school grades.

The author is inclined, rather, to agree with Terman when he says: "My experience with the test causes me to regard it favorably; but, like all others, if taken alone, it can give only a partial account of the subjects' ability. It certainly does indicate something as to the general command of language. I am inclined to think that somewhat mechanical activities like memory and association, as distinguished from synthetic or combinative processes, play a relatively more important rôle in this test than Ebbinghaus assigns to them. Indeed, verbal memory, in the broad sense, would seem to be the chief factor in success." Incidentally, ability to spell, degree of familiarity with the type of literature from which the selection is taken, and the way in which S happens to go about the test may all affect his rank. Indeed, it is possible that a very original S, one with a spark of literary invention, might fare relatively poorly.

Terman and Childs say: "We believe that it [the completion test] brings to light fundamental differences in the thought processes."

(8) *Delinquents.* Text 4 has been used by the author, together with numerous other tests, in examinations of the mental status of certain selected 'citizens' of the George Junior Republic, carried on with the assistance of Mr. Fraser, at

Freeville, N. Y. While our data (Table 135) are too few to generalize from, they reveal, as far as they go, distinct reductions from the normal performances for S's of the ages concerned, and these reductions, it is of interest to note, bring the averages in fair agreement with the standards corresponding to the *mental* ages at which these S's had been rated by the other tests. These results, then, tend to confirm the conviction that the completion method is of considerable value in diagnosis of mental status.

TABLE 135

Completion Text 4. 15-Minute Limit. Results from 'Citizens' of the George Junior Republic (Whipple and Fraser)

SEX	CASES	CHRON. AGE	MENTAL AGE	AVERAGE	M. V.
Boys_____	13	14–19	10.0–12.5	27.6	13.6
Girls_____	5	15-18	9.6–11.2	35.7	15.4

(9) *Reliability.* Coefficients of reliability computed by different investigators for varying forms of this test have as a rule been quite high; thus, Brown finds the coefficient mostly over .70, Simpson .92 to .96, Burt .68, Burt and Moore, .58, and Wyatt .89.

(10) *Correlations with other tests.* Heymans and Brugmans report the following correlations with the Ebbinghaus test: discrimination of abstract terms .54, memory for ideas .56, problem solving .56, detection of grammatical errors .72. Wyatt found correlations as follows: with analogies .85, with word-building .70, with part-wholes .75, with interpretation of fables .69, with *anos*-test. 43, with memory for nonsense syllables .61, with dissected pictures .41, with letter-squares zero. For numerous correlations discovered by Brown with six different groups of S's, consult the original texts (2b, pp. 122-123, or 2a, p. 316, or the same material may be gathered from Simpson, pp. 107-8). Simpson found correlations of .85 with hard opposites, .72 with easy opposites, .82 with memory for words, .71 with memory for ideas, .65 with adding, and .54 with the

a-test. Corrected correlations reported by Krueger and Spearman are as follows: completion test and pitch discrimination 0.81, completion test and adding 0.93, completion test and the hypothetical 'central-factor' 0.97. The completion test was not found to correlate with a test of memory span (*Auswendiglernen*). The extremely high correlation with the 'central-factor' is of special interest, since, if the argument be admitted, it demonstrates a very close dependence of performance in this test upon a certain hypothetical psychophysical capacity, presumably akin to plasticity of the central nervous system, which, in the opinion of these authors, is, for each individual, a fundamental conditioning factor in the performance of various forms of mental activity.

NOTES.—At the risk of repetition, it may be pointed out again that the outcome of the completion test hinges largely upon the degree of difficulty of the text employed: too difficult or too easy texts are alike undesirable, for the former convert the test into a blind puzzle, while the latter fail to bring out characteristic individual differences of ability.

To use the test on an extensive scale, therefore, we need to have at hand a number of texts that have been standardized by comprehensive trials with groups of S's of both sexes, various ages, and various degrees of capacity and training. In other words, we need a series of norms of performance, or 'coefficients of difficulty,' as it were, for an adequate number of prescribed texts. Tables 133 and 134 represent a contribution in this direction from the Cornell Laboratory. Any investigator can improve them by adding to them his own data.

The difficulty of making comparisons between the results of different texts applied at different times may be further reduced by always permitting each S to finish each text, and by distributing the texts to be compared in such a manner as to eliminate by subsequent computation whatever error arises from this difference of material.

The Lipmann-Wertheimer modification of the completion method is essentially as follows: a test-story is read to S to supply him with certain information which he is supposed thereafter to conceal. He is subsequently given for completion a mutilated text, the elisions of which are so arranged as to trap him into introducing facts from the test-story which he is trying to conceal.

In an endeavor to retain the essential psychological features of the Ebbinghaus test and at the same time avoid the disturbance due to dependence upon linguistic aptitude, Healy has devised a *pictorial completion test.* This is carried on with the aid of a brightly colored picture, 10×14 inches, which represents an outdoor scene with ten discrete, simple activities going on. Ten one-inch squares are so cut out from this picture as to remove 10 different objects, each of which is essential to complete one of the activities. *S* is given the incomplete picture, the 10 cut-out portions, and 35 other one-inch squares of which 30 bear other objects while 5 are blank. His task is to insert the 10 squares that he judges essential to complete the picture. Data thus far published indicate that the test is difficult below the age of 9, that performance may be as good at 10 as at 13, and that some adults make poorer scores than children (due to their more critical attitude toward the drawing). A time longer than 5 min. with more than one 'illogical' or more than two 'total' errors is suspicious of defective mental ability in *S*'s above the age of 10. This test would appear to possess many possibilities of development.

REFERENCES

(1) A. Binet et V. Henri, La fatigue intellectuelle. Paris, 1898, especially Ch. 7.

(2) W. Brown, (*a*) Some experimental results in the correlation of mental abilities. *BrJPs*, 3: 1910, 296-322. (*b*) Same material, with slight modifications, appears as Ch. 3 in The essentials of mental measurement. Cambridge, Eng., 1911.

(3) C. Burt, Experimental tests of higher mental processes. *JEPd*, 1: 1911, 93-112.

(4) C. Burt and R. C. Moore, The mental differences between the sexes. *JEPd*, 1: 1912, 273-284, 355-388.

(5) J. Cohn und J. Dieffenbacher, Untersuchungen über Geschlechts-Alters-und Begabungs-Unterscheide bei Schülern. *Beihefte zur ZAngPs*, 2: 1911. Pp. 214, especially 30-36.

(6) H. Ebbinghaus, Ueber eine neue Methode zur Prüfung geistiger Fähigkeiten und ihre Anwendung bei Schulkindern. *ZPs*, 13: 1897, 401-459.

(7) T. Elsenhans, Nachtrag zu Ebbinghaus' 'Kombinationsmethode.' *ZPs*, 13; April. 1897, 460-3.

(8)   D. K. Fraser, Unpublished investigation in the Cornell Educational Laboratory on the standardization of mental tests for the period of adolescence.

(9)   W. Healy, A pictorial completion test. *PsR*, 21 : 1914, 189-203.

(10)   G. Heymans und H. Brugmans, Intelligenzprüfungen bei Studierenden. *ZAngPs*, 7 : 1913, 317-331.

(11)   E. Kraepelin, Ueber Ermüdungsmessungen. *ArGsPs*, 1 : 1903, 9-30, especially 17.

(12)   F. Krueger und C. Spearman, Die Korrelation zwischen verschiedenen geistigen Leistungsfähigkeiten. *ZPs*, 44 : 1907, 50-114.

(·13)   O. Lipmann und M. Wertheimer, Tatbestandsdiagnostische Kombinations-versuche. *ZAngPs*, 1 : 1907, 119-128.

(14)   M. Lobsien, Ueber die psychologisch-pädagogischen Methoden zur Erforschung der geistigen Ermüdung. *ZPdPs*, 2 : 1900, 273-286, 352-367.

(15)   M. Meyer, An English equivalent of "Combinationsmethode." *JPh*, 9 : 1909, 688.

(16)   B. R. Simpson, Correlations of mental abilities. *Columbia ConEd*, No. 53, New York, 1912. Pp. 122.

(17)   Carrie R. Squire, Graded mental tests. *JEdPs*, 3 : 1912, 363-380, 430-443, 493-506, especially 442-443.

(18)   L. Terman, Genius and stupidity. *PdSc*, 13 : 1906, 307-373, especially 342-7.

(19)   L. M. Terman and H. G. Childs, A tentative revision and extension of the Binet-Simon measuring scale of intelligence. *JEdPs*, 3 : 1912, 61-74, 133-143, 198-208, 277-289, especially 198-202.

(20)   E. Wiersma, Die Ebbinghaus'sche Combinationsmethode. *ZPs*, 30 : 1902, 196-222.

(21)   S. Wyatt, The quantitative investigation of higher mental processes. *BrJPs*, 6 : 1913, 109-133.

TEST 49

Interpretation of fables.—In 1903 Swift suggested that mental ability might be measured by determining the capacity to interpret the typical situation given in a typical fable. The three test-fables employed by Swift were later (1906) used by Terman in his comparative study of bright and stupid boys. Still later (1912) Terman and Childs published a set of eight fables selected by trial from a series of 20, with the idea that responses to this test would assist in mental diagnosis in conjunction with the Binet-Simon and other tests. These authors believe that this 'generalization test,' as they term it, "will prove a usable addition to the scale. It presents for interpretation situations which are closely paralleled in human social relations. It tests the power to unravel the motives underlying acts and attitudes, to look behind the deed for the idea that prompted it. It gives a clue to the status of social conscious-

ness. This, if correct, is tremendously important for the diagnosis of the upper range of mental defectiveness." . . . "It
does not need to be unduly complicated by language difficulties,
as is always the case to greater or less degree in tests of ability
to interpret poetry." [1]

MATERIALS.—Printed sheets, containing the 8 fables selected
by Terman and Childs.

METHOD.—Instruct S substantially as follows: "I am going
to read to you some fables. A fable is a little story that is
meant to teach a lesson (convey a moral). After I have read
each fable, I want you to tell what is the lesson that you think
it teaches (the moral that it is intended to convey)." Read
each fable twice through before asking for its point. For ordinary testing use Fables I, III, VII and VIII. These four have
been specially selected by Terman and Childs from the eight
supplied, as proving in actual test to answer best the expected
requirements of due progress in scores with advance in age.[2]

It is best to conduct the test individually and to record verbatim the replies given orally by S; it is possible then to follow
up S's response by a few discrete questions if necessary to be
positive of his interpretation. If group tests are made, supply
each S with a blank sheet containing eight numbered spaces in
which the replies may be written. The norms of Terman and
Childs that follow are based upon such group tests with written replies for Fables I, III, VII and VIII.

VARIATIONS OF METHOD.—If time permits, supplementary or
control tests may be made by the use of the four remaining
fables.

TREATMENT OF DATA.—We quote as follows from Terman and
Childs: "The difficulty of finding a method of scoring which
does not give too large play to the personal equation is a serious
criticism of the fables test. After experimenting with a
number of methods the following system was adopted as the one
best suited to bring out objective differences and to call atten-

---

[1]See, for example, the test used by Bonser. p. 8.
[2]See Terman and Childs, p. 138, for the criteria upon which these four
fables were finally chosen.

tion to certain types of answers significant for clinical purposes:

"(*a*) A completely generalized and entirely relevant reply,
5 units.

"(*b*) A generalization, quite plausible, but slightly differing
from the correct one, or else a correct statement mostly generalized but not perfectly free from the concrete, 4 units.

"(*c*) Correct idea stated in purely concrete terms, 3 units.

"(*d*) An irrelevant generalization, 2 units.

"(*e*) A reply in concrete terms with just a trace of relevancy,
1 unit.

"(*f*) No response, or an entirely irrelevant concrete statement, 0."

"Elegance, grammatical correctness, spelling, etc., should have no
weight in the scoring. On the other hand, it is necessary to be discriminating as to essential thought in the response. The tendency of the inexperienced scorer is to give too much credit. "In practise there is a tendency to make sparing use of Scores 1 and 4, reserving 1 for a few replies
that are not quite bad enough for 0, and 4 for a few replies, which,
though pertinent and generalized, are not quite what is wanted.[3]

The following samples of scoring for replies to the four standard fables
will serve as useful illustrations:

Fable I. The Maid and the Eggs.

Score 0. "She wanted to be dressed nice and be praised."
Score 2. "Not to carry things on the head." "Not to be selfish." "Not
to boast."
Score 3. "If the maid had not planned so far ahead she would not
have dropped her milk." "Don't make schemes for the future while you
are carrying milk."
Score 5. "Don't count your chickens before they are hatched." "Not
to build air-castles." "Don't plan too far ahead."

Fable III. Hercules and the Wagoner.

Score 0. "Hercules was not kind." "Hercules was selfish."
Score 2. "Teaches politeness." "Teaches not to be mean." "To do as
you are told."
Score 3. "The lazy man should get out and try to push the wagon out
himself." "When you get stuck in the mud, don't call for help, but try
to get out yourself."
Score 5. "God helps them who help themselves." "Teaches us to help
ourselves before we ask others to help us." "Don't depend upon others."

---

[3]For further discussion and samples of scoring, see Terman and Childs,
pp. 135-139.

Fable VII.   The Fox and the Crow.

Score 0.   "The fox wanted the piece of meat."   "The crow ought not to have tried to sing till she had swallowed it."

Score 2.   "Not to be stingy."   "Not to steal."   "Think before you act."

Score 3.   "The crow was flattered by this speech."   "The crow was too proud of her voice."   "If the crow had not been so flattered, she would not have lost her meat."

Score 5.   "Do not let people flatter you."   "Don't listen to praise."

Fable VIII.   The Farmer and the Stork.

Score 0.   "The farmer ought to have let the stork go."   "The farmer was a bad-tempered man."

Score 2.   "To be merciful."   "Do not kill animals."   "Don't blame the other fellow."   "Never go into traps."   "Not to tell lies."   "Take what you get without squealing."

Score 3.   "The stork should not be caught with bad people like cranes." "The stork was caught in bad company and had to be treated the same."

Score 5.   "Keep out of bad company."   "You are judged by the company you keep."

RESULTS.—(1) *Norms.* The results obtained by Fables I, III, VII and VIII applied to about 350 pupils from the 4th to the 8th grades, inclusive, in 14 rooms of the Palo Alto and Mayfield, Cal., schools provide representative data for children up to 13 years of age. Table 136 shows the percentage of children of a given age that secured each of the scores from 0 to 5 for each of the four fables. Experimenters can add their own results to this distribution and thus increase the reliability of the distributions. The data in Table 137 are secured by adding together the scores of the four fables (maximal score = 20) and multiplying by 5 to bring to a percentage basis. The last column of this table may be taken as a diagnostic basis, as it indicates the score that is reached by two-thirds of the pupils of a given age.

(2) *Dependence on age.* Terman believes that "what is tested by the interpretation of fables is, in part at least, that general change of mental horizon that comes with increased experience and dawning maturity." The data thus far available indicate a fairly steady increase of proficiency with age, save that performance at 12 does not differ greatly from that at 11 years. With these four fables at least there is evidently not much chance of obtaining distributions for ages less than 9; indeed, in the opinion of Terman and Childs it would be difficult to

TABLE 136

Distribution by Percentages in Interpretation of Fables (Terman and Childs)

FABLE	AGE	CASES	SCORES						TOTAL	PERCENTAGE OF INCORRECT GENERALIZATIONS
			0	1	2	3	4	5	4 + 5	
I.	9	41	14	31	24	4	4	19	23	51
	10	53	13	22	20	4	9	30	39	34
The Maid	11	61	8	6	31	10	16	28	44	41
and	12	80	7	10	22	5	16	39	55	28
the Eggs.	13	73	5	4	18	8	15	47	62	22
	14	43	5	9	20	5	16	38	54	27
III.	9	41	14	7	19	29	12	16	28	40
	10	53	9	9	13	19	17	32	49	25
Hercules	11	61	5	6	15	13	20	41	61	22
and the	12	80	3	12	12	11	21	39	60	17
Wagoner.	13	73	0	5	15	12	18	47	65	18
	14	43	5	0	9	2	36	45	81	10
VII.	9	41	19	27	34	14	2	2	4	90
	10	53	17	26	35	2	5	13	18	66
The Fox	11	61	8	15	44	8	8	16	24	65
and	12	80	11	17	32	6	15	17	32	50
The Crow.	13	73	11	16	27	3	8	32	40	40
	14	43	14	7	34	5	14	25	39	46
VIII.	9	41	36	19	31	5	2	5	7	81
	10	53	21	24	24	2	4	24	28	46
The Farmer	11	61	16	11	21	6	11	33	44	32
and	12	80	15	15	22	5	7	33	40	35
the Stork.	13	73	8	8	14	8	14	46	60	19
	14	43	7	5	18	5	11	52	63	22

The percentage of incorrect generalizations is obtained by dividing the number of Scores 2 by the combined number of Scores 2, 4 and 5 (see explanation of scoring given above).

select any fables that would be serviceable for younger children. On the other hand, the addition of a few more difficult fables "would make the test especially valuable at the upper end of the scale and help a great deal in the difficult task of extending the scale beyond 13 years."

(3) *Dependence on intelligence.* Swift reports that the table-test showed no superiority for the 'bright' children; that, on

TABLE 137

Norms for Interpretation of Four Fables (Terman and Childs)

AGE	CASES	MEDIAN	REACHED BY 66 %
9	41	35–40	25–30
10	53	45	35–40
11	61	50–55	45–50
12	80	55	45–50
13	73	70	55–60
14	43	70–75	55–60

the contrary, with the fable of *The Fishes and the Pike*, which, he says, requires "a distinctly intellectual process," the dull group excelled the bright group, while the answers of boys in an industrial (reform) school "distinctly outranked those from both of the other groups, but especially the ones from the 'bright' division, in the penetration and versatility that they showed."

Terman's tests showed, on the contrary, that his 'dull' group was distinctly inferior to his 'bright' group, for, as he says: "in the first place, they more frequently miss the point of the story altogether," and "in the second place, the dull boys are plainly deficient in degree of abstraction. Even when they give an approximately correct interpretation, they usually express it in the concrete terms of the given situation, instead of generalizing it."

This lack of accordance is attributed by Terman to some fault in method on the part of Swift. "I should judge," he says, "that his results would have been different if he had been able to take his cases individually, instead of collectively."

By way of illustration, the following quantitative results may be quoted: Swift reports that, in the fable mentioned, 27% of his 'bright' group, as contrasted with 9% of his 'dull' group, thought the plan wise and just. Again, only 15% of the bright children, as contrasted with 30% of the dull children, pointed out that the plan would not help the fishes that were not turned into pike. When scored according to Terman's plan[4] his bright S's averaged for three fables the ranks 1.3, 3.17 and 2.83, respectively, while his dull S's averaged the ranks 1.86, 4.57 and 4.57 for the same three fables.

Swift states that "the answers from the public-school children lacked individuality; they were conventional, while those from the reform

[4]In this earlier work Terman gave the score 1 for a satisfactory answer, 5 for a complete failure.

school gave evidence of spontaneity and resourcefulness," and he draws
from this the dubious conclusion that "the question may be seriously
raised whether the schools do not train children to stupidity."

Quite on the contrary, Terman and Childs cite the following replies to
Fable VII given by pupils 13 to 17 years of age, all of whom were
retarded in school from 2 to 4 years:

Fable VII.

"The fox was slicker than the crow was."
"Not to be generous to people you don't know."
"Not to sing when you have anything in your mouth."
"To eat before you sing."
"Not to be forgetful."
"Where there's a will there's a way."
"To eat the meat and then sing."
"How to be wise."
"Don't answer if your mouth is full."
"Look before you leap."
"When you have a thing, hang on to it."
"She should not have opened her mouth."
"Teaches us to look for tricks."
"To finish one thing before we do another."
"Taught the crow to be wise and not to open her mouth when she had
anything in it."

(4) *Reliability.* No statistical constants have been reported
that might serve as coefficients of reliability. It may be mentioned, however, that "an *S*'s previous familiarity with the
fables does not necessarily increase in the least his chance of
winning a high score." In one room of the Palo Alto schools
the 35 pupils had read some or all of the test fables, but these
children made no better scores than others of their age and
school grade. Terman and Childs conclude that even had an
attempt been made to teach the moral of these fables, it would
not have been successful if the situation in the fable was naturally beyond the child's powers of comprehension.

(5) *Correlations.* Wyatt reports the following correlations
with interpretation of fables: analogies .74, completion test
.69, word-building .47, part-wholes test .56, sentence construction .53, memory for nonsense syllables .41, dissected pictures
.26, letter-squares .31.

NOTES.—For other tests that present a certain analogy to the
interpretation of fables, the reader may see Bonser's interpretation of poetry (literary interpretation), already mentioned,
Mrs. Squire's tests of supplying a suitable name to, or of ask-

ing appropriate questions about a number of pictures, and Abelson's test of interpretation of pictures.

REFERENCES

(1)   A. R. Abelson, Tests for mental deficiency in childhood. *The Child*, 3: 1912, 1-17.

(2)   F. G. Bonser, The reasoning ability of children. *ColumbiaCon Ed*, No. 37. New York, 1910.

(3)   Carrie R. Squire, Graded mental tests. *JEdPs*, 3: 1912, 363-380, etc., especially 373-376.

(4)   E. J. Swift, Standards of efficiency in school and in life. *PdSc*, 10: 1903, 3-22, especially 3-6.

(5)   L. M. Terman, Genius and stupidity: a study of some of the intellectual processes of seven 'bright' and seven 'stupid' boys. *PdSc*, 13, 1906, 307-373.

(6)   L. M. Terman and H. G. Childs, A tentative revision and extension of the Binet-Simon measuring scale of intelligence. *JEdPs*, 3: 1912, 61-74, 133-143, 198-208, 277-289, especially 133-143.

(7)   S. Wyatt, The quantitative investigation of higher mental processes. *BrJPs*, 6: 1913, 109-133.

CHAPTER XII

TESTS OF INTELLECTUAL EQUIPMENT

The tests of this chapter differ from other mental tests described in the present volume in that they measure, not the efficiency with which certain typical mental activities or mental processes can function, but rather the number of ideas that an individual possesses. In other words, their purpose is not to measure what the individual can do, or how well he can do it, but what he knows about—to take a census, as it were, of his stock of information. G. Stanley Hall's study of the content of children's minds on entering school[1] is, perhaps, most nearly allied in type and conception with the tests which are here presented.

The first test is designed to secure an estimate of the number of words in the reading vocabulary of the individual tested, the second to secure an estimate of the number of subjects (disciplines, phases of human activity) with which the individual has an exact or an approximate acquaintance.

TEST 50

Size of vocabulary.—Since nearly all thought and expression is couched in linguistic form, and since the intellectual progress of the child at school is, in a sense, a process of augmentation of his vocabulary and of refinement in its use, it seems not unreasonable to assume that the determination of the size of this vocabulary will be of significance and value in estimating his general intellectual status.

Experiments conducted by Kirkpatrick have shown that an approximate determination of what might be termed the *vocabulary-index* can be secured by the use of the relatively short and simple method that is described herewith. By extending the scope of the tests, the usual comparative study may be made, and the index may be related to its conditioning factors—age, sex, school standing, extent of reading, general ability, etc.

---

[1] See his *Aspects of child life and education.* Boston, 1907.

Kirkpatrick's original list of words has been applied by the author with some modifications of method. Terman and Childs have prepared an entirely different list, on the ground that the words should be selected from a smaller dictionary—one limited to representative and more generally employed words and not including any large proportion of technical terms. They have prepared a list of 100 test-words by taking the last word in every 6th column of Laird and Lee's Vest-Pocket Webster Dictionary, 1904 edition. This dictionary contains 18,000 words, though advertised to contain 30,000, whereas the Webster's Abridged Dictionary used by Kirkpatrick contains 28,000 words.

MATERIAL.—Two printed vocabulary tests: the Kirkpatrick list and the Terman and Childs list (modified by the author in respect to instructions for group testing).

PRELIMINARIES.—In accordance with Kirkpatrick's plan, several preliminary exercises are employed, in order, on the one hand, to obtain data with regard to S's general familiarity with words, his range of reading, etc., and on the other hand, to instill in him an attitude of caution in undertaking the vocabulary-test proper. These preliminary exercises are as follows:[2]

(1) Ask S to write the opposite of the following terms: *good, long, break, rude, simple, permanent, particular, permit, obnoxious, genuine*.

(2) Ask S to tell (orally or in writing) what the following words mean: *abductor, baron, channel, decemvirate, eschar, amalgamation, bottle-holder, concatenate, disentomb, filiform, gourd, intercede, matting, page, hodman, lanuginose, muff, photograph, scroll, tycoon*. (Where words have more than one meaning, all are to be given.)

(3) Secure from S a list of all the papers and magazines that he is in the habit of reading.

(4) Secure from S the names of the books that he has read during the past 6 months.

(5) Ask S which of these books he liked the best, why he liked it, and to give some account of what it was about.

---

[2]To follow the plan, the first two exercises, at least, should be given whenever grade pupils are tested, and all five if time permits.

(6) Ascertain the birthplace of S's parents, his school grade, and his favorite school subjects.

METHOD.—Both tests can be conducted by handing the printed forms to S and asking him to read the instructions over twice and then to mark the words carefully in accordance with them. But to secure data that will be directly comparable with those published for their test by Terman and Childs the examination of S must proceed orally. S sees the word, hears it pronounced by E, and then gives its meaning orally. E scores each term 0, 0.5 or 1. The score 1 is given when S is able to give any single correct meaning for the word, even if the meaning given is not the commonest one and even if the definition be poorly expressed. E must err on the side of leniency and make due allowance for the difficulty of definition in the case of children.

The following illustrations will indicate the degree of latitude allowed by Terman and Childs in scoring their test: Full credit (1 point) was given for: *Afloat*—"a ship floats on the water;" *civilly*—"it's when you treat a person nice;" *hysterics*—"you act funny or crazy:" *majesty*— "what you say when you are speaking to a king;" *copper*—"something you make money out of." Half credit (0.5 point) was given for: *sportive*— "to like sports;" *pork*—"a kind of meat." It will be seen that a very liberal standard has been used. "Questioning for the sake of drawing out meanings was not resorted to except in rare instances to overcome the child's timidity."

TREATMENT OF DATA.—The Kirkpatrick list supplies E directly with the number of words marked 'plus,' and this number indicates the vocabulary-index. For comparison with Kirkpatrick's and Whipple's norms based on this test, the index, taken as a per cent., is multiplied into 28,000.

The Terman and Childs list, when scored directly by E upon the oral responses of S, gives a vocabulary-index by the simple addition of points scored, and this index, taken as a per cent., is multiplied into 18,000 to make direct comparison with the absolute size of vocabulary as computed by these authors.

The Terman and Childs list, when scored by E on a basis of S's own marking (following the author's set of instructions), yields four quantities—number of words that can be defined, that can be explained, that are roughly familiar and that are unknown. The equating of these gradings with the 'points' used by Terman and Childs may be roughly accomplished by regarding each 'D' and 'E' as indicating one point and each 'F' as indicating a half-point.

VARIATIONS OF METHOD.—To study S's tendency to overestimate or underestimate his vocabulary, E may follow the plan used by the author with college students, of giving the check-definition test after the vocabulary-test.

(1) Give S the Kirkpatrick vocabulary test without suggesting that he may be called upon to justify his marking.

(2) When the marking has been completed, and the slip is in E's hands, submit to S the following list of words, with a request that each word be defined. Allow 20 min. for written definitions.

DEFINITION-LIST.[3]

abductor	interdict	amalgamation	lanugo
abet	interim	amanuensis	lanyard
baroscope	mattock	amaranth	mufti
chanticleer	maturate	bottomry	photo-lithograph
chaos	pudgy	concatenate	rejoinder
decemvirate	scruff	disentrance	skysail
eschar	scrunch	disepalous	tendinous
escheat	subcutaneous	disestablish	tendril
eschalot	tycoon	filiform	virago
gourd	tymbal	hoecake	virescent

(3) For each S, ascertain from the definition-test: (a) the number of words not defined, (b) the number of words wrongly defined. (c) Add these to find the total number of words unknown in the list of 40. (d) Consult the vocabulary test-slip to see whether any words outside the list of 40 are marked unknown.[4] (e) Consult the vocabulary-slip again to see whether any words thereon are marked doubtful and have not been cleared up by the definition-test; consider these as unknown. (f) Add all the unknown terms to determine the final corrected vocabulary-index. (g) Compare this index with the index indicated by S on the vocabulary-slip to see whether S has over- or underestimated his vocabulary, and to what degree.

---

[3]*Concatenation, lanuginose* and *lanuginous*, of the vocabulary-test, can, of course, be checked off by the definitions given for *concatenate* and *lanugo*.

[4]In a test of Sophomores and Juniors in college we were surprised to find the following words in this category: *barque, barouche, boudoir, disentomb, filigree, hodman, pagoda, rejuvenate, scroll, sub-let, tenderloin*. These words, then, it seems, would have to be added to the 40 to secure a comprehensive list of possibly unknown words.

RESULTS.—(1) Kirkpatrick's computation of the *average vocabulary* is shown in Table 138. The author's results, derived with Kirkpatrick's list applied to 70 college students (16 men and 54 women), aged 16 to 25 years, indicate an average vocabulary of 21,728 when computed on the uncorrected estimates of the students, and of 20,512 when computed on the corrections supplied by the supplementary definition-test.

TABLE 138

Average Vocabulary in Relation to Scholastic Status (*Kirkpatrick*)

SCHOLASTIC STATUS	VOCABULARY	SCHOLASTIC STATUS	VOCABULARY
Grade II_____	4480	Grade IX_____	13,400
Grade III_____	6620	High school, 1st year	15,640
Grade IV_____	7020	High school, 2d year	16,020
Grade V_____	7860	High school, 3d year	17,600
Grade VI_____	8700	High school, 4th year	18,720
Grade VII_____	10,660	Normal-school pupils_	19,000
Grade VIII_____	12,000	College students _____	20,120

The results obtained by Terman and Childs by the use of their list with individual, oral responses from 161 children, aged 5 to 13 years, are shown in Table 139. As will be understood from the explanations already given, the vocabulary-index is larger than Kirkpatrick's, but the absolute vocabulary is smaller.

TABLE 139

Relation of Vocabulary to Age: Method of Terman and Childs

MEDIAN AGE	NUMBER TESTED	MEDIAN INDEX	MEDIAN VOCAB.	VOCAB. REACHED BY 66 PER CENT.	REVISED NORMS	
					Ages	Index
6.5_____	5	13.9	2500	2300	6	12
7.5_____	14	14.4	2600	2300	7	14
8.5_____	28	22.0	3960	3600	8	18
9.5_____	35	27.8	5000	4000	9	23
10.6_____	24	33.3	6000	4500	10	26
11.5_____	29	33.9	6100	5500	11	30
12.4_____	19	42.9	7700	6500	12	36
13.0_____	7	48.9	8800	7400	13	42

The author has used the Terman and Childs list with 10 members of the George Junior Republic, ages 14 to 18: the average index was 53.8 per cent. He has also employed the same list by the written response (group method) with Sophomores at Cornell University, with the results indicated in Table 140.

TABLE 140

Vocabularies of Twenty College Students: Terman and Childs List
(Whipple)

	NUMBER	D	E	F	N	ESTIMATED INDEX
Men_____	10	65.1	20.8	6.7	7.4	89.3
Women _____	10	56.3	29.2	8.5	6.0	89.8

On the vocabularies of children below the age of 6 consult Whipple (13) for the chief studies prior to 1908, and Boyd (4), Bush (5), Ghéorgov (6) and Heilig (7) for studies subsequent to that date. For methods and results of securing vocabularies from imbeciles and other feeble-minded consult Binet and Simon (3) and Town (11).

(2) In the author's *definition-test,* no word of the 40 was correctly defined by every student, and since, as has been noted, there remained 16 other words that were unknown or doubtful, it follows that only 44 of the 100 words in Kirkpatrick's list were certainly known by every one of 70 college students.

(3) There is wide *individual variation* in the size of the vocabularies of students of the same age and scholastic status.

TABLE 141

Distribution of Corrected Vocabulary Index.   Seventy College Students
(Whipple)

INDEX	55–59	60–64	65–69	70–74	75–79	80–84	85–89
No. of cases	1	6	13	22	19	5	5

Highest index, 89%. Average index, 73.26%. Lowest index, 58%.

This variation is shown by the distribution in Table 141. The largest college-student vocabulary found by the writer with Kirkpatrick's list is 24,920 (89 per cent.) ; the smallest is 16,240 (58 per cent.), or approximately the vocabulary assigned by Kirkpatrick to the average 2d-year high-school pupil.

(4) No positive *sex differences* have been established, though there is a suggestion of superiority of boys over girls, and of men over women.

(5) In general, pupils that read the most books and magazines have the largest vocabularies.

(6) Kirkpatrick found a tendency toward positive *correlation* between class standing (teachers' grades) and vocabulary-index: "those ranking high in scholarship knew on an average about 5 per cent. more words than those ranking low in scholarship." The author found a more decided correlation ($r = + 0.45$, P.E. $= 0.06$) between the index of 58 college students and their grades in his classes in educational psychology.

(7) When no precautionary measures are taken to offset the tendency, the determination of the vocabulary-index is commonly affected by *overestimation*. Inspection of Table 142 will show that 59 of the 70 college students examined by the author overestimated, while but 10 underestimated their vocabulary: the largest overestimation was 18 per cent.; the largest underestimation was 4 per cent. Since 20, or more than one-quarter

TABLE 142

Overestimation of the Vocabulary Index. Seventy College Students
(*Whipple*)

PER CENT. OVERESTIMATED	NUMBER	PER CENT. OVERESTIMATED	NUMBER
18	1	5	7
15	2	4	6
14	3	3	7
13	1	2	10
12	3	1	9
11	1	0	1
9	2	—1	6
8	2	—2	2
7	1	—4	2
6	4		

of the students overestimated by 5 per cent. or more, it is evident that, without a somewhat elaborate definition check, the reliability of the vocabulary test is distinctly lessened.[5]

(8) The definition test reveals an unexpectedly large number of *erroneous definitions*. The source of these errors may frequently be traced to confusion with words of similar appearance or to fancied etymological derivations. The following list shows typical errors in definition by college students; the assumed source of confusion is indicated by the terms in parentheses after the definitions:

amanuensis—poet laureate, lovingness (amativeness).
amaranth—a precious stone (amethyst).
abet—although (albeit), a wager (a + bet), diminish (abate).
bottomry—the art of bottoming chairs, deceit, bottom of anything.
chanticleer—one who sings a loud song, one who leads a chant.
decemvirate—composed of five, count out by tens, formerly a group of ten men, but any number now.
disentrance—failure to enter.
disepalous—apart from the head, without shoulders (di + cephalous?).
gourd—reward (guerdon), to slash or whip (goad), morning glory.
interim—time between two reigns (interregnum).
lanugo—a kind of language.
lanyard—yard where leather is tanned (tanyard), yard about the lane.
mattock—a lock of hair (matted locks?), a kind of bird, a sort of rug, a kind of robe (cassock).
maturate—to ripen (mature), to matriculate.
sky-sail—a sail in the sky, a kite.
tycoon—a violent wind (typhoon), an animal, a silk-worm, a natural phenomena (sic).
tendril—a membrane connecting two bones (tendon).
tendinous—capable of endurance (tenacious?).
scrunch—a good for nothing person (scrug?).
virago—a kind of bird (!) (vireo), a disease, giddiness (vertigo).
virescent—sparkling (iridescent), of or pertaining to man (!) (virile).

NOTES.— (1) The greatest source of unreliability in the vocabulary tests in which S's mark their own papers lies in individual differences in the subjective standard employed by different S's

---

[5]This result may be compared with Kirkpatrick's conclusion that very young children are apt to underestimate because the isolated words of the list fail to arouse associations such as they would if they had a context. Again, when Kirkpatrick defined the words of the list to normal-school students, he found that the errors of over- and underestimation tended to cancel one another; while when college classes defined 20 words, 114 of 246 students (about 46 per cent.) correctly defined the same proportion that they had marked as known, and only 7 per cent. erred by as much as 3 in 20.

by the 'known'-or-'unknown' method: some S's mark, as known, words which are little more than familiar; others mark words as known only when they can define them accurately.

(2) This leads one to say again that, especially in the case of young children, there may be a tendency toward underestimation of the vocabulary because isolated words sometimes fail to arouse the interpretative meanings that they would arouse at once in their customary context. In so far as appeal to the ear as well as to the eye is of assistance to young children whose vocabulary is largely auditory, this source of error is partially offset by the procedure adopted by Terman and Childs of reading the list aloud to them.

(3) In grading the definition test, it is at times rather difficult to decide from the definitions whether S does or does not know the meaning of a word with sufficient exactness to be credited with knowledge of the term in question. In general, it is better, in consideration of the difficulty of accurate definition and of the short time usually available for this part of the test, to err on the side of leniency.

Thus the following definitions might be accepted: 'disestablish—to overthrow,' 'decemvirate—a body of ten,' 'mattock—a garden tool,' 'amaranth—a flower;' while the following ought, in our opinion, to be disallowed: 'lanyard—one of the spars of a ship,' 'decemvirate—Roman civil officer,' 'gourd—a hollow vessel-from which to eat and drink,' 'concatenate—to argue,' 'baroscope—an instrument for measuring something.'

(4) The pamphlet issued by Ayres (1) is of interest as showing how few words, relatively speaking, are employed in the conduct of ordinary correspondence. Out of a total of 23,629 works, taken by the method of random samples from 2,000 letters, there were only 2,001 different words.

REFERENCES

(1) L. P. Ayres, The spelling vocabularies of personal and business letters. (No. E 126, Russell Sage Foundation.) New York, 1914. Pp. 14.

(2) E. H. Babbitt, A vocabulary test. *PopSciM*, 70: 1907, 378.

(3) A. Binet et Th. Simon, Langage et pensée. *AnPs*, 14: 1908, 284-339.

(4) W. Boyd, The development of a child's vocabulary. *PdSc*, 21: 1914, 95-124.

(5) A. D. Bush, The vocabulary of a three-year-old girl. *PdSe*, 21: 1914, 125-142.

(6) I. Ghéorgov, Le développement du langage chez l'enfant. (Reprint from First Intern. Cong. Pedology.) Ledeberg-Gand, 1912. Pp. 18.

(7) M. R. Heilig, A child's vocabulary. *PdSe*, 20: 1913, 1-16.

(8) E. Kirkpatrick, Number of words in an ordinary vocabulary. *Sci*, 18: 1891, 107-8.

(9) E. Kirkpatrick, A vocabulary test. *PopSciM*, 70: 1907, 157-164.

(10) L. M. Terman and H. G. Childs, A tentative revision and extension of the Binet-Simon measuring scale of intelligence. *JEdPs*, 3: 1912, 61-74, 133-143, 198-208, 277-289, especially 205-208.

(11) Clara H. Town, A study of speech development in two hundred and eighty-five idiots and imbeciles. *JPsAs*, 17: 1912, 7-15.

(12) G. M. Whipple, Vocabulary and word-building tests. *PsR*, 15: 1908, 94-105.

(13) G. M. Whipple and Mrs. Whipple, The vocabulary of a three-year-old boy, with some interpretative comments. *PdSe*, 16: 1909, 1-22. (Contains references to 27 articles on children's vocabularies.)

TEST 51

Range of information.—The words that comprise Kirkpatrick's vocabulary test are intentionally selected by chance: some of them, like *page,* happen to be most ordinary and every-day terms; others, like *lanuginose,* are unusual, technical terms. The extent of *S*'s acquaintance with words of the latter kind depends almost entirely upon the nature of his school training, or upon the quantity and type of his general reading.

The range of information test has been devised by the author as an extension of the vocabulary test. The hundred test-words have been selected, not by chance, but by careful consideration, and in such a manner that each shall be representative of some specific field of knowledge or activity, in the sense that if *S* has made himself familiar with a given field, he will almost certainly know the word selected from that field, whereas if he has not made himself familiar with the field, he will almost certainly not know the term, or at least will not have such knowledge of it as to enable him to define it exactly. Thus, general knowledge of American history is tested by the name *Anthony Wayne,* knowledge of French by *aujourd'hui,* of chemistry by *chlorine,* of ethics by *hedonism,* of golf by *midiron,* of social usages by *R. S. V. P.,* of the technique of photography by *f-64,* etc.

MATERIAL.—Specially prepared test-blank containing 100 test-words, directions for marking them, and a request for 10 definitions.

METHOD.—Place the blank in S's hands; ask him to read the directions through twice before marking the words, and call his attention to the request for definitions as printed below the test-words. Let him take his own time.

For exact results, S should afterward be required to define every word that he has marked D, and to explain or attempt to explain every word that he has marked E or F. This check test should, by preference, be conducted orally. In practise, however, especially when testing by the group method, such careful checking may prove too onerous; erroneous definitions may then be neglected, or the quantitative data may be revised by discounting on the basis of the percentage of error revealed in the definitions actually given. Or, again, E may, after the test is concluded, define the 100 words, and let each S revise his own paper by placing a second series of marks *after* each word to indicate the manner in which he should have marked it. A comparison of the sums of the D's, E's, F's and N's of the first and of the second series will then show approximately the extent and nature of the error due to ignorance or misunderstanding of the real meanings.

RESULTS.—(1) *Dependence on school training.* Results obtained by the author at Cornell University and the Ithaca, N. Y., High School, and by Miss Smith at the University of Texas are presented in Tables 143 and 144. In both it is evident that advance in school training, together, of course, with in-

TABLE 143

Dependence of Range of Information on Academic Status (Whipple)

ACADEMIC STATUS	NUMBER	D	E	F	N
Graduates............	4	39.0	21.0	12.2	27.0
Seniors...............	5	20.6	17.2	25.2	37.0
Juniors...............	10	24.8	12.0	23.7	39.5
Sophomores.	30	17.7	12.7	17.3	52.2
High School.	52	6.8	7.6	16.3	69.3

creased maturity, is paralleled by an increase in the number
of technical terms that can be defined (D), explained (E), or
that are at least familiar (F), and by, naturally, a corresponding decrease in the number of terms that are new or unknown (N).

TABLE 144

Dependence of Range of Information on Academic Status (Smith)

ACADEMIC STATUS	NUMBER	D	E	F	N
Graduates_____	9	38.11	12.11	15.67	34.11
Seniors_____	47	24.90	16.70	19.30	39.10
Juniors_____	59	20.50	14.40	20.70	44.40
Sophomores_____	85	20.10	12.10	19.10	48.70
Freshmen _____	153	13.70	10.70	15.50	60.10

(2) *Dependence on sex.* The results obtained at Ithaca and
Austin, reclassified by sex, are shown in Table 145, where it is
evident that there exists a superiority of range of information
in the males.

TABLE 145

Dependence of Range of Information on Sex (Whipple and Smith)

	NUMBER	D	E	F	N
Ithaca men_____	44	15.79	11.98	18.22	54.02
Ithaca women__	57	12.21	9.42	17.19	61.17
Texas men_____	162	21.00	12.70	15.60	50.70
Texas women__	173	15.20	13.20	19.30	52.30

(3) The results just figured are 'raw' results; strictly speaking, these should be revised on the basis of an extended series
of definitions, as recommended in the Vocabulary Test (No. 50),
since an inspection of the definitions and explanations actually
given reveals in the majority of the papers one or more errors,

due in the main to confusion with words of similar appearance or to fancied etymological derivations. The following list shows typical errors in definition by college and high-school students; the assumed source of confusion is indicated by the terms in parenthesis after the definitions:

ageratum—an aggregation of objects: the aggragate (sic) amount.

annealed—pressed or rolled out thin: molded together.

Anthony Wayne—a historic character who was hung in the cause of freedom for the blacks: a man who fought in the Revolution on the English side.

Babcock test—a device to ascertain whether or not cattle have tuberculosis.

base-hit—when the ball is hit and strikes a base or is caught there: a ball batted over a base: when the striker bats the ball into the pitcher's hands.

Bokhara—name of a place in Austria.

cantilever—a bar with a hook in one end by which lumbermen roll logs (canthook).

catalepsy—a form of disorder of the nervous system which causes fits or convulsions (epilepsy). (Similar statements given by 15 persons.)

chamfer—the tree from which camphor gum is obtained: this is the simplified spelling of it (!). (The confusion with camphor was found in 4 papers.)

clearing-house—a sale that takes place when a store wishes to dispose of its stock (clearing sale): a place where clearing papers are given to vessels to enable them to leave the harbor (customs house + clearing of vessels): picking up everything to move; taking everything out of a house: a place used by express companies to sell uncalled-for goods: a house where goods are made ready to be delivered.

cotangent—name of one of two tangents drawn to a circle from the same point without the circle: one lying alongside of (contingent): straight line drawn to touch a circle at one point (tangent).

dibble—to get just a smattering of some subject, as to dibble in medicine or politics (dabble): to do with divided interest (dawdle).

dryad—a priest of early English times (druid).

entrée—first course at a banquet, usually soup: something in the way of food, new and out of season: when the waiter brings in a new course it is called an entré: French for 'to-day': French for 'between' (entre).

Eocene—the term applied to one of the early ages of civilization.

Euclid—a book written by Vergil (Æneid): name given to certain trees (eucalyptus): an ancient Egyptian who studied geometry: name of an avenue in Cleveland, Ohio.

f-64—means the temperature is 64 degrees above zero, Fahrenheit.

f. o. b.—cash on delivery (c. o. d): forward on board.

golden section—the section of the West most prosperous.

hydraulic press—a kind of air-pump, rather complicated, operated by suction and pressure: a machine for washing dirt from gold or from steep slopes (hydraulic mining): the force with which water flows upon or against a thing, as a paddle wheel.

impressionism—when a man imitates the looks or actions of another: the art of exciting an impression.

infusoria—a chemical herb (infusion?).

TEST 51: RANGE OF INFORMATION   [687] 321

kilogram—the greatest quantity in the metric system: French measure of distance (kilometer): French unit of liquid measure: the weight of a cube of water whose dimensions are a kilometer.

Les Misérables—a French tragedy written about the last part of the 17th century by Racine, one of the famous French writers: French work written by George Sand, author of Le Diable.

linotype—the product of a certain method of making prints from photographs.

Millet—a blind poet (Milton).

natural selection—in nature each animal selects its mate, a device for building up a stronger race.

ohm—German word for uncle (*Oheim*).

Polonius—a prominent character in Julius Caesar.

pomology—the study of the palm of the hand, used by fortune tellers (palmistry).

tort—French word for ugly (*tors?*).

triple expansion—the expanding of anything three times its normal size.

Utopia—a silk factory.

way-bill—a bill that is being considered.

Zionism—same as Dowieism.

(4) A comparison of scores made by 18 summer-session students, before and after the definition by E of the 100 terms, shows the following averages: first marking, $D = 20.39$, $E = 14.77$, $F = 18.39$, $N = 46.44$; second marking, $D = 19.77$, $E = 20.22$, $F = 19.55$, $N = 40.44$. So far as these S's are concerned, then, it appears that at first they had overestimated terms definable and, more particularly, terms unknown. The principal effect of E's explanations was to increase by about 6 per cent. the number of terms marked as explainable, and to decrease by 6 per cent. the number of terms marked as unknown.

NOTE.—Attention may be called to the suggestive method devised by Franken (1), the purpose of which is to test not so much the range of information of pupils, but rather the degree to which they overestimate their range and the extent to which this overestimation may be reduced by proper drill and instruction. A series of questions drawn from school work is propounded, first in a form that inquires as to the existence of the information and that requires merely the answer 'yes' or 'no.' After this series has been answered, the same questions are given in a second form that demands a specific answer. Examples: first form: "Do you know what city is the capital of France"? Second form: "What city is the capital of France"? For various ways of conducting tests by these two forms of questions the original articles should be consulted. Franken's method is in many features more akin to the 'Aussage' test (No. 32)

REFERENCES

(1) A. Franken, (*a*) Ueber die Erziehbarkeit der Erinnerungsaussage bei Schulkindern. *ZPdPs*, 12 : 1911, 635-642. (*b*) Aussageversuche nach der Methode der Entscheidungs- und Bestimmungsfrage bei Erwachsenen und Kindern. *ZAngPs*, 6 : 1912, 174-253.

(2) Laura L. Smith, Whipple's range of information test. *PsR*, 20 : 1913, 517-518.

(3) G. M. Whipple, A range of information test. *PsR*, 16 : 1909, 347-351.

CHAPTER XIII

Serial Graded Tests for Developmental Diagnosis

The omission from this volume of the de Sanctis tests and of the Binet-Simon tests demands a brief explanation. The reasons that have led to this omission are: first, the extension of the material of the preceding pages has brought the volume to dimensions already in excess of the original plans; secondly, the number of published investigations bearing upon the Binet tests is so enormous (Kohs' bibliography lists 254 titles to June, 1914) that the proper consideration of so much material demands more time than can be permitted; thirdly, the extensive use of the Binet tests has given rise to so many variations in method of application and scoring that there now exist numerous issues upon each one of which an authoritative presentation must take a definite and justified stand—something which is impossible without extensive comparison of the views of various writers and resolution of the conflicting views on the basis of careful first-hand investigation; fourthly, there are now available a number of pamphlets of directions prepared by competent writers (Goddard, Kuhlmann, Schwegler, Terman, Town, Winch, *et al*), so that the need for a Binet handbook that was felt when the first edition of this *Manual* appeared is now sufficiently met, and it would be only adding confusion to present still another version of the tests if it were set forth without sufficient justification to claim attention as a standardized version.

It is my hope, however, to issue later a supplementary volume that will discuss the rationale of combinations of tests into systems, that will deal with the Binet tests in a comprehensive manner, and that will include also other systems of tests, such as the de Sanctis tests and the psychological-profile method of Rossolimo. In the meantime, the selected references that follow will serve to guide the reader to some of the more important discussions in English of two of these test-systems.

REFERENCES

(1)   J. C. Bell, Recent literature on the Binet tests. *JEdPs*, 3: 1912, 101-110.

(2)   C. S. Berry, A comparison of the Binet tests of 1908 and 1911. *JEdPs*, 3: 1912, 444-451.

(3)   H. H. Goddard, (*a*) The Binet-Simon measuring scale for intelligence. Revised. *TrSc*, 8: 1911, 56-62. (*b*) Two thousand normal children measured by the Binet measuring scale of intelligence. *PdSe*, 18: 1911, 232-259. (*c*) Standard method for giving the Binet test. *TrSc*, 10: 1913, 23-30.

(4)   E. B. Huey, (*a*) The Binet Scale for measuring intelligence and retardation. *JEdPs*, 1: 1910, 435-444. (*b*) The present status of the Binet scale of tests for the measurement of intelligence. *PsBu*, 9: 1912, 160-168. (*c*) Backward and feeble-minded children. *EdPsMon*, 1912. Pp. 221.

(5)   S. C. Kohs, The Binet-Simon measuring scale for intelligence: an annotated bibliography. *JEdPs*, 5: 1914, 215-224, 279-290, 335-346. (Also sold separately.)

(6)   F. Kuhlmann, (*a*) A revision of the Binet-Simon system for measuring the intelligence of children. *Mon. Suppl. of JPsAsth*, 1: 1912. Pp. 41. (*b*) Some results of examining a thousand public school children with a revision of the Binet-Simon tests of intelligence by untrained examiners. *JPsAsth*, 18: 1914, 150-179, 233-269. (Also published separately.)

(7)   S. de Sanctis, Mental development and the measure of the level of intelligence. *JEdPs*, 2: 1911, 498-507.

(8)   R. A. Schwegler, A teachers' manual for the use of the Binet-Simon scale of intelligence. (Selected bibliography of 56 titles.) *Univ. of Kansas, School of Education*, 1914. Pp. 56.

(9)   W. Stern, The psychological methods of testing intelligence. *EdPsMon*, No. 13, 1914. Pp. 160.

(10)   L. M. Terman. Suggestions for revising, extending and supplementing the Binet intelligence tests. *Intern. Conf. School Hyg.*, Buffalo, N. Y., 1913.

(11)   L. M. Terman and H. G. Childs, A tentative revision and extension of the Binet-Simon scale of intelligence. *JEdPs*, 3: 1912, 61-74, 133-143, 198-208, 277-289.

(12)   Clara H. Town (translator), A method of measuring the development of the intelligence of young children, by A. Binet and Th. Simon. Lincoln, Ill., 1913.

(13)   J. E. W. Wallin, (*a*) Experimental studies of mental defectives. A critique of the Binet-Simon tests. *EdPsMon*, No. 7, 1912. Pp. 155. (*b*) The mental health of the school child. New Haven, 1914. Pp. 463.

APPENDIX I

Measures of Length
1 mm. = 0.0394 inch.
1 cm. = 0.3937 inch.
1 m. = 39.37 inches.
1 in. = 2.54 cm.
1 ft. = 0.3048 m.

Measures of Surface
1 sq. cm. = 0.155 sq. in.
1 sq. in. = 6.452 sq. cm.

Measures of Capacity
1 cu. cm. = 0.061 cu. in.
1 cu. in. = 16.4 cu. cm.

Measures of Weight
1 gram = 0.035 oz.
1 kg. = 2.204 lbs.
1 oz. = 28.35 g.
1 lb. = 453.59 g.

APPENDIX II

List of Abbreviations

The following abbreviations, save for a few additions, are identical with those recommended and employed in the *Zeitschrift für angewandte Psychologie*, V, Heft 5-6, VI, Heft 5-6.

AmAnt: American Anthropologist (Lancaster, Pa.).
AmJIns: American Journal of Insanity (Baltimore, Md.).
AmJPhg: American Journal of Physiology (Boston, Mass.).
AmJPs: American Journal of Psychology (Worcester, Mass.).
AmJSci: American Journal of Science (New Haven, Conn.).
AnPs: L'Année psychologique (Paris).
ArGsPhg: Archiv für die gesamte Physiologie des Menschen und der Tiere (Bonn).
ArGsPs: Archiv für die gesamte Psychologie (Leipzig).
ArPs(e): Archives of Psychology (New York).
ArPs(f): Archives de Psychologie (Geneva, Switzerland).
BuAcRoySci: Bulletins de l'Académie Royale des Sciences, des Lettres et des Beaux-arts de Belgique (Brussels).
BerlinKlW: Berliner Klinische Wochenschrift (Berlin)
BiZb: Biologisches Zentralblatt (Erlangen).
BrJPs: British Journal of Psychology (Cambridge, England).
BuSocEtPsEnf: Bulletin de la Société libre pour létude psychologique de l'enfant (Paris).
ColumbiaConEd: Columbia Contributions to Education (New York).
ColumbiaConPhPs: Columbia Contributions to Philosophy and Psychology (New York).
DMdW: Deutsche Medizinische Wochenschrift (Leipzig).
Ed: Education (Boston, Mass.).
EPd: Die experimentelle Pädagogik (Leipzig).
EdPsMon: Educational Psychology Monographs (Baltimore, Md.).
FsPs: Fortschritte der Psychologie und ihre Anwendungen (Berlin).
InMagScHyg: International Magazine of School Hygiene (Leipzig).

JAntInst: Journal of the Anthropological Institute of Great Britain and Ireland (London).

JEdPs: The Journal of Educational Psychology (Baltimore, Md.).

JEPd: Journal of Experimental Pedagogy and Training College Record (London).

JNeMeDis: Journal of Nervous and Mental Disease (New York).

JPh: Journal of Philosophy, Psychology and Scientific Methods (New York).

JPhg: Journal of Physiology (Cambridge, England).

JPsAsth: Journal of Psycho-Asthenics (Faribault, Minn.).

NeMeDisMon: Nervous and Mental Disease Monograph Series (New York).

PdPsArb: Padagogisch-psychologische Arbeiten (Leipzig).

PdSe: Pedagogical Seminary (Worcester, Mass.).

PdlJb: Paedologisch Jaarboek (Antwerp).

PhR: Philosophical Review (Lancaster, Pa.).

PhSd: Philosophische Studien (Leipzig).

PopSciM: Popular Science Monthly (Garrison, N. Y.).

PsArb: Psychologische Arbeiten (Leipzig).

PsBu: Psychological Bulletin (Lancaster, Pa.).

PsCl: Psychological Clinic (Philadelphia, Pa.).

PsMon: Psychological Monographs (Lancaster, Pa.).

PsR: Psychological Review (Lancaster, Pa.).

RepComEd: Report United States Commissioner of Education (Washington, D. C.).

RMdSuisse: Revué médicale de la Suisse Romande (Geneva, Switzerland).

RPhF: Revue philosophique de la France et de l'Etranger (Paris).

RSci: Revue scientifique (Paris).

Sci: Science (Garrison, N. Y.)

SdYalePsLab: Studies from the Yale Psychological Laboratory.

SmAbPdPs: Sammlung von Abhandlungen aus dem Gebiete der pädagogischen Psychologie und Physiologie (Berlin).

TrSc: The Training School (Vineland, N. J.).

UnIowaSdPs: University of Iowa Studies in Psychology (Iowa City, Iowa).

ZAngPs: Zeitschrift für angewandte Psychologie und psychologische Sammelforschung (Leipzig).

ZBi: Zeitschrift für Biologie (Munich).

ZEPd: Zeitschrift für experimentelle Pädagogik (Leipzig).

ZPdPs: Zeitschrift für pädagogische Psychologie und experimentelle Pädagogik (Leipzig).

ZPs: Zeitschrift für Psychologie (Leipzig).

ZScGd: Zeitschrift für Schulgesundheitspflege (Hamburg).

APPENDIX III

List of Materials

Numerals refer to test-numbers. Items starred refer to materials that are recommended, but not prescribed, or to materials for the conduct of alternative or supplementary tests.

The Materials may be ordered of C. H. Stoelting Company, 3047 Carroll Ave., Chicago, Illinois, who will quote prices on application.

I. SPECIAL APPLIANCES

Card of objects, Binet's, 32
Counter, mechanical, 36*
Demoor suggestion blocks, 40*
Kymograph drum and stand, 42, 43
Memory apparatus, Jastrow's, 38*
Pendulum, seconds', 38*
Pictorial completion test, Healy's, 48*
Pictures (lithographs), Hindoos, 31; Australians, 32; Disputed

Case, 32; Washington and Sally, 32*; Orphan's Prayer, 32*; card of 13 colored, 38
Prism, 20-D., 36*
Seconds clock, 33*, 34*, 35*, 48*
Suggestion blocks, set of 22, 40
Warmth illusory, electrical apparatus for, 44; Guidi's stove, 44
Weights, progressive, set of 15 for suggestion, 41

II. SPECIAL PRINTED FORMS

Analogies, 3 sets of stimulus cards and recording blank, 34A; three forms for group tests of same, 34A
Association, 100-word list, 33; see Analogies, Controlled association and Kent-Rosanoff test
Completion test, Ebbinghaus', set of 4 forms for, 48
Computation tests, addition book, 35; addition problems, Schulze's method, 35; addition problems, 2-place digits, 35; addition problems, 20-place digits, 35; multiplication problems, 35
Controlled association, 4 sets of stimulus cards, 20 each, for part-whole, genus-species and opposites (2 forms) tests, 34; four forms for group tests of same, 34
Fables, set of 8, 49
Information test, 51

Ink-blots, set of 20, 45
Kent-Rosanoff association test, 33A; frequency tables for same, 33A
Memory for ideas, 3 test sheets (Marble Statue, Cicero and Dutch Homestead), 39
Memory for letter-squares, set of 10 test-cards and blanks for records, 38
Memory for sentences, 2 test sheets of 21 sentences each, 38
Memory-span for digits, set of 42 test-cards, 38
Mirror-drawing, 6-pointed star, 36; set of 6 patterns, 36
Sentences for completion, 46
Substitution test-strips (Form A), 37; coverboard with key (Form A), 37; test blanks (Form B), 37; set of 4 test-sheets and cardboard key (Form C), 37
Vocabulary tests, 2 forms, 50
Word-building, 2 forms for, 47

III. GENERAL APPLIANCES AND MATERIALS

Roman numerals refer to test-numbers, italicized numerals to page-numbers.

For authors quoted, see Index of Names; for apparatus, see List of Materials; for tables and figures, see indexes following Table of Contents.

CLASSICS IN PSYCHOLOGY

AN ARNO PRESS COLLECTION

Angell, James Rowland. **Psychology: On Introductory Study of the Structure and Function of Human Consciousness.** 4th edition. 1908

Bain, Alexander. **Mental Science.** 1868

Baldwin, James Mark. **Social and Ethical Interpretations in Mental Development.** 2nd edition. 1899

Bechterev, Vladimir Michailovitch. **General Principles of Human Reflexology.** [1932]

Binet, Alfred and Th[éodore] Simon. **The Development of Intelligence in Children.** 1916

Bogardus, Emory S. **Fundamentals of Social Psychology.** 1924

Buytendijk, F. J. J. **The Mind of the Dog.** 1936

Ebbinghaus, Hermann. **Psychology: An Elementary Text-Book.** 1908

Goddard, Henry Herbert. **The Kallikak Family.** 1931

Hobhouse, L[eonard] T. **Mind in Evolution.** 1915

Holt, Edwin B. **The Concept of Consciousness.** 1914

Külpe, Oswald. **Outlines of Psychology.** 1895

Ladd-Franklin, Christine. **Colour and Colour Theories.** 1929

Lectures Delivered at the 20th Anniversary Celebration of Clark University. (Reprinted from *The American Journal of Psychology,* Vol. 21, Nos. 2 and 3). 1910

Lipps, Theodor. **Psychological Studies.** 2nd edition. 1926

Loeb, Jacques. **Comparative Physiology of the Brain and Comparative Psychology.** 1900

Lotze, Hermann. **Outlines of Psychology.** [1885]

McDougall, William. **The Group Mind.** 2nd edition. 1920

Meier, Norman C., editor. **Studies in the Psychology of Art: Volume III.** 1939

Morgan, C. Lloyd. **Habit and Instinct.** 1896

Münsterberg, Hugo. **Psychology and Industrial Efficiency.** 1913

Murchison, Carl, editor. **Psychologies of 1930.** 1930

Piéron, Henri. **Thought and the Brain.** 1927

Pillsbury, W[alter] B[owers]. **Attention.** 1908

[Poffenberger, A. T., editor]. **James McKeen Cattell:** Man of Science. 1947

Preyer, W[illiam] **The Mind of the Child:** Parts I and II. 1890/1889

The Psychology of Skill: Three Studies. 1973

Reymert, Martin L., editor. **Feelings and Emotions:** The Wittenberg Symposium. 1928

Ribot, Th[éodule Armand]. **Essay on the Creative Imagination.** 1906

Roback, A[braham] A[aron]. **The Psychology of Character.** 1927

I. M. Sechenov: Biographical Sketch and Essays. (Reprinted from *Selected Works* by I. Sechenov). 1935

Sherrington, Charles. **The Integrative Action of the Nervous System.** 2nd edition. 1947

Spearman, C[harles]. **The Nature of 'Intelligence' and the Principles of Cognition.** 1923

Thorndike, Edward L. **Education:** A First Book. 1912

Thorndike, Edward L., E. O. Bregman, M. V. Cobb, et al. **The Measurement of Intelligence.** [1927]

Titchener, Edward Bradford. **Lectures on the Elementary Psychology of Feeling and Attention.** 1908

Titchener, Edward Bradford. **Lectures on the Experimental Psychology of the Thought-Processes.** 1909

Washburn, Margaret Floy. **Movement and Mental Imagery.** 1916

Whipple, Guy Montrose. **Manual of Mental and Physical Tests:** Parts I and II. 2nd edition. 1914/1915

Woodworth, Robert Sessions. **Dynamic Psychology.** 1918

Wundt, Wilhelm. **An Introduction to Psychology.** 1912

Yerkes, Robert M. **The Dancing Mouse** and **The Mind of a Gorilla.** 1907/1926

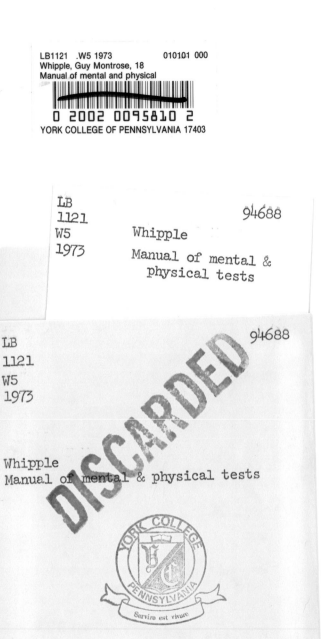